THE OPENING OF
AN ERA
1848
An Historical Symposium

Edited by
FRANÇOIS FEJTÖ
With an Introduction by
A. J. P. TAYLOR

NEW YORK

Howard Fertig

1966

First published in French in 1948
under the title *Le Printemps des Peuples*

Copyright 1948 by Les Editions de Minuit

First published in English in 1948

HOWARD FERTIG, INC. EDITION 1966
Published by arrangement with Les Editions de Minuit

First American edition

Library of Congress Catalog Card Number: 66-24344

PRINTED IN THE UNITED STATES OF AMERICA
BY NOBLE OFFSET PRINTERS

CONTENTS

CONTENTS

The essays, with the exception of those on Great Britain and the U.S.A., were translated by HUGH SHELLEY

CHRONOLOGICAL LIST OF EVENTS

before, during, and after the Revolution of 1848

THE PRELUDE TO THE REVOLUTION

1846	FEBRUARY	Massacres in Galicia
	22	Insurrection at Cracow
	MARCH 3	Capitulation of Cracow
	JUNE	Election of liberal Pope Pius IX
	JULY	Palmerston—Foreign Secretary for the third time
1847	APRIL–JUNE	Meeting of General Diet in Prussia
	JUNE 8	General elections in Belgium: gains by the Liberal Party
	JULY	First Chartist, O'Connor, returned to Parliament in England
	10	Electoral reform campaign begins in Paris
	20	Federal Diet in Switzerland decides to dissolve *Sonderbund*
	SEPTEMBER	Lord Minto sent to Italy
	12	German Democrats meet at Offenburg
	OCTOBER 4	Narvaez forms new Spanish Government
	NOVEMBER 4	Swiss Diet orders suppression of *Sonderbund* by force
	21	Hungarian Diet meets at Pressburg
	30	Swiss Civil War ends in complete victory for Diet
	NOVEMBER–DECEMBER	Communist Congress held in London: Marx and Engels commissioned to prepare *Manifesto*

THE REVOLUTIONARY YEAR

1848	JANUARY 12	Insurrection at Palermo
	18	Manin and Tomases arrested in Venice
	20	Danish Radicals demand Constitution
	27	Tocqueville's speech in Paris Chamber of Deputies: 'The storm is brewing' Naples granted Constitution

CHRONOLOGICAL LIST OF EVENTS

1848   FEBRUARY 2   End of U.S. Mexican War
- 10   Pope forms a Ministry which includes laymen
- 12   Guizot's Government gains majority of only 43 votes in Paris Chamber of Deputies
- 13   Reformist Banquet in Paris announced for 22 February
- 14   Distribution in Prague of tracts supporting Italian insurgents
- 17   Tuscany granted Constitution
- 18   Clash between students and military at Padua
- 22   Demonstrations in Paris
- 23   Further demonstrations in Paris; barricades erected; Guizot dismissed; appearance of Red Flag
- 24   Provisional Government formed in Paris; Louis Philippe abdicates
- 27   Big demonstration at Mannheim, followed by disturbances throughout Germany

  Big demonstration at Turin to celebrate Constitution
- 28   France proclaimed a Republic

MARCH   1   First session of Luxembourg Commission

Grand Duke of Baden permits formation of National Guard
- 2   10 hour working-day introduced in France
- 3   Kossuth's revolutionary speech to Hungarian Diet
- 4   Piedmont accorded a 'Statute'
- 5   Riots in Berlin. Liberal Congress at Heidelberg decides to summon a parliament

  Universal suffrage introduced in France
- 6   National Workshops organised in Paris

  King of Prussia promises periodical convocation of *Landtag*
- 10   Street demonstrations in Berlin
- 11   Big reformist meeting in Prague
- 13   Disturbances in Vienna; Metternich dismissed
- 14   Windischgrätz appointed Military Governor of Vienna; Working-class riots crushed by Civic Guard

  Rumanians granted Constitution

  Convocation of *Landtag* in Prussia
- 15   Revolution breaks out in Budapest

  Street fighting in Berlin

1848 MARCH 15 At Vienna the Emperor promises Constitution
17 Demonstrations by Parisian 'clubs' to demand postponement of elections
King of Prussia declares in favour of a federal *Reich*
18 Big patriotic banquet at Stockholm
Mieroslawski set free in Berlin
Hungarian Diet at Pressburg decides to abolish feudal dues
Schleswig-Holstein declares its independence at Rendsburg
Rising in Milan
19 Civic Guard takes over policing of Berlin
20 King of Bavaria abdicates in favour of his son
21 Formation of Danish Government—including Radicals
Kolowrat-Pillersdorf Government formed in Vienna
22 Narvaez suspends Cortes to check spreading Radical agitation
Reconstitution of Venetian Republic
23 Charles Albert intervenes against Austria
25 French Interim Government decides to form *garde mobile*
26 Riots in Madrid easily suppressed
27 Big reformist demonstration at Jassy in Moldavia
28 Students demonstrate in Barcelona
31 Meeting of *Vorparlament* at Frankfort
APRIL 2 Convocation of Prussian *Landtag*
8 The Emperor promises Bohemia a Constitution
Czartoryski arrives at Posen
Prussian project of Liberal Constitution for Posen
10 Failure of Chartist demonstration in London
11 Emperor Ferdinand ratifies new Hungarian Constitution
12 Hungarian Diet calls for reconstitution of Poland
16 Working class demonstration in Paris to demand State organisation of labour
20 *Fête de la Fraternité* in Paris
23 General Election in France
25 German Legion, formed in Paris, crosses the Rhine
Suppression of feudal rights in Galicia

CHRONOLOGICAL LIST OF EVENTS

1848 JUNE 23 Garibaldi arrives in Nice from Montevideo
25 Parisian rising quelled
28 Cavaignac appointed President of the Council in France

JULY 4 New Hungarian Assembly meets
8 Austrian Premier, Pillersdorf, dismissed
Habeas Corpus suspended in Ireland
10 Meeting of *Reichstag* at Vienna
18 Formation of Wessenweg—Doblhoff Cabinet at Vienna
23 Radetzky defeats the Italians at Custozza

AUGUST 5 Austrians occupy Milan
7 Venice proclaims sovereignty of Charles Albert
9 Charles Albert concludes armistice with Austria
12 Imperial Court returns to Vienna
21 Working class demonstrations in Vienna
26 Denmark and Prussia conclude armistice at Malmö

SEPTEMBER 2 Austrians bombard Lwow
4 Emperor reinstates Jellacic as Governor of Croatia
6 Emperor confirms abolition of feudal rights and State compensation for the landowners
11 Jellacic enters Hungary at head of Austro-Croat army
12 Rising at Frankfort
25 Rumanians of Transylvania rise against the Hungarians; Archduke Stephen flees from Hungary
28 Summary execution of Austrian C-in-C Lamberg by insurgents of Budapest
29 Battle of Velencze, near Budapest, between Jellacic and Hungarian Government forces

OCTOBER 3 The Emperor dissolves Hungarian Assembly which decides to carry on its task
6 Rising in Vienna; War Minister killed
10 Jellacic, pursued by Hungarian forces, reaches gates of Vienna
21 Windischgrätz' army encircles Vienna
30 Hungarian forces repulsed at Schwechat
31 Fall of Vienna

NOVEMBER 9 Robert Blum shot in Vienna
15 Rossi assassinated in Rome

CHRONOLOGICAL LIST OF EVENTS

CHRONOLOGICAL LIST OF EVENTS

1849   AUGUST 13   Görgey capitulates to the Russian Army at Világos: end of the War of Hungarian Independence

  23   Venice capitulates

  OCTOBER 2   Fall of Komárom, in Hungary

  6   Execution of 13 Hungarian Revolutionary Generals at Arad

THE REACTIONARIES CONSOLIDATE

1850   JANUARY 1   All associations banned in Finland

  21   Pseudo-liberal Constitution granted in Prussia

  MARCH 21   Session of *Erfurt Parlament:* plans for Constitution for German Confederation

  MAY 9   New electoral law in France

  JULY 2   Peace signed between Prussia and Denmark

  OCTOBER 1   Customs barriers removed between Austria and Hungary

  NOVEMBER 29   Austro-Prussian pact concluded at Olmütz

1851   DECEMBER 2   Louis Napoleon's *coup d'état* in France

  31   Austria's Constitution suppressed; return to complete absolutism

Re. 1848

THE OPENING OF AN ERA : 1848

A. J. P. TAYLOR

Robert Owen, on a visit to Paris, described his economic system as 'the railway which will take mankind to universal happiness'. His phrase crystallised the spirit of the year of revolutions. Movement, and a conviction that Utopia could be reached, were the essence of 1848: underlying these was a faith in the limitless goodness of human nature. The revolutionary cry, 'All change!' sounded across Europe. Hope lit the dawn of a new Europe; and mankind clambered into the trains of political and social upheaval, all of which claimed to be directed to the same terminus—the Kingdom of Heaven on Earth. New faiths, new nations, new classes announced their arrival; each was the confident possessor of an exclusive truth. Before 1848 the rights of individuals and of states were a matter of history and of settled law; the revolutions substituted the rule of abstract principle. Louis Philippe said bitterly of the revolution of 1830 which brought him to the throne: 'What perished in France in 1830 was not respect for a dynasty, but respect for anything'. This was demonstrated anew in France in 1848 and, for the first time, was demonstrated throughout Europe as well. Reason took the place of respect; and self-interest the place of tradition.

Movement was both the cause of the revolutions and their outcome: the revolutions threw down established landmarks that were already ruinous. In the preceding fifty years tumultuous development had taken the place of imperceptible change. There was an unprecedented growth of population, an unprecedented advance in the methods of industry and of transport, and an unprecedented novelty in the world of ideas: the three together composed the background to the revolutions. The old order had assumed stable populations; these ensured stability between classes and stability between states. For half a century before 1848 the increase of population had been gathering strength, and this contributed more than anything else to the illusion of progress. The increase was less in France than elsewhere in Europe; and the wise student of population figures might already guess that France, hitherto the greatest European power and the most revolutionary nation, would soon become the most conservative and the least great of the Powers. The universal growth of

telegraph

population had profound consequences. Where the peasant was already free, as in western Germany, the surplus was being pushed into the towns. In the Austrian Empire the peasants could no longer tolerate the burden of feudal dues and of feudal subordination; moreover, with the increasing demand for food, the great landowners could no longer operate their estates by the traditional methods. Both lords and peasants turned against the old order of settled obligations; both demanded freedom of movement and the rule of the market. Almost the first act of the liberal parliament in Hungary was to abolish the old agrarian social order; and the Austrian Constituent Assembly followed suit (its only effective act) on 7 September. The destinies of fifty million people were affected. The more prosperous peasants got the chance of survival; the poorer peasants lost their last traditional protection and were the victims both of the richer peasants and of the capitalistic great estates. The way was clear for the emigration to the towns and overseas which characterised the second half of the century. It was no accident that England and Russia, the only countries of Europe to escape the revolutions, had already found the way of emigration before 1848: the road to Siberia had been open since the beginning of the century, and the emigrant-steamers took the life out of Chartism when they began to sail from Liverpool in 1844. The rest of Europe had lacked the technical and social conditions for mass emigration: peasant emancipation came in 1848, and railways followed. These provided a safety valve which postponed further European explosions until the twentieth century. Modern industrial America, as well as modern industrial Europe, would have been impossible without the revolutions of 1848.

The staggering growth of towns throughout Europe was a consequence of the revolutions. Still, even before 1848, the swelling towns amazed and alarmed contemporaries; and their isolation—urban islands in a rural continent—emphasised their revolutionary character. The conscious revolutions of 1848 were all exclusively urban. 'The German revolution' is a misleading generalisation for the Berlin revolution and the Vienna revolution; 'the Italian revolution' still more misleading as a title for the revolutions in Venice, Milan, Florence, Rome, Naples, and many more. The contrast was sharpest in France. The great revolution of 1789 had been the movement of a people, the revolution of 1848 was a movement of Paris against the rest of the nation. Isolated in place, the revolutions were equally insular in idea: they had no agrarian programme and offered the peasants—troglodytes, in Marx's phrase—nothing but extinction. For the first time news of a revolution passed from one town to another by telegraph; it no longer needed to filter through, and so to affect, the countryside. The revolutionaries travelled by train from one revolution to the next; they had neither eyes nor thoughts for the country through which they passed. The revolutionaries equated revolutions with street-fighting. Their occasional forays into the countryside—from Hecker's raid on Baden in April 1848 to Garibaldi's march across Italy in July 1849—were the organised hikes of town dwellers.

Even the largest towns lacked industrial development. Labour had arrived before capital was ready for it. Only Belgium had experienced an industrial revolution; and therefore, despite its urban character, enjoyed an unique freedom from revolutionary danger. The revolutions elsewhere were not revolts against the machine; they were demands to be employed by it. The slogan of 'the right to work' was a symbol of immaturity; an industrial proletariat would have demanded the right to work less—as indeed the English working class had already done with success in 1847. 'The right to work' was a protest as much against social inequality as against harsh living condition. Nevertheless, by formulating this protest in economic terms, it launched the idea that liberty and political equality were negligible, or indeed valueless, in comparison with food and clothing. This idea was not intended by the social revolutionaries of 1848, who took up economic grievances principally in order to add greater force to their political demands. All the same the damage had been done. Continental socialism, which had its origins in 1848, wrote off political democracy as *bourgeois* and accepted the doctrine that violence and intolerance were a small price to pay for social change. Class war took the place of the struggle for political liberty, and the Rights of Man were a casualty of 'the right to work'.

The announcement of an economic programme was certainly the startling novelty of 1848; nevertheless the revolutions were not simply the product of economic circumstances. These determined the moment of revolution, not that it should occur. The economic upheaval and the upheaval in men's minds were two aspects of the same process. Certainly the age of coal and iron enforced daring political schemes and made them possible; but equally it needed a daring mind to think of the railway and the blast furnace. The great towns of modern Europe could not have been maintained without railways, steam power, and a revolution in agriculture; but the movement to the towns depended just as much on the spread of new ideas which prised men away from their traditional beliefs and traditional surroundings. The railways found people ready to move; otherwise they would have run empty. Reason was the great dissolvent force. This made men dissatisfied with their traditional homes and with their traditional place in society just as much as with the traditional methods of production. The radicals of 1848 were the heirs of eighteenth-century enlightenment: sublimely confident in human nature (except that of their fellow revolutionaries), they believed that their only task was to shake off the hold of established beliefs and established institutions. Their common programme was 'to strangle the last king with the bowels of the last priest'. The natural goodness of man would do the rest.

The old order, thus dramatically threatened, claimed to depend on habit, on history, and on established rights. No historical conflict is, in fact, fought on these easy terms. The old order was itself more rational and artificial—just as the revolutionaries were more traditional—than either side liked to admit. Revolutionary ideas had affected the upper classes before they spread to the masses; and the impact of the great French revolution had long shaken the foundations of the European system. Men were argued into conservatism as they were argued into revolution. The kings who were threatened by the movements of 1848 had less than a century of possession behind them, and many more were the creations of Napoleon. Even the house of Habsburg, the only genuine historic dynasty, had acquired a new title and new territories a generation previously and had knocked all life out of historic institutions everywhere in its dominions except in Hungary—and there from lack of strength, not of will. The 'old aristocracy' was a creation of the eighteenth, or occasionally of the seventeenth century. Most of all the territorial settlement of the Congress of Vienna was as artificial as the Empire of Napoleon which it replaced. The peace which followed the Napoleonic wars sprang from exhaustion, not from belief or from content; and the society which perished in 1848 had no moral justification other than the desire of the possessing classes to enjoy their privileges.

The kings, aristocrats, and states of the Vienna system had not even given themselves the trouble of being born; they had been conjured up ready-made by conservative theorists. Thus Metternich, to give historic character to the Austrian Empire (which had acquired legal existence only in 1804), proposed to invent for the Emperor a traditional ceremony of coronation. Metternich, symbol and chief exponent of conservatism, claimed to be building a dam against revolution. In reality, his effort to set up a universal 'system' of political ideas and institutions was typical of an eighteenth-century doctrinaire. He approached politics in the spirit of Robespierre: the only difference was in his employer. The dissolvent of reason could have been resisted only by communities with a living history; few such existed on the continent of Europe, and these few (Switzerland, Hungary, and perhaps the Low Countries) did not accord with Metternich's conservatism. As a result, the system of Metternich was not overthrown in 1848; it collapsed. This collapse astonished contemporaries, other than Metternich himself: he has always appreciated the artificiality of his own system and had never felt the faith which he demanded in others.

In 1848 Europe broke consciously with its past. This was the indelible achievement of the year of revolutions. Yet more than destruction was intended. Bakunin, most extreme representative of the spirit of revolution, once declared that if his plans succeeded he would at once begin to pull down again everything he had ever made; this did not take the zest from a lifetime of planning. The radicals of all schools were as convinced as Metternich of the need for belief; and, unlike Metternich, themselves believed in the systems which they expounded. Their systems, too, were universal and dogmatic. All assumed that reason was adequate as the sole guide in human affairs; and they assumed also that there was no limit to what reason could do. The revolutionaries differed as to the means by which the human race might be made perfect; none disputed that the goal would be attained. The radical systems provided new Absolutes for old and gave final answers in politics, in society, and in international affairs. The sovereignty of the people overthrew the sovereignty of kings; nations took the place of states; and intellect ousted heredity as the source of authority.

Though the sovereignty of the people had already served as inspiration to the French revolution of 1789, its operation had been restricted. The distinguishing mark of 1789 had been the confidence that universal principles could be limited in their application and a revolution arrested in its course. This expectation was not proved false until 1848. When all hereditary rights were repudiated, the right of private property had remained inviolate and was indeed reinforced; and the dogma of the sovereignty of the people was used to justify the franchise of the property owning middle class. In 1848 the term of this compromise expired; and the bourgeoisie, once the leaders of revolution, became the symbol of conservatism. Almost the first act of the victorious revolution in France was to abolish the property qualification and to proclaim universal suffrage. This became everywhere the most concrete expression of the revolutionary programme. Only Hungary, which combined—or perhaps stifled—revolutionary principle with historic institutions, held out against universal suffrage until the twentieth century. The events of 1848 challenged also the economic privilege of the owners of property. The June Days in Paris gave dramatic announcement of the arrival of a new revolutionary class, 'the proletariat'. The June rising was not fought to promote any practical economic change; it was a social war, a slave revolt, and its repudiation of the moral superiority of the bourgeoisie could not be wiped out by all the executions and deportations which followed defeat. Before the June Days private property had been regarded as essential for liberty; after the June Days it became the symbol of oppression, and the capitalist took the place of priest and noble as the object of democratic hostility. Henceforth the bourgeoisie was morally on the defensive, ashamed and anxious. This was true not only of the French bourgeoisie, who had genuinely experienced the 'social peril'. The alarm of the June Days spread across Europe; indeed, apprehension increased as the reality of danger became more remote. The middle classes outside France abandoned the revolutionary cause almost before they had taken it up and sought for allies against a proletariat which was still imaginary. Thus, the October revolution in Vienna, though it had a programme with no social implications, sent the German-Austrian middle classes over to the side of absolutism; and within a few years of 1848 German liberalism came to regard universal suffrage as its mortal enemy. The French bourgeoisie had pride enough to remain radical though they ceased to be revolutionary and adhered to the sovereignty of the people in the sense that they took into partnership the French peasants who had saved them in the June Days. Though universal suffrage, the work of the revolution of 1848, became everywhere a mainstay of conservatism, in France it sustained at least the Third Republic and later, in the Dreyfus case, upheld the Rights of Man. In Germany, however, it was the instrument of Bismarck; and in Austria it became in 1907 the last prop of the Empire of Francis Joseph.

In the world of nations, too, the revolutions of 1848 ended the compromise which had been the outcome of the revolution of 1789. The French revolutionaries had launched the national principle; they supposed that this would operate to the sole advantage of France and that when all else of the old order was destroyed the predominance of France would remain unchallenged. France liberated other nations as the French bourgeoisie liberated the French people: freed from their hereditary rulers, they were expected to welcome French leadership instead. The Empire of Napoleon expressed the French version of the national principle: German, Italian, Polish, and even South Slav nationalism were evoked as auxiliary weapons for the French cause. France was the only one who knew how to wield the national appeal, and remained the greatest single power in Europe even after the fall of Napoleon; the other Great Powers of the continent were states, not nations, and therefore without the strength of popular enthusiasm. Thus the French nation claimed the cultural and political heritage of Louis XIV, despite the guillotining of Louis XVI and the renewed expulsion of the Bourbons in July 1830. This cultural headship was recognised for the last time at the beginning of 1848, when the other nations of Europe waited for the February revolution in Paris before starting their own. Thereafter it was no longer enough to have taken the trouble to be born French. The laws of inheritance were repudiated between nations as much as between individuals. The lesson was not lost on the French themselves; henceforth the French nation was as much imperilled as, say, the dynasty of Habsburg by European upheavals, and France—previously the promoter of change —became the principle advocate of conservatism and of the *status quo*.

In 1848 every nation followed the example set by the French in 1789. Each claimed to be perfect: each therefore was entitled to lay down its own limits or, if it preferred, to recognise none. Moreover, each nation asserted a purity and greatness of character which made it an example to Europe and justified its bringing other less noble people under its own rule. Thus, Poland had long announced herself as 'the Christ among the nations', and her liberation was regarded as the first object of the revolutionary cause; this liberation did not, however, extend to the Ukrainians under Polish rule. Similarly Mazzini, despite his denunciations of French arrogance, set up Italy as 'God's word in the midst of the nations'. Rome was to be the capital of a new federation of nations, all duly humble, which were to be cut and shaped to suit Italy's convenience. Kossuth, too, insisted on the unique civilisation and political gifts of the Magyars. Though partly Slovak by birth, he denied the existence of a Slovak nation, and, since he could not deny the existence of the Serbs, proposed to root them out with the sword.

Magyar exclusiveness was relatively harmless, except to the subject nations of Hungary. The will to dominate was a more dangerous matter when it was taken up by the Germans, already the most numerous nationality in Europe. The revolutions of 1848 discovered 'the German mission'. This mission was simple: it was, simply, to be German. Europe was corrupt—French sophistication, English materialism, outworn institutions were all to be redeemed by the irruption of the clear-eyed, healthy German barbarian:

> *Und es soll am Deutschen Wesen*
> *Noch einmal die Welt genesen.*

A unique character was found in the German spirit (*Deutscher Geist*), and for that matter even in German rivers and trees—the one wetter and the other more arboreal than any others. Other nations based their claims on superiority of culture, as in the case of France or Italy, or at any rate on superiority of class—as Polish and Magyar nationalism sprang from their landed nobility. German nationalism was the first to depend solely on language: the future Germany was to extend wherever German was spoken. The *Volksdeutsche* were an invention of 1848. Since Germany had no 'natural frontiers'—or none that gave such an easy excuse for expansion as the Rhine to France or the Alps to Italy—national Germany used a simpler argument and claimed whatever was necessary to her existence. Thus Bohemia, despite its Czech majority, could, according to Engels, 'only exist henceforth as a part of Germany'; and the German liberal spokesman at Frankfort said of western Poland: 'Our right is that of the stronger, the right of conquest'. This phrase supplied the basic theme of German history, until it turned against Germany a century later.

Resistance to German claims was not delayed until the twentieth century; it was the motive of the Slav Congress which met in Prague on 2 June 1848. The Slav peoples of eastern Europe were individually too small to hold out against German pressure; therefore, improving on the German model which had made language the basis of nationality, they tried to find a bond of alliance in ethnography and philology. The Slav Congress had practical motives of defence against German nationalism and had no time to trouble about the virtues of the Slav character. Still, even at Prague, Bakunin, one of the inventors of Slav solidarity, found in the Slavs 'an amazing freshness and incomparably more natural intelligence and energy than in the Germans'; and he expected them 'to renew the decadent Western world'. The Slavs of the Austrian and Turkish Empires had enough to do renewing themselves and thereafter quarrelling with each other. The only contribution Russia made to the western world in 1848–9 was to crush the revolution in Hungary. But the spirit of radicalism was not permanently arrested at the Russian frontier; and pan-Slavism, which evoked little response outside Russia, became the delayed gift of 1848 to the Russian intellectuals. In the twentieth century they escaped from this ethnic intolerance only with the aid of class intolerance, which was the other legacy of 1848 to mankind.

The revolutions of 1848 dispelled the utopian dreams of the eighteenth-century rationalists. These had supposed that mankind would attain universal happiness if traditional beliefs were abandoned and traditional authorities overthrown. The experiences after 1789 did not destroy this idea. Social concord accompanied the rule of the bourgeoisie, and a true international order was established with the Empire of Napoleon; it could plausibly be argued that achievement fell short of the ideal only because success was incomplete. Had the tricolour really 'toured the world', universal happiness could have been expected to follow. In 1848 no bounds were drawn against revolutionary victory: no European country, except Belgium, escaped, and the established system lost its traditional authority for ever. The outcome was conflict, not concord. The June Days announced class war; the record of the German, Italian, and Hungarian revolutions announced war between nations. Peaceful agreement and government by consent are possible only on the basis of ideas common to all parties; and these ideas must spring from habit and from history. Once reason is introduced, every man, every class, every nation becomes a law unto itself; and the only right which reason understands is the right of the stronger. Reason formulates universal principles and is therefore intolerant: there can be only one rational society, one rational nation, ultimately one rational man. Decision between rival reasons can be made only by force. This lesson was drawn by the greatest political genius who observed the events of 1848: 'The great questions of our day will not be settled by resolutions and majority votes—that was the mistake of the men of 1848 and 1849—but by blood and iron'. After 1848, the idea that disputes between classes could be settled by compromise or that discussion was an effective means of international relations was held only in England and America, the two countries which escaped the revolutions.

Bismark.

The liberals, the moderate men, shirked the problem of authority; it was faced by the radicals. They found a substitute for tradition in 'the religion of humanity', just as their nationalism took the place of the decayed loyalty to kings. Above all, they found a substitute for the hereditary governing class in themselves. 'The aristocracy of intellect' had a limitless confidence in its right to govern; for it spoke 'in the name of the people'. The radical leaders nominated themselves to this post: none of the great revolutionaries—not Marx nor Engels, Bakunin nor Blanqui —ever secured election by a democratic constituency, and, for the matter of that, none of them was sure of a majority even among the circle of his close associates. The greatest radical effort in France was the demonstration of 16 March, which demanded that elections to the Constituent Assembly be postponed until the people were fit to exercise the franchise, that is, until they were willing to vote for the radical leaders. Blanqui, when asked how long the postponement should be, answered: 'for some months, or perhaps years.' By democracy the men of 1848 did not mean the rule of the majority; they meant rather the rule of the discontented, a reversal of the previous order of society. The essence of 1848 was belief in movement; therefore only those elements of the population who desired change were democratic. The theoretical justification for this outlook was provided by Marx; it was his greatest contribution to history. Marx found motive force of history in economic change; and this force was now impelling mankind from capitalism to socialism. Since movement and democracy were synonymous, only those who desired socialism were 'the people'. Marx could thus eliminate the peasants from his calculations, though they made up the great majority everywhere in Europe; and democracy could be turned into 'the dictatorship of the proletariat'. Marx was a man of the Enlightenment. He held that every man would recognise his own interest and follow it; therefore every

A. J. P. TAYLOR

proletarian would be a socialist. The proposition could be more usefully reversed: anyone who was not a socialist was not a proletarian. But the dictatorship was not really to be exercised even by those working men who accepted the theories of the learned Dr Marx. The workers were to be led by the communists, 'everywhere the most resolute and progressive element of the working class'. Since the communists in 1848 consisted of Marx and Engels, this was a satisfactory conclusion—and has proved a satisfactory conclusion for communists ever since. The radical theorists were led inevitably from belief in the people to belief in themselves; and so to advocacy of authoritarian government. Marx was more self-satisfied and despotic than Metternich, the other system-maker from the Rhineland.

Yet these resolute and progressive leaders never displayed their talents in a revolution. The original outbreaks had no recognised leaders; and no one knows the names of the leaders of the June Days in Paris nor of the October revolution in Vienna. The name of an individual leader in the rising of 15 May in Paris has been preserved; he is thought to have been a police spy. Only Kossuth and Mazzini experienced the practical tasks of revolutionary government; and the experience of Mazzini was not very serious. For the most part the self-styled spokesmen of the people were always trying to catch up on revolutions which had taken them by surprise, as Marx and Engels were still correcting the proofs of their revolutionary programme, the *Communist Manifesto*, when the first barricades were already built and the first shots were being fired. Bakunin distinguished himself by arriving in time for the Dresden revolution of May 1849. This was an accident—he was leaving Dresden for an imaginary revolution elsewhere and was prevented from reaching the railway station by unexpected barricades.

There would have been no revolutions in 1848 if it had depended on the revolutionary leaders. The revolutions made themselves; and the true heroes of 1848 were the masses. The radical intellectuals had supposed that, once tradition was overthrown, the masses would acknowledge instead the claims of intellect. Nietzsche expressed later this great illusion of 1848: 'Dead are all Gods. Now the superman shall live.' The masses never responded to the ambitions of the intellectuals. Though the masses, too, sought the superman, they sought in him an extension of themselves. The first of these supermen, concentrating the impulses and contradictions of the masses, was Napoleon III. He was a clever French guess at the future, not the real thing; for France remained too conservative in institutions and social structure to experience the full rule of the masses. The real superman of the masses was Hitler, in whom anonymity was personified; or perhaps even more in the enigmatical *Politbureaus* of the 'new democracies', who have put the superman into commission.

xxiv

In a deeper sense, the true superman, for whom 1848 prepared the way, has turned out to be the masses themselves. The masses have performed labours greater than those of Hercules and have accomplished miracles more wonderful than those of a divine Saviour; more than any individual superman, they have shown themselves to be beyond good and evil. The age which began in 1848 was the age of the masses: the age of mass production, of mass migration, and of mass war. In the pursuit of universal happiness everything became universal: universal suffrage, universal education, universal military service, finally universal destruction. The train which Robert Owen signalled has been driven by the masses themselves; the intellectuals have remained passengers, criticising—or more occasionally—commending the train's progress. The historic task of the intellectuals was to sever mankind from its roots and to launch it on its career of movement. This was the task which was accomplished in 1848.

*   *   *   *   *

The revolutions of 1848 were, then, of a piece; they demonstrated the unity of European civilisation. Yet, though they sprang from a common source and arrived in the end at the same outcome, they differed widely in their course. It is possible to chronicle the history of the revolution in a single town or, at most, in a single country; no one has yet managed to see Europe in 1848 with an eagle's eye and to recapture every side of the spirit of 1848. The present volume represents a new start in historical enterprise; more than a volume of commemoration, it is itself a display of the spirit of 1848, when nationalism was still possible without national hatred and democracy possible without class war. Each writer limits himself to the history of his national revolution; yet each is conscious of the wider European revolution, of which his narrative forms a part.

There is logic and pattern, too, in the arrangement of the essays. Each, though complete in itself, leads to the next; and the smaller countries are grouped round the great in the manner of modern satellites. We begin, rightly, with Switzerland; for the democratic victory in the Swiss civil war of 1847, though not strictly a revolution, destroyed the moral prestige of the old order. It was, we might say, a necessary prelude to the revolutions, as the victory of Franco in Spain was the signal for the conquest of the continent of Europe by Fascism. Moreover, Swiss democracy escaped the failures of 1848; and Switzerland has thus remained, to this day, the practical illustration of the ideals common to all the revolutionary movements. What Switzerland has become represents what the revolutionaries hoped to achieve; and the history of the revolutions would be incomplete without the solitary success among the record of failure.

A. J. P. TAYLOR

To the men of the time, however, France represented the ideal and the model. France had supplied the tradition which even a revolution needs; and in 1848 new legends were added to the old. Sensitive, prescient, and politically mature, the French did not merely recapitulate the events of previous revolutions; in the June Days they hit on the social question, and in Louis Napoleon threw up the political form of the future—the plebiscitarian dictator. The French revolution of 1848 suffers, if anything, from the excellence of what has been written about it. De Tocqueville, the greatest political writer of the nineteenth century, observed it at close quarters; Lamartine's history was without rival as an account of a revolution by one who had taken highest part in it—until his book was eclipsed by the similar history of Trotsky; and Marx devoted to the French revolution the two most brilliant (and misleading) of his historical pamphlets. It is hard for the workaday historian to break through a cloud of such genius; and the essay of Professor Bourgin is therefore of particular importance. All the same, its proportions reveal, if only unconsciously, the dwindling of France which was the most significant international revelation of 1848. All Europe had expected revolutionary France to march anew and to liberate, at least, the two martyred nations, Poland and Italy. Instead the short section on foreign affairs describes a France more resolutely pacific even than in the time of Louis Philippe. The failure to launch a general war for the sake of Poland or even to go to the assistance of Italy, in a word the foreign policy of Lamartine, marked the decisive step on the path that led to Munich and to French renunciation of her position as a Great Power.

In French eyes, the Italian revolution sprang from the French and echoed it; to the Italians, the revolutions of 1848 marked the emancipation of Italy as much from French as from German hegemony. Therefore, though the Italian chapter follows the French, it also challenges it and seeks to display an independent revolution. Certainly Mazzini was more than a translation into Italian of the ideas of the French revolution; and events in Italy had a time table independent from the main edition in Paris. Nevertheless, the fate of the Italian revolution was not determined by forces within Italy. Austria did not withdraw; France failed to intervene. These were the two decisive facts in the history of the Italian revolution; and the lesson was not lost on the Italians. Italy could be great or even independent only by balancing between France and the dominant power in central Europe, whether Austria or Germany. Hence the Italians grasped the decline of France sooner than the French themselves; and for a century they have both regretted and sought to benefit from it. France was called upon to be strong enough to expel the Germans from northern Italy, but Italy hoped then to become the predominant 'Latin sister'. Thus implicit in the events of 1848 is the aspiration towards an adventurous independent policy as a Great Power which ultimately, in the days of Mussolini, brought both Italy and Mussolini to disaster.

Still, despite jealousies, there was an underlying similarity between the French and Italian revolutions; and this similarity is even more marked in the radical movements in the countries within the French orbit from Belgium to Scandinavia. Even England, though she escaped the revolution, belonged to the world of French politics; and the foreign policy of Palmerston which Mr Bury recapitulates was essentially determined by French motives. Palmerston thought that he had achieved success when he kept France at peace; and his attitude even towards the Hungarian revolution was determined by his desire for a strong Austria which would balance France in central Europe. England was, in fact, of Europe, though not in it.

Once across the Rhine we are in a different world; and this cleavage between France and Germany was itself an outcome of 1848. Germany then opened the breach with the European tradition. It is an illustration of this that a German historian has not been found to write the German chapter. The ostensible aim of the German revolution was 'through unity to freedom'; the events of the revolution showed that unity could be achieved only by power. As Professor Vermeil shows, the effect of 1848 was to move the centre of Germany from Frankfort to Berlin. I would add that the lesson of power was not learnt only by Prussia and the liberals; the extreme radicals also lost faith in idealism and took instead the course of racial demagogy. The essential purpose of German unity was to make Germany a Great Power; and the conflict against authority was transformed into a policy of conquering the peoples of eastern Europe.

For, most of all, the revolutions of 1848 left their mark by their destruction of the moral basis of the Habsburg Monarchy. This is displayed even in this book. The Austrian revolutions had an underlying unity; yet here the Empire has disappeared, and each nationality is treated as though it had been even in 1848 an independent force. Hungary, with its genuine tradition, can survive this treatment; and the essay on Hungary is, in my judgment, an original contribution to historical knowledge. The essays on Austria, Bohemia, and Rumania—even on Poland—represent different aspects of the same events; and are incomprehensible one without the other. Even so they should, in my opinion, be completed by an essay which would deal with the Austrian Empire as a political unit. These essays confirm, too, another rule of 1848: the less mature a people, the more dogmatic its radicalism. This remains true at the present day. Hence one is not surprised to be told of 'the people's government of the new

Rumania' (which is in reality the rule of a narrow dictatorship) that it is inspired by the most dazzling democratic principles. Nor is it surprising to find the rules of Marxism applied to the history of Vienna, a city which in 1848 still lagged economically far behind any large town of western Europe. Here again: the less industry, the more dogmatic the Marxism.

Two topics are left: the romantic revolution that did not take place—the missing revolution in Poland; and the two great countries which escaped the revolution altogether, Russia and the United States. Yet the escape took place in different ways. The idea of 1848 spread later to Russia; and the Russian revolutions of the twentieth century were in the true spirit of 1848. In fact, Russia, missing the disillusionment which followed the failure of 1848, alone retained faith in the revolutionary course. America was already democratic, and therefore for her, though there was no need for revolution, there was no need for disillusionment either. For a generation after 1848, and even longer, America offered to the peoples of Europe the economic and political prizes which failure had denied them in Europe. Still, 1848 left no tradition in either Russia or America. Eighteen forty-nine has some meaning in the history of both countries. For Russia it brought a victorious repression of revolution in Hungary; for America it marked the discovery of gold in California. To the present day, the one Great Power offers Europe repression, the other material wealth. Neither can offer the liberty of spirit which was the true aim of 1848.

THE OPENING OF AN ERA : 1848

EUROPE ON THE EVE
OF THE REVOLUTION

FRANÇOIS FEJTÖ

I

'OLD Europe is dying, the old order is passing away.' So wrote the
exiled Mazzini exactly thirteen years before the February Revolution.
'But,' he hastened to add, with a revolutionary's impatience, 'it's a long
time on its death-bed.'

These words appear in an article entitled 'On the Revolutionary
Initiative in Europe', published in Paris by Godefroy Cavaignac in his
Revue Républicaine. The young author of this article had already quite a
record as a conspirator and a rebel. At the age of sixteen he had sought
admission to the Carbonari lodge at Genoa, his birthplace. He had to
kneel down in front of a man wearing a mask, who brandished a naked
dagger, gleaming in the semi-darkness, and dramatically recited the oath
he was to take. It was a period in which pomp and ceremony attended
every heroic venture, and the real dangers of the fight for freedom were
spiced with the pleasant thrill of a childishly mysterious ritual. Other
initiates had to pass much stiffer tests: in some cases a loaded and fully
cocked pistol was pressed against the candidate's temple, and if he so much
as blinked he was refused admission.

The days of the Carbonari were over, but old Europe, despite the
efforts of the 'Constitutional Brotherhood', still went on living. And yet
there were times, notably in 1830 after the 'three glorious days' in France,
when the news of the revolts in Belgium, Italy and Poland made even the
'Chief Constable of Europe', Metternich, think that it was 'the beginning
of the end'. But the prophets were wrong again: the patient obstinately
clung to life. So perhaps when studying the history of this time we should
ask ourselves not why the peoples of Europe did revolt one after the other
in 1848, but, as Mazzini and other revolutionaries of the years 1830–40
wondered, what had delayed Europe's regeneration for so long. Why had
not popular democratic revolutions broken out long before 1848?

The question is all the more understandable when one remembers that
after the Treaty of Vienna in 1815, which the diplomats considered the
final draft of the map of Europe, everything on the Continent seemed to

have changed with the exception of its frontiers. One of the most intelligent critics of the 1848 Revolution in France, John Stuart Mill, points out this fact in a pamphlet he wrote against Lord Brougham, dealing with the events in Paris. 'The arrangements' of property had changed, he wrote, and so too have 'the distinctions of ranks, the modes of education, the opinions, the manners—everything which affects the European nations separately and within themselves.' What stayed precisely the same, however, was the form of government in each country, in so far as it represented the people's collective interests and their relations with each other. It seems, and recent history appears to confirm, that political institutions are the last to change.

Who would have predicted so lasting a success for the 1815 peace treaty which, in spite of rulers' promises, took no account of the will of the peoples; officially declared null and void all the major intellectual, technical and social developments of half a century; and blandly ignored all the lessons of the Napoleonic experiment? Joseph de Maistre, who can hardly be called a revolutionary, said: 'Never before have nations been treated with such contempt, or kicked about in so infuriating a fashion.' The new map of Europe was drawn up to recreate the balance of power which had existed before the Revolutionary Wars, in contempt of public opinion. The authors of the treaty based their authority on the principle of legitimacy, preached by Talleyrand, but they did not even stick to this principle. They left Bernadotte on the throne of Sweden where Napoleon had installed him, and they let three German princes keep crowns they owed to the benevolence of the ex-Emperor. Yet on the other hand they took away the sovereign rights of the two oldest republics in Europe, Genoa and Venice, and presented one to the King of Sardinia and the other to the Emperor of Austria. The only legitimacy they recognised was that of kingdoms, and then only so long as it did not harm the dynastic interests of the Great Powers.

Yet even today there are numbers of people who admire the work of the 1815 peace treaty. Even an experienced historian like Ferrero considers that its wise provisions preserved Europe for several decades from a new major war. However, there are deeper causes than the perfection of the Treaty of Vienna to explain the relatively long period of peace which followed 1815, a peace broken only by easily localised revolts and fresh incidents marking the eternal rivalry between Russia and Turkey. Toussenal, the author of a revolutionary pamphlet which appeared in 1845, was not far wrong when he explained this long break in warmongering by the fact that the real rulers of the age, the aristocracy of wealth (whom he sometimes refers to by Fourier's term of 'mercantile feudalism') had laid all their stakes on peace. Nowadays it seems almost incredible that there could have been a period in history when the bankers and the big industrialists and even the generals ardently desired peace, whilst a great number of progressives looked to war for the realisation of their hopes. Yet that was the case between 1815 and 1848. It was this era of peace that prolonged the life of old Europe, which was not, as people have so often made it out to be, the last refuge of carefree gaiety, but a world in which royal despotism, aristocratic privilege, obscurantism and a bureaucracy, which had become almost an end in itself, reigned under the protection of an ubiquitous and all-powerful police.

Of course this monarchical Europe only appeared to be homogeneous from a distance. A close observer soon saw the political, social, economic and intellectual differences between the various kingdoms of Eastern, Western and Central Europe. The work of the peace-makers of 1814-15 already showed signs of the heterogeneous character of the coalition against Napoleon in the conflicting interests of the victorious powers: Austria, England, Prussia and Russia. All these Powers may be called reactionary, but there were significant differences in their respective attitudes towards the forces of revolution. To give an instance, ever since the Peace of Amiens, the English reactionaries had increasingly pursued a foreign policy in the interests of the upper-middle class. Russian imperialism, on the other hand, lagging far behind in capitalist and middle-class developments, was of a purely dynastic character.

It is a curious paradox that, during the first half of the nineteenth century, democrats looked upon England as the strongest pillar of reaction, whereas in point of fact she had advanced the furthest in social and economic evolution. On the other hand, the upper-middle class in Europe considered that England was the first nation to have become the model of a free country such as Montesquieu and his disciples of the eighteenth and nineteenth centuries had envisaged. England's middle-class leanings also appeared in her unwillingness to support the interventionist policy of the Holy Alliance. As for the great Canning, whose premature death was mourned by liberals in every country in the world, he used the short term of his ministry to lay the foundations of a liberal foreign policy in the interests of the upper-middle class. Canning was equally eager to help the Greek insurgents and the Spanish colonies which were fighting for their freedom. This great political innovator foresaw that the new states would be in need of money, ships, machines and industrial products, all of which they could get from England. He was not disappointed in his calculations in so far as they concerned Greece. From the very beginning, the new national state became England's client and satellite.

England, whose insular attitude aroused both anger and envy, was

never more powerful nor yet more full of social contradictions and conflicts than she was in the 'forties of the last century. Middle-class and
capitalist developments had hardly begun in Eastern Europe at the time
when in England several millions of her proletariat, already become class-
conscious, were demanding universal suffrage and social justice. Responsible English politicians, Whigs as well as Tories, had for a long time been
living in fear of a revolution. Metternich firmly believed that if revolution
was to break out, England would be the first country to be affected. The
old chancellor shuddered—though not without a thrill of malicious
delight—at the thought of the resounding crash with which that mighty
empire would fall. But English politics succeeded, thanks to the Reform
Bill, in reaching a compromise and winning the support of the liberals
among the middle class. Palmerston's foreign policy already showed signs
of such a compromise between the political conceptions of the old ruling
class and those of the bourgeoisie. That is the most reasonable explanation
of the profoundly equivocal character of his administration which led
some to believe he was in the pay of Russia and others that he was a secret
agent of the Carbonari. Marx, who looked upon Palmerston as the chief
enemy of revolution, has sketched a brilliant portrait of the British
Foreign Secretary: 'He can disguise the opinions of an oligarch with the
language of a democrat; he can clothe middle-class, commercial pacificism
with the proud speech of an aristocrat of the old school, he can feign the
offensive when he is giving way and the defensive when he intends
betrayal; he can spare an imaginary foe as gracefully as he can leave his
ally in the lurch; he knows the exact moment to take his stand with the
strongest against the weakest, and he has the art of speaking his bravest
words in full flight.'

Palmerston subordinated every moral and ethical consideration to the
task of upholding England's greatness. His policy towards France was
determined by the economic and political rivalry between the English
and French middle classes. With the full support of the English middle
class, Palmerston did all he could to hinder France's expansion, whether
it was to be through the annexation of Belgium, the strengthening of
Franco-Spanish relations, or the establishment of French bases in the
Near East.

But England's attitude of hostility and suspicion was not directed only
against that country whose form of government was closest to her own,
it was the same towards the state furthest from her in both space and time.
Palmerston was afraid of Russia. He was determined to protect against her
not only England's hegemony in Europe but also her possessions in Asia.
This fear explains why Palmerston was so eager to support Austria,
despite the antipathy which the English middle class felt for that retro-

grade State. English foreign policy needed the Austrian Empire to frustrate Russia's designs in the Balkans.

During the 'forties, Palmerston supported moderate liberal movements in every country so long as their growth did not conflict with England's imperial interests. Lord Russell, his colleague in the government, described him as doing his best to encourage sovereigns and discourage their subjects, to urge rulers towards a policy of reform, whilst preaching moderation to their peoples. In Italy and Switzerland (at the time of the conflict between the Radicals and the *Sonderbund*), as well as in Spain and Greece, England appeared as the protector of moderate reformers who admired both Britain's liberal Constitution and the immense wealth of her empire. But the Hungarians and Italians, in revolt against Austria, knocked at Palmerston's door in vain. Admittedly the sympathy of the English middle class was with the revolutionaries, but it was more important for him to hold Russia in check than to assure the independence of Hungary and Italy. Later on, England, to her astonishment and ill-concealed satisfaction, was to see Austria saved by Russia, whose interest demanded, if not the liquidation of the Hapsburg Empire, at any rate her emasculation.

On the eve of the year 1848, Metternich was not the only one watching England for the first signs of the coming avalanche of revolution. Engels was equally sure that his friend Harney, the Chartist, would replace Palmerston as Great Britain's Secretary of State for Foreign Affairs. But the social revolution, for which the ground had possibly been better prepared in England than anywhere else, flared up in France. In England it was easily forestalled by far-sighted police preparations. Metternich lost his job, but not Palmerston. The latter sat tight, carrying on even in the year 1848 a foreign policy whose sole aim was to turn the situation produced by the revolution to England's profit.

By contrast with other European States, France had reached a high stage of political and social evolution. Any Russian or Prussian who came to Paris round about 1840 must have found it hard to understand why the French should be dissatisfied with a Constitution, a free press and a degree of personal security which to a liberal foreigner looked like the realisation of his wildest dreams. But behind the façade of prosperity and freedom the will of the monarch, who leaned upon the support of the big financial interests, prevailed in France as it did elsewhere. Caricaturists fittingly drew Louis Philippe wearing city clothes over a suit of medieval armour. The old King was far from content with the purely representative rôle he had been accorded by the Constitution: his one desire was to become his own President of the Council. Guizot, far from influencing his master, merely carried out the latter's foreign policy, which was not always of the

wisest. Although Lamartine may have exaggerated a little in his denunciation of Guizot as 'a priest in Rome, an Austrian in Piedmont, a Russian at
Cracow, and a Frenchman nowhere', it is perfectly true that in his foreign
policy Louis Philippe, whilst quite out of sympathy with the French progressives, had no consistent aims. Emile Ollivier later defined this policy
in his very shrewd remark that the King 'supported the Austrian Alliance
in principle, but nearly always acted like Palmerston'. Guizot succeeded
in alienating not only public opinion in his own country, but also Metternich, who condemned his feeble attitude towards the radicals at the time
of the Civil War in Switzerland, while at the same time the Italian patriots
attacked him as a reactionary. Moreover, his proposal for a marriage
between Louis Philippe's son and a Spanish princess aroused the suspicions
of the English, who were always ready to suspect France of aiming at
world domination. As Lamartine pointed out, this marriage revealed how
little Louis Philippe really believed in his policy of peace at any price, and
proved that he was essentially as strong a defender of 'the dynasty' as any
of his predecessors.

The French people had very little to do with all this scheming and
plotting. The Chamber of Deputies consisted of the delegates of an
insignificant minority, representing an electorate of barely two hundred
thousand. It was not exactly difficult to govern with so carefully chosen
and easily corruptible a legislative body. Nor is it surprising that Louis
Philippe was so outspokenly self-confident when the German and Scandinavian Ambassadors visited him to offer their condolences on the death
of Madame Adelaide. 'Tell your masters,' he said, 'not to worry about
popular assemblies. They have only to handle them as I do mine.' It was
perhaps this very complacency of Louis Philippe in the last years of his
reign that most infuriated his contemporaries. At any rate, it is what has
made that unhappy king so unsympathetic a character in the eyes of
posterity. France owed her immense prestige in Europe, not to her
sovereign, nor even to her form of government, but to the eminence of
the Opposition leaders and of her writers and thinkers. Thanks to these
men, Paris became the centre in which the spiritual unity of 'Young
Europe' was built up. Thanks to them, observers of such widely differing
opinions as the moderate Liberal Lorenz Stein, and the communist Engels,
were able to form identical judgments on the history of France after 1789.[1]

The young Kingdom of Belgium, which had come into being at the
instigation of England and of the traditional ruling classes (the aristocracy,

---

[1] 'In France more than anywhere else, the historical class struggles were always fought to a
finish.' (F. Engels, Preface to the 3rd German Edition of Marx's *The Eighteenth Brumaire*)
'The history of France is simply the history, in its most purely national form, of the laws
governing political and social movements.' (L. Stein, *Histoire du mouvement social en France
de 1789 à nos jours*, page 184)

the upper clergy and the upper-middle class), was henceforth one of the organic elements of Western Europe and an important factor in maintaining the balance of power. The Belgian radicals who still hoped, as they had hoped in 1830, for union with France, had little influence. Besides, Belgium was unable to pursue an independent foreign policy. From the moment the 1848 Revolution broke out in Paris, Leopold of Saxe-Coburg turned to England for advice and instructions. Once revolutionaries, armed with French passports, started to cross the Belgian frontier, there would be danger of European complications, so those like Karl Marx who happened to be staying in Belgium were bustled back into France.

France, England, Belgium, Holland, Switzerland (which had only just recovered from its own domestic crisis), Sweden and Denmark began in the year 1848 in the modern form of constitutional nation States. In comparison with these flourishing States of Western and Northern Europe, Germany and Italy were mere geographical and ethnographical terms—myths, in fact. The Holy Roman Empire, which had been dealt its final blow by Napoleon, had been replaced by a federation whose thirty-eight members represented practically every form of government from the City State to Absolute Monarchy, passing through various degrees of constitutional principality. The chaos in Germany—and it is the only word to describe the situation at the time—was a miniature replica of the general confusion in Europe. The growing middle classes, seeing what was going on in France, England and America, had been fighting for years to extend their civil liberties in each of the thirty-eight States of the federation. In certain parts, such as the Southern states and Hanover, their guerilla warfare met with some success. The princes of these countries deigned, after considerable bargaining, to grant their subjects a constitution. But on each occasion the 'agreement' had to be taken before the Diet at Frankfort to be ratified. And in the Diet (at which only the eleven most important states were represented) the word of Prussia and Austria was law. The kings and princes, after pretending to become suddenly imbued with the spirit of reform, soon got the Diet to revoke their promises, their regrets on the matter being wholly hypocritical. They had gone on playing this comedy, with variations, for nearly twenty years, when the middle-class liberals in Germany realised that these partisan efforts were doomed to failure unless they could force the idea of constitutional government on Prussia. One has only to look at the size of the population of Germany to understand Prussia's predominance, as she alone possessed sixteen million inhabitants, whereas the remaining twenty-eight million Germans were divided amongst thirty-six states. That is why the whole of Germany pricked up its ears at the news that the King of Prussia had invited the representatives of his different provinces to meet in a central Diet. Up to 1847 these representatives had met separately in provincial assemblies. For some time Germany had been eagerly following the battle being waged by the middle class of Munich against Louis I of Bavaria. They were not, however, fighting for a constitution, they simply wanted to end this bohemian and extravagant king's scandalous liaison with the lovely Scottish dancer, Lola Montez. This lofty moral aim united the clergy, the aristocracy and the tax-paying members of the middle class. The convocation of the Prussian Diet, although as a feudal assembly[1] it was scarcely representative of public opinion, nevertheless gave the German people something more serious to think about: the cause of constitutional reform.

Ever since Hegel, more and more Germans had been asking themselves 'why the French put their theories into practice straight away, whereas the Germans never got beyond the theory'. A young pupil of Hegel's, Karl Marx, wondering why the German revolution had been so long delayed, came to the conclusion that in future his compatriots would never be able to bring about one which was purely political. Any revolution in Germany could lead only to a clean sweep in moral and social behaviour. Naturally, the middle classes of Prussia, Bavaria and Württemberg would be content with less than that; their object was to extend the economically successful Customs Union to all the States of Germany, and to crown their work with a moderate constitutional reform. Frederick William IV —who was rumoured to have liberal opinions when he came to the throne, but whose faith in the principles of absolute monarchy was second only to his belief in the universal mission of the Hohenzollerns—was determined to defend his privileges to the last.

Italy—so similar to Germany in her backward condition and policy of particularism—nevertheless had one advantage over her, in that she could blame a foreign conqueror for having prevented the Italian people from becoming a nation. A large part of Italy, Lombardy and the province of Venetia, was directly governed by Austria, who also exercised an indirect influence over Parma, Piacenza, Guastalla, Lucca, Modena and Tuscany. The remainder of the peninsula was divided between the Kingdom of Naples, Piedmont and the Papal States. All the Italians agreed that the expulsion of Austria was the first and principal step towards emancipation. Opinions differed, however, as to whether the people should fight on their own—with the view of establishing a republic—or with the help of the King of Piedmont, or even under the orders of the Pope. In 1847, to Metternich's great indignation, Pope Pius IX decided on liberal reform, thereby winning over to the papacy the majority of Italian patriots,

---

[1] 10,000 landowners sent 300 representatives to the Diet, whereas the 4,000,000 inhabitants of 979 towns only sent 182.

including even the most violent anticlericals. The Pope's rival, Charles Albert, who ruled Piedmont as autocratically as Frederick William IV ruled Prussia, was a man of hesitant character, who had a superstitious terror of the people, but nevertheless hoped to use the democrats to further his own dynastic ambitions.

Germany and Italy each formed a no-man's-land for the battle between the Great Powers of Europe. The determining factors in the politics of Central and Eastern Europe were Prussia, Russia and Austria. These three pillars of the Holy Alliance were united only by their determination to hold on to their common prey, Poland, and by their fear of each other. The happy thought of partitioning Poland (which had been conceived in the evil and brilliant brain of Frederick II in 1763) had for more than eighty years maintained the closest friendship between three States which, by their past as well as their future interests, were destined to come to blows. So as to safeguard her alliance with Russia, Austria renounced the House of Hapsburg's traditional policy in South-East Europe, which might easily have led to friction with the Czar. Besides, it seemed doubtful whether expansion was in the best interests of an Austria which had been so richly endowed at the Congress of Vienna. The Hungarians had already begun to feel that there were too many Slavs within the Empire, and were categorically opposed to expansion towards the Balkans.

When in 1846 Austria annexed the Free State of Cracow, which the Congress of Vienna had preserved as an independent republic, she broke a treaty whose support was the mainspring of her policy. Yet Russia denied the spirit of the Holy Alliance when, in spite of Metternich's repeated requests, she not merely refused to suppress the insurgents in Greece, but substantially helped them to achieve national independence. The appearance of an independent Greece was the one event in the period 1815–48 which shook the foundations of the Europe of the Treaty of Vienna even more than the independence of Belgium. No country was more deeply affected than Austria. The very existence of her monarchy depended on the suppression of Polish, Czech, Slovenian and Italian national feelings. If the principle of nationality which had appeared as the result of the revival of Greek independence was going to spread throughout Europe, Italy and Germany would become single nations whilst the Austrian and Ottoman Empires would dissolve into their constituent parts. The Austrian Council of State did its utmost to avert disaster by a most skilful application of the 'Divide and Rule' principle: order was maintained in the Italian provinces by Hungarian and Croat garrisons, in Hungary by Czechs, and in Poland by Austrians and Italians. Thus a natural antagonism towards an army of occupation was turned by Vienna against the different nationalities composing her empire.

But Austria did not stop at stirring up hatred between different peoples living within her borders, between the Hungarians and the Slavs, for instance; she also aroused class hatred. When, in 1846, the Poles of Austrian Galicia revolted in an attempt to win back their country's independence, Austria did not hesitate to get the Ruthenian peasants to rise against the nobles who formed the greater part of the movement. The combined forces of the Imperial Army and the national *jacquerie* smashed the revolt. This had a considerable effect on the peoples of Central and South-East Europe.[1] The Hungarians, in particular, sat up at the news of this rising. Although they lived under much better conditions, as they enjoyed a certain degree of autonomy within the Kingdom, their problems had a number of points in common with those of their neighbours to the north east. In Hungary as in Poland the nobles led the movement for reform, and the fight against Vienna was greatly complicated by the nationalities situated between the Carpathians, where national conflicts were confused by class warfare between feudal overlords and oppressed serfs.

The central position of the Council of State which controlled the affairs of the Austrian Empire enabled it to aggravate the growing conflicts between the different nationalities and classes, so that it could afterwards play the rôle of a beneficent intermediary. The radicals of the 'forties believed that if they could attack the very seat of monarchy—Vienna itself—they would be able to cut the bonds of so many nations. We shall see how mistaken they were. But then we realise today that Austria would have been in a better position if she had not won hands down in 1814, 1830 and 1848. In the end, what is the value of a power which relies not on its own strength but on its victim's weakness? After Austerlitz, Baron Gentz, the publicist and diplomat who later became a friend of Metternich, wrote a remarkable memorandum in which he advised the Emperor to take a lesson from his successive set-backs and the loss of the Imperial crown. He should transfer the capital of the Kingdom from Austria to Hungary, and form a 'federal' empire consisting of the latter country together with Bohemia, Galicia and the remnants of his possessions in Germany.[2]

With her social structure engulfed in feudalism, with her police force (in 1847 the Kingdom spent only 37,000 florins on the State schools, whereas the police cost her 1,131,000 florins), with her censorship, of which celebrated Viennese writers like Nestroy, Grillparzer and Raymund

---

[1] 'The Cracow affair had tremendous repercussions in the East', wrote the French diplomat J. Thouvenel, that same year, from Athens. (J. Thouvenel, *La Grèce du roi Othon*, Paris 1890)

[2] *Memorandum on the means of assuaging the perils and calamities in Europe and on a system of pacification.* Published in *Aus dem Nachlass*, 1838. (Vol. II, Supplement to Chap. 5, pages 96–7)

complained so bitterly, and with her inefficient and officious Civil Service, Austria was the very symbol of old Europe. Even her enemies had to admit that she was faithful to her principles. Russian policy was much less homogeneous. The Czar used the same methods as the reactionaries of Austria and Prussia in his dealings with the Poles and the Finns. But the members of the Orthodox Church in the Balkans regarded him as their protector and looked to Moscow for their liberation. How could Russia resist the passionate appeal of a people whose undying ambition was to escape from the domination of Turkey? Although Napoleon's prophecy that Europe would turn Cossack terrified a considerable number of progressives in Europe there were certainly others, particularly in the 'forties, who were beginning to feel sympathetic towards that mysterious and powerful empire. In France, Custine's book largely helped to awaken this sympathy. In England, Cobden and his friends were spreading propaganda in favour of Russia, who they felt was more susceptible to progressive ideas than Turkey, the 'sick man of Europe'.

It was a public scandal that Austrian absolutism had completely reversed the reformist policy of Joseph II, ever since 1792 when Leopold II died. But Russian Czarism, it was felt, was still at a stage when it could accomplish the major task of curtailing age-old privileges and freeing the *moujik*.

In 1848, Marx was convinced that 'the re-establishment of a democratic Poland was essential to the formation of a democratic Germany' (*Neue Rheinische Zeitung*, 7 August). The liberals and the democrats of Europe firmly believed that the freeing of Poland from Russian, Prussian and Austrian domination, even at the price of war with Russia, was an essential step not merely towards the creation of German democracy but towards the final victory of democracy in Europe. Still, there were others who wondered whether the Polish serf was not better off under the present Warsaw government than he would be in a Poland where the nobles had regained their former privileges. Proudhon himself protested against the extravagances of those friends of Poland who wanted the Russians to be barred from Europe as an Asiatic race. Anyway, in 1848, the actions of the Czar Nicholas were those not so much of the representative of Russia's imperialist interests as of the chief defender of reactionary Absolutism. Five years later, at the time of the Crimean War, he admitted himself that he had 'blundered' in supporting Austria against Hungary without asking for anything in return.

The most rotten State in the whole of old Europe was what remained of the once powerful Ottoman Empire after she had lost Bessarabia, Greece had won her freedom and Serbia semi-independence, and the so-called 'Danubian Provinces' had for all practical purposes come under the direct influence of Russia. Greece's example had shown the peoples of

South-East Europe the advantages and disadvantages of escaping from the Turkish yoke. The Greece of Otho I, which had become a constitutional monarchy in 1843, was an arena for the conflicting interests of England, Russia and France. The State's continued existence was assured by a loan of which the conditions—according to Thouvenel—were such that 'if they were put before a court of law, the three guarantor governments would be convicted of usury'. At the same time, during its twenty years 'independence', the country had made considerable technical progress. During the 'forties the question of Rumania, and even of Bulgaria, began to be raised. It was the awakening of the Slavonic world. What had happened to the Grand Duchy of Posen aroused even Albania from her lethargy. The intellectuals of Bohemia and the Southern Slavonic countries were preparing plans for the partition of Austria, which were realised in 1919 at Versailles.

All the peoples of old Europe were beginning to stir, from Denmark to Montenegro, and from Spain to Finland. But what was the young Europe? What was behind it? Whence came this new power, with its warlike songs, and oaths, and sinister prophecies? Young Europe was the dream of people who were still young themselves, with no experience in political warfare. Its godfather was Mazzini, so it was both nationalist and cosmopolitan. When, in 1830, the hero of Italy's emancipation came out of prison, the first question he asked was not about his own country: he wanted to know what had become of Poland. In the secret federation which was formed in Switzerland in 1834 under the name of 'Young Europe', there were Italian, Polish, German and Swiss sections. Another typical representative of young Europe, Harro-Haring, the Danish apostle of Scandinavianism, had fought for freedom in Greece, Poland and Germany.

One might say that young Europe consisted simply of the proud youth of old Europe, who with their faith in liberty, equality and fraternity, believed that the emancipation of each individual nation would result in the unity of the peoples. This youth suffered persecution, imprisonment and death for the sake of its ideals, and between 1815 and 1848 gave tens of thousands of lives to create a free Italy, a united Germany, an independent Poland, and a reborn Greece. Young intellectuals were in the opposition everywhere, but this was especially noticeable in France, where disillusion had been the greatest after 1830. Balzac paints a heart-rending picture of this disillusion in the words he puts in the mouth of his hero Marcas, in 1840: 'August 1830 passed by the young, supple minds. Youth has no outlet in France today, and is going to blow up like the boiler of a steam engine. . . . Nowadays, brains are on the side of the

[1] op cit., p. 38

barbarians. . . . Louis XIV and Napoleon used to, and England still does, snap up young men with brains. . . . Youth will remember the youthful representatives of the people and the youthful generals.'[1] Lamartine and Victor Hugo were at one in denouncing the rule of the 'Golden Mean', which left the young with no future, no path to follow, no ideals and no hope.

Our rapid survey of the map of Europe throws light on one of the causes which enabled the old order to keep going so long, in spite of the far-reaching changes in the material and intellectual elements of its civilisation: the solidarity of the great reactionary Powers. The nations striving for freedom had no Holy Alliance with which to counter that of Europe's rulers. From 1815 to 1848, all attempts at liberation in Europe were nipped in the bud, with the exception of the French, Belgian and Greek Revolutions, and the movement to unite Switzerland. If in a few exceptional cases insurrections were not crushed, that was because it was possible to localise them. The reactionary doctrine of intervention, which was formulated at the Treaty of Reichenbach in 1790, and finally adopted at the Congress of Troppau in 1820, could surely not have been combated except by a simultaneous rising all over the world? In his prophetic preface to his *Feuilles d'Automne*, 20 November 1831, Victor Hugo wrote that he already heard 'the dull sound of revolution, still deep down in the earth, pushing out under every kingdom in Europe its subterranean galleries from the central shaft of the mine which is Paris'.

Young Europe was a kind of intellectual striking power of the new forces which, ever since the French Revolution, had set out to demolish the rotting political structures of the continent. Before we review the currents of thought—liberalism, nationalism, democracy, republicanism and socialism—which characterise this new Europe, let us try to discover what were the social conditions and aims behind these ideas.

2

The first half of the nineteenth century was remarkable for the immense increase in means of production. The most prolific was the most important: man himself. In 1850, there were nearly 80 million more Europeans than there had been at the beginning of the century. The population rose from 188 to 267 millions, making an increase of nearly forty per cent. The proportion was even higher in Great Britain. In 1801, the United King-

[1] Balzac, *Scènes de la vie politique, Z. Marcas*, 1840

dom, excluding Ireland, possessed ten and a half million inhabitants, but in 1831 the figure was well over sixteen million. In France, the population increased by 30 per cent in the first fifty years of the century, and it is estimated that the population of Austria increased at about the same rate. The population of Hungary, between the years 1785 and 1840, rose from seven to twelve million. There are a number of reasons for this sudden increase in population, of which the most important are developments in medical science and education, and the steady industrialisation of Europe. The social importance of man's fecundity at this period can hardly be exaggerated. The simple fact of this surplus population brought about changes in existing institutions in each state as well as the creation of new ones, and generally started people thinking about social problems. It was not by chance that in the 'twenties the followers of Saint-Simon first used the word 'masses' in its modern sense. In the eighteenth century there were only communities, and groups of people. With the nineteenth century began the era of the masses. Yet this was also the era of Romanticism and its emphasis on the personality of the individual. These two trends, which seem contradictory, are, in fact, closely connected. The appearance of the masses was only made possible by an increased respect for the individual. We have just mentioned progress in medicine as one of the chief reasons for the growth of Europe's population. But what is the application of medicine other than a positive attitude towards life, the practical expression of a desire to give the individual a better chance of survival?

Progress in medicine filled the towns instead of the cemeteries. In the first instance, the big towns absorbed the surplus population of the countryside. Whereas the total population of France increased by thirty per cent in fifty years, that of Paris was doubled. The population of Lyons and Marseilles increased by seventy-five per cent, and the growth of some of the smaller industrial towns was even more striking: in 1800 Saint-Etienne had some sixteen thousand inhabitants; fifty years later, there were fifty-six thousand. Between 1820 and 1830 English industrial towns such as Sheffield, Birmingham, Manchester and Liverpool grew even more rapidly, and by 1851 half the population of England consisted of town-dwellers. At the same period in France, only ten and a half per cent of the population lived in areas of more than twenty thousand inhabitants, but the tendency was the same as in England. The industrial towns of Belgium, Italy and Germany—and even of the Austrian provinces—grew at the same rate. The eighteenth century was still a century of the market town; the nineteenth became the century of the big city. And ever since, the cities have been imposing their rhythm on the rest of the country.

All this, however, did not solve the whole problem of the countryside.

Urban influence was widely felt only in Western Europe. In the East it was no more than a vague tendency. The towns, in the modern sense of the word, merely grew up like coral reefs out of the blank expanse of the ocean, surrounded by the wastes of medieval feudalism. In France, as in Southern and Central Germany, the peasants had been freed from feudal exploitation in the eighteenth century, and both their social and material position had been strengthened. In Prussia, on the other hand, as well as in Mecklenburg and Holstein, small-scale had merely given way to large-scale exploitation by the great landowners. In most of the Austrian provinces, and in Poland, Hungary and the greater part of the Balkans, feudalism reigned with undiminished strength. The ruling class was composed of nobles, who were either landowners or in charge of the administration. In Austria, the upper grades of government service and the church were the exclusive preserve of the aristocracy. Up to the end of the eighteenth century, the aristocracy of Eastern Europe took the lead in social progress, and supported the reforms of such 'enlightened' sovereigns as Frederick II, Maria Theresa and Joseph II. Robert Endres rightly remarks that the French Revolution not only put a stop to the reforming activities of princes, but at the same time radically changed the political and social attitude of the aristocracy. In the eighteenth century the despots of Central Europe felt secure in the saddle, but in the light of the dramatic events in France, it dawned on them that the development of the middle class was a menace to their leadership. Almost automatically, they took the defensive. The less secure they felt, the more vainglorious and fatuous became their behaviour. The extent of the possessions owned by the big lay and ecclesiastical landowners was the real foundation of the old, monarchical order in Europe.

Throughout almost the whole of Eastern Europe, the peasantry was living under even worse conditions than those existing in France before the 1789 Revolution. It is true that Joseph II, by his decrees of 1781 and 1785, had abolished 'the very name of serfdom' in Hungary and Austria, but the aristocrats and the administration, which was entirely under their control, had sabotaged measures intended to improve the peasants' lot, even during the Emperor's life-time. These measures were completely rescinded after his death. According to Ervin Szabo, the Hungarian serfs in the nineteenth century lived under conditions worse than those which Joseph II, touring his kingdom half a century before, had described as 'schrecklich'—appalling. As the nobles were exempt from any kind of taxation, it was the peasants who had entirely to support the public services: taxes levied by the State, the Department and the Commune; public works; construction of roads; the expenses of sending representatives to the Diet; and the upkeep of the army by levies of men and money.

And above and beyond this, the greater part of the peasants' work went towards the payment of tithes in money and kind, and statute labour exacted by their overlords. In Moravia, the peasant had 242 different obligations towards the landowner; in Carniola the number was 123. According to Endres, even in the mountain regions of Austria, where conditions were infinitely better than in the rest of Europe, the peasant had to pay half a dozen different taxes to his overlord, on top of the rent of his land. So it is understandable that the spectre of the *Jacquerie* was ever hovering over Eastern Europe. Joseph II had already threatened to support a peasant's revolt, in order to force the aristocracy of Hungary, Transylvania and Poland to accept the administrative reforms he considered essential to strengthen the international position of the Empire. In 1831 the cholera epidemic, which ravaged Eastern Europe, caused the peasants to rise in more than one district.

Considering its growth in numbers during the first decades of the century—and the consequent increase in poverty—the downtrodden peasantry of Eastern Europe might have provided the force to smash feudalism. But there was no social class capable of starting the war and carrying it through. Although the rural population in these countries was larger and worse off than it had been in France in 1789, the middle classes had nothing like the same strength, either in numbers or in spirit. In the 'forties, the middle classes of Berlin, Vienna, Budapest and Cracow were barely out of the age of the medieval guilds; the towns of Hungary were, in fact, no more than overgrown market towns. In 1839, there were only 117,000 people engaged in industry in the whole country, but there were 136,000 noble families, totalling approximately 680,000 persons, which means that one out of every twenty Hungarians was a noble. Those who exercised the liberal professions, called in Eastern Europe '*Lateiner*' from their knowledge of Latin, were recruited not from the middle classes but from the lower ranks of the nobility. Since 1789 this class had considered itself the backbone of the nation, and assumed the rôle played in France by the Third Estate. The most intelligent of the nobles genuinely considered themselves to be liberals. Quite a number of the Polish aristocrats who revolted in 1846 held theories which were already in advance of middle-class liberalism, and bordered on socialism.

However, the reformatory ideology of these liberals and their sympathy for the people conflicted with their own material interests, which were opposed to any radical change in the social structure. The chapters of this book dealing with the Hungarian and Polish Revolutions show in detail the practical consequences of this conflict.

3

In Eastern Europe the landed gentry strove to fill the place of the middle class, but in the West, where they had been progressively pushed into the background, they were fully occupied in holding on to what they had managed to save, and had handed over the reins to the middle classes. Thus the nineteenth century which, as we have seen, was remarkable for its growing forces of production, the appearance of 'the masses', and the acceptance of the importance of the individual, may fairly be called— from 1847 onward—the Century of the Middle Class. The bankers, and the heads of industry and commerce set their seal on all the undertakings of the period. Even those who loathed their unscrupulous egoism, admired their inventive spirit and enterprise. The *Communist Manifesto*, which appeared on the eve of the 1848 Revolution, intoned a veritable panegyric of the middle classes. History has never known a social class which has so completely changed the face of the world. The origins of this change are to be found in the Industrial Revolution, which was the result of the invention of the steam engine and the power-loom and many other scientific discoveries. The middle class founded industry on a large scale. The family workshop with its tiny output was replaced by factories employing first hundreds, then thousands of workmen. The whole perspective was changed.

Ever since the eighteenth century, statesmen had attached considerable importance to economic questions, and in the course of the first half of the nineteenth century they became their main preoccupation. The astounding progress of British industry, and the efforts of French industrialists to imitate it, started a race for raw materials, labour and markets to speed the output of their products. These new needs changed the traditional aspect of imperialist rivalry. English and French interests clashed in the Middle East: in Syria, Egypt and Greece. It was more important than ever for England to remain mistress of the seas. In the interests of peace, the French middle classes resigned themselves to taking second place, and merely resolved to take their revenge at the first possible opportunity. Economic rivalry stirred up national feelings, for the capitalist becomes patriotic when he meets competition. The new ruling class did as the old aristocracy had done before, it identified its interests with those of the nation as a whole. In the backward countries too, it was the rising middle class which gave the impetus to the process of evolution whereby the divided peoples of Europe acquired national consciousness.

The concentration of banking, commerce and industry furthered developments towards political unity. The fact of Prussia's serving the interest of the German middle class by forming a Customs Union had a major influence on the future of Germany. Economic collaboration made for an understanding which formed the basis of political unity.

Capitalist nationalism was divided: one party favoured Free Trade and the other Protection. The English middle class was not afraid of competition and supported Free Trade, whereas France, dreading British superiority, favoured Protection. Besides, the French middle class's traditional desire for some degree of security curbed any urge to take a chance, so propaganda in favour of Free Trade gained little ground. Capitalists in Germany and, for the most part, in Central Europe, had every reason to welcome state protection as a means of making the consumer bear the considerable expenses of production incurred by a brand-new venture. Nevertheless, the protectionists of these countries admired England, 'the creative force of the middle-class order', as much as the free-traders. Frederick List, who founded the protectionist system in Germany, called on his compatriots to follow the example of Cobden's disciples in England. 'Great Britain', he wrote, 'by taking the lead in scientific, and for the most part, in economic progress, has attained a degree of power and national wealth, without parallel in the history of the world.' This quotation suffices to show the extent to which the middle classes in Europe thought along national lines when considering the situation of the working class. The Chartists, however, and Frederick Engels, whose study of the positions of the labouring classes in England appeared in 1845, took a rather different view of England's 'national' wealth from that held by the economists, who confused a small rich section of the middle class with the nation.

Almost everywhere, the capitalists protested against backward social conditions which hamstrung their plans, and they strove to awaken their compatriots' pride, to force them to follow England's example and speed the modernisation of their country. Thus, capitalist methods accelerated the formation of national states, whilst international commerce and progress in means of communication brought the peoples closer together. Capitalism was both national and international. Britain played a large part in the formation of new railway companies in France, and Mr Bury tells us how, in 1847, the Bank of England hurried to the aid of the Bank of France, when the latter was in temporary difficulties. The crisis in England was to have its repercussions in every European country in the process of industrialisation.

The invention of the railway and the construction of the great lines of communication made nonsense of the obstacles in the way of passenger and goods transport. Once the middle class had made it possible to travel quickly they wanted to do so as freely as they liked. On the eve of 1848, rail transport had begun in most European countries. In 1841 Austria had a railway network of 345 miles. By 1851 it covered 1,332 miles. In 1848

Italy's network covered 256 miles. Delio Cantimori gives us a picturesque detail of the early days of the railway in Italy, where chapels were built in stations so that travellers could render thanks to the Almighty for a safe arrival. The revolutions and wars of liberation in 1848 revealed the strategic importance of the railway. The French government had loyal troops brought to Paris by train, and Jean Bartier recounts the misfortunes of the Belgian republicans who in their attempt to reach the Franco-Belgian frontier and start a revolution in their own country, caught a train which bore them into the very centre of the royalist army. In 1849 the line between Pest and Szolnok and the Austrian railways were both used a great deal to transport troops.

But whereas the real significance of the railway did not appear until several decades later, the revolutionary influence of the steamship was obvious in the 'forties. The European of the nineteenth century felt he was far closer to the New World than his ancestors. It was some time before the railway was to unite Europe, but the steamship had already made a single entity of the world; China was being opened to European commerce as well as the Balkans. Middle-class civilisation began to creep into all the maritime countries through their ports, and within a few years the Piraeus and Patras were unrecognisable. The international traffic of the port of Varna was the starting point of the nationalism and subsequent liberation of the Bulgarians on the Lower Danube. Between 1830 and 1850 the volume of English and French overseas trade was doubled, and that of Germany, tripled. The sole reason Austria's increase was less remarkable (from 320 million gold marks to only 580 million) was doubtless the fact that most of her exports went to Hungary. But steam navigation, as well as being a factor leading to revolution, at the same time eliminated its causes. During the course of the nineteenth century, the steamship enabled tens of thousands of Germans, Irish and Scandinavians to find a new home in America. It is an indisputable fact that the emigration of people living under unbearable conditions relieved the pressure on the old order. Thus it is understandable that German progressives—from Heine to Marx—strove to persuade their compatriots to create the conditions of a free, happy life, not in America but in their own country.

4

The ascendency of the middle class was not only accompanied by the construction of ports and railway stations, the installation of machinery and blast furnaces, the foundation of Corn and Stock Exchanges, and the replanning of towns and waterways. There were intellectual as well as economic forces at work. At this point it may be as well to draw a distinction between England and the Continent. The French and German middle classes had become self-conscious through their intellectuals. They knew they owed their rise to power to the pioneers of the French Revolution, to men like Voltaire, Rousseau, Beaumarchais and the Encyclopedists. We find a large number of intellectuals among the leading spirits of the July Revolution, and, between 1830 and 1848, writers, scholars and lawyers formed the greater part of the revolutionary General Staff. In Germany, too, most of the mouthpieces of the political revival were poets and philosophers. Lacking a free press, and unable to play an active parliamentary rôle, the politically minded turned to literature, natural science and philosophy. The works of Hegel are saturated with political theory. The great philosophers considered the French Revolution to have played a decisive part in the evolution of mankind. 'For the first time since the sun appeared in the heavens, and the planets began to revolve round it, man took up his stand as a thinking animal and began to base his view of the world on reason.' Hegel's cautious and academic jargon was translated into plainer language by Heine and, later, by the Hegelian Radicals. They were enthusiastic over their discovery of the political implications of the Berlin philosopher's writings. Hegel expressed a conviction that before the French Revolution, the history of mankind had followed what might be termed a 'natural' course, determined by economic, geographical and intellectual factors. In 1789, however, the French middle classes, realising where their aims and interests lay, interrupted the march of history, and by the voluntary acceptance of certain laws, found a rational basis for social institutions.

The middle class on the Continent was rationalist, following sometimes Bacon, sometimes Descartes. Science had never been rated so high as it was at the beginning of the nineteenth century. Capitalism was in need of chemists, doctors, geologists, engineers, jurists, inventors and explorers. The middle class took as its motto Bacon's device: 'Knowledge itself is power'. But this same science which was deified by the free-masonry of the middle class was a dangerous force which could easily get out of hand. It is necessary, I think, to emphasise the fact that by one of those curious paradoxes of history, the middle-class intellectuals had not entirely middle-class sympathies. This intelligentsia, although it had sprung from the middle class, did not altogether share its views and feelings, and even if it only dimly understood the historical rôle of the 'Fourth (or proletarian) Estate', it frequently went further than the middle class, at any rate in theory, by adopting various principles of a more advanced radicalism. This was not only so in France. Börne, Heine and the writers of young Germany, the left wing Hegelians, whose word was read with delight by the small but enthusiastic liberal élite of the middle class, were radical democrats and atheists. By 1848, the middle-class intellectuals of Germany had long abandoned a liberalism which the bulk of the middle class had not yet wholeheartedly accepted. A small group of Germans, who were influenced by contemporary French literature, and complacently called themselves 'true socialists', declaimed against parliamentarism and Free Trade, and launched violent tirades about the freedom of the press and equality before the law, forgetting—as Marx pointed out with scathing irony—that one could not waste one's time criticising modern middle-class society in Germany before one had created it. We meet like phenomena—though perhaps in less extravagant guise—in other countries. Whilst in France, writers, political theorists, students and so forth were for the most part republicans, democrats, socialists, or even communists, the cultured middle class in Hungary (if one can call it such) raved about the poems of Petöfi, which were only middle class in the sense that their author had abandoned the pompous feudal style, and wrote verse which was almost as spontaneous as Heine's. He had not, however, the slightest understanding of middle-class interests: his political ideals were most like Babeuf's naïve and mulish utopianism. The relations between the middle classes and the intellectual élite touch on a wider problem, that of the middle-class attitude towards politics.

I have just asserted that the middle class was wholly rationalist, but the facts are not so simple as all that. The middle classes in France had already passed the first major stage of the conflict between rationalism and irrationalism, between the Church and the apostles of freedom. After the pendulum had swung between Jacobinism and the Restoration, this conflict ended in a compromise. Although the Church's position was strengthened in the first decades of the century, it was no longer possible for the clergy to recover their monopoly of education from the State. In the 'thirties, there was already a noticeable *rapprochement* between the Catholics and the middle-class liberals. Stendhal, who was one of the few writers to retain a Voltairian outlook in spite of the fashionable trend towards romanticism, was always satirising the upper-middle classes who were horror-struck when they realised that democratic opinions might lead to a democratic society. This section of the upper-middle class was so afraid of the growth of science that it wanted to put popular education back into the hands of the clergy, and, to set an example, started to go to Church again. But there was another more serious and pathetic move to reconcile the idea of freedom with belief in God. It came from the militant Catholics who, like Lamennais and Montalambert, refused to regard Christ as the exclusive property of royalty and the aristocracy. Lamennais discovered the Christ of the Poor, long before Barbusse. For the most part the intellectual élite of France in the 'forties were not the militant atheists they had been before 1789. Proudhon was one of the few who was later to write the phrase which scandalised so many believers: 'God is Evil'. As Jean Casson points out, most of the revolutionaries of 1848 were possessed by a kind of nebulous religiosity, which searched in vain for a positive form of expression. Naturally this religiosity had nothing in common with the Church; it was much nearer pantheism than belief in a personal God. The two most brilliant anticlerical historians of the 'forties, Michelet and Quinet, were religious by temperament and warmly sympathetic towards popular legends and beliefs.

The ardour of French rationalism was cooled chiefly through the influence of German writers, especially Herder. The German radicals, on the other hand, drew their inspiration from the French eighteenth-century materialists, and were only starting to attack the spiritual foundations of the Church towards 1840. The first blow was struck by Heine, who had seen the full strength of German clericalism at Munich in 1828. 'If we can weaken people's faith', said the poet, 'we will make Germany a political force.' David Strauss, Bruno Bauer and Feuerbach, and later Moses Hess, Karl Marx and his friends followed Heine's lead, by opening their case against society with an attack on religion by which they hoped to weaken the Church.

Whether they were atheists or the staunchest of churchmen, the middle classes still believed firmly in culture, and they strove to give their own children the best possible education. The French were particularly fortunate in their State system. 'No government did more to combat ignorance', writes Charléty, speaking of Guizot's ministry.[1] Public schooling was slowly adapting itself to the needs of the middle class, by coming into closer contact with realities. The classics were no longer paramount, and pupils could take up modern languages if they liked. Science played a larger part in the curriculum, and technical and commercial schools were founded. Guizot's government also did much for primary education. Although they deeply mistrusted the 'scholar gypsy', the upper-middle class realised the need for skilled workmen and better educated farmers. In the reign of Louis Philippe the number of primary schools rose from 30,586 to 63,028, and the number of pupils from 1,837,000 to three and a half million.[2]

During the same period in reactionary Austria, there had been no changes in the educational system which was a legacy from Maria Theresa. There was practically no attention paid to the positive sciences; the only

[1] S. Charléty: 'La monarchie de Julliet' in *L'Histoire de France contemporaine*, by E. Lavisse, page 217
[2] F. Ponteil: *1848*, page 108

modern language middle-class children learnt was German, and the teachers, who were regarded as outcasts, were entirely under the control of the priests.

The intellectual hold of the middle classes also had an effect on literature and the press—in fact, literature was already becoming 'middle class' in the eighteenth century. The 'realistic' approach of middle-class readers largely accounted for the abandoning of classical forms. By comparison with the rigid etiquette of the aristocracy, the middle classes behaved most 'naturally', although today we would consider their manners the height of theatrical affectation. None the less it was the rise of the middle class which banished epic poetry, although a few old fashioned romantic poets attempted to revive it, and verse drama disappeared for years. At a time when reactionary Austria was reading fairy tales, England and France had discovered that most typical middle-class product, the modern novel, which, according to Charléty, was widely read by an entirely new and diverse public. The middle-class critics no longer studied Horace and Sappho, but modern poetry, which Herder suggested should be the model for all young poets.

As soon as writers became politically minded, their work reflected it. Their most eminent representative, Victor Hugo, wrote as follows in his preface to *Feuilles d'Automne*, published in 1831.

'The political moment is fraught with danger . . . beneath the surface lie all the social problems to be reconsidered, and the whole twisted framework of politics to be melted down in the furnace of revolution or hammered out on the echoing anvils of the press . . . meantime, over the face of Europe we see mass-murder, mass-deportation and mass-imprisonment. Ireland is a cemetery, Italy a gaol, and Siberia is peopled with the Poles. At the same time can be heard on all sides . . . the dull sound of revolution, still deep down in the earth, pushing out under every Kingdom in Europe its subterranean galleries from the central shaft of the mine which is Paris. And finally, both above and beneath the surface, men's beliefs are at war and their consciences in travail; and—an evil omen—new religions are stammering out their formulas, some good, some bad, and the old religions are appearing in a new guise.'

In this restless and continually changing world the devotees of science and beauty could not stand apart from the trials of the community. Whether they were solemn prophets like Hugo or Carducci, or ironical observers like Béranger, Heine or Petöfi, they all wrote for the middle class and spoke for the people. The case of Heine is most significant. On several occasions, in both his prose works and his poems, he comes out in favour of poetry's complete independence, and bitterly satirises his young contemporaries for their 'tendentious' verse. But that did not stop him publishing his *Zeitgedichte—Poems of the Age*—which are the best that have ever been written in that genre. If, as Beaumarchais once said, everything that happened in Paris ended up as a song—the singing ended in fighting at the barricades. The 'æsthetic' period, when writers on the whole stood apart from social developments and tried to observe the life of the nation with cold objectivity, was definitely at an end. The writer of 1848, whether he was a poet or a scholar, even if he was not actually a member of any particular political party, took part in his country's social and political movements, and often played a major rôle.

As the authors of the *Communist Manifesto* have shown, the intellectual life of this period bears yet another sign of the contemporary industrial and social revolution. The peoples of the small retrograde countries of Europe acquired their national consciousness through literature. They looked for an intellectual tradition in the past, and by linking themselves to it, attempted to create a modern ideology. The first decades of the nineteenth century saw the development of modern Greek, Hungarian, Czech, Slovak, Croat, Rumanian, Austrian, and other literatures, immediately the intellectual life of each country ceased to be isolated from the rest. Goethe, in his conversations with Eckermann, was the first to point out that a universal literature was about to be born. During the 'thirties and 'forties, this universal literature made enormous strides forward. Balzac, Eugène Sue, Alexandre Dumas, Victor Hugo, Goethe, Heine and Walter Scott had already become 'universal writers' and each new work they published was translated into practically every living tongue. Lamartine's *Histoire des Girondins* was as enthusiastically read in Bucharest and Athens as in Paris. It should be added that this new universal literature was primarily French, if not always in language, at least in spirit and manner. The marvellous flowering of French literature had captivated the whole of Europe. Auguste Comte was perhaps not far wrong when he cried in a moment of exaltation: 'Paris is France—it is the West—it is the whole world!' Conscious of their industrial weakness, the French retreated further and further into economic isolation, but they were the protagonists of free trade in intellectual matters, and one could nowhere find more 'universalists' than in Paris. One review which, in the course of its brief existence, gave space to the foremost writers of France, England and Germany, called itself *Europe Littéraire*. Another, which survived up to our own days, bore the even more ambitious name of the *Revue des deux Mondes*.

The daily press played an even more important part than literature and philosophy in bringing about a revolution in popular thought. The modern press also dates from the 'thirties. The first popular daily in France was *La Presse*, founded in 1836 by Emile de Girardin. The growth of the newspapers' influence is shown by the following figures published by Charléty in his *Histoire de la Monarchie de Juillet*. In 1835 the Paris dailies had a circulation of 70,000. In 1846 the number had risen to 200,000. At this period there were no organised political parties in Europe, and the newspapers took their place. It was not a coincidence that the majority of the members of the French Provisional Government were on the editorial staff of two dailies, the *National* and the *Réforme*. Public opinion in Germany, too, was considerably influenced by such papers as the *Augsburger Allgemeine Zeitung* and the much more radical *Neue Rheinische Zeitung*, published in Cologne. In Hungary, the great democratic leader and propagandist, Kossuth, owed his popularity to the editorials he wrote in the *Pesti Hirlap* which he edited for four years. Everywhere, freedom of the press was the first objective of middle-class liberals. But at the same time there were signs—and in France, too, in the 'thirties—that the bulk of the middle class were not wholeheartedly in favour of a free press. In fact, they sacrificed it willingly enough to safeguard their political interests. In its essentials Louis Philippe's government corresponded to that type of modern government which Marx and Engels in their *Manifesto* described as 'merely a delegation appointed to manage the affairs of the middle class as a whole'. Thus after the revolts and outrages of 1834, that government decreed that any newspaper appearing more than twice a week was to give extremely high security, which in the Seine Department amounted to 100,000 francs. The same law threatened severe sanctions against anyone carrying on propaganda through the press against the system of constitutional monarchy.

5

The middle classes, like the sorcerer's apprentice in the fairy story when the spirits he had conjured up got beyond his control, took fright at the momentum of the economic and intellectual evolution they had set in motion. Their terror was nowhere more strikingly evinced than in their relationships with the proletariat. The wage earner, in the modern sense of the word, is a creation of the middle class, as he is indispensable to capitalist methods of production. His appearance was immediately followed by the birth of the modern working-class movement, which took place, according to Edouard Dolléans, between 1830 and 1836. The capitalist system brought the workers together by concentrating them in large factories, whereas previously they had worked apart from each other. Direct contact made them conscious of their common condition and interests. The results of this were particularly apparent in the course of the industrial crisis in England between the years 1837 and 1843. The English working class was enraged by the Poor Law of 1834, which was a severe blow to its dignity. The workers saw the new 'workhouses' as no better than prisons, since the unemployed were forced to work and live there, far from their families.

The English workers and the French, who revolted in Lyons and Paris in April 1834, just as the weavers in Silesia revolted in 1844, found themselves up against the combined forces of their middle-class employers and the authorities. Thiers showed no mercy in crushing the revolt of the workers which he himself had provoked. 'There must be no quarter given', he said. A few years earlier, Casimir Périer had clearly defined the middle-class attitude towards the working class. 'The workers must realise that their only salvation lies in patient resignation to their lot', was the advice offered by this banker who presided over the government.

The hypocritical indifference of the middle classes disgusted the better members of the intellectual élite. At the beginning of the 'Citizen King's' reign the Saint-Simonians had started a movement 'to raise the material and moral level of the largest social class'. From then onward a whole school of utopian writers began to criticise the rule of the middle class, which was reducing hundreds of thousands of the proletariat to penury, ignorance and physical exhaustion. Besides, the workers' condition was in flagrant contrast with all the ideas of progress on which the middle class, so prided itself. During the 'forties in England, wages barely changed, although the cost of living went up by twenty per cent. The proletariat gained little by patience and proved apt pupils for the political and social theorists who were urging them to prepare for battle.

The appearance of the working class on the political scene had a decisive effect on the attitude of the middle classes. They reacted even more strongly to the communist doctrine. It is fair to say that the tremendous historical significance of communism was understood more quickly by the middle class than by the working class who were primarily concerned. The middle class saw that communism was the logical outcome of democracy, as Balzac expressed it in *Les Paysans*, which paints a vivid picture of the war between the great landowners and the peasantry. The middle class was warned against the dangerous consequences of liberalism by the communists themselves who, like the anonymous author of the *Kommunistiche Zeitschrift*, which appeared in London in 1847, gave away their comrades' plans: 'The middle classes, to establish their supremacy, must obtain political liberties which absolute monarchy stubbornly refuses to grant them, and which we of the proletariat will be able to use later on . . . as levers to overthrow the existing order.'

The political battles of the French Revolution showed that the middle classes in fighting for their own conception of freedom found in the end that they were fighting the very principles on which they had made their stand.

The true theorists of the middle-class revolution, like Mirabeau and Mounier, shared Montesquieu's view of the superiority of constitutional monarchy, which (as could be seen in England) was the form of government best suited to the upper-middle class. Yet why should this be so? First, because in both France and England, in the eighteenth century, as well as in Prussia in the nineteenth, the upper-middle class worked in collaboration with the Crown, and although they had their differences of opinion, these never came to a head. Also, it was most unusual to find any true revolutionaries in the ranks of the middle class. That is one of the most striking paradoxes of modern social history; the middle class played a highly revolutionary part in social and economic development by demolishing outworn institutions so as to replace them by a new system of production and new institutions to meet the needs of capitalism. But just because it devoted its energies and its best qualities to economic reconstruction, the middle class was neither able nor willing to take a subversive part in politics. The upper-middle class, or its social equivalent in the more backward European countries such as the minor nobility in Hungary and Poland were, in 1789 as much as in 1848, in favour of moderate reform. The upper-middle class had no thought of undermining the State's authority. Its representatives were too busy to want to wield political power themselves. The most they wanted was to have their rights and liberties assured by law, and to exercise some control over the way the State worked, principally through its budget. The middle class considered that the ideal form of government was a monarchy whose executive power was controlled by a parliament returned by an electorate chosen according to strict property qualifications. This was the kind of government which the most forward thinking representatives of the middle class in Prussia, Piedmont and Austria wanted in the 'forties.

From the moment the working class appeared on the political scene, the middle class grew more and more suspicious of violent changes. It was even afraid of reforms, when it remembered the Terror, the Napoleonic Wars, and all that followed middle-class reform at the end of the eighteenth century. Tchernoff, one of the best authorities on French politics in Louis Philippe's reign, shows how republicanism terrified the middle classes round about 1840. It is hard nowadays to appreciate their feelings, as so many European and American republics have become entirely middle class in character. But in the 'forties, the very word 'republic' sounded as sinister as the word 'soviet' in the years following 1917. It did not simply mean government by the people: it had a revolutionary flavour savouring of the guillotine, and was always connected with the primary aim of radical democrats: universal suffrage. That absolutely horrified the upper-middle class in Europe. Even in 1848, the upper-middle class was convinced that political equality would not only sweep away the advantages of birth and wealth, but would at once abolish private property and lead to the destruction of civilisation.

We now see how the Holy Alliance managed to have such lasting success. Whether it was actually in power or striving to gain it, the class which represented the greatest economic force of the time did not dare demand even such moderate constitutional reforms as it considered essential. The upper-middle class was terrified lest its attempt at reform should provoke an open conflict with the monarchy in which it would be forced to call the lower-middle and working classes to its aid. Besides, this upper-middle class was more in sympathy with the Court than with the people, and felt a certain gratitude towards the authority which so carefully protected its interests and its position. The governments of Prussia, Belgium, Austria and a number of other countries turned a blind eye to the most shameless exploitation in industry, and in labour disputes invariably supported the employer against his employees. None of the successive governments in the reign of Louis Philippe could be reproached by the middle class for interfering with its industrial activities. And the bloody events of 1834 showed that when it came to bringing the common enemy, the working class, to heel, the army and the National Guard were at one.

In France, as in Austria, Italy and Prussia, the government played on the middle classes' fear of the people and revolution. 'Its sole instrument', wrote John Stuart Mill, 'consisted in a direct appeal to man's immediate personal interests or interested fears', and he went on to say that Louis Philippe strove to immerse all France in the *culte des intérêts matériels*, 'in the worship of the cash-box and the ledger'. Throughout Europe, the absolute governments claimed that they alone prevented mob rule. That was the reason that there could be no major change in Europe, before something happened to break the alliance formed of necessity between the middle classes and the State.

Now this alliance did have its weak spots. There were considerable differences in the interests, attitudes and ways of life of its different strata, the large and small manufacturers, the merchants, the bankers, the intellectuals, and so forth. Sometimes their differences appeared in a most striking manner. Proudhon, Marx and the Fourierist Toussenel all emphasise the financial control of the middle class in Louis Philippe's reign. Liberal France was not the only country during the first half of the nineteenth century in which the bankers had become the most powerful class. It was the same under the other monarchies. In England the industrialists and the landowners came into conflict over the Corn Laws, and the industrialists and the bankers on the question of loans. We must remember too that the middle class was no rigidly constituted and unalterable caste. In the continual fluctuations of its existence, certain elements rose to the top, founded dynasties and amassed fabulous fortunes, whereas others—for biological or economic reasons—sunk to the bottom and disappeared. The sons of the rich set out to acquire a polish in keeping with their new social status. The self-made men who were still conscious of their lower-middle class origins, took their stand as men of the people in their contest with that fraction of the middle class which held the reins. We find these 'renegades' of the middle class in almost all the reformist movements in Europe, trying to gain power by supporting democratic movements. In the case of the intellectuals, too, there were numerous examples of either political convictions or personal ambition overriding instincts of class solidarity. In the eighteenth century it had been the young apostates of the aristocracy who had given the middle class liberals their lead; now it was the latter's turn to provide a 'high command' for the democrats who, in like fashion, planned to supplant them.

In the first half of the nineteenth century, there were no sharp divisions either between the upper-middle and lower-middle classes or between the lower-middle and working classes. Artisans, shopkeepers and minor officials all considered themselves as members of the middle class. They imitated the latter's manners and, parrot-like, repeated its maxims, as in its turn the upper-middle class aped the aristocracy. At its lowest level, however, this same lower-middle class had affinities with the proletariat, and although higher social grades exercised a strong pull, their interests could on occasion set them in opposition to the authority of the State and even of the upper-middle class. Yet the upper-middle class needed their respectful submission to maintain the comforting illusion that, far from being in an isolated position, they represented the interests of the bulk of the nation.

Knowing the psychology of the middle class, one could have foreseen their attitude in a crisis. Although it had either become or was in the process of becoming the ruling class, it did not detonate the revolution, which had been fermenting deep down in society, and exploded as the natural result of the action of social and economic forces on retrograde political forms which prevented their expansion. The middle classes wanted to avoid revolution, but once it had broken out, they tried to turn it to their advantage.

Towards the end of the 'forties the upper-middle class, like the ageing Louis Philippe, had lost much of its former prestige. De Tocqueville, in his famous speech of 27 January, a few weeks before the outbreak of the Revolution, severely criticised this social class. Public opinion, he said, blamed the middle class, as the rulers of the country, for the moral decadence which had resulted in people, who had formerly devoted themselves to the common weal, now thinking and acting only for themselves. In the middle of the century there were scandalous incidents of graft among public servants in France, which revealed that the upper grades of the Civil Service were wholly without principle. But even before de Tocqueville delivered his alarming speech, both French and foreign observers had noted a decline in the upper-middle class. Its consequences were felt not only in politics but in economic and intellectual developments. Michelet, in his magnificent book *Le Peuple*, said frankly that the middle class had 'come to a standstill' and moved neither forward nor backward. Michelet blamed the middle class not merely for its selfishness—since that was what gave the impetus to its social activity—but for its weakness when it came to looking after its own interests: it was replete and comatose. This great historian also noted that fear of the future and fear of the masses were the middle class dominant characteristics. Some time afterwards, Marx, too, pointed out that the middle class could not keep its leadership as it would not accept its responsibilities and look after the interests of the people.

In France—and, under the influence of events in France, in the other countries on the Continent—the middle class as a whole could no longer be considered, on the eve of 1848, as the moving spirit behind political and intellectual progress. But what was to take its place in the eternal cycle of social change? It was not yet the ill-defined working class, the proletarian 'Fourth Estate', but simply what Michelet called *la bonne masse*—or what was loosely referred to as 'the people'. In the middle of the nineteenth century, 'the people' were the prime movers in political and social progress. But of whom did they consist? According to French writers, they consisted mostly of the fifteen million peasants, who—according to Charléty—paid forty per cent of the taxes, and who—according to Michelet—as well as paying more than 1,500 million francs in taxation, put another 1,000 million into the pockets of the money lenders every year. Besides the peasantry, Michelet included under the heading of 'the people' not only officials, tradesmen, artisans and the military, but even the small manufacturers. In the same way, the first communist periodical in German, which was published in London, included among members of the proletariat, scholars and writers, and generally speaking all those who lived neither on unearned incomes nor by exploiting the wage-earner. So in 1848 the term 'people' had the same sense as it had in 1789, with the difference that the upper-middle class, which at that time was at logger-heads with the nobility and so considered itself closely allied to the people, had broken away from them in the 'thirties. At the same period, the factory workers—especially in England and France—were already beginning to stand out from the mass of the populace. In England, where the concen-tration of capital, and therefore the numerical and ideological strength of the proletariat was greatest, a passage in Disraeli's novel *Sybil* became proverbial: England was no longer one but 'two nations, between whom there is no intercourse and no sympathy; who are as ignorant of each other's habits, thoughts, and feelings, as if they were dwelling in different zones, or inhabitants of different planets'. This division was not apparent in France even in 1840, and Michelet was doubtless alluding to Disraeli's remark when he cried to his compatriots: 'Let us never, I beg of you, become two nations. . . .'

'The people' was therefore the working population of the country, the great majority of the nation. But when we look more closely at these 'people' who were the true historical heroes of the nineteenth century, and were the authors of the revolutions in France, Italy, Germany, Austria and Hungary, and who in the first months of the year 1848—that great springtime of the people—tore up the cities' paving stones to build the barricades and gave short shrift to the counter-revolutionaries, and whose voice in 1848 became once again the voice of God, we see that they were actually the peoples of the big towns. It was 'the man in the street' of Paris, Lyons, Marseilles, London, Milan, Berlin, Vienna and Budapest who, the moment he appeared on the scene, struck terror into the hearts of nobility and middle class alike. He hoped to find an ally in the peasants to whom he was still closely bound by ties of relationship and sentiment, but, although in France as well as in the provinces of Austria he pledged himself to improve their lot, he could in no wise count upon their active support. The popular movements of the nineteenth century set out to achieve the moral and material emancipation of 'all the people', but all did not take part. That was left entirely to a fraction of the urban population.

The uprisings of the first half of the nineteenth century were also characterised by the absence of political parties in the modern sense. Parties to represent the masses had not yet been formed anywhere in Europe. This lack, combined with the absence of clear dividing lines between the different social classes, explains the continuous fluctuations of popular sympathies and political opinions and feelings. Secret societies such as the *Amis du Peuple* founded in 1836 by Godefroy Cavaignac, or the society of the *Droits de l'Homme* which followed it, had a membership of lawyers, students, teachers, cobblers, tailors and factory hands who, in perfect harmony, dreamed of the Republic which would bring happiness to each and all. Delio Cantimori recalls how, in his own country, liberating movements received their impetus not only from the lower-middle and middle-middle classes but also from the skilled and unskilled workmen of the towns, though the rural population took little or no part in them. The same author gives statistics compiled in the course of an investigation carried out by the papal police in 1849, which give an idea of the typical social composition of revolutionary movements at that time. The best-known leaders of the republican movement in Rome were apportioned as follows between the various professions. Out of 1,351 persons, there were 11 publicans, 19 café proprietors, 92 cobblers, 18 domestic servants, 24 tapestry-workers, 11 hatters, 17 carters, 19 joiners, 88 army pensioners or custom-house men, 21 carpenters, 17 street porters, 26 office employees, 22 jurists, 32 butchers, 29 serving soldiers, 46 masons, 24 shopkeepers, 22 innkeepers, 16 painters, 116 landlords, 29 tailors, 15 stone masons, 18 teachers, 24 students, 17 coachmen, 18 vine growers, and 34 agricultural labourers.

The democratic clubs of Berlin and Budapest must have had very much the same composition. People of all classes met at the same club or masonic lodge, and, on the other hand, members of the same class, and sometimes even of the same family, joined violently opposing movements. One finds among the nobles of Cracow, who revolted in 1846, as among the minor nobles in Hungary in 1848, not only partisans of freedom in the feudal sense, but nobles fighting to free the peasantry, and even some who dreamed of socialist utopias. The radical enthusiasm of the middle-class Rhinelanders verged on communism. As the social classes whose battles were to mark the years following 1848, were only in the process of formation, and since as yet there were no free and powerful political parties capable of clarifying and co-ordinating the demands of the people who were opposed to the old order, the ideological tendencies and the various movements of 1848 were neither stable nor clearly defined.

Michelet was one of the first to notice that the English and the Germans had not the same idea of 'freedom' as the French. 'Find any liberal-minded Englishman or German,' he wrote, 'and start discussing freedom. He will use the same word, but find out what he means by it. You will discover that the word has as many senses as there are nations, and that the English and German democrats are aristocrats at heart. . . .' But even different members of the same nation gave different meanings to the words 'freedom', 'constitution', 'democracy' and 'republic'. The poor people saw all these words as symbols of their burning desire for equality and social justice. Theirs was the republicanism defined by *Jeune France*[1] as: 'That hunger for equality and justice, that universally felt contempt for distinctions not based on personal merit, that urge to control his own destiny, in a word, that consciousness of human dignity which makes man rise against the despot.' The views of the middle-class liberals, on the other hand, were expressed with typically British bluntness by some who said: . . . 'Equality is not our métier.' This confusion of ideas proved of some service to the propagandists, but it concealed a number of grave dangers for the future, when it came to putting theory into practice.

We have seen the middle class mistrust of republicanism, and we have examined its causes. The French republicans of the 'forties spent a great deal of energy in convincing large sections of the middle class of the excellence of republican institutions, and in dispelling their fears that the Second Republic would produce a deluge of equalitarians of the school of Babeuf. The present problem was not so much how to popularise the Republic, as how to give it a moderate, middle-class flavour. The *Dictionnaire Politique*, the *Revue Républicaine*, edited by Pierre Leroux, and later on Louis Blanc's *Revue du Progrès*, all served this end. The author of *Organisation du Travail* took every opportunity to stress his horror of class warfare; but his proposals for State intervention were hardly calculated to calm a middle class which desired State protection only against the dangerous competition of English or Belgian goods on the market. On the whole, the orthodox republicans of the middle class had no sympathy with the social utopians who succeeded in infiltrating into their ranks, and whose excesses prevented republicanism from being accepted in polite circles. After the defeat of the Saint-Simonians, these utopians devoted less of their time to awakening the social conscience of the middle class, and more to finding some way of helping the poor to give expression to their dreams of justice. These same utopians were largely responsible for popular republicanism acquiring a mystical, semi-religious faith that the simple fact of proclaiming France a Republic would usher in an age of miracles.

But let us not be too hard on those dreamers of 1848 who, in their devotion to the people and in their idealism, strove to hasten the march of history. Let us not laugh even at the English philistine Bentham, who scrupulously examined the pettiest social institution to see what purpose it might serve. Instead of sneering at them, we should do better to follow the example of these men who were not afraid to take their innermost ambitions seriously and try to discover how life could be organised so that people should be happy. Naturally their speculations

[1] *Jeune France*, 20 June 1829, quoted by J. Tchernoff in *Le parti républicain sous la monarchie de juillet*, Paris 1901, page 43

produced some strange results. They were not so much leaders of parties as founders of sects, as faith-healers, missionaries and preachers. Nevertheless, it is they who gave the period its curiously moving, childlike quality. Take, for example, Philippe Buonarotti, Babeuf's disciple and biographer, whose philosophy, based on the ideas of Rousseau and Mably, had such an effect on the artisans and clerks of Louis Philippe's reign. Buonarotti greatly influenced even so critical a mind as Proudhon's. In fact, Buonarotti's *Egalité, c'est-à-dire justice*, became the theme song of Proudhon's philosophy which proclaimed that equality was the very essence of justice. Buonarotti taught his contemporaries that the many vicissitudes of the history of the French Revolution could be explained by the conflict, which had been latent ever since, 'between the supporters of wealth and distinction on the one hand and the supporters of equality—the mass of the workers—on the other'. These lines foreshadow the introduction to the *Communist Manifesto*, which asserts that 'the history of every society in the past is the history of the war between the classes'. It was Buonarotti who held up the austere figures of Marat, Robespierre and Saint-Just as examples to the French working class; and it was he who created the legend of Gracchus Babeuf, the model husband and father whose sons bore the names of Camille and Caius—the heroic martyr who died so gallantly on the scaffold. Before he died, Babeuf wrote a farewell letter in which he suggested that his tomb should bear the words: '*Il fut parfaitement vertueux.*'

Buonarotti's biography of Babeuf was widely read in outer Paris, where there was also tremendous admiration for Cabet, the former public attorney, who had been a member of all the societies like *L'Association pour l'Instruction du Peuple* and the *Droits de l'Homme*, and, on fleeing to London to avoid imprisonment, had come into contact with the doctrines of Robert Owen. This eager idealist was also a man of sound common sense, and his propaganda played a large part in teaching the French working class to stop putting their faith in vague conspiracies, *coups d'état* and violence, and to educate and organise themselves.

His ideas, expressed with such conviction, kept his memory alive among the working class long after the collapse of the 'Icarian' colonies he founded in America. The failure of these 'Icarian' and Owenite colonies taught the working class that it was futile to hope to make a success of tiny socialist communities in the middle of a liberal and capitalist world.

In the course of the 'forties, when he was still a regular correspondent of the *Allgemeine Zeitung* at Augsburg, Heinrich Heine wrote in his articles on the French political situation that the greatest republican speaker was Blanqui, whose attacks on the rule of the middle class had no equal in their scathing irony. This professional revolutionary, who had spent half his life in prison, and who proclaimed that the working class's only hope lay in open revolt, considerably helped to spread communist ideas. His *Critique sociale*, which summarises his doctrine, contains the following maxims which have become almost proverbial and at once caught the workers' imagination: 'Communism is the safeguard of the individual. Communists have always been the striking-force of democracy. Communism, which is the very spirit of revolution, must beware of utopias and never lose sight of political realities.'

We see in the writings of this pioneer of communism the germs of contradictions which appear later in socialist doctrine. On the one hand, he expresses his conviction that the new social order could not come into being without the aid of a dictatorship, yet on the same page he writes: 'Communism, far from imposing itself by decree, must await the free decision of the country.'[1]

The far-sighted Fourier had been dead for many years, but his disciples, the Phalansterians, with Victor Considérant and Toussenel at their head, tirelessly went on spreading their master's teachings, which they adapted to modern conditions. From 1822 until his death in 1837, the little wizened man with the features of Socrates waited each day at noon for the millionnaire, to whom he was going to explain his system for a phalanstery which would save the world. Victor Considérant, however, looked upon Fourier as a 'positive and practical thinker . . . who held all political disputes in equal contempt'.[2]

Although he always passionately denied it, the jovial Proudhon with his big round face and spectacles, who always swore it was he who said 'Property is Theft', was also a pupil of Fourier's. Marx hailed the young Proudhon as the pioneer of scientific socialism; but in 1846, when they were arguing questions of tactics, the German Hegelian dismissed his French colleague's latest work with scathing contempt. Although Considérant was not far wrong in describing the author of the *Philosophie de la Misère* as 'that strange man who was determined that none should share his views', it cannot be denied that from the end of the 'forties onward, Proudhon's works had a tremendous influence in French working-class circles.

Louis Blanc, too, created a sensation with his *Organisation du Travail*, not merely in France, but throughout Europe. The revolutionaries of Cracow must have been influenced by him in their decision to create 'national workshops' in 1846, nearly two years before the French Provisional Government published their decree. Mention must also be made

[1] A. Blanqui: *Critique sociale*, 1885, page 208

[2] Victor Considérant: *Le socialisme devant le vieux monde, ou le vivant devant le mort*, 2nd Edition, Paris, 1848

of Flora Tristan, whom Jules Janin called 'the woman of sunlight and shadow'. This tall, dark-skinned and black-eyed woman was Gaugin's grandmother, and claimed that on her father's side she was descended from the Emperor Montezuma, doubtless on better authority than Saint-Simon's in tracing his ancestry back to Charlemagne. This attractive woman (whose biography has been written by Jules L. Puech) who herself had known what it was to be poor, took up her pen in a romantic gesture to draw the world's attention to the pitiful lot of the outcasts of fortune. Four years before the publication of the *Communist Manifesto*, in a book entitled *Union Ouvrière*, Flora Tristan sounded a rallying-call to the workers of the world, both men and women. She finally fell ill at Bordeaux, while on a propaganda tour, and died in the arms of two Saint-Simonian workers: a miller, a tailor, a locksmith and a blacksmith were her pall-bearers. Another woman writer, inspired by Pierre Leroux to popularise humanitarian, republican and socialist ideas, was George Sand. There was also Liszt's mistress, the Comtesse d'Agoult, who fought for the rights of the underdog, and later wrote a remarkable history of the 1848 Revolution under the name of 'Daniel Stern'.

The 'forties open a new chapter in the history of social theory. In the eyes of posterity all these pioneers were eclipsed by the two young Hegelians—Marx and Engels—who laid the foundations of scientific socialism, as a historical philosophy of the working-class movement and its battles. Their membership of the secret society called *Die Geächteten* (The Outcasts) lends particular weight and historical importance to this movement, which was founded in Paris in 1834 by German emigrants. Later on, the extremist working-class elements broke away from it to form in 1836 the society *Die Gerechten* (The Just). According to their historian, Engels, these workers were influenced by Babeuf and proletarian communism; they believed that common ownership of property would transform society, and kept in close touch with the *Société des Saisons*, a clandestine organisation controlled by Blanqui and Barbes. After the suppression of the rising organised by the *Société des Saisons* on 12 May 1839, two leaders of the German emigrants, Karl Schapper and Heinrich Bauer were arrested and deported. Schapper, when still a young student at the School of Forestry, had taken part in the conspiracy organised by Georg Büchner. When the conspiracy was discovered, Schapper went to Frankfort, where he played a major rôle in the attempted revolution of 1833. In 1834 he joined Mazzini, and took part in the invasion of Savoy. Schapper's companion, Bauer, was a cobbler from Franconia. Later on, Engels said that these two were the first genuine proletarian revolutionaries he ever met. When they were expelled from

France, Schapper and Bauer went to London, where in 1840, they founded a cultural association of German workers. This association, which was composed chiefly of tailors and cobblers, was really a cover for *Die Gerechten*, which its leaders had transferred to London.

These German emigrants in London were extremely jealous of their radicalism; they considered Mazzini a 'bourgeois', and would not even accept the Chartists as true revolutionaries. Engels, whose book on the condition of the labouring classes in England had already come out, got in touch with these revolutionary compatriots of his in 1843. A year later he visited Marx in Paris. This year, 1844, is a date to remember, for it marked the discovery, by Marx and Engels, that communism was not a vague pipe-dream, but the essential ideology of class warfare. Marx and Engels saw that it was the proletariat's mission to engage in an organised battle to abolish private property and establish a classless society. From that date forward, both of them took an active part in radical working-class movements. Later on, Marx, when Guizot expelled him from Paris, emigrated to Brussels. Shortly after his arrival in the Belgian capital, he founded an organisation on the lines of the workers' associations in London, and brought out a paper called *Deutsche Brüsseler Zeitung*. Marx and Engels wanted to create a working-class movement on an international scale. In 1846, they formed a *Kommunistische Korrespondenz Komite* (suggested, no doubt, by the Jacobins' 'Correspondence Committees') with the object of keeping Belgian, French, German and English socialists and communists in touch with social movements and doctrines in their respective countries. In France, Marx sought the aid of Proudhon, and wrote pointing out that 'when the time comes for action, everyone will certainly want to know what is going on in other countries as well as their own'. Marx wrote this letter on 5 May 1846, and Proudhon replied twelve days later. The problems raised in this exchange of letters throw considerable light on revolutionary mentalities in the 'forties. Proudhon promised to collaborate with the committee, but he announced at the same time that they should not expect many letters from him as he had other work on hand. He took the occasion to tell Marx where he disagreed not so much with what Marx said as with what he, Proudhon, read between the lines. In the first place he warned Marx against wanting a ready-made doctrine. Proudhon distrusted all dogmas, all sectarian spirit and all cut-and-dried theories. He was also struck by Marx's reference to the 'time for action'. Did Marx believe, he asked, that the time was come to talk of revolution? Proudhon did not believe that revolutionary action was the means to bring about social reform. He wrote that the only way to achieve that was by an 'economic combine' which would 'restore to society the wealth another economic combine had taken from it'.

Marx was deeply disappointed by this letter, which revealed not only Proudhon's moral idealism, but also his lack of practical sense and his fundamental utopianism. A careful study of Proudhon's reply shows how it was that this great thinker and brilliant writer's influence on the working class was more confusing than helpful. In their centuries-old struggle, the workers needed a solid doctrine to sum up all their secret hopes and desires.

During the summer of 1847, the federation of *Die Gerechte*—'The Just'—held its first international congress in London. The German emigrants in Paris were represented by Engels; and as Marx was unable to find the fare the Germans in Brussels sent a close friend of his, Wilhelm Wolf. One of the first actions of the congress was to change the name of the federation to the League of Communists. It is interesting to examine the inner organisation of this League, which was copied from the French Secret Societies. The lowest unit was the 'commune' of three to twenty members, immediately above it came the 'section' (*Kreis*), then the 'head section', the National Council and, at the top, the International Congress. Only the last named had the power to send out instructions and elaborate a programme. The League was financed by subscription. It was decided in London to try and create public workers' cultural associations everywhere as cover organisations. These associations met twice a week; one meeting was devoted to discussion of theories, and the other—as they were of German origin—to singing. The League founded libraries and organised adult education. At the end of November, the leaders of the League met again and after ten days of debates agreed to its statutes. At the same time they commissioned Marx and Engels to produce a manifesto explaining the basic theories and practical demands of communism in simple language.

From then onward, it was a race between the communists and the sequence of events. Revolts were already breaking out in Italy, and in spite of urgent appeals from London, Marx had not yet finished his *Manifesto*. When it was finally printed and distributed its purpose was more to interpret the Revolution than to start it. In his preface to Marx's tract *Enthüllungen über den Kommunistenprozess zu Köln*, Engels was later to emphasise the extent to which the Revolution took the communists by surprise. One must not, however, underestimate their effect on revolutionary events in France and, above all, in Germany. As the communist workers' leader Stephan Born wrote to Marx in May 1848, the communists 'were everywhere and nowhere' in Berlin. Franz Mehring, the historian of the working-class movement in Germany, also expressed the opinion that: 'whenever, in the years of the revolution, the German working class showed class consciousness, it was the work of the communists.'

In 1848 the number of those who knew of the existence of the Communist League was infinitesimal. But then how many people in the reign of Tiberius knew about Christianity? The German emigrants in London had started so powerful a movement that only a hundred years later its branches were to include a great part of the workers of the entire world. Let us then pay homage to the workers of those early days who proudly wrote on their flag that revolutionary password which mankind had heard two thousand years before: 'All men are brothers.' And it was in the League's review that Karl Schapper, at the dawn of the 1848 Revolution, printed that device which should keep his name alive for ever:

'Workers of the world, unite!'

Engels later pointed out that the majority of the first communists were not factory workers, in the modern sense of the term, so that they had no connection with the industrial evolution which according to communist theory would bring about a fundamental change in society. 'These men', wrote Engels, 'were not yet proletarians in the full sense of the word. They were only that part of the lower-middle class which, whilst not yet in direct opposition to the upper-middle class, that is to say the capitalists, were in the process of becoming the modern proletariat. So it is all the more to their honour that these artisans were instinctively aware of what they were to become and formed themselves, without fully understanding what they were doing, into a proletarian party.' These anonymous workmen, tailors, cobblers and joiners had the glory of showing the way to the proletariat of the great factories. These were the men who, though peaceable by nature, were the first to take up arms in passionate defence of socialism and communism, at the barricades of Paris, Berlin, Dresden, Cologne and Milan in the years 1848 and 1849.

7

'I see the different nationalities, far from becoming obliterated, day by day turning from mere collections of peoples into clearly defined groups, each with a character of its own.' Michelet was not exaggerating when he wrote those words. During the first half of the nineteenth century, nationalism was almost visibly growing throughout Europe. In each country it had a different meaning, but as one of its best historians, Georges Weill, shrewdly remarked, 'lack of precision will contribute to its success'.

What is certain is that nationalism was originally bound up with liberalism, and in the course of time became one of the strongest weapons of the middle class in Europe. The word 'nation' received its first political blessing from the Third Estate in France which, in the course of its war

39

against the monarchy and the feudal order, transformed the States General into a National Assembly. Under these circumstances, the word 'nation' stood for the sovereign people which had acquired its political rights and the control of its own fortunes. And this nation, which had just become conscious of its rights, wanted to show a different face abroad from that of the dynasty which until then had arbitrarily ordered its affairs. The middle-class theorists of the eighteenth century, as much in France as in England, were severely critical of the foreign policy of their kings who—in their eyes—were concerned not with the moral and material welfare of their people, but solely with their own prestige and family interests. They were continually either after fresh conquests or involving their nations in squabbles over rights of succession. The idealists of the rising middle class condemned not only conquest but colonisation, and fought for free trade and peaceful co-operation between the peoples. Faithful to these doctrines, the National Assembly of revolutionary France began by declaring 'that the French Nation would undertake no war of conquest, and would never employ its forces against the freedom of any people'. Instead of family pacts, the upper-middle class, which had just declared itself 'the Nation', wanted to conclude 'national agreements' with 'honest peoples'. This desire for a moral regeneration of foreign policy is also reflected in the French National Assembly's decision that the only legitimate excuse for acquiring territory was the result of a plebiscite. Under the influence of the Jacobin extremists, the Convention adopted another resolution by which they promised to support any nation wishing to shake off the yoke of tyranny.

The peaceable nationalism of the first phase of the French Revolution became aggressive under the Directory, and imperialist under Napoleon, when it was barely distinguishable from the dynastic power-politics it had formerly attacked. In short, the Napoleonic Wars were no more than a fresh episode in the traditional rivalry between France and England. The reason why the middle class became aggressively nationalist was that it was frightened by the anarchist tendencies of the Revolution and automatically tried to relieve the growing tension between the different classes by crying: 'the country is in danger'. The Girondin, Brissot, who had a considerable hand in starting the war of the French Revolution, did so in full consciousness as a means of avoiding civil war. Fifty years later, war was still looked upon as an excellent way out of domestic difficulties. In 1847, when the political crisis was daily growing more acute in France, one of Louis Philippe's generals advised him to create a diversion by declaring war on Austria and sending the army in Algeria against her Italian possessions.[1]

[1] Henri Martin: *Daniel Manin*, Paris 1861, page 14

In every country, middle-class nationalism had two faces, a liberal one, which it showed towards the ruling house and the nobility, and an authoritarian one, which it showed towards the lower classes. In those countries in which the middle class had a hand in the government, nationalism was just another political weapon. In England, the Whigs pursued a foreign policy which the middle class considered patriotic, whereas in France the democratic, middle-class opposition attacked Louis Philippe's mean and feeble foreign policy as most unpatriotic. There was a difference, however, in the Opposition's nationalism, between the realism of a man like Thiers and the idealism of an extreme radical like Michelet, who believed in intervention. Thiers' ambitions were really those of the upper-middle class, and he simply took a bolder line than Guizot's supporters. Michelet, on the other hand—who was one day to influence Unamuno—identified his love of a personified France with his love of humanity. 'Our country,' he wrote, 'alone has the right to educate herself in this fashion, because she of all nations has identified her destiny with that of mankind.' In the eyes of all such idealists, France was the guardian of the world's great traditions, the traditions of Jewish Christianity, of Rome and of democracy, and they saw her destined to lead the nations. These men believed that to be born a Frenchman was not only a cause for pride, but entailed grave responsibilities, which the élite of France both felt and proclaimed in the course of the years preceding the 1848 Revolution. Before them, the Saint-Simonians, in their tricoloured costume, had stood under the glass roof of the great hall in the Rue Taitbout and proclaimed France 'the Christ of the nations'. The socialist Louis Blanc based his plans for the salvation of the world on the tremendous warmth of feeling and selfless spirit of the French people. Even as fierce an opponent of nationalism as Proudhon was convinced that 'France was called to set an example to the nations', and did not doubt that in her decline as in her greatness, France was 'the queen of the world'.

The grim faith of the French in their mission resulted in their desire to take up arms in defence of the oppressed. They believed it France's task to free Poland, and help not only Italy but also Germany to achieve unity and greatness.[1] They had not the slightest doubt that generosity was their best investment. Moved by France's fine and generous example, the democrats of other countries sought a mission too. Mazzini believed that the French had completed theirs with the Revolution of 1789; and that henceforth it was Italy's proud task to continue it and create a nation. Mickievicz thought on the Poles' mission in history, Széchenyi on the

[1] 'The resurrection of Italy would alone suffice to make a people's fame'—Lamartine, Speech on France and the outside world, 28 October 1847
'France's rôle in this century is to father forth the freedom of the peoples'—Thiers, Speech of 4 February 1847

41

Hungarians', and Kollar on the Slavs'. Heine, and after him the radical Hegelians, dreamed of raising Germany to the level of France and believed that the combined revolutionaries of the two countries would regenerate Europe and the world. According to Feuerbach, 'the true philosopher, who identified himself with life and humanity, should be of mixed French and German descent'. Moses Hess, in his book published in Switzerland in 1834, expressed the belief that complete individual freedom and social equality would result from a combination of French communism and German atheism.

This revolutionary nationalism was at the same time strongly inter-national. The radical theorists did not even envisage the possibility of conflict between nations freed from despotic rule. On the contrary, they entirely agreed with Manin who said, in Paris: 'There will be no peace in Europe until all the oppressed peoples have won back their independence.' The great majority of democrats dogmatically asserted that a federation of the peoples could only be achieved by the demolition of empires and the formation of national States. Proudhon was almost alone in his belief that nationalism might become an obstacle to progress, and that the people would do better to win their independence within the existing social order. The German radicals saw an evilly disguised form of nationalism behind Proudhon's anti-national theories, and thought that he opposed other peoples' struggles for freedom because he saw in Italian and German unity a threat to his own country. But perhaps they made Proudhon out to be more machiavellian than he was.

However, even if Proudhon were afraid for France, his fears were not unfounded. Italian and German nationalism were far from being as inoffensive as the Left Wing imagined. These nationalisms became a danger precisely because they represented not the will of a nation but the desire to become a nation. Hegel had once said to his French admirer, Victor Cousin: 'You French are lucky, you're a nation.' Germany was not yet a nation, and its upper-middle class, casting envious glances towards England or France, naturally felt a sense of inferiority. What distinguished German or Italian nationalism from the English with its self-assurance or the French with its warm generosity, was a wounded pride and what amounted to a national inferiority complex. The Germans held a different conception of a nation from the French and the English, who already lived an independent national life, and even from the Hun-garians who, right up to the revolution, confused the nation with its nobility. The Germans looked upon language as the foundation of nationalism, as did the Slavs, who under the influence of German philo-sophers, especially Herder, became nationally minded not as the result of fighting for political and social reforms, but through a campaign for the

42

revival of their mother tongue. In Hungary, on the other hand, the move-ment for social reforms—begun at the end of the eighteenth century, in Joseph II's reign—was only directed into linguistic channels under pressure from the conservatives who regained the upper hand in 1792. On the eve of the year 1848 the Croats and the Hungarians were arguing, not about equality of political rights, but about the choice of an official language. The Hungarian Diet wanted to substitute Hungarian for Latin which was still the legislative language, and the Croats looked upon that as a menace to their freedom and existence as a nation.

The Germans, then, took language and race as the criteria of nationality, and the natural foundation of the community formed by a State. The immense success of this doctrine of 'pan-Germanism', which was the creation of the pedants, was due to the rising German middle classes who realised that it was a miraculous means of avoiding a class war with the classes both above and below them. It was far easier to call for a Greater Germany uniting all German speaking nations, and to sing the *Wacht am Rhein* and abuse the French, than to claim universal suffrage and the establishment of assizes. In the name of pan-Germanism, the middle classes could come to terms with the aristocracy, and claim the right to control the lower orders.

Pan-Germanism even attracted certain elements among the German democrats. The first numbers of *Vorwärts*, the Paris organ of the German emigrants—which was originally edited by a journalist called Börnstein before Marx's group took it over—echoed the teachings of Dahlmann and others: 'Germany is wherever the German tongue is spoken. As soon as our beloved country realises the truth of these words, pan-Germanism will become fact. . . . Areas of Brabant, Denmark, Norway and Sweden, and even the Russian territories on the shores of the Baltic, ought to be considered as part of Germany.' At this period, the official Prussian newspaper still printed news items from Bavaria and Württem-berg under the heading 'Foreign News', but the pan-Germanists had already decided to annex Alsace, Schleswig-Holstein, Bohemia and a large slice of Poland, and were beginning to think of adding Holland to the list. The liberal phraseology of German nationalism concealed plain imperialist ambitions. On the pretext of national unity, the middle class wanted to enlarge its preserves, whilst avoiding class warfare, and stressing national interests. In France, the dissenting leaders of the middle class used the Republic as a magic formula to hold a socialist revolution at bay. In Germany, Italy and Hungary, the moderates called for 'national unity' so as to create a united front they themselves could control. One can discover this preventive use of nationalism throughout Central Europe. 'Venice can only be saved by the maintenance of law and order,' Jules Manin wrote to one of his friends on 14 January 1849. And he added that both 'might easily have been compromised by the People's Club . . . with the socialist theories they had begun to preach there'. The Frankfort Parliament, the Roman Republic, and the March Constitution in Hungary could only be saved by the maintenance of law and order, for there were popular clubs everywhere, beginning to spread socialist ideas which were a threat to the public peace. In Hungary, where the minor nobles took the place of the middle class, the only programme on which the opposition could find agreement—after months of bargaining—was one which put national, anti-Austrian aims before social reform. This nationalism of the middle class or the nobility had little in common with the heroic, generous nationalism of the revolutionary middle class of the eighteenth century, which regarded any attack on the freedom of another people as high treason and a crime against humanity.[1] This new nationalism merely played on national prejudices, in order to arouse pride and ambition; this vaunted patriotism was merely a disguise for hatred and cold-blooded selfishness.

In the preface to his book on the condition of the labouring classes in England, Frederick Engels records with joy a complete lack of chauvinism amongst the British proletariat and the Chartists.

In October 1844 Karl Schapper, the German working-class revolutionary, formed a new society made up of both his English and foreign emigrant friends. It bore the already significant name of Democratic Friends of All Nations. It is a fact that we find the purest and most human form of nationalism among the social revolutionaries. In their eyes all the nations were fighting for one and the same cause, and when the moment for action came they put into practice the doctrine they had done so much to formulate. The best and the worst were among the exponents of nationalism, of which Metternich said in his memoirs: 'it means everything and nothing, but today it sweeps the world'. Thus we find in the movements of 1848, set in motion by nationalism with all its terrible contradictions, the germs of all the clashes of interests which led to the ever increasing violence of the struggles of the twentieth century.

8

In the foregoing chapters I have been chiefly concerned with those factors which, in the first half of the last century, prevented the creation of new political forms keeping up with the rate of social and economic changes.

[1] 'Each nation is the sole possessor of the right to make and change its own laws . . . any attempt to take that right away from another nation by force, means that one does not respect it in one's own country, and is an act of treason and a crime against the human race.' Condorcet, 20 April 1792

The principal factors were, first, the close co-operation of conservative governments, and, second, the attitude of the great majority of the middle class. In one way the middle class was the mainspring of economic and social progress, but instead of leading the people against despotic governments, it was so afraid of the people that it came to terms with those governments. These two factors retarded the liberal and democratic transformation of Europe for decades. Nevertheless, the governments could not stand up for ever against the force of circumstances—against the growing force of economic, technical and intellectual advances. The observant saw that the situation was untenable: revolution was in the air. They had foreseen it and even predicted it, though admittedly without any certainty. Thiers, for instance—whose prophecies on the subject of the revolution have become legendary—proclaimed on the eve of the February risings, and in flat contradiction to his previous statements, that revolution was impossible. He argued that 'the government forces are ten times more powerful than any rioters', and added: 'the Restoration died only because it was too delicate to live. I promise you that we shall not die of the same complaint. . . . The King is quick of hearing; he will listen to reason and give in in time.'[1] Thiers' mention of the impending revolution appears to have been no more than an attempt at intimidation by a Leader of the Opposition, which he does not seem to have taken seriously himself. And this quotation shows clearly enough that the middle-class opposition's dearest wish was to collaborate with the government. Monsieur Bourgin, the author of our chapter on France, quotes at length from de Tocqueville's famous speech on 27 January 1848: 'Do you not feel the earth of Europe trembling once more! Do you not feel the wind of revolution in the air!' When de Tocqueville later wrote his memoirs, he waved aside compliments paid him on his prophetic gifts with delightful sincerity and modesty, saying: 'I did not expect a revolution like the one we had.' Monsieur Bourgin understandably wonders how it was that 'so few people at the time saw the revolution coming'. One of the causes of this phenomenon was certainly that 'society—prosaic and brutal though it was . . . lived in a state of misty exaltation'. Most people at the time had no knowledge of the laws of evolution behind social realities, and so clung to their idealism, but another cause was the equivocal position of the middle class. It had no desire for revolution, which it feared.

But if there were so many obstacles in the way of revolution, what circumstances and what forces caused it to break out? The historical materialists, like Marx, Engels and Proudhon, put it down to the critical economic situation in Europe. 'The real immediate cause of the March Revolution was the world-wide economic crisis of the year 1847', wrote

[1] Falloux: *Mémoires*, Vol. I, page 265

Engels in his preface to Marx's study. This crisis started in England and then spread to the Continent. Marx himself was convinced that 'the original process always begins in England. England is the creative spirit in the middle-class cosmos.'[1] This belief was the starting point of a very interesting concept of the philosophy of history. Marx was absolutely certain that 'even if crises provoke revolutions on the Continent in the first place, their origins are always to be found in England. . . . Violent seizures attack the limbs before the heart'. Proudhon, in his *Confessions d'un révolutionnaire*, in like fashion indicates economic difficulties as the main cause of the 1848 Revolution, but without pointing out that its roots lay in England. 'The February Revolution broke out', he wrote, 'at a time when commerce and industry, which had been in a bad way for several years, had reached complete stagnation. Agriculture was a dead loss, the workshops were idle, the shops were overflowing with goods for want of buyers, and the State handled its finances as badly as the man in the street. . . .' The subsequent findings of the economic historians (although—as Mr Bury, the author of our chapter on England, points out—they are by no means complete) entirely agree with these contemporary theories. Clapham, one of the best experts on European economic history at that period, states, in conclusion to the most detailed research, that at the beginning of 1848, the whole of Europe was hungry and restless. Mr Bury gives a detailed survey of the causes, symptoms and consequences of the crisis, so it is pointless to discuss them further here. His analysis entirely confirms the opinion of our French collaborator, who paints a horrifying picture of the sufferings the crisis caused the working class, especially the unemployed. There can be no doubt that from every angle the crisis completely undermined the position of the régime in power. On the one hand it aroused the fury of the lower-middle and working classes, and on the other it made the ruling class begin to doubt the wisdom of its own economic and political measures. The crisis widened the gap between the already divided strata of the middle class. The poor were not the only people who could not obtain credit. Business men and manufacturers, too, hated the financial aristocracy for trying to foist the unpleasant consequences of the crisis on to every class but their own. France discovered what Proudhon had already pointed out, that the 'bancocrats' or financiers who provoked the 1830 Revolution by promising a lower cost of living, had proceeded to cripple the population with far higher taxes than their predecessors. The widening gap in the middle class, and the increased pressure on the part of the Opposition, hesitant though it was, were certainly among the most important immediate causes of the Revolution. Besides the economic crisis, there were other intellectual and emotional

[1] *Neue Rheinische Zeitung*, Nos. 5–6

factors, such as individual beliefs or personal dislikes, which drove some of the middle class to join the Opposition or even the group of revolutionary and republican democrats. Others joined the malcontents for moral reasons. In France, as in Austria, corruption was widespread, and there was a succession of scandals, of which the most resounding were caused by speculation on the newly constructed railways.

The main reason, however, for the middle and lower-middle classes turning against the government towards the end of 1847, was the latter's incompetence and intransigence. It was the same in Italy, Germany, Austria and Hungary, whose arrogant governments had learnt nothing from England's example; they did not see how the electoral reforms of 1832 and the Whigs' coming to power had strengthened the Constitution of the United Kingdom. Lord Brougham, in spite of having been a fanatical supporter of electoral reform, described the 1848 Revolution as capricious. John Stuart Mill, in his pamphlet attacking Brougham, pointed out that Louis Philippe's and Guizot's policy was enough to justify the Revolution, and had almost forced the middle class to revolt, in spite of its abhorrence of any form of popular movement and any violence or disorder. After 1830 the Government in power in England had made concessions to the rapidly rising middle class, and thereby won an ally with whose help it prevented a revolution by the masses. In all probability a like move would have prevented revolution in France and other countries of Europe. But Louis Philippe, the Citizen King (whom Frederick William IV, in a letter written at the beginning of 1848, called 'the shield and buckler of Europe's monarchs') was over confident of the middle classes. He thought they were far too frightened of the people and of revolution to fail him. Also, he put too much faith in his police: Lamartine justly reproached Guizot for 'using the police to muzzle the country'.

But the revolution was not made possible only by the divisions within the middle class, nor—as happened in a 'liberal' Canton in Switzerland in the winter of 1847—by moderate reformers being forced to enlist the aid of the democrats and therefore of all the people deprived of political rights. Developments in European foreign policy also helped weaken the resistance of despotic governments to liberalism and popular movements. As Mr Bury rightly stresses, England involuntarily played the largest part in breaking up the Holy Alliance, and in weakening the reactionary policy of the Eastern Powers: Austria, Prussia, and Russia. Whether she wished it or not, England, by her very existence, by her social and political movements, by Canning's speeches and Cobden's propaganda, by the 1832 Reform Bill, and finally by the Chartists' agitation, became the very model of political and social emancipation. The most modern of 'middle-class' States also pursued a new 'middle-class' foreign policy, in the full—

and most equivocal—sense of the word. In 1846, Palmerston, the chief protagonist of this policy, once again became Foreign Secretary in the new Whig Government. This had a decisive effect on the impending revolutions. In the chapter devoted to England, readers will find an analysis of the repercussions of Palmerston's foreign policy in Switzerland, France, Italy and other countries. Everywhere, Palmerston appeared as the defender of moderate reform, and gave all encouragement to middle-class liberals. In the majority of European States, however, conditions were such that, owing to the blindly reactionary attitude of their governments, the liberals were unable to obtain even moderate reforms without the help of the people—without recourse to revolution. The spread of liberal ideas was also greatly helped by the election of a liberal Pope, and by the triumph in 1847 of the Swiss radicals, who owed their victory over the *Sonderbund* in the first place to Palmerston. This conclusively proved to the peoples of the Continent that old Europe had no longer the strength to oppose reforms and revolutions. As Marx's *Brüsseller Zeitung* said in December 1847, the victory of the Swiss radicals was 'a European victory'.

Thus the various immediate and more or less important causes of the 1848 Revolutions were as follows: lack of food; individual and national poverty; rifts in the middle class and the decrepit despotic governments (as in Austria where Metternich's opponents at Court sought liberal support to overthrow him); England's—and to a lesser extent, America's—example; the Catholic Church's spiritual revival; Palmerston's general policy; and the effect of popular movements in the 'forties in Galicia, Switzerland and Italy. The deep underlying cause, however, was social necessity, which none of Europe's outworn institutions could withstand. The peoples of Europe had to find a political form in accordance with entirely changed conditions. Their need was threefold: the new ruling middle class wanted a form of government which would look after their interests, the people as a whole wanted to create truly national States; and the industrial workers and their radical allies wanted social justice. This last need, as Marx points out, 'could not yet be widely enough felt to assure immediate success'. All the same, it had men to speak and fight for it in almost all the great towns in Europe. The working class was out to turn a political revolution into a social one. As things were, such an attempt could but go off at half-cock, but a rising class can only learn to rule by making mistakes. History decreed that there should also be a middle-class revolution to abolish feudalism and the survivals of absolute monarchy. Paradoxically, this revolution was attempted even in countries like Hungary where the middle class had little more power than the industrial proletariat in France.

The preceding paragraph shows the variety of frequently contradictory forces and movements which brought about the revolutions of 1848. Discontent was general, but it had many causes. At the beginning of 1848, in Paris—as in Berlin, Vienna and Budapest—the Opposition (or more precisely, the spirit of opposition) succeeded in producing a united front of almost all classes of society, from Legitimists to extreme Republicans. In time, the embers of resentment burst into the flames of revolution. But could those flames stay alight? Could the heterogeneous mass of revolutionaries keep their united front? The revolution had become fact. The people swarmed in the streets wearing their cockades and waving the tricolour. They brandished their shotguns and their carbines, their pistols and their pikes, and the bells rang out. Milan echoed with the shouts of *'Viva Pio Nono!' 'Viva l'Italia!'* and Paris with cries of *'Vive la République sociale, la République universelle!'* Vienna wanted to hang Metternich. Soap-box orators in the streets of Prague prophesied the coming of a great Slavonic Empire.

The Revolution broke through many other frontiers, and behind Delacroix's shining symbol of the glorious days of 1830 we can see the middle classes, whose 'own temerity scared them after the first step', as Daniel Stern remarked, marching on despite themselves. The moderates behaved the same way in every country: the Opposition in Budapest was as ready to call a halt in March 1848 as Odilon Barrot and his friends had been in Paris a few weeks earlier. On the other hand, Manin in Venice, and Kossuth at Pressburg, preferred—like Lamartine—'peril to shame'. But how long could the mass of the middle class follow these idealists? And what about the workers? Everywhere they were fighting and dying in a revolution they thought was theirs. How long would they believe fine words and promises? The 1848 Revolution had unwilling leaders at its head and was bound to fail. Yet new forces and new ideas, were, if only for a moment, at work; and they were to leave a deep impression on the conscience of Europe. Let us open the Book of Remembrance that chronicles the names and actions of the true heroes and heroines of this Revolution, and see—a century afterwards—how much they have to teach us.

THE TRANSFORMATION OF
SWITZERLAND
PRELUDE TO THE REVOLUTION
JEAN HALPERIN

May Europe be inspired by your great example!
Michelet and Edgar Quinet in a message to the members of
the Swiss Diet, 24 December 1847

*The ring of the first Austrian shot fired against Switzerland would
reverberate through Germany, Poland, Bohemia, Hungary and Italy, and
not Swiss rifles alone would answer the volleys of the armed slaves of a
detested despotism*
Fraternal greeting from the *Democratic Friends of All Nations*
in London, 13 December 1847

Even if it is a mistake to consider the achievement of the Swiss radical movement as one of the causes or determining factors of the 1848 Revolutions, it is equally wrong to underestimate its importance. The events which took place in Switzerland form an integral part of the political and social scene at that period, and it is hard to realise today what an extraordinary impact they had on all the nations of Europe.

In order to understand the extent of the transformation which took place, one must have some idea of what Switzerland was like before 1847. First of all, it is important to realise that Switzerland was the first country on the Continent to show the effects of the Industrial Revolution on the construction and, above all, on the use of machinery, which in her case was required to produce manufactured goods in exchange for much-needed cereals and coal. There were only enough cereals grown in the country to feed the population for 280 days in the year. It must also be explained, forthwith, that the Swiss, even the townspeople, still had close ties with the land; there were no big industrial cities as there were in England at that time. Swiss methods, however, were sufficiently advanced for the British Government to consider it worth while sending a representative to study them in the more important cantons. In his report to Parliament, this observer held up Swiss methods, as he had seen them in 1836, as a model for his own country.

SWITZERLAND

Towards the middle of the century, Switzerland had slightly less than 2,400,000 inhabitants; land under cultivation covered a wider area than it does today, and amounted to approximately 1,156 square miles. The textile industry, which was by far the most important, still functioned irregularly as it relied on water power in the absence of sufficient coal and wood. This economic feature of Swiss industry, which was largely confined to the towns in the East such as St Gall, Zurich, Glarys, etc, was connected with a social feature: the factory worker was still in many ways a countryman; his family often lived in the country, and he worked on the land in his spare time.

The impoverished craftsmen and home-workers, in the meantime, were rapidly forming an embryonic proletariat. The older industries of the Basle region and French Switzerland, however, were less affected by mechanical progress, and the manufacture of silks, clocks and watches, and precision instruments remained home industries. The craftsmen were proud of their skill and jealous of their great traditions and prerogatives; they were in a completely different class from the factory workers, whom they despised in many respects.

Whereas the countryside was concerned with production, the towns were mainly interested in trade, to which the ruling classes owed their wealth. The first industrialists appear to have had nothing in common with this urban aristocracy; their interests lay with the rural populace from which they had sprung.

It is common knowledge that even the briefest résumé of a country's economic life cannot afford to leave out the state of its means of communication, which affect every conceivable human activity, so it will be as well to give a general outline. To begin with, the first railway line in Switzerland was not laid until 1847, between Zurich and Baden.[1]

The first Swiss town to be connected by rail with another country was Basle, in 1844. Before then it had been developing communications with Strasbourg along the Rhine from 1839 to 1843, so it is there we should look for the greatest increase in passenger and goods traffic. In 1829, 2,000 passengers left Basle by the mail-boat; in 1835 the number had risen to 13,000, and in 1845, to 28,000. In 1821, 262,000 quintals[2] of merchandise were received; in 1845 the amount was 901,000 quintals. To complete this brief statistical survey, the population of the town of Basle went up from 22,000 in 1837 to 26,000 in 1847, whilst the population of the whole

[1] The majority of the Swiss did not want railways, which they thought would be as great a danger to health and hygiene as to economic stability: they would cause a drop in the price of cereals, lower the value of land, bring too many foreigners into the country and unsettle the people themselves, besides causing inevitable accidents, misfortunes and quarrels—in short, they would do more harm than good. These prejudices were universally held shortly before the middle of the century.

[2] A quintal is approximately a hundredweight. (Translator's note)

canton increased from 24,000 to 28,000 over the same period. The first letter-boxes—for how can one conceive of economic progress in the broadest sense without a corresponding development in the postal service? —were installed in 1840. At the same period, the number of travellers going by mail from Zurich, which was already a metropolis, increased as follows: in 1832 the number was 12,000; in 1837, 43,900; and in 1842, 61,000. The canton of St Gall had its own public postal service as early as 1836.

The conclusions to be drawn from this rapid survey are obvious: there was almost no mass movement before the coming of the railways, but one developed rapidly during the second quarter of the century. The movement had started, and it was capable of swift expansion after 1848 for reasons which will become clear in the course of this chapter.

There is another aspect of this economic and social position which is not without significance, and leads to similar conclusions. As in other European countries, social legislation was still in its infancy in Switzerland. Not only could there be no legislation for the country as a whole, but it was not until 1848 that the first canton—Glarus—passed a general law aimed at protecting the worker; Zurich and Thurgau were the only cantons to take steps—in 1815—to control child labour in the mills and factories. Even in 1858 documents mention children under ten working in the spinning mills from twelve to fifteen hours a day—from five in the morning until eight o'clock at night. Children, incidentally, were the first and most pathetic victims of the Industrial Revolution.

As the State was uninterested, one can imagine the relationship between employer and employee, with the employers carrying tyranny to the point of interference in the worker's private life. And the workers were strictly forbidden the right to combine. That was a cause of the tension and bitter antagonism between the two camps created by the economic developments of the Industrial Revolution. It was bound to influence the political issues.

Yet there was one factor which was even more decisive than the prodigious speed of industrialisation, and that was the complete impotence of economic progress in the face of unbelievable chaos in the matter of administration, customs, coinage and postal services. One of the chief historians of the nineteenth century in Switzerland speaks without exaggeration of the 'cantonal authorities orgy of sovereignty' which created a truly 'medieval' chaos in the Customs. In spite of repeated bans, seventy new customs duties had been introduced since 1803. In the same way there were eighteen rival postal services in Switzerland, with the absurd result that it cost more to send a letter from Geneva to Zurich than from Geneva to Algiers. People were aware of the economic disadvantages of this crazy patchwork at the time, and the more wide awake among them vainly tried to do something about it. Thus it was that the Italian politician Rossi, who had taught political economy at the *Collège de France*, was asked in 1832, at the instigation of fifteen cantons and one half-canton of liberal and radical tendencies, to submit a report to the Diet advocating the centralisation of postal services, coinage, tolls, and military training. This is what Rossi's report said: 'What hope is there for industry and national prosperity, if the very roads of Switzerland . . . clog the wheels of trade, and the frontiers of every canton bristle with obstacles? And as for the obstructions caused by tolls, transit dues, road dues, storage dues, cantonal customs dues, all on top of the loss of time and money caused by twenty different coinages, all more or less arbitrary, and twenty different systems of weights and measures. . . . Well, what is there left to wonder at, unless it is the fact that any trade at all is carried on in Switzerland?' A historian has put it in another way: it was worth a loss of a hundred hours' transit time to send goods on a détour which avoided cantonal frontiers.

Is it surprising that thenceforth the centralisation and economic unification of the country were first on the programme of certain political parties?

We see, therefore, that industrialisation with all its accompanying problems, and the disunity of the cantons, are the two main features of Switzerland's economic structure before the political transformations of 1847. And the economic structure is consequently the social one, a fact we must bear in mind if we want to understand the main ideological trends in politics which are our next consideration.

These are influenced by three very different factors which, to be properly understood, must be placed in their historical setting. In the years preceding the 1847 Revolution, the Swiss political movement was characterised by lack of class consciousness; by agitation by certain parties and interests for unification of the country; and by ideological influences from abroad.

We have already seen that there was no point of contact between the workers, who were separated by their origins or by their jobs; nor between what today we should call the ruling classes, as the urban aristocracy had nothing in common with the manufacturers, who were still mainly countrymen and often '*hommes nouveaux*', in the sense in which Henry Pirenne first used the phrase. As for the factory workers, some had admittedly lost their original jobs, but their still close connection with the countryside provided them with an additional source of income, and there were few real *proletarians*, in the full sense of the word with all its grave implications. One Swiss historian of Swiss socialism has gone so far as to say that even these genuine proletarians possessed a strong lower-middle class mentality. These different professional groups were lacking in class consciousness, and were unaware of having common interests to defend. They made the best of their difficulties and scarcely ever opposed their employers. The sole, isolated explosion of discontent, which occurred at Ustrer in 1832, degenerated into a 'Luddite' riot and led to the destruction of a weaving factory; it was put down in the harshest fashion.

It would be even more pointless to look for any general antagonism between town and country dwellers. The ties between them were far too close and were undoubtedly one of the main political factors in Switzerland right up to 1914. The countryman was as strongly attached to his land as to his traditions; he was persevering and dourly cautious, extremely realistic, conservative and meticulously economical; and being passionately independent he loathed all ideologies and any form of publicity. He had a marked influence on the population of the towns, with which he mingled, and his mentality is common in Swiss politics. In the course of the nineteenth century, the country people played a dominant part in political affairs as a result of an increase in rural votes. Political emancipation, encouraged by the liberals and radicals, was accompanied by economic emancipation as the result of the final suppression of the last vestiges of feudalism. The country people may sometimes have followed the radicals, but they were none the less conservative in their opposition to violent change. Here we have another case of political opinions and economic and social interests failing to create any unity. One cannot over-emphasise the way in which the population of the countryside influenced that of the towns, and the portrait of 'an average townsman' would reveal many of the countryman's characteristics.[1]

There was also a gradual change in the composition of the ruling classes. The newcomers from the country gradually began to assert themselves, and in the end succeeded in supplanting the old aristocracy and taking part in the government of the country. This change, however, was neither sudden nor systematic. The absence of any one-sided social differentiation, and all its consequences, explains the fact that the battle for a federal State was not really a social one. It was quite different with the political aspect of the matter. There the issue was much more precise—a battle for centralisation.

The revolutions of the cantons in 1830 resulted in independent, 'individualist' democrats winning the majority of seats in the governments of the more important cantons. In order to extend their political hold, they fought for centralisation, which would give them control over the

---

[1] Professor Edgar Bonjour of Basle University enumerates them as follows: 'His simplicity, which often appeared as crude, his reasonableness and ability to come to terms with life, his dislike of trifling with thoughts, his sound distrust of outward show, empty forms and hollow phrase; but also his lack of idealism, spiritual graces and decorative gifts.'

whole country. Federalism,[1] on the contrary, went hand in hand with conservatism.

As Professor William Rappard has pointed out, all the landmarks in the political evolution of Switzerland, between the attempted revision of the Pact of 1815 and the adoption of the 1848 Constitution, 'proceeded directly or indirectly from the antagonism between the supporters and the opponents of the 1830 reforms. The fact is that they were all incidents in the battle for the political emancipation of the individual in Switzerland, and his victory over the old order.'

On 25 March 1831, the representative of the canton of Thurgau demanded 'centralisation in the best interests of the whole of Switzerland'. Thus was defined the question which was to remain uppermost in political and economic debate. It immediately divided the cantons into two camps: one composed of those which were delighted with the progress they had achieved and wanted to spread it, and the other of those who were opposed to this national 'regeneration'. According to Baumgartner, who was an eye witness of the events leading up to 1847, 'it was a fight to the death between outworn traditions and privileges on the one side, and a desire for popular sovereignty based on equal rights, on the other'.

The object of this chapter is to show the significance of Switzerland's transformation, and the way in which it may have affected the course of events in other countries. Paradoxically, however, one of the factors we have mentioned as influencing Switzerland in 1847 was the impact of foreign ideas. This must not be ignored as it is complementary to the political and economic factors. None of the new doctrines had originated in Switzerland. All the Swiss precursors of socialism had some connection with either France or Germany. Albert Galeer, the founder of the Swiss *Grütliverein*, originally came from Baden and had studied philosophy at Heidelberg, before he came to live in Geneva. A short time after his arrival, he published *Le Citoyen*, which he called the organ of the Democratic Socialists of Geneva. He was influenced by Rousseau and Mazzini as well as by the Swiss Pestalozzi, and summed up his programme as follows: 'The reign of justice on earth; graded taxation; assistance for the needy; free education for all; work for all; personal security; a guarantee that what a man earns he shall keep, etc, etc.' His utopian philosophy was more a kind of liberal anarchism than socialism. Another forerunner, of whom Marx and Engels thought highly, and who played a certain part in the progressive movement, was the German Weitling, who in 1841 came from Paris to Geneva, where there were numerous political refugees from all over Europe. Weitling had been influenced by Lamennais, Fourier, Cabet and Victor Considérant, and was acquainted with the

[1] 'Federalism', in Swiss political terminology, implies the paramountcy of the canton.

theories of Babeuf. And before him there had even been a number of Saint-Simonians in French Switzerland. A whole group of young Swiss (Delarageaz, Kehrwand, Corsat and others) strove to spread Fourier's ideas. Their universalist programme included the abolition of private property and money, and a guarantee of work for all. But they were alone in their views. They may have found a hearing among foreign workers, but the Swiss lacked a truly proletarian mentality; they had their small plots of land and were as terrified of the abolition of all private property as they were of any sudden change. The Zurich government was forced to take notice of Weitling's activities, but their investigator, a conservative named Bluntschli, saw that property in Switzerland was so apportioned that there were neither poor nor *very rich*, and concluded that 'the small landowner is too jealous of his property to risk losing it for abstract theories.' Even more significant is the fact that the Liberal Party's paper announced that the communist peril was an invention of the conservatives for their own political ends. Karl Bürkli, who was also a disciple of Fourier and Considérant, was no more successful.

It was through the Swiss Johann Jakob Treichler, who had tried to found a Swiss Labour Party, that Louis Blanc's influence was felt, and that was largely because his realistic approach to reforms was sympathetic to the matter of fact Swiss. The idea of the State's economic responsibility was taken straight out of *Organisation du Travail*.

Finally, there was Pierre Coullery from the Neuchâtel Canton who was an ardent propagandist for Buchez's theories. He was a farmer's son, and had an unhappy childhood, which he later gave as the cause of his political and social attitude: 'I learnt to study society in that school', he wrote. 'I know it and its damned institutions, and I'll work until I'm dead to reform them.' His newspaper, *Le Travailleur*, had an eloquent motto: 'Work, Equality, Brotherhood and Freedom'. He had taken an active part in the radical-democrat movement in the Berne canton, just as Galeer had kept in close contact with Druey and Fazy, the leaders of the radical revolution at Lausanne and Geneva. Coullery considered that the people formed the only productive class, and that 'society should put each man in a position suited to his abilities, his capacity for work, his adaptability, his possessions and his potentialities'. The revolutions of 1848 adopted this principle, and Coullery himself stuck to it; later on, he announced: 'People say that the revolutionaries, the workers and the poor with all their talk of reform and brotherly love, are out to abolish property. That is a foul libel. In 1848, the people revolted throughout Europe and wherever they gained control, they respected private property.' This is a perfect restatement of the theme of Swiss ideology.

As for the revolutionary propaganda of the German refugees and workers in Switzerland, its main, if not its sole, object was to prepare for revolution *in Germany* where censorship and police surveillance made it impossible for them to do or write anything. Swiss territory—and in some cases Swiss printing presses—provided them with a training area and a springboard for their attack. Practically all the publishing and printing firms were run by German refugees so that they could publish their own material. The most famous and important publications were those of the *Comptoir Littéraire* at Zurich and Winterthur, of which Julius Froebel was the founder and director. One is tempted to paraphrase a recent saying by calling it an *ideological arsenal of democracy*. Karl Heinzen addressed his compatriots in a manifesto published at Hérisau in 1846 which underlined the emigrants' rôle: 'Ever since the voice of truth was silenced within our country's borders, it has always been the emigrants who kept the torch of freedom burning and one day they will bear it home!' Further on he writes: 'Believe me, a single pamphlet is a more effective weapon against tyranny, than a whole regiment of artillery against freedom.' The watchword is Freedom, a word which is, according to Rotteck, both flattering and eloquent, anathema to tyrants, meaningless to slaves, often misconstrued by fools, shamefully abused by fanatics, and nevertheless the key to justice. The German governments tried to counter this propaganda by keeping a watch on its authors' whereabouts, and by establishing a censorship to prevent it from entering Germany. In 1833 and 1834, the Frankfort Diet forbade German students to attend the new liberal universities of Zurich and Berne. But such measures only encouraged the Opposition to try even harder to keep in touch with sympathisers across the border. In 1843, there was a project to start a Franco-German circle of authors and found a paper in Paris. Future contributors included Arnold Ruge, Engels, Karl Marx and Heine. Froebel was roped in at the start and it was decided that he should open a branch of the *Comptoir Littéraire* in Paris. The plan fizzled out, but it was significant. Finally, Cabet's and Proudhon's works were translated into German and published at Zurich in 1844.

Switzerland thus became the home of revolutionary propaganda. The foreign influences at work had little effect on Swiss public opinion as a whole, but they did prepare the way for the German revolutions. It must not be forgotten, however, that their real significance lay in the way they reflected the political position, particularly of the left wing of the opposition, in Germany itself. Switzerland's main part in ideological preparations for the 1848 Revolution in Germany, was that of an accurate mirror. It was not a matter of chance that all the publishing firms, with the exception of one at Berne, were on the German border. And in 1845 and 1846—only a short time before the revolutions broke out—the Federal Diet banned the *Comptoir Littéraire*, at the request of German governments, who were not blind to its menace.

The work of the propagandists and publishers in German Switzerland was aimed at the emancipation and education of the individual; it was essentially middle class. A different kind of propaganda, aimed at the emancipation of the masses, was carried on in French Switzerland, on the French frontier, in collaboration with the socialists and the communists. Both, however, set people thinking about freedom, and enabled new sections of the populace to take their part in government.

The major political transformation was the work of a new party which had broken away from the liberals. Like the English or the French extremists, they called themselves 'radicals', for they were determined to reform existing institutions down to their very roots. Some of their leaders had been in contact with foreign politicians, in particular Jakob Stämpfli from Berne (who owed his political education to Snell), James Fazy (who started the revolution in Geneva), and Henri Druey from Vaud. Besides these three zealots, there were the equally sincere and enthusiastic Ulrich Ochsenbein (another Bernese) and Augustin Keller from Aargau. Theirs are not the only names, but they are indisputably the ones who, by the force of their personality, swelled their ranks, and won over to their ideals and their dynamic and clear-sighted policy, first the majority of the cantons, and finally the entire Confederation.

The elaboration of cantonal constitutions was frequently the cause of violent conflicts. To give but two examples, fierce feelings were roused when in 1836 the constitution of Glarus curtailed the rights of the Catholic minority, and when in 1841 Lucerne limited the freedom of the press and denied civic right to the Protestants within the canton. The debates in the Federal Diet as a result of so many decisions of this sort led to a decisive clash. The fierce battles which raged between the two major parties in nine of the most important cantons[1] were somewhat like an intensive artillery barrage put down before a full-scale offensive. The objective of this offensive was plain enough: Government 'of the people, by the people, and for the people'.

This aim was energetically pursued in every battle, especially in the fights about universal suffrage and methods of voting, the publicity of debates in the Diets, juries in the law courts, freedom of the press, freedom of worship, and abolition of privilege. The war against ultramontanism was of course part of the same policy, which was opposed to any kind of interference on the Church's part with the sovereign rights of the people. Anti-clerical excesses won the radicals some supporters but also lost them

[1] Zurich, Lucerne, Valais, Soleure, Berne, Aargau, Vaud, St Gall and Geneva.

others. The abolition of a property qualification for voters and widening of the franchise to include all social classes and a lower age-group won the support of the young and the poor. In the realms of social welfare and economics, the radicals were responsible for abolishing ground-rents; undertaking public works; and introducing new forms of public assistance, graded taxation and education within reach of all. But their opponents had no difficulty on this account in accusing them of communism and State socialism, let alone of waste and incompetence.

In conformity with their domestic programme of centralisation, the radicals pursued a vigorous national foreign policy.

As only the left wing of the liberals, the Radical Party compensated for its relative weakness in numbers by its virility and iron doctrine. It had the support of the liberals proper, who represented the interests of industry and, to some extent, of commerce, and were in favour of centralisation and the abolition of all barriers to trade for purely economic reasons, realising that there could be no progress whilst the country was divided into watertight compartments.

Behind the conservatives' passionate defence of religion was a determination to keep up all forms of tradition as bulwarks against what they considered to be the forces of moral, political and social corrosion. In their hostility towards the radicals, they became far more anti-rationalist than they had been in the past, but their support of ultramontanism and cantonal autonomy was bound to become fanatical in the face of the radicals' behaviour. The latter were fired with revolutionary fervour and were determined, by illegal means if necessary and with no attempt to compromise or mince words with their opponents, to assure the success of their cause.

Four decisive events were to prove it.

Ever since 1841, on the instigation of Augustin Keller who was himself a Catholic, the government of Aargau had suppressed monasteries and convents in the canton. There was already the possibility of intervention from abroad. In the Diet, twelve cantons and two half-cantons had denounced the secularisation law as a violation of the Pact of 1815. The law, however, was only partially withdrawn: the monasteries remained closed. Thus what had originally been a purely religious matter became first a legal, then a political one. The following seven cantons formed a Catholic bloc: Uri, Schwyz, Unterwalden, Zug, Fribourg, Lucerne and Valais.

The opposing sides had taken up their positions, and to avenge their partial defeat, the Catholics (led by Leu, Siegwart and Bernard Meyer) retorted in 1844 by bringing the Jesuits into the Lucerne canton and putting them in charge of the principal educational establishments. The radicals regarded this move as a most serious threat to the success of their aims and it created an uproar throughout Switzerland. From that moment there could be no half measures. Every Swiss was involved in a fight to the death. Even the *Gazette de Bâle*, edited by Jakob Burckhardt, an out-and-out conservative, was compelled to denounce the appeal to the Jesuits as a crime against the Confederation. The hitherto mild conflict between the ultramontanes and the rationalists reached the pitch of fanaticism. The histories of politics and literature are saturated with it, as the names of Gottfried Keller, C. F. Meyer and Jeremias Gotthelf bear witness. The alliance between the anti-clerical radicals and the Protestant masses of the countryside, which had until recently been extremely shaky, was immediately cemented.

The way was open for direct and violent action: although they did not yet imitate the medieval monarchs' '*exécutions impériales*', the governments of certain cantons gave their blessing and support to the formation of armed *corps francs* which started riots in Lucerne. The first attempt, in December 1844, was a complete disaster and the Lucerne Government showed no mercy to the ringleaders.

The issue was still primarily a political one. The revolution of 1845 at Lausanne centred round the affair of the Jesuits, and ended in the adoption of a new radical-democratic Constitution. This was the work of Henri Druey, a jurist, who had travelled widely in France, Germany and England. It was he who, with J. C. Kern, prepared the Federal Constitution of 1848.

On 30 March 1845, the Bernese Ulrich Ochsenbein led a fresh force of *corps francs* against Lucerne. His attempt failed almost as disastrously as the first, and out of 3,600 men, over a hundred were killed, and half were taken prisoner. The victors were as merciless as before. Metternich was overjoyed at the success of the Catholics, to which he attached great importance from the point of view of general European politics.

But their victory was short-lived.

On 11 December 1845, the seven Catholic cantons formed a solemn political and military pact, to defend cantonal sovereignty and to place this separate league or *Sonderbund* under a single command. This was clearly a violation of the Federal Pact of 1815, and what made it worse was that they sought willing helpers abroad. Austria and France had long been worried by the actions of the Radical Party, ever since the liberal cantons gave so warm a welcome to prominent patriots expelled by the Frankfort Diet.

An overwhelming majority of the Swiss people supported the liberals and radicals. It was a very different matter in the Federal Diet, where each canton had only one vote. The first victories were won at Zurich, where Jonas Furrer, the son of a locksmith from Winterthur, and the radicals, gained a majority; and at Berne, where the extreme radicals under Ochsenbein and Stämpfli carried the day. They immediately started to work out a new Constitution, bringing in universal suffrage and a secret, direct ballot, lowering the minimum age for voters to twenty, and separating the legislature from the executive, whilst at the same time strengthening communal autonomy. They laid down the principles of the State's social rôle, and the foundations of a strong economic policy, notably by the means of a fiscal reform introducing income tax and a capital levy.

Under the leadership of James Fazy, a young, eloquent radical, and with the aid of the Catholic country people (as only the political aspect of the conflict remained) a bloody revolution broke out (complete with barricades) in Geneva. On 7 October 1846 the revolutionaries put a new government into office, which in 1847 gave the canton a fresh constitution. Thenceforth, the State Council was elected by the citizens, freedom of education was guaranteed, and justice was assured by the introduction of juries.

In May 1847 the Radical victory in the St Gall elections created the necessary majority of twelve votes. On 20 July the Federal Diet, by the votes of twelve cantons and two half cantons, proclaimed the dissolution of the *Sonderbund* as incompatible with the Federal Pact. This parliamentary majority actually represented more than 80 per cent of the total population of the country, and over 90 per cent of its wealth. Ochsenbein, who presided over the meetings of the Diet as head of the government, made a speech in which he showed that the whole conflict centred round a simple alternative: progress or the *status quo*—if not stagnation. He went on to point out that this dilemma was not peculiar to Switzerland, it existed all over the world: hence 'the flames which are leaping up in every State in Europe to rekindle cold embers in the hearths of derelict constitutions'. According to this radical leader, '*Switzerland is a miniature replica of the rest of Europe. The participants themselves in this conflict are fully aware of the fact that the crisis in Switzerland is an integral part of the growing crisis in Europe.*' It has been said that 'Ochsenbein's confident and optimistic liberalism was in marked contrast to the attitude of the delegate from Lucerne, Bernard Meyer, whose conservative heart was filled with gloomy disgust at the state of affairs in Europe before the Revolutions'. And Bernard Meyer himself speaks of the 'demonic spirit which is determined to blow up the present political structure of Europe by undermining its legal foundations'. We see how each side, in its own fashion, felt the wind of revolution blowing across Europe on the eve of 1848, and how reactionary fury answered liberal enthusiasm. Druey gives the clearest picture of the opposing camps, in a detailed enumeration of their qualities which is typical of the age. 'On one side, democracy, liberalism, equality, brotherhood, progress, truth and unselfishness; on the other, autocracy, aristocracy, oppression of the masses, lies and egoism.' And he takes his stand with the oppressed and warns Europe 'to understand the issue if she seeks to meddle in our affairs'.

The Great Powers knew what was brewing. Metternich tried to unite what today would be called the 'Big Five', to prevent the formation of a radical Swiss Republic. In January 1847 the diplomatic representatives of Austria, Russia and Prussia pointedly left Berne. Louis Philippe and Guizot were not so definite, though they were inclined to favour the *Sonderbund*, but the republican opposition and public feeling in Switzerland made them cautious. The only opposition met by Metternich was from Palmerston and the British Government, who were sympathetic towards the radicals and opposed to any intervention. Metternich, alive to the danger, sent money and arms to his *protégés*.

Passions were roused, and fantastic rumours were in circulation. For instance, there were whispers that the radicals had made out black lists and had sent for two guillotines from Cologne and an executioner from Colmar.

Simultaneously, the two sides got ready, and both made military preparations: the seven Catholic cantons refused to dismiss the Jesuits and dissolve their coalition, and at the same time promoted a Protestant Colonel, de Salis-Solgio, to be their General.

On 4 November, the Diet declared war on the *Sonderbund*. A fortnight earlier they had put General Dufour in command of the army. This time it really was an '*exécution féderal*' and civil war—a War of the Swiss Secession, in fact. On 4 November the majority in the Diet published a manifesto in which they told the Swiss people: 'This is no war against innocent kinsfolk. It is the war of the Confederation and its legitimate authorities against the party that founded the *Sonderbund*.' One is reminded of Lincoln's words some fifteen years later, when in a letter written on 22 August 1861, he stated that his first aim in this conflict was to *save* the Union.

This was exactly the spirit in which Dufour carried out his orders. Besides, he was more of a moderate conservative than a radical by both temperament and political conviction. One Swiss historian believes that the issue at stake was even more serious for Switzerland than it would have been for the United States. 'If the South had won', he writes, 'two separate States would have come into being, but a Catholic victory in Switzerland would have meant the dismemberment of the country.' Luckily for Switzerland the overwhelming strength of the government forces decided the campaign in twenty-six days. The number of casualties was infinitesimal, and the victors showed considerable clemency, merely imposing a fine on the dissident cantons. Incidentally, the complete success of the peoples' army provided yet another political argument.

Individualism and freedom had carried the day, and the way was open for economic progress. A *new* Switzerland, of the radicals and the liberals, could be created, for the new order had won its first victory over the old.

This fact alone should be sufficient reason for devoting the first chapter of a book on the 1848 Revolutions to the transformation of Switzerland. But there is yet another reason: the immediate repercussions abroad caused by the birth of the Confederation.

There are three main facets to be discussed: the press, the attitude of the different governments, and demonstrations on the part of sympathisers.

It is true to say that all eyes were turned towards Switzerland for several weeks before the outbreak of the 1848 Revolutions, for which she had prepared the way. We have already seen how for several years German and French progressives had kept in close touch with their opposite numbers in Switzerland. But from July 1847 onwards especially in November and December of that year, events in Switzerland were front-page news in European newspapers of all colours; which plainly showed that they were of paramount interest to the general public. In November the people of Berlin and Weimar literally fought for papers giving news of Switzerland. A new paper, the *Deutsche Zeitung*, announced in its editorial on 9 July that it would give prominence to Swiss affairs, with particular reference to their significance for Germany. The *Brüsseler Deutsche Zeitung*, Marx's and Engels' paper, stated on 30 December 1847 that 'the tyrants as well as the people have fully realized the significance of the conflict in Switzerland, which was the battle of progress against a feudal past, and of democracy against the baseness of the aristocracy and the Jesuits . . . theirs was a victory for the people in every country in Europe; it was, in fact, a European victory'.[1]

The delight of the left wing newspapers is in marked contrast to the reticence of the unofficial organs of the right. The people, before they could themselves enter '*dans la carrière*', understandably transferred their emotion to Switzerland, and followed its vicissitudes as though they were their own. The defeat of the *Sonderbund* was greeted on all sides with a display of enthusiasm it is hard to imagine today. The papers are not our only source of information: eye-witness accounts, contemporary letters and memoirs all go to prove it. Michelet and Edgar Quinet, both professors at the *Collège de France*, wrote to the members of the Federal Diet as follows: 'We beg you to accept the greetings and congratulations of

[1] The most accurate documentation on the whole matter is that furnished by Professor Werner Naef in his book *Der Schweizerische Sonderbundskrieg, etc.* (Bâle, 1919).

two men who were the first to cross swords in their country with the enemy you have routed in yours. . . . You have brought solace to France.' They did not, however, speak for the whole of France. Montalambert, who in November had organised a fighting fund for the *Sonderbund*, loudly voiced his sympathies in a long speech to the Chamber of Peers. Perhaps he really did feel so strongly about Switzerland, but his chief purpose was to denounce the Swiss radicals' allies in France. Only a few days before the fall of the July Monarchy, it was the 'Swiss question' which provoked the stormiest debates in the Chamber. Opposition cheers greeted Thiers' declaration on 2 February 1848, that the Government, by supporting the counter-revolutionary party in Switzerland, had betrayed the principles of 1830.

In Rome, Florence and Leghorn, enthusiastic crowds celebrated the Liberals' victory by demonstrations outside the Swiss Consulates. They waved flags and organised torchlight processions, and—what is most significant—gave cheers for Italian as well as Swiss independence. Although its expression was curbed by the censorship, Prague's joy was no less deeply felt. Thus it was that the German, Treitschke, at the end of his *History of Germany in the Nineteenth Century* was able to speak of the war against the *Sonderbund* as a 'harbinger of the Revolution in Europe'. The conflict in Switzerland enabled foreign political parties to define themselves. For example, before March 1848, the Germans had formed Liberal, Radical, Constitutional Monarchist, Republican, Democratic and Communist Parties. To mention only Germany, the conflicting principles of the two opposing forces were almost exactly the same as in Switzerland, although the radicals in Germany were in a far weaker position; what is more, even before 1847 Switzerland was more democratic than Germany. In fact, apart from differences of detail, however great, what gave Switzerland her value as a lighthouse—a barometer even—was the alternative before her of progress or stagnation, advance or retreat. And it is because this was an universal alternative (Europe, at that time being the political universe) Switzerland's vicissitudes provided an obvious testing-ground. That is why they inevitably had such extraordinary repercussions.

That is also why the Great Powers were so anxious to intervene. This is no place to go into details of the diplomatic problems raised. Suffice it to say that in the name of law and order, the Holy Alliance—or its counterpart just before the middle of the century (that prototype of a Foreign Ministers' Council)—felt it had to forestall any political or constitutional transformation in Switzerland, otherwise a disorderly element would be introduced into an already restless Europe. The Swiss conflict was like a clash between the spearheads of two opposing armies. Professor Naef hit the nail on the head when he pointed out that Metter-

nich and his allies wanted to treat the Swiss question as a European one
—as a question of principle. That was how the peoples of Europe had
already taken it. They had seen a number of principles at stake, primarily
that of freedom, but also those of nationality and democracy with all
their logical consequences. By supporting the *Sonderbund*, the Powers themselves gave the conflict more weight and more significance and enhanced
the importance of its outcome. The victory of either party in Switzerland
would by the same token be the victory of one supporting faction, whose
gigantic shadows loomed over the tiny figures of the puppets in the spot-
light.

Metternich himself said much the same thing in a letter he wrote to
Count Apponyi, his Ambassador in Paris, on 9 November 1847: 'Switzerland is a volcano and the foreign body which will cause it to erupt is the
radical element.' He took an even more serious view (which, it must be
admitted, showed his perspicacity) of the 'progressives becoming a lawful
body'. 'Today, the Powers are faced with radicalism in control', confessed
the leader of reaction in Europe, on 12 December. He even believed that
having succeeded in their own country, the Swiss radicals would start
'radicalising' their neighbours, or at any rate help their comrades, particularly in Italy. In Austria itself, Metternich tried to counteract the influence
of the radical victory by launching a press campaign to blacken the
radicals' character and convict them of such fantastic crimes that we might
smile if we had not recently seen the effect of such methods.

Frederick William IV also saw the universal implications of the conflict
in Switzerland, where the godless radicals had won a battle in the 'general
war'. His ambassador in Switzerland had foreseen this would happen as
early as 4 November: 'It is impossible to have a radical victory in Switzerland without the strongest repercussions in Germany. They are too closely
linked. The principle of legal radicalism is one generally loved by all
enemies of justice. It will be considerably advanced by a victory here.'

The Church party in Bavaria feared that the defeat of the *Sonderbund*
might bode ill for their future: 'The foundation on which our States and
Thrones are based has been shaken much more severely than many people
believe by this defeat of the chartered and established right.' And they
drew a grim picture of the first acts of the 'communistic Jacobins', as they
called the Swiss Radical Party.

One can also understand why the Powers wanted to intervene even
after the annihilation of the *Sonderbund*, in the hopes of carving up the
cantons in the most monstrous fashion. Only Palmerston's deliberate
procrastination, followed by the February Revolution in Paris, saved
Switzerland from foreign intervention.

The peoples were preparing to counter the Holy Alliance of the absolute monarchies with a Holy Alliance of their own under the banner of freedom, as depicted by Béranger. Freedom knows no frontiers, and there were more than 5,000 signatures of all kinds and classes of people appended to some fifty odd messages of sympathy received by the Diet. The majority came from Germany, but they were also from Paris, London and Brussels, and they were all enthusiastic and often eloquent, and in many cases were sent at considerable risk to their authors, owing to the strictness of the German censorship. Furthermore, the Swiss Republic—the only one in Europe—acquired increasing value as an example. It is true that the universal revolutionary movement had been growing for a long time; nevertheless, the form the Swiss Radicals' victory had taken was 'a slap in the face for every king in Europe', and gave a new turn to European politics. As one of them said, though a trifle grandiloquently, 'the clock of the peoples marked midnight; the Swiss people advanced the hands several hours towards the dawn.'

FRANCE AND THE REVOLUTION
OF 1848

GEORGES BOURGIN

The people do not want words: they want actions
'Les Blanquistes' 17 March 1846

*In the reign of Louis Philippe you were warned to 'Beware of
dictatorship'. Now it is up to you to prevent a hunger march*
Louis Blanc to the Constituent Assembly

I

THE ORIGINS OF THE REVOLUTION

IT is said again and again that the Revolution of 1848 struck France like
a thunderbolt. That is doubly false: a whole host of causes and conditions
led to its outbreak, and countless prophets foretold it. On 7 July 1845,
Lamartine—who may have sat 'in the clouds' but none the less knew
precisely where events were leading—wrote: 'This country is moribund.
Only a crisis can galvanise it.' In the *Presse* of 11 July 1847, Madame
Girardin recorded 'political rumblings and dire predictions', and heard
people around her saying: 'We are on the eve of great events, it's going
to mean a revolution.' And Léon Faucher, too, the future Minister,
prophesied on 29 July 1847, that the prolongation of so degrading a
régime could only end in revolution; two months later he said: 'Society
is like a machine that has crocked up.' On 10 January 1848, Adolphe
Thiers said, in the course of a conversation reported by one of Guizot's
agents: 'The country is hurtling towards a catastrophe which may occur
before the King's death, if he lives to a great age, or very shortly after it.
There's going to be a civil war.' Another observer, Alexis de Tocqueville
(one of the finest minds of his time), made a speech in the Chamber on
27 January 1848, which threw a prophetic light on the immediate future:
'You say,' he told them, 'that there is no peril because there are no riots;
you argue that as the society is calm on the surface, revolution is an aeon
away. But if you will forgive me for saying so, you're utterly mistaken.
It is true there is no visible sign of disorder, but that's because the disorder

is deep down in peoples' hearts. Try to see what is going on in the hearts of the workers—who I admit seem peaceable enough at the moment. It's true they are not torn by pure political passions as they used to be. But don't you see that their aims are now social, not political?' After explaining this, de Tocqueville asserted 'that the ultimate reason for a man's losing authority is because he isn't fit to hold it.' That was why the monarchy fell in 1789—not because of La Fayette, or Mirabeau, or the deficit, or the Tennis-Court Oath, but because 'the ruling class, by its own apathy, its selfishness and its decadence had become incompetent and unfit to rule.' 'The storm is brewing', ended de Tocqueville, who in his *Souvenirs* underlines the fact that the majority of his hearers greeted his prophesies 'with sardonic laughter'.

But what was happening 'in the hearts of the working class'? Socialist or communist propaganda had shown them the remedy for their ills: a new form of society to replace one which was derelict, and stood condemned not only by its own selfishness but by the blunders of its rulers both at home and abroad.

And what about working-class distress? In 1835 Dr Guépin of Nantes summed up the whole issue by saying that to the working man 'life simply means staying alive', and the social investigators of Louis Philippe's reign—Villermé, Buret and Villeneuve-Bargemont—all agreed with him. Villeneuve-Bargemont, a Catholic too, who introduced the English word 'pauperism' into France, pointed to the appalling gulf between the rich and the poor after 1834: 'The rich', he said, 'gallop through life, without a thought for the future beyond the pursuit of pleasure. The masses, who are both morally and physically starving, demand their share of the good things of life, whether the rich will it or no.' The economists condemned industrial concentration as a new form of slavery and mechanisation as the death of craftsmanship, as well as the engagement of women, children and cripples because they were cheaper than skilled workmen.

The economists were as critical of the existing order as the socialists, from whom they differed only in their belief that Christianity was the sole way to human happiness.

Out of France's thirty-three million inhabitants in 1848, 6,300,000 persons were employed in industry, two million more than in 1826. Wages had fallen since the beginning of the Restoration, and the cost of living (according to official figures) rose by 17 per cent between 1826 and 1847. According to Agricol Perdiguier, wages had been reduced by two-thirds since 1830: the average wage for women was 77 centimes, falling to between 30 and 60 centimes for eighteen hours' work a day; the wages for men in 1848 was 1 franc 78 for thirteen hours' work; children, who were forced to save their families from starvation, were paid about

50 centimes. Physical exhaustion from working thirteen to fifteen hours a day, insufficient and bad food, alcoholism (which was on the increase despite the cost of liquor), squalor, filth, and debauchery were such that in the most highly industrialised Departments, 9,000 out of 10,000 men called up for military service were rejected as unfit. The infant mortality rate was extremely high.

Complete illiteracy was one consequence of this appalling condition of the French working class. In 1832, a short time before Guizot brought in his skeleton system of primary schooling, there were 2,895,608 children between five and twelve (that is to say two-thirds of the children of that age in the country) without any education whatsoever. 14,766,270 persons—roughly half the population—were illiterate. In 1835, these figures were even higher on account of the increase in population. Another consequence, which has received little comment, was the increase in crime: in 1841 the number of delinquents was five times what it had been in 1826.

Eugène Buret has called pauperism 'a phenomenon of civilisation'. It was the natural product of economic evolution of industry on a large scale, and might be defined as poverty felt as an injustice. Its effect on the intelligent workers was to teach them that the proletariat is as an organic whole. As early as 1832 Chateaubriand had felt the presence of 'an avenging spirit at society's back, making it tremble'. This spirit materialised in the host of secret societies, friendly societies and every other kind of society that pullulated in the reign of Louis Philippe. And each had its own system to counteract the appalling effects of capitalist exploitation.

Some, damning every aspect of modern civilisation, held that the only hope was to return to the days of trade guilds, revive home industries, and reorganise agriculture. Others, the Social Democrats, of whom Buchez was the best example, advocated the application of Christ's precept of brotherly love through charity. Liberals like Charles Dupin and Alexis de Tocqueville wanted to make conditions easier by social legislation. One law to regulate the employment of women and children had been passed in 1840 but it was never enforced; and they wished to bring in many more to safeguard contracts, legalise trade unions, and provide for all kinds of insurance. All these reformers, however, were thwarted by the champions of free enterprise, with the slogan of *Laisser faire, laissez passer*; men who had directly or indirectly benefited by the Industrial Revolution. Bastiat was their leader. They knew the Government would stop at nothing to support the reactionaries. People had not forgotten in 1847 how the King's ministers had smashed the Lyons revolt of 1831, hamstrung the working-class movement of 1834, and crushed the Paris risings. Their acceptance, after Villermé's report, of the law regulating the employment of women and children did not mean they thought it the State's business to protect the worker; the Civil Code—or, more often, the Penal Code—was sufficient to deal with such matters. Jules Bertaux demonstrates this in his book on 1848. He recalls how, in the course of a debate on sugar manufacture, a deputy who mentioned the interests of the workers drew the following retort from Sauzet, who was President of the Chamber at the time: 'We are here to make laws not to provide work.'

Yet an aristocrat, and a poet at that, could see one solution to the social problem: Lamartine had the sense to seek technical advice on such questions as sugar-refining and railways, and had enough political acumen (whatever Guizot may have thought) to realise the secret ambition which Henri Guillemin has shown that he nourished constantly from 1830 to 1848.[1] 'My theory', he wrote to Montherat on 25 April 1837, 'is that the only road to power lies in identifying oneself with the very spirit of a victorious movement at a time when no one can gainsay you.' But although Lamartine foresaw the revolution which would put him in power, he still supported the unrestricted right to private property, and favoured political but not social democracy. And he had no sympathy with labour organisation. In March 1843, as in June 1848, Lamartine revealed the secret of his ambition: 'One must harness the storm,' he said.

But Lamartine was not smart enough to fool the workers—who in February 1848 already dismissed him as a humbug. The working class, and their sympathisers in the middle class, the artisans and small shop-keepers, a large number of students and a few honest intellectuals who had not their eye on the main chance, were attracted by a bolder propa-ganda than that of Social Catholicism. In the secret societies organised between 1830 and 1840, an alliance was struck up between the lower-middle class and the proletariat, and their aims were clarified. The followers of Saint-Simon and Fourier were still far from losing all influence and the Fourierists continued to denounce 'the chaos of civilisa-tion'. In 1832, Victor Considérant and Jules Chevalier began publication of the *Phalanstère*, succeeded in 1834 by the *Phalange*, which lashed out at industrial feudalism. The Saint-Simonians were no less active, and organised centres in the provinces—particularly in the Midi. In 1830, Bazard had written: 'a new revolution is unavoidable', and shown that 'men are divided into two classes, the exploiters and the exploited'. But it was another forerunner of socialism who had the strongest influence at the beginning of Louis Philippe's reign. This was Gracchus Babeuf, who had been guillotined in 1796, but whose disciple Philippe Buonarotti had

---

[1] *Lamartine et la question sociale*, Paris, 1926

published *La Conjuration des Egaux* in 1828, in which he asserted that 'the revolt of the poor against the rich is inevitable and irresistible.'

The theories of Babeuf had a considerable effect on the members of such societies as *Amis du Peuple, Droits de l'Homme, Famille* and *Saisons,* which were continually plotting against the monarchy and continually being beaten down by the combined forces of the regular army and the National Guard. In 1832, when the *Procès des Quinze* resulted in the conviction of the leaders of the *Amis du Peuple*, Godefroi Cavaignac proclaimed that the society supported labour organisation and stood opposed to capitalist exploitation, and Blanqui declared that 'in the war between the rich and the poor . . . the rich are the aggressors, for they impose a shameful burden on the workers'. The members of the *Droits de l'Homme* went even further: 'It is not so much political changes we want as social reform. We want to see a fairer division of profits.' They demanded the suppression of the new 'aristocracy' that had sprung up from the middle class, a levelling of fortunes, labour organisation, the re-establishment of the 1793 Constitution (as it had been in the days of *Germinal* and *Prairial*) and a Federated States of Europe, founded on the sovereignty of the people; they took their name from Robespierre's bold declaration of the Rights of Man, and when they were brought to justice, their leaders were accused, like the Gracchi, of having aimed at the distribution of property. As soon as one society was disbanded, another and more violent one sprang up to take its place, such as the *Famille* in 1836, and the *Saisons* in 1837. The proletariat did not simply sit and listen to their socialist leaders elaborating plans in their secret conclaves, they took part themselves in risings, such as those in Lyons and Paris, in protest against the severity of a new law against associations, and were harshly dealt with by Thiers' Government. Auguste Blanqui planned these risings and laid down their moral aims, devoting himself to the task of freeing the people. Like both the moderate Saint-Simonians and the advanced socialists, he revealed the machiavellism of the Government. At his trial in 1836, he pronounced the following indictment: 'If a hundred thousand "bourgeois" are said to form the democratic element, then what in God's name are the other elements? Already Paul Louis Courier has pictured machinery of representative government as a kind of suction pump draining off the wealth of the nation, a pitiless machine which crushes 25,000,000 peasants and five million workers one by one in order to suck their blood and transfuse it into the veins of the privileged.'

Despite the imprisonment of Blanqui, and the slaughter of the proletariat in the Rue de la Croix-Rousse, the Rue Transnonain and the Cloître St-Merri, the people, who after 1840 had learnt to save their strength, still dreamed their dreams. Whilst their allies among the middle class turned to electoral reform, they quietly listened to yet more audacious preachers, the socialists and communists, who spoke—to use Courier's phrase—of 'the fire beneath the ashes'. The next eight years saw a widening current of revolutionary thought. Victor Considérant refurbished Fourier's theories, and attacked competition which 'led to monopolies that crushed the worker', and capitalism, with its creation of the false freedom—of 'free enterprise'. Pierre Leroux, a Saint-Simonian, hated capitalism as much as Considérant, and advocated a vast planned organisation to produce and distribute goods. Louis Blanc's dislike of competition drew him towards Considérant's doctrine, and in his *Organisation du Travail* he sought a compromise between free enterprise and complete socialism, by suggesting nationalisation of the Bank, factories, railways, insurance, and certain industries. Constantin Pecqueur was, like Pierre Leroux, obsessed by metaphysics, but he strongly supported collectivism and asserted that 'the sole landowner, contractor and capitalist in a country should be the State, representing the will of the people'. This notion of Pecqueur's is very reminiscent of Vidal. Etienne Cabet's 'Icarian' system verged on a form of communism centred round agriculture, as the sole means of achieving human happiness and security. But whereas Cabet, Considérant, Pierre Leroux and Pecqueur were all metaphysicians, deists and Christians, Proudhon was not inhibited by religion from speaking his mind on the 'brazen law' of wages, the injustice of ownership, the gulf between the middle class and the proletariat, and the illegality of paying interest on capital. Yet he was opposed to interventionism and communism, and his dialectical method, which was criticised by Marx, prevented him from seeing any means of helping the working class other than by cooperation and mutual aid.

Yet all these writers were afraid to advocate revolution, or shut their minds to it. Revolution was only in the programme of those who were later to call themselves communists, to distinguish themselves from those 'reactionary, conservative or "bourgeois" socialists', denounced by the *Communist Manifesto*. Papers like *L'Homme Libre, Le Tribun du Peuple, L'Humanité*, and *La Fraternité*, revolutionary handbooks, pamphlets written by the *Travailleurs Egalitaires*, and speeches at communist banquets spread the following simple and dynamic ideas: work alone produces wealth, so the worker should take first place; equality should mean common ownership of property, achieved by means of 'a strong dictatorship of the people', a 'provisional government', as roughed out in 1840 by the *Société Démocratique Française*, together with the establishment of 'national workshops' and an eight-hour working day.

The secret societies that prepared these bombshells were not composed solely of Frenchmen. Paris of the July Monarchy had become an international centre for revolutionaries, especially for Germans, Italians and Poles. Heine stayed there as well as Princess Belgiojoso; Karl Marx came over to argue with Proudhon, Bakunin was working on the staff of *Vorwärts*, the organ of the German emigrants in France, and Herzen there met again the comrades of his youth. And there were many foreign workers in Paris who had fought on the barricades of 12 and 13 May 1839. As Andler has pointed out, the two German secret societies *Die Geächteten* and *Die Gerechte* were formed on French models. On 29 November 1847, 1,500 Poles, Russians, Frenchmen, Swiss, Germans, Italians, Spaniards, Englishmen, Irishmen and Americans met in the Rue Saint-Honoré to commemorate the anniversary of the Polish Revolution, and as in 1863, when the First International Congress was founded in London, there was a sudden burst of enthusiasm in Paris for a federal union of free peoples. So it was in this same year 1847 that Marx's and Engels' *Communist Manifesto* was written as a result of the Communist Congress held in London. The mantle of *Die Gerechte* fell on the Communist Federation, and Marxism, unique though it may be in its methods and conclusions, would have been inconceivable—as Charles Andler has shown—but for these socialist theories, which had already stirred the French people, from Buonarrotti's to Dézamy's. The international character of the 1848 Revolution was implicit in the *Manifesto's* appeal: 'Workers of the world, unite!'

The symbol of the impending revolution had first appeared on 5 June 1832, when the funeral of General Lamarque occasioned the first rising of the reign. It took place under the Red Flag.

As Gabriel Perreux has shown, this was the Jacobin flag of the Great Revolution as well as the revolutionary socialists' emblem. Montalivet, the Minister for Home Affairs, pointed that out on the evening of 5 June sixteen years before Lamartine, when he contrasted 'the flag of anarchy' with 'the glorious Tricolour'. The Red Flag may have disappeared for a time after the riots of April 1834, when it waved in the provinces as well as in Paris, but it was not forgotten in the secret councils of the revolutionary conspirators and it is not surprising that it reappeared on the barricades of February 1848.

At the beginning of that year, it was easy for the workers of Paris to believe the moment had come to smash a tyrannous but tottering régime and build a new world on the foundations of equality and justice. On 24 January 1845, Prince Louis Napoleon Bonaparte had written to George Sand, saying: 'Day by day, France's brain shrivels, her stomach swells and her heart contracts.' A few months later, de Tocqueville wrote to Gobineau: 'The atmosphere is freezing. Every day there seems to be less warmth, less life, and there is precious little fire left in the veins of my generation. There are still some sparks in the young and the old: the twenties still have their hopes and the sixties their memories, but all that men of my age want is to be left alone to potter about in peace.'

Louis Philippe, who had hopped on to Charles X's throne with such agility, was now an old man and incapable of adjusting himself to changes of which in any case he was unaware. At the end of 1847, when he was seventy-four, he said soothingly to the forty-year-old Duc de Morny: 'Don't worry, young man, France is a country one can rule with civil servants.' And in January 1848 he said to General von Radowitz, the King of Prussia's plenipotentiary: 'Tell your master there are two things that can't happen again in France—one's revolution and the other's war.' As a head of a family once remarkable for its unity, he should have been able to see how it was cracking up. First, there was the marriage of his eldest son, the Duc d'Orléans with the Protestant Princess Helen of Mecklenburg, and then there were the liberal tendencies of the heir to the throne and the Duc d'Aumale, in complete contrast with the narrow outlook of the Duc de Nemours and the Prince de Joinville. In 1842 there was the drama of the Duc d'Orléans' death as the result of a road accident, leaving as next heir to the throne the Comte de Paris, who was but a child. In 1847, Princess Adélaide, the King's sister, died, and he lost a valuable adviser. It was all very well for street-urchins to draw the King of France as a fat-bottomed pear, and the caricaturists to picture him as a plump little bourgeois with an umbrella, but there were two attempts on his life in 1846, one on 16 April and the other on 27 July. When Lecomte, the first would-be assassin, was condemned to death, Victor Hugo made a magnificent speech against the sentence, which caused a furore, and certainly did the King no good. When, on 28 December 1847, Louis Philippe went as usual to open Parliament, he antagonised deputies and peers alike by his outspoken denunciation of 'blind opposition'. The next day, the papers recalled how Charles X had opened Parliament in 1830 with a very similar speech: 'If my government is hampered by culpable manœuvres which I do not foresee . . .'

Louis Philippe was very largely responsible for the faults of a government which he actively controlled, as was his trusty servant Guizot, whom in 1840 he had recalled from London, where he was Ambassador, to clear up the complicated Eastern affair in which Thiers had rashly engaged. Guizot did not however become President of the Council until September 1847, when he succeeded Soult as the King's right-hand man. There was an astonishing contradiction between his brilliant mind, profound knowledge of history and uncompromising Protestant honesty, and the methods he employed. First and foremost was his use of bribery, but there were also his limited outlook in matters of domestic and foreign policy,

and his daily discussions with Princess Lieven, who after all was a foreign
agent. And it is he who is supposed to have said to the French middle class:
'Get rich!'—a historic phrase which like others of its kind has primarily a
symbolic value. But the words he wrote to Pellegrino Rossi, the French
Ambassador in Rome, on 10 September 1846, sum up his attitude: 'We
are staunch conservatives. It is the first and natural responsibility of
governments. We are all the more staunch conservatives because our
country has been through a series of revolutions, and we conceive it to be
our duty to restore order and a lasting respect for authority, laws, principles
and traditions, so as to ensure the stability and endurance of society.' On
two later occasions, Guizot asserted that 'There is no need for statesmen,
barriers will do.' And: 'You need two things to govern a country: Right
and Might.'

Guizot required 'Might' only to enforce his domestic policy, for he
was a complete pacifist in his foreign policy. It was so firmly based on
friendship with Britain and understanding with Metternich that it disgusted
the French, whose patriotism was roused in 1840 by the return of
Napoleon's ashes from St Helena. Guizot was the incarnation of 'peace
at any price', and the watch-dog of the 1815 Peace Treaties.

As regards his domestic policy, he falsified the parliamentary system by
dissolving the Chamber in 1842, so as to gain an obedient majority, and
by remaining in office in 1845 in spite of a defeat in the debate on the
address to the King. Regulations concerning the incompatibility of duties
no longer applied to high officials, and 184 of the 459 Deputies held
government posts. Political allies were granted innumerable concessions,
shares in State monopolies, and lucrative appointments on the Exchanges
and in the tobacco business. There were bound to be scandals, as
in the case of Teste and Cubières; the first was Minister of Public
Works and a peer of the realm, and the second had twice been Minister
for War: they tried to rig the salt market. Then there was Duchâtel, the
Minister of the Interior, who licensed an opera house to finance a ministerial
newspaper. What could be expected of a Chamber in which the government increased its majority by such methods?

Thus Guizot was governing almost entirely in the interests of the rich
middle classes. State protection carefully safeguarded their interests against
foreign competitors; the farmers were protected by a sliding scale of
prices, the vine-growers by a tax on tea, and the manufacturers by customs
barriers. The last mentioned showed considerable initiative when it was a
question of introducing new machinery to increase production ten-fold
and improve its quality, and of constructing railways—the track increased
between 1840 and 1846 from 433 to 1,814 kilometres, so as to speed up
the arrival of raw materials and the distribution of their products. Never-

75

theless they were unnerved by the rate at which industry was progressing abroad, and they refused to come to any customs agreement with the Rhinelanders, Belgium, Prussia or Great Britain.

The middle class had the money, and the middle class was strictly orthodox in its religious views, but there were new currents in Catholicism. A handful of priests and laymen started workmen's colleges, and recommended various social reforms to relieve the workers' lot A few bold spirits, like Lamennais, succeeded after herculean efforts in fighting free of the hold of Rome and theological scruples. But the Catholic schools of the Restoration had seized their chance and produced a generation which was well under the thumb of the clergy. The Church claimed the right to form her own associations and sodalities and to teach the young, and she declared war on the University as the last refuge of eighteenth century rationalism. She accused it of 'murdering souls' and 'turning innocent children into wild beasts'. Villemain, the Minister of Education, made no attempt to counter this offensive, and even proposed a law whereby preliminary sanction was no longer required to found a free school. The Chamber did, however, reject his proposals. Thiers succeeded in having a number of Jesuit novice-ships closed, and there were anti-clerical demonstrations by students attending Michelet's, Quinet's and Mickiewicz' courses at the *Collège de France*. But these were isolated actions: the bulk of the French middle class had lost their Voltairian outlook, and provided a mass of novices for the monasteries and convents.

The middle-class monopoly was complete: prosperity on earth and happiness in heaven, and as the ruling class their energies were divided between the two. There certainly were numerous political parties. There were the legitimists under Berryer, the Bonapartists, whose candidate had escaped from the fortress of Ham and was awaiting the outcome of events in England, as was the Comte de Chambord in Austria; the liberals who supported the monarchy and moderate reform, and the republicans who sought precedents in the recent past of 1789–93. But of far greater importance were three main currents of thought representing the three main elements of society. First, there was the conservative or reactionary middle class, then the lower-middle class of artisans and shopkeepers, with sympathisers from the liberal professions, who believed that electoral reform would change the position of the monarchy, and finally there was the proletariat, silently and dourly waiting for a full-blooded revolution. Equally silent were the agricultural workers, but they were fully occupied trying to get something to grow in the tiny plots of land they had so hardly won when the big estates were sold up; they were too busy trying to get the best out of what they had to worry about the communistic bogy which politicians were later to dangle in front of them.

To sum up, the only apparent unrest on the eve of 1848 was due to the public's desire for a fair electoral system and a degree of political morality. In 1843 a new paper called *La Réforme* was founded by Flocon, the two Aragos, Louis Blanc, Ledru-Rollin, and Godefroi Cavaignac. It demanded laws to protect the worker, a ruling that no Deputy should serve as a Prefect, the lowering of the property qualification to vote to 100 francs, and the acceptance of alternative qualifications such as certain university degrees. These demands were made each year up to 1847 with the exception of 1844. They were ignored on the instructions of Guizot, who said: 'There is no excuse for universal suffrage. It is absurd. Every living creature would be granted political rights.' This unfeeling minister's obstinacy resulted in a curious form of propaganda and intimidation, the Campaign of the Banquets.

The first was held in Paris on 10 July 1847; at Châlons a special toast was drunk to the Convention; at Autun, the communist gospel of Babeuf was preached; and at Mâcon, Lamartine made a violent speech in which he spoke of a 'revolution of contempt' against the 'Bourgeois King'. There was an outburst of indignation in nearly every home in the country against 'extortion, corruption and peculation'. The movement grew like wildfire. It must have been in the course of these months that disaffection began to take hold on the National Guard—this middle-class militia force which had lost so many men in defence of the monarchy during the first ten years of the reign. In the Chamber of Deputies in January 1848, there were sharp exchanges in the debate on the King's address, finally ending again in a victory for Guizot who declared that he 'would not yield an inch'. All the same his majority fell to forty-three. Yet, when a reformist banquet of the 12th Arrondissement (comprising the Saint-Jacques and Saint-Marcel quarters) was announced for 22 February, the Government banned it. This ban was to be the signal for the Revolution.

My analysis of causes and conditions is not yet quite complete. The Society scandals of 1847 certainly had their effect; whether they were the murder of the Duchesse de Choiseul-Praslin on the night of 17 August by her husband, a peer of France, who afterwards took poison, or the murder by the Prince d'Eckmühl of his mistress; or the suicide of Comte Bresson, Ambassador in Naples and negotiator of the Spanish marriages, or the arrest and suicide of a former Minister of Justice in a brothel. It is not surprising that on 5 July when the carriages on the way to the Duc and Duchesse de Montpensier's garden party at Vincennes passed through the Faubourg Saint-Antoine, the workmen shouted out: 'Down with the robbers!'

But all this uproar and ferment stood out against a background of poverty and insecurity. An unparalleled food shortage began in 1845 with the potato famine in Ireland, and grew acute in 1846 with a bad harvest owing to lack of rain: wheat, which in 1845 was worth 17.15 francs the hectolitre, rose in 1847 to 39.75 francs and even to 43 francs. A pound of bread cost as much as 60 centimes. In the centre and west of the country, the labourers and workmen prevented grain from leaving the district, pillaged the convoys and barges, and forced the farmers to sell at a knock-out price. It was a real *'jacquerie'*, which the mounted constabulary was sent to combat and the law punished with the utmost severity. The government bought cereals from the United States, Russia and Spain, importing nine and a half millions worth of flour and grain, and willy-nilly filled the bakeries. But the food crisis, as Pouthas records, produced a chain of disastrous consequences. In the first place, the high cost of living stopped people buying manufactured goods. There were crises in the textile and metallurgical industries; workers were dismissed from the foundries and coal mines; wages fell; and pauperism increased in both town and country, where industry sought extra labour. There was also a crisis in banking. As the result of the enormous expenditure on grain from abroad, a number of countries had to approach the Bank of France, whose gold reserves fell from 80 to 59 million between 1 and 15 January 1847. The result was she had to borrow from England and Russia, call in gold from the provinces, remint silver withdrawn from circulation, and issue 25 million francs' worth of 200 franc notes. The difficulties of the most stable institution in France had repercussions on industrial enterprises, local banks and railway companies, numbers of which went bankrupt. The very foundations of society seemed to be crumbling at a time when the socialists were denouncing its misdeeds and the proletariat were preparing to smash it.

How, then, can we explain the fact that so few contemporaries saw the revolution coming? How was it that so shrewd an observer as Prosper Mérimée did not foresee it?—Mérimée who painted for the Countess of Montijo so vivid a picture of the appalling poverty in Brittany, where the poor 'lived on boiled seaweed'. The answer may be that society, prosaic and crude as it was, nevertheless swam in a sea of romanticism, and that there were few minds capable of an objective analysis of political and social phenomena. Literary romanticism as exemplified by Victor Hugo was typified in George Sand's writings by emotional and audacious content and turgid expression. Another romantic, Lamartine, said when speaking of the revolution: 'We are writing the most sublime of poems.' An eclectic philosophy, though full of truisms, was unable to discover the truth. In 1845, one Renan—who three years later was to write *L'Avenir de la Science*—refused to attend Michelet's and Quinet's lectures, because they attacked 'everything which is holy and sacred'; and the Church, to which he still belonged, was hesitating between accepting the faint democratic tendency of the new Pope Pius IX's first political writings, and the pure ultramontane tradition.

To put it briefly, the last years of Louis Philippe's reign revealed a very real crisis in France's intellectual development, whose conditions, manifestations and progress are revealed by that magnificent writer Gustave Flaubert in *Education Sentimentale*.

2

FEBRUARY 1848

On 20 February 1848, the Government and the Opposition had reached a kind of agreement about the 12th Arrondissement's Banquet, which had been banned on 13 February by a decree of the Minister of Justice, Hébert. But on the board of the *National*, Marrast, Armand Perret, Pagnerre, Havin and Alton-Shée decided to ignore this, and planned a procession to rouse public feeling. This project was published in three republican newspapers on the morning of the 21st.

The Government, seeing that the situation had entirely changed, decided that the Banquet should not take place; it was banned by order of the Prefect of Police, and a police regulation appeared on the subject of unlawful assemblies. General Jacqueminot published an order of the day forbidding the National Guard to form up without orders from their superiors, and according to the plan drawn up by General Gérard in 1840, a force just over 20,000 strong occupied the capital.

Whilst the Deputies of the Opposition (with the exception of Lamartine) acquiesced, the reformist and republican leaders met in the Rue Jean-Jacques Rousseau for a lengthy discussion which ended in their climbing down in like fashion: Ledru-Rollin, Louis Blanc and Flocon opposed 'any rash undertakings', and an article to that effect was published the next day in the *Réforme*. So 21 February seemed to end to the Government's advantage, and the King in the course of a reception at the Tuileries expressed considerable satisfaction. Generals Sebastiani and Jacqueminot, together with Duchâtel, the Minister of the Interior, decided to confine the troops to barracks, and not station them at the various vantage points in Paris, where an unnecessary display of force would only provoke the people.

Nevertheless, demonstrations began on the 22nd. At ten o'clock in the morning, workmen, students and street-urchins, who had flocked to the

Boulevards, the Rue Royale, the Champs-Elysées and the Rue Saint-Honoré—the route the procession was to have taken—were dispersed by a police charge. But there were already attempts to erect barricades in various places including the Champs-Elysées and the Rue Saint-Honoré. In the Chamber of Deputies, Odilon Barrot, with belated audacity, tabled a bill of arraignment on six counts, which Guizot accepted with disdain, adjourning the debate until the 24th. But on the 23rd the revolutionary current grew stronger: in spite of torrential rain, there were more demonstrations, barricades were erected and events took an unexpected turn. Clashes were becoming more frequent between the rioters and the regular army, when troops of the National Guard decided to come in on the side of the former; the Third Legion sent a deputation to General Jacqueminot demanding the dismissal of the Cabinet. Arms were taken up on all sides, and the Red Flag appeared for the first time on a barricade in the Rue Montmartre, in the shape of a blind torn out of an overturned cab. Duchâtel, who was growing anxious, explained the situation to the King, who—on the Queen's advice—decided to dismiss Guizot. The President of the Council was called to the Tuileries, acquiesced, and informed the Chamber that Comte Molé was to replace him.

The news of the change in the Cabinet was greeted with shouts of joy from the Opposition and imprecations from the Government benches. There was rejoicing in the richer quarters of Paris, and the houses of Thiers and Odilon Barrot were at once filled with visitors who were greeted with exuberant speeches. Other quarters, however, reacted rather differently, and someone shouted out from a barricade, 'What odds does it make if we have Molé or Thiers instead of Guizot?' The quarters of Saint-Denis, Saint-Martin and Montmartre were in ferment. A large crowd reappeared in the Boulevards; Marrast shouted encouragement from the balcony of the *National* offices, and with increased enthusiasm they made for the Boulevard des Capucines in which the Ministry of Foreign Affairs was situated. A company of the 14th of the Line blocked their way, and a Corsican sergeant, after an altercation with one of the demonstrators, shot him dead. The troops took this as a signal, and with a volley of fire, killed or wounded fifty-two. The rioters, who had first scattered, returned to collect some fifteen of their dead; heaped them on top of a waggon belonging to the *Messageries Lafitte et Gaillard*, and by the light of torches and to the sound of a tocsin, started a funeral procession from the Boulevards down to the Bastille and the Place du Châtelet.

In the light of the torches could be seen signs that the revolution had begun in earnest. Huge barricades had been erected and on all sides people were casting ammunition.

The King, forewarned by Guizot and Duchâtel, decided, reluctantly, to call in Marshal Bugeaud, who had smashed the rebellion in April 1837. 'If necessary,' he told Louis Philippe, 'I'll make these Parisians swallow the Sword of Isly to the hilt.' The Marshal immediately—at three in the morning—established contact with the troops massed in the courtyard of the Tuileries and the Place de Carrousel. Yet the King still thought it possible to rule through a parliament. After Molé had failed to form a Cabinet, he approached Thiers who promised him one by early morning.

Bugeaud, however, tried in 1848 the inopportune tactics of 1830. He split up the troops at his disposal into three columns: the first, commanded by Tiburce Sébastiani, he sent off to the Hôtel de Ville; the second, under Bedeau, to the Bastille; and the third, under Renaud, to the Panthéon. A fourth was detailed to follow the first two, to prevent barricades from being reconstructed in their rear. The Marshal decided to dispense with the untrustworthy National Guard. The announcement that Thiers and Odilon Barrot had formed a Cabinet, and the order to cease fire which was given at eight o'clock that morning, prevented Bugeaud from carrying out the whole of his plan. The troops of Bedeau's column fraternised with the insurgents, and only a handful of men marched back into the courtyard of the Tuileries in the middle of the morning. Odilon Barrot, who wanted to test public reactions for himself, came across his first barricade in the Rue d'Echelle. He crossed it all right, but he stopped in front of the one across the Rue Saint-Denis, which he saw flew the Red Flag, and whence he heard shouts of: 'Down with the bourgeois!'

When Thiers heard at lunch time about Bedeau's disastrous withdrawal, he suggested that the King should leave Paris for Saint-Cloud, and return in two days' time when the middle classes, as he thought, would have had enough of the insurgents and be prepared to support the monarchy. Thus it came about that in February 1848 the little man drafted the plan he was to carry out in March 1871. The King, however, waved aside the suggestion, declaring that he was sure of the National Guard, of which three battalions were stationed in the Place du Carrousel, and decided to go and inspect them in the company of his sons, the Duc de Nemours and the Duc de Montpensier, as well as of the Guard's new general, Lamoricière. The First Legion cheered him, but there were cheers for reform as well; when he reached the fourth, he was greeted with shouts of 'Down with the Ministers! Down with the Government!' Louis Philippe hurried back to the Tuileries, having learnt too late that his throne had begun to totter ever since the middle class had lost confidence in the Government he stood for.

Meantime, the insurgents were also moving towards the Tuileries and had reached the Place du Palais-Royal. A bullet struck a first-floor balcony at the moment Emile de Girardin, editor of the *Presse*, was advising the King to abdicate. Louis Philippe was torn between the Queen who begged him to stand firm and the Duc de Montpensier who counselled abdication. In the end he yielded to the latter, and, without appointing a regent, designated his grandson, the Comte de Paris, as his successor. Marshal Gérard, preceded by a herald and bearing a laurel branch, was sent to display to the insurgents his declaration, on which the ink had barely dried.

It was too late. The rioters had already captured the Château d'Eau, massacred the garrison, and had wrecked the Palais-Royal. The King only just escaped through the Tuileries garden in time to reach the Place de la Concorde, where three carriages waited for him and his family. An inglorious reign ended in inglorious flight.

Louis Philippe had abdicated in favour of the Comte de Paris. The latter's mother was Princess Helen, for whom the Royal family had borne little love because she was a Protestant, and also, doubtless, because she was destined to rule the country. At first she had the idea of showing herself and her children to the people, but on Dupin's advice, she set out for the Chamber of Deputies, in the company of the Duc de Nemours. Dupin was made to speak for them, and in a few words he asked the Chamber to have it recorded in the minutes that 'the cheers with which the Comte de Paris was received as King of the French, and Madame la Duchesse d'Orléans as regent made plain the will of the people'. The presence of a number of the rioters inside the Chamber, and the contradictory speeches of Odilon Barrot, La Rochejacquelin, Marie, and Crémieux must have made it pretty clear to the Princess that her son's crown was far from secure. She was lost when Lamartine, breaking the silence he had maintained from the start, stood up and asked her and her children to leave. When a threatening body of armed men broke into the hall shouting 'Dethrone him! Dethrone him!' Lamartine, after a moving speech on 'the piteous spectacle of the greatest human catastrophes', proclaimed that it was time to raise the empire of freedom above the ruins of 'a retrograde régime', to create 'that sublime mystery of universal sovereignty' on the basis of the nation's rights, and, finally, to form a provisional government.

And so it came about. As soon as the Duchesse d'Orléans had been swept aside by a flood of insurgents, and Sauzet, with the rest of the former government, had disappeared, the aged Dupont de l'Eure took the presidential chair, and the following were chosen as ministers of the proposed provisional government: Lamartine, Ledru-Rollin, Arago, Dupont de l'Eure, Garnier-Pagès and Crémieux. Ledru-Rollin opened the first session by proposing that they should adjourn to the Hôtel de Ville, so as to 'take every possible measure to put an end to bloodshed, and proclaim the rights of the people'.

The insurgents, in the meantime, under the command of two leaders of secret societies, Sobrier and Caussidières, had quite easily captured the Préfecture de Police, whilst Captain Jourdain, officer commanding the Eighth Legion, forced Rambuteau to leave the Préfecture of the Seine Department. Towards these two strongholds seized from the authorities there wound a kind of procession formed by Lamartine and his colleagues. Lamartine marched behind two drummers and four workmen in blouses, with a National Guard on his left arm and an armed workman on his right. The banks of the Seine, and the streets surrounding the Hôtel de Ville were blocked by so huge a crowd that it was with the greatest difficulty that they pushed through them. Fighting was still going on in the quarter. It was also with the greatest difficulty that they found one tiny room in the palace as the temporary headquarters of the Provisional Government. Once settled in, they immediately dealt out the various ministerial posts. Dupont de l'Eure was given the Presidency; Lamartine, Foreign Affairs; Ledru-Rollin, Home Affairs; Crémieux, Justice; Marie, Public Works; and François Arago, the Navy. The three portfolios of War, Finance and Education were allotted to the following absentees: General Sunervie, Goudchaux and Hippolyte Carnot.

At the Hôtel Bullion, however, the board of *La Réforme* had made their own appointments, and though they accepted the nomination of Dupont de l'Eure, Lamartine, Arago, Marie and Garnier-Pagès, they insisted that they be joined by the republican Flocon, the socialist Louis Blanc, and a mechanic named Martin better known as Albert. All the same, when these three arrived at the Hôtel de Ville, they were satisfied for the time being with appointments as Under-Secretaries. The Provisional Government was in the saddle.

Its first two problems were the attitude of the army, and the form the State was to take. They thought that the African, Northern and Rhine Armies might object to a new régime. Fortunately, these fears were groundless, thanks less to the proclamation immediately sent to the commanding generals, their officers and men, than to the stunning effect of the sudden turn of events. Nevertheless Paris called on them to transfer their oath of allegiance (which was rendered invalid by the monarchy's 'attack on freedom') to the victorious people, with whom friendly relations were quickly restored. But the real feelings of the officers were to be revealed four months later in June.

Another uncertain factor facing the Provisional Government was the attitude of the country as a whole towards the revolution in Paris. The insurgents demanded a republic, but they were not even the whole of Paris, and Paris was not the whole of France. Lamartine took up his pen, and produced the following text, as corrected by Crémieux:

The Provisional Government hereby proclaims the present government of France to be a republican government, and that the nation will immediately be called upon to ratify the resolution of the Provisional Government and the people of Paris.

A number of copies were made and thrown out of the windows of the Hôtel de Ville. But some workmen in the street below scrawled in charcoal on a piece of cloth the words:

THE REPUBLIC, ONE AND INDIVISIBLE, IS PROCLAIMED IN FRANCE

—a far finer and more dynamic statement than the poet's tentative announcement.

That incident alone shows that the victors were not of one mind. There were immediate clashes, and throughout the day of 25 February there were successive attempts to storm the Hôtel de Ville. On more than one occasion Lamartine and Crémieux succeeded in averting the worst. The Place de Grève remained packed, and proclamations were circularised among the mob asserting the right of 'the sovereign people' to rule in the Provisional Government's stead, and demanding a 'Paris Commune' to enable the French people to inaugurate the reign of Freedom. The windows of the houses round were decked with red, and the armed workers were wearing red sashes, for the revolutionaries had fought under the Red Flag, which had first appeared on the 23rd at the corner of the Rue de Cléry and the Rue du Petit-Carreau, and then all over Paris. It was not surprising that the Place de Grève echoed with shouts of *'Vive le drapeau rouge!'* But the Provisional Government set its face against the idea of the democratic, social republic which the new ensign seemed to herald, and would have no truck with it. That was the burden of a speech Garnier-Pagès made from one of the windows of the Hôtel de Ville, and Lamartine expatiated on the theme in another made under the very arch of the main staircase. In his famous peroration, the poet declared: 'Over my dead body shall you hoist this flag of blood. You yourselves should scorn it, for when has it ever gone further afield than the Champ-de-Mars where in '91 and '93 it trailed in the people's blood. But the Tricolour has circled the world as the emblem of France's glory and France's freedom.' As the crowd was still unconvinced, he went on: 'Very well then. So far I have spoken to you as a citizen of France. Now, hear me as your Foreign Minister. If you tear from me the Tricolour, remember that you halve your country's strength abroad. Europe sees in the flag of the Republic and the Empire the symbol of her defeats and our victories: in the Red Flag she will see but a party emblem. . . . We must fly the flag of our triumphs in Europe, for France's name and France's Tricolour are

one. Theirs is the same purpose, and the same prestige, and—if needs be—
they will strike the same terror into the hearts of our enemies.'

That evening a proclamation appeared resuming Lamartine's arguments, together with a decree adopting the 'three colours in the order in
which they were flown under the Republic'. But Blanqui and his followers,
furious at this decision, also published a proclamation to the effect that
Louis Philippe had brought shame on the Tricolour, and that 'the victorious
people would not fly his standard'.

This led to Blanqui's abortive plot to overthrow the Provisional
Government, which he abandoned, as Gabriel Perreux has shown, after
a conversation with Caussidière. He told his followers, however, that
'this revolution has been purely a matter of luck . . . even the National
Guard was only an involuntary ally . . . in order to prepare for the real
day of revolutionary might, we shall have to wait and organise the people
in clubs in revolutionary fashions'.

On 26 February, however, red flags reappeared in the Place de Grève
(though this time in the midst of a more orderly crowd) and were hoisted
on Henri IV's statue over the main entrance to the Hôtel de Ville. The
Government held a consultation. This time Louis Blanc was present, and
recalling that the Tricolour was only a compromise (the white standing
for the King), demanded the adoption of the Red Flag as 'the standard of
unity'. But he received no support after Goudchaux, the banker, had
delivered an indictment of impending terrorism. They ended by drafting
the following decree, which appeared in the *Moniteur* on 27 February:
'The Provisional Government hereby declares that the national flag is the
Tricolour, with its colours restored to the order in which they were
placed by the Republic. The flag will bear the words: *République française,
liberté, égalité, fraternité*, three words signifying the widest application of
the democratic doctrines which the flag symbolises, whilst its three colours
perpetuate their traditions.

As a sign of unity, and by way of recognition for the final phase of the
popular revolution, members of the Provisional Government and other
authorities will wear the red rosette, which will also be attached to the
flagstaff.'

By ruling out the Red Flag, the Provisional Government may have
hoped that it had succeeded in evading the social demands of the proletariat. Certainly there were echoes of 1793 and the Terror in the truculent
speeches of *club* orators, and articles in the more advanced papers. They
were no more than echoes, however, and one has only to read the *Ami du
Peuple* or *La République Rouge* to see that the insurgents of February never
intended to bring in a reign of pillage and bloodshed, as their detractors
were soon to suggest.

3

THE SOCIAL PROBLEM

The revolution of 1848 contained more ambiguities and contradictions than any other. It is true that at the beginning of their legislation, the Provisional Government appeared to be swayed by humanitarian motives, and immediately proclaimed the abolition of slavery, the death penalty and imprisonment for debt. It appeared to be bent on protecting man's freedom and dignity. At the same time it left to the Assembly, which was still to be elected, the right to ratify these decrees if it wished.

But it was in vain that the middle class sentimentalised over the worker in a spirit of brotherhood (which was not wholly a hypocritical form of self defence) and began to wear blouses and unorthodox headgear.

A genoux devant l'ouvrier,
Chapeau bas devant la casquette,

they were singing in Paris. This masquerade hid a mass of social contradictions. Four months later, the events of June were to put a stop to the idyll.

First there was the problem of the right to work. One worker put it plainly enough, when he pointed out that the working class had endured three months' destitution to create the Republic. They had to have work and food at once. The proletariat's claim to the right to work was a stumbling-block not because the middle-class Government deemed it an economic impossibility, but because they saw it as the thin end of the wedge. It may not be true that after 24 February the workers ran through the streets of Paris crying: 'Give us the right to work within the hour!' but it is a fact that on the evening of the 25th, the 'Fourierist' paper *La Démocratie pacifique* published an article in which it was stated that 'The Republic is only a means to the end, which is social reform . . . work must be guaranteed for those who honestly want it.' During the day, a workers' delegation of the same tendencies was led by one Marche to the Hôtel de Ville to demand: 'Organisation of labour, a guarantee of work for all, and a minimum living wage for the worker and his family, when he is sick or too old to work.' Lamartine's answer to these demands was to point to the cannons which were already placed at the corners of the Place de Grève, and say: 'Citizens, I should not sign a promise to fulfil those demands even if you were to stick me down the muzzle of one of those cannons. I say that for two reasons: the first is that after studying industrial conditions for twenty years, I still do not know what is meant by "organisation of labour". And I will sign nothing I do not understand.

My second reason is that we should be making you a promise that it would not be humanly possible to fulfil. And I will sign no promise to the people that I cannot keep.'

Lamartine was really voicing the feelings of the middle class which was more than ever alarmed at the turn of events. De Tocqueville later wrote in his *Souvenirs* that 'gloom and despondency had overtaken the middle class which was thwarted and threatened'—threatened perhaps, with change, but hardly thwarted. 'I do not believe,' he went on, 'that people were ever so frightened at any stage of the Great Revolution, and I think their terror can only be compared with that of the civilised communities of the Roman Empire, when they saw themselves in the hands of the Goths and Vandals.' The Vandals and the Goths of 1848 were the workers of Paris who were still carrying arms.

All the same, the workers had at least two allies within the Provisional Government itself. Among Lamartine's colleagues were the mechanic Albert, and Louis Blanc who originated the theory of organisation of labour. Torn between Lamartine and Louis Blanc, who was supported by Flocon and Ledru-Rollin, the Government produced the following declaration, which betrayed a certain confusion but was indubitably socialist in tone: 'The Provisional Government of the French Republic pledges itself to guarantee a living wage for the worker, and to guarantee employment for every citizen. It recognises the right of the workers to form trade unions to ensure that they reap the reward of their work.'

There was a codicil to the decree, to the effect that the workers would get the million francs of the ex-King's Civil List. This crumb of charity was paralleled on the 26th by the decree establishing 'National Workshops'. These had nothing in common with the 'social workshops', planned on a co-operative system of production and distribution, which Louis Blanc had made a corner stone of his 'organisation of labour'. They were merely substitutes for the 'charity workshops' of the old days—and even of recent times, whereby governments devoid of imagination and human feelings have time and again thought to remedy more or less localised distress. They were horribly like industrial England's workhouses. To cap this, the formation and administration of these National Workshops was entrusted to Marie, the anti-socialist Minister of Public Works. On the same day, another decree announced the formation of the *Garde Mobile*, a militia which, unlike the National Guard, was open to all. It was immediately joined by a mass of young unemployed who, by an irony of fate, were destined to be used against the rebellious proletariat in June.

These were not the only equivocal situations. On 28 February, which was the day fixed for the proclamation of the Republic in the Place de la Bastille, thousands of workers massed in the Place de Grève, under the banners of their respective guilds, to demand a 'Ministry of Progress', organisation of labour, and an end to exploitation ('a ten-hour working day, and no sweated labour'). The Provisional Government was still split into two factions, and when Lamartine won over the majority, Louis Blanc and Albert offered to resign. Then they hit on a compromise: the formation of a workers' commission under the direction of the two dissident members, to formulate a plan for the organisation of labour. This was no 'Ministry of Progress', as it had no powers, but a kind of proletarian study-group, which was given the grandiloquent title of 'The Governmental Commission for Workers'. Louis Blanc was made president and Albert vice-president, and it met in the Palais du Luxembourg. The document which constituted it certainly begins in a promising fashion:

'Whereas the people's revolution should benefit the people, and it is time to put an end to the age-long and iniquitous sufferings of the workers, and whereas the question of work is the primary, if not the paramount, consideration of a republican government . . .'

But no one was deceived. It was a worker who first labelled Lamartine 'a spellbinder', and the epithet was not undeserved. Anyhow, it was all very well for the Luxembourg Commission, which included 484 workers and 231 employers and maintained a standing committee of 16 workers and 10 employers, to start work on 1 March, but it was understaffed and had no funds. Louis Blanc and Albert resigned on 8 May, and the 'General Survey of Works' which the socialist deputies Vidal and Pecqueur tabled in the Constituent Assembly did not even reach a first reading. This was a genuinely socialist programme which at once went as 'alms for oblivion'. Beyond arbitrating in a certain number of labour disputes, the Luxembourg Commission could achieve almost nothing.

Still, the Provisional Government and even the Luxembourg Commission did carry out one or two valuable measures. On 2 March they promulgated a decree, prefaced by protestations of their belief in the dignity and brotherhood of man, which abolished sweated labour. But as no penalties for contravening it were laid down, it remained a dead letter until 21 March, when it was completed by a system of fines which went towards compensation for disabled workmen. The same decree reduced men's working hours to ten hours in Paris and eleven hours in the provinces. These regulations came into effect on 11 March and 14 March, together with a scale of penalties, from fines to imprisonment, for non-compliance. On 8 March free labour exchanges were set up in town halls, and on the 24th work was stopped in prisons and barracks. This removed a form of competition the workers particularly disliked and which had in places led them to attack convents. On 8 April French factories opened their gates to foreign workers, who were 'entrusted to the generosity of the people'. Similar humanitarian feeling inspired the decree of the 27th, whereby slavery was abolished in all French colonies and possessions.

Certainly all these measures sprang from humanitarian motives, and there is nothing to show that they were merely designed to placate the workers at the least cost to the government. Anyway, the workers were preoccupied by the tremendous unemployment crisis which had begun in the last days of the monarchy, and had been intensified by the revolution: capitalist anxiety, a lack of credit, the uncertain state of the nation's finances, and the fact that luxury industries had almost come to a standstill combined to reduce the amount of labour needed to a minimum.

This resulted in the above-mentioned punitive expeditions against convents, attacks by bargees on the railway yards, and smashing of machinery, so much detested because it reduced the need for manual labour. Years later, Lafargue was to fight not for the right to work but the right to leisure, but such an idea never entered the heads of the working class in 1848. They poured into the National Workshops, which were inaugurated by a decree of 6 March signed by Marie alone, and put into the dictatorial hands of the engineer Emile Thomas. But two francs a day was a strong inducement to the hungry, and by April 70,000 workers had been enrolled. By May there were 100,000, and by June 110,000. The majority, of course, came from Paris, but there were a number from the suburbs and the provinces. This influx of proletarians was marshalled into all kinds of military formations, from brigades to platoons, and employed—well, really to maintain order. In fact, some of the founders of the National Workshops looked upon them as a means of creating an organised and submissive proletariat which in conjunction with the new Militia or Mobile Guard would keep the anarchists in the Luxembourg bay. On the model (sic) of those in Paris, National Workshops were opened in Lyons, Marseilles, Nantes, Rouen and Lille.

But what did the National Workshops actually do? They were simply gangs of navvies, comprised not only of manual labourers, but of skilled workmen, clerks and artists. They worked two days a week with long pauses and in enormous gangs, at useless jobs. One can understand the workers' feeling of humiliation and injustice, which gave vent to every imaginable kind of political demonstration. On 17 March a hundred thousand men marched, under the banners of their various trades, from the Place de la Concorde to the Hôtel de Ville. On 16 April there was the first clash between the workers and the old National Guard, with the

GEORGES BOURGIN

appearance on the scene of the new militia, which had been founded on 25 March. Nearly every youth in Paris had joined it to get the magnificent pay of 1 franc 50 a day. The 20th was the Festival of Fraternity, and yet, even then, there were signs of an approaching storm. On 15 May there was an outbreak of hostility towards the Constituent Assembly over the question of Poland, which was really the excuse for a show of force on the part of the Red *clubs* which wanted to overthrow the Executive Committee which had replaced the Provisional Government. That was the day—to which I shall return later—on which the Parisian National Guard with some outside help from the provinces, broke up the riot and recaptured the Hôtel de Ville, which had been seized by Barbès and his followers.

It is said that 14,000 workers from the National Workshops took part in that riot on 15 May. How, then, could the Executive Committee continue to tolerate such an institution? Trélat, who had succeeded Marie as Minister for Public Works, wanted to clear out all unmarried men between eighteen and twenty-five and send them into the Army, and as a preparatory measure had Emile Thomas arrested and on 27 May replaced him by Lalanne of the École Polytechnique.

Three days afterwards, the Comte de Falloux, one of the foremost right-wingers of the Assembly, made a violent attack on the 'loafers' in the Workshops, and it was generally agreed that they must be disbanded. Victor Hugo gave an eloquent warning, when he said: 'You have created an army of paupers, and it is up to you to see they do not become the prætorian guard of a new dictator.' He was fully aware of the effect Bonapartist propaganda was creating in France.

On 21 June, a decree was signed abolishing the National Workshops; workers between eighteen and twenty-five were called up for the army; and the rest told they were to be sent into the provinces as navvies. People connected with the Government knew perfectly well that this was an incentive to rebellion: Lalanne said as much to Charles de Freycinet, who was then a student at the Mining College; and the Minister for War, who had foreseen it, gradually reinforced the regular garrison in Paris and speeded recruitment into the Militia. There was danger ahead, and the workers in the National Workshops came to terms with their comrades on the Luxembourg Commission.

On the evening of 21 June, bands of workers swarmed through the streets singing the *Marseillaise,* and announcing that the next day there would be a big meeting in the Place du Panthéon. They carried out their plan, and marched behind one Lieutenant Pujol, who may have been a fanatic, but was certainly a brilliant orator. He led them from the Place de la Bastille to the Palais du Luxembourg, where the Government was in session, and there was a display of verbal fireworks between him and Marie. The day ended with two open-air meetings in the Place du Panthéon. By the light of torches, Pujol announced that they must once again fight at the barricades; the mob took an oath to follow him and on 23 June rebellion broke out.

There is no point in giving the details of this rebellion. Charles Schmidt has already done so in masterly fashion, in a book written twenty years ago, but which has lost none of its freshness. I shall simply pick out one or two new details.

There was, for instance, that moment when Pujol called on the mob, singing round the column in the Place de la Bastille, to kneel down and repeat the terrible oath 'Liberty or death'. It was the drama of Lyons in 1831 all over again. Once again the barricades sprang up, and it would be interesting to find out whether the position of those erected in 1944 by the Resistance coincided (taking into account the changes in Paris) with those put up by the rebels of 1848 and 1871. In June 1848 the revolution centred round the Rue Mouffetard, the Place Maubert, the labyrinth of little streets behind the Hôtel de Ville, and the Rue and Faubourg Saint-Antoine—the area, in fact, between the Place de la Bastille and the Rond-Point de la Villette.

The insurgents were opposed by the army, the National Guard and the new militia, under the command of an African veteran, General Cavaignac, who treated the battle in Paris as an attack on a fortified position. The result, as in 1871, was a long drawn out and bloody campaign. The first blood was shed at the Porte Saint-Denis, where two women were killed by the National Guard. Whilst on this fateful day of 23 June Paris echoed with rifle fire, the Assembly was discussing Falloux's project for the immediate abolition of the National Workshops. Corbon, Caussidière and Considérant were the only ones to favour a policy of appeasement and fair dealing. The majority were too frightened and angry to listen to them, so 24 June saw a major battle.

On that day guns were trained on the barricades, and, out of class loyalty, contingents of the National Guard began to pour in from every part of France to reinforce the regular troops in Paris. A state of siege was proclaimed, and Cavaignac was given full powers, foreshadowing the dictatorship of a Bonaparte. The Assembly, however, still considered itself the mouthpiece, and Sénard, its president, addressed the insurgents in the following words: 'You have been misled; the Assembly has never dreamt of depriving you of work. They have told you lies. The Republic is here to change your lot and repair the injustices of the old order.' The workers' answer took the form of posters plastered all over the city. One read:

'When we were at the barricades in February, the men we had chosen as members of a Provisional Government promised us a democratic and social republic; they gave us their word and we abandoned our barricades. What have they done, these past four months? They have broken every promise they made.'

This poster ended with a demand for the legalisation of trade unions, the trial of the Deputies and Ministers, the immediate arrest of the members of the Executive Committee, and the removal of the troops in Paris, since 'You are the sovereign people. Be mindful of your device: "Liberty, Equality and Fraternity." '

That device had already become a mockery, and on 25 June 'that bloody Corpus Christi' as Schmidt called it—it was drenched in blood. It was a day of horror, in which fearful stories spread of bloodthirsty women hacking at the militia, convicts fighting in the ranks of the insurgents, canteen-women poisoning the soldiers' brandy, prisoners' heads on the barricades, rape and looting. But the reality was bad enough, in the operations conducted by the Government forces. These were in three columns under General Lamoricière, General Duvivier and General Bréa. The last-named was killed in an ambush on the road to Fontainebleau, and the Archbishop of Paris, Monseigneur Affre, was killed, shot (it appears) by a soldier. These were prominent men: beside them there were thousands of anonymous victims slaughtered at the barricades and by the firing-squads.

On the evening of the 25th it was all over. A sergeant of the Eighth Legion, named de Ménards, went with two insurgents to discuss terms with General Perrot, who passed them on to Sénard, the President of the Assembly. A truce was in sight, but Cavaignac had not finished, and fighting broke out again at 10 a.m. on the 26th for another three-quarters of an hour. Then the General wired the Prefects that 'order had prevailed', and published a proclamation thanking the army and the National Guard for their loyalty, and calling upon them to remain calm, as befitted men of their stature.

At the beginning of Louis Philippe's reign, a French general said after the Polish insurrection had been put down: 'order reigns in Warsaw'. Now that it reigned in Paris, Czar Nicholas sent a message of congratulation to Cavaignac. It is hard to estimate the cost of his victory, for the official figures merely state that a total of 1,460 were killed on both sides. No one could ever count those who died in hospital, or were buried on the spot, or crept away to die in the cornfields and were not found till the harvest. No one ever recorded the reprisals: the summary executions and the prisoners herded into the cellars of public buildings, of which Flaubert paints so horrifying a picture in *Education Sentimentale*; 11,671 arrests were made, followed by sentences of transportation, hard labour, and only rarely by acquittal. When all is told, 1871 was but a replica of 1848. In both cases it was a question of cold-blooded class warfare, as Prosper Merimée, who was an eye-witness, has pointed out: 'They fought only for gain and to hold on to what they had.' There was one difference, however, between the two revolutions: in 1871 there were few appeals for mercy, but in 1848 women of the middle class, in obedience to Christian doctrine, appealed to the Assembly to be merciful—as did the economist Blanqui, brother of the revolutionary, in the following words: 'If each day you saw the indescribable distress that we see, your hearts would break.' Lamennais, however, asked no quarter, but spat out at his colleagues: 'God will call on you to account for all this bloodshed.'

In the June Days Lamennais heard the death-knell of the social republic dreamt of by the socialists and proletarians of 1848.

The days of June spelt horror in other parts of the country. On the 18th there was an insurrection in Marseilles, which had a variety of causes but was mainly proletarian in origin. It was quickly stamped out, and 153 workers were sent to trial. But legal action was mainly taken against workers who were foolhardy enough to wear the red rosette (as at Béthune), or against those who voiced their opinions too loudly (as at Bordeaux).

To be sure, before the insurrection, there had been signs that the Christian-Democrats in the Assembly possessed a social conscience. For instance on 27 May a decree was published giving the workers the right to elect and be elected as members of industrial conciliation boards. But after 31 June, Charles Dupin and Wolowski started their attack on one of the Republic's first decrees, which had been to limit the number of working hours. On 9 September, they succeeded in having the decree repealed, thereby handing back to the liberal economists their precious liberty. Unions were still subject to the restrictions of the Penal Code, and nothing was done to put employees on the same legal footing as their employers.

Then there had been moves to nationalise the railways and insurance companies, introduce income-tax and reform the system of mortgage, all of which looked like a major offensive against the privileges of the middle class. But they came to nothing. The offensive was now directed against socialism, and Carnot, the Minister of Education, was attacked for permitting the publication under his auspices of Renouvier's *Manuel Républicain de l'homme et du citoyen*. Renouvier's object was 'to prevent the rich growing lazy and living on the poor'; he recommended that a limit be put on the amount of money that might be inherited or received as interest on capital and urged remedies for the harmful effects of unbridled competition. On 31 July there were only two dissident voices in the Assembly when Thiers condemned as 'an odious attack on the principles of freedom', Proudhon's advice to all debtors to demand a decree whereby their creditors should return one-third of what was owed them over the past three years, and to create a fund of 1,500,000,000 francs to restore the standard of living which had existed before the Revolution.

On 28 June, a Parliamentary Commission was set up under the Orléanist, Odilon Barrot, to investigate the causes of the insurrections in May and June. Like the Finance Committee it set out to incriminate the socialists. These naturally included Proudhon and Caussidière, but their chief quarry was Louis Blanc, against whom the Assembly, by a shameless *volte-face*, decided to institute proceedings. The Commission also proved extremely skilful in playing the remaining republicans off against each other, when it came to deciding responsibility.

Then there was the all-important question of the right to work, which dragged on, becoming less and less of a reality, throughout the Assembly's debates from 17 May onward, when the Constitutional Commission started functioning. In the first constitutional project of 19 June the right to work was still mentioned: 'The right to work means every man's right to earn a living. Society must use all the means at its disposal to provide work for the able-bodied men, who cannot otherwise obtain it.' This provision was completed by Article 9 which provided for public assistance.

After the insurrection, however, the majority first secretly, then openly came out against the original text, at the instigation of such diehards as Thiers, de Tocqueville, Duvergier de Hauranne and Goudchaux. Thiers pointed out that a right applied to everyone, and the right of a single class was no right. But even the working-class deputies, André and Corbon, began back-pedalling, and the former went so far as to assert that the right to work would encourage idleness. So it came about that the most vital demand of 25 February had disappeared from the text of the Republican Constitution which was adopted on 4 November.

The 1848 Revolution had tried in vain to be a social revolution.

It might have had some chance of success if the country's finances had been reorganised. Money was scarce at the beginning of 1848, and there was no hope of the middle class subscribing to any loan issued by the kind of Government that had come into power. On 10 February, the 5 per cent Loan fell to 118 francs, and stood at 89 francs on 6 March when the *Bourse* reopened. On 11 March the 3 per cent reached bottom at 32 francs 50. The banks had suspended payment, and the middle class was taking its silver to the Mint. Garnier-Pagès, who was a bad financier, shuddered at the memory of the *assignats*, the promissory notes issued between 1790

and 1796, and did not dare extend to the whole country the Bank of
France's monopoly as an issuing-house, which at that time was restricted
to capital. He did ask the Bank for an advance, but did not obtain it until
after the Days of June. Naturally he did not dare have recourse to a forced
loan, but he did not even attempt to introduce graduated income-tax, or
an increase in the property-tax or repurchase of the railways. He simply
stopped at increasing, on 15 March, all direction taxation by 45 per cent.
This measure did not affect the workers in the towns, but it did affect the
smallest landowners in the country, who accused the Government of
sacrificing their interests to those of the workers. The only welcome
measure was the abolition of the Salt Tax.

The solidarity of the early days of the Revolution lay shattered. On
22 September 1848, a banquet held in honour of the First Republic,
Ledru-Rollin made a speech accusing the Second Republic of having
done nothing for the people, and regretting that no Cambon had arisen
to achieve something solid. Bitterness, hatred and fear were growing up
beneath the shade of the tree of liberty, and a sort of 'Grand Panic', like
that of the Great Revolution, was spreading in this Republic doomed to
dictatorship.

4

THE POLITICAL PROBLEM

The 1848 Revolution had tried to be both social and democratic. As
Georges Renard says, whenever party-politics fade out, liberty steps in;
liberty in every form, unmarred by violence. The provinces followed
Paris' lead. Although in Lyons and Rouen, the workers rose in anger
against one or two religious communities employing labour, and although
the Red Flag waved over a number of cities, and although one or two
industrial towns doubted the success of a republican France, enthusiasts
all over the country were planting trees of liberty, and the priests willingly
assisted at their consecration. But there was bound to be a split. Those who
wanted to create a new form of society could not stay long with the
ebullient spirits who were simply carried away by revolutionary fervour,
or with the cautious ones who thought it best to cry with the pack for the
time being, whilst preparing revenge, or at any rate a way of escape.

All the manifestations of freedom were in evidence. *Clubs* sprang up
like mushrooms—145 in a month—which recalled the 1789 Revolution,
but also expressed a belief in the new order prophesied by the socialists

of the 'forties. Then there was a mass of new newspapers—171 in a few weeks—often with incendiary titles. It was not unusual for these to disappear after a few days, leaving only the memory of some fierce diatribe or rosy programme. The ranks of the National Guard were thrown open to all French citizens, and finally, in March, Ledru-Rollin sent out 'Republican Commissars', reminiscent of 1793. All this had a considerable effect on the middle class who certainly read the revolutionary newspapers and attended turbulent meetings. They were a little scared, but on the whole well-pleased. Gradually, making use of the incentive and liberty to unite and forget their former differences of opinion as Orléanists, Legitimists or Bonapartists, they constituted themselves the guardians of law and order, and a bulwark against the 'Reds' and the Communists. Meanwhile, the mass of agricultural labourers was growing uneasy at the measures taken in Paris. The Church was of course in its element: setting itself up as the mainstay of the family and the home, it succeeded in winning the support of the middle class which conveniently forgot their former rationalism. Then the conservative newspapers started both vilifying and ridiculing the republicans, 'les démoc-soc', and succeeded in stirring up fear and hatred to such an extent that they set these former comrades by the ears, as in the case of Barbès and Blanqui.

The result was that two main trends very soon appeared, first in Paris then throughout the country. Even the newly democratised National Guard split into 'loyal' and 'disloyal' battalions, which was which depending on the speaker's outlook. And whereas at the beginning of the revolution the masses had been the demonstrators, in March the middle class began to mobilise. On the 9th of that month, some 3,000 merchants and stockbrokers marched from the Bourse to the Hôtel de Ville to demand a three months' extension of the time by which bills had to be met. When the Provisional Government refused, they threatened it with a lock-out. Then on 16 March there was the 'Battle of the Busbies', when the crack companies of the National Guard demanded that they should retain a form of headgear to distinguish them from the rest of the Guard, and demonstrated with shouts of 'Down with the communists! To Hell with Ledru-Rollin!'

The next day a mighty procession organised by the *clubs* marched into the Place de Grève to demand the withdrawal of the army from Paris and the postponement of the elections. And the Government, once again at Lamartine's instigation, did agree to postpone the elections for some days, and affirmed that 'the republic needs no defender within her borders other than the people in arms'. This did not, however, prevent the poet from discussing internal security measures with General Négrier, the G.O.C. of the Northern Command, or Marrast from consulting General

Bedeau and General Changarnier about the defence of the Hôtel de Ville.

Louis Blanc, with the help of Barbès, Raspail, Cabet and Sobrier, kept the people quiet on 17 March, although with an ulterior motive, as he wanted to use them in a demonstration on 16 April. On that date, after fourteen officers had been elected on the Champs de Mars, he led them without arms to the Hôtel de Ville to present the following petition:

'The people desire a democratic Republic, they desire the end of exploitation and the inauguration of organisation of labour by means of trade unions.'

These words smelt of the Luxembourg Commission. They smelt of socialism. Once again it was Lamartine who hastily organised the defence of the Hôtel de Ville, and had the trade guilds march past shouting: 'Down with Cabet! Down with Blanqui! Down with Louis Blanc! Down with the communists!' in front of a wall of bayonets.

Thus the moderates of the Provisional Government won the day. They decided to celebrate their victory by a *Fête de la Fraternité*, and so the army returned to Paris, and on 20 April there was a march past of 200,000 troops in front of the Arc de Triomphe. They were loudly acclaimed by the friends of order.

The revolution had brought in universal suffrage. It had been promised in the early days of February, and secured by law on 5 March. But ever since the one single attempt to introduce it in the 1789 Revolution, no one had really understood its implications, and the *Réforme's* spirited campaign had been directed solely towards lowering the property qualification. Now, the vote was given to all Frenchmen over the age of twenty-one, including the armed forces and excluding only bankrupts, criminals, lunatics—and women, despite the violent agitation by the feminists under Jeanne Deroin. A secret ballot was to be held in the chief town of each canton under the auspices of the cantonal Justice of the Peace, and the 900 representatives were to be elected by each voter being called upon to choose a certain number of names from a Departmental list, the number varying according to the size of the Department. Deputies were to be paid 25 francs a day.

As soon as the electoral law came into force, every kind of political statement was heard in Paris, and candidates pullulated in the Departments. The elections for the Constituent Assembly had been announced for 9 April, but the *clubs*, whose original rôle had been to educate the politically ignorant, prevailed upon the Provisional Government to postpone them until the 23rd, when the country was suffering from a reaction to the events of 16 April. The Church played a cunning hand, and on several occasions parish priests were seen shepherding the male members of their congregation to the polls; the conservatives benefited from the panic which suddenly seized every property owner, and shamelessly distorted the phases of the Ministry of Home Affairs' *Bulletin de la République* (with which George Sand was closely connected), as well as misrepresenting the actions of the Republican Commissars Ledru-Rollin had sent to each Department, and the delegates from the *clubs*, who joined them.

The result was that the radical republicans had little success and the socialists even less. What is more, there were few genuine working-class candidates, as they were either too timid or too poor to stand. Then again, Marrast, Marie and Emile Thomas had cunningly managed to get the workers in the National Workshops to vote for middle-class representatives. Finally, there was friction between the members of the proletariat who supported the Luxembourg Commission, and those who belonged to the trade guilds. These divisions explain why neither Béranger nor Proudhon was elected. In some of the larger industrial towns the elections provoked riots. At Lyons, Limoges and Rouen the workers, angry at their defeat, erected barricades, but they were swiftly removed by General Gérard.

The composition of the Constituent Assembly plainly showed the results of the ingenuity of one side and the follies of the other. It was mainly composed of moderate, anti-socialist republicans led by Lamartine, who headed the list of successful candidates in Paris. But there were large minorities of 150 legitimists, Orléanists, and Catholics, who were led by Montalambert, Lacordaire and the Comte de Falloux. The radicals had been routed, and the leaders of the *clubs* failed to gain a single seat. Scarcely any socialists got in except Louis Blanc and Albert. It was all very well for the Constituent Assembly to open its session with shouts of 'Long live the Republic!' repeated eighteen times, and to pass a vote of congratulation to the Provisional Government, but it was as plain as a pikestaff that this assembly, which was so enormous that a new hall had to be found to seat it, was going to be hard put to it to pursue a coherent policy. The country's chaos was reflected in the confusion of its representatives.

When the Constituent Assembly first met of 4 May, it nevertheless tried to organise a government. Its tendencies soon became apparent. First, there was the nomination of a Provisional Executive Committee, consisting of five members: Arago, Garnier-Pagès, Marie, Lamartine and Ledru-Rollin—Lamartine being only fourth as a punishment for having upheld Ledru-Rollin. Then there were the refusal to form a Ministry of Progress; silence on the Luxembourg Commission's report; the repudiation of the Rouen Affair; a ban on presenting petitions at the bar of the House; and the authorisation of the President to call upon the armed forces. It was not surprising that the extreme republicans in Paris began to think of bringing these rural representatives to their senses, which they did in the middle of May, on the pretext of a demonstration in sympathy with the Poles, who were once again being martyred: they were not afraid of starting a war, which might succeed in overthrowing all the tyrants in Europe, and paving the way for a genuine revolutionary government in France.

The demonstration was planned for 13 May and took place on the 15th. General Courtais, who commanded the National Guard, did not dare order the militia to open fire on the long column of the people advancing towards them. They invaded the Assembly and chaired Louis Blanc, who had tried nevertheless to get them to leave. Raspail presented the petition on behalf of the Poles, and Barbès congratulated the people on having won back the right to do so; Blanqui demanded the abolition of poverty and the organisation of labour; then Barbès spoke again, demanding that the Assembly should declare war, soak the rich for 1,000,000,000 francs, and withdraw the army from Paris. Finally, the sinister Huber rose to dissolve the Assembly. Meanwhile, the National Guard was being mobilised, and reinforcements (summoned by telegraph) were on their way from the suburbs, and from Melun, Amiens and Caen. The Palais-Bourbon was cleared and the principal demonstrators arrested. Louis Blanc was nearly torn to pieces and Courtais nearly flung into the Seine. The National Guard closed Blanqui's and Sobrier's *clubs*. Louis Blanc and Albert resigned on 16 May, and George Sand, whose rôle had been quite insignificant, renounced any further active part in politics. Courtais was replaced by Clément Thomas. On 7 March 1849, the High Court of Bourges sentenced Barbès, Albert, Blanqui, Sobrier, Raspail and de Flotte, and (in their absence) Louis Blanc and Caussidière. But there was still an extraordinary confusion of ideas in the country. By-elections resulted in the election of Louis Napoleon Bonaparte to the Assembly by four different Departments, but also brought in the demo-crats—Caussidière, Pierre Leroux and Proudhon—and Thiers, who had now become the ally of the Church, and felt that he was destined for leadership, with the support of the *Comité de la rue de Poitiers* and the guardians of law and order, and that by himself he was capable of smiting socialism hip and thigh. It was now that the Executive Committee became wholly discredited, and that Lamartine fell with a crash from popular favour. The speed with which reaction was gathering momentum could be seen from the steady rise to power of a man like the Comte de Falloux, a pro-Catholic royalist who was out to restore the monarchy.

Falloux played the same rôle in closing the National Workshops as General Cavaignac had done in crushing the insurrection. After the victor had surrendered his powers to the Assembly, the latter hailed him as the saviour of society, and declaring that the country was in his debt, made him their Chief Executive. Thus the Republic drifted towards a military dictatorship. Cavaignac, who had surrendered his powers on 28 June, was immediately made President of the Council.

The military government settled down to weeding the National Guard of the proletariat, keeping up a state of siege, closing dangerous *clubs*, controlling public gatherings by police regulation, forbidding secret societies altogether, muzzling the press by the reimposition of caution-money (which Lamennais attacked in his famous speech 'Silence aux pauvres!'—'No say for the poor!') and by heavy penalties for writers who undermined the 'foundations of society'—by which they meant religion, private property and the family.

All the same the Assembly, which had been formed to work out a constitution for France, did—in spite of a troubled life—attain its object. The eighteen members of the committee elected on 17 and 18 May, on which Lamennais and Considérant were the only democrats, completed its draft on 19 June. It was then refused to the bureaux or commissions of the Assembly, which, frightened by the insurrection, toned down every democratic, socialist or internationalist clause. The text was debated between 4 September and 27 October, and after a second reading on 31 October, followed by a further debate lasting two days, its 116 articles were passed on 4 November by 739 votes to 30, those who opposed it being either legitimists or democratic-socialists. On the 21st it was proclaimed law in a dreary ceremony in which the people took no part. It began with a preamble which, like that of the Year III, should have been a declaration of the rights of man as a human being and as a citizen, but which in point of fact steered a careful course between the middle classes' prejudices and the peoples' aspirations. The Constitution of 1848 proclaimed freedom of worship, freedom to call meetings, form associations and present petitions, freedom of the press, freedom of education, the sanctity of the home and the abolition of slavery and of the death penalty for political offences. All these freedoms, however, did not prove inviolate: the continuance of the Concordat made a mockery of religious freedom, and Victor Hugo comments bitterly on the distortion or diminution of the remainder.

Another point is that there was no change in the centralisation brought about by Napoleon. This 'one and indivisible' Republic still kept on prefects, separate legislative and executive bodies, and also direct and universal suffrage without the guarantee proposed by one of the deputies for Tarn-et-Garonne. There was to be a single Assembly, composed of 750 deputies, elected for a period of three years by a 'multinominal' ballot in the chief towns of each canton. All deputies were to receive a salary and could not be dismissed except for flagrant offences; the question of making them ineligible for any state appointments was, however, left to be voted on when the election law came up for discussion. It was to keep an eye on the Executive that a committee of twenty-five deputies was formed to function during the recess and summon the whole Assembly in an emergency. Anxious to maintain their own control, the Constituent Assembly, opposed the principle of a second Chamber with which they were able to dispense by changing the purpose of the Conseil d'Etat. Its members, appointed and dismissed by the Legislative Assembly were given the job of preparing the text of bills with the object of making them unambiguous and legally sound.

Although the Constituent Assembly were uneasy about the Executive, they nevertheless gave it very wide powers, including the right to impose a provisional veto, the right to choose its own Ministers, who did not necessarily have to be members of the Assembly, and the right to appoint a large number of high officials. In spite of warnings given by J. Grévy, F. Pyat, Audry and Puyraveau, it was decided—after a speech by Lamartine who was not afraid to mention Louis Napoleon's candidature—that the President of the Republic should be elected by the people. It was merely stipulated that the Vice-President, who in a curious fashion doubled the President's rôle, must not be a relation or friend of the latter; and both had to swear a solemn oath of allegiance to the Republic. But as head of the armed forces, the President of the Republic had at his disposal troops which, through the maintenance of the system whereby conscripts could employ substitutes, and the lengthening of the period of service, were coming as near as possible to representing a standing army.

The presidential election was to be held on 10 December 1848. There were several candidates, including Lamartine (but he had lost all his influence), Cavaignac (but he was 'the Butcher of June') and Ledru-Rollin (to whom many Democrats preferred Raspail, who was in prison). Then there were others who secretly hoped they might be chosen: Marshal Bugeaud, General Changarnier, the Orléanist, Molé and the ambitious Thiers. But Louis Napoleon Bonaparte already had a tremendous following. This questionable nephew of the Emperor's, with his socialist leanings, promised the workers high wages and the middle class security; the country people, forgetting the huge levies of the Napoleonic era, looked upon him as the opponent of feudal oppression. An astonishing propaganda campaign by newspapers, pamphlets and *images d'Epinal*—the 'tuppence-coloured' sheets depicting the glories of the Empire—brought him supporters of every class. The wave of enthusiastic confusion which marked the early days of the revolution was followed by an even greater confusion, but of that gloomy, uneasy nature, which has so often paved the way for fascism.

The *Comité de la rue de Poitiers*, the Catholics, the Orléanists, the legitimists and the generals all held the torch for him. He promised everything to everybody, and everybody saw him as their champion or avenger. The result was that out of 7,517,811 votes, Louis Napoleon Bonaparte was elected by 5,572,836. Cavaignac obtained only 1,469,156, and Lamartine under 21,000.

The Presidential republic was just a caricature of the Republic born at the barricades of February. On 20 December, the Prince President formed his cabinet. Odilon Barrot was made President of the Council, but the principal figures were the sinister Falloux, and Léon Faucher, who as Minister of the Interior waged a merciless war on the last vestiges of democracy in the country, in particular the various Republican associations. There was a first attempt at a *coup d'état* on 29 January 1849, when troops were sent to surround the Chamber, where a debate was being held to decide the formation of a successor to the Constituent Assembly. The latter was to make two further attempts at suicide. It had shown no quarter to the insurgents of June, but quailed at deciding its own fate.

The election campaign of 1849 cleared the horizon by simplifying the issues. On one side there was the party of law and order, under the leadership of the *Comité de la rue de Poitiers* (or Liberal Union) which flooded the country with cheap booklets damning the communists (Partageux), 'the reds', and the enemies of religion and property. Henri Wallon, Louis Veuillot, Bonjean and Thiers took part in the attack on socialism, as did the economists Adolphe Blanqui and Villermé, novelists like Reybaud, who wrote *Jérôme Paturot*, variety artists, and above all a pack of utterly unprincipled journalists writing for a press which was largely subsidised. On the other side, that of the democrat-socialists, there were the factory workers, the artisans, and the farm labourers. It is true that Ledru-Rollin's programme, which he had sketched out on 22 September 1848, had been both over-ambitious, vague and rash, but socialist propaganda was a considerable force with its own booklets, songs and pictures; and with the help of Eugène Sue, Agricole Perdiguier, Michel de Bourges, Pierre Joigneaux and F. Pyat, its newspapers penetrated into the depths of the countryside. Even the rank and file of the army, and to a still greater extent the N.C.O.s, were affected by this propaganda. But the two sides were unfairly matched: the Government was on the side of law and order. The Prefects and magistrates hunted down republicans and socialists everywhere, under the pretext of eliminating secret societies. But whilst Catholic and royalist societies were untouched, the teaching profession was closely watched, and scores of teachers were dismissed.

Odilon Barrot banned the *clubs*, and Léon Faucher declared that it was a crime against the Constitution to shout 'Long live the democratic and social Republic!' The High Court of Blois was a law to itself, as it had been specially created to deal with the insurgents of 15 May and June, long after their offences had been committed. The men who murdered General Bréa in the course of the insurrection were executed in spite of the article in the Constitution abolishing the death penalty for political crimes. At the last moment before the Constitution came into force there was a wave of arrests and administrative pressure was intensified.

The composition of the Legislative Assembly was a fairly accurate guide to the feelings of the electorate. In the first place, there had been 40 per cent abstentions, due to widespread disillusionment, uneasiness and apathy. In spite of their difficulties, 180 democrat-socialists got in—to form a new 'mountain'—and several of them were elected in two Departments. Paris, Lyons, Alsace, the South-East, and the Centre voted Republican. There were seventy-five moderate republicans represented, but their leaders had gone, Lamartine the first of them. The remainder were the champions of law and order, unanimously hostile to the Republic and socialism, but split among themselves into legitimists, Orléanists and Bonapartists.

The difference between the majority and the minority could only be settled by force, and the minority had the audacity to make the first move. On 11 June, Ledru-Rollin presented an indictment of the President and Odilon Barrot's Cabinet because of the siege of Rome, and announced that he and his comrades would defend the Constitution 'by all possible means, even by force of arms!'

That was the start of the insurrection of 13 June. Paris had been purged of its more pugnacious elements by the repressive measures of the previous year, and Changarnier, the bewigged, corseted and perfumed General 'Bergamote', as he was called, had the time to take defence measures. A few barricades were erected round the Conservatoire des Arts et Métiers, which a score of *montagnards* with Ledru-Rollin planned to make their command post. Some were arrested and the others, including Ledru-Rollin, fled. The only insurrections in the rest of France took place in a few villages in Allier, and at Perpignan, Strasbourg, Toulouse and Lyons, where there was a pitched battle at the Croix-Rousse, in which more than 200 people were killed.

The consequences of the 'mountain's' defeat were quite out of proportion to the event. First, there were harsh reprisals. Countless newspapers were closed down, and the supposed ringleaders were committed for trial by the High Court. These included not only Ledru-Rollin, who had fled the country, but also Félix Pyat and Considérant. N.C.O.s and other ranks who had shown socialist sympathies were punished with detention and postings to Africa. Then there followed preventive measures: the regulations of the Assembly were altered to prevent the appearance of any more over-bold critics; Prefects and public prosecutors were ordered to keep a strict watch on *clubs*, associations and teachers, and to take action against citizens shouting the forbidden 'Long live the democratic and social Republic'; and there was a new law passed on 27 July 1849 enforcing a much stricter control of the press. The Prince President's unexpected attitude towards the restoration of the Pontiff's authority caused momentary confusion in the Government, which had acted as his handmaiden, but only Victor Hugo, who for a long time sat on the fence, abandoned a policy which was leading straight towards the annihilation of freedom.

The Prince President, however, had finally decided to let the Assembly take full responsibility for measures which were removing every obstacle to impending autocracy. On 28 October, he dismissed Odilon Barrot's Cabinet, without more ado, and replaced it by a 'skeleton ministry of mediocrities, three of whom (Parieu, Routier and Fould) were completely under his thumb'.

'I must be able to control all parties', he wrote to Odilon Barrot. Louis Napoleon Bonaparte had decided to rule France by himself, but he took one well-tried precaution. He left it to the Legislative Assembly to pass all reactionary measures, particularly those of putting education back into the hands of the Church, and curtailing universal suffrage.

Certain politicians had realised perfectly well that a wider suffrage would necessitate educational reforms so that the citizens should have the requisite knowledge to enable them to exercise their right to vote in full knowledge of what they were doing. But they had only seen these reforms as a consequence of increased freedom. Carnot, the Minister for Education when Cavaignac was President, had drawn up a report to this effect, but it did not suit the partisans of 'moral order'. They wanted to control the University and especially the anti-clerical teachers, many of whom had done much for the cause of democracy. An extra-parliamentary commission, on which Montalambert, Thiers, the Abbé Dupanloup, the Vicomte de Melun and Auguste Cochin had the greatest influence, and which comprised only a handful of university representatives, prepared a bill which was passed on 15 March 1850 under the name of the Falloux Act, although by that time Falloux was no longer Minister of Education. Its character can be gauged from the following details: the principle of compulsion was rejected, and education was free only for paupers. The curriculum was limited to the three R's. Any minister of religion or nun of a teaching order was qualified to teach in a primary school, and a degree was not essential for secondary school teachers. France was divided up into Educational Districts, with boards which were chiefly controlled by the Prefect and the bishop of the diocese: a later law enabled the Prefect to appoint school teachers. That was the manner in which France was put in an intellectual and moral strait-jacket. The poison of what Montalambert called 'intellectual communism' was powerless against the antidote of Catholic teaching. And as yet there had been no need for the more drastic measures suggested by the extreme reactionaries who wanted to eliminate history, philosophy, and even the classics from the secondary schools' curriculum. In any case, the *clubs* of the early days of the 1848 Revolution were replaced in the years 1849-51 by a host of sodalities—particularly for women—and the private (that is to say Catholic) schools were packed. That was the intellectual background of the loyal savants of the Second Empire and the 'notables' of the Third Republic.

Whereas the Falloux Act could only have comparatively long-term results, the Legislative Assembly's change in the electoral system was planned to have an immediate effect. The reactionaries had been badly shaken by the results of the by-elections on 10 March 1850, which followed the conviction of the authors of the 13 June plot: twenty *montagnards* had been returned, including Carnot, the opponent of the Falloux Act, and Vidal of the Luxembourg Commission, who on 28 April 1850, changed his constituency to the Haut-Rhin, Eugène Sue becoming member for Paris in his stead. On 3 May, the Minister of the Interior, Baroche, appointed a committee of eighteen members to work out a system for electoral reform. There was not one Republican among these *burgraves*, as they were called, and who included Montalambert, Molé, Thiers and Broglie. Even so, the committee's recommendations were too much for the Assembly which, at Léon Faucher's instigation, considerably modified them. Yet Montalambert bluntly summed up the committee's aim as 'legalisation of the war against socialism'. Thiers, speaking for 'the enlightened classes', contrasted with them 'the hoi polloi' whom they decided to deprive of their vote. Dupin laughed in the faces of the left wing deputies who claimed they were violating the Consitution. 'Not quite', he said. 'But we've lifted her skirts as high as we can.' And in spite of the efforts of Grévy, of Victor Hugo (who had finally cast in his lot with the democrats) and even of Jules Favre and Cavaignac, the electoral law was passed on 31 May. The new law debarred many more classes of people from voting, in particular men who had been domiciled for under three years in the commune or canton, members of *clubs*, journalists and politicians who had been convicted, and—above all—workmen who were forced to travel from place to place in France either on account of guild regulations or because economic circumstances forced them to change their employment. These classes totalled nearly three millions out of a population of nine and a half millions. The law of 31 May 1850, rightly called by some 'the Roman expedition on the home front', reversed one of the principal gains of the February Revolution.

But the Assembly did not stop there. On 6 June it prolonged for a year the measures in force against the *clubs*, and at the same time widened their application to electoral meetings likely to cause trouble. On 8 June the Assembly threatened political criminals with deportation, and on 16 July codified the laws concerning the press and, on top of having to pay caution-money, the publishers of newspapers and political pamphlets were obliged to affix special stamps to them as well as paying increased postal charges.

By the middle of 1850, the republican phœnix which had risen out of the ashes of the old order was a bundle of stuffed feathers. A flick of the fingers and it would crumble to dust. And that is what happened to it after a year and a half of intrigue behind the doors of the Elysée and the Palais-Bourbon. Louis Napoleon's *coup d'état* on 2 December 1851, wrote the end of a chapter. It had been a short one but full of lessons. As for the *coup d'état* itself, it is enough to say that few workers followed the *montagnards* to the barricades. Some argued a shortage of rifles in their districts since June 1848; others said they were not going to be shot full of holes for the Deputies' 25 francs. But there were a number among the dead on the streets of Paris and before the tribunals of the Joint Commissions. Above all the democrats of the countryside, who had become politically conscious after the 1848 Revolution, and—especially—after the 1849 elections, did try to break the bars of the vast prison that France had become: the insurgents in the Departments of Sarthe, Nièvre, Yonne, Hérault, Drôme, Var and Basses-Alpes, raised the battle-cry of 'Long live the Republic!' and sometimes fought under the Red Flag. But they were not only crushed, but vilified by the circulation of atrocity stories, like those which accompanied the reprisals after June 1848.

5

THE INTERNATIONAL PROBLEM

A revolution in any country is bound to have international repercussions, and thus it was in 1848. That is why Proudhon wrote: 'Keep the Tricolour if you must as the sign of our nationality, but remember that the Red Flag is the symbol of the Final Revolution. It is the federal flag of all mankind.' The preamble to the decree of 25 February which abolished the death penalty for political offences, contained the following words: 'Each revolution undertaken by the French people must establish a new philosophical truth in the world.'

The 'Days of February' had burst upon a Europe whose efforts at liberation Metternich and Nicholas had been hard put to restrain. From 1846 onward there were cracklings in Germany, the Austrian States and Italy, presaging a general conflagration. In England, meanwhile, radicals and the workers continued to join the Chartist movement, and although most of the countries in Europe were rising in the name of national liberty, they were also imbued with the spirit of equality and freedom. 1848 has been called 'the spring-time of the people'.

Besides, Paris in the reign of Louis Philippe was an international city— the centre of the world's revolutionaries. It is not surprising that delegations from every country, particularly of exiled nationals, hastened to congratulate the Provisional Government, and copied the French *clubs* in their own organisations, such as *The Italian Emigrants' Club*, *The Polish Emigrants' Club*, the *Swiss Grütli Society*, *The Iberian Democrats' Club*, *The Society of Belgian Patriots*, and *The Society of German Democrats*. The last-named combined three former German societies, and at its inaugural meeting on 6 March cried 'Long live the Republic of Europe!' And whilst Lamartine and Crémieux welcomed the foreigners who came to congratulate them with speeches reminiscent of the Girondins, Ledru-Rollin, Raspail, Barbès, Blanqui and Caussidière called for a crusade of the peoples against their kings. The German Legion formed by Georg Herwegh and Bornstedt crossed the Rhine on 25 April with the object of freeing Germany and Poland; Adam Mickiewicz left for Rome to form a Polish Legion; in Lyons the '*Voraces*' concentrated for an attack on Savoy; and Spilthoorn, from Ghent, organised volunteers to fight in Belgium.

However, the Provisional Government, or at any rate its majority, had no more intention of changing the political face of Europe than it had of changing France's social or economic structure. Peace was Lamartine's watchword in the message he sent on 27 February to all the foreign embassies: 'The proclamation of France as a Republic has changed neither her position in Europe, nor her sincere wish to maintain the most cordial relations with those countries which, like her, desire the independence of each nation and peace throughout the world.' In that circular, which is sometimes referred to as the 'Manifesto of the Fourth of March', Lamartine made no apologies for the revolution, he sought to justify it, saying: 'It is the Nation's plain right, and expresses the will of the people.' But he defined the revolution 'as an orthodox move, not an attempt to create disorder in Europe', for 'the People and Peace are synonymous'. And although France did not recognise the legality of the 1815 Peace treaties, she accepted the frontiers as they stood, *de facto*, and would never seek to change them save 'by amicable agreement'. The only occasion on which the Republic would go to war would be if Switzerland or the Italian States were forcibly prevented from organising themselves as they wished. Lamartine made no mention of either Poland, or the Slavs and Hungarians in Austria, who he well knew were preparing to free themselves.

Although the Republic's foreign policy was purely negative, the very fact of her existence and contact with the Great Powers, caused them some anxiety. On 24 February Nicholas I had promised his aid to Frederick William IV in the event of an attack on Prussia. He recalled his ambassador from Paris, and did not recognise the French Republic until 9 May, 1849. The Government of Baden asked for the support of the Berlin Government in the eventuality of a communist rising. Metternich, who was soon to be flung out by the revolution in Vienna, wrote to the Prussian envoy saying that he desired to preserve the achievements of 1815. The Czar concentrated a vast army of 400,000 men on the frontiers, and the British Ambassador, Lord Normandby, proved most uncooperative with the young Republic. Yet Lamartine never stopped warning his compatriots to be prudent and to soft-pedal the Polish and Irish questions. The Italians were the only people to whom any positive help was offered, when on 27 March he promised that 'the sword of France' would defend their country against any invader.

Nevertheless, Lamartine was worried about the Poles, and although he took no steps to help re-establish the ancient Royal Republic, he did try to win the Posnanian Poles' emancipation from Prussia, which was also in the throes of revolutionary activity. However, the Minister he sent to Berlin was the conservative Adolphe de Circourt, who loathed Poles, and at once took the side of the Prussian Government (which was beset by pan-German propaganda) against the leader of the insurgents in Posen, Mieroslawski. The pro-Polish demonstration in Paris on 15 May further alienated the Prussian Government, which would not be wooed by Lamartine's successor in the Foreign Office, Bastide. The Assembly itself gave one token of its democratic origin when on 24 May it laid down the following policy for the Government: a treaty with Germany, the reconstitution of a free independent Poland, and the enfranchisement of Italy.

Eighteen forty-eight in Germany, however, was a typical year of her history. The governments of the States of Southern Germany protested at the activities of Herwegh's legion, for which the Provisional Government had refused to provide arms, and published a statement to that effect, disclaiming all responsibility in *Le Moniteur* of 5 April. Nevertheless, Bastide co-operated with England, at the time of the Malmö armistice on 26 August 1848, in restricting Prussia's influence in the Danish duchies, and he sent repeated warnings to Frankfort on the abuses of nationalism which he realised were a menace to France.

The French Foreign Office remained merely a spectator of the upheavals in the Austrian States, but protested at the Russian occupation of the Principalities on the Danube, whereby Nicholas I hoped to forestall the immediate rebirth of a new nation, further reduce the size of the Turkish Empire, and enable his army to attack revolutionary Hungary from the rear.

France's policy towards Italy was confused and confusing, with her abortive attempt to help Piedmont, and her intervention first on behalf of, then against, the Roman Republic.

Actually, Charles Albert had never put much faith in France. On 10 March he made a point of thanking the Provisional Government for 'wishing to spread no propaganda, and leaving neighbouring countries to develop along their own lines in their own time'. On 23 March he developed this theme in his proclamation: *Italia farà da se* (Italy will work out her own salvation). All the same, the Provisional Government decided on 25 March to form an Alpine Army of 60,000 men to meet the dangers of the situation that arose when Piedmont made her lone stand against Austria. This further alarmed the Turin Government, which feared that France would annex Savoy, and that the *Voraces*, concentrated at Lyons, would cross the Alps. But when after the defeat at Custozza, the Lombards and Piedmontese (between 28 July and 6 August) called on France for help, it was too late, and all she could do was propose that she and England should act as mediators. Charles Albert forestalled them, however, on 9 August, by signing an armistice which left out Venice. This made mediation impossible, but Bastide (as Monsieur Paul Henri has pointed out) showed some fight by threatening to declare war on Austria if she blockaded Venice or attacked Piedmont. But at the same time he sent a note to Turin that if Piedmont re-opened hostilities, it would be at her own risk. When Piedmont did so, on 12 March 1849, Charles Albert was again defeated.

The confusion of French policy in North Italy was due both to Piedmont's diplomatic and military mistakes, and to the Provisional Executive Commission's unwillingness to waste lives in an expedition which might result in the creation of a new nation at the foot of the Alps to endanger France's security. The Roman expedition marked a complete reversal by the Legislative Assembly of the Constituent Assembly's foreign policy. On 14 April 1849, Odilon Barrot had asked for money to equip a 'Mediterranean Expeditionary Force' to help the Romans achieve 'real independence', after they had expelled the liberal Pope Pius IX and, on 9 February 1849, proclaimed Rome a Republic. The 'mountain' refused to vote him supplies, as the Government's explanations were most unconvincing. Anyway, General Oudinot landed at Civitavecchia and marched on Rome. He ignored the notice boards he found on his route, reproducing Article V of the French Constitution: 'The Republic will never employ its forces to deprive a people of their freedom.' Oudinot was routed by the combined forces of Rome and Garibaldi's legion on 30 April 1849.

Paris was astounded, and the President of the Republic, the Ministers, the generals and the Assembly all issued conflicting and confusing statements. Ferdinand de Lesseps had been sent as a special envoy to Rome with complicated instructions out of which he managed to prepare an agreement between the two Republics. An armistice was signed on 16 May, and a treaty on the 31st. But his actions were repudiated the day after the Legislative took over from the Constituent Assembly. From that moment, as Georges Renard said, the mask was off. On 1 June Oudinot besieged Rome, and he entered the city on 3 July. The French Republic had murdered the young Republic of Rome, Pius IX was enabled to return, and the reactionaries in France rejoiced at a 'Catholic' victory. It was all very well for Louis Napoleon, for domestic reasons, to advise the Pope to be moderate, and publish in the *Moniteur* his letter to Colonel Ney, his A.D.C. who was with Oudinot, observing that he had asked Pius IX to proclaim an amnesty and form a liberal government. No doubt the Prince President's policy towards Piedmont, Hungary, Denmark, Greece and Switzerland may have appeared to favour the rights of peoples, but the French democrats tarred with the same brush the electoral law of 31 May 1850, and the despatch of an expeditionary force against Rome. The encyclical *Hostis et nobiscum* of 12 December was a solemn denunciation of communism, socialism—and even liberalism. The Pope was never again going to deny the nature of his office.

6

THE BALANCE SHEET OF 1848

The 1848 Revolution ended in a triple fiasco: the social fiasco of the elimination of the right to work; the political fiasco of the reduced suffrage and the *coup d'état;* and the international fiasco of the expedition against Rome. The question arises, therefore, whether it is really worth while tracing the development and recording the incidents of this revolution. Is there any point in clearing the names of the men of 1848—the 'forty-eighters', the 'old fogeys'—whom history has blackened ever since Vermorel vilified them at the end of the Second Empire?

There have been many other movements in history which, like the 1848 Revolution, failed partly or wholly to redeem the vast promises made at their inception. Of course the 1789 Revolution lasted very much longer than that of 1848. It attempted to solve much wider problems, and its authors—if you like—had greater stature, but nevertheless it did not realise all its original aims; its progress was erratic, it was a mass of contradictions, and it caused the deaths of many great men and large sections of the population. The principles of 1789, however, continued to have an effect long after the revolution itself was over, and the revolutionary era gave rise to certain social phenomena which had a profound significance. Despite all its fluctuations, the history of the French Revolution was marked by the steady ascendency of the middle class, which suffered only a slight set-back at the time of the direct democracy and revolutionary government in the years 1793 and 1794. Besides this, the principal figures of the French Revolution were men who, though they may have deceived themselves or been deceived by others, triumphed in the end. Their history gives the epoch its vitality and greatness.

The Revolution of 1848 was incomparably shorter than the Great Revolution, yet Karl Marx did not disdain to remark that the 18th *Brumaire* of Louis Napoleon marked the end of the new revolutionary period, just as the 18th *Brumaire* of Napoleon I closed the first. Admittedly, the men of 1848 were not like the giants of the Year II. Louis Blanc was a little man—'small in stature but great in ambition', they said of him; Adolphe Thiers was short too, and then there was 'Napoleon—le Petit'. The gaunt and distinguished-looking Lamartine had more genius than any of them, but his political and social views were narrow and in his love of conspiracy ('like that of the lightning-conductor for the thunderstorm') he would never go beyond a compromise. Finally, there was Victor Hugo, who only overcame his prejudices in the last stages of the revolution to follow a lost cause. The leaders talked too much, and there was too much intrigue both inside and outside the Assemblies.

By way of contrast, however, there was the people—the people whose depth of feeling and whose strength had been revealed and exalted two years before the outbreak of the revolution by Michelet. And the people themselves attempted to find their spokesmen among the working-class poets who were equally confident in their cause and in their muse. Of course they had their faults, which were the legacy of an illiterate past and the age's egoism, but they showed, especially in the towns, a tremendous courage and sense of duty. Even in the countryside the day-labourers, who for generations had been under the influence of Church and Castle, began to acquire a political and almost a social sense. It was the people who came out of their slums in caps and blouses to overthrow the Monarchy and set up the Social Republic. There followed one disappointment after another: there was the banishment of the Red Flag, endless debates in the Luxembourg, the mockery of the National Workshops, the cruel reprisals after 'the Days of June', the hypocrisy of the Electoral Law, the refusal to sanction trade unions, and the legal inequality between employer and employee. The people also believed that France would go to the aid of other nations in revolt, but after Lamartine's fine words, there were only fruitless negotiations and the misdirected expedition to Rome.

But what a lesson all these disappointments taught the French proletariat! At the time when the *Communist Manifesto* was propagating the theory of class warfare, and Karl Marx was lashing out at the sentimental humbug hiding the hard facts of social antimonies, the people were experiencing their effects. Yet they had their pathetic moments of trust, which resulted in that abortion, the Second Empire, which succeeded the murdered Republic. But the proletariat did not despair, and step by step, as Georges Duveau has shown, rose up again. After 1860, the sons of the martyrs of June 1848 developed their doctrines and their bold tactics of regeneration, which were unfortunately to meet with the same lack of understanding on the part of the reactionary middle class. In 1871 the proletariat of France was to suffer its third defeat.

Thus the 1848 Revolution can be seen, if we look on the credit side, as a rich source of experience for the workers; and it saw the budding of innumerable working-class institutions, which were to flower later on. After the defeat of the revolutionaries in Europe, Ledru-Rollin, Mazzini and Kossuth formed the Central Committee of European Democrats in London, and although not all its members were out-and-out radicals, it did anticipate the First International which came into existence sixteen years later. That warm-hearted zealot Flora Tristan had the idea of an analogous organisation, and was also one of the fighters for an eight-hour working day. This attempt to reduce the hours of work was one of the revolutionaries' first objectives, but was gradually lost sight of as the forces of reaction gathered strength. In the same way, the right to work was at first accepted and finally set aside, but its principle, which originally was perhaps too vague in form, gave birth to an enormous number of working-class institutions: insurance and pension schemes, employment bureaux, and holidays with pay. All these peaceful conquests of the working class were the result of their making people realise the hitherto only dimly seen necessity for a workers' statute.

The assurance of a place for the worker in any society worthy of the name was one of the more or less conscious, more or less explicitly stated aims of the 1848 Revolution. In order to enable men to acquire a full sense of their dignity, society had to be reconstituted, and so sweated labour was made illegal, titles and the oath of allegiance suppressed, the death penalty for political offences and imprisonment for debt were abolished, as were the pillory and flogging in the navy. And to widen the sphere in which peoples' liberty was respected, slavery was abolished in all French possessions overseas. And in other countries, peoples' attempt to assert themselves as nations was not in vain. In spite of all the obstacles and setbacks, democracies did sprout from the seeds scattered in 1848, although some lay cold and low within the earth until the present day. After hearing and seeing all that was said and done at the end of February and the end of April, George Sand exclaimed in a romantic exaltation: 'How good to fall asleep in the mud and waken in the skies', and Lamartine: 'The Republic came as a surprise; we have made it a miracle'.

ITALY IN 1848

DELIO CANTIMORI

Every time you use the word 'faction', we will thrice repeat that we
are a Nation, a Nation, a Nation
Massimo d'Azeglio

I

PARTIES OLD AND NEW, AND THE NATIONAL WAR

SALVEMINI has pointed out that when even the most sanguine revolutionaries, who had achieved so much at the beginning of 1848, finally admitted defeat, Joseph Mazzini fought on. And he directed his propaganda towards the workers, in both town and countryside, and towards the young.

Mazzini acted thus because, although he refuted his socialist critics in other countries (particularly in France), he was aware that his own party, as well as other democratic parties in Italy, had too often pursued *political* rather than *social* aims.

But that is the end of a chapter, the moral to the story of the year 1848, which began with such high hopes, and ended in a victory first for Italian, then for European reaction. Yet 1848 was not a final chapter, but only the end of a phase, for long after the fall of Vienna, Rome and Venice, the spirit of revolution was still alive in Europe.

Politically speaking, the European revolution began in Italy, where the combined forces of moderate liberals and revolutionary radicals rose to obtain by force reforms denied them by despotic governments.

The liberals, if one may so speak of them today, had not so far had to choose between peaceable and violent means of achieving reform. It was only in 1848 that a distinction was drawn between the two methods which produced two separate movements. The supporters of the first, known in Italy as 'moderates', sought to induce the Governments to make a number of reforms and finally grant Constitutions; the supporters of the second were known as revolutionaries, as Jacobins, as republicans and as democrats.

It was at this period that the distinction between liberals and democrats

114

was first drawn in other European countries, and the two parties were soon to come into opposition. What is more, the majority of moderate liberals in Italy did not even want constitutional régimes, as these would lead to the formation of real political parties. The characteristically Italian neo-Guelph movement was opposed to party politics altogether, as its followers did not believe in the theory that real political freedom could only be achieved by and through divergence of opinion. This axiom of English, and even of French liberalism, found many supporters among the Italian democrats and radicals, but not among Mazzini's party *La Giovine Italia*—'Young Italy'—who on this point thought like the neo-Guelphs.

Cavour and Giacomo Durando were the only conservatives in Italy to hold this more advanced conception of liberalism. But even they were violently opposed to any form of democracy such as the extension of political rights and widening the franchise to include the 'common people', thereby enabling the whole population to take part in the life of the nation, which was the progressives' chief aim.

Besides, Cavour clearly saw that when it came to the point, the Mazzinians—unless they abandoned their fundamental aim of making the Italian States into a single, independent nation—might join up with the liberal conservatives. In 1846 he wrote:

> A democratic revolution has no chance of success in Italy. If you want to be convinced of that, you have only to analyse the composition of the party favouring political innovations. It has no great following among the masses, who apart from a few sections in the towns, are on the whole extremely attached to the country's old institutions. Almost all its adherents come from the middle classes which have too many interests to safeguard. Property, thank God, is not the monopoly of any one class in Italy and both the old aristocracy and the common people have their bit of land. Young Italy's theories have no great hold on classes which have so much to gain by maintaining a stable society. That is why (with the exception of a handful of young men, whose ill-digested theories picked up as hot-headed students have not yet been modified by experience) we can safely say that there is only an absurdly small number of people who seriously wish to put into practice the doctrines of a party embittered by failure.
>
> If the stability of society were seriously endangered, if there were a real threat to its fundamental principles, I am absolutely certain that the first to swell the ranks of the conservatives would be many of the most intransigent and idealistic Mazzinians.

Eighteen forty-seven was a troubled year for Italy. It produced a number of political developments of varying degrees of importance and primarily of an economic nature. This was due to a crisis caused by the scarcity and increased cost of bread. Reforms introduced by the rulers of Rome, Piedmont and Tuscany as a result of pressure from the neo-Guelphs and the moderates after Pius IX's election in 1846, not only did nothing to remedy this crisis, but in some cases aggravated it, as by the 'liberal' innovation of exporting wheat to England.

In the Italian States which had brought in these reforms the moderates expressed their satisfaction with their governments and the only agitation was for economic relief. In the Two Sicilies and the provinces of Lombardy and Venetia, however, although the economic factor was not ignored, the political problem was uppermost.

The salient feature of the Calabrian rising in September 1847 was its political nature; the same goes for the simultaneous revolt in Messina (although it was strangled at birth in the same month) and for the demonstrations in Milan in support of the new Italian Archbishop Romilli, who had succeeded the Austrian Gaisrück. Incidentally, Gaisrück (as Salvatorelli points out) was more liberally minded than his Italian successor, but that sort of thing counted for nothing when nationalism was at stake.

By the end of 1847, the moderates and the neo-Guelphs were proceeding from local reforms to the shaping of a national policy: from the acquisition of a more or less limited degree of freedom for the press, from a demand for a civic guard, to counterbalance the police; from respectful petitions to the Pope and regional Congresses like that of the Agricultural Association of Piedmont, to national Congresses such as the Scientific Congress for all Italy, which met regularly after 1839-40; and from celebrations like that of Ballila's centenary towards something more important. All these projected reforms were part of a move to direct the different governments' divergent foreign policies towards the goal of Italian unity.

Towards the end of 1847, there was also a move in the provinces of Lombardy and Venetia, to claim at any rate an indirect part, as consultants, in the Government: the idea was to obtain through the 'Congregations', a consultative body of Imperial origin which had been sanctioned in 1815, the nomination of commissions to investigate the causes of the economic distress and suggest remedies. The Imperial Government, however, replied with harsh repressive measures.

The political atmosphere can be gauged from the fact that the big landowners and leisured classes of Lombardy made large donations to charity in 1847; not simply because they wished to alleviate the distress caused by famine in rural and even in urban areas, but also because they feared that the Austrian Government might do what it had done in Galicia in 1846: set the countryside against the town, and the poor against the rich.

At the same time the Austrian Government, in the name of law and order and the maintenance of the *status quo*, prepared to intervene in the Italian States. In July they occupied the citadel of Ferrara, on the pretext of protecting the Austrian garrison which had been in the town since 1815; they entered into what amounted to a military pact with the Duke of Modena; and finally, in December, they sent troops into Parma.

The seizure of Ferrara made the revolutionaries, the moderates, the neo-Guelphs and Pius IX's ardent supporters pay more attention to the current rumour of a conspiracy to oust Pius IX formed between Metternich and the Gregorians, with their natural allies the Jesuits. Incidentally, there had already been demands, as in Switzerland, for the expulsion of the Jesuits.

The most important result of the seizure of Ferrara, however, was that it attracted the attention not only of the Great Powers but also of Charles Albert, King of Piedmont-Sardinia. But the hopes of successful intervention faded the moment that Charles Albert treated with reserve suggestions made from Rome and Florence—in view of a defensive alliance between the Papal States, Tuscany and Sardinia, all of which had already introduced certain reforms. Conservatives were, however, again to discuss the formation of a customs union, as a prelude to an Italian Confederation. This was the first item on the political programme of the liberals, the moderates and the neo-Guelphs. They were full of optimism now that Piedmont, the last State to adopt reforms, had shown such breadth of mind in abolishing the last vestiges of feudal privilege.

It was then that, on 12 January 1848, the revolution broke out in Sicily. It was the work not of the moderates and liberals but of the radicals and democrats, and they sought not reforms but a Constitution, which meant to the Sicilians the 1812 Constitution based on home rule. No one was surprised that Great Britain hastened to support the Sicilians against the Government of Naples. For the Italians, the rising in Palermo was a victory for the radicals, democrats, and the men who preached revolution. Its immediate result was that Ferdinand II granted not merely a handful of reforms but that very Constitution which the island of Sicily had acquired when it first won its independence, and which had been so long and so ardently desired by many moderates and every single democrat.

From a purely political point of view, the Kingdom of Naples had thus taken the lead in the *Risorgimento*. Ferdinand II, threatened with fresh risings in Apulia, Basilicata, Calabria and Naples, far out of reach of the

Austrian army, terrified lest he lose Sicily, and cut off from the rest of the world by British diplomatic action, had taken the plunge. And so whilst the principle of absolute monarchy had so far been unshaken, at least in form, on the mainland, he emerged as a Constitutional sovereign.

The plan of the projected Constitutions for Naples, Rome, Piedmont and Tuscany was substantially the same as Louis Philippe's Charter. But politically Italy had leapt into line with France, England and Switzerland.

Palmerston, swayed by public opinion in England, which had been so successfully influenced by Mazzini, gave his blessing to the Moderate movement and sent Lord Minto on a special mission to Italy. He did this partly to maintain peace, and partly as one of those concessions to reform which are necessary in an attempt to stave off radical revolution. Palmerston's encouragement spread the idea of Italy's becoming a single nation. The problem of how she was to become one, whether by union or federation, preoccupied not only Italian political movements, but the whole of Europe. But whatever decision was reached, Palmerston wanted a strong and calm Italy as a counterweight against Austria and France.

The revolutionaries of Europe hailed the Palermo rising with joy. After the moderates had failed to achieve anything by petitions and protests, it had been the radicals and Mazzinians who launched and organised it. It was at this time that the news went round that the Mazzinian conspirators behind the Palermo rising intended that it should spread first to Naples and then all over Italy. The democrats, who were newcomers to Sicilian politics, headed this movement. The moderate liberals, however, immediately gained a majority in the Sicilian Chamber, and took the reins once the rising was over. This significant fact did not weigh much on the revolutionaries, either Italian or European. They recalled with pleasure that whereas in the course of the July Revolution, a town of a million inhabitants—Paris—had defeated an army of between seven and eight thousand men, Palermo, with a population of only two hundred thousand, had routed an army of thirteen thousand. What a happy omen for the European Revolution!

'When Paris puts up barricades and Vienna is in revolt, the whole population of Milan, not merely her six hundred soldiers, takes but five days to rout Radetzky's army, which was more than thirteen thousand strong and possessed thirty pieces of artillery. The risings in Como, Moriza, Bergamo and Venice are equally happy omens.' So read one of the press reports of the time. And again: 'The Mazzinians and radicals claim that the people are proving their strength; in the five days' fighting in Milan, artisans and workmen, priests and aristocrats, merchants and manufacturers, men, women—and even children—have been fighting side by side.'

In the interests of truth, however, it should be added that when the final reckoning was made, the losses in Milan were apportioned as follows; out of 350 dead, there were only a dozen or so students, landlords and clerks; there were 40 women and 34 children of both sexes, and the rest were either artisans or workmen. But few troubled about these class distinctions. In their enthusiasm the members of Young Italy and the other secret societies came into the open. They had had a whole populace to direct towards a single goal, and the differences of age, sex and class had counted for nothing. Apparently the Italians, like the other revolutionaries, thought they saw a connection between the risings of Paris, Palermo, Milan and Vienna. As a matter of fact, up to the February Revolution in France, the moderate liberals and the Catholics (that is to say, the neo-Guelphs and moderates among them) had taken the lead, and they kept it, despite the efforts of Mazzini and Cattaneo.

Right up to February and March 1848, the dominant aim of the movement was to acquire a Constitution for each State and to see that it was respected; the Mazzinians' aim to unite the country had failed. Another point was that the Constitutions already in force were often the result of economic movements, which spread to Genoa, Florence, Leghorn and the province of Salerno. These economic movements, and revolts resulting from famine, worried the new governments, which did not know how to deal with them, and which suspected that they were the work of Austria's henchmen. The people, on their side, often failed to understand the economic liberalism which had been hailed with such delight by the rich and educated classes on the occasion of Cobden's visit to Italy. To them it often meant no more than dearer bread.

The new governments mentioned saw that Metternich and Radetzky were seeking to maintain centres of reaction against this new moderate, constitutional Italy. In February, after he had proclaimed a state of siege in Lombardy, Radetzky asked the Pope's permission to pass through the Papal States on his way to the Kingdom of the Two Sicilies. He was stopped by the outbreak of revolution in Paris and Vienna.

The 'Five Days' of Milan and the proclamation of the Republic of St Mark in Venice, transformed the Italian problem into one of national unity, irrespective of whether Italy was to be a single country or a federation. As Mazzini had already shown, this problem had existed from the moment when, while the majority of States had been granted constitutions, Lombardy, Venetia and the duchies occupied by Austria were left outside the national movement and the general upheaval which resulted in the Italian middle classes rising to power as the leaders of an Italian nation. The moment Lombardy and Venetia joined the rest of the country, the revolution was bound to lead to war—to the war for which Radetzky had been preparing when he tried to reach the South. The Italian leaders looked upon the war as one of independence against the Austrian hegemony in the country. The optimism engendered by the revolution had blinded many people to the fact that it was no easy war to wage.

Austria, although she was upset by internal disorders, was nevertheless the greatest military power in Europe. Although defeated at Milan, Radetzky's army remained practically intact. The revolutionaries in Vienna numbered few who thought in terms of democratic solidarity. The most energetic element of the people in Italy, Mazzini's republicans, had implicit faith in the happenings in France and Vienna; in the Milan rising and in the strength of the people. But the moderate liberals distrusted them.

The radicals themselves were not all of one mind, and included federalists, unionists, republicans and those who would come to terms with monarchy for the sake of national unity. It was the same with the moderates, who comprised unionists, federalists and unionist-royalists. Then there were the diehard opponents of all reform and implacable enemies of the revolution. These last were powerful and numerous in every State. They had recently held positions of authority in the Courts or at army headquarters, and hoped for the victory of the representatives of law and order, and of throne and altar, of which Austria was to them the symbol. They had no use for the neo-Guelphs' admiration for Pius IX, and disliked the moderates as much as the radicals. They were ready, moreover, to bring into play all the weapons of conspiracy and demagogy. The talk about nationalism and 'the rights of the people' they considered as dangerous doctrines, and yet it was the men who held these doctrines who were in command, and who were directing what was for the people a War of National Independence.

The evasions and waverings, the tragic weakness and at last the abdication, of Charles Albert gave an almost symbolic expression to the whole situation.

The result of the constitutional movement, as it appeared before the February revolution in France to even a revolutionary like Engels, was the exploitation of victories won, and their consolidation by the creation of a common front against Austria.

Once France had unleashed revolution in Europe, and Milan had risen, the national war against Austria would have to be fought to a finish. Cattaneo realised that fact, and right up to the last moment advised the use of legal, not revolutionary, methods. When Milan did revolt, however, he proved an excellent military leader.

The people's fervour in the two months following the 'Five Days', the intervention of the Sardinian army, and the appearance on the scene of both regular forces and volunteers from the Papal States, Tuscany, Naples and Sicily, showed the urgent need for an army capable of driving the Austrians out of Italy and resisting their counter-offensive, if 'Italy was to manage by herself!' (*Italia farà da se* was her reply to an offer of help from the democratic French Republic.) France's offer of help was refused also out of consideration for Great Britain, who had so far backed up the reformists.

The revolutionary war—for so we may well call a war of popular and national character directed by a dynasty—marks the break of a whole tradition which had recently been consolidated. It meant the acceptance of revolutionary leaders, and of the road indicated by the logic of the situation and by the enthusiastic demonstrations of the people.

This phase of the revolution implied contact with the risings which had just broken out in every part of the Empire. It took the direction indicated by Mazzini, who told the Italians that they should link up with the other young nations which appeared to be springing to birth out of the ruins of the Hapsburg Empire. It meant a natural rupture with the reactionaries, who were dubbed Austrophiles.

Mazzini had hurried over from England, and although he mistrusted Charles Albert, he promised the king wholehearted support on condition that he agreed to use the whole of the military and political strength of Piedmont to wage unrelenting war on Austria. These were the strongest forces in Italy and far more trustworthy than the troops of Ferdinand II of Naples.

Cattaneo, a federalist and republican, who was more concerned about freedom than national unity, and Ferrari, who envisaged the possibility of a revolution in Italy with the assistance of the French, both regarded Mazzini as almost a traitor. Moreover, his pact with Charles Albert meant that if the latter refrained from royalist propaganda until the war was over, Mazzini would refrain from spreading republicanism.

Charles Albert's followers, however, did not keep to their side of the bargain, and the conduct of the war and the unification of Italy was brazenly taken out of the hands of the Mazzinians, radicals and moderates, and put into those of the royalists. In fact, as we have seen from what happened at Palermo, the latter had such prestige in Italy that even the radicals could not but acknowledge it. Political authority was traditionally vested in the right wing, and all it had to do was to adopt one or two reforms.

Nevertheless, Charles Albert, the Piedmontese aristocracy and the moderates all took part in the war against Austria. And paradoxical as it was, they set the Cross of the House of Savoy on the Italian Tricolour. Their delay in beginning the campaign, however, gave Radetzky time to reform his forces which had been driven from Milan, to lead them into the Quadrilateral, and to maintain communications with the Empire through the Tyról and the Trentino. It also meant that the Italian forces were ill-prepared, a fact which soon told against them.

So far Palmerston's diplomacy had been exerted against Radetzky to prevent war. But once war had broken out, his main preoccupation was fear of French intervention or perhaps merely of an increase of France's influence in Italy, despite the francophobia of both Mazzini and the King of Sardinia. But apart from Palmerston's attempts to prevent Piedmont taking part in the war against Austria, by advising her after the Milan rising to remain neutral and not to accept military aid from the French, the moral, military and political lack of readiness became increasingly evident as the war progressed.

Palmerston's attitude and perhaps also the move to form a Northern Italian Kingdom, and the various promises of mediation, may explain why France did not intervene. And it may also partly explain the lacka- daisical conduct of this 'royal' war, which aroused so much suspicion and bitterness and finally ended in defeat. But it cannot explain how it was that the Piedmontese aristocracy thought they could defeat the Austrian armies in Italy, let alone smash Austria, with the Sardinian army which for fifteen years had been trained to fight for the dynasty and the Holy Alliance side by side with Austria, which had no sympathy for Italy's cause and which loathed her Tricolour—in those days still looked upon as a revolutionary flag. With their declaration 'that Italy would manage by herself', the Piedmontese aristocracy had spurned the aid of democratic France, and also cold-shouldered the host of volunteers which began to pour in. These were soon disillusioned by the distrust and hostility they met from the Piedmontese army who should have welcomed, organised and supplied them. Neither the heads of the other Italian States, nor the new influential groups such as the moderates, showed any eagerness to help them. The result was that in spite of isolated examples of heroism such as those of the Tuscan volunteers from Curtatone and Montara, the volunteer forces as a whole were of little use. The Piedmontese right and the moderates of the Upper Italy were prevented by political prejudice— not always entirely unreasonable—from mobilising the Italian people and which alone would have seemed to justify their announcing Italia farà da se. The townsfolk (who were the first to volunteer) met with the same treatment as the country people and I do not mean in the South but in Central and Northern Italy, starting with Piedmont itself.

The commanders of the Piedmontese army were brave enough in themselves; they were inspired by the royal tradition, exemplified by the King himself, of chivalry and courage. But for the most part they were reactionaries. Their troops' fighting spirit, which was very high at the beginning of this campaign, was gradually sapped by royalist intrigues to curtail their newly won freedom, and they saw their hopes of a democratic future for Italy fast fading away. We must also note the incompetent organisation of the commissariat and the moral isolation of the ordinary trooper.

The government itself was 'constitutionalist', and desired the nation to take part in the country's affairs as well as in the conduct of the war. The senior officers of the army, however, were royalists, and would have no truck with the nationalists and constitutionalists who could have brought in new blood. The rank and file, lacking as yet any political education, could not be expected to make heroic sacrifices inspired only by love of the monarchy, so long as the Piedmontese country people were continually aware of the fact that famine continued unabated.

It was useless to expect enthusiasm for the volunteers, however much the advantages of using them might be emphasised, and it was useless to expect enthusiasm from the peasants of Lombardy and Venetia, unless the Piedmontese government pursued a policy in their favour, which would lead all the Italian peasants and artisans to rise for the King. And yet their King had achieved a momentary unity through the enthusiasm roused by hopes of a better and more democratic future, which needed only the right moment to be realised. But neither the radicals nor the Mazzinians could help either by direct pressure or by proving their own efficiency. All their time was taken up with the struggle against the royalists and the moderates of Lombardy, who wanted fusion with Sardinia and who failed to keep their part of the bargain struck between Mazzini and Charles Albert, when Charles Albert arrived at Milan. Mazzinians and republicans alike found themselves caught up in royalist manœuvres following the plebiscite held to determine whether or not Lombardy and the Duchies should be annexed by Piedmont. They were not given a choice between union with Piedmont and the formation of some sort of independent State. The alternative presented was either that of being defended by Piedmont against Austria, or of being abandoned to Austria, and the people voted for annexation by a large majority. They suspected treason, however, at the time of Charles Albert's army's retreat, when they saw how ineptly the war was being conducted. The defence scheme, for instance, excluded the Venetian Republic, which was left to its fate. This gave the impression that the commanders' object was to reach an understanding with Austria and with the help of French and British mediators acquire the province of Lombardy. It looked as though there would be a repetition of the Treaty of Campo Formio.

The people again felt they were being betrayed, when Charles Albert forbade the inhabitants of Milan to barricade the streets and defend their town themselves. He promised that his army would protect it outside the walls and then promptly capitulated—as, it seems, he had planned to do in the first place. Rightly or wrongly, the people again suspected treason when in accepting the offer of Franco-British mediation, he abandoned the Italian people's war for diplomatic negotiations. The Italian problem had certainly become a European one, but the solution was left not to the people but to the kings.

This was the result not of a deliberate plan to betray Italy, but of the lack of a coherent policy among the various groups conducting the war. The Piedmontese right wing and the moderate liberals connected with them were as confused as were the radicals who had been forced by circumstances to leave the principal rôle to the former. Whilst Radetzky and the Austrian government were able to make use of the country people of Lombardy and Venetia who looked upon the rising in Milan and Vienna as the sport of the rich and the university students, the remainder of the rural population—from the farmers of Lombardy, Piedmont and Tuscany, to the small landowners of Emilia—took no interest in the Italian movement. The reason was that the Mazzinians, and even the most advanced radicals and republicans, ignored the countryside and looked upon the workers of the towns as 'the people'.

The politicians' indifference to the agricultural communities was largely due to the lack of sympathy shown in the country for the enthusiastic welcome accorded Pius IX. In the agricultural areas men were too busy worrying over the famine, and their priests were either 'Gregorians', that is to say supporters of Pius IX's predecessor, or they were entirely pre-occupied with parochial affairs. These priests had taken no part in the neo-Guelph movement, as had those in the towns of Piedmont, Lombardy Tuscany and the Papal States.

Murat's abolition of feudalism in the Two Sicilies—particularly in Apulia, Basilicata and Calabria—and his distribution of the land amongst those who worked it, did not, as had been hoped, create a class of small landowners. There arose instead a cartel of squireens who became increasingly powerful and deprived the poor of the common land, which by ancient law, had belonged to those who had none of their own. That is why when these squireens (*galantuomini* as they were called) began to want a constitution and to decide how the community should be governed, the poor countryfolk, who had been forced to become day-labourers, rose on several occasions to demand the restoration of their right to a share in the land. In Northern and Central Italy, the fear of a social revolution, even in spite of a number of risings in Tuscany, was really the same terror of the 'red bogy' of the *Jacquerie* and communism, which frightened all the reactionaries in Europe, as well as being the work of enemy *agents provocateurs*, whose influence was counteracted only by repeated pleas for law and order, and respect for property. In Southern Italy, however, it was a question of something more concrete than prefabricated theories spread by some socialistic journalist, or propaganda tricks to discredit the Mazzinians and radicals like Guerazzi or Montanelli. The landowners answered the demands of the rural population by organising themselves to fight revolution in the name of public order.

But if politicians in Northern and Central Italy spoke up for social reform only rarely, in Southern Italy, where a reformist movement existed, no sagacious politician would have anything at all to do with it. The only exceptions were a few utopians in the towns and the members of a handful of societies on the model of the *Carbonari*, who were by now outdated and out of touch with the people.

The right wing groups and the moderates assumed power and the radicals allowed themselves to be led. The people's war was in the hands of the royalist middle class and the liberal aristocracy—a fraction of the nation—who, despite the pullulation of popular *clubs*, and committees to recruit volunteers, left the conduct of the war to the royalists of Piedmont.

But these groups did not pursue a consistent policy. Mazzini saw the contribution to the idea of unity made by the House of Savoy's intervention. By reawakening national feeling and by conducting the war against Austria, it had become the true master of Italy. Moderates throughout Italy recognised it as such. The Piedmontese aristocracy distrusted the republicans to such an extent that they would not utilise their support. In their relationship with the other Italian States they were almost as authoritarian as Napoleon, and precipitated a crisis among the moderates and royalists who favoured federation. The attitude of the Piedmontese government and high command towards the regular forces of Tuscany, Naples and the Papal States was virtually the same as their attitude towards the volunteers. Thus these regular forces, some of whom wanted to go on with the war even against the orders of their rulers when these reversed their policy, also had in the end to withdraw from the battlefield. The fact of the matter was that Piedmont aimed at replacing Austria as the ruling force in Italy. This was shown by her hasty annexation of the Duchies, open propaganda for the ruling house, lukewarm support for the idea of a Confederation, and determination that should such a Confederation come about, Piedmont would dominate it by creating a 'Kingdom of Upper Italy'. So we can see that this royalist war was not conducted with the political and diplomatic skill that the importance of the issue demanded. It is quite clear that the Piedmontese aristocracy wanted the republicans to give up their principles and the other Italian

States to sacrifice their independence and accept the rule of Charles Albert without receiving anything in exchange. Thus the unity, which seemed to have been realised in March and April in the course of the first war for Italian independence, was soon shattered; the attempted union of the various Italian rulers against Austria was also broken; and the truce between the different political parties was over.

The royalist and Sardinian nature of the war now became more apparent. In spite of the efforts of the democratic propagandists, its national character had almost entirely disappeared. Charles Albert's army, loyal though it was, and better armed and equipped than any other in Italy, no longer had any chance against Radetzky, owing to its inferior technical efficiency and the political and military strategy behind it. The incoherent and hesitant conduct of the Piedmontese ended in making Charles Albert appear to be breaking his promises to the people, and the military high command to be mismanaging the war in the most machiavellian fashion.

Not only was there lack of co-ordination between the Italian States, between the regular and volunteer forces, and between the moderates and the Pope, but rifts also appeared between the peoples and their governments, and all the political parties were at loggerheads.

The sequence of events following the revolution in Sicily on 12 January was as follows: Constitutions were granted in Naples, Tuscany, Piedmont and Rome on 29 January, 17 February, 4 March and 14 March respectively. In each State the moderates were in power representing the middle classes or the liberal aristocracy. During the same period there was trouble in Lombardy and Venetia, beginning with the Smokers' Strike. The people of these two provinces decided to give up smoking as a protest against an increase in the tax on tobacco, so the security service sent police officers and soldiers round the towns to be seen smoking and thereby provoke trouble. This resulted in the death of several people and the arrest of Casati, the Mayor of Milan. On 18 January, the liberal leaders Daniele Manin and Niccolo Tommaseo were arrested in Venice. On 18 February, students in Padua were attacked by Austrian soldiers. Massimo d'Azeglio, one of the liberal supporters of Charles Albert, published a small book entitled *Lombardy in Mourning*, in which he stressed the nationalist and non-political character of the revolutionaries in Lombardy-Venetia. 'Every time you use the word "faction",' he said, 'we will thrice repeat that we are a nation, a nation, a nation'.

On 27 February the granting of a Constitution was publicly celebrated at Turin, and Lombardy sent delegates. On 18 March the news of the revolution in Vienna reached Milan. The Austrian viceroy, Archduke

Renier, retired to Verona. A proclamation abolished the censorship, promised a law to free the press and announced a meeting of the electoral colleges for the month of July. The middle classes demanded, among other measures, the abolition of martial law, the liberation of political prisoners and the replacement of the State police by municipal police. A delegation, accompanied by a huge crowd, took a petition summing up all these demands to the royal palace. They were met by a volley of fire from the guard.

The insurrection was led from the start by the federalist Carlo Cattaneo, who organised it with skill and energy. On the third day of the battle, he refused an armistice which Radetzky wanted in order to give his troops a breather and obtain reinforcements. A provisional government was formed of moderates and royalist sympathisers, with a radical war council. Shortly afterwards, on 23 March, Venice proclaimed herself a republic—or rather revived the old Republic of St Mark; and then Cremona and Brescia won their liberty, the first with ease, and the second only after a struggle. The towns of Vicenza, Udine, Bassano, Padua, Rovigo, Treviso and Belluno followed suit.

In the meantime Charles Albert, who had been begged to intervene ever since the beginning of the 'five days', decided on 23 March to do so. He acquired universal popularity by immediately granting a wide amnesty. Radetzky, however, succeeded in retiring from Milan in good order, as the Lombard troops whose rôle (clearly defined by Cattaneo) was to pursue the Austrians, decided they were too few in number to risk an engagement outside the city. While Radetzky was strengthening his forces with the addition of contingents from the armies occupying the Duchies, Charles Albert failed to surround and break into the ring of fortified towns, Mantua, Leniano, Peschiera and Verona, composing the Quadrilateral. He did not even take up a position on the entrances of the Alpine passes, which were defended by volunteers, but stopped on the near side of the Quadrilateral, leaving Venetia unprotected and following tactics which, as Salvatorelli says, were purely defensive and passive.

He went on sitting there for the latter part of March and the whole of April. The volunteers, whose numbers were gradually increasing, worked in conjunction with Charles Albert's army, operating on Lake Garda and the Chiese Valley, on the lower reaches of the Mincio and on the Po, and in Venetia. But they lacked arms, organisation and experienced officers. They were not properly organised until the end of the month, when groups of them were growing dispirited as the result of the heavy and unnecessary casualties they had suffered due to lack of experience. The best equipped group was one of Tuscans, but the others consisted of young men from every part of Italy. As well as Lombards, Venetians and

Emilians (the regular troops from the Duchies having been incorporated in Charles Albert's army) there were Neapolitans and Sicilians and a group of returned exiles. Many of their leaders were generals who had taken part in the attempted revolution of 1831, and some had even fought in the revolutions of 1820 and 1821. A volunteer corps was raised in the Papal States, but the Pope, frightened by Austria's threats, kept it within his borders. By the time it did finally move to the war zone, the volunteers had been thoroughly demoralised. Ferdinand II did the same with a regular corps under General Pépé, whom he kept idle on the banks of the Po.

It was this same Pépé, a veteran of the *Carbonari*, who had in vain advised his master to organise a large army, and himself direct operations. Such were the difficulties of traditional politics and antagonisms within different States which complicated a war left in the hands of the States' rulers.

The final straw was a speech delivered by the Pope on 29 April which shattered the neo-Guelphs' illusions and the understanding between the moderates, the liberals and the clergy. Just as Charles Albert had at last realised the necessity of encircling the Quadrilateral and surrounding Radetzky; just as there seemed to be a hope of the Two Sicilies sending an army complete with artillery, and even a chance of co-operation on the part of the Papal States, Charles Albert's Ambassador in Rome sent the Pope a memorandum requesting him to come to some decision.

The result was that the Pope announced that he was not in favour of war with Austria. He declared for peace and legitimacy, and thus re-asserted himself as the head of the Catholic Church. It was all up with the Pope as an Italian sovereign; the powerful alliance between the Church and the cause of nationalism fell apart to the indirect benefit of Austria, and the war hung fire. Piedmont, in the meantime, started to annex her neighbours. On 10 May she annexed Piacenza; on 29 May, Milan; on 4 July, Venice; whilst on 29 June her parliament confirmed these annexations. The annexation of Lombardy and Emilia was the signal for a renewal of the war, which was marked by several glorious victories, such as the Battle of Goïto, which was won by the Piedmontese forces, and the capture on 10 May of Peschiera, one of the fortified towns of the Quadrilateral.

The fall of Peschiera was Charles Albert's last victory, and the occasion for his soldiers to proclaim him King of Italy. The war reached a critical phase in the months of June and July. Radetzky took the offensive. Charles Albert may have hoped that the annexations would counteract the effect of the Pope's speech and of Ferdinand II's reversal of his domestic policy, by turning the war into a 'Piedmontese', 'Sardinian' or 'Savoyard' one, with a view to negotiating a peace with the assistance of France and England. Ferdinand II's *volte face*, as a result of the Pope's speech, had been as sudden as it was complete. Seizing as his excuse current disorders caused by *agents provocateurs*, he dismissed his parliament, ordered his army to sack the town of Naples, and recalled General Pépé, who had just reached Bologna. The latter returned home by way of the battlefield of Padua, but only a thousand of his seven thousand troops followed him. That is the reason why Charles Albert never had the vast army with which Pépé had dreamed of routing the Austrians.

Nevertheless, the victories at the end of May, and the annexations, seemed to augur well for Piedmont and, indirectly, for Italy. But the isolated position in which Charles Albert had put his kingdom by embarking on a war which was at once revolutionary and dynastic became apparent as soon as Radetzky began his counter-offensive. Vicenza, occupied by the Piedmontese in the spring, fell to the Austrians. It was bravely defended, but it had no fortifications and capitulated between 11 and 12 June. Treviso surrendered on the 13th, the very day chosen by Charles Albert to commemorate his attack on the citadel of Verona. The fortress of Palmanova fell on 24 June. And so from the Tyrol to the Trentino, from Cadore to Friuli, from Verona to Vicenza and from Treviso to the sea, the Austrians were masters of the situation, the lines of communication with the Empire were safe and Radetzky's reinforcements were pouring in.

Whilst Charles Albert was continuing his offensive by investing Mantua, Radetzky was preparing the attack which led to the defeat of the Italians at Custozza on 23 July, the prelude to the Italian retreat. A new offensive by Charles Albert failed owing to the disorganisation of the supporting services: the troops were ill-supplied and there was no liaison between the different units. The King withdrew from the line of the Mincio, hoping to take up fresh positions on the Adda, but his forces could not hold them. Radetzky harried them as they retreated, and terrorised the countryside, sacking and destroying the village of Sermida. The countryside was hostile to the retreating army, both because of the political hostility of the republicans in certain towns (Milan in particular) and because of fear of the Austrians, who also achieved some success by once more representing themselves as defenders of the faith, supporters of law and order, and protectors of private property. The *débâcle* was complete when no attempt was made to carry out the plan put forward by the Milanese command to defend their town in a pitched battle. The capitulation of Milan so enraged its citizens that they tried to assassinate Charles Albert, accusing him of treachery.

It was the moderates who accepted the terms under which the town was surrendered: those citizens who wanted to leave were given twelve hours in which to do so, and those who remained were assured that their lives and property would be safe. On 9 August General Salasco negotiated the armistice which ended this disastrous period.

It would take a whole book to discuss all the arguments concerning the conduct of the war, as well as the quality, numbers, value and use of the volunteers, and the various political promises made and broken, since there have been so many different views of the events and the protagonists. Garibaldi's part in the war may to some extent serve as an example. He left Montevideo on 15 April 1848, and landed at Nice on 23 June. He arrived in Lombardy to fight, and to the horror of the Mazzinians, put himself at Charles Albert's disposal as an already famous character, and as an expert in guerilla warfare. Charles Albert, however, mistrusted him and sent him to see his War Minister, who in turn passed him on to the provisional government in Milan. And so the King wasted an invaluable political and military supporter, for Garibaldi was unable to take part in the war until the situation was past hope. Incidentally, he was not the only exiled Italian to return to fight for his country and take part in the revolution. Mazzini and Garibaldi are the best-known and greatest names of the period, but there was a host of others, coming from America as well as Europe, and especially from France. There were *Carbonari* of 1821, 1830 and 1831, members of Young Italy, and generals of the Napoleonic era; there were also the professional revolutionaries, who erected the first experimental barricades; there were university professors, very youthful student volunteers and apprentices. All these held a variety of often conflicting political views, but they were fired with a tremendous enthusiasm, which flared up in that winter and spring, but as suddenly died down again and never revived.

The Italian ruling class, composed of both the most influential members of the aristocracy and the intellectuals of the middle class, could not co-operate with the Garibaldians. It could not share its responsibilities with them, considering them, sometimes with good reason, as a troop of young fanatics, madcaps, scoundrels, 'reds' and 'brigands'. They could not possibly be used or given responsibility, the ruling class thought, unless they were first tamed and disciplined. The democrats and Mazzinians were also suspect in the eyes of the ruling class which considered they had not the political maturity of the older politicians—and Cavour had not yet proved the opposite.

So at the beginning of the summer the old antagonisms revived. The war had lost its national character and the Piedmontese army was hampered by the indifference of the country people, whose livelihood had been upset by the war and who were half starving. These two facts worried the aristocracy and the middle class who were afraid of socialism and communism. Cavour was to show his political skill by exploiting this fear. The behaviour of the moderate middle class of the Papal States and the moderate and conservative aristocracy of Tuscany resulted in a political campaign, which took no account of recent changes, and differed only according to the social and economic structure of the country in which it was conducted. The Papal States were more backward than Emilia, which in turn was more backward than Tuscany. In some parts the political conflict was complicated by rebellions resulting from famine. The moderate middle class of the Two Sicilies could not create a widespread nationalist movement, owing to the presence of a reactionary Court, and they were also worried about the rural populace which expected the revolution to realise their hopes and result in their having a share in large estates. So there was no need for socialist or communist bogies to frighten the Southern middle class. They existed none the less, as did also proofs of political immaturity, which resulted in Ferdinand II's successful act of provocation on 15 May 1848. The circumstances permitted him to use the Austrian trick of setting the masses against the aristocracy, so that he could afterwards appear as the sole protector of property, law and order.

There were few liberally minded politicians opposed to Ferdinand II, and they had little strength both because of their isolation and because the reactionaries had their agents even in the liberal camp. Ferdinand's object was to alter this state of affairs so as to regain control of Sicily. There was no longer any friction there, where the revolution had first started, between the moderates and the democrats, as both parties were determined to safeguard the island's independence. Although there was discord between the aristocrats and the democrats which broke the 'Sacred Union' of the Sicilian parties, that was not much use to Ferdinand, even after the democrats, at the time of Cordova's Ministry (13 August 1848 to 23 January 1849) had been defeated when they attempted to obtain the sale of national and Church lands, which would have completely upset the still feudal system of land ownership in Sicily. The big landowners forced Cordova's Ministry to resign, and thereby quashed all hopes of agrarian reform.

Even in the Papal States, where in the course of the preceding decades a new middle class had fought for reform in the archaic political and judicial system (even if it were itself unable to have a hand in the reform), political difficulties were increased by the Pope's speech. The Pope, who was thenceforth under the thumb of Antonelli, the leader of the reactionary Cardinals, rejected the programme of the Minister Mamiani, whom his opponents accused of socialism for having mooted—among other basic reforms—the creation of a system of social insurance. Mamiani seems to have upset the clergy by attempting to withdraw the administration of charities from their control and to bring it up to date but the reason for his resignation was his opposition to the Pope's foreign policy as insufficiently 'Italian'. Shortly afterwards he was succeeded by Pellegrino Rossi, who fell foul of the reactionary clergy by subjecting them to an important tax, whereas previously they had been exempt from all taxation. Rossi was also attacked by the moderates on account of his foreign policy which was hostile to the unitary royalists. He favoured the establishment of a federal Italian League, headed by the Two Sicilies. The democrats, too, distrusted and disliked Rossi both because of his foreign policy and because of his narrow conservative constitutionalism. When he was eventually assassinated on 15 November, it was the extreme republicans and Sanfedists who claimed the responsibility. The Pope, who was forced by the threats of a crowd directed by the extremist republican club to form a new government, secretly escaped from Rome on 24 November.

On 29 December, the democratic and republican parties formed the majority in a ministry which they induced to pass a law instituting elections to the National Constituent Assembly of Italy. There was even talk of socialism and social changes in Rome and the Papal States. The popular *clubs* and secret societies produced several books on the subject. These were isolated phenomena, however, despite the fact that Count Rusconi, the Foreign Minister of the Roman Republic proclaimed on 9 February 1849, shortly afterwards published a history of the Republic in which he concluded that the future was in the hands of a securely founded socialism.

In the meantime, the Papal regular militia and the volunteers were beginning to return from Lombardy. They brought with them disillusionment, confusion and panic. The provinces, on the other hand, and the rural districts in particular, were still largely in the hands of the Sanfedists and the Gregorians. The Pope, who had taken up residence at Gaeta, was waiting for a chance to return to his dominions, with the help either of Ferdinand II, or the Austrian forces which still held the citadel of Ferrara. He counted on help from abroad to restore his temporal power which the Republic had proclaimed to have lapsed. He excommunicated the whole Constituent Assembly. The Grand Duke of Tuscany took Britain's advice and replaced his moderate government by a democratic one, with a sprinkling of Mazzinians. This new government under Montanelli and Guerrazzi, which lasted from August 1848 to February 1849, included in its programme the elaboration of an Italian Constitution and the continuation of the war against Austria. But it fell when the Grand Duke fled. Towards the end of the summer of 1848, the national revolution directed by the Piedmontese Government and the moderates, and supported by the work of such secret societies as the 'Lodge of Italian Unity' in the Kingdom of Naples, simply marked time as the result of Charles Albert's uncompromising diplomacy and the series of military defeats. Also the whole political situation in Europe had changed.

The change in attitude of the British and French governments is explained by the defeat of the democratic rising in June. Britain appeared as a mediator in Piedmont so as to secure the accession not only of Lombardy but Venetia, whereas French political manœuvres in Venice aimed at exactly the opposite result. In Naples, Lord Minto worked hard to prevent regular and volunteer forces being sent to Lombardy, and strongly supported Sicilian independence.

When, in June 1848, Britain's efforts at mediation failed, the Austrian government approached France, and in August, when Piedmont seemed likely to lose the war, she repulsed the suggestion that both France and Britain should act as mediators. The would-be mediators, meeting heavy opposition within their own governments, gave up the struggle. Further diplomatic moves, such as an attempt to get Piedmont to intervene in Tuscany, and Sardinia and Naples to attack the Roman Republic (which was finally shelved in favour of the French expedition against Rome, already agreed upon in December 1848) culminated in both France and Britain intervening in Sicily to force the islanders to submit to the House of Bourbon. Until then French policy in Italy had been to support first Ferdinand, then a republic. Britain, on the other hand, began by encouraging Sicily to keep her independence, and finished by supporting the idea of a Sicilian monarchy, with a member of the House of Savoy as king.

That was how things stood in 1849, but even towards the end of 1848 it was becoming clear that British diplomacy was quite disinterested. Attempts to collaborate with Switzerland had failed, owing to lack of co-ordination between the Lombards and Charles Albert, but after the defeat, the Swiss Confederation proved a friendly neutral by offering refuge to many volunteers and politicians. Italy also tried in vain to obtain from the new liberal and nationalist Germany the secession (on grounds of nationality) of the Trentino and the Tyrol from the German Confederation.

And the war, as a national one, with a united Italy under a constitutional monarchy, as its aim—whether a federation or a unitary state controlled by Piedmont—was virtually lost. Yet only a fraction of the people realised the fact.

Towards the end of the summer of 1848, reaction had been defeated in none of the Italian States. In fact, it was even rapidly regaining its footing, and openly triumphed in districts under Austrian rule and in the Kingdom of Naples, where Ferdinand II had counter-attacked by suspending the Constitution. He imprisoned patriots and left-wingers and welcomed to Gaeta first the Pope, and then Leopold II of Tuscany, thereby making the town a byword for reaction and even an important diplomatic centre, for the next year the first discussions on the 'Roman Question' were held there.

But the reactionaries still had to reckon with Sicily, with the democrats of Piedmont, with Gioberti, with the democrats of Tuscany, and with Montanelli and Guerrazzi. And they still had to reckon with the Roman Democrats, the Mazzinians and the popular movements such as the *clubs* which, under various names, were spread all over the country, in towns both large and small, from the Papal States to Piedmont.

The people in the towns of Piedmont, in Liguria, in both the State and town of Genoa, in Tuscany, and on the slopes of the Northern Apennines were waiting for the national war to begin again. They believed the defeat had been temporary and would soon be revenged, for to do otherwise would be to betray the cause of Italy. They were so sure that the tables would be turned, that political discussions were more often concerned with what would happen after they had won the war than with its conduct.

In 1849, after the defeat of Piedmont and the fall of Rome and Venice, people talked of 'hallucinations' and 'illusions', for that was the mood of the time. But the national revolution still lived on in peoples' hearts, and when the moderates had failed the democrats took over—as in Piedmont, Tuscany and the Papal States. Their rule was a superficial one, for the power really remained in the hands of the moderates and the monarchs (even when the latter fled their realms and waited to regain them with the help of bayonets). Yet it seemed as though the people, who had risen at Palermo and Milan, won their Constitutions, and then pushed forward the national war against Austria, were alone capable of continuing the war and assuring the Constitutional guarantees which Ferdinand II had so easily taken away from the middle-class moderates in his kingdom.

The left-wing parties (democrats, radicals and republicans, whether federalists or unitarians) had refused to accept the provisional end to the war which was brought about by Salasco's armistice. Garibaldi, for instance, disobeyed the orders to retreat and later to surrender, and continued fighting on the Verbano and at Luino. At the beginning of August he tried to contact other volunteer units in order to carry on the war.

It was at about the same time that the democrats in Bologna won a victory recalling Milan's 'Five Days'. The artisans and young radicals, with the help of the peasants of the neighbouring countryside, drove out the Austrian General Welden's troops, which, after leaving Ferrara to occupy the Papal States, had suddenly entered Bologna to restore order.

At Bologna, it was the lower classes who took the initiative in the rebellion, which was provoked by the behaviour of the Austrian soldiery. Their revolt, thanks to the solidarity of the political parties, grew into a general rebellion when they learnt that the Pope had protested against the Austrian occupation, and had appealed to the other States for support. But Bologna's gallant action had no effect on the peoples of the Legations or on Italian policy. There was no repetition of the episodes of Milan and Ferrara. No foreign armies came to their aid, and the Italian States took no further diplomatic action. The Pope refused to carry on the war begun so auspiciously by the people to defend their independence, and concluded a treaty which gave Austria Ferrara and the bridgeheads of Bondeno and Pontelagoscuro, returned to them the prisoners taken by the people of Bologna, and promised that there would be neither an attack on the Empire nor any further appeals to revolt. The result was that the extreme democrats continued their rebellion, and thus gave more weight to Mazzini's and Mamelli's theory that 'when the people rise, God puts Himself at their head'. This was the rebellion which caused the Pope to flee from Rome.

In Tuscany, following the insurrection which led to the formation of the Guerrazzi-Montanelli ministry, and for that matter at Rome, there was a renewal of the national war as a kind of 'Italian Crusade'. Many of the Italian volunteers had, in fact, fought in Lombardy wearing the Crusaders' cross. This crusade was preached by Father Barnabite Gavazzi, whose sermons dealt with patriotism and social matters as well as religion.

When Venice heard the news of Salasco's armistice and the recall of Piedmont's army and fleet, she proclaimed her independence under the dictatorship of Manin. He had been a lone fighter from the start, as France had given him little support against the intrigues of Palmerston, and he received small financial aid from the towns of Italy. In Piedmont, Gioberti assumed the leadership of the democrats, who in that province supported the Crown, but had no point of contact with the republicans of Genoa or the democrats in Florence.

The Minister Buffa openly encouraged the republicans, kept off the garrison and gave the command of the National Guard to General Avezzana (the future leader of the 1849 rebellion at Genoa), thereby providing a fresh cause for discontent. Gioberti, for his part, was trying to reopen discussions to form a federation and, with the help of the Piedmontese army, to restore both the Pope and the Grand Duke of Tuscany to their respective States. He recognised the government of Hungary, concluding an alliance with her with the object of renewing the war, and planned an alliance with the Slavs and the Rumanians, whom Italian diplomacy would have to reconcile with the Hungarians before launching an attack on the Empire. But he did not make much headway. The Ambassador he sent to Hungary was prevented by the turn of events from fulfilling his mission and took over the command of the Italian Legion which was fighting in Hungary against the combined forces of Austria and Russia.

Contact was naturally made with the suffering Poles, who won universal sympathy in 1848. Mickiewicz, Mazzini's friend, had come to Rome in March, and appealed to the Poles in Italy to ally themselves 'with all peoples fighting a national war against the common enemy'. A Polish Legion, presented with a flag by the people of Rome, went via Tuscany to fight in Lombardy, and was warmly welcomed by patriots and democrats. It fought bravely, and after Salasco's armistice, was incorporated in the Sardinian army. In 1849 it took part in the defence of the Roman Republic. Naturally, too, the volunteer committees, the political *clubs* and the patriotic societies renewed their efforts. But they failed to bring about a renewal of the war, both because of their inability to make a combined effort and because of the weary disillusionment of the returning volunteers and regular soldiers. The only hope of the revolutionaries, republicans and radical democrats lay in the resistance of Venice and Rome, the proclamation of constitutions at Rome and Florence and a projected alliance between Tuscany and Rome which was later intended to include Piedmont. Gioberti, who was planning to restore order in these regions, held the same hopes. In order to see the situation in perspective, we must remember that at the end of 1848, before the Roman Republic was proclaimed and when Tuscany's future was still uncertain, Venice and Sicily alone carried on the conflict. Piedmont was defeated. The revolution had still to be made in 1848 and the republicans based their hopes on future events. In this they resembled every other body of revolutionaries in Europe, who hoped that the Republicans in France would renew their efforts, and for a long time refused to believe that the European revolutionary movement was finished.

Like the European movement, however, of which it was only a part, the Italian revolutionary movement failed to achieve its aim.

Public opinion in Great Britain, influenced by Palmerston and Mazzini, was sympathetic towards the Italian movement, and public opinion on the Continent also gave it much encouragement, especially in the revolutionary and republican press of France and Paris, where Ledru-Rollin still kept in touch with Mazzini. When Mazzini first heard the news of the revolution in Italy, he had transformed the clandestine Young Italy association into an open, nationalist society. The many Italians abroad in

France and elsewhere attracted personal rather than political sympathies and friends. The attitudes of Germany and the countries comprising the Hapsburg Empire were most significant. I have already mentioned Poland and Hungary, and the liberals and radicals of Switzerland (the Swiss Guards of the Vatican and Naples were on the other side), but it is worth stressing the fact mentioned in the Paris paper *Le National* that when the war recommenced in 1849, the Austrians were ordered to fire on the Hungarians serving with them if they attempted to run.

Although the nationalist liberals of Germany ignored the appeal of a nationalist and liberal Italy, the democratic German revolutionaries were very much interested in events in Italy. The revolutionary Press was sympathetic though of course it had no effect on the hostility of the conservatives, who had their own romantic ideas about Italy. Marx's paper the *Neue Rheinische Zeitung*, closely followed the movement in Italy, which it considered as a national and democratic revolutionary movement of the people, who first allied themselves with the moderate middle class, then continued on their own. This paper published a remarkable letter addressed to *The Dawn*, Florence's democratic newspaper, in which it attacked the Turin newspaper *Concord* for criticising the programme of the Italian radicals and socialists. The *Neue Rheinische Zeitung* considered the Italian revolution as the vanguard of the European movement in the struggle against that citadel and centre of reaction, Austria. It pointed out that whilst Italian victories had helped the revolution, the set-back to the Italian revolution foreshadowed the defeat of the revolution in Europe. Italy did not, however, appear as the centre of the movement, which all the revolutionaries considered to be Paris. The *Neue Rheinische Zeitung* ended by attributing the Italian revolutionaries' set-back to the incompetence, ill-will and political and social treachery of the middle class in alliance with the reactionaries, and expressed its faith in the democratic movement. That was the tone of the left-wing press in Europe, which at the end of November summed up the situation as follows: 'The recapture of Milan by Radetzky constitutes the most important event in Europe since the Parisian reactionaries' victory in June. The Austrian Eagle, spreading its wings over Milan cathedral, symbolises not only the defeat of all Italy, but also the resurrection of Austria as the centre of counter-revolution in Europe.'

After the fall of Milan, Austria raised her head again. And it was from that moment that Jellacic took the offensive and the Slavs gave their full support to Austria. Finally, on 1 November, Radetzky saw the completion of the task he had begun at Custozza, for just as he entered Milan, so Windischgrätz and Jellacic took possession of Vienna.

Yet the revolutionaries still had some cause for optimism. Although in the North of Europe the people were once more at the very mercy of their rulers, and were hard put to keep what they had won, Italy suddenly rose again. Leghorn, spurred to a victorious revolution by the fall of Milan, had spread its spirit throughout Tuscany, which gave itself an avowedly republican Government, 'a government which replied to the fall of Vienna and Austria's resurrection by announcing a plan for a National Constituent Assembly in Italy'.

The enthusiasm caused by the formation of this democratic Ministry gained ground. Rome won her democratic victory by proclaiming the principle of a Constitution. 'Without a doubt', commented the *Neue Rheinische Zeitung*, 'Piedmont and Sicily will follow suit as they did last year. Then what will happen? Will this second revolution mark the beginning of a new assault by the democrats of Europe? Everything tends towards it.' But these, alas, were the illusions of observers far from the scene.

When in 1849 Italy made her second attempt to win her independence, the *Rheinische Zeitung* followed it with attention and enthusiasm. It stressed its military character, and when it failed, blamed the middle class and the Crown. It added: 'If Italy had been a republic, the fight would have been carried on to the end; the masses would have been called upon to rise as one man and there would have been an insurrection like that of France in 1793.' This newspaper's comment on Italy's future after the disaster of Novara, which ended the war, was a moving one: 'The Italians' defeat is a cruel blow. No other nation, except the Poles, has been so hatefully oppressed by so powerful a neighbour. No other people has so frequently or so courageously sought to throw off the Austrian yoke. Yet all its efforts and struggles resulted only in yet another defeat.' Some days later the *Neue Rheinische Zeitung* drew the following political conclusions from the collapse of the Italian revolution: 'The initial error', it wrote, 'was to allow the Piedmontese to put only the regular army into the field against Austria. A people determined to win its freedom cannot afford to rely on ordinary strategy. A mass rising, revolutionary and ubiquitous guerilla warfare, is the only way for a weak nation to defeat a strong one, for a small army to stand up against a better organised force. The Spaniards, between 1807 and 1812, proved the truth of this, and the Hungarians are proving it at the moment.' Like comments appeared in the democratic Press in France and in the Mazzinian Press in Italy. But it must be pointed out that newspapers in German seldom echoed such sentiments.

The command of the operations in Piedmont was given to a Pole who had been promoted to General, as the result of discussions condemning the incompetence of Charles Albert and his staff, and also because no general could be found in France to undertake the job.

Among the commanders was the notorious Ramorino, who after betraying Mazzini on the Savoy expedition, now betrayed Charles Albert. The Piedmontese war lasted three days and ended in the defeat of Novara. The initiative taken by Charles Albert and the 'democratic' government of Piedmont was later seen to have been hopeless, but it was none the less a heroic enterprise, for Piedmont stood alone and Austria was more powerful than ever. The Sardinian army, mobilised in haste, was ill-organised. It lacked tacticians and keen· officers willing to share their troops' life. The elections, the principal object of which was to recommence the war against Austria, had resulted in the formation of a Chamber which, in its answer to the King's opening speech, had asked him not to sign the armistice, as the people were prepared to accept any sacrifices for the sake of renewing the war. The conservative royalists considered that its renewal would distract the growing opposition in the country. There was already talk in Piedmont of socialism, equality, graded taxation, and so forth. This unsuccessful war was followed by the abdication of Charles Albert, who thereby proved his loyalty to the nation's cause which he had so often been accused of betraying. The result was that Piedmont was enabled to lay the emotional and moral foundations of her future policy, which aimed at restoring the prestige of the House of Savoy and creating an intellectual and political hegemony over the Italian nationalist movement, by welcoming emigrés fleeing from States dominated by Austria and Italian reactionaries. Towards the end of the 1848 movement there was widespread enthusiasm, particularly in Piedmont, for the Roman and Venetian Republics. We should not forget the gesture of Mazzini, who when a long time afterwards he was recalling the martyrs of Italian independence included the name of Charles Albert. Carducci went even further, saying: 'He, too, died for Italy.'

For the time being, apart from the personal sacrifice of Charles Albert, who was assailed by religious scruples after the Pope's change of attitude, contemporary historians attributed the failure of the 1848 movement in Italy to the following causes: the incompetence of foreign generals, chosen instead of experienced Italian commanders; intrigue; treachery on the field of battle; and the looting of the Piedmontese soldiery, which resulted in a feeling of gratitude towards the Austrian forces for maintaining order and safeguarding property.

The republican movement in Genoa marked the end of the second Piedmontese war for Italian independence. When the ancient republic learnt of the approach of the Austrian army, it recovered its former pride, nominated a Committee of Public Safety and a Triumvirate, and advised its parliament to leave Turin for the town of Genoa where it could carry on the war from the heart of the people. The Piedmontese government swiftly stopped the movement, but with clemency, on account of the hostility of the greater part of the population and thanks to the skill with which the general sent to deal with it handled the situation. As a result the French and Austrian governments' proposals to restore order came to nothing. On the contrary, Austria took harsh reprisals against Brescia, the only town in Lombardy to revolt when it heard that the war had begun again, since it expected resounding Piedmontese victories. Agents from Piedmont had come to an agreement with the towns of Lombardy whereby on a given signal they would rise unanimously. But the signal was never given. The Revolutionary Committee of Brescia, which was led by a priest, had received additional arms, supplies, and even men from the surrounding countryside, and by fighting house by house and street by street like the Jacobins, succeeded in driving the Austrians out of the town. Brescia held out for ten days, at the end of which the Austrian forces, with the connivance of their commander, General Haynau, retaliated by perpetrating the most hideous outrages. Haynau acquired such a reputation for cruelty that, when some years later he visited London, he was hissed by the crowd and driven to take refuge in a nearby house.

The disorganised and wavering democrats of Tuscany under Montanelli and Guerrazzi had been of little help to Piedmont. After the flight of Leopold, Tuscany had been left without a 'legitimate' government, and the power was in the hands of a feeble triumvirate composed of Guerazzi, Montanelli and Mazzini. Leopold II, hand in glove with Austria, acted in accordance with the instructions of Radetzky, but all the moderates of Tuscany from the unitary monarchist Salvagnoli to Ricasoli—not to speak of Lambruschini—looked upon the government first of the democrats, then of the triumvirate, as a collection of 'reds', demagogues and 'brigands'. These same moderates, instead of collaborating with the democrats, as the democrats had wholeheartedly collaborated with moderate governments, put every kind of obstacle in their way. Guerazzi, thinking to serve the interests of the country as well as the conservatives, pursued a policy on a municipal basis and gave no support to Piedmont, even though he too had proclaimed the war a national one. Not only did he refuse to unite Tuscany with the Roman Republic, but he would not even act in conjunction with it. The Tuscan Constituent Assembly met on 25 March, just when news arrived of the defeat of Novara. It made Guerrazzi dictator, and there was no more talk of a Constituent Assembly for Italy. Guerrazzi attempted to reconcile all parties, even the Grand Duke's supporters, who hoped to avoid Austrian occupation, but he had little success. The moderates preferred to plot (with the help of Florence) a peasant rising against Guerrazzi and his Livornians which would restore power to the landed nobility.

Nevertheless, the moderates gained nothing from this *coup d'état* against the democrats, because first on 28 July 1849, Austrian troops occupied the country; and secondly, when the Grand Duke did at last return, he restored his despotic rule.

The Roman Republic fell early in July 1849 after heroic resistance with the aid of volunteers from every corner of Italy. The men of the Roman Republic and the Constituent Assembly had been of little help in Piedmont's renewal of the war, in spite of their good intentions. On the other hand, the Constitution of the Roman Republic was a major event of the 1848 movement, both as a political and social transformation and as a democratic victory for Italy and Europe. In fact, as well as completing the good work of the Constituent Assembly, the government of the Roman Republic under Mazzini accomplished a real social revolution—in the democratic (not socialist) sense of the word—which followed upon the changes which had already taken place in society in Central Italy and made use of the new forces which had emerged, as Demarco has shown, in the country as well as the towns.

Mazzini's social revolution, by bringing in urgently required legislation as well as universal suffrage, gave the lower classes the chance to take part in their country's affairs. Italian democracy, whether or not Mazzini was its creative genius, proved itself highly skilled, as many foreign politicians and historians noted, in the art of government, which had previously been the prerogative of absolute monarchs or a hereditary or 'bourgeois' ruling class. But at the very moment when legislative activity was flowering in the elaboration of a Constitution, the Republic's days were numbered. It was defended, however, by young men from every part of Italy, and of every political creed from extreme Mazzinian democrats such as Pisacane to royalists like Manara.

This defence revealed a national, unitary, and clearly Mazzinian character. The Roman Republic fell after resisting to the very end an enemy superior in both arms and numbers. The enemy was the French army, which Louis Napoleon and the French conservatives had put at the service of the European reactionaries to defend French interests against Austrian interests in Italy. I must also mention the intervention of Naples, which was laughable, and that of Spain and Austria. The fall of Rome had been preceded by the failure, on 13 June, of the last attempt by the French radical democrats under Ledru-Rollin to rise in protest against the Roman expedition.

The Roman Republic was looked upon as the last refuge of the European revolution and the last rampart of the spirit of 1848. It was its glory that there were Poles; the other 'martyrs of reaction', fighting side by side with Italians in its defence. For the Italians, the heroic and desperate struggle proved the reality of Italy's existence as a nation. Sicily, which had proclaimed its independence and sought a new king from the House of Savoy, had been forced to give up the contest after Ferdinand II's flag was once again hoisted over Palermo on 15 May 1849. Rome's last defender, Garibaldi, once again tried to effect a rising by the use of guerilla tactics to aid Venice, the only republic still putting up resistance. He and his three thousand men left Rome and succeeded in avoiding encirclement by the Neapolitans, the Spanish, the Austrians and the French. But his small force rapidly disintegrated, and when he finally reached Venice, after crossing the Apennines, he was forced to dismiss the two hundred odd men who had stayed with him.

The Austrian blockade prevented any attempt to reach Venice by sea, so Garibaldi, stricken by the death of his wife, Anita, who had accompanied him, and by the shooting of his remaining troops, had to go back across the Apennines and take refuge in Tuscany. The last Italian town to capitulate was Venice, besieged on land and sea by the Austrians. The Venetian Council had declared: 'In the name of God and the People, Venice will resist at all costs to the end.' The city resisted even more fiercely than Rome, and was also aided by Italians from every province. Its fight was of symbolic importance for the independence and unity of Italy, and had something Mazzinian and democratic about it. It was the last spark of the European revolution, for by the time Venice, after suffering simultaneously from starvation, cholera and bombardment, finally had to lay down her arms, Hungary had already had to give up the struggle.

That was the end of the Italian movement of 1848. Italy was once again at the mercy of the Great Powers.

SPAIN IN 1848

J. QUERO MOLARES

The future explains the past
Balmes: 'Verdict on the Revolution of 1848'

Eighteen forty-eight is not an historical date in Spain. The outbreak of the Revolution in France, which spread within a few hours to her neighbours to the east and to the north, produced only faint echoes beyond the Pyrenees and they were soon lost in the turmoil of purely domestic politics.

Yet throughout history the fortunes of France and Spain have been so closely linked that historians have found it impossible to discuss one country without mentioning the other. Long before the middle of the nineteenth century, Du Guesclin had invaded Spanish territory to settle the succession to the throne of Castille, as a century before, Alfonso IX's daughter Blanche fought for the right of her son Saint Louis to the throne of France. Ever since the first offshoots of the Greek colony at Marseilles settled on the East coast of the Iberian peninsula, the paths of France and Spain have crossed time and again. At the beginning of the present era European history centred round a duel between the Spanish Bourbons of Austria and the Bourbons of France.

It was in 1700 that the first Bourbon, Philip V, came to the throne of Spain, and it was on the very eve of 1848 that the House of Orléans and the House of Bourbon strengthened their ties by the marriage of the Infanta Maria Luisa Fernanda to the Duc de Montpensier, which took place on 11 October 1846 at the church of Atocha in Madrid, at the same time as Isabella II, *la reina castiza*, as Valle Inclan called her, was married to the Infante Francisco de Asis. 'The Affair of the Spanish Marriages', as the historians term it, infuriated the British government which lodged an official protest. Another critic was the Infante Don Enrique, who held liberal views.

The dispute over the rightful sovereign might have been finally settled at this point, had Queen Isabella II married the Count of Montemolin, whom his supporters called Charles VI, and in whose favour the pretender Don Carlos had relinquished his claim to the throne on 18 May 1845. The repudiation of this solution on principle was a tragedy for Spain, for it

143

contained the germ of civil war which was later to poison Spanish politics.

One of the politicians connected with this affair was General Narvaez, 'the very incarnation of the militaristic spirit of nineteenth century Spain', as one Spanish historian has called him. But we must leave till later discussion of the character of this man who was to crush the Spanish Revolution of 1848; first let us look at the political scene in Spain two months after M. de Morny wrote the following passage in the weighty *Revue des Deux Mondes:*

'I repeat that I do not believe a revolution possible, unless our government makes inconceivable blunders. But at least let us have no illusions, and let the rash who feed the flames of the people's anger and the ambitious who would turn it to their profit, heed my warning: a revolution today would lead not to political reform but to communism.' De Morny proved a sorry prophet. There was a revolution and an essentially political one, for it marked the rise of liberalism. But perhaps M. de Morny's predictions concerned the distant future.

In February 1848 the Spanish Government was led by General Narvaez, Duke of Valencia, who had formed it on 4 October of the previous year, and who remained in power until December 1850.

His cabinet consisted of the following:

Luis José Sartorius—Minister of the Interior; Lorenzo Arrazola—Minister of Justice; Francisco de P. Orlando—Minister of Finance (succeeded in turn by Beltran de Lis, the Count of Romera, Alejandro Mon, Bravo Murillo and Seijas); the Duke of Sotomayor—Foreign Secretary (succeeded, on his appointment as Ambassador in Paris, by Pedro Pidal); Beltran de Lis—Minister of Marine; Bravo Murillo—Minister of Public Works; General Figueras—Minister of War (portfolio originally held by Narvaez himself); Córdova and Ros de Olano—members of the former cabinet.

Narvaez tried to set himself up as a peace-maker and a liberal to the annoyance of the ultra-conservatives such as Pidal, their spokesman, and Rios Rosas, who demanded a repressive policy. But Narvaez's ideas were fashionable at the time, now that the Pope, Pius IX, was liberally inclined, as were the two foremost Spanish Catholic writers, Jaime Balmes and Donoso Cortés. Narvaez had given certain proofs of his conciliatory attitude, of which the most important was restoration of his former honours to General Espartero, whom he made a senator and permitted to return to Spain. Equally significant was Narvaez's approval of the Duke of Rivas' conduct when, as Spanish Ambassador in Naples, he made a speech to the Neapolitan revolutionaries congratulating them on their victory over their King, Ferdinand II, whom they had forced to grant the country a liberal constitution. But if Narvaez did not actually want to be a dictator, the idea did not fill him with horror, for he liked to 'seize the cudgel and lay about him' (*empuñar el garrote y pegar fuerte*). The 1848 Revolution was to give him scope for his personal predilections.

As soon as the February Revolution broke out in France, the minority party of progressives in the Cortes split into two groups. The larger group consisted of all the right-wing deputies, such as Mendizabal, Madoz, Infante, Cortina, Sancho and others, who were afraid of revolution in Spain. Opposed to them were the left-wingers, such as Sagasti, Orense, Rivero, Puig, Lopez Grada, Jordán and Ordax Avecilla. From this split the Radical or Democratic Party later emerged, whereas the Progesssive Party was descended from the old 'idealistic' constitutionalists who had opposed the *Doceañistas*. The *Doceañistas* were the ancestors of the Moderate Party, to which Narvaez belonged. Both the moderates and the progressives supported the principle of constitutional monarchy. The most famous progressive was General Espartero, Duke of Vittoria, who was the Spanish regent. When he retired from public life in 1856, the Progressive Party disappeared, and the Liberal Union under General O'Donnell appeared on the political scene.

The most active revolutionary group was composed of a number of army men under the leadership of Colonel Joaquín de la Gandara, who, according to his contemporaries, was an extremely honest and intelligent man, but somewhat vague in his political ideas. His party, which included Joaquín Clavijo and Ramón Lopez Vazquez (who were later shot at Barcelona), Manuel Buceta, Ricardo Muñiz, Francisco Serrano Bedoya and Victoriano Ametller, operated both inside and outside Spain. Colonel de la Gandara sent a deputation to Paris which got in touch (through a former emigré named Bernardo Iglesias) with Armand Marrast, Mayor of Paris and President of the Constituent Assembly, who in 1837 had been condemned to death in Spain for writing a satirical song against the Regent. But a far more serious threat to the Spanish Government was the effect of de la Gandara's propaganda on the Madrid garrison, where he had succeeded in forming an organisation of six sections, each consisting of over a hundred army officers.

General Narvaez tried to check this underground revolutionary movement, and he drew Mendizabel's and Sagasta's attention to what he had learnt of the conspirators' plans. As a proof of good will, Narvaez offered to advise the Queen to form a new, Progressive government, and at the same time promised not to suspend constitutional guarantees, and to modify the projected law on printing. These offers were useless, for Colonel de la Gandara had already given Muniz the task of making ammunition for his revolutionary groups. Four arsenals were set up in

Madrid, and so as not to attract attention, the revolutionaries got their wives to purchase the gunpowder in small quantities. There is one story of those days which is worth recalling not for its political significance but as a nice example of the quickness of Spanish wit. One of de la Gandara's agents was carrying an enormous trunk full of ammunition, when, as it was a public holiday, he was stopped by a suspicious policeman. Asked about it, he replied: 'It belongs to a general's A.D.C., who is about to leave by coach.' He was immediately released.

While de la Gandara's friends were planning their revolt, one of the progressives, José María Orense, approached him with the suggestion that they should work together. Orense, Marquis of Albaida, was a seasoned revolutionary and his particular programme was the corner-stone of the progressives' and later of the republicans' platform. He had explained it to the Cortes in 1844 when he stated that 'the foundations of a proper constitution are: sanctity of the home, respect for all property, the unrestricted right to hold meetings, complete freedom for the newspapers (whose editors should be responsible to no one and pay no caution money) and universal suffrage.' In 1848, the left-wing progressives completed this programme with freedom to choose one's employment, the right of petition, free primary schooling, equal political rights, openings for all in every profession and the institution of juries. Orense was one of the first Spanish republicans, and his name should be remembered along with those of Pi i Margall, Figueras and Castelar. As President of the Cortes, however, after the proclamation of the Republic in 1873, he was converted to cantonalism, a caricature of federalism which proved the death of the young republic.

Orense's friends decided to start the revolt on 26 March, in spite of opposition from de la Gandara, who asked for at least an extra week to complete the arming of the revolutionaries. Next, the conspirators organised their forces, and appointed ringleaders for the various quarters of Madrid. It would be impossible to explain Orense's haste, had there not taken place in the meantime an event of major importance. England had taken the side of the progressives against Narvaez's Government. In fact Lord Palmerston, the British Foreign Secretary, had written a letter on 16 March, which arrived in Madrid on the 21st, in which he suggested that it would be wise for the Queen of Spain 'in the present critical state of affairs to strengthen the executive Government by enlarging the basis upon which the Administration is founded, and by calling to her councils some of those men who possess the confidence of the Liberal Party.'

In his letter to Mr Bulwer, Queen Victoria's fiery and violent Minister, he made the following comments:

SPAIN

The recent fall of the King of the French, and of his whole family, and the expulsion of his ministers, ought to teach the Spanish Court and Government how great is the danger of an attempt to govern a country in a manner at variance with the feelings and opinions of the nation, and the catastrophe which has happened in France must serve to show that even a large and well-disciplined army becomes an ineffectual defence for the Crown, when the course pursued by the Crown is at variance with the general sentiments of the country.

This letter marks the beginning of a tension which ended in Spain breaking off diplomatic relations with Great Britain. She took umbrage at what she considered to be unwarranted interference although Great Britain merely considered it to be friendly advice.

One can easily understand the influence such an attitude would have on men already disposed to overthrow their government, particularly when the British Ambassador openly communicated with them. That at any rate is what is implied in a report submitted by the Chief of Police in Madrid to the Government. Anyway, it was evident that ever since the beginning of the nineteenth century, certain other nations had their eyes on Spain. At the Court of Isabella II, both France and England fought to establish their hegemony, and supported their pet political parties. Thus the moderates came under French, and the progressives under British influence. Great Britain had not forgotten the dangerous strengthening of family ties by the Infanta Maria Luisa Fernanda's marriage to the Duc de Montpensier, nor the ex-regent Christina's plot to marry the Queen of Spain to the Duc d'Aumale. Although the situation had changed and although for the time being the fact that Marianne had once again donned the Phrygian cap of liberty led to a decline in French influence in Spain, England nevertheless thought it worth while to support the Spanish liberals and her attitude encouraged them to overthrow Narvaez's government by force.

We are a long way from the policy of non-intervention in Spain which England was to pursue a century later at France's instigation. But we must not forget that in 1904 the ancient rivalry between France and Great Britain was superseded by the *Entente Cordiale* which enabled the democratic nations to defeat the pan-Germanism of the Hohenzollerns and the imperialism of the Nazis. It was at that later period that Lord Grey declared that the real aim of British foreign policy was to maintain peace throughout the world, and said that in consequence non-intervention was the great guiding principle which the Government of which he was a member wished to adopt. That did not prevent Palmerston interpreting non-intervention in a most peculiar fashion, which was doubtless the result of that pragmatical quality which is the strength if not the virtue of British foreign policy.

The first rising of the Revolution took place in Madrid on 26 March, but it did not go according to plan. What happened was that at zero hour, when everyone was ready, the man whose task it was to give the signal for the revolt to start, sent a message to the revolutionary headquarters in the *Café de San Sebastián* saying that as most of the men under his command had gone to their lunch, he would have to wait a bit. On receiving this message, the rest of the revolutionaries stood down. A few hours later occurred an incident which wrecked the revolt. In the *Café Español*, a revolutionary named Narciso de la Escosura started calling the leaders traitors and cowards. Another revolutionary, whose job was to guard the arms belonging to de la Gandara's group, overheard him and put the arms in his charge at de la Escosura's disposal. So six hundred men, without their appointed leaders, went out to face the police, the army and the gendarmerie. In spite of their barricades, which, according to the Marquis of Miraflores, were erected for the first time, they were completely overwhelmed by the Government forces.

Foreseeing what might happen, Narvaez's Government had on 28 February induced the Cortes (by a majority of 148 votes to 45 in the Chamber and 88 votes to 13 in the Senate) to suspend the laws for the protection of individuals, and had obtained authority to levy taxes to the extent of fifty million pesetas to meet any extraordinary expenses necessitated by circumstances. Further, on 22 March, he suspended the sittings of the Cortes since they provided a platform for progressive propaganda. The dictatorship lasted for nine months, for the Cortes did not meet again until 15 December. It was then that Nicolas María Rivero formed a new political party, the Democrats.

These preventive measures were at first accompanied by a leniency that was shown in the Royal Decree of 31 March, which greatly reduced the penalties awarded by the War Council set up to suppress the rising. This leniency was a rare phenomenon in Spain, where the rebel often paid for his independence with his life.

In spite of this victory, the air was not cleared. On the contrary there were visible signs of political unrest, and it was at this time, on 9 April, that the British Ambassador sent a copy of Lord Palmerston's letter to the Spanish Foreign Secretary. Its contents were already known to the public, as it had been published some days previously in the opposition newspaper, *El Clamor Público*. Palmerston's letter was accompanied by another from Bulwer, in which he expressed a strong wish that the Government of Her Catholic Majesty would consider returning without delay to the ordinary forms of Government established in Spain, calling a session of the Cortes, and explaining away the impressions given both in the kingdom and abroad by the arrest of certain men and the apparent intention of deporting them. There were among them some of the most distinguished members of the Cortes, and they had neither been given trial nor accused of any offence. Bulwer went on to remind the Duke of Sotomayor that Queen Isabella's cause had been distinguished from that of her royal adversary primarily by the promise of constitutional liberty inscribed on Her Catholic Majesty's banners. He concluded by remarking that this promise had been an important factor in determining Great Britain's sympathy with and support of Her Catholic Majesty. He supposed, therefore, that the Duke would not be surprised by the opinions expressed in his letter, which were to the effect that the European situation, and public opinion everywhere, made it clear that the best guarantees for the safety of a throne were to be found in the liberty and justice dispensed under its authority.

The Duke of Sotomayor was surprised, and most unpleasantly so, judging from his reply. In fact, the Spanish Foreign Secretary began by expressing his astonishment that the opposition paper, *El Clamor Público*, should have published 'in advance the substance' of the British Foreign Secretary's note. He went on to say:

> On 16 March, when Lord Palmerston sent you this note, the Spanish Cortes were still meeting, the press was completely free and Her Majesty's Government had adopted a line of conduct that even her enemies and opponents were forced to admit was conciliatory in the extreme. I am at a loss to understand what motive could have led Her Britannic Majesty's Foreign Secretary to take it upon himself to interpret the feelings and opinions of this country, and, furthermore, to interpret them in so improper a fashion, seeing that he is treating with the Government of a free country. From what motive did he recommend that Government to act in a legal and constitutional fashion as though that were not already the case in Spain, and permit himself to advise her to modify the basic principles of her administration and admit men of this or that persuasion to the Crown Council?

After pointing out that General Narvaez's Government still enjoyed the confidence of the Queen and the Cortes, the Duke of Sotomayor answered Lord Palmerston's 'extraordinary claim' to interfere in the domestic affairs of Spain, by asking:

> What would Lord Palmerston and what would Your Excellency say if the Spanish Government were to pronounce judgement on the administrative actions of the British Cabinet and recommend them

to modify their system of government, or advise them to adopt more efficacious and more liberal measures to ameliorate the appalling conditions in Ireland? What would he say if Her Catholic Majesty's representative in London were to criticise (in Your Excellency's terms) the exceptional repressive measures the British Government is preparing to take against an aggressor within her own borders? What would he say if the Spanish Government demanded, in the name of humanity, more respect and justice towards the hapless peoples of Asia? And finally what would he say if reminded that recent events on the Continent served as a salutary lesson for every government, not excluding Great Britain, and that consequently the reins of government should be handed over to the illustrious Peel, that able statesman who, after winning the general favour of his countrymen, has earned the sympathy and esteem of every government in Europe? Lord Palmerston would say what the Spanish Government has the right to say now: it denies the right of any foreign Power to make such observations, which it rejects as an insult to the dignity of a free and independent nation. Actuated by feelings natural to the Spanish nobility and to any self-respecting government, Her Catholic Majesty's Cabinet cannot but make the strongest possible protest at the content of Lord Palmerston's and Your Excellency's communications; and whereas it would be undignified to retain them, returns them herewith. At the same time it declares that should Your Excellency's official communications again go beyond the bounds of international law, and intentionally meddle in the private affairs of the Spanish Government, I should find myself in the unpleasant position of having to return such communications unanswered.

After such an exchange Bulwer's position at the Court of Madrid clearly became extremely delicate. The explanations with which he furnished the Spanish Government were insufficient to relax the tension created, as is evident from the letter from the Duke of Sotomayor to the British Ambassador, dated 15 April 1848.

Madrid was still restless in spite of the Government's victory. On 28 March the military had to be called out to deal with the students of Barcelona University, but as General Pavia wrote in his Memoirs: 'the trouble died down at once, without any unpleasant incidents or any need for punishment, at a mere show of force, which was necessary to frighten these young men, who were certainly more thoughtless than malicious.' Catalonia remained calm, but there was a certain amount of anarchist propaganda in Barcelona and a number of other important towns, such as Reus, Figueras, Tarrasa and Tarragona. The fact that danger did exist is proved by the fact that Ferdinand de Lesseps, the French Consul-General at Barcelona, acquainted the military authorities with his intention of requesting his government to send a warship to protect French interests in the event of a revolt. De Lesseps was dissuaded from making this request by General Pavia's attitude of serene confidence.

There were also a few incidents at Valencia, but this revolutionary activity was less important than that which was helped financially by a former minister and financier named José Salamanca, who was friendly with Bulwer. Señor Salamanca's attitude is explained by his animosity towards General Narvaez, who at a meeting of the Congress in November 1847, had permitted (with evident relish) an attack by Señores Pidal and Seijas Lozano on this banker with political ambitions. The enmity between Salamanca and Narvaez shifted from the rostrum to 'the boards', when the former took up a French dancer called La Guy and the latter an Italian known as La Fuoco. Both danced every night at the *Circo de Pablo* to the applause of their respective political supporters. It is even said that Salamanca was shamed by the unfounded rumour that La Guy had been to bed with General Narvaez.

The result of this agitation was the mutiny on 7 May of the 'Spanish' Regiment under the orders of Buceta who, together with Velo and Muñiz, had made his plans with Salamanca, and had induced a number of sergeants to open the barrack gates. On the death of General Fulgioso, the government appointed General Juan de la Pezuela as the Madrid Area Commander, and he ordered the harshest reprisals. That very night he had shot one sergeant, two corporals, five other ranks and five civilians, after Lersundi's troops had surrounded the mutineers. For the first time, shouts of *Viva la República!* were heard in Madrid.

The collapse of all these risings should have warned Narvaez's opponents that resistance was useless. To make assurance doubly sure, the head of the Government published a decree on the subject of suspects, and over two thousand were deported to the Canaries and Fernando Po. Nevertheless a fresh revolt broke out at Seville on 13 May. The ringleader was an army officer named José Portal, who used the Second (Guadaljara) Battalion of which he was second-in-command. Portal was also a friend of Bulwer's, and a member of the Progressive Party, whose interests he served. There was later an attempt to give this rising a republican bias, but if we are to believe the Spanish historian Antonio Pirala (who had the story from Portal himself), there was never any talk of a republic among the planners of the rebellion.

Portal's troops, reduced to one battalion of infantry and one squadron of cavalry, were chased from Seville right into Portugal, where on 12 May they laid down their arms. So the Government emerged victorious from each battle. It strengthened its position by arresting Manuel Somoza y Gambero and his friends, who had hatched a conspiracy in Galicia, and by sending General Zavala and General Ros de Olano to stamp out a revolution planned by Ceuta.

It was at this point that Narvaez's Government took a grave decision, which attracted considerable attention abroad. On 17 May the Duke of Sotomayor sent the following letter to Bulwer:

> I am obliged by considerations of the utmost importance to acquaint you with a decision Her Majesty's Government has regretfully been compelled to take in the interests of honesty.
>
> You are aware from the newspapers and other sources of the weight of public opinion against you in Spain as the result of recent events. The Government's efforts have been powerless to restrain the outbursts of indignation on the part of every honest citizen of Madrid, and of every soldier of the garrison, and we entertain grave fears for the safety of your person, which—as the representative of the British Government—we should be unable to protect in the unhappy event of a repetition of such scenes as have twice already afflicted the Capital.
>
> Your conduct, doubtless dictated by your instructions, has been censured by public opinion and by press and Parliament in England. Her Catholic Majesty's Government cannot presume to defend it when it has already been condemned within Her Britannic Majesty's realms.
>
> This being the case, your presence in Madrid is considered here, though naturally without foundation, as a proof of our weakness, and if this belief were to gain ground, it would result in a conflict which it is our duty to prevent at all costs.
>
> These, therefore, are the motives, the honesty of which must be plain to the British Government and people, which have compelled the Government of Her Majesty Queen Isabella to put an end to so disagreeable a situation by sending you your passports and inviting you to leave the capital within twenty-four hours, or, if possible, even earlier, as your departure is a matter of urgency and we should regret any delay in your preparations.
>
> We are discharging a painful duty. In sending you so disagreeable a communication, I am commanded to proclaim in all sincerity that it is by no means the intention of Her Majesty's Government to cast a slur on the dignity of the British Government or the British people. I am to inform you, on the contrary, that not only will your departure, at any rate from our point of view, create no rift between two

nations which have so long been united by ties of friendship which are of the highest value in the eyes of the Spanish Government, but it can be the only means of strengthening those ties, in view of the turn of events in Europe.

The Spanish Government flatters itself that Her Britannic Majesty's Government will fully appreciate the honesty of its intentions, particularly when the Court of St James has received a satisfactory explanation.

I have, therefore, the honour of sending passports herewith for you and your staff, together with the necessary permits to enable post horses to be put at your disposal on your journey.

I have thought it worth while reproducing this letter in its entirety as a rarity in the history of diplomacy. Bulwer's expulsion created a considerable stir at the time, for ever since Lord Aberdeen had sent him to Madrid towards the end of 1843, he had enjoyed high prestige, as was testified by his appointment as arbiter between Spain and Morocco on the occasion of the peace treaty in 1844. The affair was thoroughly thrashed out in the House of Commons. The debate opened with a long speech by Mr Bankes in support of the Spanish Government's action. Mr Sheil then put forward arguments on behalf of the Foreign Secretary's attitude. Other M.P.s to take part in this discussion were Viscount Mahon, Sir R. H. Inglis, Mr Hume, Mr Urquhart, and even Lord John Russell, Viscount Palmerston, Mr Disraeli and Sir Robert Peel. Whilst there was general approval of Bulwer's conduct, Lord Palmerston was the object of several attacks, and defended himself by emphasising that he never intended the whole contents of his letter of 16 March to be communicated to the Spanish Government. Disraeli's attitude is worth noting. While strongly criticising Spain's action, he attacked liberalism as the cause of all the trouble. The Quadruple Alliance he described as a triumph of liberalism, which he looked on as fatal to liberty, whether in home or foreign affairs, and which he said had characterised British foreign policy for too long. His objection to it was that it substituted philosophical notions for political principles in its approach to the most important practical affairs. This meant that when a representative was sent to Madrid, for example, he would not try to govern his conduct according to the best interests of Great Britain's relations with Spain, but would attempt to introduce certain philosophical principles into a particular political party, probably the weakest in the country, and that these principles would establish a bond with one small political faction which would, perhaps, never have existed without such encouragement.

Shortly after Bulwer's departure from Madrid, the British Government sent Señor Isturiz, the Spanish Ambassador in London, his passports, and diplomatic relations were broken off. Lord Palmerston had refused to receive the Count of Mirasol, whom the Spanish Government had despatched with all haste to the Court of St James to explain the situation. The Foreign Secretary justified his refusal, which had been censured by some members of Parliament, on the grounds that the Count of Mirasol was not a diplomat and his explanations had no official weight. As a personal envoy, it was unwise to receive him, as between 1832 and 1847 Spain had had thirty different Presidents of the Council and thirty-eight different Foreign Secretaries. What Lord Palmerston could not explain so easily was the letter he wrote to Bulwer on 20 April in which he asserted that Her Majesty's Government thoroughly approved the representations which Bulwer had just concluded with his communication of the 7th, as well as of 12 April.

The result of this affair, as I have already noted, was the breaking off of diplomatic relations between Spain and Great Britain. It must be admitted that General Narvaez had acted in a somewhat off-hand manner, but then he was no respecter of conventions, and he had the support of Spanish public opinion. It was also at this time that, after he had put down the rising in Madrid on 7 May, he looked round for Salamanca. Discovering that he had recently taken sanctuary in the Belgian Legation, he ordered the Chief Commissioner of Police, the Marquis of Villahermosa, to arrest him there in spite of the fact that he was on ex-territorial ground. He broke the law in vain, for the whole time the police were searching the legation, Salamanca lay hidden inside a sofa in the hall, on which the Chief Commissioner himself (whether by accident or design) sat waiting to hear the result of the search.

On the other hand we must not forget that Lord Palmerston was an autocrat and a fire-eater. In the course of the debate in the House of Commons on the expulsion of the British Ambassador in Madrid, Mr Urquhart did not mince his words when he declared, in Palmerston's presence, that his continuance in office was a threat to peace in Europe, and made agreement between Great Britain and the foreign powers impossible. His opinion was shared in France. 'It is exactly the opposite in Spain and Greece,' wrote Alexandre Thomas in the *Revue des Deux Mondes*. 'Mr Bulwer and Sir Edward Lyons seem to look upon it as their task to emulate Lord Palmerston as a warmonger. They are fundamentally on the side of every kind of conspirator or rebel. Sir Edward has not yet been caught in the act like Mr Bulwer . . .' Lord Palmerston was to bear a grudge against Spain for a long time to come, and the British press of the time took advantage of it to wage a ceaseless war against Narvaez's government.

SPAIN

In this breaking off of diplomatic relations between Spain and Great Britain, which lasted until the middle of 1850, there were signs of an independent spirit in the Spanish Government's policy, which on the whole satisfied the patriotic sentiments of the country. General Narvaez's position abroad did not suffer from it, as it was strengthened externally by the recognition of Queen Isabella II by the governments of Austria, Prussia, Sardinia and Tuscany; and internally by a petition over sixty thousand Spanish nobles addressed to Her Majesty, putting their lives and fortunes at her disposal. The Papal Nuncio was solemnly received by the Queen of Spain on 23 July. This change in the Vatican's attitude was a great triumph for the Government.

But we must not forget when we review the events in Spain which immediately followed 24 February 1848, that there was still one problem to solve: the curse of Spanish politics, civil war. It is true that General Narvaez had announced to the Cortes that the *partidas* operating in Catalonia had been wiped out. General Pavia, who was in command of the government forces, had in fact begun a report to the War Minister, dated 6 January 1848, with the following words: 'The factions which, for over a year, have flown the standard of revolt in the mountains of Catalonia, and who a few months ago totalled over two thousand men, have ceased to exist.' But the wish was father to the thought, as the report itself showed by mentioning that 'certain rebel leaders (who on being deserted by their followers, have not been taken prisoner, and have neither escaped into France nor given themselves up) have hidden in the densest parts of the forests. But the arm of the law will follow.' From a private letter from Narvaez to Pavia, dated 9 December 1847, which the latter published in his Memoirs of the Catalan War, we know that despite Pavia's protestations to the contrary, the report to the Cortes was simply the result of a desire to please the head of the government.

Political unrest was favourable to the outbreak of a fresh civil war in Catalonia. One of the first proclamations was written by Rafael Sala, of whom Planadamont has told us, and another appeared from the pen of José Masgoret. They were dated 21 March, and 1 April 1848 respectively, and proclaimed Carlos Luis de Borbón as King under the title of Charles VI. Even more remarkable was Francisco Ballera's manifesto of 2 April, in which he said: 'The cry of the citizen Enrique María de Borbón will be echoed in every province in Spain. All free men will rally to the flag of the Republic to fight for freedom, and once and for all smash all the plans of the tyrants who hold us in bondage.' This manifesto, which contained certain allusions to its author's merits, ended with the triple apostrophe: 'Eternal glory to the Free! Long live the Republic! Long live Liberty, Equality and Fraternity!' This political pact between those who styled

155

themselves 'legitimists' and the Republicans was—to put it mildly—unusual. The Spanish Republican Movement at this period was only a pale reflection of the régime which was being set up for the second time in France. In the parallel political currents on both sides of the Pyrenees, the Spanish stream almost always tends to flow more slowly, for obvious economic and social reasons. Nevertheless it is an important historical fact that a Spanish Republican Party did take part in the political struggle in April 1848. Whilst we are discussing republicans, we should not forget the name of Abdon Terradas, another Catalan republican, who on 1 July sent his friends a passionate letter from Paris in which occurred the following passage:

'In this age, now that the French people have proclaimed the sole political system in conformity with human dignity, any man who does not come right out in favour of a republic must be considered an enemy of the people, no matter how he disguises his opinions, whether he talks about constitutional Cortes or the vague scheme for a central Junta. The first essential is to accept the principle of democratic republicanism, and then establish a revolutionary government, composed of known democrats, to educate public opinion, render powerless the enemies of equality and create a constituent assembly of the entire nation.' These words have a modern ring, which is not surprising. Spain's political ills have long been the same, as have the remedies which have never been applied.

As I have brought up the name of Abdon Terradas and also as we have just celebrated the fourth centenary of Cervantes' birth, I cannot resist mentioning one incident in this politician's career. In his home town of Figueras there was a man named Vicente Perxas, who was feeble-minded, and who, after reading Don Quixote, imagined himself to be the heir of Princess Micomicona. Terradas thereupon organised King Perxas' Court, complete with a 'Royal Gazette', with the object of ridiculing the monarchy and Court etiquette, and putting into practice his principle that 'hatred of kings is the first civic virtue'.

The Republican Movement, although it had supporters in Catalonia and Valencia, presented no real danger to Narvaez's Government. Its armed rebellions were no more than skirmishes. Its leaders, Ballera, Coma, Molins and Baldrich possessed little real military knowledge, although as they knew the ground they were skilled in field craft. This republican agitation assisted the work of the Carlists.

Civil war again broke out in Spain, this time after preparations and with help from abroad. On 23 June a veteran and experienced leader of the first civil war, named Cabrera, crossed the Spanish frontier at Osséja, accompanied by Carlist partisans who were scattered throughout France, and took over command of the rebel forces in Catalonia. He was joined by the other Carlist leaders: Masgoret, the brothers Tristany, Caletrus, Castells and Borges. Forcadell directed operations in Aragon and at Valencia, and Alzaa and Royo organised the revolt in Navarre and Castille. Within a short time there were Carlists in action not only in the above-mentioned districts but also in the Basque country and Estremadura.

Although this situation created a state of confusion, neither the throne nor the government was seriously threatened. This recrudescence of civil war had little force behind it: the Republicans and the Carlists were too few in number. Cabrera, without the promised help from abroad, was reduced to organising his forces in small bodies and was unable to put a regular army into the field. None the less it was in Catalonia that the civil war attained its greatest proportions. The rebels in Estremadura, Andalusia and Aragon were easily defeated; their leader in Aragon, El Cofo de Cariñena, accepted the Government's pardon. In Navarre, General Villalonga scattered the forces of Zabaleta, Ripada and Zurbiri. In Guipuscoa the rebels' plan miscarried, and the Carlist leader Alzaa was shot.

The result was quite different in Catalonia. Cabrera and Borges won decisive victories over the government forces. But whilst fortune smiled on the Carlists, one of the Republican's leaders, Ametller, was defeated by General Nouvilas, and General Fernandez de Córdova discovered a Republican plot and court martialled and shot the conspirators. General Pavia was relieved of his command in Catalonia and General Córdova succeeded him for a short while but had little success, and was replaced, on 8 December 1848, by General Manuel de la Concha. From that moment Cabrera's position grew increasingly difficult. After the Count of Montemolin had made an abortive attempt to enter Spain, and been arrested by the French Customs officers and taken back to Perpignan, the Carlist General retreated into France in April 1849. It was a great success for General Narvaez and his Government, and he celebrated it by the decree of 8 June proclaiming a general amnesty.

Another important event, which has been variously interpreted, also took place under the Narvaez Government. Cardinal Antonelli appealed to the Catholic Powers (Austria, France, Spain and the Two Sicilies) to re-establish Pius IX, who had fled to Gaeta and been removed from office by the Constituent Assembly of the Roman Republic. On 5 February, 1849, Spain sent a squadron under Admiral Bustillos and an expeditionary force of five thousand men under General Fernando Fernandez de Córdova. The Italian revolutionaries made use of the latter's name, which was also that of the 'Great Captain', who had won fame in Italy in the days of the Catholic Kings, to reinforce their attacks on the Spaniards. Spain's gesture had only a limited effect, as the French, with an army of thirty thousand men under General Oudinot, fought the war on their own, and entered Rome on 3 July 1849. Austria, for her part, occupied Venice, and thus re-established her position in Italy. The Spanish troops occupied Terracina and other unimportant places in the poverty-stricken countryside round Rome. Although it was on so small a scale, Spain's expedition against Italy proved that she was not indifferent to European politics, and was determined to remain in the picture.

Speaking of Spain's activities abroad, we must not forget that on 6 January 1848, General Serrano (known as 'the charmer' on account of his having taken the romantic fancy of the Queen) captured the Zafferines, and that Captain-General Claveria conquered the Sulu archipelago in the Philippines. Piracy in the waters round these islands endangered the lives, trade and industry of the Spanish there. In spite of fierce resistance from the natives, who in Fort Sipac killed themselves rather than surrender, the Sultan finally recognised Spanish sovereignty.

We must also remember, too, how in 1847, Spain, with the approval of France and England, intervened in Portugal to consolidate the position of Queen Maria la Gloria. On 21 May, General Manuel de la Concha crossed the Portuguese frontier and soon brought the rebel leaders to heel. Portugal's domestic situation, which was more or less the same as Spain's, explains why the 1848 Revolution had no direct effects on her political evolution. The eyes of the public were fixed on the battle for supremacy between General Saldhanha and General Costa Cabral. The former was victorious in 1847, the latter in 1849, and the former again in 1851. Saldhanha's entry into Lisbon on 5 May 1851 was rapturously received by the people, who saw him as the saviour of the country. The reality was not quite so satisfactory. Saldhanha, who whilst he was planning his revolt had linked up with liberals like Ferrer, Souza, Pestana and Herculano, once he came to power supported a group of financiers headed by Rodrigo and Fontes.

Nor had the Revolution of 1848 any echoes in Spanish America. Mexico had just emerged shattered from her experience of unprovoked aggression on the part of the United States, which ended in the treaty of Guadalupe-Hidalgo whereby she lost Texas, New Mexico and Upper California in return for an indemnity of fifteen million pesos. The Argentine was under the dictatorship of Rosas, who ruled the country for twenty-two years according to his personal whim, and who since 1843 had been at war with Uruguay, under Joaquín Suarez. The other republics had military heads of Government: General Belzu in Bolivia, Castilla in Peru, Carrera in Guatemala, and Bulnes in Chile. That was the beginning of an independent political existence for peoples with so rosy a future. In the West Indies, Spain remained in Cuba, and General Narvaez repulsed an American effort to buy it.

Narvaez's political successes did not prevent the formation of an opposition, which grew out of his own party and the military High Command. Generals like Pavia, Serrano and Prim, and politicians such as Gonzalez Bravo, Benavides and Rios Rosas, did not spare their criticism of the government which was suffering from unbalanced budgets. On top of this, there were intrigues at Court. Sor Patrocinio and Father Fulgencio, the King Consort's confessor, were behind the formation on 19 November 1849 of the 'Lightning Ministry', so-called because it only lasted twenty-seven hours. But Narvaez returned to power and stayed there until 10 January 1851.

Narvaez won great renown abroad, and when he resigned his leadership of the Spanish Government and went to Paris, his reception by Louis Napoleon proved it in a striking fashion. This man, whom his enemies called *El Espadon de Loja* ('the Sword of Loja'—his birthplace) left a mark of brutality and economic chaos on Spanish political history. The imprisonment of Salustiano de Olozaga, who had to flee to Portugal and France, the countless people sent into exile and the number of convictions by his government stigmatise Narvaez as the epitome of reaction. But I will quote in his favour the little-known testimony of the French Ambassador, Ferdinand de Lesseps, who tells us in his *Souvenirs* that he never intervened in vain on the behalf of Narvaez's political enemies. 'After the reputation for cruelty so many people have foisted on Narvaez, my remarks may astonish; it has even been said that when the man was on his death bed and his confessor asked him if he forgave his enemies, he replied: "I've no call to, since I've had them all shot." This saying is a shameful calumny, for I have known few men of such a straightforward and generous nature. Narvaez was always ready to lay down his life, either to defend his country against another, or to keep the peace at home.' This panegyric presents Narvaez to us under an aspect often neglected by historians. Like all men of his time, he was half beast, half angel, for it is only our age that has produced, in the fascist, the man devoid of every human feeling.

BELGIUM IN 1848

JOHN BARTIER

The honourable member (Monsieur Castian) has just told us that the ideas behind the French Revolution will tour the world. I would tell him that to do so they need not pass through Belgium
Monsieur Delfosse in his speech to the
Belgian Chamber on 1 March 1848

Political constitutions are simply the collection of institutions and guarantees whereby one class secures its economic hold over the rest. So if we are to change the social conditions of our way of life, we must first of all smash these constitutions which shackle us
Victor Tedesco: 'Le Catéchisme du prolétaire,' 1848

In the last months of 1847, Belgium's future was a matter of grave concern for the prophets of Europe. They hesitated to accept a State born of revolution and endowed with so infamously liberal a constitution; they felt they should arraign its government for criminal negligence in allowing the country to become a refuge for every hot-head in Europe, and for refusing to muzzle the democratic *clubs*. Metternich had always shown himself hostile to the thought of an independent Belgium and on 14 November 1847 his ambassador in Brussels wrote: 'The Belgian liberals are blind; they will all be swallowed up by the communists.' Louis Philippe trembled for the fate of his son-in-law Leopold I, and on 1 December his ambassador wrote: 'The reformists in Belgium are blundering on like a bull with its head down.'

As we know, the future was to give the lie to these dire predictions: it was not Leopold but Louis Philippe who lost his crown, and Metternich who fled to Brussels, not Charles Rogier to Vienna.

I recall these inaccurate predictions not for the idle amusement of pillorying their authors' lack of perspicacity, but, on the contrary, to show how even well-informed observers saw the situation in Belgium early in 1848. On the face of it there was nothing absurd about their pessimism. When King Leopold, his ministers and official circles learnt what had happened in Paris, they were terrified lest the movement spread to Belgium. The King was so dispirited that at one point he thought of abdicating. The deputy d'Elhougne tell us that the sitting of the Chamber of Representatives on 26 February, 'had a funereal aspect, and all the members looked like mourners'. Another eye-witness, Thonissen, did not hide the fact that the news from France had produced 'a universal feeling of the deepest despondency', and added: 'We were all waiting to see the republican flag run up in Flanders and Hainault'. The radical leaders thought their hour had come. Victor Considérant, who was in Belgium at the time, wrote on 26 February to Charles Rogier: 'The kings have had their day . . . go to Leopold, explain the position to him, and get him to send a message to the Chambers to the effect that if Belgium wants the new order, he will not stand in her way.' He added, in a postscript: 'Before two o'clock tomorrow afternoon, the streets of Brussels will teem with a hundred thousand men, all agog with enthusiasm, and shouting "Long live the Republic!" ' The same day Lucien Jottrand, one of the heads of the *Association Démocratique*, called an emergency meeting of the leading party members in Brussels.

But the crisis quickly subsided. There was no Belgian Revolution in 1848. Our only problem is to discover how it was that people should have hoped—or feared—that one would break out. It should not be necessary to point out that the European crisis in 1848 had many facets. It will simplify the position if we isolate the three main forces at work, sometimes in conjunction with and sometimes independently of each other: they were nationalism, liberalism and socialism. In one place the subject peoples were fighting for their independence. In another, the middle classes were denying their King's 'divine right' to rule, and elsewhere, there was the proletariat, attempting (clumsily it is true) to destroy the capitalist system which was throttling it. Among the 'Forty-eighters' were Kossuth and Mazzini, Gagern and Ledru-Rollin, Marx and Blanqui. There was no fear of a nationalist rising in Belgium, since the successful insurrection in 1830 had won her independence.[1]

As for the Flemish movement and the Walloon claims to which it gave rise, they had not yet begun. The political problem was of a different order from that of France or Germany. The 'old order' had long been abolished. Belgium's charter represented the revolutionaries' ideal in many other countries.[2]

The King had never interfered with the workings of parliamentary institutions, and autocrat though he was by nature, he had adapted himself remarkably well to the rôle of a constitutional sovereign. The monarchy

[1] 'Of course the nationalist movement which is now gaining impetus in Italy achieved its object in this country eighteen years ago.' (*Considerations sur les Révolutions de 1848 au point de vue belge*, Brussels, July 1848, page 23)

[2] Belgium was even further removed from Germany, which was almost totally lacking in parliamentary institutions and civic rights. 'The constitution Belgium has acquired is rightly considered the most liberal in Europe; other countries frequently point to it as an example.' (*Ibid.* page 22)

may have been anathema to some, but not the King. The only uncertain quantity was the extreme left wing. The system of a property qualification for voters meant that the rich held the reins. Out of a population of four million, there were less than forty thousand with a vote. Not only the people but even the lower-middle classes were excluded from the electorate.

Industry on a large scale was beginning in the towns. The workers of Ghent, Liége and Verviers were as poverty-stricken as their fellows in Rouen and Manchester. Mareska's and Fossion's investigations revealed conditions as horrifying as those discovered by Villermé, Villeneuve-Bargemont, and Engels. For instance, one of the Belgian investigators, Dr Schoenfeld, wrote: 'As a rule the miner does not live to old age.' And one of his colleagues said of the workmen in Ghent that 'destitution brutalises them and fills them with hatred for society'.

Yet the workers in the big modern factories were privileged beings compared with the flax workers. The flax industry, which had long brought wealth to Flanders, had not changed with the times, and no one had bothered to mechanise it. Out-of-date methods of production and a hopeless sales organisation had lost it markets abroad. It held its ground within Belgium, but only because each successive government subsidised it so as not to antagonise a section of the electorate. It was moribund from 1840 onward. The workers, unconscious of the evolution which was steadily crushing them, remained faithful to their traditional craft. Their wages fell and they began to lose their jobs.

By 1847 in East Flanders, the number of destitute had reached roughly 25 per cent in the towns and 30 per cent in the country. In the neighbouring province of West Flanders, one out of every three inhabitants had to be given public assistance.

The picture was dark already, but famine and epidemics were to make it even blacker. After 1845 the potato crop, the mainstay of the people's diet, was deplorable. The scientists tried in vain to discover the cause. The next year the people of Flanders, weakened by hunger, fell an easy prey to 'famine sickness' and then typhus; the recruiting offices in West Flanders had to turn down a third of the conscripts. Between 1846 and 1848—a significant period—the population of the flax-growing districts fell by five per cent.

But who was to exploit these causes for discontent? Was there a revolutionary party in Belgium?

The fact of the matter was that the Opposition was heterogeneous in the extreme. Socialist propaganda had made some converts. First the Saint-Simonians and later the Phalansterians had sent their propagandists into Belgium, and they found eager listeners. The poet Weustenraad, one of the great names—in comparison with the rest—among the Belgian Romantics, freely admitted his debt to Fourier. Old Buonarotti, who lived in Belgium and published Babeuf's *Conspiration* there, left a certain following behind him. Louis de Potter, one of the authors of Belgium's independence, had been converted nearly ten years before to Baron de Colins' collectivism. Eugène Sue's *Le Juif Errant* and Lamartine's *L'Histoire des Girondins* were as enthusiastically read in Belgium as in France. Newspapers such as *Le Radical*, *L'Uylenspiegel* and *Le Débat social*, and periodicals like *La Revue démocratique* attempted to spread the new doctrines. For simple people these were summed up in almanacs, pamphlets and songs, and there appeared a whole crop of books under such naïve titles as *Souvenir d'un vieux prolétaire*, *La Propagande du père Libertas* and *Le Catéchisme démocratique*. The progressives took advantage of the liberties assured them by the constitution, and formed *clubs*. One of these, the *Association démocratique*, became especially well known, for its members included both the leading Belgian radicals and a number of famous refugees, such as the Pole Lelewel and Karl Marx. The majority of members were intellectuals: lawyers, doctors or engineers, but there were two working men of importance, Jacob Kats and Pellering. The first was a former weaver and the second a cobbler. Both understood the people and spoke their language. There was also one member of parliament who sympathised with the *Association*, Adelson Castiau, the deputy for Tournai; and there were a number of influential members of the Liberal Party, particularly the two lawyers Faider and Bartels. The *Association* was strongest in Brussels but it throve too in the provinces under the energetic leadership of Spilthoorn at Ghent, Braas at Namur and Tedesco at Liége.

The progressive movement did not lack men of action. Belgium, too, had her half-pay list. In the great days of 1830, the Provisional Government had built up an army in a hurry, and had shovelled out commissions and promotions with little thought for the moral or military competence of their recipients. When the revolution was over they tried to instil discipline into the Army, and to do so had to dismiss and pension off a number of officers. It is easy to imagine the discontent this produced. The first years of Leopold I's reign were marked by an unbroken succession of military conspiracies. Louis Leconte has usefully pointed out that the majority of their authors were on the side of the Opposition in 1848. General Mellinet and General Le Hardy de Beaulieu were both in the *Association démocratique*. Lieutenant-Colonel Grégoire and the ex-officers Hérode, Becker and Fosses were soon to come into the limelight.

Yet even the combined forces of the advanced Liberals, the various kinds of socialists and the group of former officers did not in themselves represent a serious threat to the government. Their worry was what would happen if this opposition were to win the support of the French Republic, or if the masses were to catch the Parisian fever.

The issue was decided within a month. Whilst the *Association démo-cratique* held a number of violent meetings and sent a delegation to see which way the wind was blowing in Paris, the Belgian middle class formed a 'holy alliance'. The Catholic Opposition at once stopped hampering the liberal government. The President of the Council, Charles Rogier, showed foresight, firmness and prudence in this time of crisis.

A forced loan, voted on 26 February, enabled the Treasury to meet any eventuality. On 2 March, the property qualification for voters was lowered, and the electorate went up from 46,636 to 79,360, thus removing the lower-middle class from the ranks of the malcontents. The government also hastily took steps to appease the advanced liberals by suppressing the stamp tax on newspapers, regulating the King's power to nominate burgomasters, and passing a law making members of parliament ineligible for government posts. They tried to alleviate the people's sufferings, too, by embarking on major public works, granting assistance to the destitute, and reforming the workhouses and municipal pawn-offices. At the same time the army, the civic guard and the whole of the judicial and adminis-trative machinery were kept in readiness. Finally the government avoided all international complications.

During this period, the revolutionaries were daily losing ground. The list of riots is significant. They took place in Brussels on 27 February and 1 March; at Bruges on 10 March; again in Brussels on the 15th; then at Vaulx, near Tournai, on the 18th. Between 17 and 19 March the Red Flag flew over Virton. There were further demonstrations in Brussels on the 26th; at Saint-Nicolas-Waas on the 27th; and in the Borinage district on the night of the 28th.

These riots were nothing like those in Paris or Vienna. The rioters erected no barricades and were dispersed with the minimum of force. They worried the government far less than the formation in Paris of a Belgian Legion, whose commanders openly announced their intention of invading the kingdom. They were known to be in communication with the revolutionaries in Belgium, and the police secured copies of the proclamation they were circulating under cover. Its authors apostrophised their compatriots as follows: 'Now you have seen the glorious example of Paris—of France, how long will you sit down under an anti-national government which has lost you Limburg and Luxembourg? Will you be the last to join the Republic of Europe?'

The government also discovered that the legionaries were supported by Caussidière, Ledru-Rollin and even Lamartine. The last-named sent two agents into Belgium to get in touch with local democrats in Brussels, Ghent, Antwerp and Liége. Naturally the police followed their move-ments and watched them closely, on the look-out for an opportunity to expel them discreetly. Lamartine's choice of agents, incidentally, was typical. One was Tony Johannot, the illustrator of so many Romantic works, and the other, Hetzel, Jules Verne's publisher and himself a children's writer. There was a large number of Belgian workmen in Paris who were out of work as the result of the revolution, and they proved willing recruits for the Legion when they were shown all the advantages of returning to Belgium as soldiers of a victorious army. The Legion was soon two thousand strong. The Belgian authorities grew increasingly anxious when they learnt that it had left Paris. The first column reached Valenciennes on the 24th. But they never had the chance to fight. Two bold engineers were sent to the railway station and coupled an engine on to the rebel's train. Before the latter realised what had happened, they were whisked away to Quievrain, where they were disarmed without attempting to resist. A second column, after bivouacking at Seclin, crossed the frontier near Mouscron on the 29th. General Fleury-Duray scattered them at Risquons-Tout. A major load was off Rogier's mind: the revolutionaries had lost their army. Once the French Republicans saw that a revolution in Belgium had little chance of success, they withdrew their support. From April onward, there were only completely harmless demonstrations. The defeat at Risquons-Tout gave the government a pretext for reprisals. They were careful to pull in all the most violent republicans without worrying too much about their actual complicity. Forty-three accused, including Méllinet, Spilthoorn and Tedesco, were sent for trial at the Antwerp assizes. The jury accepted the prosecutor De Bavay's conclusions and recommended seventeen death sentences, which—I hasten to add—were never carried out. By June the government was sufficiently sure of public opinion to risk an election. It was a triumph. The radicals were out of the running. During the last months of 1848 and in 1849 there was the odd meeting or democratic banquet at which toasts were drunk to the 'Universal Republican', but the spirit had gone. In Belgium, as in the rest of Europe, socialism had taken a beating from which it would not recover for years to come.

Our final problem is: why was the revolutionaries' failure so complete? Charles Rogier was an adroit and subtle man, unlike the stiff-necked Guizot, and he steered a clever course. It is only fair to add that the deputies showed an undeniably well-developed political sense in supporting him to a man, and accepting essential concessions to public opinion whilst there was still time. The lowering of the property qualification for voters was objectionable to most politicians. One of them, Frère-Orban, had even exclaimed that so tiny a qualification would produce not an electorate but a staff of servants. Yet this electoral law was passed easily enough. Rogier's task was made easier by the wisdom of the Catholic

Opposition. In this connection, I must point out that the gulf between Catholics and Liberals was nothing like so deep or so wide as between Legitimists and Orléanists. The two became separate parties only in 1846, and the bridges between them had not all disappeared: many people still hoped for a return to Unionism. The Belgian government played its hand well, but its opponent was a weak one. In the first place, France's support was infinitesimal, and more of a hindrance than a help. The spirit of independence fought against party loyalty. The nation identified the republican cause with that of a foreign power. On the other hand, the radical leaders themselves were timorous. They could not rid themselves of respect for the law. Castiau, the sole republican deputy, resigned because he felt he had not his party's support. De Potter quarrelled with his socialist master, Colins, because he wanted only a peaceful revolution. Jottrand was of the same opinion, and clung so firmly to it that he could not be sent for trial with the others after Risquons-Tout. Of course if from the beginning the republicans had felt that they had the masses behind them, they might have stopped worrying about the legality of their actions. But the masses did not follow them, and men like Kats and Pellering were exceptions. The Belgian proletariat was not so advanced as the cabinet-makers of the Faubourg Saint-Antoine or the English Chartists or the German tailors of Weitling. The reasons for their apathy are obvious. City life, which was to destroy tradition, had only just begun. The majority of workers still lived in semi-rural boroughs or villages which socialist propaganda reached only with difficulty, and where any agitator received short shrift. Besides, how could the Belgian workmen be expected to understand the new theories? They were crassly ignorant. Three-quarters of the miners were illiterate. Usually the intellectual reformists spoke only in French, whereas most of the workers knew only Flemish or, in Romans, a Walloon dialect. And whether the socialist propagandists were deists or atheists, they offended the workers' loyalty to the Church and their deep-seated piety. Their faith helped them to bear their poverty with resignation. Their passivity was astonishing, as can be seen from a glance at M. Jacquemyns' fine book on the subject. In the darkest days of the crisis in Flanders, the starving poor never went further than smashing a few bakers' windows.

The ease with which Belgium came through the 1848 crisis had major consequences. It gave her her prestige abroad, and strengthened her people's confidence in their liberal institutions. One even wonders whether it was not the memories of 1848 and Risquons-Tout that taught later socialists like Vandervelde and Anseele their preference for legal methods, and their hatred of violence which so shocked Georges Sorel.

THE EVENTS OF 1848 IN SCANDINAVIA

LOUIS TISSOT

*Freedom is an old friend of mine, for I am a Swede and we
grew up together*
E. Tegner

ALTHOUGH the Scandinavian countries are so remote geographically
from continental Europe, their political and social evolution has followed
a parallel course. Frequently their liberal views have been even more
advanced. It is therefore not surprising that so many Nordic voices echoed
the call to action in 1848. We must examine whether the very bitterness
of the conflict did not prevent the realisation of those liberal aspirations
which dawned with the 'year of revolutions', and see how far social aims
gradually gave way to national ones.

At the beginning of the nineteenth century, two great changes took
place in Scandinavia. The first was Russia's acquisition of Finland, which
for five hundred and fifty years had been united with Sweden. This was
the result of the ambitious Colonel Sprengtporten's activities, ending in
the Treaty of Fredrikshavn on 17 September 1808. The second change
was Sweden's annexation five years later—by the Treaty of Kiel—of
Norway, which she received by way of compensation.

Denmark was the great loser, for although Sweden had compensated
her for the loss of Norway by the cession of Swedish Pomerania and
Rügen, she in turn had ceded these to Prussia in 1815.

That was still the position in Scandinavia in 1848. Norway, although
she had kept her own national institutions, was dissatisfied with a union
which prevented her pursuing an independent foreign policy. As for
Finland, ever since 1808 she had been allowed a governor-general, in the
person of Sprengtporten, and she had been granted a parliament. Furthermore, the Russian government had promised to respect the Finns'
religious beliefs and traditional liberties.

LOUIS TISSOT

I

LIBERALISM IN SCANDINAVIA

At the end of the first half of the nineteenth century, reform was the subject of many heated discussions in Scandinavia. In Denmark, the theologian Grundtvig had conducted several campaigns from the pulpit against too superficial a conception of Christianity: he succeeded in producing a genuine religious revival. Grundtvig's influence was felt in the nationalist movement whose apostles included such well-known writers as Oelenschläger and Bertil Thorwaldsen. The reformists appeared in the 'thirties, when they vainly attempted to exert pressure on their unwilling king. They remembered how Norway had acquired a liberal constitution in 1814, though admittedly not by virtue of her new ruler's generosity or liberalism: it had been a purely political manœuvre to forestall possibly violent agitation for a separation.

When Christian VIII died on 20 January 1848, the Danish Radical Party decided that it was time to act. Its leaders since 1840, Clausen and Schouw, announced that a constitution, which was barely deemed desirable in 1839, had become a necessity, and that under it Schleswig should be reunited with Denmark. Thus the issue at once became one of national prestige; Herr Hvidt, the leader of the middle-class party, supported the Radicals.

When Frederick VII was proclaimed as the new king, the delegation from the municipality of Copenhagen was cheered with optimistic enthusiasm. A projected constitution was tabled immediately, and the *Kjöbenhavnposten* commented: 'Absolute monarchy brought in by Frederick III has been abandoned by Frederick VII, but as absolute power was vested in the former with the tacit approval of the people, it should now revert to them. Frederick VII should be a democratic king.' On 14 January there were seven thousand two hundred and forty signatures to be seen on a petition to the King by a peasant deputation. Ideological discussions continued unabated. Some forty patriots met regularly at the house of Professor Clausen, and at the end of February denounced the idea of a unitary state. They wanted the Danish islands as well as Jutland and Schleswig to be united under the same constitution, with a separate Diet for Schleswig, which itself should be separate from Holstein.

This was the first mention of what was to become the Danish Radicals' primary aim, to establish Denmark's southern boundary on the Eider, the river into which Charlemagne is supposed to have flung a javelin, exclaiming: 'This is the Empire's frontier!'

The Paris riots gave the Copenhagen Radicals their opportunity to demonstrate: crowds surged through the streets shouting 'Denmark to the Eider!' and associations of patriots sprang up.

The question of Schleswig was soon to take the centre of the stage and push the democratic and social problem into the background where it was to remain for many months. The constitution was finally adopted only on 5 June 1849. It brought in universal suffrage but shelved the question of Schleswig, which by then was in a state of revolt.

In Finland, national aspirations were paramount as a result of Russian domination, but already a number of intellectuals were becoming interested in social problems. From 1842 onward, the influential writer Snellmann had attempted to bridge the gap between the educated minority and the masses.

The events of 1848 were received with joy, in the first instance, by the writers (especially Topelius), but the whole nation rejoiced when the Hungarians, too, entered the conflict. The people recalled how once in the Urals and Altai Mountains close family ties had linked the Finns with those far off Finno-Ugrians who after their long odyssey had settled on the banks of the Danube. Finland's heart went out to the people of Budapest. But within their own country the Finns could only express their nationalism in a negative—or at the best in a purely intellectual fashion. In December 1848 there appeared in Helsingfors Runeberg's *Tales of Stal the Standard-bearer*. One of these, entitled *Our Country*, was set to music by the composer Pacius and sung at the Spring Festival. This song was to become Finland's national anthem.

Desire for reform in Sweden had not waited until 1848 to find an outlet. As far back as 1830 the leaders of the democratic party, J. G. Richert and C. H. Anckarsvard, had campaigned for a revision of the system of representation in parliament, which was still based on the antiquated division of the nation into four Estates—or classes.

In the Diet of 1834, electoral reform had headed the agenda. First, the Opposition succeeded in obtaining the universities' right to send their own representatives to parliament. Then a Bill was tabled proposing that each Estate should have an equal number of electors who would send their representatives to a single Chamber. There they would vote by a show of hands, and—among other prerogatives—would have that of electing an Upper Chamber. When the first *Riksdag* met in 1844–5 (in the reign of the 'Liberal King', Oscar I), Baron Nordenflecht declared the reform an urgent one. Liberal hopes revived, but the systematic opposition of the clergy and the nobility led to the rejection of the Bill. All the liberals obtained was the abolition of trade guilds in 1846, and the first Poor Law in 1847.

The year 1848 began calmly enough. Nevertheless, when news of events in Vienna and Berlin arrived in March, the Swedish democrats began to make certain claims. A patriotic banquet was organised in Stockholm on the 18th, and there were as many speeches as they were noisy demonstrations. Although feeling did not run high enough in Sweden to provoke serious trouble, there was turmoil enough for the government to call out the military. Besides, at this democratic banquet, which was held under the auspices of the liberal leaders, Lars Hïerta, Franz Schartau and Richert, streamers were flown and leaflets distributed bearing the words: 'Five thousand citizens are met tonight in the Brunkeberg Square. Long live Reform and the Republic!'[1]

There were a number of people killed as well as wounded in the subsequent fray between the demonstrators and the military, and the capital was restless for several days. But order had been quickly restored, and St Petersburg was most gratified. The Czar embraced General Nordin, the Swedish Ambassador, and through Baron Krüdener, his own Ambassador in Stockholm, congratulated King Oscar on his firm attitude towards the 'revolutionary disturbance in the streets'.

Nevertheless liberalism was gaining ground, and the newspaper *Aftenposten* stoutly repelled the attacks of the reactionaries' leader Hartmannsdorff. The Society of the Friends of Reform had a number of branches in the provinces, and held a national congress at Orebrö in June 1849. The final motion it passed declared: 'National representation depends on universal suffrage with no distinction between the different Estates or classes.'

Although her Eidsvold Constitution had always been looked upon as a pattern of liberalism, Norway had none the less felt the after effects of the War of American Independence as well as the July Revolution in France. Then came the spring of 1848.

There had been a revival of nationalism since 1845, due to the work of C. Asbjörnsen and Bishop Jörgen Moe, who had collected and published some of the popular sagas. The liberal movement had a large following in Oslo. On its extreme left wing there was a section—which some said even flirted with communism—led by Marcus Moeller Thrane, a picturesque character who, together with a band of students, sought to form a third party, which he named *Det Demokratiske Eller Folkiepartiet* (the Democratic or People's Party). The liberal newspapers, in particular *Morgenbladet*, applauded the work of the progressives in other European countries.

---

[1] Quoted in Hallendorf's *Sveriges Historia* (Tofte Delen), Vol. XII, page 45

2

SCHLESWIG: A SPECIFICALLY NATIONAL PROBLEM

It is worth while to investigate the origins of the Schleswig problem. Lord Palmerston said he had known only three men who were capable of understanding it: one was dead, the second had gone mad because of it, and he himself, the third, had forgotten what it was all about. The facts, however, were as follows: out of Schleswig's 330,000 inhabitants, there were 180,000 Danes, 120,000 Germans and 25,000 Frisians, who spoke a dialect akin to Low German. The rule of the German landed nobility had resulted in the predominance of German, 'the master tongue', in the schools.

Now since 1460 the Kings of Denmark ruled both the Duchy of Schleswig and that of Holstein, as successors respectively of the Duke of Schleswig and of the Count and Duke of Holstein. These Duchies had always enjoyed certain special privileges and these had been recognised on various occasions: for instance by Waldemar III's constitution *Ne unietur* of 1326, which had proclaimed that Denmark and Schleswig-Holstein were never to be united under the same monarch; by the privileges of 1460; by the declaration of Christian of Denmark, elected Duke of Schleswig and Count of Holstein, not because he was King of Denmark but as feudal lord of both Duchies; and finally by the Letters Patent of 1846 which stated: 'The Duchies are independent states and have nothing in common with Denmark except the person of their sovereign.' The author Lallerstedt considers this clause a clumsy one, making it appear that all the faults were on the side of the King of Denmark, for since Schleswig was a Danish fief, there was no need to give a ruling on the right of succession. As for Holstein, the King had no right to change a fundamental law on his own initiative.

When the Holy Roman Empire collapsed in 1806, the two duchies were reunited with Denmark, but the Congress of Vienna revoked this decision and in 1834 Denmark gave them a separate government and a Supreme Court at Gottorp. This concession did not, however, satisfy German dynastic ambitions, which were implacable. The position was that the Duke of Augustenburg was head of the male, or 'royal cadet', line of the Oldenburg family, which in the sixteenth century had divided into two branches: the Holstein-Gottorps and the Royal House of Denmark. Now Holstein did not recognise succession through a woman, which was likely to occur on the death of Frederick VII who would be succeeded as King of Denmark by Prince Frederick of Hesse, the son of King Christian's sister Charlotte. The Duke of Augustenburg therefore reserved his rights, hoping also to bring Schleswig-Holstein into the German Confederation.

As early as 1834 the Germans in the Duchies wanted the union of Schleswig and Holstein; in the session of the Estates of 1842 they wanted the combined duchies to be separated from Denmark, and in 1844 the Estates had decided that: (a) the Duchies were independent States; (b) succession was through the male line; (c) the Duchies were irrevocably united.

These three principles were later to be the articles of faith of the insurrection. Rebellion had thus been brewing for a long time among the Germans of Schleswig, and particularly among the middle classes or 'Philistines', who 'hung the portrait of the Imperial Vicar in their drawing rooms and ostentatiously wore the black, red and gold rosette'.

In February 1848 the Schleswig question was to the fore in Copenhagen. It was not only a constitutional but also a national problem, and therefore a social one, since the aristocrats of Schleswig were anathema to the democrats of Denmark. One has only to compare the Assembly of the German Estates which met in the Duchy on 3 April with the 'Casino Ministry' in power in Copenhagen to understand that side of the problem.

Henceforth, in Denmark, Schleswig was to oust the Constitution as a topic for discussion, and all parties appeared to take the same view of it. On 11 March, Herr Hvidt of the Bourgeois Party and editor of the paper Fadreladet spoke in the Casino attacking Schleswig-Holstein's influence, and was applauded by an audience of two thousand. At this same meeting Professor Clausen was loudly cheered when he said: 'Our King thinks and feels like a true Dane. We must stand behind him.' On 12 March another meeting—again two thousand strong—was held at the Hippodrome, and there were demands for a wider franchise and the maintenance of Denmark's frontier on the Eider.

The Duchies replied on 15 March by a meeting at Altona to demand a constitution for Schleswig-Holstein and Schleswig's accession to the German Confederation. There were also demonstrations at Kiel, which go to show that it was always Holstein, and her aristocracy in particular, which spoke for Schleswig. On 18 March, the independence of Schleswig-Holstein was declared at a meeting at Rendsburg.

Whilst Denmark took certain defence measures, the 'Casino Party' held a meeting at which five resolutions were passed, among them one demanding the maintenance of the integrity and of union of Denmark with Schleswig under a common constitution, based on a truly popular franchise. These resolutions were signed by Hvidt, Clausen, Orla Lehmann, Tscherning and Schouw, and were passed unanimously, except for the fourth which provided for Schleswig's independence as a province, and for that reason received only fifty-odd votes. The speeches which preceded the voting were particularly vehement. Orla Lehmann declared: 'The King is not up to his duties, the Duchies are in a state of revolt, and our country is in danger.' Hvidt emphasised the national side of the problem, saying: 'We must incorporate Schleswig'. The session ended by the members sending a petition to the King, holding out the threat of a popular rising: 'We beg Your Majesty not to drive the nation to such a pitch of despair that it is forced to take the matter into its own hands'.

A contemporary observer wrote of these days preceding the fall of the Government: 'Copenhagen was in a state of intense agitation, and it was easy to keep it so. There were no outrages, but that was because no one crossed the people, who were in sole control. Thousands thronged the streets, and every other wall was plastered with posters. The whole scene, in fact, was set for an insurrection.'

21 March was the day which decided the victory of the 'Casino Party'. At a Cabinet meeting presided over by Bardenfleth, the Ministers, overwhelmed by the turn of events, handed in their resignations. At the same time there was a demonstration, organised by a so-called 'People's Deputation', which was run by a committe of four under the leadership of one Fredriksen. The Cabinet was replaced on 22 March by one headed by Count G. Moltke of Bregentveld, whose name made possible the inclusion of a number of radicals. It included Count Knuth (Foreign Secretary), Monrad (Minister for Ecclesiastical Affairs), Tscherning (Minister of War), and Bluhme (Minister of Commerce), as well as Hvidt and Lehmann (Ministers without portfolio).

The King hoped that Moltke and Bluhme would prove restraining influences, but the extremists in the government were determined to realise their ambitions to the full. Orla Lehmann stated quite clearly: 'We are in the middle of a revolution which will have even more widespread effects. To all intents and purposes we no longer have a King but only a provisional government.'

Naturally the masses welcomed such a statement and crowds thronged the streets. At the port they stopped the boat service to Kiel.

The atmosphere of the first Cabinet meeting evidently distressed one contemporary historian, who commented bitterly: 'Plates of bread and butter and glasses of port were to be seen on the conference table.' His final verdict on this Ministry was typical of his time: 'They are busy trying to make respectable King's Ministers out of the raw revolutionaries foisted on them by the Casino meetings and the counsels of despair.'

The government's first action was to draw up a declaration which left no room for doubt: 'Schleswig will be reunited with Denmark by a common, liberal constitution.' Immediately all Germans working in

Copenhagen started for home, either overland or on board the *Hekla* and the *Skirner*.

One can see that the political development of Schleswig was on the same lines as that of Denmark, with the difference that the Germans in South Schleswig had for many years been waiting for the chance to prove their loyalty to their mother country. They had been greatly attracted by the Young Germany movement.

On 24 March 1848, the King of Prussia promised his unconditional support to the Duke of Augustenburg, and on the 31st the Frankfort Assembly admitted Schleswig-Holstein into the German Confederation. In the meantime Schleswig's military preparation proceeded apace; head-quarters were established at Rendsburg and locomotives were kept under steam on the line to Kiel, where a provisional government had been formed. It consisted of Prince Frederick of Schleswig-Holstein Noer, Beseler, Count Reventlow, a business man from Kiel named T. Schmidt and a Flensburg lawyer named Bremer. Its first action was to send the Duke of Augustenburg's army to capture the fortress of Rendsburg—the strong-hold of the country—which the Danish High Command had neglected to put in a state of defence and which fell without much difficulty.

The Confederation held another meeting on 3 April of sixty delegates, with an imposing majority of aristocrats: Count Reventlow, former ambassador in Berlin, Count Hahn, attaché at the embassy in Vienna, Count Otto Rantzau, former ambassador in St Petersburg, and Baron Blom von Falkenberg, former ambassador in London. One has only to compare this assembly with the 'Casino Ministry' to see the difference between the opposing sides. The provisional government announced: 'Our Duke's hand is forced and the country is without a government', to which Copenhagen replied: 'Whosoever has taken or shall take part in the revolutionary movements in the Duchies, thereby failing in his duty as a loyal subject, will have to bear the full consequences of his actions.'

Then the guns spoke.

3

THE RESULT OF 1848: A SET-BACK

The year 1848 ended for Scandinavia, as for the rest of Europe, in a wave of reaction.

Denmark's 'Casino Ministry' did not last out the year: in November its more advanced elements, Lehmann, Monrad and Tscherning, saw that they could not count on France and England to support their claim to

Schleswig, and so resigned. Shortly afterwards, as a result of Russian intrigue, the liberal 'Casino Ministry' was replaced by a national unionist ministry under Bluhme, which prepared the naturally far from radical constitution submitted in 1849.

This constitution was sympathetically, but not enthusiastically, received by such liberal newspapers as *Fadreladet* and *Kjöbenhavnposten*. Events justified their caution, for in 1854 Oersted's government replaced the 1849 Constitution by a new charter which stopped short at the creation of a National Council.

This body was entirely in the hands of the King, as will be seen from the following details of its composition: Royal nominees, 20; provincial representatives, 30 (Denmark 18, Schleswig 5, Holstein 6, Lauenburg 1); representatives elected indirectly by voters with an income of over 1,200 Rdl (*Rigadaler*) or paying over 200 Rdl in taxes, 32 (Denmark 17, Schleswig 7, Holstein 8). As a Danish historian points out this was the constitution of a 'unitary and conservative State'.

Eighteen forty-eight in Denmark resulted in a triumph for nationalism at the expense of the reformers.

It was the same in Sweden, where in 1848 the right wing repulsed all attempts at reform. King Oscar, influenced by ideological developments and by the turn of events in Europe, instructed the Minister for Ecclesiastical Affairs, Genberg, to table a Bill providing for the abolition of the Estates, and the creation of two Chambers of Representatives. The Bill went as a matter of course before the 1851 Diet and the conservatives defeated it. The liberals had first abstained from voting, then half-heartedly supported it, and the general opinion was that the King did not really wish it to become law.

In Finland, too, there was a set-back, for Russia of course reacted vigorously to any display of liberalism there. Already in the course of 1848 a ukase had been published declaring the Finnish women liable, by commutation of sentence, to deportation to Siberia, where they could be employed in the imperial factories.

After the publication of a Finnish translation of *William Tell*, the Czar (who was already perturbed at a crop of nationalist literature) decided on 4 June 1849 to ban 'literary, scientific and economic societies of all denominations, whether benevolent or otherwise, with the exception of small trade associations'. A further law forbade the publication of any work in Finnish, with the exception of 'books on religion or domestic economy'. It also forbade the raising of funds for any purpose other than the aid of an individual, as well as subscriptions to periodicals other than government publications. As from 1 January 1850 all existing associations were banned. Even the Finnish Literary Association had to give up announcing its meetings. In every sphere the Finns had to have special permission 'to think, or even to console themselves by talking over their memories together'.

Thus the fetters of reaction were felt more drastically at the end of 1848, even by Finland, who had never been in a position to attempt a revolution.

4

THE PROBLEMS OF NATIONALISM AND
SCANDINAVIAN SOLIDARITY

Excepting in Sweden, the nationalist aspect of the movements of 1848 was to the fore in Scandinavia.

Norway had not welcomed the 'uneasy union', as it has been called, of 1814, and she grumbled at the terms under which Bernadotte, at the Treaty of Kiel, had decided she was to pay the Danish Debt. Also she resented the Swedish nobility, and the Oslo *Storting* thrice voted the abolition of their rights and privileges, which thus became law without the need of a royal proclamation. On the whole, however, the Eidsvold Constitution left room for conciliation and 1848 passed in Norway without a violent upsurge of nationalism.

In Finland the nationalist problem was a much more complex one, for in allowing Finland a certain degree of autonomy, Russia had favoured the ruling class, in other words the Swedish nobility, so that the Finns grew resentful of Sweden. The result was that the Finns (assisted too by the liberal measures of Alexander II) became conscious of themselves as a nation, and so in a round-about fashion at once turned against Russia.

Besides the various nationalist stirrings as a result of territorial claims, there was also the revival of a Scandinavian nationalism in 1848. An instance of this is King Oscar's attitude towards Denmark.

On 4 May 1848 the King of Sweden declared that his country would consider the entry of German troops into Jutland as an act of war, and when, after the Malmö Armistice on 2 July, General Wrangle did decide to invade Jutland, King Oscar planned to send an army against him. The Convention of 26 August, however, put an end to hostilities, and Sweden had no occasion to intervene. A few years later Swedish aid would have been invaluable, but in spite of all her promises, Sweden then let Germany take both Schleswig and Holstein from Denmark. This produced a rift in Scandinavian relationships which it took many years to heal.

Eighteen forty-eight can be considered a 'decisive' year for Sweden, insomuch as she began to drift away from Russia towards the West, and so again become conscious of herself as a Scandinavian country, and therefore as a nation.

This Scandinavianism (which was purely defensive and had none of the aggressive characteristics of German nationalism) had already become apparent in 1845, when Norwegian, Danish and Swedish students held a reunion at Upsala, and for the first time sang the National Anthem of Scandinavia, which proclaimed the unity in diversity of their three nations (*Skjont han er Tremde*).

When the Germans invaded Schleswig-Holstein, many Swedes and Norwegians (especially students stirred by the 'Nordic Renaissance') rallied to defend the frontier of the 'Scandinavian Fatherland' on the River Eider. It is estimated that the Swedes had concentrated some eight thousand men in Scania for eventual operations, and in the last campaign the Danes were assisted by a squadron of Norwegians and Swedes under the command of the Duke of Uppland. The King of Sweden, on the other hand, had helped to prepare the Malmö Armistice Treaty and had agreed to share the occupation of Schleswig-Holstein with the Germans until 1850. So faith in Scandinavian unity was somewhat premature.

The liberals in Norway and Sweden stood out against German imperialism, as they detested its authoritarian and feudal character, but their opposition was a purely intellectual one. Norway and Sweden were not threatened by any foreign power and Denmark alone fully appreciated the fact that the Germans of Schleswig-Holstein had behind them the full support of the King of Prussia, and therefore the whole weight of *Deutschtum*.

Thus in spite of their memories of the Union of Kalmar in 1363, the great defect of Scandinavianism in the nineteenth century was that the northern nations did not season their ardent ideals with the salt of realism. But could it have been otherwise? Scandinavia appeared to be more or less a geographical unity, it is true, and her peoples had certain racial and linguistic affinities with each other, but—it is a big 'but'—each of the Scandinavian countries had fought long and hard for its own independence. And there were geographical and political factors which tended to separate them. Finland had Russia on one flank, who used her as a buffer; Sweden was a Baltic nation and so a long series of conflicts with Russia had put her on the defensive; and Denmark was semi-continental, semi-peninsular, controlling the entrance to the Baltic and also looking out on the North Sea, so she had to beware of Germany. Norway's problem was again a different one. A wholly maritime nation, she seemed to be for ever seeking allies and outlets across the seas. Has it not been said, incidentally, that the Arctic Ocean and its territories are Norway's natural hinterland? The Norwegians bore a grudge against Denmark for having dragged them into a war against England at the beginning of the nineteenth century, for apart from their pro-British sympathies, the people of Christiania wanted to protect their merchant fleet, which, since the suppression of the Hanseatic League's monopoly in 1757, had grown from 80 to 1,150 vessels.

Each country, too, had a different social structure. In Sweden, due largely to the chancellor Axel Oxenstierna in the seventeenth century, the nobility reigned supreme both in their own country and even in Finland. In Norway, on the other hand, despite the mildness of Sweden's rule, their feudalism was fiercely resented. Not only were the Norwegians liberals by nature, but they had acquired a considerable degree of autonomy when under Denmark, and their social classes were highly advanced. In Norway a liberal middle class had developed as a result of international trade. It was the same in Denmark, for since the 1720 treaty with Sweden, Copenhagen had become a port of call for ships sailing between the Baltic and the North Sea and also for those of the West India Company. The Norwegian peasantry, being less heavily taxed than in the other countries, were also more advanced. The peasants of Finland, however, were kept down first by the Swedish nobility and then still more by their Russian masters.

After 1814 Sweden had given up taking any part in European wars, and the peninsula had profited by peace. Trade flourished and liberal theories grew. But the Romantic movement, which indirectly assisted the rise of nationalism, found the Scandinavians lost in their dreams and their illusions. Although a Swede, Tegner, attacked the Stockholm paper *Phosphorus* (the counterpart of the *Globe* in Paris) when it appealed for an understanding of Germany and her philosophy of *Sturm und Drang*, his protests were purely intellectual. 'The conflict', he wrote, 'is between the Germans and Reason—between the ephemeral and the eternal.' Some decades later a German, Arndt, replied by threatening the Danes: ' . . . hatred will rebound on the heads of this vain and vicious little race which is germinating in our midst like a deadly seed.'

Germanism had indeed been born, and it did not need a *Turnvater* [1] like old Jahn as a wet nurse: it had the support of a whole dynamic race, the course of whose political and social development had been largely changed by the Napoleonic Wars. The Scandinavian countries had not developed in the same way, for, with peace assured and with their Lutheran sense of order and discipline and their capacity for hard work, they had been able to make striking moral and material progress. This in its turn made them

[1] Teacher of gymnastics (Tr.)

increasingly peace-loving; besides which they imagined that their geographical features alone protected them from any would-be invader.

That then was the situation in Scandinavia in the early days of 1848. Its component countries were united by their common memory of the Union of Kalmar, and also by their conflicts one with the other, which led in the end to mutual understanding. On the other hand, their geographical positions and consequent interests divided them when it came to dealing with Germany, their common enemy in the years to come, for there was no longer a sovereign capable of uniting them as Princess Margaret had done in 1389, when she won the victory of Falköping over the German forces of the Prince of Mecklenburg. That had been a victory of the North over Germanism.

But the spirit of the peoples of Scandinavia was no longer the same.

GREAT BRITAIN
AND THE REVOLUTION OF 1848
J. P. T. BURY

*However terrible the storm of the moment may appear to the younger men
among us, I am firmly persuaded that the times are in our favour, that is, in
favour of the cause of constitutional freedom under the aegis of Monarchy.
Therefore it now behoves us here in England to come forward as an exemplar,
and to prove to Europe that the monarchical constitution is the
strongest bulwark of genuine possible freedom*
Sir R. Peel to Baron Stockmar, *cit.* T. Martin, 'The Life of
H.R.H. The Prince Consort', ii, 30

WHEN the revolutionary movement on the Continent had laid
prostrate almost all its Governments . . . England alone displayed that
order, vigour and prosperity which it owes to a stable, free and good
Government.' [1] Thus wrote Queen Victoria in December 1851 with
pardonable pride. During the great year of revolutions, 1848, Great
Britain and Russia alone among the Great Powers had stood fast amid
the upheavals which had shaken nearly every other European state save
Sweden and Belgium. Yet her ties with the Continent were too close for
England to view the revolutionary wave without anxiety. As one of the
Great Powers and one of the signatories of the Treaties of Vienna she
could not look with indifference upon changes which threatened to
transform both the character of government and the balance of power.
For a moment, indeed, the repercussions of those changes appeared to
menace her own good order. Traditionally hospitable, she gave asylum
to countless refugees of high and low degree, and all of these brought with
them their hopes and fears and passionate interest in the vicissitudes of
continental politics. Moreover, some of the most illustrious of these
exiles, men such as Metternich and Guizot, alleged that it was the mis-
guided policy of Great Britain which was in large measure responsible
for the disorders of which they were the victims. Thus, although Great
Britain herself had no revolution, it is not inappropriate to include in this

[1] Lord E. Fitzmaurice: *The Life of Granville George Leveson Gower, second Earl Granville*, I,
page 48

volume some brief survey of her relations with the Continent during these stirring times; to enquire whether by accident or design she contributed to the revolutionary movement; to examine its influence upon her foreign policy; and to ask how far it affected events at home.

Upon the conclusion of the Napoleonic wars Great Britain had once again renewed contact with the Continent, from many parts of which she had long been more or less wholly isolated, and in the years after 1815 Europe and the island kingdom were more than ever aware of their interdependence. As an example of a constitutional monarchy which had survived the storms of the great Revolution England and English institutions enjoyed a new prestige; as one of the principal victors in the war she was necessarily concerned to uphold the peace settlement which she had had a large share in making; as the pioneer of the industrial revolution she sought continental markets for her manufactures, while Western Europe went technically to school in Britain or learnt the new industrial secrets from skilled British workmen who visited the mainland.[1] Economically and politically, therefore, she was linked to the Continent perhaps more closely than at any time since the surrender of the last of her dominions in France. Very recently, indeed, the French Revolution of 1830 had shown how sensitive she might be to political change on the mainland, for the passing of the Great Reform Bill in London in 1832 owed not a little to the upheaval in Paris in 1830. In view of these considerations we might therefore expect that an economic depression of some severity in Great Britain in 1846 and 1847 would leave its mark upon the Continent and that the continental revolutions of 1848 would have serious repercussions in Great Britain.

If, however, we first examine the economic crisis, we shall find it extremely difficult to assess the extent to which it contributed to the continental unrest that culminated in the 1848 revolutions. Much more detailed work by economic historians will probably be necessary before its effects can be accurately gauged. None the less, the broad outlines are fairly clear. There can be little question that the most widespread and fundamental causes of European suffering and unrest in 1846 and 1847, as in 1946 and 1947, were bad weather and shortage of food. The European corn harvests of 1845–7 were generally poor and the blight which befell the potato crops of the northern part of the Continent from Ireland to Silesia aggravated the widespread suffering. In France these misfortunes accentuated a financial crisis which was already brewing as a result of

[1] As a result of the economic crisis in France after the Revolution of February 1848, many of these were obliged to return to England and did so in a very anti-French spirit. (*vide* E. Halévy, *Histoire du peuple anglais*, IV, page 231)

over-speculation in railways and of an excessive absorption of capital by State loans and public works. The outcome was an industrial and commercial depression, owing to a shortage of capital for investment and to the shrinkage in markets at home and abroad. Between 1 July 1846 and 1 January 1847, the gold reserve of the Bank of France fell from 252 to 80 million francs and something like a panic ensued. The Bank was obliged to follow the example already set in Britain of raising the discount rate to 5 per cent and to obtain a credit of £1,000,000 through Barings from the Bank of England. In Great Britain, however, similar causes were at the same time leading to similar results. Exceptionally large imports of corn and heavy calls on railway shares, many of them foreign railways, led to a drain of gold abroad, and the treasure in the Bank of England decreased by £4,000,000 during the first quarter of 1847. In the autumn of that year several firms which had speculated in corn went bankrupt, others engaged in colonial trade came to grief, and a number of private and joint-stock banks were obliged to close their doors. The crisis was such that the Government was forced to suspend Peel's Bank Charter Act of 1844 which limited the issue of bank notes.

There is no doubt that this English crisis, with its consequent tightening of the British money market, led to a sharp decrease in Continental investments by British stockholders and thus worked to Europe's detriment. British capital was no longer as free as it would otherwise have been to come to the aid of French and other enterprises, and the industrial and commercial depression in Europe was therefore intensified, particularly in France. In so far as the English crisis had this result it certainly contributed to increase the sense of instability and lack of confidence which infected some even of the staunchest adherents of the Orléans monarchy on the eve of the 1848 revolution. But it would on present evidence be difficult to claim that its influence was decisive or to say more than that it added one further disturbing element to a situation which was already disturbed for other reasons. In the less industrialised countries which were to suffer from revolution, such as Germany and Italy, its effects were undoubtedly still less important.

If England's involuntary economic contribution to continental revolution is thus difficult to assess, what of the contribution of that revolution to England's economic difficulties? The short answer is clear and with it we must be content in this brief survey. It introduced no new element into the situation, but only served to prolong the already existing depression. The French Revolution had a paralysing effect on business in France and so reduced imports of British goods and intensified unemployment in Great Britain. This and the political stimulus of upheaval abroad contributed to a renewal of the Chartist agitation at home which in turn was further discouraging to a speedy revival of trade. Moreover, the upheavals abroad still further postponed the return of the British investor to the field of continental enterprise.

We must now turn to the social and political, as distinct from the economic, aspect of Great Britain's relations with the European continent during these troubled years. Did she wittingly or no contribute to the social and political unrest of the Continent and how far did that unrest disturb her own political and social structure?

Perhaps her main and quite involuntary contribution to social unrest lay in the fact that during the years preceding the revolutions her own society came in for increasingly critical examination by foreign observers. Its defects served as a text for social reformers, and when those reformers were men as influential as Louis Blanc and Friedrich Engels this fact was not unimportant; for the revelation of British ills ably expounded in such books as *Die Lage der arbeitenden Klasse in England* contributed not a little to the growing continental consciousness of social wrongs and to the desire to redress them. At the same time England's liberality in providing a refuge for foreign exiles meant that numerous social as well as political revolutionaries found their way to London where they constituted societies of their own, and maintained correspondence with like-minded brethren abroad. Thus, in addition to groups of Poles and Italians, whose main aspirations were political and national rather than social, there were societies like the Parisian Fédération des Justes, largely Swiss and German in its original membership, which reformed in London after 1839 and later merged in the Communist League. It was on English soil that this Communist League was founded in 1847, and in London that the famous *Communist Manifesto* was first printed in 1848. It was from English soil that many of these revolutionaries, from the German communist, Joseph Moll, to the Italian patriot, Joseph Mazzini, set sail in 1848 to take part each in his own revolutionary struggle. Moreover, many of the social revolutionaries had been in touch with the English Chartist agitators. They had studied the ideas and methods of the Chartist movement[1] and approved or rejected them according to their temperament. So, too, the political revolutionaries had been able to observe English constitutional government at work and to watch the operations of those who pressed for further constitutional reform. Thus in this way also, as a refuge and pattern to continental exiles, Great Britain involuntarily contributed to the European revolutionary movement. How far at the same time voluntarily and of set purpose she contributed to it by official advocacy

[1] The Chartist Movement developed towards 1838, its main programme being set forth in the People's Charter with its six demands: (1) universal male suffrage, (2) voting by ballot, (3) redistribution of constituencies, (4) annual Parliaments, (5) abolition of the property qualification required of candidates for Parliament, (6) payment of M.P.s.

of constitutional reforms we must consider later when we come to review her foreign policy.

In the two most highly industrialised of the Great Powers of Europe the economic crises of these years were, as we have seen, perhaps still more striking for their parallelism than for their interdependence. To a certain extent the same may be said of the development of organised working-class movements to obtain redress for social and political grievances. There were similar trends in both Great Britain and France, although the proletariat in Great Britain was much more important than in France where the majority of workers were still artisans or home workers. In general these movements followed national lines and the programmes of English Chartists or Trade Unionists and French Socialists were formulated independently. If the British workman of the nineteen forties is still strongly insular, even more so was his forebear of the eighteen forties, and it is probably true to say that the majority knew little and cared less about foreign countries. None the less, as we have already seen, some of the Chartist leaders entered into contact with the foreign refugees. Not only this, but some of them had continental connections of their own. Feargus O'Connor himself was nephew to a naturalised Frenchman who had married a daughter of Condorcet, and it has been said of him that he was influenced almost as much by the French revolutionary tradition as by his Irish nationalist antecedents. James O'Brien had glorified Robespierre and Babeuf in writings which had a wide circulation. Ernest Jones was born and bred in Germany and had many connections with German revolutionaries; and Lovett had helped to found the society of 'Fraternal Democrats' at whose meeting in November 1847 to commemorate the Polish Revolution Marx made a celebrated appeal for a 'Congress of Nations, a Workers' Congress in order to establish liberty throughout the universe'. In consequence the leaders at least had begun to develop a sense of the international solidarity of the working classes, and it was the pride of Lovett that the message of goodwill to the workers of Belgium sent by the Chartists of the Working Men's Association in 1836 was the first of its kind. Since that time contacts had multiplied and it could be said that many Chartist leaders were in close touch with revolutionary developments on the Continent and that their own movement was watched with increasing interest by would-be continental reformers.

The Chartist movement had declined in the early 'forties as a result of internal divisions and a return of prosperity, and although in July 1847 O'Connor had been elected as the first Chartist member of Parliament its fortunes remained at a low ebb. In view of their continental connections, however, the Chartists were increasingly sensitive to disturbances in Europe, and it was therefore by no means surprising that they hailed the

February Revolution in Paris with enthusiasm and that it gave an immediate and powerful stimulus to their activities, all the more so since the French Provisional Government promptly introduced universal suffrage, which was one of the main points of the English Charter. Congratulatory delegations were promptly sent to greet the new régime. The *Northern Star* declared that 'as France had secured for herself her beloved Republic, so Ireland must have her Parliament restored and England her idolised Charter'.[1] Throughout March, Chartist meetings and demonstrations took place all over the country; tricolours were displayed, cries of '*Vive la République!*' were heard, and sentries at Buckingham Palace were invited to shake hands and 'fraternise as the French have done'. In some towns in the North, notably Glasgow, the demonstrations were accompanied by food riots and serious disturbances which caused much alarm. The climax came early in April when the leaders summoned the Chartist Convention, which decided that a National Assembly should be convoked and remain in session until the Charter had been adopted and that a mass meeting should take place in London on 10 April and convey a third monster petition to the House of Commons.[2] 'Elaborate plans for the constitution of the Chartist Commonwealth', writes the main English historian of the movement, 'were now in the air. The aim of the zealots was a revolutionary assembly that would secure the extension of the Republic from France to England. Even before the Convention had met, O'Connor had sketched in the *Star* an ideal polity which had many affinities with the French Constitution of the Year Three.'[3]

All this agitation naturally caused the authorities grave concern and, warned by the events on the Continent, they took elaborate precautions in case the manifestation of 10 April should lead to serious disturbance or an actual attempt at revolution. Some 17,000 special constables were enrolled to reinforce the ordinary police, among them the future Emperor of the French, Prince Louis Napoleon, and several thousand troops stood by under the command of the aged Duke of Wellington. No attempt was made to prevent the meeting on Kennington Common, but there the Chartist leaders were informed that a procession to the House of Commons would not be allowed. Feargus O'Connor was no revolutionary, but still exercised great sway over his followers. So it was that without any difficulty he could persuade them peaceably to disperse while he himself undertook to present the petition on their behalf. Thus the great demonstration ended in fiasco and in ridicule, which increased when it was found that the petition contained far fewer signatures than the Chartists

---

[1] M. Hovell: *The Chartist Movement*, page 288

[2] The first Petitions had been presented in 1839 and 1842

[3] M. Hovell: *The Chartist Movement*, page 289

alleged and that many of these were humorously bogus, such as 'Victoria Rex' and 'Mr Punch'. The relief was immense and widespread. 'Yesterday', wrote Lord Palmerston joyously on the 11th—he had turned the Foreign Office into a fortress the day before—'was a glorious day, the Waterloo of peace and order . . . the result . . . will produce a good and calming effect over all this and the Sister Island. The foreigners did not show; but the constables, regular and special, had sworn to make an example of any whiskered and bearded rioter whom they might meet with, and I am convinced would have mashed them to jelly'.[1]

Although there were still to be a number of Chartist meetings and disturbances in various parts of the country throughout the summer, the *débâcle* of 10 April effectively spelt the end of Chartism as a social and political force of any consequence. Its demonstrations in 1848 were the most striking repercussion in Great Britain of the revolutionary movement on the Continent, yet it was in a sense killed by that movement, for without the examples of revolution in Paris, Berlin and Vienna before them the Government might have been much less thorough in their precautions. Although individuals among them advocated violence, the Chartists as a whole were neither prepared nor organised for the use of physical force, and, when it was seen that they could achieve nothing by mere agitation, men began to weary of their methods. They were not on the whole vindictively treated by the authorities, but various efforts to inject new life into the movement met no success. The majority of workers fell back on other organisations such as the trade unions, which were virtually unaffected by the continental revolutions, and looked to them for the fulfilment of their most urgent aspirations.

Thus England stood fast. Immediately perhaps the main effect of the Chartist disturbances of 1848 was to discourage concessions to radicalism, and when in 1852 Lord John Russell, influenced by events on the Continent, made electoral reform a chief plank in his programme he met with little response. On the other hand the renewed social agitation among the poorest classes reminded all others who had a sense of responsibility that the 'condition of the people' was still a serious problem. Thus 1848 led J. S. Mill to modify the second and third editions of his *Principles of Political Economy* and inspired the formation of a new group of Christian Socialists under Charles Kingsley. Moreover, it did not put an end to further attempts at social legislation, as witness the Factory Act of 1850 and the Act of 1852 legalising the formation of industrial and provident societies. Politically, however, English stability owed not a little to the fact that, in the words of Elie Halévy, 'the Reform of 1832 . . . had been

[1] E. Ashley: *Life of Palmerston*, I, page 93

so bold as to go beyond the real desire of the population.'[1] Even the conduct of the Chartists themselves to some extent bore witness to the truth in Peel's belief that it was 'confidence in the generosity and justice of Parliament' which in no small degree enabled England to pass triumph- antly through the storm. And, to quote Halévy again, 'there is no doubt about the general feeling. Everybody, irrespective of party, was proud to belong to a nation which had, for more than a century, escaped the opposite excesses of revolution and reaction, and in particular the peril of reaction through revolution; proud to belong to a nation strong and stable enough to receive all those who fled from Paris, Louis Philippe . . . and Guizot, and Louis Blanc some months after, and Ledru-Rollin one year later, all in their turn the victims of the passing moods of the crowd.'[2]

England and Scotland, however, were not the only parts of the British Isles to be disturbed during the revolutionary year. 'I look homewards', wrote Lord Minto from off the coast of Sicily in March, 'with some anxiety and impatience lest Ireland should catch fire from France.'[3] It might indeed have been expected that the risk of serious trouble in Ireland would be grave, for the 'Sister Island' had now for some years been the scene of a powerful movement for repeal of the parliamentary Union with England, it had witnessed the growth of a nationalist party called 'Young Ireland' which went further and aimed at complete independence, it was embittered by a war between landlord and tenant which, according to Lord John Russell, had gone on for eighty years, and it had just been ravaged by the most terrible famine. Yet here, as in England, the attempts of the disaffected to make a bid for power ended in miserable fiasco. As was to be expected, the news of the Paris Revolution at once inflamed the hopes of the nationalists. Hitherto the Young Irelanders had been divided upon the issue of using armed force to attain their ends, but the European upheavals put an end to the hesitations of the more cautious. On the morrow of the French outbreak, they hastened, like the Chartists, to send a deputation to the Provisional Government, not merely to convey greetings, but also undoubtedly in the hope that the Republic in France would supply material aid for the establishment of a Republic in Ireland. This hope proved vain, for Lamartine, who had already been warned by Palmerston of the risk of jeopardising Anglo-French relations by receiving deputations and giving direct encouragement to political agitators, would offer no help. The March Revolutions in other parts of the Continent, however, gave the men of Young Ireland fresh heart. The call went out to their supporters to arm and drill, and plans were made for the formation

---

[1] A. Coville and H. Temperley: *Studies in Anglo-French History*, page 55
[2] *Ibid.* pages 56, 57
[3] G. P. Gooch: *Later Correspondence of Lord John Russell*, I, page 323

of an Irish National Council and an Irish National Guard with which to carry through the eventual revolution. All this was not unobserved by the Government, who naturally took precautions and increased the number of troops in the island. John Mitchel, one of the most fanatical of the Young Ireland leaders, was arrested, prosecuted for sedition and sentenced to transportation for several years, and in July the Habeas Corpus Act was suspended. These measures led the conspirators to act prematurely. Smith O'Brien, like Feargus O'Connor a member of Parliament, joined two others in the south and planned to capture Kilkenny and raise Tipperary. But, in the words of an Irish historian, 'Kilkenny was not ready . . . In Cashel no one stirred'.[1] Only a handful of people answered the rebel call and the rising was crushed with ease. Those of the Young Ireland leaders who escaped capture fled into exile, there to nurse their grievances and eventually to hatch the next subversive movement in the shape of Fenianism. With their removal Ireland entered upon a quieter period and in 1849 the Queen and Prince Consort were able to visit the island with safety and success. So, in August 1848, ended the only definite attempt at armed revolution within the British Isles. Hopelessly ill-prepared, mis-timed, unsupported by the majority of Church and people, it had no chance of success.

The repercussions, economic, social and political of the continental revolutions were thus comparatively slight so far as the United Kingdom was concerned and Queen Victoria might well look with satisfaction upon the stability of her realm. More important was the influence of British foreign policy upon the course of events in Europe. With this the Queen was by no means so well pleased, and to some consideration of its character we must now turn.

Foreign policy during this period meant in general the policy of Lord Palmerston, the dominant personality in the Whig Cabinet formed by Lord John Russell in 1846. It was a policy which earned him great popularity with the majority of Whigs and Radicals, but which was much disliked by the Tories, by a large section of upper class society and often by the Queen herself. Yet such was his position in the Cabinet and in the country that she was seldom able to overrule him and struggled vainly to secure his removal to some other office.

Lord Palmerston was nearly sixty-two when in July 1846 he became Foreign Secretary for the third time, but his vigour was quite undiminished. He had held his first ministerial post as long ago as 1809 and had been in charge of the Foreign Office almost continuously from 1830 to 1841; thus he combined a long experience of home politics with a knowledge of foreign affairs unrivalled by any other British statesman of the day. As

[1] S. Gwynn: *History of Ireland*, page 457

one who had been minister while Great Britain was still in the throes of the Napoleonic struggle, he was profoundly convinced of the blessings of peace and of the necessity of maintaining them upon the basis of the Treaties of Vienna; but this did not mean that he was a blind advocate of the sanctity of existing forms of government. On the contrary he believed no less profoundly that constitutional reform was the most efficient barrier to revolution, which like Metternich he held to be the greatest danger to European peace. Minister in a Whig Cabinet, he was still primarily a Canningite, and in foreign affairs that meant that he was heir to what Metternich with high disapproval called the 'Aeolus policy' of Canning. In other words he was opposed to interference by the autocratic and conservative powers of Europe in the affairs of lesser states which sought, peaceably or not, to modify their form of government, and he was inclined to sympathise with or patronise constitutional states and parties. For Metternich and men of his views this meant the encouragement of revolution. The opposition between Palmerston's general principles of constitutionalism and non-intervention and the 'system' of Metternich was complete.

Palmerston's return to the Foreign Office in 1846 was thus a cause of dismay to European conservatives and of hope to European liberals. Disquiet was not confined to the Eastern Powers. It extended also to France, for although in the 'thirties it was Palmerston who had helped to make the Anglo-French Entente, which had done so much to preserve the peace of Europe and to maintain the prestige of the two western constitutional states, in 1840 he had helped to break it by his attitude towards France in the Eastern Question. Much of the damage had been repaired by his successor, Lord Aberdeen, but the rupture of 1840 had sown seeds of distrust which were hard to eradicate, and soon after Palmerston's return to office the Spanish Marriage question came to a head, reopened the breach and, aggravated by suspicion and misunderstanding on both sides, made it wider than ever. Lord Aberdeen might be rightly convinced that 'a good understanding with France is just as necessary now as it was at the moment when the Entente was most cordial and intimate', and rightly add that 'This marriage is not an adequate cause of national quarrel'[1]; but a good understanding between the France of Guizot and the England of Palmerston had become impossible. Palmerston was furious because he believed he had been tricked, and an acute observer deduced from a conversation with Lady Palmerston that her husband's 'fixed idea was to humble France and make her feel her humiliation'.[2] Guizot for his part was no less resentful. While Palmer-

[1] R. W. Seton-Watson: *Britain in Europe 1789-1914*, page 246
[2] *The Greville Diary*, ed. by P. W. Wilson, II, page 260

ston, afraid of a French invasion, vainly urged his colleagues to create a big militia, Guizot contemplated the formation of a Quadruple Alliance against England. Relations could hardly have been worse.

Can it be said that this unfortunate breach and the hostile policy now pursued by Palmerston towards France in any way contributed to the French Revolution of 1848? There can be little doubt that the rupture of the Entente was a blow to the Guizot Government. France was now isolated and her policy abroad too often failed owing to British opposition. Moreover, although Louis Philippe and Guizot were ready enough to seek escape from isolation by forming closer ties with the Eastern Powers, such co-operation was far less palatable to public opinion in France, which was beginning to be highly critical of the Government on other counts. The importance attributed to Britain's attitude is remarkably emphasised by a passage in the memoirs of the Baron de Barante: commenting late in 1847 on the growing criticism of the Guizot Government, he remarks that 'the circumstance which would have the greatest influence would be a change of ministry in England'.[1] It is also true that, not content with humiliating Guizot abroad, Palmerston sought to attack him at home. It is known that he had indirect contact with Thiers, both through Panizzi, the future Librarian of the British Museum, and through the British Ambassador, Lord Normanby, who became intimate with various leaders of the French opposition. He provided material at one time for an opposition attack upon Guizot in Parliament and he and Normanby certainly both personally sympathised with the cause of parliamentary reform in France. It is equally certain that the reform campaign was inspired by the example and methods of British reforming movements such as the Anti-Corn Law League. All this, however, hardly justifies Guizot's complaint to Disraeli after the Revolution that 'Palmerston had done it all by his patronage of Thiers and the encouragement that Normanby etc gave to the Reform Banquets'.[2] Palmerston's conduct may have been very questionable; he certainly aimed at the discomfiture and possibly at the overthrow of the ministry; but this was a very different matter from working for the revolutionary overthrow of the régime.

In fact, Palmerston was too much concerned for peace to play any such dangerous game. The treaties of 1815 might not be permanently operative, but where their arrangements broke down he held that they should be modified only by the peaceful agreement of all the powers concerned. Unfortunately in 1846 the Eastern Courts had seized the opportunity afforded by the rift between England and France to override the Vienna settlement and to connive at the Austrian annexation of Cracow without

[1] Baron de Barante: Souvenirs, VII, page 273
[2] W. F. Monypenny and G. E. Buckle: The Life of Benjamin Disraeli, I, page 993

reference to the Western Powers. Palmerston was justly indignant and, although his official protest was surprisingly mild, he cogently pointed out that the Eastern Powers had infringed their own principles. 'The Treaty of Vienna', he said, 'must be respected as a whole. If it be not good on the Vistula, it may be equally bad on the Po'.[1] In the following year, by taking a firm stand on the Treaty, he was able to prevent foreign intervention in Switzerland, with the dangers to European peace which might have resulted, to turn the tables on the Eastern Powers and to give successful support to a liberal cause.

Religious and constitutional difficulties which had long been growing in intensity came to a head in Switzerland in July 1847, when the Federal Diet, which sought to expel the Jesuits and to reform the federal constitution in a liberal sense, pronounced the dissolution of the *Sonderbund* or League which had been formed by seven Catholic cantons for the defence of their religious and political interests. Thereupon the seven cantons seceded and civil war followed.

This breakdown in the constitutional arrangements of a state whose neutrality and independence had been guaranteed at Vienna was a matter of immediate concern to the Great Powers. Metternich was eager to intervene, for as the asylum of many objectionable political refugees Switzerland appeared to him to be a hotbed of conspiracy and its Diet a dangerously radical body. But Palmerston stood out against any interference to meddle with the revision of the Federal Compact, and his stand enabled the Federal troops to win a decisive victory before a European Conference could be called. Thus on the small but central stage of Switzerland there was a trial of strength between the forces of liberalism and conservatism which was watched with extraordinary interest by the rest of Europe; and, although Austria was Switzerland's immediate neighbour and the sympathies of Russia and Prussia were with the *Sonderbund*, it was the liberals and Palmerston who won.

Nowhere did this contest arouse greater passion than in Italy. Elie Halévy has said that the revolutions of 1848 originated not in France but with the civil war in Switzerland in 1847.[2] They might, however, be ascribed to a still earlier event in Italy, the election in 1846 of a liberal Pope in the person of Pius IX. That remarkable occurrence, the only thing which Metternich said he had not foreseen, aroused extraordinary enthusiasm, and was the signal for a wave of liberal activity throughout the peninsula.

Palmerston had been quick to perceive that the situation in Italy was dangerous. 'Italy', he had told Lord John Russell in July 1846, 'is the weak

[1] R. W. Seton-Watson: *Britain in Europe, 1789–1914*, page 250
[2] A. Coville and H. Temperley: *Studies in Anglo-French History*, page 54

part of Europe, and the next war that breaks out in Europe will probably arise out of Italian affairs'.[1] His policy was clear and characteristic. It was to encourage the Pope and the other Italian sovereigns to follow the path of reform and to exercise such British influence in the peninsula that they should be able to do so undeterred by the hope or fear of intervention by France or Austria. Austria appeared most likely to be the chief obstacle to this policy, for already in July 1847 Metternich had caused Austrian troops to occupy the Papal city of Ferrara. Thus in his language to Austria, while carefully avoiding any specific threat, Palmerston sought to convey the impression that any further military pressure would oblige Great Britain to take similar measures. In this he had the warm support of a large section of British opinion which had long been extremely sympathetic to Italian liberal and national aspirations. Furthermore, in order to make the British attitude still clearer and to strengthen British influence still more, he despatched a Cabinet Minister, Lord Minto, on what Disraeli was to describe as 'a very peculiar roving mission . . . to teach politics in the country in which Machiavelli was born'.[2] In fact, he was to advise the reforming sovereigns upon constitutional questions, to give them the impression that Britain would support them, and at the same time to restrain the impatience of the more ardent liberals.

Minto's tour was a triumphal progress. Many upper-class Italians had long been strongly Anglophil; several of the nobility took the English aristocracy as their model, and economists and business men looked to England as the Mecca of material progress. Now, not long after an unofficial visit by Cobden, the hero of free trade, came the journey of the Lord Privy Seal, which for every Anglophil and liberal Italian was the confirmation that Britain was Italy's foremost champion. Vainly did the Austrian Ambassador represent to Palmerston that British policy was serving French not British interests. As the future Duke Albert de Broglie, then a young diplomat in Rome, was sadly to note in his memoirs, Lord Minto had 'no sooner put his foot on Italian soil . . . than . . . every one believed or said that he had come to give Italian liberals and patriots the support refused them by M. Guizot'[3]; and Lord Minto himself wrote in January 1848 that Louis Philippe was 'almost forgotten'.[4]

'From what I am told', Minto reported at the end of September 1847 from Turin, 'I see little reason at present to apprehend any extensive or serious movements for Italian unity';[5] and nearly six weeks later he wrote with satisfaction from Rome of 'the sober and orderly progress of the

[1] H. C. F. Bell: *Lord Palmerston*, I, page 412
[2] W. F. Monypenny and G. E. Buckle: *The Life of Benjamin Disraeli*, I, page 999
[3] *Mémoires du Duc de Broglie*, I, page 169
[4] G. P. Gooch; *The Later Correspondence of Lord John Russell*, I, page 320
[5] *Ibid.*, l, page 312

great Italian revolution'.[1] This was exactly what Palmerston wanted, the orderly reform of institutions without foreign intervention, war, or territorial upheaval; but it was not to last. Switzerland saw the first armed struggle of the 'forties between the forces of liberalism and conservatism; Italy, not France, produced the first armed revolution of 1848; and within a few months there was war in the peninsula and a new prospect both of foreign intervention and of sweeping territorial change.

Lord Minto was still in Italy when the first revolution broke out. His visits to the North Italian courts had been brief, but in Rome he stayed for no less than three months. This was important, for whereas neither Austria nor France was as yet inclined to intervene in Piedmont or Tuscany, both were disposed to step in to save the Papal States from what Metternich regarded as anarchy; and it is probable that Palmerston deliberately prolonged Minto's stay in order to discourage such intervention. It was not, however, in the Papal States, but in a part of Italy not yet visited by the British Minister that revolution first occurred. On 12 January 1848 the Sicilians broke into revolt and demanded that the King should grant them the Constitution of 1812 which they had enjoyed under English occupation at the close of the Napoleonic wars. Within a short time they had cleared the island of Neapolitan troops, and King Ferdinand in alarm had granted a constitution to both Naples and Sicily, but not the Constitution of 1812. Palmerston's policy in face of this emergency was wholly characteristic. He discouraged Austrian intervention by once more conveying the impression that England would be forced to take the opposite side and that a general war would ensue; he seized the opportunity to point out to all British representatives in Italy that the revolution might have been averted had the King of Naples been willing to grant moderate reforms; and he despatched Lord Minto to try and bring about a settlement between the King and his discontented subjects. Minto did his utmost to secure an arrangement which would preserve the allegiance of the Sicilians to the Neapolitan Crown, but Palmerston not unnaturally refused to underwrite it with a British guarantee; and then, in Minto's words, the February Revolution broke out in Paris and 'turned the heads and raised the demands of the Palermitans'.[2] They became intransigent and Minto was obliged to abandon his task. In fact, the French Revolution not only complicated the Sicilian situation but also speedily transformed the European scene. The greater part of the old European order now came tumbling down, half the capital cities were engulfed by revolution, half the statesmen known to Palmer-

---

[1] G. P. Gooch: *The Later Correspondence of Lord John Russell*, I, page 315
[2] *Ibid.*, I, page 322

ston were in hiding or flight. He had at once to adjust himself and British policy to new problems and new men.

But before we see how Palmerston reacted to the new situation we must pause to enquire how far he had contributed to bring it about. For Metternich and others of his way of thinking it was largely 'the infernal rôle' of Palmerston which was responsible. Enough has been said to show that the avoidance of revolution and all the dangers which it might unleash, through the encouragement of timely reform was the whole aim of his policy; and up to a point it was successful. He had prevented foreign intervention in Switzerland and in Italy and he had helped to secure a considerable measure of reform in orderly conditions. His very success, however, to some extent increased the danger he wished to avoid, for excitable southern liberals were more easy to encourage than to restrain, and Minto, the ardent Whig, was perhaps not the best man to exercise restraint in the Italy of 1847. There is no reason at all to suppose that either he or Palmerston desired or connived at the Sicilian revolt, although Palmerston sympathised with it more strongly than with any other revolutionary cause—not least, perhaps, because of the discomfiture it was likely to cause M. Guizot—and later supplied the Sicilians with arms; but it is highly probable that Palmerston's policy in Switzerland and Italy together with Minto's visit raised in the minds of the Sicilian rebels both the confident expectation that they were sure of British support if they rose to demand the 'British' Constitution of 1812 and the belief that there could be no better time for doing so than when Minto was at Rome. In so far as it failed to prevent revolution before February 1848, Palmerston's policy was thus a failure; but in so far as it had averted a general war it was a success, and, as we shall see, it continued to be a success.

The victory of the Republicans in Paris not only excited liberal and radical enthusiasm all over Europe; it also called up visions of a new crusade by a revolutionary France for the emancipation of peoples and the overthrow of the 1815 settlement. Metternich hoped that Great Britain would at last see reason and join with Austria in reforming the Grand Alliance, but Palmerston replied by once more drawing the moral that only reform could avert revolution and by suggesting that Austria should grant liberal institutions to Lombardy. At the same time he urged the King of Prussia to lose no time in completing his constitutional arrangements, suggested that the Tsar should give Poland 'a good constitution',[1] and invited the Queen of Spain to take in some more liberally minded ministers, with the result that the British Ambassador was requested to leave that country within forty-eight hours!

In fact, although he grieved at the prospect of a Republic in France,

[1] E. Ashley: *Life of Palmerston*, I, pages 84, 91

because it increased the danger of a general war, Palmerston was more cautious in his attitude than Metternich and more perspicacious. He sensed that the France of 1848 was more like the France of 1830 than that of 1793, and accordingly he hoped to repeat the tactics of 1830, to strengthen the hand of the moderate elements in the new Government, and by the exercise of tact and patience to avoid war instead of provoking it. 'Our principles of action', he told Lord Normanby on 26 February, 'are to acknowledge whatever rule may be established with apparent prospect of permanency, but none other. We desire friendship and extended commercial intercourse with France, and peace between France and the rest of Europe. We will engage to prevent the rest of Europe from meddling with France. . . . The French rulers must engage to prevent France from assailing any part of the rest of Europe. Upon such a basis our relations with France may be placed on a footing more friendly than they have been or were likely to be with Louis Philippe and Guizot'.[1] Accordingly the British Government's attitude was conciliatory, although Palmerston at once emphasised that they would tolerate no meddling with Belgium. It is perhaps questionable whether the Tories would have been equally accommodating had they been in power. At any rate, they were reported to be highly incensed by Lamartine's famous circular referring to the 1815 Treaties, whereas Lord John Russell agreed with Palmerston that they should ignore the provocative passages and 'take M. Lamartine's professions in the most pacific sense without relying too much on his power to make good his means'.[2] Such indeed was the force of Palmerston's coolness at this time and so evident was his zeal to keep the peace that even the King of Prussia could write to Queen Victoria thanking Providence 'for having placed Lord Palmerston at the head of your Foreign Office, and keeping him there at this very moment'.[3] Queen Victoria's reply is unfortunately not recorded! None the less, although the peaceableness of the new French régime soon became apparent, the situation in France continued to give anxiety. Thus on 26 April Palmerston wrote to Lord John Russell that 'a procession of 300,000, or even of 200,000 armed men in Paris augurs but ill for the future peace of Europe. I trust that we may be able to keep out of war, but there can be no doubt that there exists in France a feeling of hostility to England'.[4] Above all he was concerned lest Radical pressure should compel the French to intervene by force in the affairs of Italy.

Italy was still as he had called it in July 1846, 'the weak part of Europe'; and in that letter he had expressed the fear that 'the ascendancy of the

[1] E. Ashley: *Life of Palmerston*, I, page 77
[2] G. P. Gooch: *The Later Correspondence of Lord John Russell*, I, page 293
[3] *Cambridge History of British Foreign Policy*, II, page 308
[4] G. P. Gooch: *The Later Correspondence of Lord John Russell*, I, page 294

liberal party at Paris, whenever it may happen . . . will soon be followed
by an outbreak in Italy. That is the point to which the French liberals
look; they know that if they tried to get back to the Rhine they would
have against them all Germany united, Russia, and more or less England;
but in supporting an insurrection in Italy . . . they would stand in a very
different position'.[1] Such intervention, however, would inevitably produce a counter move by Austria: 'France and Austria would then fight
each other in Italy, and France would have all the Italians on her side.
But the war begun in Italy would probably spread to Germany, and at
all events we can have no wish to see Austria broken down and France
aggrandised.' This acute diagnosis also betrayed Palmerston's old distrust
of the France which had overrun Europe in the time of Napoleon and
the importance he attached to Austria as an essential factor in the European
balance of power.

The danger of French intervention seemed more than ever acute during
the months following the February Revolution, and one of Palmerston's
last communications to Metternich was to adjure him to concert joint
measures with Sardinia in case of a French attempt to invade North Italy.
But on 13 March Metternich himself was overthrown and the paralysis
of government in Austria was speedily followed by risings in Austrian
Italy and the expulsion of the Austrian garrisons from Venice and Milan.
The call for an Italian crusade to drive the foreigner from the peninsula
for ever was now irresistible, and the Lombard revolt was soon followed
by a Sardinian declaration of war. Palmerston had done his best to dissuade
the Sardinian Government from such a course, but the King knew only
too well that, if he did not give the lead which all Italy awaited, a Republican movement within his own dominions was likely to gain such
force as to sweep him from his throne.

Events now moved so swiftly and the Italian forces made such headway
against the Austrians that Palmerston was obliged to reconsider the whole
Italian situation. As ever concerned primarily to avoid the risk of a general
war, he now came to think that Austria 'would be much better out of
Italy than in it',[2] and that the best solution would be for 'the whole of
Northern Italy to be united into one kingdom'. Such an arrangement, he
told the King of the Belgians, would be 'most conducive to the peace of
Europe by interposing between France and Austria a neutral state strong
enough to make itself respected, and sympathising in its habits and
character neither with France nor with Austria'.[3] It is interesting to note
that he did not entertain any notion of a united Italy and that he did not

[1] H. C. F. Bell: *Lord Palmerston*, I, page 412

[2] E. Ashley: *Life of Palmerston*, I, page 102

[3] E. Ashley: *Life of Palmerston*, I, page 98

GREAT BRITAIN

believe that relinquishment of her Italian dominions need entail any real diminution of Austria's strength. The maintenance of the Austrian Empire was still 'an object of general interest to all Europe and to no country more than England',[1] and he was soon advocating the abdication of the imbecile Emperor Ferdinand in order that the Empire might have a real head and be strengthened thereby.

Now that war had broken out Palmerston hoped that it might be brought to a speedy conclusion by a decisive Italian victory. Each week's prolongation of hostilities increased the risk of French intervention and at the beginning of May a menacing proclamation to his troops by the Commander of the French Army of the Alps and a resolution passed by the French National Assembly suggested that such a move was imminent. In point of fact the alarm passed and the French authorities were soon preoccupied by fresh internal difficulties; but it was sufficient to induce the Austrian Government, already favourably impressed by the expressions of goodwill conveyed by one of Palmerston's special envoys, to send a representative to London to seek British good offices for the negotiation of a settlement. After a struggle between Palmerston and the more strongly pro-Italian members of the Cabinet it was agreed to inform Baron Hummelauer that Her Majesty's Government would be ready to set on foot a negotiation on the basis of the cession of Lombardy and of 'such portions of the Venetian Territory as may be agreed upon between the respective Parties'.[2]

This proposed British mediation came to nothing, not only because the basis was hardly attractive to the Austrians, but also because the Italians insisted on the cession of South Tyrol as well as the whole of Lombardy and Venetia. In these circumstances Austria preferred to continue to try the fortune of war. Meanwhile, after the suppression of the June rising the French Government appeared to have attained a great stability, but it had not lost interest in Italy. In fact, both the French and the British Governments were in a very similar position. Neither wished to be involved in war, yet both wished to exercise influence in the peninsula. The main difference was that the French opposed while the British favoured the establishment of a strong North Italian kingdom. Not wanting war, the French Government now also considered offering mediation and, having first sounded Austria without much success, they approached Palmerston about a joint move. After an initial refusal, Palmerston quickly fell in with the idea, for on 25 July it was the Austrians, not the Italians, who won a decisive victory at Custozza. At once the danger arose that the Italians would send an urgent appeal to France for

[1] R. W. Seton-Watson: *Britain in Europe, 1789–1914*, page 259
[2] A. J. P. Taylor: *The Italian Problem in European Diplomacy*, page 110

aid which the French Government would find impossible to withhold. Normanby, indeed, seeing 'no means of preventing a war that might become European, except in the combined action of the British and French Cabinets to reach an arrangement between the belligerent parties',[1] committed Palmerston on his own responsibility to such a combined action and was warmly approved. Although the later conduct of the Cavaignac Government certainly supports the argument that France never intended to go to war in any event, this was far from obvious from the state of French opinion and the state of mind of some of the French rulers at the time, and Palmerston therefore had some justification for his subsequent claim in the House of Commons that he had 'joined France in a mediation which prevented European war'.

This new Anglo-French 'Entente', as it was ironically called by Queen Victoria,[2] who could not so soon reconcile herself to the idea of co-operation with French Republicans, also came into effect at this time in the affairs of Southern Italy. The King of Naples had by now begun a reconquest of Sicily which was accompanied by such barbarities that French and British Admirals combined to enforce an armistice and the two Governments tried once more to bring about a settlement. Sicilian intransigence, however, once again proved too much for them. Their mediation in the north was scarcely more successful. Although the offer to mediate was accepted with alacrity by the Sardinians, who concluded an armistice on 9 August, the Austrians were far less eager, and their delay was no doubt encouraged by the knowledge that Queen Victoria and an important section of British society strongly disapproved of Palmerston's policy. Moreover, the French were to be further embarrassed by the action of the Venetians in repudiating the armistice, re-establishing a Republic and appealing to them for aid. Once again the danger of armed intervention by France loomed in view. Palmerston's reaction was characteristic: 'For my own part, thinking that the Austrians are intruders in Italy and that their expulsion would be no real injury to them and a great blessing to the Italians, and believing that if the French were to enter Italy the Austrians would be swept clean out of it, I should on that account be rather glad than sorry to see a French army cross the Alps; but then if it went in on its own account it would of course turn its success to its own account, and would settle all matters as the French Government might choose. We should be put upon the shelf and England would cut but a sorry figure in Europe. My own opinion is that, if France is to act anywhere in Italy she ought to be tied up by a previous agreement with us as to the extent of her action'.[3] But Palmerston's colleagues

[1] A. J. P. Taylor: *The Italian Problem in European Diplomacy*, page 138
[2] *Letters of Queen Victoria, 1837–61*, II, page 186
[3] G. P. Gooch: *The Later Correspondence of Lord John Russell*, I, page 340

overruled him: they were alarmed at the prospect of any deeper commit-
ment in Italy and would hear of no such previous agreement for limited
action, so that when Cavaignac suggested a joint Anglo-French occupation of Venice Palmerston was obliged to be evasive. The French were
only saved from the awkward necessity of going to Venice alone or of
refusing the Venetian appeal outright by the sudden decision of Austria
to accept the offer of mediation.

But the peace negotiations hung fire, first of all because of Austrian
tactics, and then because of the presidential election in France, which
brought Louis Napoleon to power, and of a new revolution in Austria
which placed Schwarzenberg in control of Austrian policy. Schwarzenberg had no intention of ceding any territory and quickly realised that
France had no eagerness to secure Lombardy for Sardinia. He therefore
aimed at courting France, not England, and eventually at finding a
pretext for renouncing the mediation altogether. The British proposals
of June 1848 were now a thing of the past, and Palmerston was gradually
and reluctantly convinced that his dream of a great North Italian kingdom
had vanished, that Austria could not be induced to yield any part of her
Italian dominions and that no one could force her to do so. His only
object now could be to bring about a mediated peace as soon as possible.
But the Brussels Conference designed for this purpose never opened,
because Palmerston's refusal to accede to a brusque demand from Schwarzenberg for a written assurance beforehand 'that the territorial limits
recognised by the treaties (of 1815) were recognised'[1] gave the Austrian
the excuse he desired to withdraw from the negotiation. It was of course
impossible for Palmerston to give any such assurance; not only was it
incompatible with the rôle of mediator, but it would have had a disastrous
effect upon Italian opinion and greatly angered the English liberal public
on whose support the British Government mainly depended.

Meanwhile, as month succeeded month and peace negotiations were
continually deferred, the Sardinians became increasingly impatient and
eventually on 12 March 1849, in spite of strong British and French efforts
to dissuade them, they renewed hostilities only to meet with a swift and
crushing defeat at Novara. Once again they appealed to Britain and
France, but both had by now had enough of mediation and neither was
prepared to go to war on behalf of the Sardinian King. They contented
themselves with urging greater moderation upon Austria in the pro-
tracted peace negotiations which now at last ensued. It is true that there
was one further alarm in July, when a new French Foreign Minister
displayed interventionist tendencies and suggested a joint Anglo-French
expedition to Genoa to defend Sardinian interests; but the British Cabinet

[1] A. J. P. Taylor: *The Italian Problem in European Diplomacy*, page 211

was no more inclined for such a venture than it had been in the previous September. 'The Queen's Government wants Italy pacified as soon as possible. All our efforts are towards that end'[1]—such was the final word of British policy in the tangle of Italian affairs which had resulted from the 1848 revolutions. But in the North it was Austria who effected the pacification by force of arms and on the basis of the territorial settlement of 1815; and in the Papal States, where the murder of the Prime Minister in November 1848 had led to the flight of the Pope, anarchy and the proclamation of a Roman Republic, the 'pacification' was effected by the forces of the very nation whom Palmerston had striven so long to keep out of Italy. In April 1849, French troops occupied Civita Vecchia and two months later they entered Rome. This time, however, the danger of a clash with Austria, which might have been still more grave than in 1848, was averted because the Austrians were fully occupied by a serious revolt in Hungary. France was left with a free hand and Palmerston could only urge her not to permit the Pope to return to his capital unless he gave adequate constitutional guarantees, and attempt to persuade the Pope to confirm the Constitution he had granted in 1848. These exhortations were vain, and in private letters Palmerston did not conceal his irritation. The French Government was able to go its own way and England now seemed really to be 'on the shelf'. Yet there was an important difference in the circumstances of the French intervention of 1849 and the threatened interventions of 1848. Then France would have entered Italy as a liberator, now she posed rather as a guardian of order anxious to maintain French influence by hook or by crook. There can be little doubt that Palmerston appreciated the difference and foresaw that her new rôle might give France more embarrassment than profit. This was perhaps his main consolation for not being able to exert British influence to more effect.

We have dwelt so fully upon the Italian question because it more than any other was a source of continual anxiety to the British Foreign Secretary and because British public opinion was so keenly interested in it. Moreover, it illustrates very clearly the aims and methods of British policy during the revolutionary period and the difficulties with which Palmerston had to contend both at home and abroad.[2] Before we turn in conclusion to consider the effect of this policy as a whole we must first glance briefly at the two other main storm centres of Europe in 1848–9.

The Hungarian revolt, which began in March 1848, and helped to divert Austrian attention from the Papal States, was also to lead to events which roused strong feelings in England. For Palmerston, however,

[1] A. J. P. Taylor: *The Italian Problem in European Diplomacy*, page 230

[2] This summary has been largely based on Mr. A. J. P. Taylor's excellent study: *The Italian Problem in European Diplomacy, 1847–1849* (Manchester, 1934)

Hungary and Austrian Italy were very different matters. Lombardy and Venetia were Austrian by virtue of the Treaty of Vienna which was an European concern, but Hungary he regarded as an integral part of the Austrian Empire whose maintenance, as we have seen, he strongly believed to be 'a European necessity'.[1] Thus despite strong Liberal sympathies in England for the Hungarians' cause he would give them no encouragement and rebuffed all their endeavours to enter into official contact with the British Government. Moreover, when in April 1849 Kossuth imprudently deposed the Hapsburgs and proclaimed a Hungarian Republic, Palmerston's aloofness turned to active disapproval. He had no wish to see another Republic in Europe or Austria fatally weakened by a separation which could redound only to the profit of Russia. So he hoped that the Hungarians would see reason and come to terms, but if they did not he was prepared to see their rebellion crushed even by the means of Russian aid. This was what in fact happened, and at the end of August 1849 he expressed his relief that the rising was over and his hope that the Austrians would know how to use their victory with moderation, and re-establish the ancient Hungarian constitution. Privately, however, he shared the deep and widespread English indignation at the brutality of the Austrian repression; and publicly he was able to show this by his effective backing of the Turkish refusal to comply with a curt Austrian and Russian demand that the Turkish Government should surrender Kossuth and a number of Hungarian and Polish rebels who had taken refuge on Turkish soil. This was not only a matter of showing disapproval of Austrian and Russian harshness; it was also another incident in the Eastern Question which gave Europe so much trouble. Russia had already taken advantage of the Hungarian revolt to encroach upon the Principalities without Turkish consent and Palmerston was determined that her pressure upon Turkey should go no further. He secured French co-operation and the despatch of the French and British Mediterranean squadrons to the Dardanelles, and supported the Turks with such energy that the two Eastern Powers withdrew their demand. It was one of Palmerston's most striking successes and it was largely due to the fact that he had the British fleet behind him.

There remains one other important region which was disturbed by liberal revolutions, by a surge of nationalism, and by a local war; and of Germany also a word must be said. Towards the introduction of 'good constitutions' in German as in other states, Palmerston was, as ever, sympathetic, and he did not hesitate to say so. But of German attempts to achieve unity he appears to have been sceptical. In general, he had told the Prince Consort in 1847, he believed that England and Germany had a

[1] H. C. F. Bell: *Lord Palmerston*, II, page 14

mutual interest in assisting one another to become 'rich, united and strong',[1] because both were in danger from attack by Russia or by France or by a combination of these two Powers; but he seems to have had no clear policy of supporting any particular solution of the problem of German unity. His coolness was probably due partly to the complexity of the whole problem, partly to the fear that any unity which implied an extension of the Zollverein would be detrimental to English commercial interests; and above all to the unwelcome trend of German nationalism which threatened to produce European complications in Schleswig-Holstein. Here, as we shall see, he acted with energy; but apart from this one instance it cannot be said that the attitude of the British Government had any direct influence upon the course of events in Germany.

The Schleswig-Holstein imbroglio had led to a popular German demand for the incorporation of both duchies in the Germanic Confederation and their severance from Denmark, to a revolt in Schleswig, and to an invasion of Denmark by Prussian and Federal troops. This German advance was halted only by the menacing attitude now adopted by Russia and Sweden, who both viewed with alarm any extension of German control in the Baltic. The problem from Palmerston's point of view was in many ways very similar to that presented by Northern Italy and he tackled it in similar fashion. Having failed to prevent the outbreak of hostilities he aimed at bringing them to an end as soon as possible in order to prevent the danger that the war would spread. He therefore offered British mediation and his offer was accepted by both sides. In fact, however, his own sympathies and those of British opinion as a whole, though not of the Queen, were strongly pro-Danish and his attitude was well summed up in a letter from the Prince Consort to Stockmar: 'The fixed idea here is that Germany's only object in separating Holstein with Schleswig from Denmark is to incorporate them with herself, and then to draw them from the English into the Prussian commercial system; Denmark will then become a State too small to maintain a separate independence, and so the division of European territory and the balance of power will be disturbed'.[2] This no doubt gives an important clue to Palmerston's German policy as a whole. While the unification of Germany might usefully strengthen the balance of power by interposing a stronger force between Russia and France, it was still more important to prevent German nationalism from disturbing the balance of power in the north to the detriment of British commerce and with the risk of provoking a general war in which Russia and Sweden would take a hand. The eventual settlement of the question after long and laborious negotiations

[1] T. Martin: *The Life of the Prince Consort*, I, page 447
[2] *Cambridge History of British Foreign Policy*, II, page 323

under the auspices of the mediating power was, much as in Northern Italy, a virtual return to the *status quo*. As such it could not be more than a temporary expedient, but Great Britain had achieved her main aims: the general war was averted and the balance of power was preserved.

In conclusion we can claim that after the outbreak of revolution in 1848 Great Britain exerted herself as an effective force for peace and that she was successful in the attainment of two main objects, the prevention of a general war and the maintenance of the balance of power. On the other hand, she was unable to prevent war entirely, as Palmerston had wished, and she was obliged to look on at the overthrow of many of the constitutional systems whose erection she had welcomed so warmly. The reason for this was very simple: she herself was essentially pacific and had neither the wish nor the means to exert military force upon the Continent. The success of her foreign policy, therefore, in so far as it was successful, was due to a well-conducted diplomacy, and to the awareness of other Powers that if Britain had no army to speak of she did possess a powerful navy. The British people might well be grateful for a Government which handled Chartist demonstrations and Irish rebellion with firmness and kept the country at peace in a time of singular turmoil.

THE UNITED STATES AND THE
MID-CENTURY REVOLUTIONS

ARTHUR J. MAY

Peace, plenty and contentment reign throughout our borders, and our
country presents a sublime moral spectacle to the world
President James K. Polk—5 December 1848

Oh, joy to the world! the hour is come,
When the nations to freedom awake. . . .
Thomas Buchanan Read—1848

I

As the nineteenth century moved to its mid-point America was in a period of general prosperity, which fostered a feeling of smugness and contentment. Virgin lands in the Middle West were being occupied and worked with labour-saving machinery, a network of railways was being constructed in the East and Middle West, small-scale manufacturing was flourishing and so was foreign trade. Having just adopted a low-tariff policy for itself, the United States was alert to the advantages for commerce if other nations should lower their duties, particularly on agricultural products.

Business and manufacturing, as yet, were carried on by individual 'captains of industry', though large private fortunes had started to accumulate in the North and many a Southern plantation owner was comfortably fixed. The philosophy of rugged economic individualism was deeply embedded in the American soil. Yet the establishment of scores of adventures in social experimentation—about thirty communitarian socialist colonies on the Fourier plan alone—testified to the popularity of other ideas on the best economic order. Agitation for improvement in the standards of wage earners had given rise to trade unions and the principle of a ten-hour workday had been adopted for employees of the federal government and written into the statutes of a few states.

Humanitarian social forces and agencies were actively at work, being stimulated in some degree by currents operating in Western Europe at the time. The idea, for example, that it was the responsibility of govern-

204

ment to furnish elementary schooling for all children had won general application in the states of the North. Pressure for more humane treatment of criminals and the mentally ill, pressure for the abolition of imprisonment for debt and for legal restraints on the consumption of alcoholic beverages, were gaining ground. Similarly, there were growing campaigns for equality of women and for the elimination of war to settle international quarrels, though the latter movement was dwarfed by the prestige of military power which had been enhanced by the recent defeat of Mexico and the splendid territorial dividends that had been earned.

Overshadowing, of course, all other issues with social implications was the perilous problem of Negro slavery. In the South 'the peculiar institution' shaped attitudes on virtually every public question that arose; militantly anti-slavery societies in the northern states had already enlisted thousands of adherents, but the propaganda lacked the depth, the intensity, and the momentum it was to acquire in the next decade.

From the beginning a land of unique promise and offering wider personal freedoms than prevailed in Europe, the United States in the years just before 1848 had attracted throngs of immigrants. About one in ten of the inhabitants of America in 1848 was of European birth, Irish and Germans predominantly, but there were contingents of other nationalities too. These folk, or some of them, cherished affections for their homelands, followed unfolding events abroad, and through correspondence with relatives and friends in Europe spread sentiments sympathetic to American political institutions and hostile to monarchism and social antiquarianisms.

On the other side, an occasional radical crusader drifted from Europe to the United States to stir up interest in revolutionary movements among immigrants and to solicit financial support.[1] By reason of naturalisation, many foreign-born Americans had been enfranchised. Much the larger part of these new voters identified themselves with the Democratic Party, whose name possessed a certain magnetic quality. Professing to be the champions of the lowly and the immigrant, moreover, and opening lesser public offices to immigrants, the Democrats consolidated their hold on newcomers. Whig Party strategists tried on occasion to outbid their rivals for the favour of immigrant voters, though without much success.

At 1848 the tides of nationalism and territorial expansion were running high in the United States. Rich expanses of land had just been joined to the national domain: Texas, the Oregon Country, and areas in the Southwest ceded by Mexico after swift defeat by American arms. All told, the newly acquired territory covered an area four times as extensive as France.

[1] Carl Wittke: *Against the Current: the Life of Karl Heinzen* (Chicago 1945) pages 44, 53–7

Small wonder, then, that the conviction that it was nothing other than 'manifest destiny', the march of history, for the United States to lord over all of North America crowded to the front. It was symptomatic of the mood of the hour that both major political parties nominated soldiers for the presidency in 1848; the victor at the polls, General Zachary Taylor, though he was unfamiliar with affairs of state, personified the exhilarating triumph over Mexico. Suspicions that America had further designs for expansion caused consternation in more than one European capital. Self-assurance and self-consciousness were expressed on another level in the emergence of a literature that was national in character.

In the realm of political ideology the basic attitudes of the United States were firmly solidified by 1848. The heritage of 1776, frequently and passionately invoked in press, on pulpit, and platform, and the marvellous material progress under a régime of republican democracy, deepened and strengthened popular attachment to the Constitution and the political institutions of the country. The emotional capital of America was heavily invested in ideas of freedom and equality (with a reservation to be entered in the case of the Negro), in ideas of republicanism and federalism, and national self-determination. Folk memories, after all, abounded in affirmations of personal liberty. The Pilgrim Fathers, the War of Independence, the Westward Movement were all concerned with facets of human freedom.

It was inescapable, therefore, that the European convulsions of 1848–9 should evoke a hearty, even a buoyantly optimistic response in the trans-atlantic Republic. Devotion to democratic ways and institutions was matched by widespread detestation of monarchy and authoritarianism. These were looked upon as vestiges of an outmoded age which Europeans of courage and enterprise would do well to cast into the discard. Few were the Americans who through personal experience in Europe had come to the conclusion of Albert Brisbane 'that the American Republic was simply a new dress on old institutions. It remained the same system of social relations, the same system of commerce, the same rights of property and capital'.[1]

Outside of official circles familiarity with the actualities of European politics was decidedly limited. An increasingly more mature press, it is true, kept readers posted on current happenings in the Old World, but it seems fair to say that perspectives on Europe were faulty, and that hopes were often substitutes for facts. There was a marked tendency to view the mid-century revolutions in a haze of romantic sentimentalism. But tempering that feeling was abiding faith in the conviction of the 'Father

[1] Arthur E. Bestor, Jr: *Albert Brisbane—Propagandist for Socialism in the 1840s*, 'New York History,' XXVIII (1946–7) pages 134–5

Founders' of the nation that American interests would best be served by holding aloof from the turmoil of Europe. It is against this many-coloured texture of American life that popular and official interest in the European upheavals of 1848–9 must be set.

2

Of all the nations of continental Europe France has enjoyed the longest and widest popularity in the United States. Recollections of the indispensable assistance which royal France rendered the revolting colonists in 1778 grew dim at times, but that chapter of history ensured a sympathetic interest in French affairs whenever French governing institutions approximated those of the United States. Only the Hungarian revolution of 1848 caused greater excitement in the United States than the French. Unaware of an earlier outbreak in Southern Italy, Americans believed that the French had actually started the campaign to replace monarchism by republicanism.

Popular sympathy for the French insurgents of 1848 was more restrained than for their forerunners who had driven Charles X from the throne in 1830. Leading American cities witnessed mass meetings and celebrations hailing the proclamation of the French Republic and expressing fervent hopes for its success. In New York city, for example, a throng estimated at 100,000 saluted the revolution and adopted resolutions of gratitude for the triumph of freedom in France. It was remarked, however, that prominent civic leaders had absented themselves from the meeting. Very few public men participated in a similar gathering in Washington, though both houses of the Congress suspended their deliberations for the day. Spokesmen of immigrant groups lauded the French rebels and predicted that the flame of revolt would sweep into their own native countries. 'Fraternal congratulations' were dispatched to the young French Republic by the national convention of the Democratic Party.

At the start of the revolutionary storm, the press of the United States, regardless of political affiliation, heaped praise upon the French revolution, with Whig papers somewhat less sanguine over the outcome than the mouthpieces of the Democratic Party. The comparatively peaceful manner in which a Republic had replaced the monarchy of Louis Philippe elicited widespread and sympathetic commentary. Yet doubts soon arose in the minds of editorial writers in the conservative newspapers, more than one of whom pessimistically prophesied a recurrence of the terrorism of the Great Revolution. National self-esteem was, however, touched by information that French law makers were studying the American

Constitution and might borrow from it for the new political system of France.[1]

Men of letters in the main applauded the apparent triumph of republican and democratic principles beyond the Atlantic. John Greenleaf Whittier, whose Quaker pen was ever at the service of freedom, enthusiastically greeted the French developments, while James Russell Lowell in an *Ode to France* ascribed the revolution to the maleficent rule of the 'bourgeois king'. Never did the altars of freedom, he sang, burn 'with purer fires than now in France'.[2] 'So long as a king is left upon his throne', commented Henry Wadsworth Longfellow, 'there will be no justice in the earth.' On the other hand Ralph Waldo Emerson, who was in Paris in the spring of 1848, preferred to withhold judgment, as befitted a philosopher, until it was clear whether 'the Revolution was worth the trees' that had been chopped down to make barricades.

At Washington, meanwhile, general satisfaction over the turn of events in France had been manifested. President James K. Polk, while studiously holding aloof from the Washington meeting that acclaimed the French Republic, alluded to the revolution as an 'interesting and sublime spectacle'. The administration promptly approved the action of the minister in Paris, Richard Rush, who, on his own responsibility, had recognised the provisional government on 28 February, a mere four days after the beginning of the revolution. To the criticism of fellow diplomatists that he had been too precipitate, Rush retorted that he desired to aid a noble cause and that he had acted in keeping with the spirit and the wishes of the United States.

Applauding the initiative of Rush, the Secretary of State, James Buchanan, instructed him to render all possible help to the Republic in fashioning a new government, which he hoped would incorporate the federal principle that had worked so well in the United States. Buchanan asserted that 'it was with one universal burst of enthusiasm that the American people hailed the late glorious revolution in France in favour of liberty and republican Government . . . Liberty and order will make France happy and prosperous. . . .'[3]

To the Senate, Allen, a Democrat, representing the state of Ohio, offered a joint resolution expressing 'the congratulations of the American to the French people upon the success of their recent efforts to consolidate the principles of liberty in a republican form of government'. That proposal afforded senators an opportunity to disclose their thoughts on France in a formal way. Such respected public men as Stephen A. Douglas,

[1] Actually the French Constitution in its final form contained few clauses that could be traced directly to American precedents. Eugene N. Curtis: *The French Assembly of 1848 and American Constitutional Doctrines* (New York 1918) pages 325–30

[2] Elizabeth B. White: *American Opinion of France* (New York 1927) page 119

[3] John B. Moore, editor: *The Works of James Buchanan* (12 volumes, Philadelphia, 1908–11), VIII, pages 33–4

Lewis Cass, Henry Clay, and Daniel Webster, all alike distinguished for their talent in assessing the drift of public opinion, spoke approvingly of the resolution, the last with somewhat less warmth than his colleagues. Other senators friendly to the resolution remembered with gratitude the assistance France had furnished in the colonial revolutionary struggle. But spokesmen of the South, of whom Senator John C. Calhoun carried the greatest weight, were as distrustful of the outcome of the French revolution of 1848 as they had been of the 1830 predecessor. Calhoun gravely questioned whether the movement would promote the cause of liberty, more likely it would prepare the way for a military despotism.

Nonetheless, on 3 April 1848, the Allen Resolution was adopted by the Senate. The House of Representatives concurred in the measure with only two dissenting voices, though before the vote was taken the hall of Congress rang with fiery exchanges on the subject of Negro slavery, which the proposal called forth. Members of the Whig Party tended to be less hearty in their support of the resolution than their Democratic rivals, but attitudes were determined more by convictions on the slave question than by party ties.[1]

Newspaper criticism of French revolutionary policy-makers increased as time progressed. Men who were strongly attached to *laisser faire* economics were distressed by the law setting up National Workshops. Southern editors remarked caustically on the act emancipating Negro bondsmen in the French Empire, though the anti-slavery press rejoiced. The bloody excesses of the 'June Days' seemed to confirm the prophecies of men who doubted whether the French possessed the inherent qualities necessary to organise a durable republican democracy on the style of the United States.

The subsequent course of events in France bore out the forebodings of pessimists. In particular the candidacy of Louis Napoleon for the presidency and his election provoked distrustful and resentful expressions of feeling. Would not the new Napoleon, eager to emulate his famous uncle, seek glory by the sword and push for the restoration of monarchy? Sympathy for France and the French touched bottom in December 1851, upon Louis Napoleon's *coup d'état*. There indeed was proof positive that French allegiance to sound principles of government was of a superficial nature. Any nation that gloried in a man on horseback was deficient in the traits of mind and character prerequisite for a lasting Republic. The French 'are lacking in morale', Emerson lamented, and he echoed the sentiments of a multitude of his countrymen. Only after the capitulation of Napoleon III at Sedan did American faith in France start to revive.

[1] Eugene N. Curtis: 'American Opinion of French Nineteenth Century Revolutions', *American Historical Review*, XXIX (1923–4) page 263

3

As the home of the Renaissance in its fullest and fairest flowering the Italian peninsula was highly esteemed by educated Americans. Yet strivings for freedom and unity among Italians never excited the deep passions that Greek struggles to win independence roused in Philhellenic circles.[1] Part of the difference is no doubt to be ascribed to the circumstance that the Greeks fought against infidel Turks and the presence of the Papacy in Italy confused feelings in the United States.

Strongly Protestant America watched Italian developments involving the Pope with caution and reserve. On the other hand, the bulk of the Roman Catholic minority, which in 1848 must have been about 1,500,000, could be relied upon to rally to the support of the Vatican if papal interests were in jeopardy. The leading spokesmen of Catholicism was the Bishop of New York, John Joseph Hughes, militant polemicist and sturdy defender of Church interests.

Forward-looking innovations which Pope Pius IX inaugurated in secular administration soon after his election in 1846 were favourably received in America. Public assemblies in New York City and in other large communities felicitated the Pope on the reforms and he was spoken of as the predestined leader in the unification of the Italian states. 'He seems', remarked the Secretary of State, James Buchanan, 'to be an instrument destined bỳ Providence to accomplish the political regeneration of his country'.[2] Doubters, however, wondered whether Pius IX could be at once the head of an international Church, a temporal ruler, and the leader in a movement to unite Italy.

Risings in 1848, from Palermo to Venice, appealed strongly to the heart of freedom-loving America. The small Italian colony in New York City celebrated the Palermo outbreak with due solemnity. From the tone of the press comment it is evident that grants of constitutions by Italian kings and princes were thought of as foreshadowing a brighter and happier history for the Italian nation as a whole. Newspaper reports were particularly full and generally optimistic on the struggle directed by King Charles Albert of Sardinia, to break the Austrian hold on Lombardy and Venetia. Yet there were reservations on the personality of the monarch. Did he possess ingenuity and resolution? Was he singlemindedly devoted

[1] Edward M. Earle: 'American Interest in the Greek Cause, 1821–7', *American Historical Review*, XXXIII (1927–8) pages 44–63
  Arthur J. May: 'Crete and the United States, 1866–9', *Journal of Modern History*, XVI (1944) pages 286–93

[2] Howard R. Marraro: *American Opinion on the Unification of Italy, 1846–61* (New York 1932) page 7

to the welfare of Italy or was he bent upon the aggrandisement of his personal fortunes?

When Italian forces won victories over Austria, the American press applauded. When they retreated before superior Hapsburg armies there was, nevertheless, praise for the courage and martial qualities the Italians demonstrated. Even after the fighting had stopped completely and Charles Albert had abdicated, friends of Italy still declined to concede that all was lost. Division of mind among policy-makers, the inadequacies and limitations of Charles Albert, the unwillingness of France to help, the unpreparedness of Italians for liberty, each was assigned responsibility for the failure to attain the goals of freedom and unity. But the victory of Austria, it was freely declared, would only be transitory; the spirit of Italy would flare up anew in due time and sweep the nation into the ranks of progressive powers.

The revolution in the Papal States, attended as it was by the expulsion of Pope Pius IX from Rome, roused mingled emotions in the American mind. As interpreted by one school of Protestant thought, there was nothing surprising in the departure of the Pope from Rome, for that coincided with certain prophecies in the Book of Revelation. Wide sections of opinion and mass meetings registered sympathy for the Roman Republic and hoped that it would prove permanent. It was even proposed that the exiled Pius IX might emigrate to the United States and set up the papal dignity there. 'Let him come', cried a Boston newspaper, 'and we will convert him into a good democrat'.[1]

That attitude was not, however, shared in American Catholic quarters where it was felt that His Holiness had been grievously wronged by the insurgent Republicans. Bishop Hughes delivered an especially violent assault on the rebels. Churchmen summoned the faithful to pray for the physical well-being of the Pope and for his restoration to his estates. An appeal by Hughes for contributions to sustain the Pope in his exile brought on a heated controversy with Horace Greeley, editor of the New York *Tribune*, who insisted that such funds would flow into a papal war-chest for use in combating the Roman Republic. Upon his restoration, Pius IX expressed gratitude for the 'sympathy and contributions of pecuniary assistance' that had come from the United States.

It was, of course, the armed power of Louis Napoleon which re-established papal authority in Rome. That act was hotly criticised in broad sections of the press and in public gatherings called together in scattered cities of the United States. Bishop Hughes, on the other hand, ordered special services to celebrate the return of Pius IX to the Holy City.

The official policy of the United States toward rebel governments in

[1] Boston *Daily Evening Transcript*, 12 January 1849
  Marraro: *op. cit.* page 57

the Italian states was notably less cordial than in the case of France or Central Europe. American consular authorities, in Palermo, in Venice, and in Rome bestowed their blessings on the forces of revolt with the same alacrity that Rush had done in Paris. But the consul in Palermo was rebuked by the State Department, albeit in mild language, for recognising the revolutionary régime, and Washington would not receive a representative who claimed to be the official agent of the Palermo government. The consul in Venice, thinking to encourage the republicans by his commendation, exultantly cheered the return of 'the Queen of the Adriatic' to the sisterhood of republics. It must have been pleasing to American eyes to read an address dispatched by the Republic of Venice to the Republic of the United States saying that 'we have much to learn from you; and, though your elders in civilisation, we blush not to acknowledge it'.[1]

The response of Washington to the action of the consul in Rome in heartily congratulating the republican insurgents and assuring them that the United States would recognise them as the legitimate authority was prompt and unmistakable. The consul was called home.

Only so recently as March 1848 the United States had for the first time decided to establish a legation at the Papal Court. Prominent churchmen in Rome, the Pope apparently among them, had requested that an American diplomatic representative be stationed there. President Polk, on 7 December 1847, recommended to the Congress that a mission be set up in Rome which would be of value, he said, in diffusing knowledge of American institutions and might be helpful in the promotion of trade. After a spirited, full-dress debate in the Congress, in which pride and prejudice were mingled and the fundamental political philosophy of Pius IX was subjected to searching criticism, a law was passed authorising a legation in the Papal States.

The first appointee to the post at the Vatican, Dr Jacob L. Martin, a veteran of the State Department, was definitely instructed not to place a religious interpretation on his assignment. Martin died soon after reaching Rome and before his successor arrived the revolutionaries had taken command.

Washington hesitated to extend official recognition to the Roman Republic, though, as noted above, the consul in Rome, who had indicated warm friendship for the rebels, was recalled with scant ceremony. Party strategists warned the President that Catholic citizens might answer recognition of the Republic with reprisals at the polls. But more persuasive perhaps was the well-grounded suspicion that the revolutionary government rested on extremely shaky foundations and would not last

[1] Marraro: *op. cit.* page 37

long. That interpretation was communicated to the State Department by the newly designated chargé to the Papal States, Lewis Cass, Jr. Cass, who was in Rome, was forbidden to present his credentials to any government without explicit instructions from Washington.

America, quick to admit revolutionary governments in France and Germany into the family of nations and on the verge of recognising the Hungarian insurgent régime, withheld that honour from Mazzini, Garibaldi, and their Roman republicans.

4

It was appreciated in the United States that the uprisings in Central Europe formed an important phase of the general revolutionary storm. Opinion on developments in Germany, while less lively and less widespread than in the case of France, was vocal along the Atlantic seaboard and in inland communities with German populations. Editors saw in the insurgencies in Germany 'the Revolution of 1776 extending itself across the seas'. Meetings in major cities, organised mainly by Germans, though not by them alone, listened to speeches, drank toasts, and passed resolutions of sympathy for the cause of republicanism and national unity in Germany.

When the defeated revolutionary hero of Baden, Friedrich K. F. Hecker, came to America in the autumn of 1848 to appeal for help for the revolutionaries, New York City welcomed him as though he were a conqueror and effervescent gatherings in Philadelphia and provincial cities paid him honour. Less buoyant, however, was the receptions accorded to Professor Gottfried Kinkel, who, for his revolutionary faith and works, had been sentenced to life imprisonment. With the help of an admirer and former student, Carl Schurz, Kinkel dramatically escaped, and appeared in the United States late in 1851. He addressed audiences in many of the larger cities and collected a small sum of money for revolutionary purposes. But his mission was overshadowed by the thundering welcome given to the Hungarian chieftain, Louis Kossuth.

The idea of a federal union for the German states met with a ready response in the transatlantic Republic, for it argued imitation of the pattern that had worked so well here. It was a source of pride, too, to know that the Declaration of Independence and the Constitution of the United States were being extensively studied by Germans. Asked for suggestions of use in preparing a constitution for a united German state, Senator Calhoun drafted a detailed commentary on the projected fundamental law for Germany. His colleague, Webster, once thought of going to Germany to aid in the organisation of a federal government.

As the deliberations at the Frankfort Assembly proceeded on their dreary way, doubts arose in America as to whether anything of value would result. The decision of the Assembly to bestow the imperial German crown on the Prussian king called forth the lament that the Germans had abandoned democracy and republicanism for a mess of monarchical pottage.

Disillusionment concerning the political capacity of Germans had long since set in. Direction of affairs had been assumed by unpractical visionaries and professional theorists, it was felt, rather than by men trained in the practicalities of statecraft. Instead of frittering away invaluable time in chauvinistic addresses against Denmark on the Schleswig-Holstein controversy, instead of indulging in socialistic vagaries, the revolutionaries should have concentrated on dethroning kings and the establishment of republicanism. Yet mingled with pessimism were expressions of confidence that some day the forces of democracy and liberalism would inevitably trample tyranny in the dust, and Germany, free and united, would take her proper place among the nations of Europe.

The policy of the Government on revolutionary Germany sounded a bolder note than in France or Italy. In fact, alone among the Powers, America granted official recognition to the abortive German national régime which was set up at Frankfort.

At the court of Prussia the United States was represented by Andrew Jackson Donelson, nephew of the man whose name he bore and like him a staunch believer in the values and universal applicability of democratic government. Upon the outbreak of revolutionary disturbances in Berlin, he warned his fellow-countrymen in Germany against taking part; he strongly felt at first that the democratic ideology would triumph, though his faith ebbed as the might of authoritarian tradition asserted itself.

Soon after the convocation of the Frankfort Assembly, Donelson requested power to enter into official relations with the new Government, if he thought recognition wise. Such authority the State Department granted him in July 1848, hoping that trade might benefit. Then, taking another step, President Polk, the Senate concurring, appointed Donelson as Minister to the Frankfort government. He would, however, continue to represent the United States at Berlin; only when Washington was sure that the authorities in Frankfort had full jurisdiction in German foreign affairs, would the mission in Berlin be discontinued.

Friedrich Ludwig von Roenne, who had served as Prussian Envoy in Washington, was officially received by Polk, in January 1849, as the representative of the central German state. Subsequently the American missions in Frankfort and Berlin were separated, but a change in administration at Washington and more important, the dwindling prestige of the central government, nullified the decision. Although the United States kept a minor representative at Frankfort until the central régime was wholly extinct, Donelson himself was recalled. Spokesmen of the Democratic Party in the Senate sharply criticised the Whig administration of President Taylor for suppressing the Frankfort legation just when it might have proved serviceable to the cause of a United Germany on a democratic foundation.

Partisan attacks were also levelled at the Whig executive for neglect to assist Germany wholeheartedly in the building of a fleet. At the request of German officials, the United States sent Commodore Foxhall A. Parker to Germany to ascertain how he could be of help in creating a navy. Brief consultation with German officials and the prospect of a German war with Denmark convinced Parker that it would be inadvisable to give technical aid to Germany. Washington readily endorsed that view.

On the other hand, Commodore Matthew C. Perry acted as adviser to a German agent in the purchase of the merchant steamer the *United States*. And the commandant of the Brooklyn navy yard was instructed to permit the use of the facilities of the yard in converting the ship into a war vessel. Work was almost finished when Taylor and the Whigs replaced Polk and the Democrats in the management of the Government.

Fearing that the *United States* might be used in war with Denmark, which would infringe international law, the Whig cabinet declared that the ship might not leave America unless and until satisfactory guarantees were given that she would not fight any country with which the United States was at peace. Democratic Party critics condemned the Whig decision as a mark of sympathy 'with tyrants and aristocrats of Europe in their struggle with the people'. The proper retort, of course, was that the Government had acted in harmony with orthodox prescriptions of international law. Politicians in the know considered the partisan wrangle in the press over the *United States* as a huge joke.[1]

5

So limited was American interest in the risings in Vienna, Prague, and other centres of the Austrian Empire proper that it may be dismissed without remark. On the other hand, the Hungarian rebellion against the Hapsburgs attracted the most impassioned and sustained attention of the entire revolutionary epoch, being crowned by the tumultuous reception

[1] Arthur J. May: *Contemporary American Opinion of the Mid-Century Revolutions in Central Europe* (Philadelphia 1927) pages 32–3

accorded to Louis Kossuth in 1851–2. More than once, popular and official manifestations of sympathy for the Magyar insurgents produced head-on collisions between Washington and Vienna, representing two radically divergent concepts of the good life, politically speaking, and threatened to bring about a rupture of diplomatic relations.

Towards the end of 1848 metropoli an newspapers, ignorant of some decidedly unpleasing features of Kossuth's principles and administration, started to praise the gallantry of the Hungarian rebels. They were lauded as the Americans of Europe, the only Europeans in fact qualified for freedom. It was fashionable to liken Kossuth to Washington and to pray that the one might be as successful as the other. News that the Hungarian chief had published a declaration of independence was received with transports of delight. Americans took to studying the history and topography of Hungary, which became as well known as those of any European country.

Public meetings all across the United States, in city and town, listened to and cheered resolutions of sympathy for the Hungarian insurgents and called upon the Government to recognise Hungary as a free and independent nation. At a popular gathering in Illinois, for example, an obscure politician named Abraham Lincoln offered a resolution asserting that Hungary commanded the highest admiration in the United States and ought to be admitted to international society. Former President Martin Van Buren professed to have greater interest in the fortunes of Hungary than of his own country, while ex-President John Tyler believed that if Hungary should win her freedom, more would be accomplished for the cause of humanity than anything that had happened since the American revolution. As Senator Webster read the public mind, 'the sympathies of everyone are with Hungary'.

Always partial to the underdog, American opinion, for the most part, hotly resented the thrust of the armies of Nicholas I into Hungary. Except for the Russian intervention, the Hungarian republicans, it was confidently assumed, would have made good their bid for independence. The news of the collapse of the revolt rolled over America like the tolling of a funeral bell. It was recommended that Kossuth and his aides, who had taken refuge in Turkey, should be brought to the United States either under the auspices of the Government or by funds raised by popular subscription.

Agents of the Government, meantime, and the Government itself had been more or less faithfully reflecting the popular interest in the Hungarian cause. For instance, at one point in the civil war when a representative of Kossuth asked the minister of the United States in Vienna, William H. Stiles, to intercede with Austrian authorities to secure a truce,

Stiles promptly did so. His overture was turned down but his initiative was approved by the State Department.

In response to resolutions of public meetings, to the importunities of influential politicians, and to the requests of Hungarians domiciled in the United States, the Government decided to make a gracious but rather unorthodox diplomatic gesture. On 18 June 1849, the Secretary of State dispatched secret instructions to A. Dudley Mann to proceed to Hungary, study the situation, and, if in his judgment it appeared that the insurgent régime was likely to prove durable, he should formally recognise it and negotiate a commercial treaty. The United States, though concerned not to transgress accepted rules of neutrality, was eager to be the first country to welcome Hungary into the family of nations. A representative of the revolutionary government who appeared in Washington was assured that recognition would be forthcoming as soon as his country had won its independence.

The man to whom the delicate and unusual mission to Hungary was assigned knew his way about Central Europe. Appointed consul in Bremen in 1842, Mann had roamed around the German states collecting data on emigration and arranging commercial treaties. His dispatches to Washington on the Frankfort Assembly had heightened his reputation for sagacity and prudence. A warm partisan of the democratic creed, Mann had watched the Hungarian struggle with keen interest.

In Paris at the time he was ordered to go to Hungary, Mann started off, but before he could reach his destination the insurrection was crushed. Somehow or other the Austrian government got hold of a copy of the Mann instructions, very likely through an Austrian subject who was employed in the legation of the United States in Vienna.

After the defeat of Hungary, mass meetings in the United States and sections of the press strongly urged that the legation in Vienna should be discontinued, as a mark of condemnation of despotism. Half in keeping with that feeling, half with the object of building political capital among naturalised immigrants, Lewis Cass proposed in the Senate, on 24 December 1849, that an enquiry be undertaken to ascertain the desirability of suspending diplomatic intercourse with the House of Hapsburg. The resolution provoked a lively debate in official circles and in the newspaper world, Whig partisans arguing that the proposal was impolitic, and it was dropped.

Annoyed by the Mann mission and irritated by the Cass Resolution, the Austrian government fairly boiled over in the spring of 1850, when the documents in the Mann case were presented to the Senate for examination. Vienna dispatched instructions to its chargé d'affaires in Washington, Hülsemann, to protest the actions of the United States in connection with the Hungarian uprising. Well acquainted with the United States, where he had been stationed since 1838, Hülsemann was personally resentful of official Washington tactics and of the popular exuberance for the rebel cause. Only the conventions of diplomacy and the dictates of prudence had restrained him from speaking his mind long before.

In a note full of sharp language Hülsemann upbraided the United States for what he called the indefensible interference in the domestic affairs of the Hapsburg realm. Mann's errand, he said, laid him open to arrest as a spy.

Daniel Webster, who had moved into the office of Secretary of State, answered the Austrian protest in a document which in spite of its arrogance and bombast is one of the notable American diplomatic papers of the nineteenth century. In composing the reply, Webster was minded to impress all the world with the growth and majesty of the United States, and, by assertive nationalism for home consumption, to lift the mind of America above the divisive slavery controversy. He would acquaint everyone with the genuine American interest 'in the extraordinary events which have occurred, not only in Austria, but in many parts of Europe since February 1848'. It was entirely proper, he said, for Americans to cherish an 'interest in the fortunes of nations struggling for institutions like their own'.

Paragraph by paragraph, Webster eloquently combated the Austrian complaints, declared that the United States had never contemplated interfering in Hapsburg domestic affairs, and bluntly stated that if Mann had been treated as a spy the United States would not have hesitated to unsheathe the sword.[1] Webster's vigorous exposition of the national creed and hope elicited general and generous endorsement from press and politicians.

In the meantime, the government had harkened to popular pressure to secure the release of Kossuth and his colleagues from their Turkish exile and bring them to the United States. So early as 12 January 1850, the State Department had instructed the American Minister in Turkey to seek permission for Kossuth to depart for the New World. But the Turks temporised. Early in 1851, a joint resolution was passed by the Congress empowering the President to send a national vessel to Turkey to bring Kossuth to America.

Negotiations with the Turks now yielded the desired result. On 10 September 1851, Kossuth and a large retinue embarked on the U.S.S. *Mississippi*. Hülsemann had warned Webster that if Kossuth came to America, he would engage in political activities deterimental to Austria,

---

[1] Webster to Hülsemann, 21 December 1850, U.S. National Archives, Department of State MSS 'Notes to German States', Vol. VI

but the Secretary of State insisted that he would come simply as a settler and would be treated as a private person. That interpretation of his trip Kossuth himself challenged by declaring, aboard the *Mississippi*, that in the United States he did not seek 'an asylum for exiles . . . but an avenger . . . against the oppressors of a holy cause'.

Friction between the captain of the ship and his 'inflammatory cargo' developed at several ports along the Mediterranean. At Gibraltar, Kossuth and his immediate party quitted the *Mississippi* and proceeded to England. The enthusiastic welcome extended to them in England, lavishly recounted in the American press, intensified the already great excitement which the impending visit had aroused.

After caustic debate in which allegiance to the tradition of non-intervention in the politics of Europe was reaffirmed and criticism was expressed of the way in which anti-slavery zealots might exploit Kossuth for their special ends, the Congress voted by overwhelming majorities to receive the Hungarian chief officially in Washington. Without exception the negative votes were cast by men from the South.

On 5 December 1851 Kossuth landed in New York. The advance publicity could scarcely have been better contrived. Here, in the feeling of much of America, was the symbol, the living image of the sacred cause of liberty, humbled but not broken by the might of autocratic despotism. Here indeed was the apostle who might one day lead Europe out of the darkness of tyranny into the bright light of freedom and liberty.

Saluted on his arrival with military honours, Kossuth received an ovation from New Yorkers without precedent in the history of the community. A cross-section of the political, intellectual, religious, and workingmen's organisations of the city called to do him honour. The metropolitan welcome was a foretaste of the effervescent enthusiasm with which he was hailed in all parts of the nation, except the South. Whether malady or nobility, 'Kossuthism' gripped a large part of America.

Kossuth had acquired a remarkable command of the English language and in oratory and forensic skill he had few peers. In all his appearances, he stressed his intention of using 'every honest endeavour to gain your operative sympathy and your financial, material, and political aid for my country's freedom and independence', and he emphasised the need for funds either as a gift or a loan for the revolutionary cause. These themes, with variations, he was to iterate and reiterate in more than five hundred addresses in the course of his progress up and down the United States.

Rapturous crowds enthused over the 'Magyar Demosthenes' in Philadelphia and Baltimore. In Washington he was received at the White House by President Fillmore, who was taken aback by Kossuth's straightforward request for intervention on behalf of Hungary.

The high points in the Washington visit were formal receptions in the Senate and the House of Representatives, Kossuth being welcomed in the same language that had been used in greeting Lafayette a quarter of a century before. At a Congressional banquet, Secretary of State Webster, in a piece of rhetoric which he later regretted, spoke up for 'Hungarian independence, Hungarian control of her own destinies, Hungary a distinct nationality among the nations of Europe'. That utterance so thoroughly incensed Austrian authorities that they came very close to breaking off diplomatic relations.[1]

From Washington Kossuth and his party took a grand tour round the Republic. Excitement ran high in the western and northern states, and some money poured in, but the South reacted to the presence of 'the foremost soldier of freedom in this age', as Emerson called him, in a frigid manner. Among public men, too, and the more conventional editors, the Kossuthian appeals for intervention in the maelstrom of European politics chilled moral sympathy for the man and the cause he had close to his heart.

Having made the circuit of the country, Kossuth returned to New York City and dabbled a bit in partisan political waters. Then on 14 July 1852, under the pseudonym of Alexander Smith, he sailed back to Europe. He who had entered the metropolis seven months before as a roaring lion, left it as the meekest lamb, almost unnoticed.

6

The experience of Kossuth in the United States reflected the mercurial quality in the trends of thinking on the revolutions. Impulsive, uninhibited fervour, rightly to be described as lyrical, caught hold of large masses of the population in the North and West, only to give way to a sense of apathy or momentary indifference. For the American mind in the broad the risings of 1848 seemed a melancholy catalogue of hopes aroused and hopes deferred. Yet appeals for patience concerning Europe and notes of optimism for the future were sounded in many quarters.

Among well-to-do citizens and beneficiaries of the slave system a tendency to scepticism, if not downright hostility, characterised reactions to the 1848 movements. Evidences of departure from orthodox economics by revolutionary governments or leaders were severely condemned. In a similar way Bishop Hughes (Archbishop after 1850) and the churchmen

---

[1] Merle E. Curti: *Austria and the United States*, 1848–52 ('Smith College Studies in History', XI, Number 3, 1926) pages 185–97

for whom he spoke consistently denounced reformist and radical currents in the European movements.

Conservatism, too, largely directed official policy. At no time was there any really widespread support for change in the traditional policy of abstention from the politics of Europe. A cry was raised, it is true, for the use of the physical power of the United States to promote and uphold republicanism in the Old World. That theme was expounded by a few Middle Western senators and was placed on the agenda of a short-lived 'Young America' movement.[1]

But the predominant national faith was proclaimed by President Fillmore in his annual message to the Congress of 1852:

> ... We cannot witness the struggle between the oppressed and his oppressor anywhere without the deepest sympathy for the former and the most anxious desire for his triumph. Nevertheless is it prudent or is it wise to involve ourselves in these foreign wars? ... Our policy is wisely to govern ourselves and thereby set an example of national justice, prosperity, and true glory as shall teach to all nations the blessings of self-government and the unparalleled enterprise and success of a free people.[2]

Up to a point, the political, economic and cultural life of the American Republic was enriched by the coming of refugees fleeing from oppression and autocracy in the Old World. Some of the fugitives, to be sure, sought only a temporary asylum; an enterprising matron in New York City, soon after 1848, might have invited to a dinner party, Garibaldi, Lamartine, Ledru-Rollin, and less well-known revolutionary worthies of German or Magyar nationality. After eking out a humble living in the United States, these transients returned to more dramatic scenes in Europe.

A company of Hungarian political refugees, under the leadership of Ladislaus Ujhazy, landed in the United States before the visit of Kossuth. A flattering reception was given to them in New York and other eastern cities, and they were greeted in Washington by President Taylor and other prominent public men. They proceeded to the Middle West, founding a small agricultural community in Iowa appropriately called New Buda. Without skill as farmers, and finding the climate too rigorous, they soon moved on to Texas.

From Germany almost a million emigrants crossed over to the United States in the decade after 1848. But it is erroneous to imagine that any

---

[1] Merle E. Curti: 'Young America', *American Historical Review*, XXXII (1925–7) pages 34–58

[2] J. D. Richardson, editor: *Messages and Papers of the Presidents*, 10 volumes (1789–1897) V, pages 179–80

large proportion of these newcomers set off for America because of the attractiveness of the democratic political atmosphere. It has been amply established by historical scholarship that the great mass of the German emigrants were seeking release from enchaining economic restraints.[1] It is a revealing and remarkable fact that when the government of Baden offered to transport imprisoned revolutionaries to the United States at no cost to themselves, almost every one of them chose to suffer in chains at home.[2]

Authentic German political exiles, a few thousand of them, of whom Carl Schurz became the most eminent, emigrated because of admiration for the liberties and ideology of the United States. Men of cultivation, of superior social standing, and leaders in their homeland, many of this minority attained places of distinction in the New World. It was perhaps natural for descendants of other German immigrants to identify their own pioneering ancestors with the political 'Forty-eighters'.

Intellectual radicals by conviction and desperately concerned about the rights of man, the outlook of many a 'Forty-eighter' was not changed by the collapse of revolutionary visions nor by the passage to the New World. It is not at all surprising that such minds sharply denounced the prejudice against aliens, the puritanical social conventions, and the mockery of slavery which they discovered in America. Some even talked of organising a German state in the Federal Union whose way of life would conform to their own concepts of the good, the true, and the beautiful. But in the main the 'Forty-eighters' soon channeled their reformist energies and talents into the campaign against slavery.[3]

Hungarian and German exiles were not the only defeated revolutionaries of 1848 who fused their destinies in the American melting pot. Several hundred French, Italian, Czech, and a few Polish fugitives added to the richly variegated tapestry of civilisation in the United States.

---

[1] Marcus L. Hansen: 'The Revolutions of 1848 and German Emigration', *Journal of Economic and Business History*, II (1929–30) pages 630–58

[2] Marcus L. Hansen: *The Atlantic Migration, 1607–1860* (Cambridge, Mass. 1940) pages 272–3

[3] Carl Wittke: *We Who Built America* (New York 1940), pages 187–97. At the time of his death on 11 January 1947, in Washington, Professor Veit Valentin, the distinguished authority on the German revolutions of 1848–9, was engaged in a study of the impact of the 'Forty-eighters' upon the life of the United States.

AN HISTORICAL PARADOX
THE REVOLUTION OF 1848 IN GERMANY
EDMOND VERMEIL

Race can mean more than the State
Dahlmann

Prussia is determined to enlarge her cramped quarters, and the German theory of nationality provides her with the means to do so
Metternich (June 1847)

IF one investigates the reasons for the dramatic and disastrous climax to the events of 1848 and 1849 within the German Confederation, one discovers that they lie not so much in external causes as in the mentality of the German people. The peculiar aspects and developments of German romanticism provide the clue.

The period was not only a golden age for the arts. The Revolutionary and Napoleonic Wars had developed to a remarkable degree the future guiding principles behind German thought and action. There had taken shape a clearly defined view of the world, which explains the gradations, the strength and the curious weaknesses of the conservative and liberal viewpoints which at that time were in conflict throughout the length and breadth of the Confederation.

The intellectuals of this era, influenced by the classical philosophers, claimed to understand the fundamental laws of nature, and believed that the living organism represented the only reality. Going further than the sceptic, Kant, they saw a direct relationship between the whole and the parts of the living being, whether as a single unit or as a group.

Thus they considered any society worthy of the name as an organic whole, composed of separate elements, each contributing to the general harmony. This led to the conservatives, who were concerned with maintaining governmental unity, accepting certain liberal theories which justified the relative autonomy of individuals, families and social groups. Inversely, the liberals, who upheld the importance of this autonomy, made certain indispensable concessions to the authority of the executive. With the exception of a handful of radical republicans, they continued to support the monarchical idea.

223

Authoritarian conservatism and emancipatory liberalism therefore existed side by side in the great majority of German minds. The thirty-nine states of which the Confederation had been composed since 1815 were invulnerable against both the masses, who were wholly unaware of their weakness, and the élite of dons and jurists, who were united by no common aim and were naturally inclined to accept any compromise.

What, then, did the honest German want? He wanted *unity* and *liberty* in a new democratic monarchy. The final result was Bismarck's pseudo-liberal Empire, which meant Prussia united with the rest of Germany under a king supported by the industrialists and the army. That was a disaster both for Germany and for Europe. German unity was henceforth dependent on cohesion through force and force through cohesion—on the *Reich* for the *Reich*—with the object of establishing a German hegemony in the old world. The extraordinary weaknesses of German liberalism caused it to bow before the work and will of pure power politics, which could not be reconciled with liberty.

I

THE EUROPEAN PREDICAMENT

The vast drama was staged in a kind of empty amphitheatre, left by the collapse of the Holy Roman Empire in 1806 and of Napoleon's Empire in 1815, in the middle of Europe as it was reorganised by the Congress of Vienna.

What was the German Confederation? In the north there were small Lutheran states and in the south there were the Catholic provinces of Austria—both conservative fiefs. In the south-west there was a bloc of seven states which had been enlarged by Napoleon; they were liberal in both politics and religion, and were cautiously assimilating western ideas. Between the two groups was Prussia with her four eastern and two western provinces. Her object was to co-ordinate the agriculturists east of the Elbe, and the rising industrialists on the Rhine, and she therefore steered a course between the conservatism of the former and the liberalism of the latter.

Since the states composing the Confederation were all entirely self-governing, and were linked only by a modicum of conventions, the field was clear for every kind of influence.

The diplomats of 1815 had constructed the peace treaty on the basis of an equilibrium between the eastern and western powers. The eastern bloc consisted of the nations forming the Holy Alliance, which with its monarchist and particularist prejudices was the sworn enemy of liberal radicalism. The rivalry between Austria and Prussia weakened this eastern bloc, but the moment it was joined by Russia it was able to exert considerable pressure on the states of the Confederation. The western nations lacked unity and so could present no alternative influence. England was self-satisfied and France was busy licking her wounds.

Austria and Russia, then, had only to combine their efforts to ensure the predominance of absolutism. Germany, whether the Small Germany later desired by Bismarck or the Greater Germany hoped for by many members of the Frankfort Parliament, could only achieve unity under the conservative aegis. Prussia, strengthened by the Customs Union and her military victories, and after refusing to accept the Imperial Crown at the hands of the Frankfort Assembly, had only to defeat Austria, and Germany's destiny would be fulfilled.

Between 1815 and 1818 Austria and Russia had for a moment been rivals when the Czar supported and Metternich persecuted the liberals. But in 1819 the Congress of Aix-la-Chapelle and the decisions reached at Carlsbad provided the eastern nations with a common programme. Between 1819 and 1823 began the sinister policy of intervention inspired by Metternich's memorandum on the causes of the revolution.

It took the Affair of the Spanish Colonies and the Eastern Question to rouse Canning's England, bring her closer to Russia, and—between 1823 and 1830—force her to take steps to counteract the activities of the eastern powers. Then, between 1830 and 1836 the western nations did make a strong concerted effort to check the Holy Alliance. But towards 1840 Britain and France were again divided over the Eastern Question; in 1846 the Affair of the Spanish Marriages created further difficulties; by 1848 western unity was shattered and the reactionaries triumphed. They were steadily to strengthen their position between 1848 and 1852, up to the appearance of the French Second Empire.

This lack of balance in Europe explains the remarkable evolution of the German Confederation between 1815 and 1850. From 1816 to 1820 there was a first wave of liberalism, followed—from 1820 to 1830—by a violent reaction, international in its origins. From 1830 to 1833 there was a second wave of liberalism followed by a fresh reaction, this time German in origin, between 1833 and 1845. Finally a third, and the most far-reaching wave of liberalism swept the Confederation between 1847 to 1849, and was finally checked by a rigorous restoration in the years 1850 to 1860.

The reason why the shock was comparatively great between 1847 and 1850, and the élite of Germany was able to devise a programme of unity and democracy such as the nation—even under the Weimar Republic—

has never equalled, was that the upheaval was a European one. Events in England, France, Switzerland, Italy and finally in Hungary were of a nature to raise the highest hopes in the hearts of the liberal middle classes.

One remembers Heinrich Heine's verdict on France. The Saint-Simonian poet thought that the July Monarchy would frustrate the social revolution which seemed to be growing within the womb of France. He exclaimed at the madness of 'these egalitarian workers, devotees of Communism, the Leveller', and accused the French people, with an élite too rotten to guide them, of following only their baser instincts. When the storm broke in February and March 1848, he was no longer capable of appreciating either its extent or its limits.

The revolution was very much a Parisian one like that of 1830. France reacted to it with more passivity than enthusiasm. Only the workers, who were in control of the capital, recommended the Provisional Government to adopt socialist formulas, which were as yet ill defined. The executive remained in the hands of the middle class. Nevertheless the 1848 movement did bequeath to the French people some essential political institutions: freedom of the press; the right to hold what meetings and form what associations they wished; and universal suffrage together with multinominal voting by Departments. Moderate republicans formed two-thirds of the Constituent Assembly. But the moment the workers showed signs of revolt after the closing of the National Workshops, they were quickly crushed. Cautious liberalism was the winner. The *coup d'état* of 2 December 1852 was close at hand. Heine was to have plenty of time to discover that his fears of social revolution were hardly justified. And he was to regard the *coup d'état* as an opportune check. He did not, however, see the profound difference between this revolution and similar movements in Germany.

The course of events in Britain was not as simple. These consisted of a rural rising which was put down without mercy, and an electoral reform, in 1832, which the Chartists, supported by the proletariat, vainly attempted from 1835 to 1845 to have modified. But what else could one expect of a British movement which more or less imitated the French? The English were to be quite content with free trade and the Poor Law.

Events in Switzerland more closely affected the German Confederation. Since 1830, the conflicting elements there had formed two opposing camps. The strongly conservative country people were in opposition to the liberal townsfolk. The conflict was much more violent than it was in Germany. The agrarian cantons formed the Catholic *Sonderbund*, anathema to the other cantons, which aspired to political liberty and were hostile to the Church. The only possible outcome was civil war ending in the later part of 1847 by a victory for the liberals under General Dufour.

What Germany was really interested in was the new Swiss Constitution, for it tackled the problem of federalism. The Swiss Charter vested sovereignty and supreme power in a Federal Assembly, composed of a Federal Council of cantonal, and a National Council of popular, representatives. This was not unlike the system evolved at Frankfort. Anyway, it was the first attempt in Europe to put the accent on centralisation within a federal framework.

Another important point about the transformation of Switzerland was the distress it caused the King of Prussia. Frederick William IV was also the ruler of Neuchâtel, whose industrial population had joined forces with the Swiss cantons regardless of Prussia's say in her affairs, with the result that he was henceforth the sworn enemy of all popular elements.

Italy was painfully seeking to acquire political unity, and radical changes had taken place since 1845. In the north, particularly in Piedmont, there was a tremendous press and literary campaign for political liberties, which however relied the whole time on the support of the Church. When Pius IX succeeded Gregory XVI in 1846, the Papal States suddenly acquired a modern guise, with laymen sharing high office with the clergy. And in August 1847 the Pope stood up to Austria, the most formidable enemy of Italian unity.

Pius IX became a national hero, but unity and liberty were not to be won with his support: he was first and foremost the head of the Catholic Church, and it was only to her greater glory that he encouraged liberalism. The Church did indeed profit by it to break down territorialism and regain autonomy. But democratic unity presented a new danger for her. It is not surprising that Pius IX reversed his policy, withdrew his support from the liberal and national movement, and, in April 1848, effected a reconciliation with Austria, Italy's mortal foe.

This remarkable recantation imperilled all the hopes of Young Italy. It was to be explained by the local revolts first in the south, then in the north, where the Governments of Parma and Modena frantically sought support from Austria. It also resulted in the declaration of a state of siege in Lombardy, whilst in Piedmont, the centre of the nationalist movement, Charles Albert decided to satisfy a legitimate ambition by uniting Italy under the House of Savoy. In April 1848 he crossed the Austrian frontier without even declaring war. The rest is common knowledge: how the Italians lost the war at Custozza on 25 July. All the same, Austrian influence had perceptibly diminished in Italy. Austria wanted a more complete revenge, and won it in the autumn of 1849 by smashing the movement in Upper Italy. From 20 March to the 24th, Charles Albert was defeated for the second time by the veteran Marshal Radetzky; Venice surrendered on 30 August; and Charles Albert's successor, Victor Emmanuel II, had only to come to terms with Austria.

Events in Hungary had more serious consequences for the Hapsburgs. Austria had had to grant the Hungarians a personal union under the dynasty. (Among the members of their liberal Ministry was the lawyer Louis Kossuth.) The Hungarians, imbued with the spirit of nationalism, had quarrelled with the Slavs in the south, who wanted Austria to form a kingdom uniting the Croats, Slovenes and Dalmatians. The result was, of course, that Austria played off the Slavs against the Hungarians. Kossuth thereupon organised a resistance movement with the object of winning Hungary her independence. But the moment he saw victory in sight, and announced the end of the Hapsburg-Lorraine dynasty, Austria called Russia to her aid. On 13 August 1849, the Hungarians capitulated at Világos and were brutally punished.

This résumé of the situation in Europe enables us to understand the background of the German revolution. It was bound to suffer from the unequal contest between the reactionaries and the democrats. In England and France, both centralised and heavily industrialised countries, the social problem appeared on the horizon and transcended the limits of middle-class democracy. In the centre of Europe, in Switzerland and Italy, political unity was of more consequence than the acquisition of funda-mental liberties. In Hungary the battle was purely one for independence. All these risings were doomed to failure; in England owing to the solidity of the conservative tradition, in France through the advent of Louis Napoleon, in Italy owing to an Austrian counter-offensive, and in Hungary owing to the alliance between Austria and Russia.

The German revolution was to share these vicissitudes. Liberal democracy and the social problem were to figure in Germany as in the west, though to a lesser extent. But then there was also the question of political unity linked up with the acquisition of fundamental rights. Finally, there was the fight to maintain independence in the face of Austrian pressure.

And all ended in disaster, followed for Prussia by humiliation at Olmütz and for the Confederation by the fierce reaction from 1850 to 1860.

2

ECONOMIC AND SOCIAL CAUSES

Round about 1815 the states of the German Confederation were com-paratively poor, being under-populated and relying on agriculture for their subsistence. Economically speaking, Germany had no fixed frontiers and was paralysed by the numerous territorial divisions and by archaic methods of farming. The old mercantilist system had left a heritage of conflicting legal systems and customs barriers. The peasants were apathetic and industry was in the hands of trade guilds and home workers. Communications throughout the country were in a lamentable condition.

The hapless Germans turned to the west for new economic theories and practices. They, too, had to be spurred on either by England's example or by the impetus of the Revolution and the Empire in France. It is well known how much some of Napoleon's measures accelerated Germany's material recovery.

The spirit of a new era struck German society like a rock flung into a stagnant pond. Between 1815 and 1850 the Germans started breaking up their medieval inheritance. The line their future was to take soon became plain. The feudal aristocracy in the east and in the west took to large-scale agriculture and connecting industries. A middle class of business men, manufacturers, shopkeepers, the professional classes and office workers in both State and private employment grew rapidly. In contrast to these two classes, which were soon to produce the future rulers of the country, there appeared an entirely new proletariat, both industrial and agricultural in character.

This transformation explains the remarkable modernisation of Germany, marked by unprecedented progress in means of transport and communication, and a host of new inventions. Towards 1850, after the set-back in 1848, the industrialisation of Germany proceeded apace. Between 1816 and 1850 she developed her first system of road transport and a postal service worthy of the name. Towards 1835 she began to construct railways, and by 1840 had laid 282 miles of track; by 1850, 5,134 miles; and by 1860, over 6,600 miles. Internal and external trade was slow to develop and only expanded to any extent between 1850 and 1870.

Nevertheless throughout this period Germany remained an agricultural country. Prussia's example in freeing the peasantry in 1870 was followed by the other states, but they encountered stiff opposition. The feud between the big landowners and the peasantry did not come to a sudden end. Nevertheless, after 1820, thanks to the work of such agricultural experts as Thaer and Liebig, German farming began to make tremendous strides. The sugar beet industry started round about 1830, and modern machine methods were introduced between 1847 and 1850.

Whereas England was already using a considerable number of steam engines by 1810, Germany relied on home industries until 1830. There was much more rapid progress in mining, particularly for coal and iron. In 1850 Germany produced 208,000 tons of iron; by 1860 the figure had risen to 1,391,555.

Capitalism had flourished in the days of men like Fugger and Welser, but the impact of the Reformation on the Holy Roman Empire had destroyed its foundations. Two centuries passed before it revived under the patronage of intelligent rulers. The middle class was to do the rest. In the old days the capitalists had concentrated on trade, leaving agriculture and industry far behind. Certainly seventeenth and eighteenth century commercialism had paved the way for the manufacturers, but it was only in the nineteenth century that capitalism in its modern form transformed both agriculture and industry. The discovery of gold in California and Australia accelerated the process, which between 1850 and 1870 also led to the large-scale organisation of industry in France.

One must not, however, exaggerate Germany's economic success and strength before 1850. The principal phenomenon of the period was rather that of the economic unification of the German states by the extraordinarily successful Customs Union promoted by Prussia in 1818. In that year a deputation of important Rhenish employers prevailed upon the Chancellor Hardenberg to abolish internal customs and transfer the barriers to the boundaries of the Confederation. Thus the Prussian Customs Law began the new movement. At the same time an attempt was made to break into the English market, which, however, put up a strenuous resistance. Then in 1819 the economist List laid the foundations at Frankfort and Nüremberg of a commercial union which he considered would accelerate the creation of the Customs Union. The latter's history is well known. Conferences were held in 1821, 1823 and 1825, which led to the movement gaining ground rapidly between 1830 and 1840. After 1846 there was no stopping it.

The Germans, as we know, almost invariably act according to a preconceived theory, and after 1815 their advance in economic thought was as striking as their material progress.

Towards the end of the eighteenth century, religious—especially Lutheran—conceptions of economics and finance still reigned supreme. The Physiocrats were almost exclusively concerned with agriculture, which they looked upon as the only profitable industry. It needed the influence of Adam Smith and his system, which had crystallised round about 1789, to open new perspectives to the Germans. Adam Smith showed that agriculture, industry and trade were equally important factors in production, granted the existence of free enterprise.

Henceforth the Germans were forced, though it went against the grain, to recognise a sharp line of demarcation between the State's province and the sphere of private interests.

This phenomenon greatly helps us to understand the drama of 1848. Germany was to lead even England in the field of economic liberalism.

At this strangely complex period of transition, the whole German nation seems to have swung right round on its own axis, dragging itself out of the slough of the past to create an economic system on a scale unparalleled in modern European history. Economic liberalism was thus to have far greater attractions for the Germans than political liberalism, particularly under the republican form which the latter assumed in France.

In order to maintain power the monarchies of the Confederation and later the Imperial monarchy kept the middle-class democrats and the proletarian socialists out of public life. They were relegated to purely material occupations, though without the requisite form of education. Materialism rapidly took hold of the mass of the middle class, which grew increasingly indifferent to the cultural achievements of the past.

There were two main currents of thought in Germany at this time. Adam Smith's theories had taken root between 1800 and 1850—Stein and Hardenberg had attempted to put them into practice between 1807 and 1811—and economic liberalism gained ground between 1815 and 1850; but we must not forget that state socialism had made its appearance in France in the years 1800 to 1830, and that the famous Romantic theorist Adam Müller had fiercely attacked Adam Smith's individualism. Later on List's protectionism and Rodbertus' theories were to provide state socialism with a strong case. From then onward, German capitalism was to differ from western capitalism. It was to have far more official weight, as it was bound to the State by interests which would one day favour the intensive military preparations of the Second Reich.

The new economic theories and practices were accompanied by a corresponding change in the social hierarchy.

In 1815 Germany was divided into three main classes: the nobility, the educated middle class, and 'the people'. The last was a vague term designating all those whom the middle class considered its social inferiors: peasants, artisans and shopkeepers, domestic servants and the proletariat. Class consciousness was little developed (except among the nobles) in a society with so few strata. The only differences of any importance were between people of different education, religions or professions. This remained the case until about 1850. It took the sudden development of industry and capitalism to create antagonism between the nobility and propertied or salaried middle class and the proletariat.

Nevertheless some changes took place between 1847 and 1850. The nobles lost their essential privileges in 1848, and were no longer looked upon as a class apart, with the exception of those who had held titles under the Empire. The great families of ancient lineage were to uphold the Crown and the Church, whilst the squireens of the east, and the landed middle classes, were to maintain their judicial and police rights over their peasantry.

It was towards 1850 that the middle class, benefiting by the changes which had taken place in the past decade, became the chief propertied class. It turned, almost to a man, to business, and thanks to industrialism was to produce a monied aristocracy—an oligarchy which, by virtue of its vast resources, was capable of exercising an uncanny and almost irresistible control over the country. The genuine democrats and radicals in its ranks could only emigrate in a body after 1850. The middle-class liberalism that flourished between 1820 and 1848 disappeared almost completely under Bismarck.

By the side of this middle class there appeared a proletariat which from 1850 onward grew steadily. The big industrial towns were filled with landless peasants as the result of a Prussian law authorising the large land-owners, when a small landowner died or his lease expired, to dispossess his family. The result was that the nation lost one of its most valuable elements, which could have done so much to enrich the countryside. So Germany found herself without a responsible middle class or a firmly rooted rural populace.

The German family of the eighteenth century, as we read of it in both religious and secular literature, with its original characteristics resulting from the Lutheran patriarchal system, pietism and a host of foreign influences, retained its characteristics in spite of the comparative speed of modernisation. Between 1815 and 1850 (in what is known as the Bieder-meier period) it still kept its faith in the value of family ties and the inner life, although after the Revolutionary and Napoleonic Wars it lost much of its rigidity. In spite of the alarming changes of the years 1840 to 1848, Germany stayed content with her picturesque little medieval towns, her simple houses, clothes and customs, and her sheltered domestic existence. This doubtless explains the apathy of the masses, and the gulf between them and the handful of intellectuals striving to build a united and free nation. This élite, which saw what the future would bring, lived a life apart. It could not inject the spirit of nationalism into a conglomeration of little states dozing under rulers whom, as Heine remarked, one could hear snoring.

THE POLITICAL EVOLUTION

The Confederation's system of government was reactionary by nature. It was based on particularism, as the only ties the states would accept were pacts to ensure their security. Admittedly the general will of the Confederation was not the same thing as the sum of the wills represented by each of its states, but unanimity of opinion in the Diet was required before any decision could be taken, and that was a permanent obstacle in the way of any unitary movement.

Austria looked upon a *rapprochement* between Prussia and south-western Germany as the real danger, and in fact German unity did depend upon it. There were two courses open. Traditional federalism could be replaced either by a centralised Greater Germany, mediatising the states including Prussia and Austria, or by a federal and national state of Lesser Germany under the control of Prussia.

The problem was an extremely complex one, for Germany—like Italy—was a national 'civilisation'. Had she to become a 'political' nation —a national state like France and England? And, if so, was she able to become one without the guiding hand of Prussia? There was nothing to prevent the Confederation from coming under a strong central authority, leaving its thirty-nine states a reasonable degree of autonomy. But would one of those states have to be Prussia, comprising two-thirds of the nation's territory and population?

To put it briefly, was Prussia to be absorbed by the *Reich*, or was the *Reich* to be absorbed by Prussia—particularly if Austria were not included? The connection between the federal problem and the political problem is obvious. Prussian hegemony would guarantee the maintenance of the monarchical states with their semi-absolute rule tempered by a minimum of concessions to liberalism and democracy. A Great Germany both unitary and federal would assure the establishment of parliamentary democracy, but it would mean the exclusion of those rulers who refused to grant fundamental rights. That was how at least some of the legislators of 1848–9 saw the problem, although they were unable to solve it.

Since 1815 there had been growing opposition between the political State of Prussia, which looked like expanding into a German nation, and the virtual nation, which, not content with merely representing a particular form of culture, wanted to become a political state. The tragedy of Germany was being prepared well in advance. Fichte hoped Germany would absorb Prussia. Stein went so far as to hope she would absorb

Austria as well. The historian Niebuhr, on the other hand, looked upon Prussia as the quintessence of Germany.

Between 1830 and 1848, at the time when the constitutional movement was gaining in the north, the burning question was: 'Will Prussia turn liberal?' Pfizer[1] believed it would, and wondered whether the Prussian people would not impose institutions of a partly monarchical and partly democratic nature on the states of the Confederation. Should freedom be put before unity, or unity before freedom? In his heart, Pfizer hoped that Rhenish Prussia would counterbalance East Prussia, and their rivalry would lessen the danger of an aggressive Prussian hegemony. How could the Prussian State and national autonomy exist side by side? In 1848, Friedrich von Gagern, more liberally and unitarily minded than Pfizer, was to demand that the King of Prussia, on becoming head of the new *Reich*, should have no realm of his own, and that Prussia should be divided into equivalent provinces.

The Confederation supported not only particularism against unitary proposals, but reaction against liberalism.

Now, a number of political advances had been made in the German States by virtue of an evolution which throws an interesting light on the problem of unity. In fact, Prussia's political position was analogous to that she took in the matter of unification.

A number of important events, all of the same origin, mark the history of these years: violent criticism of the Confederation; a youth movement; the Wartburg festival in 1817; the assassination in 1819, by a student, of Kotzebue, the playwright who went over to the reactionaries; the parliamentary movement in the south-western states; the spread of liberalism to the north; the Hambach festival in 1832; the Frankfort affair in 1833; the growth of liberalism in Saxony; the appearance, after 1848, of radicalism; and the turmoil created by the influx of western ideas. Yet this list does not bring out the real aim, the concrete objective of the movement.

This evolution took different forms in different states. Also, it was a fairly slow process. There were more compromises than bold solutions, and there was the mixture of monarchical traditionalism and parliamentary liberalism whose significance we have already discussed.

To see concrete results, we must look to the south-western states, which tried the first compromises. The constitutions acquired by Baden and Bavaria in 1818, by Württemberg in 1819, and by Hesse-Darmstadt in 1820, all have this in common, that they were the gifts of the respective monarchs to their subjects. Their dynasties remained hereditary, but they held their authority under the Constitution. Each of these constitutions also provided for a representative Parliament consisting of two Chambers,

[1] Author of the famous *Correspondence between Two Germans*

one for the nobles and the other for the middle class. This Parliament had some control over the budget, ensured equal treatment for all religious denominations, equality in the eyes of the law and fundamental rights for all citizens. The object of these constitutions, which roused no violent political passions, was to make the State an organic whole.

One can clearly see here the origins of the German parliamentary system. Parliament was no creation of popular sovereignty. Election of representatives to the Assembly did not destroy its position as a State body. Parliament, in a word, was simply an instrument of unification in the hands of each monarch. The so-called 'popular' representation simply brought to light the various conflicting political and economic interests, and so enabled the ruler to govern accordingly.

The evolution of the south-west had its counterpart in the states pullulating in the northern plain which was on the way to becoming part of Prussia. As they were mostly Lutheran and reactionary, they were slow—if not reluctant—to become modernised. Changes only began to take place after 1830. Sudden and violent swings of the pendulum cancelled the effects of revolutionary disturbance.

Prussia was divided between the eastern provinces and those on the Rhine—between conservatism and liberalism. Western ideas, and indeed French institutions, had made considerable inroads since 1789. The Rhine-landers' growing resentment of the bureaucrats of Berlin, the defence of their Civil Code against the Prussian *Landrecht*, and their passionate love of equality were all signs of the gulf between the two halves of the kingdom. Between 1840 and 1848, Hansemann, Mevissen and Camp-hausen promoted in the Rhenish Diets a form of national liberalism which was the prototype of that which flourished under Bismarck. The national liberals had confidence in Frederick William IV, and business circles were encouraged by the success of the Customs Union. Shortly after 1840, economic preoccupations gradually began to overrule principles of political morality.

Prussia thus presented a curious combination of contradictions and compromises. Seen as a whole she was less liberal than the radicals in the west and less reactionary than the states in the north. She made an increasing number of friends through the Customs Union, and right up to 1871 Germany was to owe her a certain degree of gratitude. She had, too, made some attempt at constitutional reform, following the example of the south-western states, with the difference that between 1820 and 1830 her reactionaries had swept away all wish for innovation, so that she was satisfied with her provincial assemblies. When the new King came to the throne in 1840, he reviewed the constitutional programme. Although he distrusted parliaments, and was anxious to reconcile the Rhenish Catholics with the eastern Lutherans, he nevertheless decided to call the Provincial Diets to a *Landtag*, which met in 1845 and 1847.

This Assembly, in which a large number of talented representatives (including Bismarck) gathered together, was the natural clearing-house for all the opinions of the period. It was in 1850 that, under the pressure of circumstances and in order to save Prussia's cohesion at all costs, the King granted his people a Constitution. This stressed the unity of the crown lands, gave the citizens their fundamental rights, granted the different religious denominations a wide degree of freedom, and, whilst vesting the executive in the Crown, allotted the Government a certain degree of responsibility by creating a Chamber of Peers and a Chamber of Deputies, with an electorate based on a property qualification. The text of this constitution greatly helps us to understand Bismarck's Constitution.

These facts throw a surprising light on the position of the different political doctrines and on the formation of the first political parties.

Conservatism was on firm ground, whether Catholic or Lutheran in conception, for the ruling classes of the Confederation were its staunch supporters. Liberalism and radicalism took their inspiration not only from western sources, but from those provided by the critics of the dogmas and institutions of Christianity. Between these two extremes was a vague state of mind which combined both tendencies in a curious fashion. Economic factors and conflicting religious interests complicate the picture. The German theorists, being protagonists of the golden mean, accepted the Crown and balanced its power by introducing a Parliament of two Chambers, which played off the old nobility against the new middle class, and consequently effected a compromise between conservatism and liberalism. That is how western ideas came to take a form of their own in Germany. Much the same thing had happened in the era of rationalism, which as soon as it reached Germany had become bogged in religious disputes.

The policy of the different religious denominations of the time clearly shows the traces of this curious political syncretism. The Catholics assured Rome of their loyalty and gradually began to assert themselves until by 1848, thanks to Papal support, they were holding their own assizes at Mainz. But they took advantage of the liberal movement to start a campaign for the liberty of the Church, weary of its long subservience to the laws of the country. It claimed a certain degree of autonomy and especially an equal footing with the Evangelical Church. This was an example of corporate liberalism. Although the liberals made unexpected concessions to the reactionaries, it would be a mistake to regard the philosopher Stahl's conception of a Christian State, which directly inspired Bismarck, as simply a return to absolutism. The German Catholics made concessions to both the monarchists and the democrats, and were careful to swing neither too much to the right nor too much to the left. The Lutherans, faithful to Hegel and Stahl, followed suit. Every theorist asserted that in the State of the future, the whole and its component parts would be 'organically' linked. Had not the romantics always contrasted this conception of the State—this organic *Reich*—with the fluctuations of French politics?

Before 1850 Germany had had no political parties, properly speaking. Metternich in Austria, and the kings of Prussia, had bitterly opposed 'factions'. Doctrinal tendencies made their appearance, but contributed to no definite programme of action or organised groups. Yet in this comparative confusion the historian can discover the origins of the future parties.

At this time the Lutheran conservatives were led by the brothers von Gerlach, friends of Bismarck, who however was to break with them when they opposed unification in the name of Prussian particularism. It was the 'Independent Conservatives' who were to help the 'Iron Chancellor' to achieve a national unity based on the hegemony of Prussia.

In the years 1845 to 1850, liberal middle class and industrial circles began to take to the idea of national liberalism, which favoured free trade, but had little use for parliamentary democracy. This ideology was still close to conservatism but supported the Customs Union and industrialisation.

Progressive, or radical, liberalism, which left its mark on the 1848 Revolution, was to be the natural inheritance of the educated middle classes, particularly the university professors and jurists, who were sympathetic to western ideas.

The future social democracy was still very much in embryo. Nevertheless it was in 1848 that the first Workers' Congress met in Berlin, and the first Syndicates and Co-operative Societies were formed.

The Centre, with its right and left wings, its aristocratic elements and servile masses, was a miniature replica of Catholic Germany. It was the future 'pivot-party' whose compromises would always be justified in the eyes of the so-called 'Christian' democrats.

When the era of political realism dawned, tendencies became proper parties, and Bismarck was faced with an admittedly complex but efficient political organisation.

Our picture of the 1848 Revolution in Germany would, however, be incomplete without an account of cultural developments. In the thirty-five years between 1815 and 1850, Germany became a relatively homogeneous land, where modern techniques enabled the Germans for the first time to use all their energies to a single end. The intellectual and moral evolution of these years explains the collapse of liberalism and the appearance of a gulf between the *Reich* and her western neighbours.

We know Heine's prophecy. From 1834 onward he drew France's attention to the philosophical and religious trends in Germany, where, with remarkable perspicacity, he observed a general offensive against Christianity and the rule of the middle class. Once Christianity was destroyed, demonic forces would be unleashed, which might one day destroy European civilisation. The Churches would not be saved by their political parties.

There was, in fact, a concerted attack on humanism, and therefore on liberalism, so it is worth our while to study the powerful forces at work.

Historism, Hegel's conception of the course of events as a historical, spiritual process, naturally flourished more in Germany than anywhere else. Geology and geography, the necessary preliminaries to the study of geo-politics, made rapid advances. It was between 1845 and 1848 that Alexander von Humboldt was engaged upon his book *Cosmos*, a summary and elucidation of the Copernican theory of the world. Henceforth all the intellectual sciences were studied only through their historic evolution. The laws, it was argued, have been formulated throughout the course of centuries, and represent the customs and potentialities of the communities of mankind. There is therefore no standard rule of conduct, for no civilisation lasts for ever. God may make immutable natural laws, but then He is eternal. Whilst German industrial technique forged ahead, German scientists were hard at work making their inventory of the heritage left us by the past.

What were the scientists' conclusions? Their conception of Greek and Roman antiquity was radically changed. The old ideas gave place to a picture of fierce, warlike civilisations, which produced their famous art only after a series of bloody conflicts, and were doomed to decay once they became rationalist. Orthodox Christianity naturally defended its positions and its Churches, but on one hand it was used to promote nationalism, and on the other, in the universities, it met violent opposition. D. F. Strauss' *Life of Jesus* appeared in 1835. B. Bauer, Arnold Ruge and Feuerbach violently attacked the dogma of transcendent values.

This atmosphere helped to intensify the war on liberal doctrines in the years 1830 to 1850, which laid bare the major problem of the time: was Germany to follow her own traditions or those of the west? Liberalism has never made more headway nor suffered such bitter attacks as it did at this period. As ill luck would have it, France gave signs after 1840 of wanting to take back the left bank of the Rhine, with the result that liberalism became confused with the cause of nationalism, thereby losing its strength and integrity. And what hatreds it aroused! It was no longer a case of romanticism versus rationalism. Two political systems were at grips. And when liberalism made a reappearance in Bismarck's system, all it had in common with the former doctrine was the name.

Socialism suffered a similar fate. In Marx's day and before Lassalle's advent, it copied the western model and drew its inspiration from Babeuf, Saint-Simon, Fourier, and Proudhon. Marx germanised it and Lassalle nationalised it. Little by little it began to lose its original international and humanitarian character. The structure of social democracy was to recall that of the Catholic Centre.

What then did the Germans look upon as the ideal *Reich?* What was their conception of the religious, racial and political community of Greater Germany? The German Revolution was eclipsing the French Revolution, and the moment was not far off when Prussia's conquest of Europe would be a very present fear. Goethe's was the voice of the Universe, Hegel's of Prussia and Schlegel's of Austria. But Constantin Krantz and Paul de Lagarde were the real pan-Germanists. It was they who made German nationalism a religion and considered that Germany should destroy France and Russia, the military states of western and eastern Europe.

During these years, Germany acquired three new advantages: economic unity, the alternative between Greater and Lesser Germany and the vision of a German hegemony in Europe. It was against such a background that the events of 1847–50 took place.

4

THE REVOLUTIONARY MOVEMENTS

The 1848 Revolution was in preparation from 1840 to 1848. Feelings were roused by books, songs and plays of a political nature. Radicalism produced a number of exponents who largely contributed to the sporadic explosions of the period 1845–8. As for the moderate liberals, France's policy both in the east and in the Rhineland caused them to throw in their lot with the nationalists. Their comparative enthusiasm was roused not by their fidelity to western ideas, but by that patriotism which produced the *Wacht am Rhein.*

At this time it seemed as though there was no one capable of standing up against the established authorities, and yet the Confederation gave way without a struggle before the first outbreaks. It revoked the tyrannous laws it had passed and adopted the very colours (of black, red and gold) which it had imprisoned so many young enthusiasts for wearing, thereby leaving the way clear for the unitary and liberal movement. It was a wonderful chance for Austria and Prussia to step in. They played the rôle of bulwarks against revolution, since they were in the greatest danger. In order to have a complete picture of the complexity of the situation, it is important to know what events took place within the Confederation, for they had a greater influence on the unitary movement than had the Frankfort Parliament.

Austria's part had scarcely fitted her to take the lead in these years of universal turmoil. Metternich was still in power, but the moment the first demonstrations took place in Vienna, he abandoned the struggle in weary despair. There was no one to take his place. The Emperor Ferdinand, who had not yet come of age and was, furthermore, a weakling, was a complete anomaly among the monarchs of the Confederation.

Thus from the beginning Prussia was in the centre of the movement, and no one questioned her predominance. From 1840 onward her position depended entirely on the personality of her king, Frederick William IV. Towards 1842 Metternich had shrewdly said of him: 'He is a curious mixture of outstanding qualities and undeniable weaknesses, including a passion for displaying his talents to the full.' Metternich, in fact, was afraid that the King of Prussia would upset the established order in both his own country and every state of the Confederation. The King's ambition was to make Prussia a nation capable of taking its place beside the Great Powers. 'After all', he declared, 'she possesses all the virtues: the thirst for truth, honour, loyalty, and the determination to build anew by combining the wisdom of the old with the brave enthusiasm of the young.'

He had started to introduce reforms from the day he came to the throne, but—as the unfair punishment inflicted on the poet von Fallersleben proves—he was not particularly well advised. Nevertheless he introduced a series of popular measures, such as the amnesty of 1840, relaxation of the censorship between 1841 and 1843 and vague attempts at parliamentary organisation. All these had compensated for a number of mistakes. In 1841 an ordinance on the subject of the permanent committees of provincial Diets had decided that these committees should meet together in Berlin so as to work in collaboration.

But towards 1844, there was a sudden change in the King's policy. Tschesch's attempt on Frederick William IV's life led to a restriction of the magistracy's independence, and the Silesian weavers' revolt retarded parliamentary and constitutional progress. Conflicts within the General Synod of the Evangelical Churches, and the uncertainty of the foreign situation which made Prussia dependent on Austria and Russia, also provided an opening for reaction which in conjunction with that in Austria presented a grave threat to the unitary and liberal movement.

Yet the King considered himself bound by the law of 1820 (under which all loans had to be sanctioned by the future Parliament) to ask the country for money needed for the construction of railways. This led to the convocation, in 1847, of the united *Landtag*, which, although a hastily improvised affair, was really the first Prussian Parliament. It sat in Berlin from 11 April to 26 June 1847. It was, incidentally, a remarkable body, containing numerous partisans of German unity. The King's opening speech, however, was a great disappointment, for he asserted his 'divine right' to rule, and so scotched in advance any other solution to the parliamentary problem. The debate on the loan had barely begun before the united *Landtag* declared itself unqualified to deal with the matter, as its composition did not conform to the conditions laid down in 1820. The King dissolved the *Landtag* at the very moment when the first risings took place.

They broke out all over the Confederation at the same time as the revolts in France, Switzerland, Italy and Hungary.

Political agitation had been on the increase since the end of 1847 and especially since the rise in the cost of living. Karl Marx had judged the situation with his usual insight.[1] He considered that the middle class was fully aware of its strength, and was determined to rid itself of feudal and bureaucratic despotism which was hindering the development of industry and trade. The landed nobility were beginning to produce for the market and so were on the side of the middle class. The lower-middle class was burdened by taxes and had many other causes for complaint, but had no clearly defined programme of reform. Finally, there were the peasants who were weighed down with feudal dues, and at the mercy of money-lenders and lawyers; and the working class in the towns who were equally unhappy and were receptive to socialist and communist propaganda. So although opposition was widespread, it was heterogeneous, and the interests which followed the lead of the middle class were varied.

The small revolution at Wiesbaden in Nassau was a sign of the times. On 2 March 1848, a popular assembly there had taken advantage of the Duke's absence to present its demands to the government. The Duke returned post-haste, and conceded all the liberal measures they asked for.

In Bavaria, local circumstances resulted in the insurgents gaining a temporary victory over the military authorities. Since the beginning of 1846 there had been trouble in Munich, where the students—at the instigation of the clergy—had noisily demonstrated against Ludwig I and his

[1] In his study of the Revolution and the Counter-Revolution (1851–2)

mistress, the Scottish dancer Lola Montez. They resulted in Lola's departure and the King's abdication in favour of Max.

The events in France had immediate repercussions in Baden, Württemberg and Saxony. There, as at Wiesbaden, the revolutionaries demanded freedom of the press, trial by jury, the abolition of feudal dues and other reforms. In all three states, liberal Ministers were included in the government. A mild form of anarchy reigned in the smaller principalities, which had little aptitude for parliamentarism, and the Frankfort Diet, Prussia and Austria were powerless to check a movement enabled by particularism to take the form of a host of small and scattered revolts.

Prussia was extremely disturbed by the course of events in France, and later in Vienna. The Government seriously considered following Radowitz's advice by reconstituting the Confederation and introducing reforms in Prussia. It went so far as to enter into negotiations with Austria. Russia gave her approval, and even urged haste. On 6 March 1848, the King promised to call the *Landtag* at intervals; on the 8th he changed the law on the press; and on the 14th he ordered the *Landtag* to sit until 27 April whilst awaiting the decision of the States' rulers who were in conference at Dresden.

These measures were taken too late. Public meetings became more frequent in Berlin, and after 10 March they were accompanied by street demonstrations. The army was mobilised, and its commanders' brutality angered the masses who had still kept their faith in the Crown. The result was the skirmish of 15 March with the Uhlans driving the mob from the Palace Square, the erection of barricades and the shooting. On the 17th the government decided to make certain concessions. The King declared in favour of a federal *Reich*, with an elected Parliament, a national citizenship and a national army, freedom of the press, and other liberal measures. He summoned the *Landtag*, and the crowd cheered; but the sight of troops massed in the courtyard of the Palace aroused its fury, and it demanded their withdrawal. A clash was inevitable, and when the military opened fire on the unarmed mob the situation was changed in an instant. There were cries of treason. The middle class was enraged, and the ordinary people, who had so far taken no active part, ran to erect barricades; from that moment it was a battle to the death between the populace and the army.

The King made a speech to his 'dear Berliners' and promised to withdraw his troops. He did not know at first whether to seek the protection of his soldiers or his subjects. Then a deputation from the people arrived to assure him that order would be restored. Next, the mob marched into the courtyard and forced the King to bare his head before the bodies of the victims; a civic guard was formed despite the angry protests of the regular army; and the King rode through his capital. Finally, the hundred and eighty-three victims of the massacre were buried with full rites.

The King formed a liberal government under Ludolf Camphausen, the best-known of the Rhenish liberals. A Constituent Assembly was then elected, but, as the most capable men were then at Frankfort, it proved an apathetic body. On 21 October 1848, it tackled the problem of elaborating a Constitution. There were fantastic scenes. The left wingers violently objected to the terms 'King of Prussia' and 'by Divine right'. The liberal government resigned without reaching a decision, and in November were succeeded by a so-called Ministry of Public Safety. The military elements united against the Assembly. The Civic Guard was disbanded; the clubs were closed; meetings were banned. Reaction had triumphed, and on 5 December the King dissolved the Constituent Assembly.

Nevertheless, Frederick William IV granted his people a Constitution. When order was restored in 1849, the new Chambers met on 26 February. The parties, however, were deeply divided, with the result that proceedings ended in April without any conclusions having been reached. New elections were held and new Chambers elected, more subservient than their predecessors. The Constitution was promulgated on 31 January 1850, and on 6 February the King swore to observe it.

If this new Charter was not as liberal as that of 5 December 1848, it at least made Prussia a constitutional monarchy.

The two Chambers and the grant of fundamental rights were what the south-west had acquired. But the system of voting according to a property qualification, the strength of the Crown's position and the lack of any guarantee for the rights granted were the antithesis of liberalism. Bismarck was to make use of this state of affairs after 1862, and the military victories of 1864–71 were to do the rest.

The effect of events in Catholic Austria had created more confusion and uncertainty.

Nowhere had the revolution taken a more violent turn. The Hapsburgs had to contend with their conglomeration of different races, and were intimately affected by events in Hungary and Italy. Schwarzenberg had just succeeded Metternich. Czechs and Hungarians were all demanding freedom and independence. Metternich's system was exposed in all its weakness. In May 1848 the first draft of a Constitution was deemed inadequate and trouble followed. The Emperor retired to Innsbruck. The National Assembly met on 22 July and, under the presidency of Archduke John, began to discuss the constitutional plan. The Ministry, for its part, decided to reform the State, dissolving the Assembly in March 1849, and taking the power into its own hands. It tried to justify this action in a series of edicts, then granted Austria a Constitution, which turned her into a highly centralised *Reich*, without dualism, but with provincial Estates according to the different nationalities. When the system was working, a single *Reich* Parliament was to be summoned. As in Prussia, the Crown retained wide powers.

The constitutional movement achieved the same results throughout the Confederation. Everywhere the Crown retained the lion's share of the executive, and everywhere the formation of two Chambers perpetuated the divergencies of society. In the end the people acquired the minimum essential concessions, and the various Christian denominations once and for all gained equal status.

The nationalist movement began even before the February Revolution, in Baden, whose Parliament, the most advanced in the Confederation, took the initiative. On 12 September 1847, the radical association, 'The Sincere Friends of the People', held a public meeting at Offenburg, at which they demanded that the Frankfort Diet should grant parliamentary representation to the whole of Germany. Welcker had already made the same demand in the Baden Parliament, and in October, a meeting of the moderates at Heppenheim followed suit. On 12 February 1848, Basserman tabled a motion in the Baden Parliament to the effect that the German parliaments should send representatives to the Diet. A few days later the news from Paris gave added weight to these claims.

Finally, on 5 March, some fifty liberals (including Heinrich von Gagern, Welcker, Hecker and Struve) met at Heidelberg and decided to summon a German Parliament. To prepare the ground, they nominated a committee of seven which established contact with several governments, before creating a central provisional government. Von Gagern thereupon devised a Constitution, in which Prussia was to play the leading rôle. Baden, Württemberg and Saxony approved these measures. Berlin was to be consulted, but by means of a meeting held at Frankfort of all the members of the different parliaments and other notables.

It was at this moment that revolution broke out in Berlin and Vienna. As Austria was out of action, the King of Prussia declared his willingness to head a nationalist movement. But then, as usual, he hesitated, recanted and decided to wait and see what would happen. He missed his only chance. In the meantime, the Frankfort Diet had recovered from its fright. It promised to raise Germany to the level of the western nations, and invited seventeen outstanding liberals to revise the Statute of the Confederation. It was also decided, on the other hand, to summon the provisional Parliament on 31 March. But the Diet, so as to restrict its activity, promulgated a law whereby one deputy would be elected for every seventy thousand inhabitants, by way of forming a national Constituent Assembly, which was to work in collaboration with the different governments. The Provisional Parliament, consisting of five hundred members, achieved no major results, and the Diet fixed the elections for 7 April.

The radicals, well aware of their weakness beside the moderates, tried to force an issue by means of an armed rising. But the troops of the Confederation defeated their *corps francs*. Meanwhile, the seventeen liberals were hard at work under the chairmanship of the historian Dahlmann. They proposed that the Austrian part of the *Reich* should consist only of the German-speaking provinces, and that the rulers of the different states should become merely hereditary presidents, with the Hohenzollerns of Prussia at their head. The Diet and Frederick William both opposed this scheme. Austria claimed that her Emperor should rule the *Reich*, with a Hohenzollern as the 'German King', elected by the Frankfort Diet and crowned by either the Archbishop of Mainz or a German Lutheran primate. So the work of the seventeen liberals was set aside, and the National Assembly met at Frankfort without either a plan for a Constitution, or a provisional government.

Towards the middle of May the first session was held in the Church of St Paul in Frankfort. The six hundred deputies were the political élite of Germany, and its president was Heinrich von Gagern, a forceful personality and a good diplomat, who was well able to express the feelings of the people.

From the beginning, it could be seen that the difficulties were almost insuperable. Were they to create a Lesser Germany under Prussian leadership which would form an alliance of international importance with Austria? That would mean the King of Prussia acquiring the status of an Emperor. Or were they to create a Greater Germany, including either the whole of Austria or only her German-speaking provinces? That solution would create a religious problem, for it would enable Catholic Austria to rise up against Lutheran Prussia. And an even more serious danger was that it would enable her to continue the old methods of 1815–48 in the heart of the future *Reich*. The only way of avoiding this danger was to accept the paramountcy of Prussia.

Then there was the question of a provisional central authority. The left wing wanted the Assembly to be supreme, which would mean the formation of a provisional government in which the states' governments would have no say. The moderates and the right wing wanted collaboration between the two. Next came the problem of the form this central authority was to take—whether its power was to be vested in a directorate or in a single man. They decided to appoint a single man, a *Reichsverweser*, a provisional head of the *Reich*. The Assembly decided against discussing his appointment with the Diet, and on 28 June elected Archduke John of

Austria. On the Diet's ceasing to exist, the *Reichsverweser*, who was responsible to no one, was authorised to form a ministry responsible to himself, but was only permitted to declare war with the Assembly's approval. Furthermore he was not permitted to interfere with the drafting of the Constitution, which was the prerogative of the Assembly alone. The unitary and nationalist movement was so strong at this moment that neither the Diet, the States' governments nor the Archduke questioned these decisions.

But the position of the provisional head of the *Reich* was a dangerous one. He was both empowered by the Diet and elected by the Constituent Assembly, but he chose his own Ministers. Hence the beginning of the conflict within the Assembly.

The radicals, led by Blum, wanted a republic, and being supported by the people of Frankfort were extremely active. Their theorists were Vogt and Ruge. The right wingers, too, were in the minority. They were led by Prussians such as Prince Lichnowsky, von Vincke and Radowitz.

The majority of the Assembly were middle-class nationalist moderates, with their own right wing of moderate liberals such as von Gagern, Dahlmann and Gervinus and left wing of South Germans who were prepared to sacrifice the states and their dynastic interests to the idea of popular sovereignty.

As the Assembly found it had to start off by deciding the principles on which the central authority should be founded, on 4 July 1848 it tackled the problem of fundamental rights. A heated discussion finally achieved satisfactory results, and after years of bondage the Germans were accorded certain essential liberties. But the time it took to reach a decision lowered the Assembly's prestige.

When later on the Assembly was forced by circumstances to tackle the question of military supremacy, the States' Governments overrode the Assembly's decisions and it was rudely awoken to the fact that the states were not as amenable as it had thought. Now, by the time the states had recovered from the first shock, the Assembly had blundered in its foreign policy. The left wing supported an alliance with France and Poland, thereby antagonising Prussia, which was already dissatisfied with Archduke John's election and unwilling to surrender her military supremacy to him. The Schleswig affair showed John the insecurity of his position, for he could hardly agree to Schleswig's entry into the Confederation when the Great Powers were taking Denmark's side against Prussia. Nor could the Assembly prevent Prussia accepting the humiliating armistice of Malmö, although she no doubt reserved the right to revenge, such as she took in 1864. Hard facts brusquely disputed the Assembly's theoretical sovereignty.

GERMANY

The left wingers tried in vain to influence the majority by provoking popular risings. When they accused the majority of treachery, the Minister Schmerling called in several battalions of troops from Mainz. Clashes took place, and the Assembly declared a state of siege, but the troops stayed. Little by little the left wing began to abandon its military and nationalist programme in favour of an inefficient form of particularism.

These were the lamentable conditions under which the Assembly tackled the problem of the central authority. The main question was the relationship of Prussia and Austria to the future *Reich*. If the whole of Prussia lay within the Confederation, part of Austria was outside it. Would Vienna consent to a division of its Empire? This difficulty caused a split in the majority in the Assembly. Its right wing, with Dahlmann and his supporters, declared itself categorically in favour of the exclusion of the non-German provinces. Von Gagern, von Vincke and a number of others wanted a restricted Confederation without Austria. On 27 October 1848 the Assembly passed Dahlmann's motion, for its principle aim was to destroy the Austrian legitimist policy.

Order was restored by Schwarzenberg after the rising in Vienna. On 2 December Francis Joseph came to the throne. Schwarzenberg, who was determined to see Austria a unitary State, opposed the decision reached at Frankfort. There, the provisional central government had fallen and von Gagern had exchanged the presidency of the Assembly for the premiership. He boldly suggested that as Austria did not wish to become part of the future *Reich*, she should form an alliance with a Lesser Germany. But, he added, that was a matter for the diplomats, not the Assembly. The Church party, the particularists and the idealists protested. Austria, for her part, obviously wanted only to restore the old Confederation. But von Gagern refused to be intimidated, and on 13 January 1849 obtained full powers to negotiate with Austria.

The creation of Lesser Germany, however, meant that the Assembly had to approach the King of Prussia, and they did not know whether he would be amenable. They discussed the functions of the future head of the *Reich*, and von Gagern went to see Frederick William IV. His visit was unsuccessful, as the King wanted at all costs to keep in with Austria. This was the moment the Assembly chose to tackle the problem of a Parliament. They decided on the creation of a *Staatenhaus* (or Federal Chamber) and of a *Volkshaus* (or People's Chamber). In January 1849 they decided that the head of the *Reich* should be one of the princes with the title of Emperor of the Germans. Frederick William IV's answer to this was to continue negotiations with Austria. Schwarzenberg rejected the proposal of an alliance between Austria and Lesser Germany, as he dreamed of a Hapsburg ruling a Greater Germany of seventy million people. There were many patriots, not to speak of pan-Germanists, who would gladly have followed him.

On 24 January 1849 the German governments accepted the Frankfort Assembly's projected Constitution on the advice of Prussia, who wanted it to be made law at their instigation. The Greater-Germanists thereupon combined with the left wing in an attempt to discourage Frederick William IV by making use of the electoral law which had brought in universal suffrage with a direct and secret ballot. But their machiavellian plan miscarried. They imagined that Austria would permit her German-speaking provinces to join the future *Reich*. On 4 March, however, the Emperor granted his subjects a unitary constitution. Hence the paradoxical situation in the Assembly. On the one hand there were the partisans of Little Germany and the left who now wanted the support of the King of Prussia, and on the other, the radicals who upheld the electoral system and the supremacy of the People's Chamber over the future Imperial monarchy. Anyway, no one doubted that the King would accept, and the bells of Frankfort rang out for the new Emperor. Then, as we know, Frederick William IV refused to accept the Crown at the hands of the Assembly. He wanted to form a Lesser Germany with the approval of the states and Austria. He followed the advice of his own conservative Court. Furthermore he, too, did not think he was expecting the impossible in hoping for an understanding with Austria.

Any attempt to revise the Frankfort Constitution would have been in vain. Its fate was sealed, and the Assembly's rôle had ended. Every sign of revolt was stamped out. The Assembly moved to Stuttgart, but it did not stay there long. On 18 June 1849 the military occupied its Chamber, and its last minutes declared that the Assembly had succumbed to force.

5

THE CONSTITUTION OF 1849

When in 1919 the Weimar Assembly had reached the third reading of the new Constitution, a Populist member, Herr Heinze, asserted that whilst it repudiated Bismarck's 'organic' and 'realist' Constitution, it slavishly followed the one of 1849, which was a purely ideological affair. To be sure the two Constitutions followed the same plan, but whereas the Constitution of 11 August 1919 was born of defeat and a half middle-class, half socialist movement, the 1849 Constitution was the work of a movement which was wholly middle class and comparatively revolutionary in character. Its aim was to promote German unity on a parliamentary basis. It failed to do so, and Prussia was the sole beneficiary of the parliamentarianism of the period.

How could its makers have foreseen that after half a century of Bismarck's régime, the Weimar Assembly's main preoccupation would be the dismemberment of Prussia? In 1849, Prussia had not yet begun to hasten its formation. The western provinces were for the most part liberal. The 1849 Constitution only mentioned possible rearrangements of the different groups, letting it be understood that the composition of the Federal Chamber would be altered in the event of a fusion of a number of provinces.

The 1849 Charter was designed to establish a balance between the central authority and the federal authorities, going much further towards a unitary State than the Statute of the Confederation. It provided for a federal *Reich*, making the most of the old divisions. Centralisation as it existed in France, could only be won at the price of an unprecedented conflict, and people said at the time that a single, indivisible Republic 'would cost too much blood'. The *Reich*, in return for the authority vested in it, was to guarantee the Germans their basic rights. These rights, being the same for every state, would put an end to particularist and reactionary federalism. With this in mind, legislation and administration were combined. The *Reich* had almost complete authority and the states only the necessary minimum. Entirely absorbed in their theories, the deputies of 1849 cared little whether or not the states were contented, as Bismarck did. Certainly the die-hard conservatives did not consider a single monarchy sufficient compensation for the loss of their states' sovereignty.

What was the relationship between Crown and Parliament? The 1849 Charter aimed at creating a unitary monarchy. The liberals, as well as the moderate conservatives, though not the radicals, were in agreement on this point. The head of the *Reich* was to be a hereditary monarch like the King of England.

But what was his position in regard to the People's Chamber? The 1848 movement was a major episode in the history of German parliamentarianism. Between 1815 and 1848, as we have seen, the states of the Confederation had used popular representation to achieve unity and cohesion. Did the 1849 Charter go no further along the road towards popular sovereignty? The electoral system had already brought in universal suffrage with a direct and secret ballot. The head of the *Reich* had only a suspensive veto. The Charter saddled him with not only the

People's Chamber, but also the great *Reich* Ministeries, which were such a menace to the states' autonomy. The moderate liberals would willingly have granted the head of the *Reich* wider powers, doubtless to appease the conservatives, who bitterly fought for the rights of the traditional sovereign. In fact, the Assembly tried painfully to strike a mean between the old absolutism and democratic parliamentarianism. It tended towards a kind of parliamentarism on the English model, which would to some extent weight the scales of Parliament against the Crown. The People's Chamber voted the budget and so held the monarchy's fate in its hands.

The real sovereign was the *Reich*. Its power was divided between the head of the *Reich* and the *Reichstag* with its two Chambers. The powers of the former were no greater than those of a president. On the final count, the national monarchy and the states were much weaker than this *Reichstag*, at once unitary and federal in character, with extremely wide legislative powers. The Frankfort Assembly by no means sacrificed the King's personal authority to the representatives of the people. But it did establish a balance between them which might break down at any moment.

What was the exact significance of the fundamental rights? The Assembly was trying to consolidate the ideological victories of a new era. It tackled economic, social, ecclesiastical and scholastic problems and defined the rôles of groups and individuals.

Its first aim was to assist agricultural, industrial and commercial progress in the newly unified State. The conditions of landownership were stripped of the remaining vestiges of feudalism, and freedom of trade came in with freedom of travel. These were, of course, purely middle-class innovations, but then the proletariat was still in embryo.

There were many changes in the affairs of the churches and the schools. The various Christian communities lost their privileges, and the State Church disappeared. People were free to believe and teach what they liked, the schools being undenominational and subject only to state control. Education was made compulsory, and the teachers servants of the state. Primary schooling and education in the smaller technical schools was made free so as to enable talented but poor children to succeed in life. These state schools, except for religious instruction, were taken entirely out of the hands of the clergy, and the day of the church schools was over. The relationship between the Church and the State was equally boldly resolved: neither had any obligations towards the other.

As for the liberties of groups and individuals, they were especially valued in an age when they had known such violation. They consisted of freedom to hold meetings, form associations and present petitions; communal autonomy; openings for all in government service; equality before the law and as regards conscription; and freedom of movement and emigration.

One can easily see the stumbling-block in the way of the Assembly's very considerable progress. To the dynastic principle it opposed a unitarism which would be hard on the states' rulers and would deprive the *Reich's* future sovereign of a number of his traditional prerogatives. The parliamentary system was as advanced as it could be in Germany at that time.

It would still have been all right if the Assembly had had a number of similar states to deal with. But on top of a patchwork of extremely varied states there were Prussia and Austria, the first composed of both Catholics and Lutherans and the second of both Germans and Slavs. Prussia could not possibly have been absorbed in the future *Reich*, nor could Austria have suffered the loss of her Slavonic provinces.

If Greater Germany had come into being, it would have given German Catholicism a new importance in the *Reich*. Above all, it would have established in the very centre of Europe a comparatively unified Empire of about fifty million people, already ripe for industrialism. Would it have continued the peaceful traditions of the Holy Roman Empire?

The Assembly prepared the idea of a Lesser Germany, in close alliance with Austria. It depended, however, on Frederick William IV, and as he refused to sacrifice Prussia to the *Reich*, the plan was bound to fail.

German historians have reproached the Assembly with a lack of realism, because it wanted to turn the King of Prussia into a hereditary German Emperor chosen by itself and dependent on a Parliament elected by the entire populace; and also because it demanded an impossible sacrifice from Austria. These same historians add that from 1849 the German states had triumphed over the revolution. There lies the key to the situation. This triumph was to turn against the Assembly, for the very reason that it was too easy a victory over what was merely a handful of revolts scattered all over the Confederation. Once the people, who did not realise their own weakness, failed to overthrow their rulers there was nothing to prevent the latter from getting the better of the Assembly. They had retained the effective power together with their armies. With their aid the reactionaries of the Confederation were enabled to defeat a powerless parliament.

It was then up to the strongest state to impose its will on the others with a view to unification. The only real problem facing Germany in the years 1848 and 1849 was that of Prussia's attitude to German unity. Austria's position was not so important. Now, the Prussian state was faced with two hostile movements: one was liberal and unitary and the other Catholic and provincial. Both sought to dismember her. Prussia could no longer retain her isolation. She had either to be absorbed by, or establish her hegemony over, Germany.

In the interval, Prussia had been preparing a parliament and a constitution which was to come into being in 1850. The liberals rejoiced, not realising that the Prussian state could not both acquire a parliament and be dismembered. They did not see that Prussia, endowed with a perfect instrument of internal unification, would not dream of being absorbed by the *Reich*. Destroying Prussia was no way to use her to achieve this unification. To support a constitution for Prussia meant putting liberty before unity, and to oppose it meant putting unity before liberty, and betraying liberalism.

The result could only be rivalry between the parliamentarians of Frankfort and Prussia. After all, von Gagern, the South German liberal and President of the Assembly, had gone to Berlin to protest against the promulgation of the Prussian Constitution. And the Catholic Rhinelanders were not the last to fight against Prussian centralisation.

Now, the Prussian state, motivated by a sound instinct of self-preservation, wanted a Constitution so as to remain a state like the others and establish a hegemony. Prussian particularism was both conservative and liberal in origin. It resolved the constitutional problem to its own advantage. The King preferred Prussian liberalism to that of Frankfort. The Prussian Constitution smashed the Frankfort Constitution. Frankfort wanted to use Berlin, but it was Berlin that used Frankfort.

But the problem of German unity had not yet been settled. Prussia by saving her existence endangered her position as a unifying factor. She paid for her safety in 1850 by the humiliating defeat at Olmütz, when she had to give in to Austria, who opposed her projected Union of the German States. The dream of unity under Prussia's aegis suddenly vanished, and the Frankfort Diet picked up the broken thread of her traditions.

Nothing shows the true nature of German liberalism more clearly than this political tragedy. It was in the name of liberalism that the Assembly tried to build the *Reich*, and in the name of liberalism that Prussia kept her comparative independence. But Prussia, in spite of her set-back at Olmütz, had strength on her side. The day was not far off when Bismarck was to unite Germany, no longer in the name of democratic liberty, but by force, by blood and iron, after winning three military victories. So the tragedy of 1848 already foreshadowed Europe's tragedy in the twentieth century.

1848 IN AUSTRIA

ROBERT ENDRES

There is only one effective weapon against democrats: the army
W. von Merckel

Freedom: there is a word that echoes round the world
Anastasius Grün

I

VIENNA IN THE MONTH OF MARCH

THE news of the fall of the Bourgeois King of France reached Vienna in the first week of March. It had a profound effect on the people. A new hope filled all the opponents of the régime, who had been growing more and more determined to end a situation which had now become intolerable. This opposition was drawn from all sections of the populace: proletarian, upper- and lower-middle classes, the liberal nobles and certain factions in the Court. But they had only one object in common, which was to remove the Chancellor, Metternich. Apart from that, each class had its own particular aims.

The proletariat were living in the appalling conditions created in every country by the growth of large-scale capitalism. They suffered from low wages, long working hours in bad conditions, and the employment of women and children. The lower-middle class was afraid of being wiped out altogether by the increasing use of machinery, and was angry with the government for not heeding their plea for protection. The upper-middle class wanted a share in legislation and administration, so as to reform the State to meet the needs of capitalism. The liberal nobles wanted to introduce reforms to forestall a possible peasant rising. Finally, Metternich was hated in certain Court circles for his influence over the weak-minded and weak-willed Emperor Ferdinand.

The universal feeling of unrest gave vent to a flood of petitions which poured in on the Court from every quarter. One had been drawn up by the students, who decided to present it to the Lower-Austrian Diet, which was in session at the *Landhaus*. They planned to support their demands by organising a mass march. On 13 March, therefore, in the early hours of the afternoon, a long procession of students accompanied by a crowd of interested spectators, made their way towards the *Landhaus* and the Kerrengasse. They stopped in the *Landhaus'* courtyard, where a young doctor named Fischhof made an impassioned speech and read aloud the address spoken by Louis Kossuth on 3 March to the Hungarian Diet. His ardent words further inflamed the crowd. After a lengthy parley, the students finally prevailed upon the Diet to present their petition to the Emperor, and the entire crowd followed deputies to the Hofburg.

When they arrived, the guard would admit only the deputies, so the crowd spread out in the adjoining streets and squares. Shortly afterwards numbers of workmen began to arrive from the suburbs. The authorities grew alarmed and ordered the area surrounding the palace to be cleared. Archduke Albrecht, the military commander of Lower-Austria and Vienna, told the palace troops to take no half measures, with the result that, without more ado, they opened fire on the closely packed crowd. Five people were killed, and the crowd, in a paroxysm of rage, rushed the guard. But they were armed only with sticks and stones and were easily driven off. In the meantime another clash had taken place outside the city gates, which had been shut to prevent a further influx of workmen. But there, too, the troops easily defeated their unarmed opponents. The workmen thereupon returned to their own districts, where they looted several shops, and set fire to a number of factories whose owners were notorious for exploiting their employees.

When evening came the glow of these fires could be seen from the Hofburg where discussions were in progress. The Emperor, who would have to make the final decision, was ill and incapable of performing any act of government. So the negotiations were left to the State Council headed by Metternich and Archduke Louis. The Court itself was divided. An important faction led by the Archduchess Sophia wanted to sacrifice Metternich to the anger of the populace and declared that he should resign. The Archduchess Sophia, the Emperor's sister-in-law and the mother of the heir presumptive, hoped to use the troubles to be rid of the Chancellor whom she hated and who blocked all her efforts to make the Emperor abdicate. Her influence was doubtless the cause of the police not immediately dispersing the students, for until the month of March the government had not been in the habit of allowing that kind of demonstration to grow to such proportions.

The other faction, which included the Archdukes Louis, Albrecht and Maximilian, as well as Metternich himself, was in favour of taking strong action. That is why the deputies from the Diet, the students' delegations and the middle-class militia had to wait so long for an answer. There were endless arguments over their two demands, which were Metternich's resignation and the formation of a National Guard. However, when the menacing glow of the fires in the suburbs was seen, the Archduke Louis decided to grant both demands. So the first day of the revolution ended in a partial success. Its future development resulted from the Court's unwillingness to make further concessions. The first day also broke up the united front presented by Metternich's opponents. The middle class, terrified by the proletariat's revolt, was prepared to be content with a few minor concessions; it was far more anxious to safeguard its factories than acquire the reins of government. The Court was satisfied with Metternich's departure, and saw no reason for taking any further part in the revolution. In the suburbs, the middle-class militia and the National Guard took shameful toll of the workers, thousands of whom were arrested and imprisoned. Several, too, were killed—not in a war against the old feudal and bureaucratic system and the soldiery defending it, but by the upholders of middle-class rule, who infinitely preferred freedom to exploit their employees to political and religious liberties.

Without the sacrifice of the proletariat, however, the middle class could not succeed in their object of replacing bureaucratic absolutism by a system of popular representation, so when the government tried to rescind the concessions it had made, the consequence was that it reformed the united revolutionary front.

On 14 March the news went round that the Archduke Albrecht, who had been responsible for the shooting on the previous day, had been replaced by Prince Windischgrätz, a notorious reactionary. He was henceforth in complete control of both civil and military authorities. This change was bound to increase the people's resentment, and all day long a tumultuous crowd thronged the streets round the Hofburg. There were no clashes with the troops, however, who simply manned the fortifications and guarded the city gates to prevent entry from the suburbs.

The numerous delegations of citizens, students and National Guard which came to demand a Constitution all met with a categorical refusal. The Court added insult to injury by offering them in its stead a 'Permanent Central Committee', entitled merely to make recommendations to the Government. An outbreak of violence seemed unavoidable, for the crowd appeared to be bent on assaulting the Hofburg, when at the last minute the Emperor intervened. On his express orders, an announcement was made on the afternoon of the 15th to the Viennese and all the Emperor's subjects that he had granted them a Constitution. This proclamation was received with transports of delight and that night the whole city was illuminated.

But the people's joy was premature, for the official communiqué stated merely that the Emperor was to summon the Diet, with additional middle-class members, to discuss this Constitution. No mention was made of popular representation, universal suffrage or any other important matter. Furthermore, even after 15 March, a state of siege existed in Vienna. The garrison had been doubled by reinforcements from the provinces and now totalled twenty thousand men. The strongpoints were manned and there were troops under canvas on the waste ground between the fortifications and the suburbs. In the suburbs themselves arrests became more and more frequent. Anyone who still did not see where events were leading had only to study the composition of the Cabinet, which was made public on 21 March. It was composed exclusively of reactionaries and bureaucrats—'the old gang', in fact. Three of the seven ministers were counts, three were barons, and only one was a member of the middle class. The reactionaries had retreated a pace or two before revolutionary pressure, but they were determined to recover the ground lost at the first possible opportunity. The new government was to be their means of doing so.

The Kolowrat-Pillersdorf Cabinet was too weak to quell the revolutionary movement by force of arms, but on the other hand it was too reactionary to make a firm stand for the Constitution. It continually wavered between the revolutionaries' demands and the reactionaries' instructions, with the result that it soon became universally distrusted and the democrats gained fresh impetus. Ever since the abolition of the censorship on 15 March, the Court circles—the *Camarilla*, as they were known—had been working on a new law which would enable them to muzzle the press. Pillersdorf was afraid that it would provoke a new rising, so decided not to introduce it, but his revised version, which he brought in on 31 March, was scarcely more liberal. The Imperial House, high officials and certain State and ecclesiastical institutions were protected by special regulations; publication of a newspaper entailed the payment of a large deposit as caution money; and the public prosecutor could order the confiscation of any edition he considered might endanger the safety of the State. Finally, journalistic offences came under the jurisdiction of professional judges. The students, who after 15 March had taken over the lead of the liberal movement—a proof of the middle class's political immaturity—agitated against these press laws and forced Pillersdorf to rescind them. This sign of the government's weakness gave the radicals renewed confidence.

The only sections content with the outcome of 15 March were the nobility and the upper-middle class. The artisans and workmen had made no essential gains and, above all, there had been no improvement in their economic position. The democrats were not satisfied either, for the concessions they had obtained were no proof that Austria was to become a constitutional monarchy. But the radicals had neither a clearly defined programme nor an energetic leadership to take its place should the need arise.

So a leaderless revolutionary movement was confronted with an aimless government. No one knew how to escape from this dilemma, for the provinces were in no better position than the capital to undertake a revolution.

In the capitals of the Alpine provinces there existed an intellectually and politically undeveloped middle class which, although far from content with its lot, had not even envisaged the possibility of violent upheaval. It welcomed the news of the Vienna revolution, but made no serious effort to help the Viennese. After a few days of disturbances, daily life returned to its normal course in the Alpine towns. The same old officials carried on in the same old way, and to all appearances no change had taken place.

The peasants, who might have been expected to give some active support to the Viennese revolutionaries, merely waited and hoped. The conditions of those in the German-speaking provinces were, in fact, much better than among the Slavs and Hungarians. They had owned their own plots of land since the reign of Joseph II (1770–80), and feudal dues, although heavy, were bearable. But although Joseph II had given them their personal freedom and abolished serfdom, they were still tied by their duties towards the great landowners. Two generations after the French Revolution, the Austrian peasants owed absolute obedience towards the landed nobility and their bailiffs. These landowners represented the State in the countryside, and the main powers of administration and primary jurisdiction were in their hands. Their bailiffs saw that the peasants paid their taxes, carried out land surveys, and acted as guardians for orphans; the administration of forests, fire services, labour, constructional works and public security was in their hands; and they published and enforced the imperial decrees. The peasant certainly had the right to appeal if he considered he had been wronged, but in actual fact he was very rarely able to exercise it. For all practical purposes, the peasants were the slaves of complete despotism, which is why one might have expected them to seek their emancipation through the revolution. Events were to show, however, that they could not improve their lot by themselves, but needed assistance from the towns as they had neither leaders nor organisation.

The Vienna revolution was to meet much more sympathy from the Czechs than from the people of the Alpine provinces. Prague might have become a second revolutionary stronghold had the mutual enmity of Czechs and Germans not caused the energies of the revolutionaries to be diverted by a fruitless nationalist quarrel. The antagonism between the two races came to the surface when the inhabitants of the Alpine provinces and the Sudetens, who until 1806 had formed part of the old German Empire, were invited to send deputies to the German National Parliament at Frankfort. The Czechs quite rightly refused, as they were not Germans, but they thereby enraged the Sudeten Germans. National feelings ran so high that the revolution in Bohemia was paralysed, and Vienna could expect no support from that quarter.

As for Hungary and her dependencies, and the Italian provinces, they were all busy with their own revolutions, which had only an indirect influence on events in Austria.

For the greater part of the time, therefore, the revolutionary movement in Vienna was at a standstill for want of a coherent programme, intelligent leadership and support from the provinces. But the Government, by its equivocal behaviour, time and again set it once more in motion.

2

REVOLUTION AND REACTION

In the course of the tumultuous days of March, the Viennese had, as we have seen, overthrown absolutism and forced their Emperor to promise them a Constitution. Henceforth everything depended on the way the promise was fulfilled. The Pillersdorf Government did not follow the course laid down by the imperial proclamation of 15 March. It did not call upon the Diet to elaborate the new Constitution, but simply copied the Belgian Constitution of 1831 and published part of it on 25 April. It was significant that this charter, which was to establish the relationship between the sovereign and his people on a new footing, already broke the terms of the Emperor's promise by being promulgated without reference to the people's representatives. What was even more serious was that the principal aim of this charter appeared to be to restrict the people's rights. Furthermore, it took no account of the special needs of the Empire with its incongruous medley of eleven different nationalities. Neither Hungary and her dependencies, nor Italy, was even mentioned. Admittedly Italy was in chaos, but Hungary had already acquired a privileged position within the framework of the Empire and forced Vienna to recognise her own Constitution.

The wishes of the Poles and the Czechs, who were striving to obtain constitutions like Hungary's, had not been taken into consideration any more than had Austria's relations with the German Confederation, whose reorganisation was under discussion at Frankfort. The new Constitution

AUSTRIA

was a centralist one, that is to say, that it centralised the legislature and the executive in the hands of a Parliament and the Imperial Government. That was a grave mistake, to start with, for it was extremely hard to govern the heterogeneous Austrian Empire from a single capital. None of the seven races in Austria proper—excluding Hungary and Italy—was numerically strong enough to rule the rest. For centuries the German-speaking Austrians had been the ruling race; and the administrative and judicial authorities used German in their official correspondence. The other races objected to this monopoly and claimed equal rights for their own tongues. If at this point each province and its legislative body had been granted a *Landtag*, wider liberties and a stronger influence over the legislature and the executive, it would have been much easier to overcome the difficulties presented by the existence of seven different nationalities in a relatively small area. But the Government had not even considered the question when it was elaborating the Constitution. Pillersdorf was far more concerned with curtailing popular representation as much as possible. And he was wholly successful.

The Imperial Parliament was to consist of two Chambers, a Senate and a Chamber of Deputies. The first was to be composed of both life-members and members elected for the length of a legislative session. The first group was to consist of Imperial Princes who had attained their majority and a certain number of nobles, and the second of members elected by the great landowners. In fact, the Senate was to be monopolised by the nobility and become a kind of Chamber of Peers. The electorate sending members to the second Chamber was to be subject to so high a property qualification that the proletariat, peasantry and lower-middle class were virtually excluded, and the Chamber of Deputies was therefore accessible only to the upper-middle class, the bankers, big business men and industrialists. So the phrase 'popular representation' became a mockery. Furthermore, the government had provided for a system of indirect elections, and invented various other obstacles.

This reactionary electoral law delighted the nobility and the upper-middle class, but aroused fierce resentment among the other classes and led to violent demonstrations, particularly on 2 May. Once again the Government gave in to popular pressure. On 9 May there appeared a new electoral law, without the property qualification, so the lower-middle class and the peasants were able to vote. But workmen were still ineligible. There was a clause stating that 'workmen paid by the day or by the week, domestic servants and persons receiving public assistance are not eligible to vote for candidates standing for the Chamber of Deputies'. The government expected this clause to break the revolutionaries' united front.

ROBERT ENDRES

It seemed at first as though it had succeeded, for Vienna remained calm after 9 May. Pillersdorf, emboldened by the lull, decided to strike another blow at the revolution. On 14 May the 'Central Committee' was dissolved. This committee had been born in the course of the May demonstrations, when the proletariat and lower-middle class, led by the students, protested against the property qualification for voters. At that time the National Guard and the University Legion, formed after 13 March, had elected trustworthy representatives to a 'Central Political Committee of the Viennese National Guard'. The government disapproved of this body and ordered its dissolution, which led to the *Sturmpetition*, or 'Storm Petition', of 15 May. The students and the National Guards, accompanied by thousands of members of the proletariat and lower-middle class, marched through the town to the Hofburg. At many points on their route, the army fraternised with the demonstrators, with the result that the government was obliged to give way. The demonstrators presented the following five demands: the Central Committee should be restored; strong points in the city should be jointly occupied by regular troops and National Guards; the army should be called in only at the request of the National Guard; universal suffrage should be introduced; and parliament should consist of a single Chamber. The first three demands came from the students and the two others, which were far more ambitious, had been added during the course of the demonstration. Here was further proof that the revolutionaries lacked a programme and leaders who could see further ahead than the needs of the moment. The complete success of the *Sturmpetition* produced a wave of enthusiasm in Vienna, which extended even to the nobility and the upper-middle class, who certainly had no cause to rejoice. But when the Court left the capital for Innsbruck, the enthusiasm died down.

The reason the Court gave for its departure was that the Emperor's health was seriously endangered by the permanent state of turmoil in Vienna. In point of fact, Ferdinand, who had never ruled of his own accord, was very little affected by the course of events, as he had no idea where they were leading. This insignificant and slow-witted monarch had not left Vienna of his own free will, he had simply been abducted by the Court. His entourage, composed of out-and-out reactionaries, could not bear to see Austria under a Constitution which would deprive the nobility and the bureaucrats of their exclusive control. They were wholly determined to restore absolutism. The leading spirit of the *Camarilla* was the Archduchess Sophia, who had joined the ranks of the reactionaries after the fall of Metternich, when she realised that the revolutionaries were pursuing their own ends instead of serving hers. Around her were the other members of the ruling House, the high Court and government officials and the Generals, who had their own views on politics and who followed Prince Windischgrätz. At this time he was in Prague as the military commander of Bohemia. He had at his disposal an army of forty thousand men and was waiting to seize the first opportunity to use it to quell the revolution. He kept in close touch with General Hammerstein, the military commander of Galicia, as well as with Marshal Radetzky, the Commander-in-Chief of the Southern Army fighting in Italy, and every other opponent of the new régime. He corresponded frequently with his friend Count Latour, the War Minister, who kept him informed of the state of affairs in Vienna as well as the situation at Court. That was how the reactionaries concentrated their forces and awaited the moment for a counter-attack.

The first blow struck at the revolutionaries was the abduction of the Emperor. The result surpassed the reactionaries' hopes. All the waverers who had been led by the events of the last few weeks to acclaim the revolution, now tried to make amends by protestations of loyalty, and countless petitions arrived at Innsbruck begging the Emperor to return to his capital. The Viennese have since been blamed for their weakness of character, but we must not forget that only certain sections of the populace behaved in this shameful manner, and they were chiefly the nobles, the upper-middle class and the government officials as well as those opportunists who always back the favourite. We must also remember that the people of Austria had suffered for more than ten centuries under an absolutism which, although superficially less tyrannous than that of France, had had far deeper effects and had broken the people's spirit.

In Austria, as in France, the eighteenth century had seen the victory of bureaucratic absolutism over the feudal system. And the government had the support of a single Church, for the Counter-Reformation had banished every denomination except Catholicism. In Western Europe, which was economically far more advanced, the middle classes had been quick to seek control of the State. Their battle for power against the nobility had produced the new ideas in statesmanship, law, economics, religion, art and science which mark the age of enlightenment; so the era of absolutism in Western Europe was marked not by an intellectual set-back but by continual progress. It was the very opposite in Austria and Central Europe, for their backward economical conditions had resulted in trade shifting from the Mediterranean to the Atlantic, so the middle, commercial, class was infinitely weaker than it was in the West. The appalling destruction created by the Thirty Years War, and the wars with Turkey (which had laid waste whole provinces of Austria), and finally Austria's conglomeration of backward peoples almost without tradition, had retarded her development. Furthermore, the Church forbade freedom of thought and the State barred any influx of new ideas from the West, so between the two of them they purposely kept the people in a state of abysmal ignorance.

Admittedly the era of reforms between 1740 and 1792 had seen attempts to remove the worst evils, and in Joseph II's reign Austria had almost surpassed France in the way of reforms which included the emancipation of the peasantry, religious freedom and the introduction of public assistance. But in the course of the next two generations Austria marked time while the rest of the world went ahead increasingly rapidly. Before March 1848, she was far behind Western Europe both economically and intellectually, and the very words liberalism and socialism were almost unknown. Children were given only the most elementary education, and even educated people found it hard to keep in touch with cultural developments in the West and to obtain the German classics. Austria's two centuries and more of subjection had atrophied any desire for political or intellectual freedom, and had quickly killed the spirit of Austrian nationalism, which had appeared when Austria was fighting in defence of her own territory against the Turks, the Prussians and the French. In the end the Austrians were forced to become as secretive, wily and subservient as those oriental races who have known similar oppression. It must be frankly admitted that the Austrian has less dignity and pride than people of other nations, but before reproaching him with it, we should remember that his lot has been far harder than that of the Western peoples. Both nation and national characteristics are the result of the destiny each people has experienced in the course of its evolution.

No one will deny that these national characteristics, formed by the influence of absolutism and a single Church, were particularly apparent in the Viennese. Unlike the Bourbons, the Hapsburgs had always lived in their capital, with the result that close relationships had been established between its citizens and the Court. When the latter left Vienna so unexpectedly, taking the Emperor with them, the Viennese felt it was a severe but not undeserved blow. They were filled with anger and remorse—anger against the men who had forced their 'good Emperor' to leave them, the students and National Guards who had presented the *Sturm-petition* on 15 May. For two days the whole of Vienna had acclaimed and fêted them as national heroes, but now the wind had changed and they were shunned. The members of the Central Committee no longer felt safe; many of them feared reprisals and would no longer have any part in the revolutionary movement, so in the end the Central Committee dissolved itself. First the nobles and upper-middle class had left the movement, and it was now the turn of the students and lower-middle class. But once again Pillersdorf's blundering government united its opponents against it.

Pillersdorf had clearly seen that public opinion was turning against the students, so he decided to dissolve the University Legion of the National Guard. On the morning of 26 May the population of Vienna were presented with a grandiloquent proclamation explaining how the events of 15 May had led to the Court's departure. It then went on to assert that all the provinces entirely disapproved of the conduct of the Viennese, which might mean, the people feared, that the new Diet would meet not in Vienna but in some provincial town. The proclamation ended with violent accusations against the University Legion and announced its dissolution. This ingenious mixture of fact and fiction was calculated to make the Viennese believe that their city was likely to lose its position as the capital and frighten them into withdrawing their support from the students, who would thus be easier to deal with. The Court forgot, however, that the students were the most active revolutionary element, being followed by the mass of the working class and the majority of artisans, and possessing a great influence over the National Guard. The reactionaries were right in thinking that the dissolution of the University Legion would deprive the revolutionary movement of its guiding body, but they acted a week too late. The emotion caused by the Court's departure had already died down; and the Viennese were angered by its refusal to return in spite of their humble plea for forgiveness. They also saw the hand of the *Camarilla* in the Emperor's departure, and it was already rumoured that he had been abducted. Finally, a number of people had lost their faith in Pillersdorf, who on account of his shilly-shallying was now looked upon as an ally of the reactionaries. These factors contributed to the failure of the attempt to isolate the students, which was equally due to the courageous attitude of these 'citizens of the University' themselves.

In the early hours of 26 May Count Colloredo, the commander of the Legion, appeared in front of the University accompanied by a number of professors and ordered the guard to stand down. Although he repeated his order three times, the students refused to obey. When troops arrived on the scene to enforce the government's decision, the students, under the leadership of their military chaplain, Professor Füster, entrenched themselves in the University and prepared for a desperate resistance. From all sides workmen and National Guards hurried to their assistance; barricades were erected throughout the centre of the city; and within a few hours the whole of Vienna was up in arms. Once again Pillersdorf gave way, and the order disbanding the legion was rescinded. The barricades, however, remained up until the 29th, for no one trusted the government any longer.

26 May had marked a new victory for the cause of freedom. The Government's insane attempt to take a strong line had been a complete

failure. But this time the victory had no tangible results. In March the revolutionaries had obtained the dismissal of the universally hated Metternich, the abolition of the censorship, the right of the people to bear arms again, and the grant of a Constitution. 15 May had brought in universal suffrage and the single Chamber. Both days, which had begun with demonstrations of a defensive kind, had ended in gains which the revolutionaries had not even thought of at the outset of the riots. But now, unless they started claiming social reforms, which neither the students nor the middle class would hear of, the revolutionaries had nothing further to fight for. The proletariat, which alone would benefit from a social upheaval, was totally unorganised and so could not carry on the revolution on its own.

The months of March and May 1848 had none the less given the workers some advantages. Freedom of the press and freedom to hold meetings had to some extent lightened their burden; also, wages had risen in certain industries, and—at any rate for a time—they were more humanely treated in the factories as their employers were growing afraid of them. But none of these improvements had any great significance. There were still neither trade unions nor working-class newspapers and, above all, the tremendous conception of socialism was unheard of. Wilhelm Weitling (1808–71), one of the first fighters for the emancipation of the proletariat, had tried in vain between 1834 and 1836 to form a vast working-class movement; and Karl Marx himself, who visited Vienna in August 1848, thought it too soon to start one. Under existing conditions, the right to vote did not mean much to the working class and they did not return a single representative to the 1848 *Reichstag*. Long working hours, the employment of women and children, starvation wages and lack of security all long outlived the fall of absolutism. It was of all the more importance to the working man that the Government at any rate recognised the 'right to work'. It tried to reduce the growing unemployment first by road construction then by reclamation of waste land, but when the costs grew far too heavy, the government contemplated cutting them down.

The Pillersdorf Cabinet had been dismissed on 8 July, as it had lost the confidence of the Court as well as the people by its shilly-shallying. The new Wessenberg-Doblhoff Cabinet was looked upon as a liberal one, which meant that it was slightly less reactionary than its predecessor. It demonstrated its liberalism principally by refusing at all costs to interfere with the country's economy. This was in an extremely bad way owing to closed markets, lack of raw material and commercial instability. The chief sufferers, as usual, were the manual workers who were near starvation, but Schwarzer, the Minister for Public Works, was less concerned with remedying their plight than with finding the money to pay for the works undertaken to reduce unemployment. As he was a firm believer in the principles of economic liberalism, he was convinced that the best way of increasing production was to lower wages. So his first action was to reduce those of persons employed on public works.

On 19 August, therefore, the Government announced that women and children so employed were to receive 15 instead of 20, and 10 instead of 12 kreutzer respectively, whilst the men's wage of 25 kreutzer would remain unchanged for the time being. As there was no work done during bad weather, and as Sundays and holidays were unpaid, even the old rates had been insufficient to provide the bare necessities of life, so the fall in wages hit the working class extremely hard.

Nevertheless, the first few days passed without incident, as the workers were waiting to hear the results of negotiations with the Government. But Schwarzer was implacable. He followed the example of his French colleague Marie, who by similar methods had provoked the June riots which had been quelled in a bath of blood by Cavaignac. And Schwarzer reminded the workers' delegation of the fact. He achieved the desired result: the Battle of the Prater on 23 August. It began with an absolutely harmless demonstration, but the police attempted to intervene and fighting ensued. The police were reinforced by the National Guard, but when the workers too received reinforcements, the skirmish turned into a pitched battle. The workers being unarmed suffered heavy losses, and when the National Guard returned that evening as the victors, they were greeted with the cheers of the propertied middle class, which had had its revenge for the terror it had felt for months past. The Court, too, expressed its thanks to the 'valiant Guard', and with good reason, for the Battle of the Prater had been a decisive victory for the forces of reaction.

It seemed on that black day of 23 August, when the National Guard had massacred the proletariat, as though the revolutionary front was broken once and for all. Recently, too, the Court had received good news from all the battlefields where its armies were counter-attacking the revolutionaries. The national risings of the Poles in Galicia and the Czechs in Bohemia had long been overwhelmed. Count Stadion, the governor of Galicia, and Lieutenant-Field-Marshal Count Castiglione, the commander of Cracow, had nipped the Polish revolution in the bud. Stadion had set the peasants against the landowners, telling them that dues in land and forced labour were to be abolished; Castiglione forced the people of Cracow to surrender by shelling the town. In Prague, Windischgrätz ended the Czech freedom movement by smashing the Whitsun Rising of 12 to 16 June, Radetzky subjugated Milan, after having won a decisive victory over Charles Albert near Custozza on 26 July, forcing him to ask for an armistice. And now the Battle of the Prater had broken the revolutionary front in Vienna. Only Hungary and Venetia were still in open revolt. But the reactionaries had found an invaluable ally against the Hungarians of Budapest in the Serbs and Croats of the south, who hoped one day to realise their national ambitions with the help of the Viennese Court. Their leaders, Jellacic, the Governor of Croatia, and Stratimirovic, the champion of Serbian freedom, saw too late that they were merely tools of the reaction.

Anyway, the Court had no intention of creating a new Austria in which the eleven nationalities could live at peace. The Emperor was clay in its hands, and its sole aim was to restore the old bureaucratic absolutism in its entirety. After the Poles, Czechs and Lombards had been subdued, it turned its full strength against Hungary. The Budapest Government was already at war with the Rumanians of Transylvania, the Serbs and the Croats. A second front in the west was bound to be its undoing, and the Court had only to find a pretext for opening one.

The Court had always been in close touch with Jellacic, but had not dared support him too openly. In the course of a visit to Innsbruck, Count Batthyani, the President of the Hungarian Council, had obtained an imperial decree depriving Jellacic of the command of the Croat army and his position as Governor of Croatia. Not that Jellacic had worried, since he was sure of the Court's secret support. But after the fall of Milan on 6 August, and the Battle of the Prater, the reactionaries considered they were strong enough to drop their mask: on 4 September Jellacic was reinstated, and a week later he crossed the Drave and prepared to march on Budapest.

In their distress, the Hungarians called on the Austrian *Reichstag* to intervene. One could then see how far national hatreds and prejudices had prevented people from taking a rational and calm view of the situation.

The *Reichstag* did not realise that if they crushed the Hungarian revolution it would be the end of constitutional rule in Austria. With the exception of the Poles, the Slavonic deputies, out of racial sentiment, supported the Croats. The Poles, on the other hand, wanted autonomy for Galicia on the lines of the Constitution acquired by the Hungarians at the beginning of the revolution, so they supported the Hungarians. The German deputies were divided into two groups. The centre party, which wanted a Greater Austria with a unitary empire governed from a single capital, were against the Hungarians, whom they considered were digging the Empire's grave. These 'peoples' representatives' of noble and upper-middle-class birth did not see that Austria's future lay not in centralisation and German predominance, but in a looser federation of the eleven nations. This federation would certainly have to have a united foreign policy, but within its boundaries each nationality should have had the right to develop its own culture in peace and freedom. Many of the ills for which the people of the Empire were to suffer were due to the Centre Party's obstinacy in clinging on to the idea of a Greater Austria. As for the democrats, although they saw the need for helping the Hungarians in their distress, they had no influence over the conservative majority. So the Diet refused to touch Hungary's affairs and intervene in her favour. Once again the reactionaries benefited and the Court knew that in the case of war with Hungary it need not fear the inopportune intervention of the Austrian *Reichstag*. The reactionaries were finally given their pretext for armed intervention by the assassination on 29 September of Count Lemberg, whom the Court had sent as an intermediary to Budapest.

3

THE OCTOBER REVOLUTION

At the end of September, Austrian regiments were sent off to help Jellacic. This was undeniably an interference in a neighbour's affairs such as the Diet had shunned some weeks earlier, when it came to helping Hungary, but the conservative majority refrained from pointing out the fact to Latour, the War Minister. The democrats, on the other hand, were afraid—and not without reason—that if Hungary was subdued by force the days of Austria's freedom were numbered. They were determined therefore to prevent the departure of any more troops, so on 6 October, when the Richter battalion was due to move into Hungary, they started demonstrations on a large scale. They began at dawn outside the Gumpenhof barracks, then spread to the Northern Station, where the rails were unbolted and the telegraph wires cut, and finally reached their height on the Tabor bridge. There, the students had entrenched themselves behind barricades so as to hinder the force. The War Minister threw in additional units against them, but with the aid of the Gumpenhof National Guard they resisted these as well, and in the course of the fighting captured three guns.

In the city itself there were clashes between the radicals and the reactionary municipal section of the National Guard, known as 'Black-and-Yellows'. The Wieden Guard had driven them back as far as the Church of St Stephen, where fifteen men were killed and ninety-five wounded. Fresh troops arrived and were again repulsed by the masses, whose fury turned against Latour, who had been responsible. They captured the War Ministry and strung up Latour himself on a lamp-post. Immediately afterwards they attacked the Renngasse arsenal which fell the following morning, thus the workers were able to obtain the arms they had previously been denied.

The events of 6 October were somewhat similar to those of 13 March and May, for once again the Government tried strong-arm tactics and enraged the mob by its intransigence. Then it gave way, capitulated to the revolutionary forces and was forced to make much larger concessions than had originally been asked for. The *Reichstag* was partly responsible for the fighting on 6 October. It was well aware of the atmosphere in Vienna, and yet carefully refrained from reminding the War Minister of the constitutional limits to his powers, for the majority of members were secretly on Jellacic's side and would not have been sorry to see Hungary humbled. On the other hand, there is nothing to support the hypothesis which has long been held that the Court intentionally provoked the rising in order to find an excuse to subdue Vienna by force of arms.

This does not mean to say that the new revolutionary outbreak seemed to it to be inopportune. On 7 October, the Court fled to the fortress of Olmütz in Moravia and put itself under the protection of the Bohemian army under Prince Windischgrätz, who immediately took over control of the operations. On 16 October there appeared a proclamation from the Emperor to his subjects, threatening the Viennese with harsh reprisals and announcing Windischgrätz's appointment to the command of all the Austrian armies with the exception of Radetzky's in Italy. Vienna was to be taught obedience by force of arms.

The Czech deputies who remained loyal to the Government protested against this proclamation, for they were horror-struck at the thought of so much power in the hands of a man like Windischgrätz. The Government yielded, for Prince Schwarzenberg, who was tipped for the presidency of the Council, and Count Stadion, the future Minister for the Interior, were on the side of the opposition. The proclamation was replaced by another calculated to have a pacificatory effect, for it guaranteed to disencumber the estates and uphold the Constitution. By a regrettable mistake, or perhaps on purpose, Prince Windischgrätz was sent not the new proclamation but the one of 16 October.

There ensued a long argument as to which was the valid proclamation between the Prince and the 'Rump Parliament' in Vienna, so called because the majority of deputies had left the capital on 7 October, some following the Court to Olmütz and others returning to their homes. This paper war was, incidentally, quite pointless, for legal arguments had little weight with a reactionary of the Prince's vintage. Force was the only argument he understood, and only a popular rising could have saved the cause of freedom at this juncture. Nor would an appeal to the people have fallen on deaf ears: this time the Alpine provinces were with the Viennese, and small detachments from Linz, Salzburg and Graz arrived to aid them in their fight against the reactionaries. Furthermore, even if the Czech politicians were loyal to the Government, the masses would certainly have answered an appeal from the *Reichstag*, for the name of Windischgrätz was hated throughout the length and breadth of Bohemia. In fact, peasant risings in the Alps or Sudetenland would have delayed the Imperial Army's march on Vienna and obliged the Government to change its tune. But the Parliament did not seize its last chance to save freedom. It insisted on acting in a legal manner. It was certainly democratically minded, but it had no breath of the revolutionary spirit.

This explains why the 'Rump Parliament' and the 'Permanent Committee' it elected to organise the defence of Vienna shirked their obligations. The Permanent Committee and the Municipal Council both spent all their energy in negotiations with Windischgrätz. The Municipal Council, composed entirely of reactionaries, did not even consider taking part in the battle and hoped for an early end to the revolution. The majority of the middle class—or at least that section of it which had not left the city—was in the same frame of mind. Only the working class, the University Legion and a handful of the lower-middle class was prepared to fight it out. But most of the leaders of the National Guard were from the upper-middle class, and the revolutionary spirit of the rank and file had no chance to develop. That is why indecision reigned in Vienna.

The Permanent Committee had ordered the Commander of the National Guard to take the necessary steps to ensure the defence of the capital, but the original commander, his successor and his successor's successor resigned their command. Finally, on 12 October, the Committee approached a retired Lieutenant named Messenhauser, who was prepared to give himself heart and soul to the defence of his native city; but he was neither an organiser nor an army commander and his good will was not enough for him to overcome all the obstacles put in his path. His Chief of Staff was the former Polish revolutionary General Bem, who had proved his military ability in 1831 and later in Hungary: but he too was unable to manage his subordinates.

The force defending Vienna consisted of the National Guard, the University Legion and the militia. The National Guard, which in the summer had been 42,000 strong, had lost half its number by the departure of the municipal section, the 'Black-and-Yellows'; the University Legion had only a thousand men, one-fifth of its strength in May. The militia, on the other hand, which had been embodied shortly after 6 October, was a considerable force; its nucleus consisting of workmen and regular troops sympathetic to the revolution, most of them from the Richter battalion, but there were also men from many other units. The militia was inadequately armed and under-trained, but its morale was good and its determination made it a valuable addition to the defence force. But the total force did not exceed 40,000 men, hardly enough to man the fortifications; and there was a shortage of artillery, ammunition and every type of weapon. Vienna, therefore, could not hold out long unless outside help arrived.

As the *Reichstag* had failed to call upon the peoples of the Empire to join the war for freedom, the only possible ally was again the Hungarian army. But the Hungarian Defence Committee hesitated to order its intervention, since it too did not want to act illegally and was waiting for an appeal from the representatives of the Austrian people. So the Imperial Army was able to advance on the capital in perfect safety.

Since 6 October the Vienna garrison had been stationed in the Schwarzenberg Park and the Belvedere, waiting for the situation to develop. On the 10th Jellacic, who had retired to Presburg after the battle of Velencze, arrived outside Vienna. The events of the 6th had come at an opportune moment for him, as they gave him an excuse for leaving Hungary where his position was untenable since he was cut off from Croatia. The Bohemian Army arrived on the 21st, so there were now 70,000 men and 200 pieces of artillery threatening the capital. After a few skirmishes between the outposts, the battle was joined on 23 October on the line Hernals-Nussdorf. Two days later the Imperial Army launched their first major offensive; they penetrated as far as Leopoldstadt, which was then a suburb, and on the 28th captured it. By that time they had reached the city walls at two points, and after taking the Southern and Eastern railway stations and the eastern suburbs had reached the fortifications.

The fortifications consisted of a double ring: the city proper (the modern district 1) was surrounded by its ancient walls which had already withstood the Turks; then there was an outer ring of fortifications, dating from the eighteenth century, round the suburbs (the modern districts 2 to 9). This was composed of an embankment thirteen feet high and the same distance across, with a deep ditch in front; it stretched from St Marx to Liechtental and was reinforced at two points by the natural barrier of the Danube.

On the 29th the negotiations between the Viennese Municipal Council and Windischgrätz resulted in a truce. Everything was prepared for a capitulation when on the 30th the sound of gunfire was heard to the east: the Hungarians under General Moga had crossed the Leitha. They had halted, however, between the rivers Fischa and Schwechat, waiting to establish contact with Vienna. They failed to do so, with the result that the Hungarians and Viennese failed to take Windischgrätz's army in a pincer movement, and the battle on the Schwechat ended in the retreat of the Hungarians. In the city, on the other hand, there was a change of heart: the radicals no longer talked of surrender and the Guards in the suburbs recommenced the battle. In spite of this, the next day the Municipal Council sent a fresh delegation to Windischgrätz, agreeing to show they were willing to surrender by hoisting a black and yellow flag on the tower of St Stephen's. But a group of radicals prevented their doing so, and the Imperial Army attacked. They occupied the suburbs in the morning and the city itself in the afternoon without meeting serious resistance. On the 31st Vienna was in their hands.

The effect of Windischgrätz letting his troops loose on the capital was appalling. For months the officers of the Bohemian Army had been inciting their men against Vienna with denunciations of its inhabitants' 'shameful conduct' and descriptions of the city's legendary wealth. Thus the troops were inflamed with anger and greed, and looting began the instant they entered the suburbs. But as they found little of value in the houses of the poor weavers and petty artisans, their disappointment turned to rage and they slaughtered the inhabitants. We have the testimony of an eye-witness that in a single street of the 5th district fifty-seven people, none of them armed, were massacred. There must have been several thousand killed in the whole of Vienna, but of course there are no official figures to record the shame of the Imperial Army, which behaved in a more bestial fashion in the capital of their own country than the Huns or the Janissaries.

Excuses might be found for the atrocities of a band of brutal soldiers, following the example of their own officers, who took part personally in the looting and murder, but not for the legalised slaughter which followed. From November to April, 1849, 2,400 people were thrown into prison, not counting those who were freed after a short period. Seventy-two death sentences were pronounced and twenty-five carried out; 460 prisoners were condemned to long prison sentences, and 1,320 were acquitted only after several months' detention. Among the victims were Messenhauser, the commander of the Viennese forces, and Robert Blum, the member of the Frankfort Assembly, who fell victim to a personal vendetta.

Behind this vicious revenge lay the fear of a new rising by the Viennese. That is why a state of siege continued for several years and in the spring of 1849 people were still being shot for possessing arms. Many men were forcibly enrolled in the army in spite of being acquitted by the tribunals. The members of the University Legion were the worst sufferers, for out of pure cruelty they were put as private soldiers in units composed of the coarsest, most degraded illiterates. The civil authorities were put under the Generals, among whom Gordon (the future War Minister), Welden and Kempen were the most hated. The radical press was suppressed and the remaining journals were subjected to the strictest censorship. All democratic and workers' associations were banned after November 1848. A flock of stool-pigeons settled on Vienna, denouncing everyone who dared speak too freely. Long hair and bushy beards were a dangerous luxury for their wearers, who were immediately hauled off to the police station and shaved. Wide-brimmed hats were equally offensive to the guardians of the peace, whose truncheons were in constant use. And yet Austria was still under a Constitution guaranteeing her citizens their fundamental rights.

The Parliament in the meantime had moved to the little Moravian town of Kremsier, whilst the Court and the Government were still at Olmütz, and dared not criticise the shameful conduct of the Generals, who ruled the city as despotically as an ottoman of Turkish pashas. The democrats themselves had earned ironical comments from their opponents by dissociating themselves from the October Revolution. The *Reichstag* had certainly not fulfilled its part in the political evolution of the country, but it did do two things of importance: it suppressed feudal rights over the land and it produced the Kremsier Constitution.

4

THE REACTIONARIES' RETURN TO POWER

On 21 November, three weeks after the fall of Vienna, a new Cabinet was formed. The Government, headed by Prince Schwarzenberg, Windischgrätz's brother-in-law, was much more reactionary than its predecessors, but it did include some valuable experts. Among these were Count Stadion, Minister of the Interior; Bach, Minister of Justice; Bruck, Minister of Commerce; and Krauss, Minister of Finance. They were responsible for the reforms which gradually transformed the half-feudal, half-bureaucratic Empire into a modern middle-class State. Schwarzenberg was determined to dissolve the *Reichstag* at the first possible opportunity, but the revolution was far from over in Hungary, the battle for hegemony in Germany was still being fought, a fresh revolt might break out any minute in Italy and in Austria itself the spirit of the revolution was not yet dead. He thought it best therefore to allow the Parliament a few months' grace. It profited by the respite to draft the Constitution, for it had already completed its other task of freeing the land.

On 26 July 1848 the deputy Hans Kudlich had moved the abolition of serfdom, together with its accompanying rights and obligations, and raised the question whether or not the landowners should receive compensation. The matter was debated from 6 August to 6 September, when the *Reichstag* voted the proposed reform, and compensation for the land disencumbered, leaving it to the Government to decide how the law should be enforced. They thereby completed the emancipation of the peasantry begun by Joseph II in 1781.

The Parliament's draft for a Constitution, however, contained so liberal a definition of civic rights and so many allusions to popular sovereignty that it set the reactionaries against the representatives of the people and on 7 March, only a few days before the final vote on the Constitution, Schwarzenberg dissolved the Parliament. At the same time, the Government promulgated a new charter, which applied to the whole of the Austrian Empire including Hungary. Actually, this charter was never put into force, but its publication was designed to give the impression abroad that Austria was a Constitutional monarchy.

But revolutions have their own laws. One may suppress them by force of arms, and oppress their makers, but the fact remains that they have taken place, and it is impossible to pick up the old way of life exactly where one left off. The Schwarzenberg Government was obliged to introduce certain so-called 'liberal' reforms. In point of fact, Stadion, Bach and Bruck were 'liberals' only in so much as they were less narrow in outlook than the Court and the advisers of the new, eighteen-year-old Emperor Francis Joseph, in whose favour Ferdinand had abdicated on 2 December 1848. The latter abdicated under pressure from his *entourage*, in particular the Empress and Archduchess Sophia, who was determined to see her son on the throne so that she could rule in his name. Francis Joseph took an oath on the Constitution, but that did not prevent him from governing, after 7 March, without the help of the representatives of the people, or, on 31 December 1851, from reviving complete absolutism.

This retrogression was due to the nobles, who hoped that a restoration of absolute rule would also restore their economic and social privileges, the very foundations of which had been shaken by the revolution. Serfdom had been suppressed, and the landowner had also lost his right to levy dues in kind and the 'robot' or forced labour from the freed peasants. Furthermore the nobles had lost their special judicial powers, for the principle of equality before the law had been enforced even in Austria. But what annoyed them most was that riches had gradually come to replace birth in the social hierarchy: a man was no longer esteemed for his ancestors' valorous deeds, his title or his name, but for his wealth. True, the nobles were still the topmost class in society, were accorded precedence on certain occasions and were received at Court, but they were no longer given, as a matter of course, the key posts in the army and the civil administration. They found themselves on the defensive against the rising middle class, so they naturally opposed a Constitution which gave this class even a modicum of influence in the legislature and executive of the State.

The upper-middle class was extremely pleased with this revolution, although it had continually betrayed it. It was the first to benefit by it because, in Austria as elsewhere, the year 1848 marked the end of feudalism and the rise of capitalism. What was more, officialdom became a preserve of the middle class, and this easily consoled it for the lack of representation in Parliament. Finally it was once again master of its factories, for the Government had suppressed the workers' newly won rights.

The peasants, too, benefited by the revolution: their lands were freed from the control of the nobility and they themselves were no longer at the mercy of the nobles' arbitrary whims. Yet only those who had large and medium-sized holdings benefited, for the smallholders and day labourers found no appreciable improvement in their economic situation. But as capitalism, freed from the shackles of feudalism, had made tremendous strides, the young peasants were able to earn a living in the towns, and their exodus removed the surplus population which had hitherto been such a burden on the countryside. The workers and lower-middle class, on the other hand, who had made the greatest sacrifices, lost the fruits of their fight for freedom. The lower-middle class suffered from the devaluation of manual labour; and, threatened by a drop in the social scale, they were frightened into joining the ranks of the reactionaries. They denied the ideals of 1848 and sought help and protection from the rich middle class, whom they were henceforth to support politically. Finally the workers had returned to their old bondage, and their emancipation was not to be won until half a century later.

These changes in the social system were a major result of the revolution, but the reforms introduced were equally important. The first of these was the freeing of the land, which had to be effectively done if another revolution were to be avoided. An imperial decree applying the law of 7 September 1848 and releasing the peasants from all feudal obligations was published on 7 March 1849, but it was applicable only to the Alpine provinces and Sudetenland: special measures were required for Hungary, Galicia and the Bukowina. This law laid down the following principles:

the landowners were to receive no compensation for the loss of their police and judicial powers; a 'minimum' compensation was to be paid for the loss of the right to levy taxes and command forced labour[1]; dues in kind were considerably reduced and the value of the land for purposes of taxation was taken into consideration: and money dues were reduced by one-third. The total expense incurred by the State was considered to be equal to the interest on capital twenty times greater, which was to be repaid not in cash but in special 'liberation bonds' redeemable in forty years. In the Austrian half of the Empire two hundred and ninety million florins (£29 million) were paid in this way, and thus 2,872,000 peasants were enabled to own their land.

This law ended the era of the great landowners. In their place appeared the rural 'commune', created by the law of 17 March 1849. It enforced the laws of the State, and was solely responsible for looking after the poor and sick, keeping up the roads, controlling the commune's finances, fighting fires. At the same time it maintained a police force (also responsible to the State authorities) to patrol the fields and roads and keep the peace. The commune's affairs were in the hands of a municipal council, elected by the taxpayers, which appointed its own mayor and officers. Each commune possessed two or even three bodies of electors according to the scale of taxation.

This system of communes worked extremely well and its general principles are still in force today. The communes were under the District authorities, who enforced the regulations made by the *Statthalter*, or Imperial and Royal governor of the province. The Governors were primarily concerned with police, commercial and industrial matters; religious and educational affairs; agriculture and public works. All local government officials were State servants, and the old administrative departments of the Court were replaced by eight ministries: Foreign Affairs; the Interior; Justice; Finance; Commerce; Education; Agriculture and War. The first six were created in 1848 and the last two in March 1849.

The reorganisation of the State was completed by a revised judicial system. The civil and criminal courts of first instance became district courts, empowered to deal with minor offences and disputes. Major offences, crimes and important lawsuits were dealt with by District 'Collegiate' Courts (*Bezirks Kollegial-Gerichte*), called Provincial Courts (*Landesgerichte*) in the capital of each country. Above these were the

---

[1] This was worked out as follows: three days of forced labour were considered worth the wages for one day's voluntary labour: a third was deducted, representing the cost incurred by the landowner in supervising the work; and the remainder was divided equally between the State and the peasants.

Provincial High Courts (*Oberlandesgerichte*), and at the top was the Supreme Court. Under the new system proceedings were open to the public and evidence was given verbally both in criminal cases, before the Public Prosecutor, and before a jury.

The disencumbering of the land and the reorganisation of the administration were major achievements. A third was economic and customs unification. Here, too, the reforms introduced had been begun in the eighteenth century. Maria Theresa (1740–80) had already abolished the customs barriers within the hereditary States (Erbländer) and between Hungary, Transylvania and Croatia. But they still existed between the eastern and western halves of the Empire. Their justification was that taxes were much lower in Hungary than in Austria; so the duty imposed on goods sent between the two halves of the Empire not only protected the Austrian farmers but also partly compensated the State for the small revenue from Hungary. In 1849, however, the Hungarian nobility's exemption from taxation was abolished, and income and other taxes were made applicable to the whole of the Empire. The interior customs barriers had therefore lost their value, so they were abolished and economic unity was achieved over an area of 625,000 square kilometres, thereby permitting Austrian capitalism to industrialise the country on a grand scale. Lastly, in November 1851, new tariffs were fixed for foreign trade.

Bruck, the Minister of Commerce, had planned to link up with the German Customs Union, but Prussia objected. This episode was no more than an incident in the struggle for hegemony in Germany which was then taking place between the Hapsburgs and the Hohenzollerns.

5

AUSTRIA AND THE GERMAN QUESTION

When the representatives of the German people met for the first time at Frankfort to decide Germany's future, one of the items on their agenda was its relationship with Austria. From 1438 to 1740 the Hapsburg, and from 1745 to 1808 the Hapsburg-Lorraine, dynasty had worn the German Imperial crown. Austria's representative had precedence in Germany, and as in Italy, the Hapsburgs held a dominant position. Yet the German-speaking peoples formed only a minority in the old Austrian Empire, and furthermore—ever since 1526 and the Counter-Reformation—they had followed a very different path from that taken by the other Germanic peoples; their future was interlocked with that of the other Austrian nations and Hungary. The ties between these countries, which had been strengthened in the wars against the Turks, the French and the Prussians, on the battlefields of Hungary, Southern Germany and Bohemia, had led in the eighteenth century to dreams of a Greater Austria. Austria's eleven races had certainly not combined to make a single nation, but they had grown to feel some kind of solidarity between them. This idea of a Greater Austria conflicted before March 1848 with the nationalist aims, first of the Czechs and Magyars, and later of the other Austrian peoples.

This latent conflict came to light when the Frankfort Diet began to discuss which parts of the Hapsburgs' Empire should be incorporated in the new German Empire. The Diet's appointed task was to create a German national State, which by itself meant the exclusion of Slavonic, Magyar and Italian territories, and Article 2 of the projected Constitution stipulated that: 'no part of the German Empire shall combine with non-German lands to form a single State'. It went on to add that: 'if a German land is under the same ruler as a non-German land, the relations between the two shall be established solely on the basis of a personal union'. This meant in practice that the Austrian Empire would be broken into two halves, whose only connection would be a common sovereign. The question was whether or not such a tie would be strong enough for the Hapsburgs to hold on to Hungary.

The majority of German Austrians did not worry about this dilemma when they extolled the advantages of Austria becoming part of the new Germany. In the spring of 1848, a wave of enthusiasm swept Vienna, Graz, Innsbruck and the rest of the Alpine towns. They flew the black, red and gold flag of the German Empire, sang national songs and toasted the future Empire in gallons of liquor. The Sudeten Germans were eager to see Bohemia incorporated in it, hoping by union with their blood-brothers to re-establish their tottering dominion over the Czechs, since they were in the minority in Bohemia, Moravia and Silesia. Nevertheless they held the key positions in the country. Whereas the propertied middle class and many of the nobles in Bohemia considered themselves Germans, the Czechs were for the most part peasants, petty artisans and workmen, so that class differences were behind the clash of nationalities. These two antagonisms have always been so closely interwoven in Austria that the racial problem has been exceptionally hard for the foreigner to unravel.

Under these conditions, it is easy to understand that the Czechs fiercely resisted the movement to incorporate Bohemia in Germany: their aim was to develop their own national culture. That was why they refused to take part in the elections to the Frankfort Parliament, which increased the Germans' bitterness. The Slovenes of Southern Styria and Carniola, on the other hand, were almost indifferent to these events, for they were a peasant people with no history, who had not yet developed national feelings.

The Czechs met with wholehearted sympathy from the Austrian Government. The Viennese Court saw no advantages in the creation of a German Empire, for even if the crown were to fall to a Hapsburg, the dynasty would gain no additional prestige or power; the ruler of Austria was already an Emperor and his delegate presided over the German Confederation. Nevertheless the 1848 revolution had profoundly shaken the countries of the Empire, so Vienna tolerated the Frankfort Parliament' which had voted for the exclusion of non-German lands from the new Germany four days before Windischgrätz entered Vienna. That was the end of the Austrian revolution, but Austria did not break off relations with Frankfort until February 1849, after the battle of Kapolna, when the Schwarzenberg Government saw that Hungary was on the verge of collapse.

The Austrian reactionaries' contempt for the German Parliament was shown in their execution of Robert Blum, and the reasons they later gave for it. Schwarzenberg declared that 'the Austrian Government had not been officially notified of the decision reached on 30 September that German deputies were legally immune, so did not feel themselves bound by that decision'. Then on 7 March, the day on which it dissolved the Kremsier Parliament, the Austrian Government issued their new Constitution which they had 'granted'; making it applicable to every country in the Empire without exception. It was in complete contradiction to Article 3 of the Frankfort Constitution; and it strictly forbade members to be returned to the Frankfort Parliament.

The Frankfort Parliament, for its part, renounced the idea of creating a Greater Germany. On 26 March Frederick William IV of Prussia was chosen as the German Emperor, but he refused to accept the crown at the hands of the people. The creation of a United Germany was, however, one of Prussia's aims, which is why—on 9 May—she asked Austria to leave her *carte blanche* to create a smaller German Confederation under her own aegis, comprising all the German nations except those in the Austrian Empire. By way of compensation, she offered Austria a perpetual alliance with this Confederation, which was to be known as the 'Enlarged Confederation' or 'German Union', and a guarantee by the Union of Austria's right to Hungary and the Italian provinces. But as the Czar had promised his unconditional support against Hungary, and the Italian campaign had been successfully concluded, Vienna was in no hurry to consider this particular proposal.

Prussia then tried to form a Lesser German Union independently of Austria and in the face of Vienna's disapproval. She found a glorious opportunity in the risings in Upper and Central Germany which necessitated the intervention of Prussian troops, at a time when the Austrian army was fully occupied in Hungary and Italy. Twenty-eight small and middle-sized German states joined this Union. However she met strong opposition within her own borders. The dominant Junker class would not hear of a German Empire, for they considered themselves Prussians not Germans and felt a loyalty to their own country which, formed by the fusion of a number of different elements, had acquired its own national spirit in opposition to that of Germany as a whole.

We must not forget that whereas Spain, France, Russia, Sweden and other countries had, in the course of the sixteenth, seventeenth and eighteenth centuries, welded together their conglomeration of principalities, free towns, seignories and so forth into unitary States, Germany was still split up into these independent divisions. Then the Counter-Reformation had divided the country into Catholic Germany and Protestant Germany, and the Germans had lost any consciousness of themselves as a nation. On the other hand, the domains of the Hapsburgs and Hohenzollerns had developed, in the course of the eighteenth century, into European Powers under the leadership of Prussia and Austria respectively. This had created a Prussian and a 'Greater-Austrian' spirit. The first was by far the stronger, since national feelings had been aroused in the countries composing the Austrian Empire before the March revolution.

The Junkers' resistance, however, had prevented the Prussian government from taking the golden opportunity, in the summer of 1849, to carry out its plans. Schwarzenberg, who had his hands free after August, was able to win over the Central German countries of Bavaria, Württemberg, Saxony and Hanover. He suggested that Germany should be divided into six zones under the influence of Prussia, Austria and these four Kingdoms. This scheme looked as though it would create a balance of power, but in point of fact it would have meant Austria's supremacy in the German Confederation. A further suggestion was that the whole of Austria, including Hungary and the Italian provinces, should be incorporated in the Confederation, and that they should also share in the German Customs Union.

Prussia, for her part, summoned a new Diet at Erfurt, which between 20 March and 15 April devised a Constitution providing for a hereditary Emperor and an elected Parliament. The assembly of the Princes in Berlin, in May 1849, was intended to promote the King of Prussia to Emperor, but now the revolution had been quelled, the majority of them no longer wanted a German Empire.

Austria and Prussia then approached the Czar, Nicholas I, but their meetings in Warsaw from 28 to 30 May were unsuccessful, as he refused to arbitrate between them. That summer, two events strengthened Schwarzenberg's position in his dispute with Prussia. The London Protocol, concluded between France, England and Russia to decide the succession to the Danish throne, had to be ratified by Austria, Prussia and the German Confederation. Austria immediately agreed to the decision reached in London, whilst Prussia hesitated. This annoyed the Czar, but what made him even more angry was Prussia's taking the side of the Hessian Parliament in its quarrel with the Prince Elector. Austria, on the other hand, had joined with Bavaria in coercing the Hessian Parliament in accordance with the decision reached by the Assembly of the new German Confederation, which had been sitting at Frankfort since 2 September. Prussia had taken no part in this Assembly and refused to recognise its decision. The result was that at the second Warsaw meeting in October 1850, the Czar gave his full support to Schwarzenberg. Austria was now powerful enough to force Prussia to recognise the new German Confederation, and to sign the Treaty of Olmütz on 9 November 1850. Prussia had to submit to all her demands.

After winning this victory, the Austrian reactionaries felt they were in a particularly strong position. They immediately stopped their reforming activity, and legislation was modified accordingly. And when Louis Napoleon Bonaparte, President of the French Republic, risked the *coup d'état* of 2 December 1851, the Austrian reactionaries too dropped their mask: the Council of Ministers and the Imperial Council—composed of members appointed by the Government, and neither better nor worse than an elected assembly—decided at a combined session to withdraw the Constitution. Their decision was announced by ordinance on 31 December. There was no longer any need to pretend that the Hapsburg Empire was a Constitutional State.

Once the bureaucrats no longer had to fear the control of an elected Assembly, the administration fell back into the bad old ways of before March 1848. The problem of nationalities was still unsolved, and the Empire had missed its last chance to change with the times. Yet absolutism was finally to collapse in 1859 and 1866 on the battlefields of Italy and Bohemia. One can slow down the march of history but not halt it, and twenty years after their defeat, the ideals of 1848 were to triumph—even in Austria.

BOHEMIA

ARNOST KLIMA

I

SOCIAL AND ECONOMIC CONDITIONS

THE first half of the nineteenth century was of great importance in Bohemia. It was a time of rapid change in her economic structure. A large number of factories were built, and the manufacture of textiles, which until then had been a craft-industry organised on a family basis, was becoming industrialised. At the most, until then, there had been but few manufactures. Machines from the west, chiefly England, were being introduced, and the use of steam which by 1823 had become general, revolutionised conditions of production in Bohemia as it had done in Great Britain.

When, in 1763, the Silesian war between Frederick II and Maria Theresa ended with Prussia's annexation of a territory which was economically the most advanced in the Empire, Bohemia took its place as the textile centre of the Austrian Monarchy, and Austrian textiles began to appear on foreign markets.

To begin with, the work was done on the farms of Bohemia and Northern Moravia. The flax was spun on the spinning wheel and the finished products were bought by the wholesalers from the big towns, to be marketed abroad. Obviously such a primitive method of production could not meet the daily increasing demand. Yet, in the existing conditions, with the restrictions of the guild system in the towns and with serfdom in the country, economic developments were impossible without drastic social changes. Those responsible for the economic life of Austria were faced with a serious problem: that of serfdom.

Maria Theresa and Joseph II realised that the necessary measures were grave ones, but saw their inevitability. Thus, during their reigns, the various prohibitions imposed by the guild system came to an end and economic life became freer. In 1781 Joseph II took another decisive step in the same direction by decreeing the abolition of serfdom. The serfs were then able to leave the feudal estates and migrate to the towns, where they began to work in the new workshops, and later in the factories. The

281

young peasants, however, who came to the towns, and especially to Prague at the end of the eighteenth century, were not only workmen. Many of them entered the schools and the University. The University was German, but to meet the demands of these Czech students a chair of Czech language and literature was founded in 1791.

The young countrymen, passionately proud of their language and their Czech origin, were deeply struck by the German character of the towns, and particularly of the capital. They saw clearly enough the imprint of the Hapsburgs, and realised that they were no more than citizens of a province of the Austrian Empire. Their own invasion of the towns, in large numbers, necessarily did much to modify this German character. These young students of history, literature and philology were soon to become the moving spirits behind an awakening of national consciousness.

This awakening is closely connected with the rise of Czech industry and the birth of a new social class. It is at this point that the first Czech newspapers appeared; poets began to write of their country and its glorious traditions; and the Czech theatre came into being. These 'partisans of the awakening' at the end of the eighteenth century anxiously questioned the fate of the Czech people oppressed by German rule; the following century made it clear that this race-consciousness was steadily increasing.

The Napoleonic wars and the Continental System made it possible to sell out the products of the growing cloth and cotton industry. On the Continent the supply of English goods, better in quality and less costly, was irregular. As against that, linen goods reserved for export glutted the home market. After the fall of Napoleon, the Czech textile industry went through a difficult period. Local production was unable to put up a fight against the flood of English goods. The only answer to this influx of cheaper material was to revolutionise methods of production and meet British competition by mechanisation. This began to take place in 1823, and it was then that the factory workers' first great struggle began.

An industry carried on in the home or in workshops produces work done by hand and is extravagant in man-power, whereas the machine age is characterised by increased production obtained with fewer workers, and those workers can include a large number of women and children. The Czech working class now began to see the danger threatening them, as the English had seen it a few years earlier, and they turned with hatred against the new 'iron monsters'. They began to break the machinery and wreck the factories. The first outbreak of this sort took place near Bydzev, in 1840, but it reached its height in Prague, in 1844, when all the textile workers were carried away by it.

In 1829 new customs duties were imposed in the territories under Austrian domination. They were intended to meet a difficult financial situation. They hit all essential foodstuffs: potatoes, grain, bread, meat. They affected particularly the poor of the towns. This, aggravated in the 'forties by the rise in prices and the growing number of unemployed, led to the issue of free soup to the needy of the towns from December 1846. Rumours ran round the capital that the people were in revolt against the high cost of living all over Bohemia. From 1847 the unemployed were to be seen massed in front of the Prague bakeries. These working-class demonstrations were aimed at the whole political system, which the proletariat considered responsible for its plight.[1] The situation continued into 1848. The Chief of Police in Prague wrote to his superior in Vienna, Count Sedlnitzky: 'It is feared that the present unrest may eventually lead to communistic ideas among the lower classes'.[2] Count Frantisek Thun, one of the most important nobles in the opposition, wrote to his elder brother that the greater part of the people lived on rotten plums and roots: 'The mine is buried here! If the whole system is not *completely* overhauled very soon, I can foresee a black future . . .'[3] That is a picture of life as it was in the towns. What of the country?

In 1781, Joseph II had passed a law enabling the peasants to send their children to school, and even to apprentice them to trades, without having first to ask the landowner's permission. He had also repealed the age-old law against the peasants leaving their place of residence, but only a small number of them had moved to the towns and those staying behind had quickly fallen back into slavery. The history of Bohemia from the sixteenth to the eighteenth centuries is packed with peasant revolts, and their causes were still valid in the first half of the nineteenth century. That is why fresh rebellions occurred in 1821. The question of statute labour, which the nobles were doing their utmost to prevent coming to a head, was still the root of the trouble.

On 14 December 1846, there appeared a decree providing for the replacement of statute labour and feudal rights by certain taxes which it was hoped would lead to an amicable arrangement between the land-owners and their serfs. Instead, it produced a storm of protests. The people were hoping for the complete and compulsory abolition of statute labour, but this measure did not bring about any real change in their situation and the economic and social condition of Bohemia was as I have described it when the great revolutionary conflicts took place in 1848.

[1] Kazbunda, 1848 *in Bohemia*, page 22
[2] *Ibid.*, page 25
[3] *Ibid.*, page 24

2

THE TWELVE ARTICLES OF ST WENCESLAS

Bohemia was greatly stirred by the outbreak, at the beginning of 1848, of the Revolution in Italy. The papers published articles expressing sympathy with the Italian people, and posters appeared in various parts of Prague calling upon the Czechs to follow the Italians' example and show the world what a nation can do when it is determined to win its freedom.

Metternich did his best to form a bloc to isolate the Italian revolutionaries, and he was counting on the aid of Louis Philippe, when on 24 February the revolution which was to sweep away the monarchy broke out in Paris. Contrary to Metternich's expectations, the revolutionary movement spread rapidly, and a few days later news reached Bohemia of risings in the Grand Duchy of Baden and in Bavaria.

The Governor President of Bohemia at the time was Count Rudolf Stadion. When he assumed his appointment in February 1848, he considered what was known as the 'feudal' opposition as a much more important political factor than the popular movement. Ever since the reign of Joseph II, the Bohemian nobles had been at loggerheads with the Vienna Government, because its centralisation affected their feudal privileges, particularly when the Emperor set out to combine the executive with the judiciary and set his authority above that of the nobles, which had been limitless.

Thus the nobles jealously defended the ancient Czech laws which for centuries had given them the right to exercise a variety of privileges; but they were indifferent to the national question and proclaimed themselves 'neither Germans, nor Czechs but true Bohemians and good Austrians, loyal to God, King and Country'.[1] Right up to 1848 they formed the only political body in Bohemia.

The year 1848, however, saw the end of their privileged position, for they were to cease to be the chief spokesmen of Bohemia as a nation. The middle class of the towns was to take their place, for since the end of the eighteenth century, Bohemia had become economically the most important part of the Austrian Empire. However it was not the Czech but the far more powerful German middle class that controlled the country's economic life. Its centres were in the districts along the northern frontier, where lay its big textile factories, and where the Liebigs and Leitenbergs lived. It was a long time before Czech enterprises could compete with their German rivals.

[1] Krofta: *Under Austrian Rule*, page 374

In 1833 there had been founded in Prague the Union for Industrial Development, the Czech section of which contained a whole group of patriots who looked upon the Union as a means to prepare for future political activities. It also contained a second group composed of men of lower social status, who used to meet at the Sign of the Golden Goose. This group consisted of artisans and guild and factory workers, and, adopting a more radical attitude, stressed the need for social reform. It was this group that thought of holding a huge people's meeting for which they prepared the agenda. Besides freedom of the press, freedom of worship and freedom to hold meetings, their demands included matters which clearly showed that they expected the support of the working class: the more important of these were the organisation of labour, the fixing of wages and the abolition of taxes on essential food-stuffs.

After they had drawn up their programme, the radicals approached two members of the national-liberal group, Doctor Brauner and P. A. Trojan, who was then the secretary of the Czech section of the Union. These two politicians played an important part in drafting the demands of the Czech movement in 1848. Then, on 8 March, bills were posted all over Prague inviting the people to attend a meeting to be held on the 11th at the St Wenceslas Baths. The meeting was to be held on a Saturday evening and in a working-class district, as the organisers particularly wanted the workers to attend.

Government circles were alarmed. Count Stadion realised that it would only make matters worse if he were to ban the meeting, so he stifled his fears and decided to take no action. Heyde, the Chief of Police, was certain that the consequences would be disastrous for public order. The Mayor of Prague used his influence over the masters of the trade guilds to prevent them from letting their workmen and apprentices out on Saturday evening. The rich were terrified of an attack on their property. And so the great day drew near on which the Czechs, for the first time after years of oppression, were to claim their political rights. Prague talked of nothing but the meeting.

On 11 March there gathered outside the St Wenceslas Baths an immense crowd, of which only a tiny percentage could get inside the building. After speeches by the radicals who had organised the meeting, P. A. Trojan rose to explain the object of the meeting, and to ask the crowd to behave in an orderly fashion. When he had finished, it was decided to present a petition to the 'King of Bohemia' (i.e. the Austrian Emperor), asking for satisfaction of the country's pressing needs. This petition was to be framed by a committee of representatives of all classes, which is why it included three members of the 'feudal' opposition, although in the beginning the organisers of the meeting had been very chary of having anything to do with them.

The Assembly then passed what became known as 'The Twelve Articles of St Wenceslas'. These began with certain national claims, in particular Brauner's demand for a single executive to administer the Czech crown lands, together with a parliament and responsible Ministers who would sit in Prague. Then came demands dealing with complete equality between the Czechs and the Germans in the schools and in government service; and finally there were a number of social claims, but containing no mention of organisation of labour or fixed salaries.

After these articles had been passed, the meeting broke up and Count Stadion, who was impatiently waiting in his nearby palace to hear the result, immediately informed Vienna that it had gone off very satisfactorily, and that it would be wise to satisfy public opinion by granting the more moderate demands that had been made. It was the job of the committee elected on the 11th to see that the resolutions taken at the meeting were carried out. It had been decided that the petition should be displayed at prearranged places on the following Wednesday and Thursday, so that every citizen could sign it. Although the Imperial Government in Prague hoped that the committee, or at least the whole of it, would never meet again, its first session took place on 12 March, and the following officers were appointed: Count Deym, as President; Peter Fastr as Vice-President; Trojan and Doctor Gabler as secretaries. It is noticeable that already the radicals, who had started the movement, were taking a back seat and that the national liberals and the 'feudal' opposition were coming to the fore. This became plain immediately the committee commissioned Gabler, Trojan and Pinkas to speed up the elaboration of the petition. In the end Gabler and Trojan accepted the version made by Pinkas, one of the most conservative Czechs.

Two days later the revolution broke out in Vienna; Metternich resigned and the Government promised to grant the people's basic demands. The abolition of the pre-censorship of the press resulted in Prague in a shower of pamphlets attacking Metternich, the old order, and Müller, the Mayor. The workers, who had been suffering from the high cost of living, bitterly complained that in spite of the new Constitution the price of food was exactly the same. Unemployed from the country districts poured into Prague.

The petition bore several thousand signatures, and the departure of the delegation which was to take it to Vienna was fixed for 19 March. The streets of Prague were gay with bunting and there was a spirit of carnival in the air. Many people had demanded that the petition should insist on an improvement in the peasants' lot, the abolition of statute labour and of the landowners' judicial powers. The inhabitants of the Karlín district, who for the most part belonged to the working class, demanded that they be guaranteed work and wages, so that 'the unfortunate poor people should not be driven to despair through hunger and misery'.

3

THE DECREE OF 8 APRIL

The political movement in 1848 drew its strength from the economic development of the Czech provinces. It had both the Czech and the German middle classes behind it. That is why we find them making not only economic but also important political claims such as the demand for an Imperial Diet to give Bohemia a Constitution. They considered that Austria should become a constitutional monarchy. The middle classes were all the more insistent as they knew their own strength, and some of their representatives even demanded that the monarchy should be replaced by a republic.

The great majority of the Czechs took part in the revolutionary movement, for it was predominantly nationalist in character. But as the lower classes mainly consisted of Czechs, social demands were indivisibly linked with national ones. The German middle class in Bohemia soon gained the impression that the Czechs wished to combine with the workers against the Germans, and Count Stadion openly voiced this fear in a report sent on 22 March to the Archduke Ferdinand Charles, in which he wrote: 'the middle class is terrified that there will be a rising of this nature'. These fears increased when large numbers of Czechs joined the St Wenceslas Militia, their National Defence force.

We can see what tension existed at this time from Count Stadion's decision to have elected a council of a hundred members whose task it would be to appoint a provisional municipal council of twelve. Stadion's own explanation was that: 'the Court feels that the course of events makes it a matter of urgency that Prague should have a freely elected body of representatives'. But it is obvious that this sudden decision was inspired by Stadion's wish to weaken the position of the St Wenceslas Committee, which had the backing of the people, and took every opportunity to point out that it was a popularly elected body. As the Assembly which had elected the committee was mainly composed of radicals, so the radicals were in the majority on this Committee, a state of affairs which Count Stadion was anxious to remedy.

ARNOST KLIMA

The delegation which had left for Vienna on 19 March returned on the 22nd, bringing back only vague promises. The Government's reply was badly received in Bohemia, and it was decided to send a second deputation to the Imperial Capital, bearing a fresh petition which would put the Czech's demands more forcibly. This led to the first serious differences of opinion. Whereas the representatives of the militant German middle class, such as Ruppert, asked that their demands should be couched in the strongest and most unequivocal terms, the delegates from the nobility, realising the full significance of these demands, declared that they could not give them their approval *in toto*, for they would bring about too radical a change in the existing state of affairs. The second petition was drawn up on the 29th and a mass deputation of the people forced Count Stadion to sign it and make it clear that he was expressing the wishes of the people of Prague. Tracts were distributed calling on the military and the peasants to stand shoulder to shoulder with the citizens of the capital under the flag of freedom. One of these in particular invited the peasants to mass their forces, take up arms and start training so as to be able to stand up against their enemies; it also spoke of 'complete freedom', which gave the country people hope of speedy relief from their present misery.

The deputation which arrived in Vienna with the petition at the beginning of April was received in a most friendly fashion by Baron Pillersdorf. This was principally because Austria was faced with a grave situation in Northern Italy, where a revolt had broken out and the Governor General, Radetzky, had been forced to retreat. Austrian dominion was also collapsing in Venice, which had proclaimed itself a republic. On top of this Pillersdorf was worried by the situation in Hungary, where Batthyany had formed a responsible government. He therefore greeted the members of the Czech delegation warmly, and asked them to prepare a suggested reply for the Emperor, which would serve as the basis for further negotiations. The delegation presented their draft reply the following day, and on 8 April a decree containing the following concessions was published:

1. The promise of a Czech Diet, freely elected from representatives of all interests and social classes
2. The obligation on all Government officials to know both German and Czech
3. An equal footing for German and Czech in the schools
4. The abolition of landowners' courts and judicial powers
5. The grant of citizenship from the age of thirty

But the demand concerning autonomy and an independent government for the Czech provinces was turned down.

The decree of 8 April was for a long time to be the basis of Czech politics, which were concerned with putting its provisions into practice. I have already mentioned that ever since the formation of the St Wenceslas Committee, Count Stadion had been trying to create another body to replace it and to act as his mouthpiece. When he was convinced that a municipal council could not fulfil this rôle, he decided on 1 April to organise a special consultative commission, with twenty-four members, appointed by himself. They included Count Deym, a moderate, who was the Czech President of the St Wenceslas Committee, and the great historian Frantisek Palacky. The formation of this Commission caused the resignation of several of the members of the St Wenceslas Committee, such as J. B. Riedl and Pinkas, who from the start had disliked the over-democratic and radical nature of that popular body. Count Stadion then struck another blow at the Committee by ordering the rooms of the Union for Industrial Development, which it had been using, to be returned to their original purpose.

On 10 April, the radicals of the Committee organised another mass meeting at the St Wenceslas Baths. They were too small to hold the crowd that turned up. Among the proposals put forward, two are of especial interest: the one claiming the right, subject to no property qualification, of all citizens over twenty-five to vote; and the other, supported by the moderates who wanted the Committee to be combined with the Consultative Commission, demanding the creation of a 'National Council'. This second proposal, which cunningly anticipated Count Stadion's and the moderates' objectives, met with violent opposition from the poor people. There were shouts of 'The National Council must have our confidence!' Count Stadion thereupon did on his own authority what the moderates had failed to do at the meeting: on 14 April a government proclamation announced the formation of a National Council which was to embody the Consultative Commission. Thus Stadion crowned with success the attempts he had been making since March either to suppress or weaken the Committee of the peoples' representatives.

4

CZECHS GERMANS AND HUNGARIANS

We know that the great democratic movement of 1848 had also shaken Germany. In March, representatives had been summoned to Frankfort to discuss the creation of a strong, united Germany. This meeting resulted in the formation of a 'Preparatory Parliament' of fifty members which was later enlarged. Frantisek Palacky was invited to join it as the Czech representative for Bohemia. The Czechs were invited to Frankfort as Bohemia formed part of the German Confederation.

Palacky, in a letter dated 11 April, formally declined, since he realised that the creation of a strong, united 'Greater Germany' must of necessity imperil the existence of the small Slavonic nations. That is why he wrote, quite frankly: 'If the State of Austria had not already been in existence for centuries, we should be forced, in the interests of Europe and even of humanity, to create it.'[1]

The moderate Czech politicians were convinced of the necessity of preserving Austria. They believed that the most advantageous solution to the Slav problem was to transform the absolutist Empire into a federal state of nations possessing equal rights, as they believed that the Slavs, who outnumbered the Austrians, would be in the majority in an Imperial Diet. This doctrine, known as Austro-Slavism, led them in the course of 1848 to uphold the Austrian point of view on all occasions, and oppose anything which might harm Austria and weaken her authority. We know today how wrong they were to trust in their numerical strength and in the Hapsburgs' good will to reform their ways. Later events were to show how the rulers of Austria used the Slavs to help them out of their difficulties over the revolutionary movements in Italy, Vienna and Austria. Once they had succeeded in mastering them, they turned against those who had helped them in the hour of danger. The fact that the centres of national risings were in Germany and Vienna had seriously perturbed the Czechs and had thrown them into the arms of the counter-revolutionaries. It was the same in Slovakia, where the Magyars headed the revolutionary movement, and the Slovaks, justifiably fearful of Hungarian oppression, joined the reactionaries.

Neither the Germans nor the Hungarians succeeded in winning the sympathy of the Slavs, although they were so oppressed, because they would not grant them the independence they sought only for themselves. That is the crux of the 1848 Revolution in Austria and more particularly the tragedy of the rising in Bohemia and Slovakia.

The refusal of the Czech moderates to go to Frankfort was followed, in the early days of May, by the resignation of the German radicals from the National Council in Prague.

[1] Palacky: *Radhost*, Vol. II, page 14

5

THE CONSTITUTION OF 25 APRIL

The Constitution promised after the fall of Metternich was granted on 25 April. It was based on the principle that the monarchy was indivisible. It guaranteed respect for the different nationalities and the free use of their own languages; freedom of the press, freedom to hold meetings, and freedom to present petitions; an independent judiciary, public trials and the institution of juries. The Government was made responsible to an Imperial Diet, which was to consist of two Chambers. The Upper Chamber, or Senate, of two hundred members at most, was to comprise, besides the Imperial princes and other life members, a hundred and fifty delegates chosen from among the great landowners, who were to hold their seats for a period of five years. The other Chamber—of Representatives—was to consist of three hundred and eighty three members returned by an electorate subject to a property qualification.

This Constitution was criticised not only in Austria but also in Bohemia. Whilst the Viennese demanded a Constituent Assembly, the Czechs violently opposed the system of two Chambers. At this moment the Empire was in a delicate situation. On 30 April, after the battle of Pastrenga, Radetzky had had to retreat a second time, and Austria's position in Northern Italy was again critical. Cracow had revolted on 26 April, and the Hungarians were fighting fiercely for complete independence. These events and the revolutionary spirit of Vienna caused the resignation on 3 May of the premier, Count Ficquelmont. He was succeeded by Baron Pillersdorf, the Minister for the Interior. In Bohemia, Count Stadion also resigned and was replaced by Count Leo Thun.

The proclamation of the Constitution on 25 April had caused an uproar in Vienna. The Viennese objected to the Constitution being granted by the Emperor, not made by themselves, and to the two Chambers, one of which, the Senate, naturally represented the conservative views of the feudal nobility. That is why there was increasing agitation for a Constituent Assembly elected by the whole nation. More and more people supported these demands, and at the beginning of May delegation upon delegation hammered at the Government to grant the people what they wanted. As a result of this onslaught, Baron Pillersdorf promised to summon a Constituent Assembly of the kind they wanted. Vienna, at this point, had the appearance of a besieged town: some people even demanded the creation of a republic, and it was then that the Emperor decided to leave his capital and seek a safer abode. On 17 May he left for his usual excursion to Schönbrunn but did not return: he had gone on from there to Innsbruck. The atmosphere cleared in Vienna and the revolutionaries were left in control.

There then took place in Bohemia a major political event. On 20 May Count Thun, the Governor President, attended a meeting of the National Council to announce that he was prepared to act without Vienna's approval and, if necessary, contrary to Vienna's wishes. Two members of the Council, Trojan and Baron Wurmbrand, thereupon proposed that the Governor President should surround himself with men whom the public trusted and form a kind of provisional government. Count Thun at first refused, but when the Viennese revolution gained ground he changed his mind. He began by asking the advice of the high government officials and of General Windischgrätz, the military commander. When the National Council met on 29 May he announced the creation of a provisional government council of eight members of which he was to be the President. This body was to be more powerful than a State Council, and would be in a position, in an emergency, to take decisions concerning the administration of the country. Thun also gave the names of the members of this Council: the Germans on it were to be Counts Nostitz and Wurmbrand, an industrialist named Herzig, and a municipal expert named Borrosch. The Czechs were to be Palacky, Rieger, Brauner and Strobach. Thun wanted the Emperor to ratify his proposal, so Wurmbrand and Rieger left for Innsbruck to put it to him.

The Vienna Government, however, held a very different view of the situation. They considered the existence in Prague of an autonomous government as a danger for the future centralised State. The Ministers Doblhoff and Wessenberg were given the task of informing the delegates to Innsbruck that they could not count on the Government's recognising this Council. When Wurmbrand and Rieger set out on the return journey to Prague on 13 June, they had no idea that the situation had completely changed and that the capital of Bohemia had become the centre of popular riots.

6

THE SLAV CONGRESS

The Czech provinces were not the only ones to be effected by the great political movement of 1848. In March of that year there was a major demonstration at Liptovsky Svaty Mikulas. Its object was to claim the rights of Slovak nationals and agitate for the use of the Slovak language in the schools and the law courts. The Hungarian Minister replied by declaring in March that Hungarian was the sole official language. This naturally produced violent reactions not only from the Slovaks but also from the inhabitants of another country that suffered equally from Magyar oppression, Croatia. It is remarkable that the idea of a Slav Congress was first thought of by the Slovaks and the Croats. It was a Slovak, Ludovit Stur, who worked for it in Prague from the middle of March onward, and strove to interest the Czech politicians. On the 20th Ivan Kukuljevitch wrote an article on the subject in the newspaper *Narodni Noviny*.

The Czechs soon took to the idea of this Congress, particularly as they saw that it would express the point of view of the Austrian Slavs on the decisions reached by the Frankfort Parliament. A preparatory committee met in Prague and it was agreed that the Congress of the Slavs of the Empire should meet on 31 May.

The inaugural meeting took place on 2 June. Prague's whole life was coloured by it, and Slav costumes, flags and emblems were everywhere in evidence. The populace was delighted. The Congress, presided over by Palacky, consisted of three sections: Czechs and Slovaks, Serbs and Croats, Poles and Ruthenians.

The first agenda produced by the provisional committee of 27 May consisted of four items: the formation of a Slav group inside Austria and the study of means to provide mutual assistance; the elaboration of a scheme for an Austrian federation; the question of relations with the other Slavs in Europe and of the revival of Slavonic arts and sciences; and finally, discussion of the decisions reached by the Frankfort Parliament concerning the Slav provinces of Austria.

This agenda, which was to be the basis on which the various sections were to work, was radically changed when, on 5 June, the Polish delegate Libelt proposed that the Congress should produce three appeals: a manifesto to the peoples of Europe; an address to the Emperor, and an appeal to the Slav countries to unite and maintain their unity. The Congress agreed to Libelt's proposal, but only the manifesto to Europe was actually drawn up. It began with the significant words: 'We Slavs repudiate all special privileges, all abuses of authority and all political inequality; we unanimously demand equality before the law and equal rights and obligations for all.' This manifesto took up the defence of the Poles fighting to regain their independence; condemned the oppression of the Slavs in Hungary, Prussia and Turkey; and demanded a European Congress to study the international aspect of the Slav problem.

The second item on the agenda was fiercely debated. The proposal to create a Slav bloc presupposed the constitution of a federal Austria composed of a number of States of equal status. But whereas the Yugoslavs wanted to be completely independent of the Hungarians, the Slovaks simply wanted equal rights, and the Czechs were satisfied with the promises contained in the Imperial Decree of 8 April.

Before an agreement could be reached on this item, the first session of the Congress was marked by a tragic occurrence, On 12 June street fighting started in Prague and went on for several days, considerably influencing the course of events in Bohemia.

7

THE PRAGUE RISING

The events in Prague immediately following the February Revolution had led to a series of military conferences taking place from March onward to formulate plans for dealing with possible trouble. Particular attention had been paid to the citadel of Vysehrad, from which guns could be trained on the working-class district of Podskali, where the first big political meeting of 1848 had taken place.

During the second half of May, General Windischgrätz, the military commander of Prague, returned to the Czech capital. The object of his return was to scare the people, who connected his name with reprisals against the workers in 1844 and the quelling of the revolutionary movement in Vienna in March 1848. He was notorious as the staunchest supporter of Austrian absolutism and the most obsequious servant of the Hapsburgs, and for his bloodthirsty delight in smashing popular risings. So it was not surprising that Prague feared his reappearance. And Windischgrätz soon proved that their fears were well founded. He planted batteries on the two heights of Vysehrad and Petrin commanding the town, and then decided to hold a grand military review on 7 June, which he felt should kindle excitement. Bodies of troops continually patrolled the capital and the atmosphere was one of a state of siege.

Windischgrätz was particularly loathed by the students, who in Prague —as in Vienna—were the most ardent lovers of freedom and the most revolutionary-minded section of the populace. Windischgrätz refused their request for arms and ammunition for the University Legions, and when, on 10 June, they called upon the citizens to erect barricades, it was clear that there would soon be an explosion.

On 12 June a solemn mass was to be celebrated to mark the holding of the Slav Congress, and the students decided to make it the occasion for a grand Czech demonstration. To ensure its success, they made a special appeal to the workers to join this demonstration *en masse*. The workers, together with the students, constituted the most enthusiastic element in the nationalist movement, and they detested Windischgrätz. Their presence at this mass gave the gathering a formidable air, and it needed only a spark to set off the explosion. At the end of the ceremony the people marched in two columns to Army Headquarters to demonstrate their strength. Immediately the troops marched out of their barracks and advanced on the mob with fixed bayonets, raking it with fire.

Thus the battle began between the people of Prague and the army, with the radicals in the forefront of the insurgents. It lasted five days and ended with the capitulation of the town. The people were defeated, first, because the rising was restricted to Prague (which proved the political ignorance of men like Ruppert who declared that Prague was Bohemia), and secondly because only a section of the middle class mistrusted Vienna's promises and favoured an armed attack on Austrian absolutism. The majority had faith in the Vienna Government, and were willing to come to a compromise over disputed issues since—like their allies of the nobility—they supported the conception of a united Austrian monarchy. This defeat was indicative of the general situation in Bohemia, where the Czech middle class, struggling to gain power, was economically and politically too weak and too divided.

After the capitulation of Prague, however, the Czechs still had an important political rôle to play. Doblhoff's government, which had summoned an Imperial Diet, came into conflict with the German left wing, and it was seriously embarrassed by the revolutionary movement in Hungary. The Czech representatives in the Diet, who were for the most part moderates, proved Doblhoff's chief supporters, particularly in September and October 1848. The Bohemian deputies violently opposed the Magyar revolution. On 19 September a deputation from Budapest, led by Deak and Eötvös, appeared before the Imperial Council to ask the Diet's assistance against the Hapsburgs who were using Jellacic, the governor of Croatia, to break the Hungarian revolution.

The German conservatives and the Czech moderates who formed the majority in the Diet refused to admit the Hungarian delegation. The result was a fresh revolutionary outbreak in Vienna, particularly directed against the Austrian army's being set against the Hungarian liberals.

This revolt broke out in Vienna on 6 October, and its first victim was the War Minister, Count Latour. The members of the Diet who had shown hostility towards the Hungarian revolutionaries knew that the revolt was aimed at them as much as at the Vienna Government. Nearly all of them, including the Czechs, hurriedly left the capital, and only four radical deputies stayed behind. The attitude of the Czech representatives in the Diet was far from meeting universal approval in Bohemia. There were many people, particularly among the radicals, whose sympathies were with those deputies who, instead of fleeing, had remained at their posts. It was difficult for the Diet to carry on in such an atmosphere, and on Palacky's suggestion it adjourned until 15 November, when it met again at Kromeriz (Kremsier) in Moravia.

In these black days for the Imperial capital, the Emperor sought sanctuary in Moravia. It was a tragic paradox for the Czech nation that, at the most critical moment of its history, it should shelter the Hapsburgs. According to Marx, the Czechs' tragedy is explained by the fact that as Germany and Hungary were the centres of the Revolution, they were compelled to become counter-revolutionaries. The Czech moderates were frightened by the risks they would incur in seeking independence, and of the growth of Germany and Russia in the event of Austria breaking up. That is why the Czech members of the Diet fled with their German colleagues, after the Viennese Revolution, to continue their work in Moravia. But the defeat of the Viennese insurgents and the signs of a weakening of Hungary's resistance enabled Schwarzenberg's government, which had replaced Doblhoff's, to set out to recapture the ground won by the revolutionary movements. Schwarzenberg strove to substitute for the Constitution passed by the Diet one devised by the Government, and then to dissolve the Diet.

At Kromeriz the Diet was continuing to work out the details of the Constitution. But the government counted on a change in the political situation and was no longer prepared to give in to middle-class pressure. This became clear the moment the principal clause of the new Constitution was published. 'Count Stadion, the Minister for the Interior, objected to the theory expressed in the first paragraph of the clause dealing with fundamental rights, which proclaimed that the State's authority was based on the will of the people. The ministers opposed the wishes of Parliament in this matter and declared that a constitutional monarch ruled by divine right.'[1]

The Vienna Government was already counting on the return of the old absolutism. It at once began to prepare a new Constitution without the Diet's assistance, and presented it to the Emperor Francis Joseph on 25 January 1849, a few days before it decided to publish it and to dissolve the Diet.

On 27 February 1849, the Austrian army defeated the Hungarians at Kapolna. Schwarzenberg thereupon decided to take immediate and decisive action. On 6 March, Count Stadion informed a number of the foremost representatives at Kromeriz that the Emperor had decided to

[1] Tobolka: *Czech Politics*, No. III, page 153

dissolve the Diet and grant a Constitution. This was done the next day. The Constitution, which was to apply to the entire Empire, was dated 4 March 1849.

This was the final blow to the Czech moderates' hopes of a reconstituted Austrian State, based on the equal status of every nation composing it, and on an Imperial Diet, or *Reichstag*. Everything pointed to Austria's resuming her old absolutist policy of oppressing her component nationalities. The defeat of the Hungarian revolutionaries had contributed to this development, which was to plunge the Czech nation back into darkness for another ten years. There was no more political life, the chief national organisations were barred, arrests became frequent, and the intellectuals were subjected to a thousand restrictions. The *coup d'état* of 2 December 1851 in Paris encouraged the Emperor Francis Joseph to curtail the last of the liberties won in the course of the preceding years.

The Constitution granted on 4 March 1849 was abolished on 31 December 1851, and Austria became once more an absolute State.

THE RUMANIANS IN 1848

MICHAEL ROLLER

The Rumanian revolutionaries of 1848 wanted not only to be free but to own their land, otherwise the words 'liberty and equality' would have been meaningless. That is why they added the word 'fraternity' to their motto, as an essential condition of human progress. Theirs was a social revolution
Nicholas Balcesco
'The March of the Revolution in Rumanian History'

I

THE PRINCIPALITIES

THE three Principalities which today form the country of Rumania were subjected in 1848 to social and national upheavals like the rest of Europe.

We find common characteristics in the histories of Moldavia, Wallachia and Transylvania, as for centuries each was under the rule of a foreign empire—Moldavia and Wallachia under the Turks and Transylvania under the Austrians. Foreign domination retarded their economic and cultural development, particularly as both empires were feudal in structure. Both replaced the old feudal system of command by one which placed the armed forces in the Principalities under their respective Imperial governments.

Neither Austria nor Turkey encouraged the development of the Principalities, and their natural resources were only used to satisfy the economic needs of these two empires, which found them a source of considerable wealth, especially after their expansion was stopped.

Another characteristic common to the three Principalities was that their inhabitants resisted both their foreign rulers and their State religions.

In Moldavia and Wallachia, the Orthodox Rumanians came into conflict with Islam, the official religion of the Turks, and they were even more hostile, in Transylvania, to the Catholic Church. This explains the religious character of many of the peasant revolts.

The people were also mercilessly exploited by the local nobility and the

Imperial tax collectors. Their situation was extremely precarious, for they wanted to break free from both foreign rule and the tyranny at home. The events of 1848 were preceded by the great peasant rising of 1785 in Transylvania, under the leadership of Horia, Closca and Crisan, and by the Wallachian revolt of 1821 led by Tudor Vladimiresco.

However, in spite of these common characteristics we have just mentioned, Moldavia and Wallachia, being under the Turks, suffered a different fate from Transylvania. The decline of the Ottoman Empire, particularly in the eighteenth and nineteenth centuries, made it more difficult for capitalism to make any advance in Moldavia and Wallachia than in the Empire of the Hapsburgs.

That is why these two Principalities made slower progress. Transylvania, on the other hand, developed more rapidly by reason of its geographical position and its economic wealth (its gold mines and so forth) and because the Austrian Empire had introduced capitalist methods sooner.

But there was also another difference: whereas in Moldavia and Wallachia the ruling class was Rumanian and Turkish rule relatively unitary, the Rumanians of Transylvania were governed by Hungarian and Austrian nobles, who used their position to divert the Transylvanians from their true aims and keep them under the control first of the Hapsburg and then of the Austro-Hungarian Empire.

It must also be pointed out that Moldavia and Wallachia had a different system of legislation from Transylvania: both being subject to the 'Organic Statute' of 1830–2, which brought them still closer together.

In spite of all these differences, however, capitalism had been introduced into the Principalities long before 1848. It had appeared in Wallachia and Moldavia in the second half of the eighteenth century, when the first industries began to make headway and the export of cereals became more important. All three Principalities began to take a part in international trade, the volume being greatest in Transylvania on account of her more advanced economic development.

Before 1848, Wallachia, Moldavia and Transylvania were the theatre of a brisk trade in ideas, combined with revolutionary activity.

It is enough to mention, in this connection, the advances made in education and national culture thanks to the work of Peter Maior in Transylvania, Asachi in Moldavia and Lazar in Wallachia, and the new currents of thought introduced by Kogalniceano in Moldavia, and by Balcesco and Laurian in Wallachia and Transylvania.

At the same time there were the 'federative conspiracies' of Moldavia in 1839 and Wallachia in 1840, and the popular risings in Transylvania between 1841 and 1847.

In Moldavia the conspirators, headed by Leonte Radu, planned to reorganise the country by abolishing the hierarchy of *Boyars* (the privileged class in Rumania), removing the censorship, confiscating the land owned by the monasteries, encouraging the development of national industries, emancipating the Gypsies, founding a bank to be financed by foreign capital, and so forth.

The rather clandestine movement in Wallachia in 1840 was controlled by Dimitrie Filipesco. At its head was a committee of a group of patriots (including the historian Nicholas Balcesco; the French professor J. A. Vaillant[1]; Eftimie Murgue; and the peasant Sotir) composed not only of merchants and intellectuals but also artisans and workmen. This committee drafted a Constitution under which the *Boyars* would lose their privileges, the land would be divided amongst the serfs, a powerful national army would be organised, and a Republic would be established. The conspiracy was discovered, and the ringleaders, among them Nicholas Balcesco, were imprisoned for periods of between three and ten years.

In Transylvania, particularly in the Apuseni Mountains, the oppressed miners, led by Catherine Varga, the Hungarian heroine, fought for years, first for their 'traditional rights' and then as revolutionaries. They continued the battle even after the Austrian authorities, with the help of Bishop Andrei Saguna, had arrested Catherine Varga, who died in prison.

There was organised action in Wallachia, in the years 1843–5, to encourage the peasants to arm and rise for the furtherance of revolutionary, middle-class and democratic ideas. It was at this time that Balcesco and Ghica formed the society known as *Fratia* (the Brotherhood).

All these activities were the result of the Principalities' economic and social development. Agriculture, feudal in character, was still predominant but industry, commerce and the different trades were making rapid progress.

The social forces consisted of the *Boyars* (some of whom were in the cereal trade), the serfs, a small number of free peasants, the factory owners, the traders and the workers. All were affected by the great middle-class revolution in France, whose ideas assisted the development of nationalism and—throughout the nineteenth century—gave impetus to the struggle to create an independent, unitary State.

The influence of the Encyclopædists had already been felt in the Principalities in the eighteenth century.

Even before the outbreak of the Revolution in France, French revolu-

[1] Called to Bucharest in 1820, to organise public education, he founded the Boarding College of Bucharest and the girls' free school. He taught at the National School of St Sava, and among other works published a Franco-Wallachian grammar (1836) and a book on Rumania (1844).

tionary ideas had come into the country in the wake of trade. Their influence grew, after 1789, by the enterprise of Frenchmen sent into the Principalities and the increasing number of Consulates. These ideas inspired the national revolutionary organisations of the *Hetairia*, which sprung up in the Principalities and of which Tudor Vladimiresco, the leader of the peoples' revolt in Wallachia in 1821, had been a member.

The ideas of the Revolution came in under all their different forms—Girondin, Montagnard and Socialist—and they were sometimes spread by Russian officers and intellectuals, such as the Decembrists, passing through the Principalities in the course of the Napoleonic wars. Students, belonging to rich families who had studied in France, were also propagandists. One of the poorer ones, Tudor Diamant, studied under Fourier in Paris, and after taking part in French Fourierist societies tried, in 1832 and 1833, to create a Phalanstery near Ploiesti.

The rise of the revolutionary movement in France on the eve of 1848 had its effect on the Rumanian students in Paris. In 1839 there appeared there the Society of Rumanian Students, possessing a library and reading room kept up by donations from people in Rumania and from French sympathisers. The members of this nationalist society, who had close ties with France, started to bring the Rumanians' situation and aspirations to the attention of the outside world. Thanks to the friendly support of Quinet and Michelet, and their relations with *La Réforme* and *Le National*, the organs of revolutionary middle-class opposition, they succeeded in interesting French public opinion in Rumania's problems.

The part played by Rumanian students in helping to found Louis Blanc's newspaper, *Les Ecoles*, on 1 June 1845; their contributions to *La Réforme*, *Debats* and *Le National*, where they published articles in the form of correspondence sympathetic to Rumania's social and national demands; the examination of the Rumanian problem at the Collège de France; the entry of several Rumanians into the Masonic Lodges; their attendance at the banquets organised by the revolutionary opposition; and finally the active participation of several Rumanians—particularly Nicholas Balcesco—in the battles at the barricades in February 1848, and in Ledru-Rollin's demonstration, all show the influence of French revolutionary ideas on young Rumanians.

It was these students who formed the delegation which in March 1848 went to the French Provisional Government to express the Rumanian peoples' solidarity with the French Republic. It was then that they voiced one of the claims which was beginning to be heard at this period: 'The Wallachians, the Moldavians and the Transylvanians all declare that they are Rumanians and that their land, which has so long been witness of their distress, is called Rumania'.

Thus these young students, by keeping in close touch with the conspirators and revolutionary organisations of the mother-country and of France, drew the world's attention to the aims of the inhabitants of the Principalities and taught their compatriots what was being thought and done in France.

2

THE REVOLUTIONARY MOVEMENT IN MOLDAVIA

The first Rumanian revolution broke out in Moldavia shortly after the 'Days of February' in France.

Contrary to what happened in Wallachia and Transylvania, the Moldavian revolution was nipped in the bud before it could spread throughout the province. The rising took place on 27 March as a result of the discontent caused by the way Prince Michael Stourdza abused his authority.

On that day there took place at the St Petersburg Hotel in Jassy a meeting of several hundred people. The historian Xenopol mentions the presence of several *Boyars*, the Metropolitan and his clergy, important merchants of various nationalities, small landowners, professors, lawyers and scholars. One of the most remarkable men present was Alexander Ion Cuza, who was later to be the first ruler of the United Principalities.

The Assembly commissioned a committee of sixteen people to draw up a memorandum which was to be presented to the Prince. This memorandum contained thirty-five items, among the most important of which were the establishment of a national system of education; the removal of the export tariff on cereals; the publication of accounts of the Assembly's meetings and of trials in the law courts; the formation of a National Guard; and removal of the censorship. The memorandum stressed the point, however, that its authors supported the Organic Statute in its entirety. This showed that the *Boyars* concerned were anxious to limit the application of their claims.

The Organic Statute, ratified by the Turkish Government under pressure from Russia, was the Principalities' first Constitution. It contained a number of articles, the object of which was to assist their progress, but at the same time to safeguard the *Boyars*' privileges. Now, the main problem in 1848 was to abolish these privileges, so as to ensure the economic and social development of Moldavia. But the very fact that the memorandum upheld these privileges by supporting the Organic Statute, shows the weakness of the middle class and of the minor nobles whose interests none the less demanded their abolition.

It must be added that the memorandum made no mention of sharing out the land, which from the start deprived the movement of the support of the peasants, who could have assured its success.

Michael Stourdza easily dealt with the feeble attempts to erect barricades and the resistance of a handful of the leaders of the movement entrenched in the house of the *Boyar*, Navrocordat.

The movement in Jassy had a few minor repercussions in the villages, where the peasants, believing their moment had come, tried to obtain satisfaction for their own demands which had not been touched by the memorandum. But their efforts were quickly nullified.

The revolutionary movement in Moldavia was chiefly the work of the *Boyars* who were dissatisfied with the Prince, and wanted to gain certain advantages without losing any of their privileges. It did not seek major social and political changes that could have been accomplished only by a middle class with the support of the oppressed masses of the towns and the villages, who were looking for a lead.

Later, in the years following 1848, a middle-class policy on these lines was formulated in the National Party's programme. This programme was the work of Kogalniceano and was devised to produce national unity.

3

THE MIDDLE-CLASS AND DEMOCRATIC
REVOLUTION IN WALLACHIA

Unlike Moldavia, Wallachia in 1848 was the scene of a powerful rising of the masses who were determined to carry out a revolutionary, middle-class and democratic programme.

The moving spirit behind this Wallachian revolt was the great patriot and historian Nicholas Balcesco (1819–52). We have already mentioned the rôle played by the organisation known as 'the Brotherhood' in preparing for the revolutionary movement in Wallachia, which—on the eve of the revolution—had expounded its programme in what historians later called 'the Islaz Proclamation'. The clandestine revolutionary organisations of this province were composed of merchants, workmen, and officials in groups of between ten and twenty, each member knowing only the leader of his own particular group. At the head of all these groups was a revolutionary committee which carried out the instructions of a supreme committee of three men: N. Balcesco, A. Golesco and I. Ghica.

These organisations made intensive preparations for an armed rising, and collected arms and ammunition. They planned to act in April 1848. The revolutionary committee established contact with the French Provisional Government and put off the date of the rising solely because Lamartine, the Foreign Minister, promised he would help them if they did so.

But as Prince Bibesco had scented danger and decided to arrest the revolutionary leaders, and as French help was slow in coming—Michelet himself had said that France could only weep for those who trusted her and to whom she gave no aid—an earlier date was fixed for the rising.

The revolutionary committee sent its representatives into the different districts of Wallachia to stir up the people. Balcesco went to Ploiesti, where he won the support of the army and the workers in the salt mines. Eliade, Major Tell and A. Golesco went off to Islaz (a village in Oltenia) where the garrison was on the side of the revolutionaries, and where they were to mass the peasants, who still had vivid memories of Tudor Vladimiresco's rising. C. Boliac, C. A. Rosetti, N. Golesco and I. Bratiano had the task of stirring up the people of Bucharest, particularly the merchants. All these actions were to be carried out in the name of the principles laid down in the Proclamation drawn up by Balcesco and toned down by Eliade. The essential aims presented by this proclamation were as follows:

1. Autonomy in internal affairs
2. Equal political rights
3. An Assembly representing all classes
4. A prince elected (for a period of five years) by all classes
5. Ministers responsible to the people
6. Freedom of the press
7. Emancipation of the serfs, who would share in the division of the land
8. Emancipation of the Gypsies
9. Abolition of feudal dues
10. Abolition of the death penalty
11. Emancipation of the Jews
12. A Constituent Assembly, representing all classes, with the task of drawing up a Constitution in accordance with the above principles

On 9 June, the revolution began with a mass meeting of the peasants at Islaz. The Proclamation was read to them, and the Tricolour, a symbol of national independence, was blessed.

The revolutionaries, followed by a small army and groups of peasants, then set off for Bucharest.

The troubles in Bucharest had started with an attempt on the life of the ruling Prince, although the news of the revolt at Islaz did not arrive until 11 June.

On that day the Bucharest mob, formed of shopkeepers, workmen and a host of men and women wearing cockades and brandishing the Tricolour, forced their way into the palace and tried to make Bibesco dismiss his Cabinet, form a provisional government and accept a new Constitution based on the Proclamation. Prince Bibesco, realising that the army would not act against the people, gave way.

A Provisional Government was formed with Balcesco as Foreign Minister, N. Golesco as Minister for the Interior, Magheru as Minister for Finance, Eliade as Minister for Ecclesiastical Affairs, A. Golesco as Minister for Justice, and Colonel Odobesco as War Minister. Cretulesco was made President of the Administrative Council, and Rosetti, Prefect of Police in Bucharest.

Two days later Prince Bibesco fled from Wallachia in terror. Eliade and his group hurried to Bucharest, and on 15 June, on the Filaret Field on the outskirts of the capital, the Constitution was submitted for the people's approval, and was accepted.

When Eliade's group arrived in Bucharest, the provisional government was reorganised. Up till then, Balcesco's radical group had been the strongest, but now the moderates took the upper hand. The Metropolitan, Neophite, who was a reactionary, was made head of the Provisional Government. Heresco became Minister for Finance and Odobesco remained War Minister—although both of them had been Ministers under Prince Bibesco.

The more progressive elements, Balcesco, A. Golesco and Rosetti, were reduced to positions of Secretaries of State in a purely advisory capacity.

The reactionaries, defeated but not broken, hatched several plots to overthrow the Provisional Government. But their conspiracies came to nothing, thanks to the intervention of the peasants' forces which were drawing near the capital. It is interesting to note that Colonel Obolesco and the Metropolitan, Neophite, were both implicated in the conspiracies, although they were members of the Provisional Government.

Still, Eliade's group of moderates took no action against them and even let them keep their posts after they had solemnly promised to respect the Constitution.

So as to plead its cause, the Provisional Government sent representatives to Constantinople, Vienna and Paris.

As to its domestic policy, the Provisional Government, composed mostly of moderates, was careful to avoid putting into practice the basic principles which would have ensured the success of the revolution. It tried to postpone indefinitely the summoning of the Constituent Assembly after there had been serious differences of opinion as to the way the elections should be run: Eliade's group wanted a property qualification for voters, whilst Balcesco's wanted universal suffrage, as laid down in the Proclamation.

Against the wishes of Balcesco, who wanted the immediate emancipation of the serfs and the parcelling out of the land, the Provisional Government decided to shelve this problem by appointing an Agrarian Commission, which was to sit interminably without reaching a decision. This commission, which started work on 9 August 1848, was composed of representatives from the landowners and the peasants of each district. Their discussions were frequently extremely heated. The *Boyars* were determined to stone-wall, and had no intention of ever giving up their property. What was more, the Government granted their request that, until a solution had been reached, the peasants should still carry out their feudal obligations. The peasants, on the other hand, insistently demanded that the terms of the Proclamation should come into force, and answered the landowners' claim to the inviolability of their property by saying: 'We'll see it's inviolable, but first share it out.'

The peasants, worn out by this procrastination, ended by agreeing that the landowners should be compensated for the loss of their land; but the *Boyars* would not even accept this solution. 'Why are the *Boyars* so intransigent?' asked Balcesco. 'Do they feel they are being unfairly treated? Are they attached to their land? Of course not. The *Boyar* has no love for the land; he does not live on it and work it. . . . He looks upon the land as a penal settlement in which to keep the peasant so as to exploit him with the help of his farmers . . . he does not hate the revolutionaries because they wanted to take the land from him: he hates them because they wanted to deprive him of the privilege of living a life of leisure on the sweat of the peasant's brow. He has sold his country's freedom to save his rights of tyranny. . . . The peasant represents the *Boyar's* capital.'

In the end, Eliade dissolved the Commission. The landowners won their case and the problem of the peasants was shelved indefinitely.

The Provisional Government's domestic policy, then, was a purely negative one. Its foreign policy, too, contradicted the principles of the Islaz Proclamation.

The Turks, on the advice of Nicholas I, sent an army under Suliman Pasha into Wallachia. The radicals, under Balcesco, insisted that the Government should mobilise its forces and arm the people.

But the Government thought otherwise. It started to negotiate with the Turks and strove to 'convince' them that it was essential to recognise the aspirations of the peoples as expressed by the Proclamation.

Once the Government had started on this path there was no going back. It gave way to the Turks when they demanded that the Provisional Government should be dissolved and replaced by a lieutenancy formed by three members of the former government. Balcesco later commented that by their submission, the Government had lost 'the country its freedom in spite of our opposition. The failure of political revolution followed the failure of social revolution, for our right to revolt was based solely on our autonomy. . . . The revolution was finished.'

What happened was that the Turkish troops, who were then at Giurgiu, occupied the whole of Wallachia, under the orders of Fuad Effendi who replaced Suliman Pasha. A feeble attempt at resistance put up by the firemen of Bucharest failed to prevent the Turks from committing atrocities and looting.

There was a slightly more serious attempt at resistance in Oltenia under the leadership of Magheru, who, at the head of an army, wanted to attack the invaders. 'But, on the advice of his old friends and the British Consul, not to lead the country blindly into so unequal a contest, he disbanded his forces—though not without sending a protest to Fuad Effendi against such an attack on the rights of the Rumanian people, and such a violation of their territory' (Xenopol).

That was the end of the Wallachian Revolution. It failed because Eliade and his friends' moderate and temporising policy had quenched the revolutionary spirit of the people, who, given neither rights nor land, had nothing to defend.

But although Wallachia's revolution was unsuccessful, the ideas behind it, championed so courageously by Balcesco, slowly took hold of the masses.

4

1848 IN TRANSYLVANIA

May the very word serfdom and all its associations perish
G. Baritiu
'The Transylvanian Gazette,' No. 46, 1848

The Rumanians' revolutionary struggle in Transylvania is closely linked with the Hungarian rising. But this did not immediately produce a purely Rumanian movement. For some time, there were merely isolated disturbances in different parts of Transylvania, as among the Rumanians in Pest, for no clearly defined reasons. This slowness to take up a definite attitude exasperated some of the revolutionaries, such as Laurian, who impatiently exclaimed: 'Ripe fruit doesn't pick itself. . . . It's high time we acted!'

Meetings took place in various parts of Transylvania (such as Tg-Mures, Blaj and Brasov) in the course of which three main tendencies became apparent.

The first of these was shown by Bishop Andrei Saguna, who kept up friendly relations with the Viennese Court, tried to make a success of collaboration with the Austrian Empire, and spread the theory that there lay the sole solution to Rumania's problems.

A second plan, put forward by Simion Barnutiu and Avram Jancu, was to form close ties with the Hungarians, but on condition that they recognised the Rumanians as the fourth nation composing the Hungarian State, the other three being the Hungarians, the Saxons and the Széklers.

Baritiu, however, foresaw the creation of a federated Transylvania, an alliance with the Hungarians, equal legal status for each of the four nations, the reconstruction of the cantons on a racial basis, and universal suffrage for citizens over twenty-one.

The partisans of these three theories argued violently among themselves, and it was not until the meeting of the Blaj Assembly on 3 May 1848, which had been organised as the result of a number of local Rumanian meetings, that they succeeded in agreeing upon a minimum programme. The promoters of this Assembly, who belonged for the main part to the leisured classes, had tried to win the co-operation of the middle class who were extremely dissatisfied with the fact that the Hungarian Constitution had made no provision for the Rumanians as a nation. The Government banned this Assembly, which was fixed for 21 December, and would not permit it to be held until 3 May.

To the great surprise of the organisers, who had expected only the delegates and especially the ecclesiastical representatives, numbers of peasants arrived that day in Blaj. Although in theory they had been freed from serfdom as a result of the great peasant revolt led by Horia, Closca and Crisan in 1784, in point of fact they were no better off. When they heard of all the revolutions taking place in the spring of 1848, the Transylvanian peasants began to hope that they too might at last win fair treatment.

That is why they arrived in Blaj from every corner of Transylvania. Their appearance completely changed the character of the Assembly, and its organisers, who had originally had the purely political aim of freeing the Rumanian nation, found themselves fighting to free the peasants.

On 2 May 1848, the day before the Assembly opened, there was a preparatory meeting in Blaj Cathedral, attended by the revolutionary leaders of Wallachia and Moldavia. Simion Barnutiu made a speech explaining the revolutionaries' programme, in which he demanded that the Rumanians should be granted their national liberties.

The whole of that night there was a lively discussion centred round the text of the resolution that they were to put to the vote of the Assembly the next morning. The argument for tightening relations with the Hungarian revolutionaries, in order to fight for a common freedom which would help to solve the Rumanian national problem, met with little success. On the contrary, Saguna's group led the Assembly to frame its resolution as follows: 'The Rumanian Nation declares that it will always remain faithful to the Emperor of Austria.' Thus the Rumanians' struggle was separated from that of the Hungarian revolutionaries, and the Rumanian people were ranged under the standard of the 'oldest, most infamous and most pitiless of the despots', as Balcesco said.

It was from this moment that the Rumanian revolutionary movement in Transylvania began to slide towards disaster. After the Assembly's session on 3 and 4 May, the following further demands were added to the Resolution: the use of the Rumanian language in all matters pertaining to the nation, administrative as well as legislative; the Church's independence from all the other denominations and its equal status as regards rights and benefices; the abolition of serfdom and feudal dues without compensation; freedom for the press and freedom to hold meetings; personal freedom; the formation of a National Guard; proportional taxation; the foundation of State-supported secondary schools and a national university; and various other items. These demands show the justice of the Rumanians' cause, and shame those of their leaders who betrayed their hopes.

The Assembly appointed two delegates to take the resolution to the Emperor and to the Transylvanian Diet. As a result of the Diet's procrastination, it took several weeks for the Resolution to reach the Emperor who had fled from the revolution in Vienna and had gone to Innsbruck.

This method of presenting their claims, which Saguna wanted to keep strictly within the bounds of legality, did not produce the expected result. The Emperor, whilst making promises to the Rumanians in order to sow discord between them and the Hungarians, at the same time recognised the Hungarian Constitution which united Transylvania with Hungary. The revolutionary committee elected by the Blaj Assembly was astonishingly inert. Nevertheless, the peasants, who considered they were freed from serfdom and their obligations towards the Hungarian nobles, refused to do statute labour. This resulted in a series of risings which soon grew widespread.

The political blunders committed by the Hungarian Government under Kossuth, who failed to provide a truly revolutionary solution to the nation's problems, further widened the gulf between the Hungarian and Rumanian insurgents. They also facilitated the task of the Viennese Court, which was to use the Rumanian movement against Hungary.

After a second meeting at Blaj on 25 September, 1848, General Baron Plüchner, the Imperial Army Commander, ordered the Rumanian Revolutionary Committee at Blaj to disarm all the Hungarians and to defend the Emperor's cause. 'Thus', writes Xenopol, 'the Rumanian counter-revolution broke out in all its violence'. It would be false, though, to say that all the Rumanians fought for the Empire against Kossuth's Hungary.

The Hungarian revolutionary forces under Bem met the Austro-Rumanian army at Ciucea and defeated it. They then occupied Cluj, started a rising among the Széklers, entered Brasov, and became masters of nearly the whole of Transylvania.

The brilliant General Bem organised a new army of thirty thousand men, mainly composed of Széklers but also of Rumanians, which proves that there were some to join the Hungarian revolutionaries. A number of them were given Magyar ranks and decorations in recognition of their valour. Another group of Rumanians, led by Avram Ianco, still insisted that they would only co-operate with the Hungarians if they were recognised as the fourth nation composing the country.

The Wallachian leaders, however, remained faithful to their revolutionary ideals despite set-backs, realising, as Balcesco said, that 'national freedom is not given away by Emperors and despots out of the kindness of their hearts: it can only be won by a united effort of all Rumanians, who must rise as one man and show their solidarity with all oppressed peoples'.

This is why the Wallachians, with Balcesco at their head, turned towards Transylvania and tried to effect a reconciliation between the Hungarian revolutionary army and the Rumanian forces under Avram Ianco, who had put themselves at the Emperor's disposal. Balcesco had interviews with Bem and Kossuth and arranged one between Avram Ianco and the Hungarian envoys. But neither party would give up their narrow nationalist outlook. Balcesco went on trying but the two armies continued to fight.

At the beginning of 1849 they were just starting to reach a compromise, but it was too late. The combined Austrian and Russian armies were already on their way to smash the revolution.

Most of Casimir Ralikovski's Russian troops, who went over to the Hungarians, died because they would not 'stain their hands with the blood of the defenders of freedom'.

After the capitulation of Hungary, the Imperial Court forgot its generous promises. It was much later on, after fresh fierce conflicts, that the Rumanians triumphed. They realised then that, despite their revolutionary ardour and desire to fight for freedom and their national rights, they had been betrayed by certain of their leaders into serving the cause of a Power which was oppressing, among so many other races, the Hungarians as much as the Rumanians.

It is the understanding of these realities that today makes it possible for the Rumanians and Hungarians to live side by side in peace in Transylvania, each respecting the others' national and individual liberties.

Although the events of 1848 in Moldavia, Wallachia and Transylvania did not lead the Rumanian people to achieve their hopes, they nevertheless had great historical importance. They helped to spread democratic ideas, strengthened the Rumanians' conception of themselves as a nation, and—above all—proved that a truly democratic movement can only succeed if the masses combine under an effective leadership.

HUNGARY

THE WAR OF INDEPENDENCE

FRANÇOIS FEJTÖ

The future of Hungary will remain uncertain and insecure . . . so long as the Magyar people submit to their rulers' will and own no political rights
Louis Kossuth to the Pressburg Diet on 29 November 1847

I

THE NEWS FROM PARIS

It was on the night of 29 February that the news of the fall of the House of Orléans reached Pressburg, the legislative capital of Hungary, and thence spread rapidly throughout the country. The first reaction was a financial panic. The merchants of the Hungarian free towns, which were mostly German-speaking, had vivid and most disagreeable memories of the two occasions, after the 1789 and 1830 revolutions, on which the Bank of Vienna had gone bankrupt. According to the *Pesti Hirlap*, it was hard even by 3 March to find a shop which would accept banknotes; on the 5th, which was a Sunday, huge crowds braved torrential rain to besiege the State Bank in Buda, and try to exchange their notes for silver. By midday this crowd had grown to such proportions that it took a squadron of cavalry and a battalion of infantry to control it; and there was an equally large mob outside the savings banks. The price of gold rose visibly. In the Pressburg Diet, one of the deputies proposed that they 'very humbly' petition the King-Emperor 'to enlighten the country as to the position of the State Bank and give an assurance that banknotes would be honoured, so as to restore the peoples' confidence'.

The Hungarian Diet had been sitting since 12 November 1847. The moderate members of the Reform Party (such as the men who directed the policy of the newspaper *Pesti Hirlap*) considered it a stroke of luck for the country that the Diet should be in session at a time when momentous events were taking place in the West. They believed that the effect of the 'Days of February' would be the speedy realisation of reforms which the Diet had been considering for several years.

Still, the opposition had no illusions about the Hungarian Diet, which was no representative National Assembly in the modern sense of the term. In the first place, instead of being in the centre of the country it was situated in a frontier town, where it was quite out of touch with public opinion. Secondly, it represented only the nobility, a minority of the population. Admittedly there were also deputies from the free towns, but they did not enjoy the same privileges as the nobles who had a vote each, whereas they had only one between them. In point of fact, even if the members from the sixteen free towns had had a larger say in the Diet's affairs, they would not have been much help to the progressives there, for they represented the interests of a still feudal middle class, which staunchly upheld the guild system.

2

FEUDAL HUNGARY

This country, whose people were to be so violently affected by the news of the February Revolution, was still fast sunk in the feudal bog. The nobles who owned most of Hungary paid not a single tax, whereas the peasantry were burdened by tallage, tithe and statute labour, and had no political rights whatsoever. A member of one of the greatest families in the country, Count Stephen Széchenyi, who (after several visits to France and England, where he had become imbued with the ideas of Adam Smith and Bentham) had given much thought to his country's lot, made the following calculation: 'There are among us men who own a five-hundredth part of Hungary, others who own a hundredth, and yet others who possess one seventeen thousandth of the universe, one eleven hundredth of Europe, one eightieth of the Austrian Empire and one thirtieth of our unhappy country.'

The magnates, or great landowners, looked upon the high offices of the State as theirs by right of birth, and held in fee the Council of the Lieutenancy, the Chancellery and the Chamber of France. They governed the Counties, and they alone sat in their own right in the Upper House or House of Magnates, which traditionally threw out every bill produced by the progressive opposition in the Lower House which threatened their privileges. Ever since the eighteenth century when Austria had crushed Rákoczi's insurrection, the aristocracy had lost its critical tendencies and the spirit of independence, which had been identified with that of the nation. It had merged its interests with those of the Viennese Court and the nobles of Austria and Bohemia, and strengthened its ties by marrying into their families.

Most of these magnates could not even speak Hungarian, which they despised as the vulgar tongue, and as one of their own kind, Count John Pálffy, said, 'they have ceased to be the upholders of Hungarian nationalism and are become strangers in their own land'.

When the news of the great happenings in France reached Pressburg, Hungary had for twenty years been torn by an ever-growing conflict between the magnates and the minor nobles. The latter, partly of their own accord and partly under the influence of events in Europe, 'clothed their old social and national ambitions in coats of a French cut'.[1] These minor nobles who wanted to rule the country formed no homogeneous class. Half their strength of 680,000—no mean figure for a population of twelve million—were poor and worked their own little plots of land, sometimes even paying rent for it, but for all that they were jealous of their social superiority over their commoner neighbours. The fifty-two County Assemblies, which administered the country, were in the hands of the middle class of nobles, owning between twelve hundred and twelve thousand acres. This social stratum included a number of well-educated people, who were prepared to sacrifice wealth and even privileges to assert their right to rule the country. Francis Deák, an extremely level-headed man, was the political spokesman of this class of nobles, which, in spite of its conservatism, wanted to bring in certain basic reforms, and was to have led the great reformist movement on the eve of the 1847 elections. But the man who took over the lead was a son of the impoverished nobility, the lawyer and publicist, Louis Kossuth. How was it that this man, who from the moment he entered public life suffered humiliation upon humiliation at the hands of the contemptuous aristocracy, succeeded in becoming the spokesman of the Diet and the undisputed head of the Hungarian nation?

This frail and sickly looking creature, with his melancholy blue eyes and pale face, was one of the most powerful forces of the century. A tireless worker, with an indefatigable brain, he was by nature ambitious. But he had no illusions as to the difficulty of winning the confidence of the nobles, who so mistrusted him, in order to use them in the realisation of his political ideals. Kossuth had an inflexible will, and neither set-backs nor disappointments nor betrayals daunted him. His stormy eloquence equalled that of Lamartine and O'Connell, and he was capable of every mood from calm deliberation to passionate rhetoric. Yet although he possessed such power to sway the masses, he never let it get the better of him: he could control his own emotions, suppress his private hatreds and delight in making generous gestures.

When the Diet met on 3 March, no one was surprised that this Louis

[1] Ervin Szabo: *Class Warfare in Hungary in 1848 and 1849.*

Kossuth, whom six months previously his own party had refused to send as its representative to the Assembly, now rose to voice the hopes of the nation. He owed his success to his powerful protector Count Louis Batthyán, who spent several hundred thousand florins on convincing the electorate. This great noble was one of the few magnates who espoused the cause of their country's independence.

In his speech, Kossuth clearly outlined the reformists' programme, which had been such a labour to produce owing to the divergence of interests in the opposition. By a curious paradox, the Vienna Government drew from it several ideas for its own programme, thereby spiking the Austrian opposition's guns. The Austrian opposition was further disconcerted by the events in Galicia in 1846, when Vienna tricked the peasantry into rising against the Polish nobles who were themselves in revolt against Austrian domination. This tragic episode in the history of Poland furnished Kossuth with an excellent argument to persuade the Hungarian nobility to head the anti-feudal movement instead of allowing it to overwhelm them. 'Let the nobility act', he cried, 'or it will fall a victim to those whom it should free, and that day of massacre will spell death to the Constitution and to the Hungarian nation.'

3

NATIONALISM AND LIBERALISM

To this day the Hungarians still argue among themselves whether Kossuth simply represented the nationalist nobles, or whether he was—if not, as he himself claimed, a true democrat—at any rate a true liberal, in the European sense of the word. The Marxist writer Joseph Révai seems to take the latter view in a recently published article. My own belief is that Kossuth only became the spokesman of the nobles so as to use them to carry out what he considered to be necessary reforms. Although many of his speeches are full of panegyrics on the past glory and present mission of the aristocracy, we must realise that he was not deceived by his own flattery. That is why we should not be surprised that he posed as the champion not only of national independence, but also of constitutional autonomy for the nobles' beloved Counties, which I have already mentioned. The Government of the country depended on the fifty-two counties whose administrative officers were elected by the local Assemblies of nobles. Joseph II had had violent disputes with those 'fortresses of Magyar feudalism', which rejected all reforms that might benefit the peasantry, but patriotically fought against the germanisation of Hungary.

Kossuth, who had read the works of Guizot, Thiers, Lamartine and Cobden, and was an admirer of the parliamentary battles of England and France, had a very different conception of the fatherland from these conservative patriots. Nationalism in his eyes could not be separated from liberalism. He objected to the State Council of Vienna on account of its 'policy of bureaucratic conservatism', not because he was afraid of a violent change in Hungary's social structure.

In fact, since the failure of Joseph II's vast scheme of reforms, the Vienna Government had made no further attack on feudalism. Thus, from being offensive and expansionist, its policy had become purely defensive and conservative. The only link between the different provinces of the Empire was a powerful, officious bureaucracy, backed by a meddle-some police force and a heterogeneous army whose officers were mostly imbued with monarchist principles. Kossuth, in his speech of 3 March, contemptuously remarked that 'bayonets and red-tape are pretty despicable ties'. Count Széchenyi, Kossuth's great rival, was seen to frown as he listened to this condemnation.

Széchenyi never tired of warning his compatriots of the danger they ran in provoking, out of national pride and a desire for legitimate reforms, a desperate conflict with the machinery of the Empire and the various nations within Hungary's borders. He was moved not solely by his class instincts but also by a genuine anxiety for the future of the Hungarian nation. He looked upon Kossuth's nationalism—not without justice—as essentially 'emotional', and lacking in political and social realism. But then nationalism is bound to arouse peoples' passions.

Middle-class nationalists everywhere looked upon national unity as a miracle worker which would prevent class warfare and a popular rising. The moderates and even some of the radicals at the time of the French Revolution had looked to the wave of patriotism produced by the national war to resolve domestic disputes, and had found it a powerful preventitive against class warfare. In Hungary in 1848 resentment against foreign reactionaries and their Hungarian henchmen united men of such different temperaments and outlooks as Batthyán, the reformist magnate; Deák, the spokesman of the middle class of nobles; and Kossuth, who represented the intellectuals of the minor nobility.

Kossuth was aiming at Vienna when in his speech of 3 March he said: 'Unnatural political systems sometimes have a long life, for it takes a long time to exhaust a people's patience. But some of these political systems do not grow stronger as they grow older, and there comes a moment when it would be dangerous to extend their life because they are beginning to decay. Their death cannot be circumvented, but it can be shared. I know that it is as hard for an old system as for an old man to give up the habits of a lifetime, and see a life's work crumble away, but when the foundations have rotted, the building is bound to collapse.' Never before had so damning an indictment of Austria been pronounced in the Hungarian Diet.

4

REFORM OR REVOLUTION

Kossuth followed up his condemnation of the Austrian régime by urging that the political system of the monarchy should at once be changed by the grant of Constitutions not only to Hungary but also to the hereditary provinces. He then read a draft edict summarising Hungary's own particular demands, which consisted of universal taxation; the abolition of tallage and statute labour, with compensation for the landowners; the transfer of control of the Budget and conscription to the nation's representatives; and the formation of a government responsible to them. The House passed Kossuth's proposals and sent them to the Upper house, which, following its old dilatory tactics, discussed them word by word and phrase by phrase without admitting their urgency. These aristocrats did not take seriously the news from Pest that the students there, under leadership of the revolutionary poet Alexander Petöfi, were preparing a grand reform banquet, on the French model. The nobles relied on the strong garrison across the Danube at Buda, the seat of the Government, which could easily make a hundred or so young hotheads see reason. Then, during the night of 13 March, some terrified bourgeois from Vienna reached Pressburg with news of the fall of Metternich. And Kossuth had been indirectly responsible, for it had been his speech to the Diet with which the young Dr Fischof had inflamed the students' demonstration that began the Vienna Revolution.

The next day Kossuth gave the Diet a commentary on the events in Vienna. He stressed the fact that his party wanted reform and not a revolution. But the revolution was at Hungary's gates, and if they lost time in idle discussion it might spread to their own country. 'It is our duty', he told the unconvinced nobles, 'not to lose control of the movement and not to let ourselves be overwhelmed.' It is important to remember Kossuth's determination to preserve for the nobility the lead of the reformist movement, for therein lay both his greatness and his limitations.

317

Kossuth had not sufficiently succeeded in forgetting his noble birth. His sentiments were only partially 'middle class' in the western sense of the phrase, for he was an aristocrat filling the rôle of a middle-class man in a country where virtually none existed, and his environment and the interests of his class which he had to safeguard to secure his ends, prevented him giving full rein to his beliefs and feelings.

This was equally true of the Hungarian opposition and even of the whole Pressburg Diet of which Kossuth was a member. They were outspoken enough on the subject of Hungarian independence, but they hesitated when it came to changing the feudal system. And yet this was an urgent matter. The peasants' wrongs had to be righted, and it was necessary to reconcile the nobility with the disinherited masses.

Count Sztáray, although a conservative, had said several years previously that 'half measures were no longer any use, and radical changes were needed to lighten the people's burdens'. Yet the nobles saw no other way of abolishing tithes and forced labour than that of the purchase by the peasants of their own freedom, without any help from the State, at a price laid down by commissions mainly composed of landowners. They retained this attitude right up to 13 March, the day on which the revolution broke out in Vienna. On the 14th, a deputy named Szentkirályi suggested to the Diet that the Government should pay the compensation to the landowners for the abolition of their feudal rights, and his proposal was carried unanimously. Fright had awoken the Diet's social conscience, for its members were afraid not only of the Viennese revolutionaries, but of the inhabitants of Pest. Increasingly alarming rumours of their activities were going round Pressburg.

5

THE IDES OF MARCH IN PEST

Public rumour had it that a hundred thousand peasants armed with scythes had assembled on the Rákos Field just outside Pest, prepared for a vast *jacquerie*. The truth was much simpler: the crowds reported in that area were merely collecting for the great annual fair on 15 March. The only signs of unrest in the town itself were to be found in the cafés, where people read and loudly discussed the Paris and Vienna papers. They talked of freedom of the press, and criticised the Diet for its halfheartedness. The most influential of these café politicians was the poet Petöfi, son of an innkeeper and a peasant woman, who was a great admirer of Béranger and Burns, whom he translated, and was passionately fond of both Heine and Byron.

Petőfi found his inspiration in popular poetry and introduced new forms and rhythms into Hungarian verse. Some years before he had written some prophetic stanzas on the liberating effects of revolution.

I dream of days of bloodshed
In which an old world dies,
And see from smoking ruins
A phoenix world arise.

Petőfi, as well as most of his friends of the *Café Pilvax* in Pest, had found their political and human ideals in the history of the French Revolution and the literature it produced. Robespierre, Danton and Lamartine all inspired them; *L'Histoire des Girondins* was their Bible; and they were familiar with the teachings of Babeuf. Petőfi envied the French intellectuals who had the chance of fighting for the Universal Republic, shoulder to shoulder with the masses. The artisans of Pest and the Hungarian peasants did not even know the meaning of the word 'republic'. Besides, out of a population of twelve million there were only a hundred and ten thousand industrial workers, and they were mostly artisans.

Petőfi was in the country when he heard the news from Paris. He was quite overcome and hurried to Pest, feeling the same restlessness that Heine had experienced when he left for Hamburg on hearing of the July Revolution. When he arrived there, Petőfi decided with his friends to organise a great banquet on the Rákos Field to celebrate the success of the February rising. He had written a poem which he wanted to become a national anthem like the *Marseillaise*, and which he proposed reciting at this banquet, as well as reading out the 'Twelve Points' which summed up the young radicals' programme.

The moderates in the capital, afraid of being overwhelmed by the revolutionaries, had this demonstration postponed and demanded that the 'Twelve Points', which will be enumerated further on, should first be circulated throughout the country as a petition so that it should bear a great number of signatures before being solemnly borne to Pressburg.

That was how things stood when on 14 March the youth of Budapest learnt of the events in Vienna, and decided to take direct action too.

When later on the press was freed, it celebrated the day of 15 March as a bloodless revolution, and in point of fact it was more like a popular fair than a revolt. Széchenyi ironically called it the 'Umbrella Revolution' for it was raining that day in Pest (as it had rained on the first day of the revolution in Paris, Palermo and Vienna). The young people met in the garden of the National Museum, to hear Petöfi's poem and the 'Twelve Points', under a forest of umbrellas.

Thanks to the rain, this youth demonstration attracted the mob, for the peasants had abandoned their fair and came to see what was going on. They were impressed and their enthusiasm spread to the rest of the populace.

The 'Twelve Points' were as follows:

1. Freedom of the press and abolition of pre-censorship
2. A Government responsible to the people
3. An annual meeting of a Parliament elected by universal suffrage
4. Equality for all before the law
5. The formation of a National Guard
6. Equal taxation for all
7. The abolition of feudal rights
8. The election of juries to try criminal offences
9. The creation of a national bank
10. The formation of a national army
11. The liberation of political prisoners
12. The union of Hungary and Transylvania.[1]

Apart from its force and clarity of expression, this programme, so like the liberal demands being made all over Europe, differed little from that of the legal opposition under Kossuth.

The young radicals there and then set about putting into practice the first of these points, which according to Petöfi was 'logically the first step and the principal duty of the Revolution'. They forced the largest printing house in Pest to print their revolutionary song and the Twelve Points, of which they distributed thousands of copies throughout the town. By the afternoon the whole of Pest was in the streets. The municipal council, to the delight of the crowd, accepted the Twelve Points and had them posted on the walls of the capital. A Committee of Public Order, composed of fifty members, was chosen from members of the municipal council and the revolutionaries. The crowd then set off towards the Buda prison, where they freed the sole political prisoner they found there. There was a second, a Rumanian democrat, but they did not know of his existence, and it was several days before he was let out. The prisoner released by the crowd was a Hungarian named Táncsics, like Petöfi, a pioneer of democracy and socialism in the country.

Táncsics, with his high domed forehead and large placid face framed

[1] Transylvania, after the Austrian Army had freed it from Turkish rule, had a government responsible to Vienna. The Hungarians, in the name of the traditional rights of the Crown of St Stephen, wanted to end this relationship.

in whiskers, looked like a gentleman of leisure. But he had led an eventful life. The son of a peasant, he had begun life as a farm servant, then became in turn weaver, journeyman, assistant teacher and student in the Arts School of Pest University. This self-taught man, who had learnt from the works of Volney and Rousseau, took up his pen at the age of thirty to defend—like Proudhon, whom he admired—the interests of the little man against the nobility. He went abroad, visiting Vienna, Paris—where he met Cabet—and London, where he made his first contact with modern industry on a large scale. Táncsics was not an original writer—his work is diffuse and his ideas confused—but his *Catechism for the People*, published in 1846, was a remarkably clear presentation of the peasants' demands. The main point he made was that feudal rights should be abolished without compensation for the landowners.

It was for this pamphlet that he had been imprisoned, and the crowd went mad with joy at the chance to release him. They carried him in a cab, pulled by the young revolutionaries, to the National Theatre. There the orchestra played first *The March of Rákoczi* then the *Marseillaise*, and actors recited revolutionary poems. Petöfi later exclaimed with pride that 'our ancestors did not do as much in a century as we did in twenty-four hours'.

The next day began the organisation of a National Guard. Marshal Lederer, the Austrian garrison commander, at first refused to allow arms to be drawn from the arsenal, but in the end he gave in to threats. That evening Buda and Pest were illuminated. After the Committee of Public Order had quelled an anti-semitic demonstration by middle-class Germans, who objected to Jews being admitted into the National Guard,[1] it sent a delegation to inform the Pressburg Diet of the course of events and present it with the text of the Twelve Points.

6

PRESSBURG'S VICTORY OVER PEST

Kossuth had just returned from Vienna, where he led a delegation from the Diet. He had been loudly cheered by the people of the Imperial capital, and the Emperor Ferdinand, lest worse befell, had accepted the Hungarian proposals and called upon Count Batthyány to form a Government. On 17 March, Kossuth appeared on the balcony of his hotel in

[1] The Hungarian Jews gave their wholehearted support to the movement, which they hoped would free them from age-old bonds. Numbers of them distinguished themselves in battle, and one of the Kossuth Government's last acts was to decree their emancipation.

Pressburg and, calling for silence from the entire populace assembled in the square below, removed his hat and in dramatic accents cried: 'Gentlemen, greet with me the dawn of Hungarian freedom!' Yet this man, whom the Viennese workers had hailed with shouts of *Unser Erlöser!* (Our Deliverer) when he returned to Pressburg would not even see the revolutionary delegates from Pest. Under the influence of the other moderates and even some of the radicals in the opposition, he kept carefully within the bounds of legality. He would not tolerate the smallest spontaneous rising of the people; the mob was there only to cheer him and heed his instructions; 'I'll break you', he was heard to mutter.

The law-abiding opposition of Pressburg easily and peacefully defeated the revolutionaries of Pest, who made use neither of the workers of the town nor of the peasantry. When the Government moved from Pressburg to Pest and began to lay the foundations of a new régime, the Committee of Public Order, which had been in existance for barely a month, disappeared and the majority of young men who had taken part in the rising of 15 March were absorbed into the administration for the newly created army. The mob was occasionally to grow angry when their hard-won liberty was endangered, but their leaders had gone.

This easy victory of law and order had a harmful effect on the cause of liberalism in Hungary. The young revolutionaries under Petöfi had been laughed at for their utopianism, but they had a clearer idea how to solve the country's social and national problems than the majority of professional politicians. Petöfi had reason to smile at the self-importance of the latter who at Pressburg discussed means of abolishing, in principle, feudal rights, whilst continuing to make the peasants carry out statute labour. Petöfi, Táncsics and their friends demanded immediate abolition of all feudal rights without compensation. The young men of Pest were nationalists as Kossuth was, but their nationalism had no aristocratic bias. They won the support of the Serbs in the South of Hungary, and the Rumanian democrats of Transylvania under Jancu. They realised that a Hungarian Constitution would only be practicable if it gave the peasants their freedom and took into account the particular interests of each of Hungary's various nationalities, such as the Slovaks, the Croats and the Little Russians who still looked upon the Hungarian Government as the aristocratic oppressor. These nationalities formed seven-twelfths of the population.

7

THE LEGISLATIVE WORK OF THE DIET

During the three months following the 'Days of March', the Pressburg Diet passed thirty-one bills. But their Constitution was far from extremist. The law freeing the press contained so many restrictions that the disappointed youth of Pest ceremoniously burnt the text of it. The bill introducing popular representation contained a high enough property qualification to exclude the majority of artisans, domestic servants and peasants from the electorate. Only the nobles had a free vote. The law abolishing forced labour and tithes did not apply to the *métayers*, or farmers paying their rent in kind: vine growers still had to pay tithes, and a number of feudal rights were retained, such as tolls, grazing rights, fishing, hunting and hawking rights. The payment of compensation to the landowners was guaranteed on 'the nation's honour'. Kossuth hurried this bill through, warning the Diet of the danger of delay with the country in its present state of unrest.

Some days after his return from Vienna, Count Batthyány formed his Government with Kossuth as his Finance Minister and Kossuth's rival Széchenyi as Minister of Communications. Except for Kossuth and Szemere, the Minister of the Interior, the Ministers were all chosen from among the moderates in the opposition. Francis Deák, the Minister for Justice, stood for keeping in with Vienna; the Defence Minister, Colonel Mészáros, was an officer of the Imperial Army, and the Minister for Austrian Relations was Prince Esterházy, the greatest landowner in the country, who was known for his loyalty to the dynasty. Batthyány was obviously determined to keep on good terms with Vienna. Yet a week later the Austrian Government sent a note containing a number of amendments to the decisions reached by the Diet. The gist of the note was that Austria wanted to retain control of Hungary's finances and army, which the Emperor had unwillingly put in her hands some days previously.

The patriots of Pest, when they learnt the contents of the Imperial note, vehemently protested against this unexpected hardening of Austria's attitude. 'The whole world runs blood, stars fall from the heavens, Kings and their Ministers are swept away; the entire universe seethes with portents, and yet Vienna will not see them', wrote the *Pesti Hirlap*. It echoed the exasperation of the youth of Pest, who had gained fresh impetus from the spread of the freedom movement to the rest of the country. The middle class of every town carried arms, and in several districts the peasants had freed themselves from a number of feudal obligations without waiting for the agrarian laws.

Then the news arrived from Italy that the patriots had driven back Radetzky's forces.

At a stormy meeting called by the Committee of Public Order, a resolution was adopted whereby in the event of Vienna refusing to ratify the March laws and dismissing Batthyány's Government, a provisional government would be formed in Pest itself. The result of this announcement was that within twenty-four hours Vienna had recognised the Hungarian Government.

Kossuth hastened to reply to this concession by assuring the Emperor 'of the Hungarian nation's complete loyalty', and that they would continue to recognise the validity of the Pragmatic Sanction of 1711 (whereby Hungary was indissolubly united with the hereditary provinces of the Hapsburgs).

But Kossuth, at the same time as reassuring the Court, was unwise enough to point out in the same speech that as 'an ordinary citizen' he had been in the position to decide the fate of the Austrian throne. 'If I had rejected then, and if I was to reject now, the propositions put forward by Vienna, blood would flow', he said. It was all very well for him to add that he would never gamble with the lives of his compatriots and the nation's peace, and that 'freedom is only truly won if one voluntarily uses the minimum of force': but his first statement struck the traditionalists of the Viennese Court 'like a slap in the face'. And the moderates in the Hungarian opposition were equally shocked—not only Széchenyi, but also Batthyány, Deák and Baron Eötvös (the Minister of Education, and an ardent admirer of Montalambert), who did all they could to appease the Austrians by repeated assurances of their loyalty. They accused Kossuth of nullifying all their efforts with his conceit. But it is hard to believe that any protestations of loyalty could have succeeded in disarming the suspicions of the Viennese Court.

8

THE ARCHDUKE STEPHEN AND VIENNA

The Emperor was represented at Pressburg by the Archduke Stephen, whom his contemporaries described as a weak-willed and narrow-minded popularity seeker. 'The cowardly viceroy of an idiot king' was what the Transylvanian magnate, John Pálffy styled him. The aristocracy later criticised him for not taking a stronger line from the start with the revolutionaries, for allowing himself to be frightened by 'the noisy urchins of the Pilvax district' (as they called Petőfi and his friends) and for being scared of Kossuth instead of rendering him harmless.

But the Archduke was neither as cowardly nor as stupid as his detractors made out. The day on which Batthyány published the list of Ministers, the viceroy or *Nádor* sent a secret despatch to his uncle the Emperor, giving him his views on the situation in Hungary. He said that there were three alternatives open to the Austrian Government. The first was to evacuate Hungary and leave the nobles and the peasants to fight it out on their own; the second was to negotiate with Batthyány; and the third was to send a High Commissioner at the head of a considerable force to punish the rebels and to restore order.

The Austrian Government accepted the Archduke's advice to take the second course, but did not rule out the possibility of adopting one of the others. Two months later, in September, the Emperor declared the laws passed in March invalid as he had signed them under pressure. The Court had known all along that Austria could not afford to lose control of Hungary's finances and the Hungarian army, but it had not been strong enough that spring to assert itself. This was the explanation of the double game Austria had been playing all that year, recognising the Hungarian Constitution but doing her utmost to curtail its powers.

She had been forced, however, to avoid an open conflict because an important part of the Imperial Army fighting in Italy and garrisoning Bohemia, Moravia and Galicia, was composed of Hungarians, and she could not risk their desertion. On the other hand the military command in Hungary was in the hands of senior Austrian officers—which gave the Hungarian Government food for thought.

9

THE ATTITUDE OF THE DIFFERENT RACES IN HUNGARY

There was, first in the Pressburg Diet, then in the Assembly which met in July, a strong majority which, either out of class interests, a feeling for tradition or opportunism, wanted to avoid a complete break with the Austrian Court. It preferred to come to terms with the Imperial Government rather than achieve independence with the aid of the peasants or the peoples of other races. Batthyány's Government tried half-heartedly to do both. The conservatives and the moderates were the ones who advised firm resistance to the demands of the subject nationalities. Széchenyi insisted that the nobility constituted the essence of the Hungarian race, and if it were to lose its privileges, the six million Magyars would be swamped by the Slavs.

In this aristocratic bias lay the tragedy of the Hungarian Revolution. Hungarian nationalism, in spite of its generous intentions and democratic spirit, appeared to the Serbs of Bánát and Bácska, the Rumanians of Transylvania, the Slovaks of Upper Hungary and, above all, the Croats, as an aristocratic movement, a family squabble between the Hungarian nobles and the Court of Vienna. Nevertheless, the news of the risings in Pressburg, Vienna and Pest, had a considerable effect on these different races.

The Yugoslavian historian, V. Bogdanov, asserts that the spontaneous Serbian revolts towards the end of March in the south Hungarian towns such as Pancevo, Zimun and Kikinda, where the Serbs were in the majority, were not anti-Hungarian. The youth of the middle class—the students, intellectuals, lawyers and priests—who led them, strove to ally themselves with the Hungarian radicals. They too wanted to abolish the last vestiges of feudalism. The Serbs had sent a delegation to Pest bearing a message of friendship to the young revolutionaries. The first assembly of the Transylvanian Rumanians had agreed to their province forming part of Hungary, and asked for adequate Transylvanian representation in the central Parliament, the administration and education. Only the Croats adopted from the start a hostile attitude towards the Hungarian liberal movement. Under Doctor Gaj they had been the enemies of the Hungarian progressives for several decades.

Croatia, although possessing a large degree of autonomy and a provincial Diet, formed part of the Hungarian crown lands and sent deputies to the Pressburg Diet. Now, the Hungarian liberals wanted a closer control over all Hungary's dependencies. This angered the Croats, who particularly objected to their introducing Hungarian as the official language instead of Latin, which had hitherto been the *lingua franca* of the Empire. The Croats were to the Hungarians what the Hungarians were to Austria, with the difference that the Croats were not liberals but only ardent nationalists full of bitterness against those who refused to recognise that they constituted a nation.

At the beginning of April a delegation of Serbs from Novi-Sad arrived at Pressburg to present their national and social claims. It was a crucial moment in the Hungarian Revolution. The Serbian delegation, headed by the liberal Kostic and the young revolutionary Stratimirovic were well received at Pressburg. Kossuth made a point of welcoming them, but the speech he made on this occasion showed how little he understood the issue. They explained that they wanted autonomy for the province in which they formed the majority, but Kossuth replied that true freedom knew neither rank nor privilege but only citizens who, whatever their language or religion, shared common liberties.

This was the Magyar attitude towards not only the Serbs but all the other races in the country. Although they were prepared to recognise their right to speak their own languages and practise their own religions, even the Hungarian progressives refused to accept them as nations. They pointed to France where, they said, Bretons, Flemings, Alsatians, Catalans and Provençals considered themselves Frenchmen and had no objection to French as the official language once it had been used for the Declaration of the Rights of Man, and the laws framing its principles. They thought that the other races in Hungary, whom they considered to be less advanced than they were, should stand together with them in the defence of a common cause. They were sadly disappointed. Three months later Kossuth had to admit to the Assembly that the Hungarian nation had acted too late. Whilst it was preparing to free the peoples within the country, the latter instead of uniting to form a common front against Vienna followed their own individual and political ends.

The harm done by so many centuries of injustice could not be repaired within a few months except by extreme measures which the moderate Batthyány Government and the traditionalist majority in the Diet were not prepared to countenance. The Slavs and the Rumanians in Hungary remembered that the first measures to prevent their exploitation by the Magyar landowners had been taken by the Viennese Government. Although the Hapsburgs of the nineteenth century did not carry on the anti-feudal work of Maria Theresa and Joseph II, the Viennese Court was careful to put the full responsibility for these peoples' sufferings on the Magyar nobility. The Slavs and the Rumanians now refused to believe that the Hungarian landowners represented the forces of progress besieging a citadel of absolutism and imperialism.

In 1848, the intellectuals of the non-Magyar races were as resolute nationalists as the Hungarian nobility. It is true, as Ervin Szabó has said, that their nationalism originated in social antagonisms, but from the beginning of the nineteenth century it became an independent force, constituting the official doctrine of the middle class. It was the weapon of the small but dynamic intelligentsia and was in favour with the Orthodox clergy who combined religious with patriotic fervour.

The Serbs under Stratimirovic, Kostic and Knizanin, the Rumanians under Jancu, the Slovaks under Stur and Hurban, and the Croats of the Illyrian coast all identified freedom with national autonomy. But whereas they did not realise that the Hungarian State was their ally and Vienna the common enemy, the Hungarians did not understand that peoples whom they had hitherto looked upon as so many backward serfs, had acquired national consciences.

After the failure of the Pressburg discussions, the revolt began in the towns, and in April spread to the countryside. It was only then that it took an anti-Hungarian turn. In the eyes of the peasants who assembled at Kikinda to demand not only the abolition of feudal dues but also a share in the land, the Hungarians were the squireens who oppressed them. They looted the houses of the rich, tore down the Hungarian flag over the Prefecture and ran up the Serbian colours. They were against every landowner, whether he was a Hungarian or a German, a reactionary or a liberal.

The Serbian middle class and the Orthodox Church under the Patriarch Rajacic were also pulled into the movement and strove to give it a national rather than a social character. The harsh reprisals, often carried out by Hungarians of Serbian origin such as Baron Jovic or Sebö Vukovics, also helped to poison relations between the two races.

Thus Batthyány and Kossuth blundered irreparably, as the historian Horváth (who had himself taken part in these events) later remarked, 'by thinking it sufficient to proclaim the principles of equality and freedom without bringing in laws guaranteeing their application to the different races living on the soil of Hungary'. Furthermore, the Hungarian Government showed little intelligence in putting the Serbian districts under great landowners such as Ernest Kiss and Count Alexander Esterházy, who were particularly hated by the peasants.

The Batthyány Government's blunder was all the more inexcusable because it knew that Stratimirovic, the leader of the Serbian rising, was staunchly opposed to absolutism. Garachanin, the premier of an independent Serbia, wrote of him: 'He is so contemptuous of the Emperor and his officers, that one would think that he had a large enough army to take on both the Hungarians and Windischgrätz'. This 'dangerous' man was to make the Serbian National Assembly, which he summoned on 13 May at Karlovitsi, accept so revolutionary a programme that it frightened Rajacic, whom they had elected patriarch, and his lieutenant Shuplikats.

Rajacic, supported by the whole Orthodox Church, and Stratimirovic, backed by the masses and the small Serbian army, who respectively represented the conservative and democratic sides of the nationalist movement, were soon to come into open conflict. The Hungarians missed yet another chance to create a permanent rift between them.

The Viennese Court immediately took advantage of the tragic misunderstanding which had arisen between the Hungarians and the Slavs. An Imperial officer of Croat origin, named Jellacic, who was a violent pro-Austrian and anti-Hungarian, was appointed Governor of Croatia. He convinced Doctor Gaj of the necessity of co-operation with Vienna. He would not recognise the new Hungarian Assembly, and accused Batthyány's Government of wanting secession from Austria. Batthyány, surprised and indignant at Jellacic's hostile attitude, asked the Court to disavow him, which it did only after long negotiations. On 10 June the Emperor signed a manifesto to the Croats condemning Jellacic's policy and replacing him by another officer of the Imperial Army, General Hrabovszky. Jellacic asserted that the Emperor had acted against his will, and Batthyány realised that in point of fact the Court supported Jellacic, and that he himself was impotent in the face of such machiavellian intrigue. Nor was he able to prevent the Serbian movement from turning into an anti-Hungarian revolt, under the auspices of Rajacic.

The Hungarian Slovaks looked towards Prague, where on 1 June was to be held the first Slavonic Congress. The Transylvanian Rumanians merely voiced their social demands whilst waiting for the Hungarians, the Saxons and the Austrian garrisons to take up their positions. There were rumblings of the storm to come when a delegation from Kolozsvár (the Rumanian Cluj) came to Pest to meet the Magyar reformists. The head of this delegation, Baron Nicholas Wesselényi, an old friend of Széchenyi's but more of a radical, interrupted the enthusiastic speeches of welcome by announcing: 'The days of rejoicing are over. The alliance between the Hungarian progressives and the democrats of other nationalities has ended.'

10

THE POLITICAL HORIZON

In the meantime, the Government proceeded with the elections after taking care to remove 'agitators spreading tendentious rumours about the legislation devised by the former Diet'. These elections were far from free —liberal institutions cannot be improvised in a country which has never known them—and one could quote a host of cases of pressure and fraud. The main platform was a national front against the Viennese reactionaries and aggression by the Serbs and Croats.

The *Pesti Hirlap* complained on 13 May: 'Racial warfare is bad enough, but what will become of us if we also have class warfare?' Táncsics, Petöfi, Arany (another poet) and numerous democrats and republicans were refused the right to speak. So Kossuth's prediction that the composition of the Assembly would not differ essentially from that of the Diet came true. The majority of the four hundred and forty-six deputies elected were nobles, and there were a good number of lawyers, doctors, magistrates and solicitors; but there were only two peasants. In the newly elected Austrian *Reichstag*, on the other hand, ninety-two out of three hundred and eighty-three members were peasants, and there were many middle-class representatives.

The new Assembly held its inaugural meeting on 4 July. Eight hours later, Kossuth made the most pathetic speech of his career, when he proclaimed 'the country in danger'. The situation, already difficult, had become critical: a government Commissioner had to be sent to Upper Hungary to restore order; Croatia was in turmoil; at Karlovitz the Serbs, encouraged by the Austrian consul at Belgrade, Mayerhofer, proclaimed the independence of their territory, and Jellacic refused to negotiate with the Hungarian Government, unless Hungary's financial and military affairs were put back in the hands of Austria. The Austrian Government informed Batthyány that, if he failed to reach an understanding with the Croats, it would be obliged to abandon its neutrality.

Faced by this complex crisis, Kossuth pondered on possible allies.

England? 'She will only help us so far as is necessary to defend her own interests.' In fact, a few months earlier, when the envoy from Budapest (László Szalay, the famous expert on international law) arrived in London, Palmerston refused to receive him, saying that he did not know of Hungary but only of Austria-Hungary, whose ambassador was Baron Koller.

France? 'Poland relied on French sympathy: the sympathy is still there, but not Poland.' The French were equally sympathetic towards Hungary. At the Collège de France Michelet made an impassioned speech in her favour, and when Count Teleki arrived in Paris in September as the representative of the Batthyány Government, he achieved a brilliant social success. The left wing read with understanding his pamphlets on the imminence of the pan-Slavonic menace. But the Government of the Second Republic, as cautious as that of Guizot, did no more than make a few platonic representations to the governments concerned.

Russia? The concentration of Russian troops on the banks of the Pruth caused the Hungarian Government a good deal of anxiety. Baron Eötvös was instructed to ask the Czar's ambassador their purpose. He replied that it was to maintain order in the provinces placed under the Czar's protection and that Hungary had nothing to fear provided that she gave no encouragement to any concentration of forces against Russia. The Czar was fully aware of both Hungary's traditional friendship with the Polish nobility and the presence in Hungary of a large number of Polish

HUNGARY

émigrés, who hoped to profit by Austria's difficulties to try and free their country.

Turkey? After what had happened in Moldavia and Wallachia, she had shown her inability to pursue an independent policy.

Germany? The Germany of the Frankfort Assembly was rather a chaos of potential power than a present help. Nevertheless, the radicals who were so frightened of Russia, showed no apprehension at the thought of a unified and powerful Germany. They looked upon the pan-Slav movement as a major peril to civilisation, but they were prepared to consider the huge Confederation of the German States, which they would have liked Austria to join, as a safeguard of their own security. This attitude, which may seem strange to us, is explained by the fact that they saw the Slavs as powerful allies of reaction, and the pan-Slav movement as a cover for Russian imperialism. In comparison with the Slavs, the German-speaking Austrians and the Germans of Frankfort were democratically minded.

There was also a strong dash of traditionalism and aristocratic prejudice in this friendship between Hungary and Germany. The Hungarians did not realise how much they exasperated the Slavs by emphasising the cultural superiority of the two nations, which they considered was bound to prevent the Slavs from coming to an understanding with Vienna. Thus the so-called 'reconciliation' between Hungary and Austria in 1867, whereby they were to create a dual monarchy to the detriment of the Slavs, was already in germ.

But let us return to Kossuth's speech. After discussing possible allies for Hungary, he was forced to admit that she would have to defend herself. He therefore asked the Assembly to vote at once an extraordinary credit of forty-two million florins (£4,200,000) and an army of two hundred thousand men, forty thousand to be recruited immediately. A scene then occurred which appears in every school history book in Hungary, and which actually was an impressive occasion. One of Kossuth's opponents, Paul Nyáry, the member for Pest, shouted out 'We grant your demands', and the whole Chamber rose to echo his words. After the tremendous applause had died down, Kossuth clasped his hands in sign of gratitude, and in a voice shaken with emotion said simply: 'You, Gentlemen, have risen as one man. I bow before the nation's greatness, and I say to you: show as much zeal in carrying through my motion as you have shown patriotism in accepting it, and the Gates of Hell shall not prevail against our will to defend the fatherland.'

These 'exceptional measures' had to be approved by the Emperor, and there was the expected delay. The reactionary front headed by the Archduchess Sophia, Windischgrätz, Jellacic and Rajacic was ready to go

331

into action; and the Viennese middle-class liberals were not as pro-Hungarian as they had been. As Doctor Endres has shown in his chapter on Austria, they were strong monarchists and had been greatly upset by the Emperor's flight from the capital. Also many of the merchants and industrialists were angered by rumours of Hungary's refusal to send further reinforcements to Italy and support her share of the National Debt, and were even disposed to block imports of Austrian goods.

Vienna's demand for reinforcements provoked a significant crisis in the Pest Assembly. When Batthyány's Government proposed to accede to the demand, a number of radical members, supported by the mob which demonstrated in the streets, protested against a decision which would be in such flagrant contradiction to the principles of the Government's domestic policy. Kossuth argued that policy could not always be made to conform to principles as it has to meet the needs of the moment. 'If, as a matter of principle', he said, 'we have to help the Italian revolutionaries, we should also help the rebels of Croatia and Bohemia.' He finally turned towards the radicals and exclaimed: 'Let us silence this insignificant minority which would have recourse to violence.' Nevertheless, it appears to us today as though this 'insignificant minority' had a sharper sense of reality than the Government, for Italy and Hungary had the same aims. In the end Kossuth made the Assembly agree to providing Austria with forty thousand men, who were on no account to be used 'against the freedom of the Italian nation'. This pleased neither the Hungarian democrats nor the Austrians.

II

THE EVENTS LEADING TO THE BREAK WITH AUSTRIA

At the end of August Batthyány and Deák, the Minister for Justice, left for Vienna to make a final effort to reach an understanding. They principally wanted the Emperor to ratify the 'exceptional measures', whose adoption was urgently needed to enable the Government to meet the danger presented by Jellacic's movement. The two Ministers were unlucky. Now that Radetzky had taken Milan and Windischgrätz had 'pacified' Bohemia, the Vienna Government felt strong enough to settle its relations with the Hungarian Government to its own advantage. Ignoring the Hungarian statesmen's presence in Vienna, it sent a note to Pest asserting that the laws of March 1848 were in contradiction to the fundamental principles of the Empire as laid down by the Pragmatic

Sanction. It invited the Hungarian Government to send a delegation to Vienna to discuss, in Jellacic's presence, a fresh solution to the Hungarian problem. At the same time it published an Imperial manifesto rescinding the decree of 10 June, which 'for no valid reason, had disowned our loyal and faithful servant, General Jellacic'. Thousands of copies of this manifesto were distributed amongst the Hungarian troops guarding the frontier between Hungary and Croatia, along which Jellacic had concentrated his forces.

Vienna's treachery resulted in tumultuous demonstrations in Budapest. The people demanded protection against Austria's aggression, but Kossuth replied that 'Hungary's future is not to be decided by the mob'. Nevertheless he profited by the Assembly's terror of these demonstrations, to force it to pass at once the laws authorising mobilisation and the issue of paper money.

This decision, which dispensed with the Emperor's ratification required by the Constitution, marked a new stage in the history of the Hungarian Revolution. After this, it was hard to keep up the fiction that the March Constitution accorded with the Emperor's will, although the reasons for such a fiction were still valid. Kossuth himself had had to admit that the Hungarians were still ultra-royalists. When the commander of a division stationed in Northern Hungary heard the false rumour of a republic being proclaimed at Pest, he at once decided to march on the capital and smash it. Kossuth felt that in the end the partisans of Hungarian Independence would break with the Imperial House, but he knew that in September 1848 an attempt to dethrone the Hapsburgs could only lead to civil war. Mainly out of consideration for the royalist convictions of the army officers, the fiction of loyalty to the Hapsburgs was maintained. As the Imperial note mentioned the Emperor's ill-health, the Hungarians were able to invent the new theory that the 'enemies of the Crown were taking advantage of the King's[1] illness to make him sign decrees in contradiction to his former promises to Hungary'. Now that the Hungarian Assembly was to defend the Crown, the viceroy, the Archduke Stephen, became indispensable, but he no longer knew which way to turn. Realising the hopelessness of his efforts to bring about a reconciliation with Austria, Batthyány then resigned, and Széchenyi, seeing his fears realised, went out of his mind and had to be shut up. Kossuth, on the contrary, rode on the crest of the wave: never had his brain been so lucid or his attitude so practical as when the Assembly listened in terror to the shouts of an angry mob. He declined, however, the Assembly's offer of the presidency and suggested that Batthyány should form a new Cabinet, considering that he himself was best employed in organising the country's defences.

[1] The Emperor of Austria was King of Hungary

FRANÇOIS FEJTÖ

12

THE 'LEVEÉ EN MASSE'

On 11 September, Jellacic's forward troops crossed the Drave. The
Hungarian army, which should have opposed this act of aggression, committed under the pretext of restoring law and order in Hungary, made no
resistance. Its commander, Adam Teleki, declared to the Government
Commissioner that his oath to the Emperor and King forbade him to fire
on Imperial troops. He withdrew his men, and even threatened to
join Jellacic if he did not receive supplies in time. This act of treachery
caused panic in Budapest and a number of deputies began packing their
bags.

The Batthyány Government was later criticised for not having taken
the necessary measures to organise a trustworthy army. But its failure to
do so was the result of Batthyány's general policy which was to abide by
the law. He could not remove the various commanders of the troops
stationed in Hungary, who were mostly Austrians, without bringing
about a break with Vienna, which he wanted to avoid. The consequences
were disastrous. Several regiments went over to the Croats, and in
Southern Hungary strong-points were surrendered to the Serbs. There
were even certain officers of the purely Hungarian Hussars garrisoning
Pest who at one time thought of rejoining the Austro-Croatian army.

One of Kossuth's greatest claims to fame is the rapidity with which he
formed a popular, national army. Wearing a tri-coloured sash, and carrying a flag of the national colours—red, white and green—he toured the
towns and villages of the great Hungarian plain—the cradle of the
Magyar race—and aroused such enthusiasm that the problem was not
how to get recruits, but how to find enough arms and equipment for the
future *Honvéd* (or 'Home Defence') regiments.

13

28 SEPTEMBER

In spite of Kossuth's defence measures, the Hungarian moderates made a
final attempt at reconciliation with Austria. The middle class of nobles,
who formed the bulk of the moderate party, wanted Hungary's independence, but they did not want to pay too dearly for it. These squireens

thought that if they could get rid of Kossuth, they would reach an understanding with Vienna more easily. Batthyány tried to form a government without his former Minister for Finance and without Szemere, the former Minister for the Interior, a zealot who, like Kossuth, was firmly resolved not to compromise on the essential principles of independence.

The viceroy, the Archduke Stephen, who in the meantime had agreed to relieve Teleki of his command of the army on the Drave, had taken only twenty-four hours to obtain the Emperor's approval of Batthyány's new rôle. But Vienna had demanded the complete list of the new Ministers to be submitted for approval before it was confirmed. At the last minute Batthyány drew back, and the left wing of the Assembly again appealed to Kossuth. But Kossuth stood aside for the second time in Batthyány's favour, declaring that appeasement of Austria could be achieved only by a man who had the confidence of both the Viennese Court and the Hungarian Assembly. But whilst protesting his desire for peace and his loyalty to the King, Kossuth pushed ahead with his defence measures. 'Let the politicians argue', he said. 'The *Honvéd* will repulse the invader.'

The Vienna Government, realising the weakness of Batthyány's Cabinet in the face of Kossuth's immense popularity, decided to precipitate matters. Baron Nicholas Vay, a Transylvanian politician who had deserted the Hungarian cause, was given the task (which, incidentally, he never succeeded in fulfilling) of forming a puppet government. At the same time, General Count Lamberg, Commander of the garrison at Pressburg, was appointed Commissioner Extraordinary, with full powers to dissolve the Hungarian Assembly as an illegal body. We do not know what would have been the deputies' reaction to Lamberg's appearance in their midst to read out the Rescript of Dissolution, for once again the mob in Pest settled the problem. When, on 28 September, they heard of Lamberg's arrival, thousands of men armed with swords, old shotguns and scythes started to march on Buda. They met the Imperial Commissioner as he was crossing the bridge between Buda and Pest, dragged him from his cab and killed him on the spot. They then carried his corpse in triumph round the town.

This summary execution caused a panic in the Government. Some, such as Baron Eötvös, former Minister for Education, left the capital on the spot and fled either to Vienna or to their own estates. It was no good the Assembly expressing its horror at the crime and ordering a thorough investigation: the Viennese Court proclaimed Kossuth and his colleagues personally responsible. Lamberg was replaced by Jellacic, who was appointed Commander-in-Chief of all the Hungarian armed forces, including the National Guard and the *Honvéd*.

Jellacic's appointment was an insult to the whole nation, and instead of intimidating the Hungarians, as Vienna had hoped, it caused many moderates to join Kossuth. The latter was now in complete power: he was nominated President of the National Defence Committee of nine members, which the Assembly appointed to deputise for a Cabinet.

14

THE SACRED UNION

Vienna's intransigence had resulted in a war which hurt the traditional feelings of an important section of Hungary. When the Austrian General Schlick invaded the North, the squireens of the County of Sáros not only made no attempt to defend their territory, but welcomed the Austrian troops, who they hoped would rid them of both Kossuth and the anti-feudal laws passed by the Assembly. Although this was an isolated incident, it showed what obstacles lay in the way of patriotic nobles who would embrace the national cause. Kossuth, who was a realist and understood the landowners' misgivings, pronounced a serious warning in the Assembly to all who would 'turn the country against the nobility, the magnates or any other class of society'. His words were principally aimed at Táncsics, Petöfi and a number of other radicals in the Assembly, who insisted that the legislative work begun in March should be completed by measures abolishing the last vestiges of feudal practice, which caused discontent among the peasants without being of any great advantage to the State. Kossuth's answer was that 'exciting the people over questions of common-land and vineyard dues meant diminishing the forces needed to save the country'. 'All domestic quarrels must cease', he said. But the nobles were not satisfied with these proclamations which extolled the 'sacred union'. They regretted the concessions they had made in March and had little faith in the previous Government's promises of compensation for the loss of their feudal rights. So they applauded Kossuth when he announced that he was immediately going to pay them an advance of fifteen million florins (£1,500,000). This announcement won over a number of waverers.

That was the key to the internal situation in Hungary in 1848 and 1849. Kossuth needed the nobles to form the nucleus of the new State and army in process of formation. He had constantly to lure them with concessions and to refrain from scaring them by too radical reforms which he himself considered necessary. The peasants, for their part, although they showed some qualms at the time it was taking to carry out the new legislation, trusted the Government and answered Kossuth's call to arms. They showed more disinterestedness than the nobles. The people had faith in Kossuth, whom, despite his reservations, they recognised as a revolutionary.

And Kossuth, although he had deferred the social and economic aims of the revolution, showed himself a true democrat when it came to the defence of his country. He wanted to repel the invader with the whole might of the people, not merely the regular army. He remembered how the scythes of the Poles under Koscziusko, had been more than a match for Suvarov's guns. He even quoted the example of the Russian peasants harrying Napoleon's army on the retreat from Moscow. 'I expect the people to rise in their millions,' he said, 'not to fling themselves against the enemy's batteries, but to harry the invader without respite. . . . Let them scorch the earth where the enemy would quarter. . . . Let them show that no one can lay a finger on Hungary with impunity, for a nation that rises as one man to defend its existence is invincible.' Kossuth proclaimed the Sacred Union for this holy war, and taught the people that they must conquer or perish.

His peoples' army halted Jellacic's well-led troops at the beginning of October, and a few days later defeated them at Pákozd, forcing them to retreat towards the Austrian frontier.

Jellacic's defeat resulted in the most tragic episode of the Revolution in Central Europe. When the Vienna Government wanted to send Jellacic reinforcements, the Viennese democrats once again rose to prove their solidarity with the Magyars. They seized Latour, the War Minister, and hanged him from a lamp-post.

Windischgrätz, who had smashed the Prague revolution, immediately ordered his troops to march on Vienna, and Jellacic's forces, too, closed in on the Austrian capital. The victorious Hungarian army might have been able to repay the Viennese democrats for their help, but when General Moga, who commanded it, arrived at the Austrian frontier he dared not cross it: the royalist tradition among his officers was too strong. Kossuth was furious at their hesitation which, he said 'lost Hungary a chance of victory which would never be repeated'. He hurried to Moga's headquarters and called a Council of War. Moga and the majority of his officers said that they could not advance on Vienna without risking the destruction of their untried army. Only one officer, Arthur Görgey, disagreed. His fervent patriotism and energy so impressed Kossuth, that he put him in command of the force. But three precious days had been lost. The army marched on Vienna but was halted at Schwechat, a few miles from the capital, and forced to retire. The Viennese Revolution was shattered.

337

After this defeat, Görgey tackled the difficult business of reorganising the Hungarian revolutionary army. He had not yet succeeded in doing so, when Windischgrätz, who had reformed his troops, attacked him on the whole length of the Austro-Hungarian frontier. The order for this attack had been counter-signed not by Ferdinand but by his nephew, Francis Joseph, who had succeeded him as Emperor after a Palace revolution. The Hungarian Assembly refused to recognise the new Emperor and Görgey continued the battle in the name of King Ferdinand V.

15

THE POLITICAL CRISIS IN HUNGARY

Windischgrätz's rapid advance into Hungary created a panic in the political circles of the country. In order to understand it, we must analyse Kossuth's relations with the Assembly.

John Pálffy, one of Kossuth's opponents, later said of him: 'He alone made the Hungarian Revolution'. This was not meant as praise, but it was the truth. Kossuth was a great deal more than a party leader, fighting against the peacemakers of the Assembly. In any crisis, he knew how to foil his opponents and win a parliamentary majority. He owed his success both to the opposition's lack of a leader, and to his own magnetic personality and eloquence. One of his tricks was to repeat that he was only the humble tool of an all-powerful Assembly, and time and time again the deputies would be hypnotised into doing his will.

At the end of December 1848, when Windischgrätz's forward troops were nearing Budapest, many of the deputies thought that when the capital fell any further resistance would be useless. But how could they rid themselves of Kossuth? Batthyány suggested that the Assembly should remain in Budapest and that only the Defence Committee should take refuge with the Army Headquarters. Kossuth and his radical supporters knew what that meant: once he was out of the way, the Assembly would disown the Defence Committee and come to terms with Windischgrätz.

Kossuth repudiated both this suggestion and Pálffy's proposal to adjourn the Assembly. He needed to control the legislature so as to represent himself to the army as the servant of national sovereignty vested in the Assembly. He therefore demanded that the Government and the Assembly should both retire to Debreczen, and once again they did his bidding. He did, however, make one concession to the 'peacemakers' by agreeing that a parliamentary delegation of five members under Batthyány should be sent to Windischgrätz's headquarters to discuss the March laws.

Windischgrätz refused to see Batthyány, whom the Court considered to be chiefly responsible for Hungary's separatist tendencies, but he told the rest of the delegation, which included Deák, that he had but one answer to give the Hungarian people—'unconditional surrender'.

The Assembly, which indignantly rejected Windischgrätz's insulting suggestion, was no more than a 'rump parliament'. Many deputies had not followed the Government to Debreczen. The exact number of the deserters is unknown, but when some weeks later the Defence Committee decided to expel those who had deserted for no valid reason, the number of absentees was, after lengthy debates, fixed at a hundred and seven.

The Upper Chamber had only twenty-eight members left. All the magnates gradually left the revolutionary movement, and some (such as the Counts Louis Károlyi, Anthony Forgács and Maurice Almássy) even accepted appointments as Commissioners under the Austrian forces of occupation. Yet others (such as Szirmay) went so far as to recruit Hungarian volunteers for them. A certain Count Edmund Zichy was arrested at one of the national army's outposts and found to be carrying leaflets printed by Jellacic, inviting the Hungarians to surrender. On Görgey's orders he was summarily executed. Another Count Zichy later approached the Czar to beg his help against the 'rebels'. A civil war among the Magyars was avoided, thanks not to the aristocracy but to the patriotism and sense of honour of the minor and middle-class nobles who followed Kossuth to the end although often disagreeing with his policy.

It was their desperate courage which won for the Magyars the admiration of the liberals and revolutionaries of Europe, and Karl Marx was later to call them 'the heroes of '48'. It was a moving spectacle to see this little nation, after the defeat of all the other revolutionary movements in Europe, refusing to be discouraged by their defeats but flinging themselves again into battle and, as Petőfi said, preferring 'a grand death to a miserable life'.

The difference between the 'last-ditchers' and the 'peacemakers' did not consist only in the fact that the former still hoped for final victory. Kossuth continually repeated that the nation had no choice, and that capitulation would mean the end of freedom. His chief desire in the black days of January 1849, when Budapest fell, was that the Assembly should stand together, and on the 15th his eloquence compelled its members to swear an oath that they would not break up.

The course of the war forced Kossuth to pay frequent visits to Army Headquarters. His presence was essential to inspire all ranks of his young

<

army which at the end of January began a counter-offensive. His frequent absences from Debreczen were used by his opponents to make contacts, found their own newspaper and even combine to overthrow the majority in the Assembly. Each time Kossuth returned, he had to reassert his influence over the deputies and he began to lose patience. A new parliamentary crisis occurred at the very moment when the Hungarian forces were gaining the upper hand—when Görgey was advancing on the Danube, when the Polish General, Bem, was reconquering Transylvania, and the Serb, Damjanich, was battering the Serbs. A number of deputies, who had disappeared when things looked black, now returned to Debreczen, where the radicals, fearing that they would strengthen the opposition, asserted that their unjustifiable absence had caused them to lose their seats. A storm broke out in the Assembly, and Kossuth, who had just returned from Army Headquarters, vehemently demanded that his Government's policy should not be attacked every time he left Debreczen for the war zone. He still declared that he was only the Assembly's servant, but he added, threateningly: 'The Assembly must remain what it was when it first came to Debreczen, that is to say, the spirit of resistance. If the Assembly decides to change colour, national unity will be broken and civil war will be the result.' The spectre of civil war again had its effect. The 'peacemakers' once more gave way and waited for a more favourable opportunity, but their position had been weakened by Vienna's refusal to treat with them. Francis Joseph's answer to their expressions of willingness to come to terms with the Court on the basis of the March laws, was to promulgate a new Constitution for the whole Empire, which took no account whatsoever of Hungary's traditional rights and still less of the independence which she now claimed. This intransigence justified Kossuth's 'back-to-the-wall' policy, and war was the only possible answer to the Olmutz Constitution.

16

GÖRGEY VERSUS KOSSUTH

Kossuth had his difficulties not only with the Assembly but with his military commanders, of whom General Görgey gave him the most cause for anxiety. Görgey, a thirty-year-old noble, had little use for the National Guard recruited by Kossuth to reinforce the army, and dismissed it on the pretext that it lacked discipline. A regular soldier, he was hostile to Kossuth's conception of a national army, and having risen to high rank too quickly, his chief aim was to be acceptable to the senior officers, all of whom detested Kossuth as an upstart.

The first clash between Görgey and the Defence Committee came at the time of Windischgrätz's successful offensive in January 1849. Görgey wanted to put the responsibility for his retreat on to the Defence Committee, which he said had asked him to hold a wider front than was practicable with the forces at his disposal. Then, on the very same day that Kossuth reproached the army for making no attempt to defend the capital, Görgey published a proclamation, which was more of a political manifesto than an army order of the day, attributing his defeat to the Committee's contradictory orders and a lack of adequate supplies. After stressing that the Army of the Danube would stand by its oath to defend the Constitution ratified by King Ferdinand V, both against its enemies abroad and against the republicans who would overthrow the monarchy, Görgey declared that henceforth he would only take orders from General Mészáros, Batthyány's former War Minister, who was the only military member of the Defence Committee. This was a serious act of insubordination to Kossuth, the President of the Committee. Görgey later explained it in his *Memoirs*, by his wish to keep in the army those officers who had grown dissatisfied as the result of the series of defeats.

It was true that desertions were becoming more numerous. Later on, a battalion in Dembinsky's army, after entering the town of Kápolna in triumph, thereupon—to the horror of its commander—went straight over to the Austrians, complete with its arms and equipment.

Pro-Austrian officers continued to desert to the enemy throughout the course of the War of Hungarian Independence. Görgey, although a poor politician, was a staunch patriot and obviously had nothing in common with such traitors. He was a fierce little man, who could not bear anyone to contradict him; but ambitious though he was, he could never make up his mind whether to become the Cromwell of revolutionary Hungary or the defender of the 'peacemakers' with their loyalty to the dynasty. A few days after his act of insubordination, he gave proof of his patriotism by indignantly refusing—in the presence of his entire staff—a secret offer from Windischgrätz to the effect that if he laid down his arms he would receive a full pardon from the Emperor. Kossuth did not want matters to come to a head, so instead of calling Görgey to order, as he deserved, he sent him money, ammunition and supplies. Görgey, for his part, seeing that his defeat had resulted neither in the army collapsing nor the country losing heart, assured the Defence Committee of his loyalty.

When it became necessary to unite the Hungarian armies under a single commander, Kossuth's choice fell not on Görgey but on Dembinsky, one of the leaders of the 1831 rising in Poland, to whom Count Teleki, when envoy extraordinary in Paris, had offered a command in the new Hungarian Army which was short of senior officers with battle experience. Görgey and his friends considered Dembinsky's appointment as an insult both to Görgey and to the nation. The first time that the Pole lost a battle, they made it an excuse to refuse to obey his orders. This revolt of the Generals, in the face of the enemy, reached such proportions that Szemere, the Government Commissioner, had provisionally to appoint Görgey Generalissimo, and send for Kossuth.

Kossuth, accompanied by Mészáros, the War Minister, hurried to General Headquarters, and on seeing that officers and men were unanimously in favour of Görgey, did not dare call a Council of War, but at once put him in command of an Army Group. Another Army Group was formed under Damjanic, and General Vetter, the former Chief of Staff, was made Generalissimo. Dembinsky grudgingly accepted the command of an independent force operating in North Eastern Hungary. Shortly afterwards, Vetter fell sick, and in the end it was Görgey who planned the combined offensive, which resulted in brilliant victories for the Hungarians.

I have analysed these military intrigues in detail so as to illustrate the countless difficulties with which Kossuth was faced. Nearly all the Hungarian Generals behaved like suspicious feudal overlords, jealous of their prerogatives and always prepared to object to the instructions they received from the central authority. That was why Kossuth had to keep Szemere permanently at Headquarters to see that the Defence Committee's orders were carried out.

Kossuth's meekness towards Görgey was due to his fear that the irascible General might at any moment go over to the 'peacemakers'. It was only Görgey's political ignorance and the 'peacemakers'' clumsiness that prevented their coming together until the end of the war, when it was too late for any serious political consequences to follow.

17

THE PROCLAMATION OF INDEPENDENCE

On 13 April Kossuth returned from the front to Debreczen, where he called a secret meeting of the principal deputies and told them that the next day, at a full session of the Assembly, he would ask for a solemn declaration of Hungary's independence. This unexpected decision paralysed the 'peacemakers' with terror. The next day rumours of sensational happenings went round the town, and the entire population surrounded the Protestant College which temporarily housed the Assembly, and invaded the lecture hall. The Assembly then moved to a large disused Calvinist Church which gave them more space, and there Kossuth launched an attack on the Hapsburgs. He condemned their crimes without number against the Hungarian people, their attempts to wreck the Constitution, and their alliance with Jellacic, the avowed enemy of Hungary. 'In the name of the Hungarian nation', he said, 'I hereby declare the House of Hapsburg-Lorraine to have forfeited all sovereignty over Hungary, Transylvania and all the districts and enclaves comprised in these Territories.' Assembly and crowd rose together to say 'amen' to this pronouncement.

Later, the opposition was to reproach Kossuth with forcing their hand by allowing the crowd to invade the church and swamp the Assembly. Although the newspapers supporting Kossuth had been preparing public opinion for such an eventuality ever since the new Austrian Constitution had been proclaimed on 4 March, the country as a whole was taken by surprise. This proclamation was considered to be Kossuth's single-handed work. One of the reasons why he chose the middle of March to announce this decision, which he had been thinking over for some time, was the successful progress of the war. Görgey, Damjanic, Klapka, Aulich and Gáspár had won the victories of Hatvan, Gödölö and Isaszeg (to mention only the more important battles) over the combined forces of Windisch-grätz, Schlick and Jellacic. Before he came back to Debreczen, Kossuth had spent Easter night at Gödölö in the very bed from which Görgey's Hussars had chased Prince Windischgrätz. Hungarian troops had just reached the outskirts of Pest, and good news came in from the other theatres. In Southern Hungary General Perczel smashed the Austrians, who received little support from the Serbs.

The break between the Hungarians and the Austrians in September had, in fact, strengthened Rajacic's authority: he wrote to his old friend Jellacic that 'the Serbs no longer talked of justice or national organisation or religion but only of the war'. Still, the Patriarch, who was afraid lest he be overruled by the people to whom he owed his election, asked the Viennese Court to give its official recognition to the decision reached by the Karlovitz Assembly regarding the Serbs' secession from Hungary. He received only vague promises, however, and when at the end of the year Austria occupied Pest and again felt she was mistress of the situation, her attitude towards the Serbs hardened. She had used them against the Hungarians, but had no intention of granting them the autonomy which they demanded as the reward for their sacrifices. Shortly afterwards, she sent back the Serbian volunteers, disarmed the civil population in the

Voïvodina and replaced Serbian Army Commanders and high officials by Austrians. The 'anarchist, Jacobin, revolutionary and republican press' was suppressed. It is understandable that the Serbian poet Nenadovic should have cried in bitter disillusionment:

> Hell take the Serb who sheds his blood
> To serve a foreign cause!

In Transylvania, General Bem, after he had scattered the Austrians, drove out the Russian troops whom the citizens of the Saxon towns had called in to save them from the Revolution.

All liberal Europe applauded the Magyar army's brilliant feats of arms. But their ephemeral character did not deceive the far-sighted, and perhaps they did not justify Kossuth's gesture. Some of the 'peacemakers' thought, on the contrary, that they might make it easier to come to terms with Vienna. In the course of the secret meeting which preceded the proclamation of independence, Kossuth had asserted that the army had demanded it; and he had in fact discussed the matter with the Generals. Some, such as Klapka, were in favour of breaking with Vienna, but others—Görgey, in particular—disagreed, not out of love for the dynasty, but because they were opportunists and feared repercussions from the people or at any rate the royalist element. However, they all accepted the proclamation once it was made. When some weeks later General Hentzi commanding the Austrians in Buda began pouring red-hot shot into Pest which had been retaken by the Hungarians, Görgey wrote to Kossuth in indignation: 'The whole town is in flames. But they have lit the funeral pyre of the dynasty'; and went on to say that the Imperial House had not a friend left in Hungary. That did not prevent him, though, from later blaming Kossuth for all the country's misfortunes—particularly the intervention of Russia.

Kossuth, in a letter addressed immediately after the defeat to the members of his diplomatic corps, explained the reasons for his decision to break with Austria. He thought that the moment had come for the nation to make a final effort, and that the only way to ensure it was for the Hungarian people to show the world that they stood for freedom and independence. He rightly saw that such a gesture would lead to an exaltation of Hungarian patriotism for centuries to come. A more immediate reason was that he felt that the repudiation of the dynasty would confound the 'peacemakers' and finally cut their links with Vienna.

After the proclamation of independence which left the future form of government undecided, Kossuth, who was elected Regent, asked Szemere to form a government.

344

Some days after the fall of Pest, Windischgrätz had to hand over his command to General Welden, who ordered a general withdrawal— Görgey's forward troops had captured a courier of his, who was bearing to Vienna a despatch containing the information that the Austrian Generalissimo had only forty-five thousand exhausted men under his command. It was the moment to smash the enemy, but Görgey, instead of following up his advantage, spent a month trying to take Buda, so the Austrians had time to regroup their forces and receive reinforcements from Italy. Görgey later made out that his tactics were dictated by Kossuth, who wanted to create an impression abroad by retaking the capital. Kossuth indignantly denied the charge, and the majority of Hungarian *émigrés*, who afterwards entered the controversy, stated that Görgey had been actuated by political considerations. Daniel Irányi, in a book published in France, wrote that: 'Görgey's intention was to have the proclamation of independence annulled, and its author, Kossuth, removed, so that he could open negotiations with Austria on the basis of a modified form of the 1848 Constitution'.

But perhaps this was an exaggeration. It was only later on, after Görgey had recaptured the capital, that he actually contacted a number of 'peace-makers' there, although he had already been in touch with them through General Klapka.

Whatever the facts were, it is certain that Kossuth would have preferred Görgey to follow up and smash the enemy. From now on, while the Regent represented the will of those Hungarians whose whole heart was in the winning of their independence, Görgey—perhaps in spite of himself—came to be the hope of those who saw and feared the disaster that lay ahead.

18

THE RUSSIANS INTERVENE

Kossuth was in his zenith on the day he entered the newly liberated Budapest as the Regent of Hungary. But in the midst of the crowd's acclamations, he tasted the bitterness of a victory that could lead nowhere. He was aware of the vast forces which were combining to shatter Hungary's independence. Austrian reinforcements were pouring in and the troops of the Czar were marching towards the Hungarian frontier. Kossuth was accused of having provoked the Czar's intervention by his proclamation of independence, but in point of fact the Czar had been discussing the matter with the Emperor long before 15 April, and it would seem that Kossuth's action had only provided him with the pretext for an intervention already decided upon in principle. After the Austrians had been defeated at Isaszeg, Schwarzenberg had asked Paskiewicz, the Commander-in-Chief of the Russian forces in Poland, for three hundred thousand men to quell the rebellion which, he said, was a menace not only to Vienna and Austria, but to Germany, Poland and the whole of Europe.

On 1 May, the Russians' forward elements entered Cracow, in Austrian Poland. On the 8th, the Czar published a proclamation to the effect that he was sending his armies into Hungary, where 'the Polish traitors of 1831, together with refugees and outlaws from other countries, had seized power'. Russia intervened, not only to maintain the balance of power on the Continent and retain absolute governments in Eastern Europe, but also because the Czar was afraid, in the event of a Hungarian victory, of Transylvania and Northern Hungary being used as military bases for operations to free Poland. St Petersburg suspected a secret alliance between Hungary and Poland, whereby the Hungarians would repay the Poles for the help they had given them by assisting Poland to recover her own independence.

From the moment that Russian intervention became a serious threat, the Hungarian Revolution began to show the signs of disintegration that precede every *débâcle*. Kossuth and his handful of supporters remained faithful to the end to their principles and their aim of independence. Knowing that all was lost, they tried to do the impossible. And it was Kossuth who, faced by a combined offensive of the Russians and the Austrians, proposed the only reasonable tactic of concentrating all the armies into a single force of approximately two hundred thousand men. This force would still have been capable of inflicting heavy losses on the enemy, and would eventually have been able to fight through to the Turkish provinces in Europe. The prolongation of Hungary's resistance might have brought off a last-minute political *coup* by turning to her advantage what Budapest believed to be the inevitable discussions between the Russians and the Austrians. There might even have been a chance of England and France coming to Hungary's aid.

This intelligent scheme was wrecked by the Generals' lack of discipline. Each thought it best to follow his own plans. Görgey, who wanted to regroup his forces on the right bank of the Danube, continued to try and do so even after the revolutionary Government had ordered him to fall back rapidly on Szeged. General Perczel, whose task was to stop the advance of General Haynau, Welden's successor, also refused to obey Kossuth's instructions.

Whilst the Hungarian Army fought to hold off the Russians, the Government lodged a formal protest against their 'unjust intervention', announcing to the civilised world that 'the Hungarian people would not yield to the aggressor but would fight on to their last drop of blood'. Europe listened to this poignant appeal to international justice in embarrassed silence. The democrats and the revolutionaries of the world were powerless to help this handful of heroes against the combined forces of the two greatest powers on the Continent. Heine, in his moving poem, *1849*, echoes the distress of the 'good Europeans', and Palmerston, averting his eyes from this shameful spectacle, said to the Czar's ambassador: 'finish as quickly as possible'. The French Foreign Minister simply sent a mild protest to the Courts of St Petersburg, Vienna and Berlin. When the left wingers expressed their dissatisfaction with the inadequacy of his action, Drouin de Lhuys exclaimed: 'If you want war, appeal to the country.' But who would have dared to ask Frenchmen to die for far-off Hungary?

At the end of June 1849 Kossuth issued a second proclamation, passionately reproaching England for allowing the policy of non-intervention, of which she had been the champion, to be set at nought, and France for denying the principles of her Constitution by abandoning first Poland, then Italy and now Hungary to their fate. 'You are repudiating all those who, putting their trust in you, have taken the bloodstained path of liberty.' But there was no reply to his despairing appeals.

19

THE LAST DAYS OF HUNGARY'S INDEPENDENCE

The Austrian Army, joined by the Russians at Pressburg, marched swiftly on Pest, which the 'rump parliament' had just left for Szeged, in the south of the great Hungarian plain. The Czar's armies also invaded the north, the north east and Transylvania, and Kossuth's star began to wane. His own Ministers had already begun to turn against him. He made another attempt to get rid of Görgey who, at the approach of disaster, was growing even more sarcastic and contemptuous than before. He wanted to replace him by the War Minister, Mészáros, but nearly every officer, deputy and minister objected so strongly that he had to give way. Kossuth was openly criticised, and his most violent critics were those who a short time before had been under his spell. Numbers of his oldest supporters rose against this new Pied Piper who had led them to disaster. Not only did they think further resistance useless, but the cruel absurdity of the revolution itself was now revealed to them.

In these tragic days when their hopes lay shattered, Görgey and the terrified politicians saw Kossuth as a tragi-comic figure, who had deceived himself and those who had believed him. Had he not shouted a thousand times that the Gates of Hell would not prevail against the courage of the Magyars? Where, now, were his fine words?

Szemere, the Minister for the Interior, was the only man to keep his head. Some time later, commenting on Görgey's growing importance, he remarked that 'as the régime dissolves in chaos, the civil population instinctively turns to the soldier for protection'.

Nevertheless, the main Magyar army under Görgey retired southward in good order to link up with Dembinsky's forces. But Dembinsky, instead of making for the agreed rendezvous, put the main part of his army under Bem and retired on Temesvár, probably to cover the flight into Turkish territory of the marked men among the politicians and army commanders. Görgey informed the government that if he succeeded in making contact with Bem's troops, he would join battle with the Austrians; otherwise, he would immediately set about negotiating a surrender.

Görgey had already made formal contact with the Russian Head-quarters. When the Russian Generalissimo, Paskievitch, invited him to capitulate, he replied that Hungary, in her present desperate situation, would rather have a Romanoff on the throne than be oppressed once more by the Hapsburgs. When the Hungarian Government was informed of Görgey's reply, they decided to follow it up by offering the crown to Grand Duke Constantine, thinking to split the reactionaries. But the Czar dismissed their offer as 'fantastic'.

Bem, instead of joining forces with Görgey, decided in a rash moment to take on the Russians by himself, and his forces were scattered. Events began to move fast. On 11 August, Kossuth had to step aside in favour of Görgey, whom the failing government appointed Generalissimo and Dictator. Görgey's first order of the day, warning the country that capitulation was imminent, contained an attack on Kossuth's character and policy, thereby tarnishing the tragic grandeur of this heroic defeat. But it was a blow to Görgey's pride to be made dictator only to preside over the débâcle.

He was forced to surrender unconditionally to the Russians who assured him that the Czar meant to spare the lives of those who threw themselves on his mercy.

The epilogue of this tragedy took place some days later. For the last time Görgey reviewed his troops, who had already piled their arms.

Officers and men alike wept, and only Görgey, eye-witnesses said, 'preserved his habitual cold and sardonic mien'.

Kossuth and thousands of patriots fled abroad, whilst those who had no chance to do so hid in the countryside. The prisons were filled, and the Czar's promise of mercy was swept aside by the Viennese Court. Count Batthyány was condemned to be hanged,[1] and only escaped so ignominious a death by attempting to commit suicide. Seriously wounded, he was taken out and shot.

The Austrians' reprisals were directed by General Haynau, who was already notorious for ordering the mass murder of Italian patriots at Brescia. Hundreds of Hungarians, both soldiers and civilians, paid for their loyalty to the cause of independence with their lives.

Palmerston intervened to ask the Viennese Government to treat their luckless enemies with clemency, but the Austrian Ambassador replied that his government was the sole judge of the way it should treat the rebels. Some days later, thirteen of the best Hungarian Generals were hanged in the courtyard of the citadel of Arad in Transylvania. That black day of 6 October is still observed as a day of mourning by the Hungarian people, who on 15 March celebrate the anniversary of the revolution. Finally, Petöfi, the poet of this war, which Karl Marx called 'the heroic epilogue of 1848', was killed by a Russian lancer at Segesvár. He lies in an unmarked grave.

[1] The military tribunal was disposed to clemency and returned this harsh verdict only because it was told that a condemnation in principle was required and because it had the Archduchess Sophia's assurance that a pardon would be granted.

POLAND IN 1848

BENJAMIN GORIELY

Poland can recover her independence by becoming a democratic nation
Slowacki

*Poland proclaims her freedom and independence, and holds out the hand of
friendship to all Slav peoples*
Mickiewicz

THE 1848 Revolution put the Polish problem in the forefront of the
international political scene. The masses, in sudden revolt against the
tyranny that gripped Europe, believed that 'the peoples' spring' would
repair the injustice done to torn and trampled Poland. Paris and London
were hourly expecting the outbreak of a Polish revolution, and it is not
surprising that 'the shameful silence' of the twelve million Poles under the
heel of Nicholas I should have disappointed not only the revolutionaries
but also the governments of Western Europe.

During the course of that stormy year 1848, Poland's cause linked with
that of the Revolution became an instrument of blackmail in the hands
of the diplomats, and a stimulant for the revolutionary masses.

The demonstration in France on 15 May 1848, when a hundred
thousand Parisians, led by Blanqui, marched from the Place de la Bastille
to the Place de la Concorde, waving Polish flags and shouting *Vive la
Pologne!* shows that the Polish problem played an essential part in the
foreign policy of revolutionary France.

By carrying a petition in favour of Polish independence to the National
Assembly, Blanqui showed that he thought it necessary for France to
undertake a war to liberate the peoples of Europe in order to strengthen
her own position. Lamartine, on the other hand, who from the start of
the revolution favoured a peace policy, was driven by the radicals into
playing a double game. This consisted of making the country believe that
he was prepared to re-establish Poland's independence by force of arms,
and at the same time assuring the Prussian and Russian governments that
he would maintain the balance of power in Europe and remain friends
with Russia.

Hatzfeldt, the Prussian *chargé d'affaires* in Paris, wrote as follows in a report to his government on 15 May 1848:

'Yesterday evening I had an opportunity to see Monsieur de Lamartine. He spoke to me of the Polish question which is to be debated today in the Chamber. He told me that a sympathetic attitude towards Poland is used here to influence the masses, and that in the Assembly former deputies try to win popularity by posing as wholehearted defenders of the Polish cause. He himself, he said, was opposed to any rash decision, but should the Assembly decide to make a declaration or pass a motion expressing sympathy with the Poles' national aspirations, he would raise no objection; particularly as even under the old government, both Chambers used to pass annual motions protesting against Poland's treatment. . . .

'. . . I do not consider France's interest in the cause of Polish nationalism excessive, and I think that it is true that certain parties are merely using it to further their own domestic political ends.'

On 15 May, Raspail read out to the Assembly a petition demanding the re-establishment of Poland, even, should diplomatic methods fail, at the cost of war. The revolutionary government formed the same day by Barbes just had time to draw up a manifesto demanding the restoration of Poland, under the threat of a declaration of war. The failure of their *coup d'état* and the arrest of the 'imposters' marked a victory for the reactionaries and hence the abandonment of the Polish cause.

'Our cause has suffered a serious set-back as the result of the demonstration and subsequent events of 15 May', wrote Prince Czartoryski to Dudley some days later.

And on 18 May 1848, Hatzfeldt commented:

'The moral result of the 15th was, as is always the case with unsuccessful risings, a victory for the forces of law and order no less than for the government—if it decides to profit by it. . . . But another, quite independent result, has been to show a lot of people the worth of the so-called public sympathies for the Italians and Poles, and to weaken what little inclination the masses had for a war on behalf of either nation.'

Lamartine's double game, which was at last exposed, was typical of the middle-class attitude of all those governments put in power in 1848 by popular risings.

But why should the governments of Paris, Berlin and Vienna have supported the Polish insurgents, and why should they have counted, with however many reservations, on a restoration of Poland? The reason is quite simple. The governments of '48 were afraid, with a terror that sometimes amounted to an obsession, that Europe's *Gendarme*, the Czar, would fight to restore reactionary régimes amongst his neighbours. That is why the Berlin government promised Mieroslawski, the leader of the

Polish revolutionaries, who had been freed from the Moabit prison by the Berliners, that it would support the Poles in their revolt against the Czar and would guarantee their independence and their former boundaries.

The Grand Duchy of Posen became the centre of the Polish rising, and the King of Prussia made no attempt to prevent the Poles organising and arming themselves. For a few months the Poles and the Germans were on good terms, but their relations gradually deteriorated until there was frank hostility between them, particularly when the whole of the Frankfort Parliament, with the exception of a hundred democratic deputies, betrayed its high mission by confirming the new partition of Poland.

Berlin's material and moral support to the Poles in the early days of the revolution is easily explained by Prussia's fear of Russia. She was hourly expecting an official proclamation announcing the independence of the Grand Duchy of Posen, which would have been bound to start a war. Now, Nicholas I, in these critical days, showed himself a first-class diplomat. On 31 March 1848, the *St Petersburg Journal*, the government organ, published an official communiqué outlining the Czar's foreign policy. This communiqué stated that, in spite of provocation and in spite of attacks from abroad even in semi-official newspapers, Russia had no intention of interfering in the domestic affairs of other States; but that she would not tolerate any invasion of her territory 'on the pretext of reconstructing nations which had ceased to exist'.

'Russia will not attack unless she herself is attacked', proclaimed the manifesto. 'She will respect her neighbours' independence and territorial rights so long as they respect hers.'

This pacificatory communiqué, which made Russia's neutrality subject to Berlin's refraining from reconstituting Poland, was a master stroke. And the Frankfort Parliament, reassured on the subject of German unity, was able to cease worrying about the solution to the Polish problem, which had already taken on a new aspect as the result of the brutal intervention of the Prussian generals, and the activities of the German elements in Prussia's Polish provinces. From that moment even the Grand Duchy of Posen's autonomy was in danger.

The Polish historians, especially those with German sympathies, willingly admitted that of the three countries among which Poland was partitioned, Prussia's policy towards her was the most liberal. And it is true that there was less persecution in the area under Prussian rule; in 1846 and 1848 its inhabitants had regained almost complete freedom, and a Polish army had even been organised. But on the other hand, neither Nicholas I's deportations to Siberia nor the hangings at Lwow had harmed Poland so much as the germanisation and colonisation of Prussia's Polish provinces. By 1848 the Poles were faced by an accomplished fact and the process of germanisation was increasing in intensity. The Grand Duchy of Posen, as early as 1833, contained 790,000 Poles, 450,000 Germans, and nearly 80,000 Jews. These figures were produced by certain deputies in the Frankfort Parliament as a reason why the German part of Posen should be incorporated in Prussia. Marx bitterly criticised this first manifestation of German Imperialism when he wrote in the *Neue Rheinische Zeitung:* 'They systematically planted German settlers in the State lands of Poland, in the forests and the remains of the nobles' former estates, with the object of driving the Poles and their language from their own territory so as to create an essentially Prussian province which would rival even Pomerania in its fanaticism. After the Polish rising in 1846, there was founded in Berlin itself, under the patronage of the most eminent persons, a society to buy up Polish estates for the German nobility.'

In Austrian Poland, fear of Russia and fear of the populace obliged the moderates to veer between reaction and revolution. Reaction won in the end. So long as the Vienna Parliament was still in existence and the Hungarian insurgents were undefeated, there was still hope for Polish nationalism. The Poles of Galicia and Cracow, helped by all the peoples under the rule of the House of Hapsburg, could have stood up to the Austrian Government, but in 1848 it was the 'unifying' constitutional policy that prevailed.

There were several possible reasons for the Austrian Poles' failure to unite against Austria: the nobles may have feared a repetition of the peasant revolts of 1846; the economic development of the country may have bred moderate tendencies; the Poles may have lost faith in their own strength. Whatever the true reason, there was a large section of the Polish population which was satisfied with the liberties granted under the April Constitution to all the peoples of the Empire: racial, linguistic, religious, and personal liberties; free speech and a free press; and the right to form associations and present petitions.

A Polish National Council had been formed at Lwow, but Stadion, the governor of Galicia, immediately countered it with his *Beirat,* or Consultative Council. The Polish reactionaries who formed it had Austria's official support, whilst the National Council was too frightened of the growing proletariat to seek its aid.

So the 1848 Revolution in France was followed by no Polish rising. The Russian provinces did not stir, the Austrian provinces behaved as though they were an integral part of Austria, and the Prussian provinces, although ready to strike, dared not risk a European war by provoking a sudden attack by Russia. This hesitancy disappointed even the British Government, despite its disapproval at the spread of the popular movements on the Continent. In the course of the debate in the House of Commons in 1848 on the Polish question, Lord Palmerston made the famous pronouncement that England had no lasting ties with any particular country and did not identify her policy with that of any other. She had no natural enemies and no eternal friends, but when she found that another country was pursuing the same policy as she was, that country would for a time become her ally.

At this period a *rapprochement* was beginning to take place between Britain and Russia. This new orientation of English policy spelt the end of sympathy for Poland's 'folly'.

Palmerston was aware of the danger of Austria's collapse. He was afraid that the French would invade Northern Italy to drive out the Austrians, and that then Russia would absorb the Slav nations, which would bring her armies to the gates of Constantinople.

He was pleased therefore to find himself in agreement with the Czar over both issues. Nicholas violently opposed any expansion on the part of revolutionary France and was determined to save Austria from being dismembered. In return, Palmerston's Ambassador Extraordinary to Berlin supported Frederick William IV against his Minister, von Arnim, whose policy favoured the Poles' anti-Russian attitude. Britain's special representative advised the Prussian Government to do nothing that might be construed by Russia as a hostile act. Furthermore, the Schleswig question still more closely united the only two European powers outside the revolutionary movement: neither Russia nor Britain wanted the appearance of a fresh rival on the shores of the Baltic, so they both exerted pressure on the Prussian Government. Count Meyendorff, Russia's representative, wrote: 'British diplomacy is doing its utmost to prevent the Prussian Government from giving us any cause for mistrust, or forcing us to become involved with the Poles.'

When the first disturbances took place in Posen, Palmerston's representative went to inform von Arnim that he would hold him responsible for the lives lost.

Besides the international considerations which caused Britain to support the Czar, she was afraid of the movement in Ireland. The effect of Palmerston's sacrificing Poland was to damp Irish aspirations.

We see, therefore, that the policy of the Great Powers, and the fears and equivocal behaviour of the revolutionary middle class in 1848 warred against Poland. All that the Poles could have done was to seek the help of the insurgent masses, which they failed to do—or at any rate to do adequately. We must go back some fifteen years to discover the reason why there was no Polish Revolution in 1848.

POLAND

From 1831, when Nicholas I quelled the Polish rising, until 1846 when Galicia and Cracow revolted, Poland was partitioned between Russia, Austria and Germany.

It was in 1833, at Münchengrätz, that these three nations decided to crush any attempt at independence and to rid themselves of dangerous revolutionaries. The Republic of Cracow, which had been granted a semblance of independence, was nearly suppressed as the result of the Toeplitz meeting in 1835. But it was merely saddled with an Austrian garrison. Posen's autonomy was curtailed, and Paskievich instituted a reign of terror in Russian Poland. The young men were deported to Siberia, the Diet was suppressed, the Constitution was abolished, the *emigrés'* property was confiscated, the universities and secondary schools were closed, the United Greek Church was banned and its members were forced to become members of the Orthodox Church. The use of the Polish language was discouraged, and the wearing of the local costumes of Mazowice and Cracow was forbidden in 1839 by the Governor-General.

Finally defeated on 5 October 1831, at Ostrolenka, the insurgents retreated into Prussia and thence escaped to France.

This 'Great Emigration', as it was known, soon spread throughout every country of western and southern Europe. Among the *emigrés*, apart from the members of the National Government, represented by Prince Adam Czartoryski and Generals Bem, Dniernicki, Dembinski and others, were the most eminent members of the nation: the historian Lelewel, the composer Chopin, and the poet Mickiewicz.

The insurgents re-formed and reorganised their ranks and impatiently waited for an opportunity to recommence the revolution.

After they had analysed the reasons for their defeat and worked out a basis for a future national movement, the Polish *emigrés* formed three centres in Paris.

The first, a royalist body, had its headquarters at the Hotel Lambert in Paris, from which it took its name. Its leader was Adam Czartoryski and it represented the feudal nobility, who wanted Poland to be a monarchy with the territory it had held before 1772. The Hotel Lambert was hostile to and fearful of a rising of the people and jealous of its privileges. It believed in the possibility of reconstituting Poland by diplomatic means with foreign assistance. Its members, whom their opponents ironically nicknamed 'the Resurrected', as they were always talking of the 'resurrection of the Fatherland', refused to learn the lesson of their defeat in 1830 and 1831, and confused Poland's future with their own. Thus they objected, either openly or in secret, to the abolition of serfdom and any agrarian reform.

I must mention at this point a major incident in Polish history, which largely explains the failure of the revolution both in 1830 and 1831 in the Russian provinces, and in 1846 in Galicia and Cracow.

The nobles had promised the peasants at the beginning of the revolt that they would abolish forced labour; but the moment they realised that the peasants were winning victories over the Russian troops, they changed their minds and postponed this reform indefinitely on the entirely false grounds that the army would run short of food. Naturally, the Polish peasantry was extremely bitter.

Niewenglowski, one of the insurgents at the time, spoke as follows at the thirty-first anniversary of the 1830 rising, organised in Paris:

'All those who signed the petition demanding the abolition of forced labour were asked:

' "Do you want the army to go without food?"

'I remember noticing the expression on the face of a young gunner in my battery, and how I said to him:

' "What's wrong with you? Don't you know we're fighting for our country and for freedom?"

' "Yes, sir," he said, "for freedom. But at this moment my old father may be being dragged out to do forced labour." '

The second group, the Polish Democratic Society, more commonly known as *Centralizacja*, severely criticised the policy of the Szlachta (the gentry). Its members, impregnated with the revolutionary theories of the century, realised that independence could not be achieved without freedom, and that no rising could succeed if it evaded the social issue, and— above all—the problem of the peasantry.

'Poland can recover her independence,' said Slowacki, 'by becoming a democratic nation. As an agricultural country, she can guarantee the future happiness of the people by providing them with land.'

All the democrats of the Democratic Society realised that they could not create a new Poland without deciding on her social and democratic structure. The chronicler Seweryn Goszczynski's deductions were as follows:

'Unconditional independence would be a lifeless life, a formless form, an unreal reality; it can be imagined as an abstraction, but not realised . . . the people want concrete conditions.'

The Polish Democratic Society was a young, dynamic, revolutionary organisation, which set out to influence all social classes. But it could not rouse the apathetic mass of the peasantry without giving them land. Several proposals for agrarian reform were put forward. Some were not concerned to solve the social and economic problem, but saw in the distribution of land a useful political weapon. Other economists objected to sharing out the land, and proposed that it should be the property of the

POLAND

future State. The principle exponent of this point of view was Mickiewicz, who had great moral influence among the *emigrés*.

Nevertheless there were large sections of them who did not agree with him, and when he went to Rome in 1848 for an interview with the Pope Pius IX, very few people joined his Polish Legion.

Before leaving Rome on 29 March 1848, Mickiewicz produced his political and social credo which, although impregnated with semi-political, semi-Christian mysticism, none the less reveals him as the most progressive Pole of the period. The full text in his own characteristic style is as follows:

1. The Christian spirit manifested in the Holy Catholic and Roman faith is embodied in free actions
2. The divine word of the Gospels becomes the law of the peoples, both as nations and societies
3. The Church, guardian of the Word
4. The fatherland is the field of life given to the divine Word upon earth
5. The spirit of Poland, servant of the Gospel; the soil of Poland and her people are one. Poland resurrected with the body in which she suffered and descended into the tomb a hundred years ago
Poland declares herself to be a free and independent person and holds out her hand to all the Slav peoples[1]
6. In Poland: freedom for worship, for every faith in God and every Church
7. Free speech, freely revealed and judged by the law according to its fruits
8. Everyone belonging to the nation is a citizen, every citizen is equal before the law and the institutions of government
9. For every post: everyone eligible—freedom of choice, freely given and freely accepted
10. *To Israel, the elder brother—respect and brotherliness, with aid for his well-being, temporal and eternal. Equal rights in all things*
11. To woman, man's life companion—brotherliness and citizenship. Equal rights in all things
12. To each Slav dwelling in Poland—brotherliness and equal rights in all things
13. To each family—domestic activity protected by the community
14. All property—safeguarded and inviolable under the protection of the national administration

[1] All italics are mine—B. G.

15. Political aid—the aid of a member of a family from Poland to her Czech brother and to the parent Czech peoples and to her Ruthenian brother *and to the peoples of Russia*. Christian aid to each people, as to one's neighbour

Towards 1835 several social and economic problems had had to be solved, for the industrialisation of Poland at this period was progressing at a remarkable speed. She found a vast market for her goods in Russia, so it is not surprising that textile factories sprang up everywhere, and completely transformed such towns as Bialystok, Pabianice and Zyrardow into important industrial centres. The modern proletariat came into being at the same time. So the Polish Democratic Society strove to reconcile a number of contradictory political tendencies, but it failed to achieve unanimity except on certain abstractions such as independence, revolution, the people and freedom; and on one concrete aim: land for the peasants.

The Democratic Society differed little from Young Poland, the third and most radical of the Polish organisations, which formed part of Mazzini's Young Europe. Its members, influenced by the doctrines of Saint-Simon, stressed the social aspect of the problem.

It banked on a Europe-wide revolution, and it was its faith in an imminent social upheaval that separated it from the Democratic Society. According to Young Poland, a rising of all the people would result in the liberation of Poland, and this rising, it believed, was near at hand. But the Democratic Society no longer believed in a general revolution.

Victor Heltman, a member of the Democratic Society, delivered a famous speech in 1838 in which he expressed his party's scepticism:

'First weeks, then months, then years passed and still the universal revolt of the peoples did not take place. Little by little our eyes were opened, and we began to realise that our hearts so full of warmth towards our foreign friends no longer beat in unison with theirs, which had grown colder and colder.

'We felt the people turn from impatience to disillusion and from enthusiasm to indifference. Soon, all around us was cold, dark and silent. And the silence was rarely broken. And then only by weak, impotent voices, like a feeble echo.

'In our disillusionment, we turned our eyes, half-blinded with tears, to Poland, our poor mother. And she replied:

' "Why seek help abroad, my children? Can I not raise myself unaided?" '

It seems natural that it should have been the Democratic Society which took in hand the organisation of the Polish rising. It counted only on the patriotism of the entire nation. From 1838 to 1839, the Society's agents in Posen, Galicia, Warsaw and Vilna feverishly set to work to muster their forces for an immediate rising.

Young Poland, too, sent agents—even before the Democratic Society—but with the object of spreading propaganda and educating the people. So as to prepare the ground for revolutionary activity, they spoke to the poor people of the towns and villages of a radical change in the social and economic system.

Their appeal for solidarity with the oppressed peoples had its effect. The Russians, regarded as oppressors, were particularly affected by this propaganda and rallied round the famous member of Young Poland, Konarski.

In fact, when he was arrested and condemned to death by the Czarist tribunal at Vilna, the Russian officers stationed in Lithuania decided to rescue him. But two Poles who were in the conspiracy, Orzesto and Bylewski, were arrested and broke down under torture. Their treachery resulted in the arrest of six hundred Russian officers, including the revolutionary leaders Korovaiev (the head of this conspiracy), Ogon-Doganovski, Barkwitz, Guerassimov and Demosene. Two hundred of them were detained in a fortress and the others reduced to the ranks and sent to the Caucasus. The Russian revolutionaries' plan was similar to that of the Decembrists in 1825. It consisted of seizing the forts of Modlin and Vilna, and then, with the help of the people of Poland and Lithuania, marching on St Petersburg. So as to prevent a rising in 'the Western districts of the Empire', the Czar promised to improve the lot of the rural population.

Young Poland, confident of the peoples' solidarity and their revolutionary spirit, carried their propaganda into every country in Europe. And the absolutist governments looked upon every Pole abroad as an agitator. The majority of the Poles who played such a large and enthusiastic part in the 1848 revolutions in France, Italy, Germany and Austria were members of Young Poland, and put their faith in a free society without exploiters or exploited.

The Polish Democratic Society, on the other hand, turned its back on Europe and, after calling several meetings of the Central Committee, decided that the unaided revolt of the Polish people should take place simultaneously in the three divisions of the country. After long discussions, the Central Committee, having already provided its military and administrative leaders on the spot, planned the rising to take place on the night of 21—22 February 1846. The plan, worked out in every detail, was that hostilities should begin in Prussian Poland as a spring-board for an attack on Russia.

Mieroslawski, the chief of the conspirators, wanted to win the friendly neutrality and even the support of the Berlin Government. His diplomacy, which had the backing of the Central Committee, was not lacking in finesse. King Frederick William IV did in fact openly show his sympathy towards the Poles of Posen and even of Pomerania, especially in the first years of his reign, that is to say, after 1840. The removal of Flotwell, the late King's chancellor, who had germanised Polish territory, the formation of a Catholic department in the Ministry for Ecclesiastical Affairs, the authorisation of the use of Polish in the courts and in the primary and secondary schools, the foundation of a Polish theatre at Posen, and the definite promise to found a Polish University, all led the Polish patriots to believe that the King of Prussia, impatient to free himself from the tutelage of the Czar, wanted to win their sympathy and support. Mieroslawski and the Democratic Society were not mistaken: Frederick William IV hoped to rule over a united Poland. The *rapprochement* between England and Russia, which appeared to be directed against Turkey, resulted in frequent diplomatic contacts between the three monarchs. The King of Prussia's ambition seemed to be taking shape: he would rule the whole of Poland and compensate Austria with Turkey's Slav provinces and Russia with the Dardanelles. But his plan was doomed to failure from the start, not only because Britain was strongly opposed to Russia's having an outlet on the Mediterranean, but also because Hungary repulsed any proposal to include too many Slavs in the Danubian monarchy. Throughout the nineteenth century, the Hungarians prevented Austria-Hungary from becoming a 'triple' monarchy in which their influence would be necessarily reduced.

Nevertheless, whilst the project of a Prussian Poland was still under consideration, Frederick William thought it wise to win the sympathy of the Polish people and, in the meantime, tolerate the Polish revolutionaries' semi-open preparations for a fresh revolt.

Furthermore, feeling ran high among the German democrats on the eve of the 1848 Revolution, and Frederick William was forced to include several liberal Ministers in his Government, one of whom was von Arnim, a staunch friend of the Poles, who became Minister for the Interior. There was an increasing number of demonstrations by the German people in favour of the reconstruction of an independant Poland. Von Arnim forbade his Prefect of Police in Posen to search premises which were publicly known to be used by the Poles for subversive activities.

Everything was in readiness for the revolution to break out in the three parts of Poland. It was to start at Kolo on the River Wartha. The Prussian army on the Russian frontier consisted of only three thousand men; and the *Landwehr*, the German militia, had previously been won over to the insurgents' cause. The patriots in Galicia, under the command of Colonel

Babinski, were, it is true, confronted by an army of twenty-five thousand men, but these were dispersed throughout the province.

The plan was for the Polish troops to march on Kowel. So two armies were to invade Russian Poland, occupy the fortress of Deblin and join up with their brothers-in-arms in Warsaw, who were to operate behind the Russian lines, under the command of Bronislav Dombrowski, the son of the famous Commander-in-Chief of the Polish Legions.

Mieroslawski, however, made mistake after mistake by acting quite openly, and the Czarist police sent messages to Berlin demanding the arrest of the revolutionary leaders, enclosing their names and addresses.

Who was Mieroslawski? The leader of the 1846 conspiracy was the son of a Polish father and a French mother, and was born at Nemours in 1814. He came to Poland at the age of seven, and was sent to school at Lomza. He entered the Military Academy in 1828, and as a Lieutenant, took part in the 1830 rebellion. After its failure, he settled down to study the rebellion from the military point of view, and became a distinguished strategist.

In planning the triple rising he neglected to take the masses into consideration, and the success or failure of a revolutionary war depends, first and foremost, on the people. Mieroslawski's blunder was no mistake; it was part of his plan. Although even the absolutist governments realised the importance of the people's support in an armed conflict, Mieroslawski concentrated on the purely military aspect and adopted a reactionary political attitude. He put far too much faith in Frederick William's loyalty, and repulsed the invaluable offers of help given by the Slavs, especially the Czechs. Although he had once planned a Slav Federation, when he was in the dock in Berlin in 1837, he said that his object was to halt 'the dangerous rise of pan-Slavism'.

'It would be absurd', said Mieroslawski, 'for the Polish revolutionaries to count on a genuine alliance with Prussia. But although in the past she has been Poland's enemy, she now looks to a future when her pan-Germanic policy must sooner or later lead her to combine with the only power capable of halting the rising tide of pan-Slavism.'

The Czechs felt they were not strong enough to break away from Austria. The southern Slavs looked towards Russia. So Mieroslawski refused the help of both Slav nations.

The Czechs, with their political clear-sightedness, said: 'What would become of our national spirit and our national culture, if Russia, the only great Slav power in the world, were to cease to exist? We should be finally absorbed by the Germans.' And Vladimir Soloviev was later to refer to Moscow and Prague as the two eyes of the Slav movement. For some of the Polish democrats, however, Russia was fast sunk in the slough of reaction. The members of the Polish Democratic Society considered that the Czar's Slavist policy had nothing in common with republican and progressive Slavism. They ignored the deep-seated disturbances beneath the surface of Russian society, and underestimated the Russian people's revolutionary aims, as represented by Bielinsky, Granovsky, Stankevich, and many others. They looked upon Bakunin as an isolated figure, out of touch with his own country.

Under pressure from the Czar, the King of Prussia ordered Miero-slawski's arrest on 12 February. He was taken to the Moabit Prison in Berlin. His rashness bordered on levity, for when he was arrested, they found on him a complete list of the revolutionary leaders in Posen, who were all arrested and imprisoned; this disaster threw the insurgents into a state of complete confusion, particularly in Russian Poland, where the plan depended entirely on Posen. The confusion grew, some demanding the cancellation of the revolt, and others that it should start sooner. The frequent movements of the revolutionaries in Austria, where the disturb-ance was greatest, alarmed the authorities, and on 18 February 1846, the Austrian General Collin occupied Cracow. After Mieroslawski's arrest, the leaders of the Democratic Society began to quarrel among themselves. They could not agree whether or not to postpone the rising. Time pressed, and the rank and file of the movement would not hear of any delay. Seeing the gravity of the situation in Cracow, once it had been occupied by General Collin's forces, the National Council—the supreme head of the movement—met to make an official decision to postpone the revolt. Later, the Democratic Society was to condemn their folly. Seeing the distances that would have to be covered to inform the local revolutionary leaders in the far-off provinces of Galicia and Lithuania, this tardy decision was bound to wreck the revolt from the start. At the height of the battle in Galicia and Cracow, workmen arrived at Siedlec, Vilna and other towns, with orders to stop the fighting. The Polish Generals, sent from Paris by the Democratic Society, learnt of the postponement of the rising *en route* and returned to France at the very moment when the insurgents, already in the thick of the battle, most needed them.

Whilst all this was going on, the absolutist governments were on the alert, and in order to prevent the revolt of a powerful nation which it would not be easy to bring to heel if it presented a united front, cunningly exploited the already existing antagonism between the nobility and the peasants.

In Galicia, the Vienna Government's agents spread the rumour that the Polish nobles were planning a revolt against the Emperor, because he was producing a law whereby the peasants would gain both land and liberty. The Polish nobles paid dearly for their treachery in 1831, when they had broken their promises, for the Galician Peasants' Revolt in 1846 was terrible in its effects.

'On the morning of 19 February', writes the historian Limanowski, 'the peasants, on a given signal, launched their attack on the properties of large and small landowners alike. Even the presbyteries were not spared.'

An eye-witness, Walenty Chlebowski, tells us that 'the barbarity of the Galician massacres surpassed that of the Sicilian Vespers and the Eve of St Bartholomew. . . . In our own district armed peasants guarded the whole area as far as Dukla. No one could move. News came in every minute of fresh atrocities. The peasants carted the corpses and the wounded (tied hand and foot) off to police headquarters, where the officials congratulated them and even rewarded them with money. The masses, gone berserk, had taken the law into their own hands, whilst the army and the civil authorities stood aside, calmly watching and encouraging them. There was no longer any government, we were at the mercy of the peasantry.'

It must be added that the Austrian Government succeeded in setting the peasants against the nobles not only by exploiting the serf's age-old detestation of his master, but also by stirring up racial hatred: the population of Eastern Galicia consisted of Ukrainians, whereas the landowners were Poles, whose estates stretched beyond Kiev in the Ukraine.

The Galician massacres had a considerable effect in Berlin and Paris, where the Austrian diplomats succeeded in convincing Louis Philippe that 'the peasants' revolt was simply the natural result of the oppressed's hatred of the oppressor'. Metternich was furious when the Prussian *State Gazette* accused the Vienna Government of having a hand in the affair. His attitude was that if at the start the Prussian Government had not tolerated the Poles' activities on Prussian territory, the Galician massacres would never have occurred. Apponyi, the Austrian Ambassador in Paris, wrote on 15 March 1846:

'. . . His Majesty refuses to believe in the atrocities which are laid at the door of even the most humble Austrian officials in Galicia. He is deeply distressed that the *State Gazette* of Prussia should demean itself by publishing in its columns these exaggerated and without doubt frequently erroneous accounts. Whilst appreciating the benevolent rule of our Government, and recognising the fact that it is one of the principal motives behind the Galician peasants' methods of expressing their grateful loyalty, His Majesty considers that recent events are also largely due to the peasants' deep-rooted and implacable hatred of their overlords, who treat them with brutality, make them do forced labour and ravage their land with their hunting.'

Naturally, the Polish nobles were thrown into great confusion, and to understand how firmly these 'overlords' stood by their privileges, we need only recall how Prince Czartoryski himself petitioned the Emperor of Austria to restore his lands which had been confiscated as the result of the events in Galicia, and how he promised to retire from public life if his request were granted.

In order to prevent the spread of these peasant revolts into Russia, Nicholas I strove to win the support of the peasants of the 'Western Provinces' of the Empire (meaning the Polish peasants) by publishing in 1846 the following decree:

1. The landowner may not banish a peasant from his estates on his own authority
2. Deserted land may not be requisitioned by the noble
3. Deserted land must, after a lapse of two years, be given to other peasants
4. It is forbidden to increase forced labour arbitrarily
5. The procedure of litigation between nobles and peasants is to be simplified

This decree was published at the same moment as the news arrived from Cracow (which had been occupied by the Austrians) that serfdom had been abolished.

Whatever the details of the case may be, it is clear that it was the absolutist governments and not the nobles who relieved the Polish peasants' misery. That is the chief reason for the comparative peace that reigned in Poland from the 1863 revolt (which also failed) up to the World War of 1914.

Let us return to the events of 1846 in Cracow, where the Polish democrats nearly triumphed. With the help of the poorer people of the town, between six and eight thousand insurgents defeated Collin's troops on 21 and 22 February, in the course of a battle which lasted all one night and all the next day. On the evening of 22 February, General Collin's garrison realised that it was encircled by the peasants who had come in from the neighbouring countryside, and therefore evacuated the town and fled through the night with the revolutionaries hard on their heels.

Once the Austrians had left the town, the middle class, frightened by the rule of the people, called upon Joseph Wodzicki to form a 'committee of public safety', but the masses decided otherwise, and forced the democrat Tyssowski to take control. A National Government was formed at eight o'clock that evening. Its first action was to publish a manifesto announcing to all the provinces of Poland that the revolution had begun:

'We are twenty million strong. If we rise as one man nothing can stand in our path. We will gain such freedom as has never been known on earth. We will win for ourselves a society in which each one of us shall enjoy worldly goods according to his merits and capabilities. There shall be no special privileges of any kind, and every Pole shall find security for himself and his family. Anyone physically or morally handicapped by his birth shall receive, without any humiliation, the help of the whole community. Land conditionally held by the peasants shall become their own unconditional property. Usury, serfdom and all kinds of feudal dues shall be abolished without compensation. Sacrifices made for the nation's sake shall be rewarded by distribution of the nation's wealth.

'From henceforth there shall be no distinction amongst us; we are brothers, the sons of one mother, our country; and one Father—in Heaven. Let us pray for His aid, and He will bless our aims and grant us the victory. But that He may hear our prayers, let us not soil ourselves by drunkenness and pillage; let us not foul our blessed weapons by despotic behaviour or by the murder of members of other creeds, other nations; for it is not against the people that we fight but against their oppressors.'

After the publication of this manifesto, the revolutionary movement achieved a breadth of purpose that surpassed its leaders' wildest hopes. It did not stop at promising the abolition of serfdom, usury, forced labour, and dues in kind, but guaranteed the farm workers that they would share in the distribution of the State lands; and the workers in the towns, the formation of national workshops. An official decree announced the abolition of the nobility and all titles. All these revolutionary social reforms undertaken at the instigation of the masses produced a wave of indescribable popular enthusiasm. It is easy to understand that the minor nobles and the middle class in the towns were terrified out of their wits, and that even the new government grew anxious and began to curb further revolutionary activity.

So as to forestall any attempt at a reactionary coup, Tyssowski, supported by his energetic secretary Dembowski, became dictator when the national government resigned.

But Tyssowski was not up to the job. He was a typical 'Forty-eighter'— indecisive, and much too mild and ineffectual. He was a well-educated, good-looking man with a flair for oratory, but in no way outstanding, and he only held his position thanks to the support of Dembowski, who could deal with difficulties as they arose. Later, Dembowski's premature death in battle caused the defection of several honest democrats, who were idealists without any practical sense.

When he became dictator, Tyssowski published another manifesto in which he confirmed all the promises made in the first one: land for the peasants; recompense for the agricultural workers fighting with the insurgents; national workshops; equality for all citizens; abolition of privileges and titles. This proclamation threatened all offenders against the new regulations with sanctions. A special decree granted equal rights to the Jews.

Tyssowski's reforms aroused great indignation amongst the middle class of Cracow. It was at this point that Michael Wiszniewski, a professor at the University, accompanied by his students who had previously obtained arms, broke into the meeting hall of the National Council and, with the moderates' approval, dismissed the government and proclaimed himself dictator. And Tyssowski made no attempt to prevent him: he withdrew after receiving a vague promise that the peasants' freedom would be respected. Dembowski, however, would not be so intimidated: he arrived in front of the National Council's building at the head of a large crowd, and restored Tyssowski to power. Wiszniewski fled into Prussia.

Later events clearly proved Tyssowski's incompetence. The most immediate task was that of organising the country's defences against invasion, which demanded prompt and vigorous action. It was plain that the Poles could not make a frontal attack on the three partitioning Powers. The patriots' only hope was to split up into small units and spread out over the country to wage a guerilla war. But the National Council had caught Mieroslawski's passion for war on a grand scale, and had concentrated all its armed forces at Cracow. It did not need a military expert to see that the insurgents could not even defend themselves in a pitched battle against armies superior in numbers and equipment—much less defeat them. The postponement of the rising, decided upon at the most critical moment, also had its effect. The insurgents lacked capable generals and technicians, and the only man who might have saved them would have been Dembowski. Once he had gone, Tyssowski lost his last flicker of energy. So what with the revolutionaries' failure to make use of the masses, fear of the peasants (although those round Cracow had supported the rebels), lack of technicians, the feebleness of the military commanders, the want of initiative and revolutionary ardour, and the desertion of the moderate elements, the revolution was doomed to disaster.

Thanks to Tyssowski's tactics—or rather lack of them—General Collin was able to join forces with the troops under Benedek, and the Russians were able to advance on Cracow without meeting the slightest resistance from the partisans. The middle class in Cracow took heart at the approach of the imperial armies and forced Tyssowski to capitulate. He resigned himself to leaving Cracow with a thousand of his men.

Tyssowski and his followers made for Prussia instead of dispersing in the mountain regions of Kielce and the Tatras, where the Democratic Society's propaganda had won them two thousand supporters. Had Tyssowski joined up with them, the guerilla warfare, frowned on by the theorists of the Society, could have been carried on longer. The revolutionary forces could easily have obtained help not only from the local population but from the Czech and Hungarian neighbours, who were already ripe for revolt. The very presence of armed and properly organised partisans would have brought the masses to swell their ranks.

But instead, Tyssowski, indecisive as usual, arrived at the Prussian frontier, which he crossed when Berlin, alive to the dangers of a partisan war, promised him that his troops would not be handed over either to the Emperor of Austria or to the Czar of Russia.

General Collin himself afterwards admitted, when he had quelled the rising, that his position would have been extremely precarious had the insurgents started guerilla warfare.

Cracow capitulated on 3 March 1846 after a ten day revolution. The Cracow Republic was dead. It was incorporated in the Austrian Empire at the very moment when the news of the insurrection was spreading from mouth to mouth throughout every country in Europe. In France, the Polish Revolution was greeted with tremendous enthusiasm by the people of Paris on 4 March 1846. Democratic and even reactionary newspapers such as *France* hailed this awakening of the Poles. Montalambert and Victor Hugo spoke up for Poland, and Guizot protested against the Vienna Government's decision to abolish Cracow's independence.

But the sacrifices made by the people of Cracow in 1846 were not in vain. The Polish insurrection precipitated events in France, and two years later a new hope was born in the world.

From the beginning of March 1848 onward, the revolutionary fever that had crossed the Rhine, came nearer and nearer to central Europe. On 13 March the revolution broke out in Vienna. On the 20th the Austrian Government proclaimed an amnesty for all political prisoners who had been involved in the 1846 conspiracy in Galicia and Cracow. Two days before, the people of Berlin had freed Mieroslawski and all the other Polish prisoners from the Moabit Prison, and carried them in triumph through the streets of the capital. When the mob reached the royal palace they called for the King, who appeared on the balcony and bared his head in respect for those whom his courts had condemned to death or life imprisonment a year earlier.

This even had a galvanic effect on the Polish masses in the Prussian provinces, and three days later a Polish delegation, headed by Archbishop Pvzyluski, appeared before the King to present a petition on behalf of the Polish citizens.

Frederick William granted the delegates an audience, in the course of which he recognised the validity of their claims, and promised to 'reorganise' the Grand Duchy of Posen to satisfy their nationalist ambitions, on condition that the interests of the German citizens of the province were safeguarded.

Not only the Poles in Poland but also those in France grew impatient. Moved by Lamartine's words ('Your country is yours. Return to it!') Adam Czartoryski, his Ministers and his Generals, took the road for Posen via Germany. They were warmly welcomed by the people of Cologne and Berlin, who greeted them with shouts of 'Long live the new-born Poland!' Czartoryski and his suite arrived at Posen on 8 April, whilst the Generals Dwernicki, Dembinski and Bem went off to Lwow. Following the example of their leaders, the mass of *emigrés* left their families and their jobs and hastened to their native land.

In the meantime, the royal commission charged with the reorganisation of Posen decreed the formation of a Polish National Army, and ordered the general mobilisation of all Polish citizens. The German people approved this measure, and young men arrived in numbers from Russian Poland to enrol under the national flag. There was even a fund started in Berlin to help to finance the new army because, as has been already mentioned, the German democrats who feared a Russian invasion hoped that Poland would eventually act as a buffer between Russia and Prussia and so become an invaluable ally of the revolutionary peoples of Europe. This active support of Poland's independence was a reply to a formidable manifesto published by the Czar, who declared that he was determined to stem 'the tide of anarchy which threatened to overthrow lawful authorities and the whole order of society'.

On 4 April, the *Vorparlament*, or 'Preparatory Parliament', of Frankfort passed the following motion:

'The German Union proclaims the partition of Poland to be a shameful injustice, and considers it the sacred duty of the German peoples to do their utmost to achieve her reconstitution. The Union hopes that the German Governments will allow the free passage of unarmed Poles through their territory, and that they will give them any assistance they require.'

The Austrian Government, for its part, published a similar declaration in the *Vienna Journal* of 6 May:

'Free Austria will bring freedom to Poland, and with the support of Europe, will not hesitate to fight Russia in order to realise so high an ideal.'

The Hungarian Diet, too, demanded Poland's reconstitution on 12 April. On 23 March, Lamartine, equally afraid of Russia, sent his diplomatic representatives abroad a circular stressing his interest in Polish independence.

Falkowski, in his *Memoirs*, summed up the situation as it appeared at the beginning of 'the peoples' spring' as follows:

'In March and April 1848 the Polish question, which had been brought to the bar of Europe, took a turn that gave us cause for the greatest optimism. It was up to the Poles to work out the final solution, or at any rate to keep their problem on the agenda of European politics by linking it closely up with the problem of German unity. But in order to do that the Poles had to show considerable perspicacity, moderation and tact, which, alas, are rare virtues among us, particularly since they demand a combination of civic sense and strength of character.'

Nevertheless, the Polish forces rallied at Posen until they formed an army of twenty thousand men. Their fervent nationalism upset the *Junkers* who immediately protested to the Berlin Government against Polish 'anarchy'. Then the Germans in Posen, who were alarmed when the Polish National Committee refused to accept their representatives, inundated Berlin with their complaints, accusing the Poles of being anti-German. Finally the Czar demanded the recognition of the Münchengrätz agreement.

As a result of all this agitation, a state of siege was declared in the town of Posen, and the Polish volunteers were forbidden to rally there. This soon caused bloody encounters between the Prussian patrols and the Polish volunteers crossing the Russo-Prussian border.

The King of Prussia then entrusted General Willisen with the delicate task of reorganising the Grand Duchy. Willisen angered his compatriots by making public on 8 April his plan not merely to make Posen autonomous but to permit the creation of a Polish National Army composed of a militia and a volunteer force. Furthermore he promised to withdraw the troops from other German provinces who were garrisoning Posen.

Willisen's proposals produced a violent reaction from the *Junkers* and the Germans in Posen. General Wedel, who commanded the Prussian forces in the Grand Duchy, categorically declared that he would prevent Willisen from carrying out his programme. At that moment the Polish Army was already thirty thousand strong, whereas the Prussians had only twenty-eight thousand men. As the Poles were forbidden the town of Posen, they massed their forces near Sroda. Twelve thousand Poles were concentrated in the Forest of Krotoszyn. The situation was growing steadily worse, and there was likely to be a clash between the two armies at any minute. Falkowski said afterwards that 'Mieroslawski acted like a dictator, sending his Chief of Staff to Berlin to treat with the King as between one power and another'. It is not surprising that Willisen ended by being removed from his post and that the conflict between the *Junkers* and the Polish troops could no longer be avoided. The Poles' victory turned Mieroslawski's head and he called on the people of Posen to rise against the Prussians. On 9 May, after a week's fighting, Mieroslawski capitulated and gave his word that he would never again take up arms against Prussia. On 14 March he returned to France—at the very moment when the antagonism between the Polish and German populations of Posen was at its height. That was the sorry end of the career of a leader who had enjoyed immense prestige not only among the Poles but also among all sections of the German people.

There has been a great deal of criticism—often unfair—of Mieroslawski. But he did commit one serious blunder, which shows the narrowness of his outlook, and which for a long time compromised the Democratic Society's policy: he made no attempt to start a general war against the Czar by attacking the Russian Army, at a time when the whole of Europe was behind the Polish independence movement and when Russian Poland was empty of troops and von Arnim himself was expecting a war between Germany and Russia.

When the revolution broke out in Berlin in March, the Russian forces in Poland did not exceed twenty-four thousand men. And it had been proved in 1846 that they were in part influenced by democratic propaganda.

Paskievich, the Governor of Warsaw, wanted to evacuate Poland when he heard that the prisoners had been released from the Moabit, knowing that by the beginning of April between twenty and thirty thousand men from Posen would be free to invade Russian Poland.

The Russian Government hourly expected such an invasion. Meyendorff, the Czar's Ambassador in Berlin, wrote to Paskievich: 'I would draw your particular attention, Your Highness, to the warning I have received that the people of Posen may invade the Kingdom on 5 or 6 April.'

And in point of fact, several Polish leaders demanded from the beginning a sudden attack on Russian Poland, but Mieroslawski, surprisingly enough, was opposed to the idea. He gives a lengthy explanation in his *Memoirs* of what he was trying to do, which, incidentally, is not hard to imagine. He wanted to wage war on a grand scale, with a large, well-trained, well-armed and well-disciplined army. He planned a vast campaign based on both Posen and Galicia. With his abhorrence of small-scale partisan warfare, and his refusal to make use of the people, Mieroslawski was the victim of a curious political aberration. And yet in his *Memoirs* he writes of his foresight, his prudence and his political sense. Fundamentally, Mieroslawski was a little man with illusions of grandeur. But what was even more serious was that a whole section of the *emigrés* had similar illusions, and one is tempted to agree with Proudhon when he writes:

'Although it is true that the partition of Poland was a crime on the part

370

of Catherine, Frederick and Maria Theresa, it is equally true that the Poles virtually committed suicide. The soul had departed before the body was dismembered. Politically and morally, Poland was already dead. Now it is a law of history—almost, I should say, a necessary part of civilisation—that when a nation collapses it is immediately absorbed by its neighbours.'

The failure of the Polish insurrection in Posen was followed by severe repression. At the beginning of June, just when the Frankfort Parliament was holding its first session, the Polish *emigrés* were expelled from Posen. We know that the Frankfort Parliament's reactions did more than anything else to harm the cause of German democracy. The defeat of Poland resulted in a new alliance between Russia and Prussia. Bakunin, referring to this alliance as a 'marriage of convenience', wrote of it as follows:

' Since the partition of Poland, and precisely because of it, Russia and Prussia have become mutually interdependent. They cannot fight each other without letting go of the provinces they have taken, and neither can do that as the strength of each lies in her Polish possessions. As they cannot fight, they must willy-nilly be firm allies. Poland has only to stir for Prussia and Russia to fall over themselves in protestations of love for each other. Their enforced intimacy is the fatal result—which is often unfortunate and always painful—of their criminal assault on noble, hapless Poland.'

Once the Posen rising had been put down, the Polish patriots moved their centre to Lwow. Revolution was boiling up in all the Austrian provinces. A National Committee was set up at Cracow (which had not yet become an indivisible part of Galicia). This Committee had only local demands to make as it considered Cracow a dependency of Vienna.

The lessons of 1846 taught the nobles and middle class of Cracow and Lwow to go carefully. Furthermore, these propertied classes were divided among themselves. Some wanted democratic reforms and national autonomy, and others, openly relying on the support of the reactionaries, followed the Governor, Stadion, who emboldened by the law-abiding behaviour of the National Committee at Lwow, demanded its dissolution on the grounds that it was 'unconstitutional'. Whatever may have been the case, the nobles sent petitions to Vienna, defending their national rights. But they still would not take a unanimous decision to declare, through the medium of the National Committee, that serfdom was abolished. In December 1848 the *Polish Democrat* complained:

' Either because we felt that we were not politically mature, or because of the disastrous chain of events, we have always chosen the legal, constitutional path.' This, the *Polish Democrat* stigmatised as the unnatural, incomprehensible and monstrous result of all the follies committed in 1848.

Out of fear of the people, the privileged classes had made the nationalist

movement dependent on Vienna. This same fear caused them to hide
behind Stadion every time 'the mob' grew ugly and demanded its rights.
It was not in order to abolish Cracow's autonomy that General Castiglione
('without any apparent reason') decided to bombard the town on 26 April
1848: he aimed at smashing the social revolution. In the same way, the
bombardment of Lwow, on 2 September, was the reactionaries' method
of trying to curtail its liberties, and intimidate the revolutionary *emigrés*
from France and Russian Poland, who at last realised that revolution
alone could restore Poland's independence, and that it was their duty to
help it wherever it broke out. Thus the patriots of Lwow sent delegates
to Hungary to ask them for help, not as mercenaries, but as allies fighting
for the same aims and the same ideal: freedom.

The traditionalist Polish historians criticise the revolutionaries of 1848
for their political immaturity; without going to the root of the matter,
I should say that the Polish revolutionaries systematically refused to learn
from the past, although the similarity between the situation created in
Galicia and that created in Posen was self-evident. Whilst in Posen the
Germans ended by causing a civil war, in Galicia trouble might break out
at any moment between the Ukrainians and the Poles. The National
Committee had done nothing to remedy this state of affairs; it had even
sided with the reactionaries. It neither gave the Ukrainians autonomy nor
promised them that their national rights would be respected. The whole
problem was closely connected with that of pan-Slavism. The projects
for a Slav Federation remained a dead letter. Furthermore the Slavs, a
race of agriculturists, had not obtained the abolition of serfdom, and as
minorities in Poland and Hungary they had been actually persecuted.
Kossuth, the great Hungarian revolutionary leader, had said, alluding to
the Slovaks and the Croats: 'The Hungarians form the only nation: the
other races are merely dependents.' The result was the historical paradox
whereby the House of Hapsburg, which had defended the peasants
against their Slav overlords, now protected them from the Polish and
Hungarian nationalists who had not yet even succeeded in winning their
own freedom. The Slavs of Austria, who were often illiterate and were
under the thumb of the clergy, became the upholders of the monarchy
and the counter-revolution because the frightened middle-class revolutionaries of 1848 would have no dealings with them. The Poles turned
their backs on the Slavs, including the Czechs, even when Austria had her
hands tied in Hungary and Italy. They wanted an alliance with the Hungarians as they hoped to create a triple monarchy of Poland, Austria and
Hungary.

Kossuth, the very incarnation of the Magyar Revolution, appears to
have favoured an alliance with the Poles. In March 1849 he clearly

stated: 'Hungary's freedom hangs in the balance until Poland has achieved hers.' The Hungarian General Görgey frequently reproached Kossuth with 'his passion for the Poles'.

However, the thesis of the French historian Desprez does not fit in at all with this story. His theory is that Kossuth supported collaboration with Poland only after the March revolution, and then simply in order to obtain further concessions from Vienna. At the beginning of the revolution he had no thought of destroying the Austrian Empire. Desprez also recalls how Kossuth—admittedly with reservations—had pushed through a bill voting money and troops for the war against the Italian revolutionaries, in the hope that Vienna would support him in return in his dispute with the Croats and the Rumanians. It was only when the Viennese Court decided to choose the Croat, Jellacic, as their defender that Kossuth and his followers turned once more to the Poles.

According to the Polish Colonel Bulharyn, who was commanding a number of Polish detachments in Hungary, Kossuth placed no reliance on the solidarity of the two peoples.

Nor did Kossuth immediately accept the help of the Polish Army, although it was in Hungary's interests that it should operate in Galicia. Bulharyn's view was shared by Teuseman, who was sent to ask Kossuth's help for the defenders of besieged Vienna.

Kossuth saw that the Imperial forces after bringing the Czechs to heel, and conquering the Italians, would quickly turn against the Hungarians as soon as they had dealt with the Viennese. It was only then that he realised that in 'the solidarity of the peoples' lay the only hope for the Hungarians, the Germans and the Poles. In spite of his fear of Russia's intervention, he yielded in the end to the Poles' arguments, and allowed the formation of a Polish army in Hungary. He had finally decided to do so as the result of the Viennese Court's stupidity in refusing to withdraw their support from Jellacic, even when Kossuth promised to abandon Poland as he had previously abandoned Italy.

So Kossuth accepted the assistance of senior Polish officers and Polish technicians, as well as arms sent by Polish *emigrés* from France and Galicia. It was shortly after this that he agreed to the formation of a Polish army.

The gates of Pest were opened to the young volunteers from Galicia, who arrived in considerable numbers, and General Bem became Commander-in-Chief of the Hungarian armies. He was 'the spiritual descendent of the Polish revolutionaries of 1831', as Kossuth himself said to Falkowski, for he had the highest opinion of both Bem and Czartoryski. Kossuth was also extremely interested in Mieroslawski and wanted him to come to Hungary.

The young Polish democrats of Pest, under the leadership of Wysocki,

were openly hostile to Bem as a representative of the Hotel Lambert and
the Polish nobility. And Bem, for his part, opposed the formation of
purely Polish legions. As supporter of Czartoryski's Slavophil policy, he
wanted a Polo-Slav Army to be formed in Croatia, with the object of
reconciling the Magyars with the Slavs. His letter to Czartoryski of
29 September 1848 (published in 1877) expresses this point of view:

'The Hungarians, with whom the Poles have been on the most friendly
footing since time immemorial, are at present in a critical position. The
Croats, who like the other Slav races have been united with the Hungarians for centuries, have been stirred up by the Germans and even by
the Russians to revolt against them. The country is threatened with civil
war. We Poles are the only people capable of making the peace between
the opposing parties by advising the Magyars to guarantee the Slavs all
constitutional liberties, and persuading the Slavs that union with the
Magyars would be to their advantage.

'I have persuaded Your Excellency's son to lead this important mission,
which will also include Prince Sanguszko, Prince Jerzy Lubomirski and a
number of other distinguished members. We are going first to Tarnor
and Vienna, where we will decide upon our plan of action, and thence
proceed to Pest. The formation of a Polo-Slav legion, comprising all the
emigrés, will enable us to form a detachment in Hungary which will lend
our offer of mediation more weight, and will at the same time form the
nucleus of a future Polish Army.'

Bem's offer of mediation, which angered the Hungarians as much as
the Croats; his refusal to create an all-Polish legion on Hungarian soil;
and his high-handed behaviour in intriguing against Wysocki, the Democratic Society's representative, all infuriated the democratic emigrés. One
young Pole, excited by what he had heard Wysocki say of the matter,
went to the house where Bem was staying, and fired a revolver at him,
wounding Bem in the cheek. He was rescued, however, by the Polish
emigrés and the Hungarian democrats. The free press of Pest started a
campaign in the young hot-head's favour and the Hungarian crowd
started a demonstration with shouts of 'Down with Bem!' Kossuth
yielded to public opinion and the young man was set free. Bem was not
made Commander-in-Chief and Wysocki was appointed as Polish
representative to the Hungarian Government.

Falkowski, a delegate of the Galician Youth Movement, decided that
the Poles had no future in Hungary. Having decided to leave Hungary,
he wrote a farewell letter to Kossuth. The next day Kossuth asked him to
come and see him. 'You're mistaken', he told him. 'Your plan hasn't
failed. I give you my word of honour that there will be Polish legions in
Hungary, only we have partially accepted General Bem's wise and

practical advice. For the moment we are forming two Polish companies only, as the formation of whole legions would mean war with Russia. When these two companies are up to strength and fully equipped, we shall move them into the provinces and, under cover, start forming two more in Pest, and so on. I've spoken with Colonel Bulharyn. He's an old soldier, an honest man without any political prejudices, and will be the permanent organiser of these Polish companies. At first, all Polish infantry, cavalry and artillery units will be scattered throughout the Hungarian army. Then at any given moment they can be combined under one command. So we shall have a Polish Army Corps ready to attack the Russians from the rear if they decide to invade Hungary and start a revolt here and in Galicia. That is my plan.'

The Austrian offensive shook the Poles' confidence. All the Hungarian Generals retreated, and only Bem held his positions. On 5 January 1849 Windischgrätz occupied Budapest and the Hungarian Government moved to Debrecen. 'The whole of Vienna', Marx said, 'knew that the war against Hungary was in reality a war against the Constitution.' But just when the Hungarian revolution seemed to be in its death-throes, Kossuth began to show more energy and initiative. He made Bem civil and military governor of Transylvania, which had been almost completely occupied, and entrusted the supreme command to the Polish General, Henryk Dembinski.

Without a shadow of doubt, the Poles were of immense help to the Hungarians. Polish troops were everywhere in the forefront of the battle, never losing heart despite a chain of disasters, and on occasion saving entire divisions by their bravery. The Austrians were under the impression that there were huge numbers of Poles—thirty thousand was one estimate —whereas in point of fact there were a thousand at the most.

The whole world rang with the story of the Poles' heroism, and when the Polish legion left Buda for Miskolc, where a Polish division was being formed, the Hungarian troops promised 'that they would not lay down their arms until Poland was free'.

We must not forget either that the counter-revolution, which had the advantage in the winter of 1848-9, contributed to the *rapprochement* between the Slavs and the Hungarians. The Austrians restored the old order everywhere, germanising the schools and the government institutions, and putting in their own officials. The Slovaks' disappointment was particularly bitter. So the victories of the revolutionary forces in the spring of 1849 were hailed with joy by all the oppressed peoples. Their excitement reached its zenith in Galicia, and numerous Poles from that province, in spite of the state of siege, took up arms in Hungary's support, and the Czar feared a rising in Russian Poland.

When Kossuth reviewed his troops he bared his head before the Polish legion and Bem's prestige eclipsed that of the Hungarian generals.

In the meantime, events were taking an increasingly revolutionary turn, for the Hungarian Parliament declared the Emperor of Austria no longer King of Hungary. Görgey, who was appointed Commander-in-Chief and War Minister, had no love for the Poles who brought a revolutionary spirit into the army. According to the Polish historians, he loathed Dembinski, who had offended him by criticising his strategy. Görgey finally got rid of Dembinski on account of his sympathies with the Slovaks and his impatience to enter Galicia. It is true that Dembinski, when he saw that the formation of the Polish division was being delayed, had planned to cross the Carpathians and enter Galicia with eight hundred men. Görgey considered that this would provoke the Russians, and this he wanted to avoid at all costs. In June he removed Dembinski from his command and replaced him by Wysocki. A few days later, the Russian Army invaded Hungary. The last citadel of the revolution fell, and with it died Poland's last hope of winning her independence in 1848.

HELLENISM AND 1848

MICHAEL SAKELLARIOU

$\mathbf{A}$LTHOUGH the Greek people took no direct part in the great intellectual and social maelstrom of this year of 1848 which had so decisive an effect on the world's history, and although they did not experience the full effects of the dramatic events which took place at the time in eastern and western Europe, we should nevertheless be wrong to think that they were entirely unaffected by them. The object of this brief essay is to relate what did happen in Greece in 1848 in relation to the rest of Europe, and to form an appreciation of its real significance.[1]

Eighteen forty-eight found the Greek nation divided into three parts: the young Kingdom of Greece covering an area of 37,612 square kilometres inhabited by a population of 950,000; the tiny State of the Ionian Islands (2,695 square kilometres and 200,000 inhabitants); and three million Greeks still under Turkish rule. As I have found it impossible to discover the reactions of the Greeks in Turkey, I shall deal only with the Greek Kingdom and the Ionian State.

I

THE KINGDOM OF GREECE

It must at once be stressed that the events of 1848 in Greece were of a totally different character from those of western Europe. Economically, Greece was very backward. Trade, hampered by inadequate purchasing power, was on only a small scale. Apart from primitive handicrafts, industry was non-existent. The merchant service, it is true, was making steady progress, but it was still of limited importance. The middle class was in its very early stages, and there was as yet no proletariat.[2]

Consequently, Greece knew none of the social problems of western

[1] Unfortunately the subject has not yet been even touched on, and I have had to collect my material from original sources, so this study does not pretend to be exhaustive and must be considered as merely a preliminary outline of events.

[2] The following figures are significant: in 1840, out of a population of 850,000, Greece had only 18,296 merchants, 15,343 artisans, 13,679 seafarers, and 276 bankers and money changers.

377

Europe. But there was social and political antagonism between the masses, who were for the most part peasants, and a small number of landowning families which sought to conserve and increase their economic, social and political supremacy.

The burning problem of the period was what to do with the huge body of men who had fought for national independence and, now that the country was free, found themselves out of a job. The new State did not want them as soldiers. The only means of setting them up consisted in giving them land that had previously belonged to the Turks, but this scheme was blocked by the upper classes who wanted it for themselves. These war veterans, however, did not constitute a homogeneous class which could play a revolutionary rôle. Some took to the bush, and started a terrible reign of banditry, made famous by Edmond About; others became social parasites, the shock-troops of party politics; but the majority formed an inert mass, an easy prey to the demagogue.

Finally, we must remember that the political régime of the new State had been decided upon when it was first created, by the three Great Powers of Britain, France and Russia in the London Protocol of 1830. The new monarchy was foreign to the nation's political tradition, for there had previously been two opposing forces: the oligarchs and the democrats. The oligarchs were the most affected by Greece becoming a monarchy, for the system of representation that had been in existence under the Turkish occupation and during the revolution had enabled them to set themselves up as the elected rulers of the people. They were therefore in the forefront of the movement to make King Otho grant a Constitution. They were the leaders, and chief beneficiaries, of the insurrection on 3 September 1843. So in 1848 Greece already possessed a Constitution which, with Great Britain's, was one of the most liberal in the whole of Europe. This fact, which made Greece one of the most progressive nations, deprived the Greeks of the strongest motive for large-scale political revolution in 1848.

But the Constitution was not put into practice. The King had been forced to accept it, but he had no intention whatsoever of complying with it. He very soon got rid of Metaxas and Mavrocordatos, the two politicians who had imposed it on him, and put in power Kolettes, who had not taken part in the constitutional movement. Kolettes was a true friend to the King, who trusted him completely. When he died, in September 1847, Otho made Tzavelas his Prime Minister, but in fact ruled himself. From 1844 to 1848 the Government persecuted the constitutionalists, rode rough-shod over the Constitution (especially as the King refused to hold himself responsible to his subjects) and rigged the elections. The authorities were corrupt and tyrannical. This régime had the support of the most reactionary powers in Europe at that time: France, Austria, Prussia and Bavaria; but came up against the open and intransigent hostility of Great Britain.

So although there was a Constitution, it was violated by this corrupt and despotic régime and there would therefore seem to have been sufficient cause for a popular revolutionary movement.

In reality, however, the situation was not quite so simple. In actual fact the Government Party, Kollettes' 'French Party', was the very one the masses supported. The 'Russian Party', led by Metaxas, represented the small landowners, and the 'English (or Constitutional) Party', under Mavrocordatos, represented the old oligarchs, Greeks who had returned from abroad, and the intellectual élite.[1]

The 'French Party' had a genuine democratic tradition behind it, but it was under the influence of Kolettes, whose theatrical protestations of love for the masses misled the people and the democrats. Thus there was the paradoxical situation of an anti-constitutional régime supported by the masses, and an opposition consisting of the naturally conservative sections of the populace.

The opposition, which had very little influence in parliament, waged war through the newspapers, but with little effect.

It was a different story, however, with the 'rebels' in the 'French Party', which grew in size, particularly in 1847. The active members of this party, who were former generals and officers of the army of liberation, started a number of insurrections during that year. Those that took place in June in Acarnania, and in August in Euboea were easily enough put down, but the revolt in Naupactus—also in August—was a more serious matter: the movement spread to Phtiotis and was not suppressed until November. The year ended with the Patras rising. It is characteristic that the rebels never stated that they were against either the King or the régime.

At the beginning, the rebels were in agreement with the opposition, which hung back and stopped at comment in their newspapers. Whilst putting the responsibility for what was happening on the Government and the Court clique, they refused to support the revolutionaries openly.

These were the conditions in Greece when the revolution broke out in Europe. The first news from Italy produced a wave of enthusiasm. The newspapers were filled with addresses of sympathy, and the students

[1] See Thouvenel, *La Grèce du Roi Othon*, pp. 132–5, 144; cf. 11, 13, 14, 19. The 'French Party' owes its name to the period preceding the Greek Revolution of 1821, when the people, excited by the French Revolution, formed democratic groups in the self-governing Greek communities. They called themselves by such names as *Gallophrones* ('people who think like the French') as at Kozani, or *Carmagnoli* (after the French revolutionary soldiers) as on Samos. The conservatives of that time counted on help from Russia. In Otho's reign, the 'English Party' made a third party.

celebrated in style. But the fall of Louis Philippe and Guizot deprived the Greek régime of its main supporters abroad, and its importance was not lost either on Sir Edmund Lyons, the British Minister, or the opposition, which gave a banquet at which they toasted Thiers. The King and Queen, seeing the fall of the royal house which had been their strongest ally, were extremely worried.

Like the King, his political godfathers, the Ministers of Austria, Bavaria and Prussia, as well as Thouvenel, the French *chargé d'affaires*, felt that the situation was dangerous, and that some concessions in matters of detail should be made so as to save the whole. That meant dismissing the Government, the scapegoat of the régime, and calling in the opposition. Then the question arose as to whether or not the parliament should be dissolved. Apart from the fact that the opposition did not look upon parliament as representing the will of the people, it was laid down by the Constitution that parliament should be dissolved once a minority was asked to form a Government. But the King and his foreign advisers would not hear of it. The fact was that the parliament contained a number of members who were in with the Court and would vote for the new Government if it asked them to. So if the King agreed to retain the parliament, it would be completely in his hands, and he would still be the real ruler of the country. Apart from these considerations, the February Revolution in France had so disturbed the people that new elections might endanger public safety. It was Thouvenel who advised most strongly against putting in a Government that insisted on the dissolution of parliament.

The first attempts to win over Sir Edmund Lyons were made immediately after the news arrived that the French monarchy had fallen—and even before the governmental crisis. The Bavarian and Prussian Ambassadors made several efforts to stop Lyons from attacking the parliament, and even went so far as to hint that if a dissolution were prevented, he might be allowed to nominate the members of the new Government himself. But Lyons was inflexible.

Nevertheless, King Otho did in the end dismiss the old Cabinet. It is worth remembering that for some time his relations with his Government had not been very friendly. The Cabinet attributed its financial and other difficulties to the interference of the Court. The King refused to approve the appointment as senators of fifteen Government supporters whom they had proposed in order to recover the majority they had lost in the Upper House. It was this incident that caused the Cabinet to resign on 15 March.

The news only came out two days later, when the King started summoning prominent politicians to the Palace. Convinced that the leaders of the two opposition parties would accept office only on condition that parliament was dissolved, he started by approaching two moderate members of the 'English Party': G. J. Kountouriotes and S. Trikoupes, in the hope that one of them could form an apparently constitutional and pro-British government. The first declined; and the second, who had come to terms with the opposition leaders, demanded the dissolution of parliament and an amnesty for the rebels of 1847, and said he would accept only on condition that he could include Metaxas and Mavrocordatos in his Cabinet. The next day, therefore, the King summoned the two opposition leaders who also made the dissolution of parliament a *sine qua non*. The King then approached Kountouriotes again, and this time succeeded in persuading him to form a Government without dissolving parliament. Kountouriotes failed to get any of the members of the 'English Party' to take office under him, so he surrounded himself with men connected with the Court, and chose three of his Ministers from a small group within the 'French Party'. The new Government was not essentially different from its predecessor. It, too, merely served as a convenient cloak for the policy of the King and the Court clique.

By this conduct Otho not only failed to conciliate the opposition but aroused the hostility of a whole section of the 'French Party'. This party, which—as we have seen—represented the masses and the former revolutionary combatants, had always been in favour of democratic solutions. Only Kolettes, abandoning his former principles to help the King to ride rough-shod over the Constitution, had tried to transform the party into a governmental, royalist one. But the party had refused to follow him. After his death, his successors in the Government started to object to the King's frequent interference in their business. The Government's resignation put a stop to this unnatural collaboration, but at the same time antagonised those who thereby lost office.

There was an immediate reaction. On 17 March, the day on which the King began summoning the various political leaders, armed supporters of the old Government started democratic demonstrations.

The opposition's supporters, who were conservatives by nature, grew alarmed and hastily armed themselves too. That night was an uneasy one and there was a constant threat of a clash. Some days later, on 16 April, the national holiday provided the occasion for a fresh demonstration. This day, the anniversary of the 1821 Revolution, was celebrated with exceptional enthusiasm: the people hailed the freedom won and the constitutional changes gained in Europe, and also demonstrated in favour of democracy in Greece. On the Constitution Square the cavalry charged demonstrations of students who were swarming through the streets shouting: 'Long live Democracy!' Among them was Delegeorges who some years later played a prominent rôle in the movement directed against Otho, and became Prime Minister of Greece. Other demonstrators were 'French Party' members, who even had the support of the police.

One of the men behind these demonstrations, apart from the ex-Ministers, was D. Kalliphronas, President of the Chamber, a staunch liberal who had been elected Mayor of Athens in 1835, though the King had refused to ratify his appointment. His brother, who acted as Mayor of Athens and Chief of the Municipal Police, continued to be very active behind the scenes.

All these disturbances had repercussions among the people and produced extremely serious unrest. The Government thought of forming a militia, but hesitated to do so as it feared it might get out of control. The opposition, too, was anxious. One of its newspapers demanded the creation of a national guard, formed 'not of the homeless' but of property owners, merchants, artisans, lawyers, professors and students. In spite of all these reactions, the Deputy Mayor of Athens continued to take bold action. He even went so far as to send four policemen to organise a democratic peasant rising at Phyli, a village near the capital. The Government suspended him, and dismissed his brother, who was Secretary General of the Ministry for Foreign Affairs. It then held new municipal elections in Athens, and formed a National Guard under the command of Makrygiannes.

The democratic movement alarmed the foreign powers. Baron Brunnow, the Russian Ambassador in London, hastened to instruct the Russian *chargé d'affaires* in Athens to inform the Greek Government of Russia's attitude. The *chargé d'affaires* sent a circular to each of the consuls instructing them to underline in their conversations the fact that 'Greece's political existence was bound up with that of the Monarchy', and that any attack on the monarchy would annul the international acts which had created the Greek State. This document was widely circulated by the Greek Government and through the press.

Anyway, Greece's internal situation was not favourable to the development of a genuine and permanent democratic movement, which was not to appear for a long time to come. The events I have just mentioned had no social basis and no political consistency. They were really connected not with the régime but with individuals. Once the excitement of the early days had died down, the men behind these demonstrations appeared in their true guise as personal opponents of King Otho. Such they remained until fourteen years later (in 1862) when they turned him out of Greece.

Whilst these premature democratic demonstrations were taking place in Athens, there were a number of successive revolts in the provinces.

The new Government realised that the rebels of the previous year—
whether they were in prison or had fled into Turkey—constituted an
'open sore' and might create fresh complications and keep the spirit of
revolt alive. They therefore published an amnesty on the national holiday.
But the rebels of Naûpactus and Phtiotis (Velenzas, Papacostas, etc), who
had fled to Thessaly, which at this period belonged to Turkey, had a
number of supporters. These crossed the frontier, and on 22 April started
a new insurrection. They were joined by government troops and peasants,
and so were able to advance as far as Phocis and Euboea. Although they
were not greeted with unanimous enthusiasm, they found quite a large
number of partisans, even among the local authorities. Some days later,
on 16 May, an officer named Perrotis mutinied at Kalamata with all his
men. At the same moment another officer, Cheliotis, also mutinied. Next
came the revolts led by Rentis, Mayor of Perachora in Corinth, and by
Vilaetis, who had considerable political influence in Elis. But their movements gained little support and soon fizzled out. Two other risings, at
Naupactus and Nauplia, also failed. Finally the mobilisation of the considerable government forces succeeded, after five weeks, in quelling the
revolt on the Greek mainland.

What were the rebels' political aims? Local authorities' and the Government agents' reports call them 'democratic', but their own proclamations,
which were reproduced in the papers, contain no attacks on the régime
or on the King. The rebels on the Greek mainland demanded that the
Constitution be upheld, that the Court cease interfering in the government of the country and that the Chamber be dissolved. One of their
appeals even invited the people to ask 'His Majesty, our respected sovereign,
for a general reform of the country's affairs'. Rentis' and Cheliotis' proclamation asked for the collaboration of the King and the nation, and for a
National Assembly. Perrotis, as well as making various demands concerning the Constitution and the Parliament, etc, expressed several
nationalist aims, calling for the suppression of political parties, the formation of a Government composed of the pick of the nation, rearmament
and national unity so as to ensure the safety of the country and the Crown.

It is plain from all these proclamations that none of the provincial
insurgents was in contact with the Athenian democrats. The Government's assertion that all the provincial movements took their instructions
from the British Legation and the opposition parties, would seem to be
without any foundation, when one thinks of the diversity of their claims.
The opposition was certainly behind the great movement on the mainland, as it had been the previous year, and its newspapers, without openly
supporting the rebels, at least defended them as individuals. It was the
opposite with the other movements, and the paper *Elpis* violently con-

demned the demands of the Corinthian rebels. 'The season of National Assemblies', it said, 'is one of dangerous fever.'

All these little upheavals were so many spontaneous signs of a revolutionary spirit and a real desire for change, but they lacked a political objective. It is also characteristic that the opposition mistrusted and disliked these provincial demonstrations as it had the democratic demonstrations in Athens. The 'English' and 'Russian' parties were opposed to unconstitutional monarchy, but they would not tolerate any subversive activity.

It was this very conservatism of the opposition that not only made it afraid of revolutionary demonstrations, but weakened it and made it incapable of attaining its own ends, modest though they were. The King hurriedly called in Trikoupes, who, when Mavrocordatos refused, agreed to go to Munich in April as the King's envoy. On his return he became the King's right-hand man. Mavrocordatos, henceforth on his own, began talking of overthrowing the monarchy but never made a political issue of it.

So Otho succeeded in overcoming all opposition at home (without worrying about incurring the displeasure of the British Foreign Office), and in retaining his personal authority, although ancient kingdoms crashed all round him. Nevertheless, the events we have just discussed marked a turning point in the country's internal history. The unnatural collaboration between the popular party and the royal house had come to an end and it was this party that was to produce the main leaders in the fight against the monarchy.

At this time there was also the problem of the unredeemed territory. The greater part of the Greek community was still under Turkish domination. All the Greeks, whether or not they had won their freedom, were obsessed by the 'Great Idea', by a passionate desire to free their compatriots from the Turks. For many of them this also meant something much more ambitious, the revival of the Byzantine Empire and the re-establishment of Greek supremacy over the whole of the Balkans and the Near East. Kolettes had been the principal protagonist of this scheme, urging the necessity for immediate action without waiting—as Mavrocordatos advised—for the State to be organised first. He hoped that Greece, with the help of France, would establish her supremacy in the Near East within ten years. Kolettes' aims were enthusiastically supported by all those who had fought to win Greece her independence. Between the war and 1848, societies were formed, funds raised, and contact made with the Greeks and other races still under Turkey. Kolettes had also given his support to revolutionary movements in Albania.

It was natural that the news of the national movements in Italy should be sympathetically received by the Greeks. The 'French Party', which had been putting out democratic propaganda, now added nationalist aims to their programme. Their ambitious plan was 'to take Constantinople', but they had no means whatsoever of doing so, and there was no limit to their ingenuousness. Their proclamations were popular with very simple folk, but they caused grave anxiety among the more intelligent, who clearly saw the dangers inherent in such rash designs.

It was at this point that Makrygiannes started a new secret society, with the object of making serious preparations for actions which would be taken only when the moment was ripe. We have already seen that Perrotis' revolutionary proclamation contained irredentist proposals. It was also at this moment that the poet Soutsos wrote *The Greek Awakening*, in the preface to which he expressed the general belief in an imminent Greek Revolution; and *The Political Scene in Greece* in which he stated: 'There is only one way out of the prison in which we are rotting, and that is to extend our frontiers.' Soutsos urged the rebels to unite and attack the Turks without waiting for an order from the Government. The naïve writings of a Macedonian patriot, Zissis Sotiriou, are equally illuminating on this subject.

The Government, threatened by the democratic movement in Athens and the revolts in the provinces, also began to talk of the 'Great Idea', partly in order not to leave the field clear for its opponents, and partly so as to distract the peoples' attention from domestic problems. But feelings ran so high that it almost lost control of the situation and was perilously near war with Turkey. The rebels who had escaped into Greece from Turkish occupied territory were accompanied by a small number of Turco-Albanians. The Government, wanting to use this fact, published a communiqué in the press on 4 May, declaring that the rebels had the support of the Turks, 'the enemies of our faith and of our country'. The very next day, under the direct influence of this announcement, a Greek, who was a Turkish subject and was employed by the Turkish Legation, attempted to assassinate the Turkish Minister, and wounded him in the hand. The newspapers continued to talk of the Turkish invaders and the atrocities they were committing, and further inflamed public opinion. Soutsos, in his *War Song*, accused the Turks of being the first to begin the war by invading Greek territory, and sounded a national call to arms.

This was the state of affairs when, on 2 June, Sir Stratford Canning arrived as a special envoy to 'advise' King Otho, and suggest that he should pursue a constitutional policy, and calm the anti-Turkish feeling. Sir Stratford was still in Greece when certain elements of the 'French Party', then in the opposition, made a violent attack on the Government, accompanied by warlike speeches. They believed that they would bring about an immediate political change if they profited by the public's anger at the news of fresh atrocities. The Government answered that it considered local authorities in Thessaly and not the Turkish Government to be responsible for these atrocities. The Foreign Minister was forced to admit that the news of the Turks joining the rebels to invade Greece, had been designed for domestic consumption.

Greece at this period was far too weak to risk a war with Turkey. All thinking people knew it perfectly well, and they had watched the thoughtless gestures of certain 'patriots' with concern. Mavrocordatos produced a memorandum at the King's invitation in which he declared that he was opposed to any declaration of war without the fulfilment of two preliminary conditions: first, adequate preparations, and secondly a suitable occasion offered either by a war between Russia and Turkey or by a Russian-aided rising of the Slavs in the Balkans. In fact, the feeble Greek State was unable to realise even some of her national ambitions, although the public wanted war, secret societies had armed bands in Epirus and collected funds even from the Greeks in Moldavia and Wallachia, contacts could have been made with representatives of other Balkan countries, and the Greeks still under Turkish rule were impatiently awaiting the hour of their deliverance.

This sketch would not be complete without some indication, however brief, of the Greek people's reactions to the revolutions in other countries, and the liberties they had won. I have already mentioned the way the press and the public hailed the news of the movements in Italy, and of the February Revolution in Paris. News items, leading articles, and commentaries on the course of the first revolutionary movements in Europe filled the larger part of the newspapers, which overflowed with enthusiasm and excitement. It was the same, though to a lesser extent, when they heard of the risings in Austria, Prussia and Bavaria, and finally those of the Slavs and the Hungarians.

These revolutions also inspired the Greek political muse. The poems of Soutsos, Voulgaris, the anonymous 'Constantinopolitan' and Karasoutsas have little poetic value, but they bear witness to the Greeks' passionate love of freedom and the warmth they felt towards France as the champion of democracy. There were as well a number of Greek translations made of works inspired by the Revolution, such as Landremont's *Brève histoire de la dernière Révolution française*, the *Débats a l'Assemblée Nationale Française*, Duvergier de Hauranne's writings on *La Réforme parlementaire* and *La Réforme électorale*, and Thiers' treatise, *Du droit de propriété*.

GREECE

2

IN THE IONIAN ISLANDS

In the Ionian Islands, social and political conditions and differences were more clearly marked than they were in the rest of Greece. The events that took place there were, although on a smaller scale, much more sharply defined.

In the middle of the nineteenth century, the social conditions of the Ionian Islands were still completely medieval. The few old families dating back to the time of the Venetian occupation kept their economic and social privileges intact. They possessed estates worked, under the most precarious conditions, by peasants without any land of their own. These aristocrats looked down not only on their labourers but on the entire population, even the merchants, the professional classes and the intellectuals. They were hated by the people, especially the peasants who had been nursing their anger for centuries. Those of Zante had rebelled in 1628 during the Venetian occupation, and there had been fresh peasant revolts in 1817 and 1819 in Leucadia (Santa Maura) and elsewhere.

Since 1809, after a short occupation by the French following the long occupation by the Venetians, the islands fell into the hands of the British. The Treaty of Paris, on 5 November 1815, had recognised the Islands as a State under the name 'United States of the Seven Ionian Islands', and had put them under the protection of Great Britain, which was given the right to maintain troops there, occupy the citadels and the ports, and control the legislature and the executive. The narrow margin of freedom left to the Ionian States by these restrictions was still further reduced by the Constitution Britain produced in 1817. This gave the British High Commissioner complete control over the legislature, the executive and the judiciary, with the right to veto any decision taken by the legislative and adminstrative body and uncontrolled power over the finances. The right to vote was given only to inhabitants possessing an annual income of over 365 thalers. The deputies were elected from a list drawn up by the Government with the approval of the British authorities. The Chamber, in its turn, elected the Ministers, whose appointment had to be ratified by the High Commissioner. There was no freedom of the press.

The inhabitants of the Seven Islands were violently hostile to both foreign occupation and the illiberal constitution. They wholeheartedly threw themselves into the fight for Greek independence. It was an Ionian, Deny Solomos, the first great figure in Neo-Greek lyricism, who wrote *The Hymn to Freedom*—that freedom which was then being born again in

387

Greece—and condemned the British occupation. The year 1830 opened the period of the great national and political conflicts, for it was the year the Greek State came into being, and henceforth the Ionian Islands strove to join it. In that same year Ionian students took part in the July Revolution in Paris and in the battles on the plains of Italy against the Austrians. When they returned home, they plunged into the fight for freedom. National and political aims went hand in hand: they demanded free elections and a free press, and at the same time sent out nationalist appeals for union with Greece.

The movement was strongest in Cephalonia. Pamphlets were in circulation there even in 1831; and in 1833, when the elections were held, a revolt occurred because the lists of candidates did not contain the name of a single liberal. The conflict reached its height between 1835 and 1843. The few liberal deputies made bold demands for reforms, and when they met with firm opposition from Douglas, the High Commissioner, they began sending memoranda to London and writing in the British press. Douglas thereupon took strong measures. He dissolved one parliament after another, so as to silence the liberals; banned the distribution of Greek newspapers; and exiled the most influential liberals. In spite of these measures there were disturbances in Cephalonia in 1843, when the news arrived of the constitutional revolution in Greece.

In this conflict, the majority of the aristocrats sided with the British, and together with the class of officials which had arisen under the occupation, strengthened the British reactionaries by opposing all concessions and reforms, to secure their own personal ends. They objected to any form of freedom. Thus there was complete antagonism on all fronts, social, national and political, between the two opposing sets of interests.

Lord Seaton, who became High Commissioner in 1833, radically modified British policy. He made friends with the liberals, appointing some of them to official positions, and at the same time developed State education and social insurance, authorised the distribution of Greek newspapers and the foundation of a printing house to publish non-political works, subject to pre-censorship; finally, he left the door open for other reforms. The liberal élite—both intellectual and social—of Corfu (the most prominent being the poet Jules Typaldos, the philosopher P. Vraïlas-Armenis and the jurist N. Zampelis) started to establish friendly relationships with the High Commissioner and his son (who spoke Greek), and seeing their first demands granted, began to believe in the possibility of further improvements.

However these measures made no difference to the situation of the peasants and the other sections of the masses, who remained in a wretched condition in all the islands, especially Cephalonia, the most barren of the seven. Cephalonia had been ruined for several years by a terrible economic crisis. The price of currants, the chief product of the island, had fallen extremely low, and all the landowners—particularly the poor farmers—were completely destitute. The merchant fleet, which had been very flourishing at the time of the Russo-Turkish War, had vegetated since 1830. Taxes and stamp duties were a heavy burden on these impoverished people, and they were skinned by the moneylenders. Their possessions were frequently sold by auction and several went to prison for their debts. Their powers of physical and moral resistance were almost exhausted, and the Government did nothing to lighten their burden. What was more, they saw what was happening in Greece and noticed that everyone there had equal rights, and that social distinctions and privileges were unknown. So the Cephalonians even more than the other islanders wanted union with Greece rather than interior reform.

As, in Cephalonia, this frame of mind extended to the middle class and the handful of liberal aristocrats, that island, unlike the others, had a certain homogeneity.

When the intellectual élite of Corfu heard of the liberal movements in Europe, they thought the moment had come for them to win the fundamental rights and liberties the Ionians lacked. N. Zambelis, the jurist, drew up and sent to the Colonial Secretary a memorandum describing the Islands' pitiful situation, and supporting the people's demands for a free press and an unrestricted electoral system.

The judge and poet J. Typaldos sent a similar memorandum to his friend Edmund Seaton, the High Commissioner's son. But the reformists wanted to give their petition a more official and general character, and also, perhaps, to show their loyalty to the Queen. If their demands were represented as coming from rebels against the protectorate, they would doubtless be rejected. Therefore, despite the disapproval of the aristocracy and officialdom, the 'Booklovers' Society', a club composed of Corfu's intellectual élite, organised an official banquet in Seaton's honour, for 4 April 1848. It was the perfect occasion for the liberals to state their case. The President of the Society, P. Vraïlas-Armenis, began by proposing the Queen's health, and after a number of other toasts, he proposed one to Greece, phrased in the diplomatic words: 'to the good fortune and prosperity of our beloved Greece, to the nation that protects us, and to all civilised peoples'. Afterwards a letter was sent to the Colonial Secretary demanding freedom of the press, a direct and secret ballot for the elections to the legislature, and the creation of an army composed of Ionian citizens. The people of Corfu, however, were not satisfied with the tone or the content of either the toasts drunk at the banquet or the letter to the Colonial Secretary. They considered them humiliating, and inconsistent with their ardent desire to proclaim union with Greece. A crowd formed outside the Society's headquarters, and demonstrated against its members and their line of action.

In the meantime the High Commissioner, who was in favour of reform and saw the necessity of making certain concessions, reduced a number of taxes and lowered the salaries of government officials, which had rankled with the masses. He also got the British Government to grant freedom of the press and permit the Chamber to vote expenditure. But Seaton did not summon a General Assembly (which would have modified the Constitution), but only the Chamber itself, which at a special session in May 1848 passed both measures in the form laid down by the British Government.

In Cephalonia, the news of the European revolutions fell on willing ears, and the revolt which broke out shortly afterwards aimed at the immediate expulsion of the British. The revolutionary leaders came from the urban population, and were for the most part lawyers, merchants, artisans and priests, as well as a few liberal aristocrats. The leading personalities were G. Livadas, a jurist, who had been one of the fighters for Greek Independence, and J. Typaldos, another jurist, who had previously been a member of the Supreme Court of Appeal in Greece; Elias Zervos, a barrister, who had been behind the risings in 1843; K. N. Phokas, known as 'The Republican', a Doctor of Law, and another ex-soldier of the War of Independence; Pretenteris, a priest, and J. Metaxas-Loutsos.

Their revolutionary campaign had considerable effect, and numbers of citizens came to join them, expressing both their hatred of the British and their collaborators and their selfless patriotism. The peasants were particularly swayed by the movement, for they hoped that a revolution would abolish bankruptcy proceedings and I.O.Us, and exterminate the aristocracy and the moneylenders.

From the beginning of March the people were visibly in a state of ferment. The British and their friends were openly attacked in the clubs and at patriotic banquets. A series of organised incidents showed that the revolutionaries were resolute and determined to accept no compromise. On the first Monday in Lent, which is a holiday in Greece, drunks staggered through the streets insulting the aristocrats who collaborated with foreigners and oppressed the people. On 18 March, Livadas, Phokas, Zervos, Pretenteris and Metaxas publicly burnt an announcement made by Zambelis, to the effect that he was going to publish in England a newspaper upholding the rights of the Ionians. As they did so they shouted: 'No truck with the British!'

There was a rumour that on the Feast of the Annunciation—6 April, the Greek national holiday—the peasants were going to descend on the town, loot the banks and the archives and open the gaols. Nothing of the sort occurred, but the people's patriotic fervour found another outlet: a vast crowd accompanied the Greek consul through the streets of Argostolion to the church, where a *Te Deum* was sung. The majority of the clergy, and even a number of aristocrats, rivalled the people in all the ways in which they expressed their national and political feelings. As the procession passed, the Greek flag and the Tricolour fluttered out of the windows of clubs and houses. At every moment there were shouts of 'Union with Greece! Liberty and Fraternity! Long live the French Republic!' That evening a banquet was held, and toasts were drunk to the Union and to Freedom. The national holiday was celebrated in the villages by hoisting the Greek flag and by illuminations. Some days later, on Good Friday, when the procession bearing the Holy Sindon (Christ's shroud) stopped in front of the British Residency, and the Bishop was preparing to say the prayer for the Queen, the same revolutionary leaders mentioned above leapt upon him, cursed him for a flatterer, and snatched the Holy Sindon from him.

Whilst all this was going on, the news reached Cephalonia of the banquet held and the memorandum sent by the reformists of Corfu. The Cephalonians were furious and declared that the reforms were a mockery, and that they made no basic difference to the Ionians' wretched condition.

Unrest continued throughout the months of May, June, July and August. The revolutionaries completed their organisation and the movement spread; its leaders contacted Cephalonians in Greece, and political societies in France and Italy. There was talk of help from France: if the patriots could hold out for a month in the countryside, French troops would then reinforce them. . . . Town and country people began to amass ammunition. The movement was so widespread that it was no secret to the police and the British Resident, Baron Everton. He informed Lord Seaton, but the High Commissioner was sceptical and told him to keep his head.

The revolution had a triple aim: national, political and social. The oath taken by the revolutionaries was as follows: 'I swear by the Holy Virgin and by Jesus Crucified, my Christ, to give my life for the love I bear my country, and to do my utmost to drive out the tyrant that I may live in freedom.' 'Free the isles and drive out the English' was the propagandists' slogan, and their anthem called for 'freedom and union with Greece'. Their political object was to do away with the British local authorities and form a provisional government. Their social aim was to seize the law-courts and the archives, burn the documents relating to their debts and mortgages, and free people in prison for their debts.

The revolution broke out on the morning of 26 September. It was precipitated by the reactionaries who, alarmed at the prospect of a revolution, and dissatisfied with Seaton's proposals for reform, thought that by causing a premature outbreak of the revolution they would on the one hand ensure its failure, and on the other throw cold water on the High Commissioner's liberal ardour. At the break of day, two bodies of peasants marched on the two small towns on the island. About two hundred revolutionaries marched on Argostolion. Immediately the Resident was informed, he sent to deal with them an N.C.O. and twelve men who arrived in time to occupy a bridge and bar the insurgents' way. In the engagement that followed the British casualties were two killed and one wounded, and seven of the rebels were killed and a number wounded. The Resident had the time to bring up fresh British troops and the constabulary, who dispersed the rebels. Thus five hundred conspirators who were waiting to rise in the town had to remain inactive.

Lixuri, the other town, had no garrison, and forty peasants entered it without meeting any resistance. They were led by a man carrying the Greek flag, followed by priests carrying a cross, and shouting: 'Long live Freedom and the Fatherland!' The peasants marching behind sang a translation of the old revolutionary song of the Girondins:

> *Fais-toi aussi de ta poitrine*
> *Un bouclier pour la Patrie.*

When they reached the centre of the town, they disarmed the few police they found there, occupied the law-courts and freed the prisoners. The moneylenders and the rich people, as they had done at Argostolion, gathered up their papers and their money and fled across the sea. In the meantime the Resident, having dispersed the rebels at Argostolion, concentrated his forces and attacked Lixuri by sea. He drove back the rebels from the shore with his guns, and forced them to evacuate the town. They held out for two days in the mountains, but were then defeated as the British were better armed. Lord Seaton arrived in the interval, and called upon the people to remain calm. Afterwards he imposed a fine of 1,600 thalers on them to cover the cost of quelling the revolt. British troops and the constabulary took money and belongings from the peasants' houses to make up the sum, Some of the revolutionary leaders escaped to the Peloponnese, and the rest were captured.

The British were merciful towards the instigators of the rebellion. Although they accused them of high treason, they decided to try them by a civil, not a military, court and in the end there was no trial. An amnesty was granted some months later on the occasion of the arrival of a new High Commissioner.

A month after the rising, a law was passed granting freedom of the press. The first paper to appear in the Ionian Islands was Elias Zervos' *Phileftheros* ('The Liberal'), in Cephalonia. It immediately started a violent campaign against the British rule. Other newspapers followed in 1849.

The new High Commissioner, Sir Henry Ward, did not follow his predecessor's policy. He restricted the press, deported journalists and opposed electoral reform. The result was that in August 1849 there broke out a more serious revolution than that of 1848. It lasted several days and much blood was shed. The military courts condemned twenty-one people to death by hanging and inflicted severe penalties on dozens of others. The Ionian Islands continued to fight until 1864, when their wishes were granted and they were united with Greece.

THE RUSSIA OF NICHOLAS I
IN 1848

BENJAMIN GORIELY

According to the Soviet historian Tarlé, Nicholas I felt that revolution was imminent not because he appreciated the revolutionaries' strength or the aspirations of the masses, but because he realised the weakness of the European monarchs and their governments.

In 1846 he said to a Danish diplomat: 'We used to be three sovereigns in Europe; now there are only one and a half: I no longer include Prussia, and Austria only counts as a half.'

When Nicholas received the first news from France, he exclaimed to the officers of the Guard: 'To horse, gentlemen! The French Republic has been proclaimed.' He knew in his heart, though, that he was too isolated to intervene in the affairs of Europe. He was lonely and discouraged, and the only person he entirely trusted was Paskievich; although he told him to 'crush the rabble', it is clear from his letters to the Viceroy of Poland that he neither could nor would declare war. In the middle of 1848, when he felt danger threatened, he put a sanitary cordon between himself and Europe. Besides his alarm at the sudden turn of events in Berlin, Vienna and all the States of the German Confederation, and the threat of a Polish rising and an invasion from Posen, he was apprehensive of Great Britain: since the Whigs had come into power in 1846, she had opposed Russia's influence in Europe. Nicholas I remembered what Palmerston had told the Russian Ambassador, Pozzo di Borgo in 1837: that Europe had been asleep too long, and was now waking up to prevent the series of aggressive actions for which the Czar was preparing on various frontiers.

On 3 April 1848 Nicholas sent Queen Victoria a letter inviting the only power still unaffected by the revolution to come to terms with Russia in order to restore order and save Europe from disaster.

When the wave of revolution swept on unchecked, Nicholas published a proclamation which, whilst it condemned all attacks on lawful authority, announced that Russia would not interfere in European affairs 'unless anarchy crossed her frontiers'. Once Nicholas had silenced the voices in France and Germany calling for war against his own people, he was driven by the events of 1848 to pursue a policy of such cruelty as Russia had never known before.

And yet from the moment Nicholas I came to the throne he had introduced so ferocious a reign of terror that historians refer to his epoch as 'the cruel century'. Men were arrested on the slightest hint of liberalism; they were deported for the most trivial offences, sentenced to a thousand or two thousand strokes of the rod for a subversive statement, and hanged for the smallest act of insubordination. The élite of Russia was decimated, and especially the intellectuals. The Czarist police closed the club formed by the first utopian socialists, who, from 1845 onward, banded together under Petrashevsky. Towards the end of 1848, Petrashevsky hit on the idea of transforming his literary club, which studied foreign authors, into an active revolutionary organisation. All its members were arrested on 23 April 1849. They included Dostoevsky, Plestcheiev, Durov and many other writers and scholars. The charge read:

'The dangerous doctrines which caused disturbances and riots throughout Western Europe and threatened to destroy the peace and well-being of the nations, have unfortunately had a repercussion in our own country. A handful of nonentities, the majority of them young and immoral, has tried to ride rough-shod over the sacred rights of religion, law and property.'

On 16 November 1849 all the accused were condemned to death, but at the moment they were mounting the scaffold, their punishment was commuted to imprisonment in Siberia. Dostoevsky, who was sentenced to four years in prison, gives a picture of conditions there in his novel *The House of the Dead*. Petrashevsky himself, an enthusiastic disciple of Fourier and Saint-Simon and a great champion of the peasantry, was sentenced to deportation for life, and died in Siberia. The Czar persecuted not only the revolutionaries and the liberals, such as Herzen, Ogarev, Belinsky, Chernyskevsky, Dobroliubov, Turgenev and Saltykov, but even Slavophiles like Khomyakov, although he opposed the 1848 Revolution. It was forbidden to print the name Belinsky and the newspapers used instead the periphrase: 'critic of the school of Gogol'. All criticism of the government and government institutions was forbidden. The Czar scented hatred of the régime on all sides, and suspected everyone. Even reactionaries and royalists, like Bulgarin and Pogodin were watched; and Count Uvarov, himself, Nicholas's Minister and the theorist of autocracy, in time became suspect: the Czar, for whom discipline meant blind obedience, abhorred all intellectual activity. On one occasion he read a report which ended with the word 'progress'. 'Progress!' he stormed, 'What Progress? That word shall be struck out of the official vocabulary.' This war on the intellect was all the more fantastic as it was at that period that the Russian intelligentsia, imbued with the theories of freedom of expression and argument, was at its most brilliant. Alexander Hertzen, speaking of the 'era of cruelty' from 1825 to 1855, described it as one of 'outward slavery and inner freedom'. It must be appreciated that Nicholas I's unexampled repression of any attempt at emancipation was the logical outcome of his political beliefs. The Czar's rage was uncontrollable, and though he was temporarily successful when he smashed the Hungarian Revolution, that was largely due to the hesitancy of the moderates and the European middle-class liberals' fear of the peoples' fight to free themselves from economic and national slavery.

Nicholas I gave Uvarov the task of systemising his policy, and as a belated answer to the three principles of the French Revolution, Uvarov summed up his programme, in the words: 'Orthodoxy—Autocracy—Popular nationalism.'[1]

The first paragraph of the *Fundamental Principles of the State*—a kind of government catechism published at this period—explains the conception of Autocracy:

'The Czar of all the Russias is the fearless and omnipotent sovereign ruler. He must be obeyed not only through fear of him but through fear of God, for He ordains it.'

The relations between the Czar and the Church were defined as follows (paragraph 64): 'The Russian Czar is a Christian Sovereign. He is the supreme guardian of the faith of the Orthodox religion. He watches over the worship and good order of the Holy Church. In that sense he is the head of the Church.'

Nicholas I considered the Church as an instrument of his obscurantist policy, as a means of exerting pressure on the masses and creating the conception of a double duty to God and to himself. It is not surprising, therefore, that he condemned Professor Solntsev, who in his lecture at Kazan University had developed the thesis that the Law was based on reason and not on the Scriptures.

The students at the Military Academy were taught that Christ's greatness consisted in the fact that He was a 'model of discipline and obedience to the secular government'. Recruits at the beginning of their twenty-five years in the army were told that God had placed men in their respective careers according to His will. 'You, too, were chosen by the Divine Will to be soldiers. God is the Great Czar. He ordained that you should be soldiers before you were born.'

Children in the towns and the villages were rounded up for the army by government agents, and their families were unable to correspond with them once they had been conscripted.

[1] The Russian word *narodnost* corresponds to the German *Volkstum*, but there is no exact English equivalent.

So as to prevent the faithful from escaping the control of the Church, Nicholas I organised religious homogeneity in Russia, persecuting the schismatic Raskol, the Dukhobors (who later greatly influenced Leo Tolstoy) and all the other sects. The peasants of the western provinces, that it to say of White Russia and Lithuania, were forcibly converted to the Orthodox Church. Flogging, deportation or prison were the lot of the recalcitrant.

Nicholas I loathed State education. He looked upon the University as the source of all evil ideas. He suppressed the Chairs of Philosophy, and Uvarov introduced theology and church history as obligatory subjects in all the faculties. Frightened by the ideas spread by the revolution he stopped the teaching of European law; logic and psychology had to be taught by theologians; and the historian Granovsky was prevented from finishing his course of lectures on the Reformation. The University's task consisted in forming 'faithful sons of the Orthodox Church, loyal subjects of the Czar, and good and useful citizens.'

In 1847, Uvarov began reforming secondary schooling. Latin and Greek were suppressed, so that 'young people shall not be corrupted by the Greek authors'. The Russian writers Pushkin, Lermontov, Gogol and Griboedov could only publish their work subject to a strict pre-censorship. There were twenty-two different censorship authorities.

Nicholas I's policy and Uvarov's theories were spread by official publications, particularly the review, *Maiak* (' The Lighthouse'), which appeared from 1840 to 1850. *Maiak* attacked European culture as being contrary to the Scriptures. Western Europe, it claimed, continued the Roman pagan tradition whence sprang the revolutions, free thought, the Reformation and the Papacy. The Russian and Christian East would build the Kingdom of God on the ruins of the West. Incidentally, this idea of 'the degenerate West' was shared by the Slavophiles. *Maiak* condemned the whole of Russian literature and first and foremost the works of Belinsky. Pushkin was influenced by the French Encyclopedists, and his language was a synthesis of French constructions and the vernacular; so he became unpopular as a result of the campaign against French and English influences. Soon, Uvarov also attacked the influence of German culture, which, through Madame de Staël, had made a great impression on the men and women of the 'forties.

The Russian intelligentsia in Nicholas I's reign was no longer recruited solely from the nobility. More and more students came from the families of merchants, the liberal professions, artisans and, especially, the lower clergy. This was due both to the beginnings of industrialism in Russia and to the influence of revolutionary ideas coming from France. The young Russian intellectuals were eager to learn, and they formed numerous societies to study French and German authors. The result was that the Universities, with the exception of one or two professors who supported the régime, immediately took the lead in the revolutionary movement. It is plain that the young intelligentsia was formed by the great Russian classic writers whose masterpieces crown the highest point of her cultural development. In spite of police persecution, literary societies, the first clandestine newspapers and forbidden books went on spreading in Czarist Russia. Nicholas I, believing that the revolutionaries consisted of a number of agitators and demagogues, put Count Benckendorff at the head of his Intelligence Department, as an attaché to the Imperial Chancellery. Count Benckendorff had distinguished himself in the suppression of the Decembrist movement.

All the Russian revolutionary movements followed the theory and practice of the Decembrists. At the beginning of the nineteenth century, the young Russian aristocracy, mainly composed of educated officers who had served in the Imperial Guard in the war against Napoleon, had been greatly impressed by European culture and democratic institutions. They therefore formed the first secret society on the western model. Masonic Lodges already existed in Russia and numerous Free Masons helped form the Society of Salvation, or 'the society of true and loyal sons of the mother country'. In 1818 this organisation turned into the 'Common Weal Society' and gained an increasing number of adherents, but it lacked homogeneity. A congress of delegates, which met in Moscow in 1821 to reorganise the society, wanted to get rid of the lukewarm hangers-on, so the leaders decided to dissolve it and form a new one with a more clearly-defined programme. N. I. Turgenev took charge of the movement in St Petersburg, the two brothers Fonvizin in Moscow, and Jakushkin in Smolensk.

The 'Common Weal Society' was divided into a northern and a southern section. A new association was formed in 1825 under the name of 'The United Slavs', and comprised delegates from the Slav peoples of the west and the south: Czechs, Slovaks, Croats, Slovenes, Ruthenians, and Serbs from Lusatia. It was affiliated to the 'southern section', which was also in close contact with the 'Patriots' Society' of Poland.

In his book *Zur Russischen Geschichte und Religions-Philosophie (Soziologische Skizzen)* T. G. Masaryk wrote of the Decembrists:

'At the start, the aims of all these societies were confused; they were a mixture of humanism, rationalism and demands for literary, political and social freedom. Little by little they became more defined. The decision to murder the tyrant grew stronger and stronger until on 14 December (whence the name 'Decembrists') the revolution broke out. It was the first attempt at a mass rising in the new Russia, but it was primarily an aristocratic venture. The war against Napoleon had created a general feeling of strength and independence. And so on Alexander's death the revolt began.'

The majority of the Decembrists were liberals, who favoured a constitutional monarchy. They demanded several reforms: amelioration of corporal punishments (not their abolition), a reduction of the twenty-five year period of military service and relaxation of the censorship. The most important reform demanded by the secret societies was a judicial one: the introduction of juries, officially recognised counsels, and public trials.

Both the northern and southern sections had their 'intellectuals' and their 'emotionalists'. The 'intellectual' in the north was Nikita Muraviev and the 'emotionalist' the poet Ryléev. In the south, the 'intellectual' was Pestel and the 'emotionalists' Muraviev-Apostol and Bestujev-Riumin. The emotionalists, eager for action, blamed Pestel for his dilatoriness and he blamed them for their haste. But there were more serious divergencies of opinion between Nikita Muraviev and Pestel. The 'northern' theorist supported a constitutional and federative monarchy, with Russia divided into thirteen States like the United States of America. The capital, they decided, should be transferred to Moscow. Each State should be completely self-governing, and there should be only four Ministries representing the whole federation: a Ministry of Foreign Affairs, a Ministry of War and Ministries for the Navy and Finance. This plan of Muraviev's was widely approved.

Pestel, however, was still the most prominent figure in the Decembrist movement. Among the numerous plans drafted, Pestel's were the most carefully and clearly worked out. He advocated not only political but also social reform. He made a thorough study of the social movement in France and England, and arrived at the conclusion that a revolution was essential to reorganise outworn institutions. He pointed to France's example, where the Restoration had been obliged to retain the new institutions created by the Revolution.

Pestel was a German by birth, and had received his education at Dresden. In Russia, he helped edit *Russkaia Pravda* ('Russian Truth'), in which he often expressed his own point of view. He believed in a republic with a strong central government, and strongly opposed the idea of a federation. His idea was that revolution would give Russia a transitory régime preparing the way for a republic, so that he decided it would be necessary to form a provisional government and even chose possible Ministers from among the leaders of his secret society. This provisional government was to have full executive powers but no authority to make laws. Its objects would be to bring about:

1. Equal rights for all classes of society
2. The formation of municipal, departmental, regional and State councils
3. The creation of a 'People's guard', or militia
4. The introduction of the jury system
5. Equal periods of military service for all classes
6. The abolition of a standing army
7. Preparations for elections to a Constituent Assembly which would devise the future form of government and legislation

Pestel proposed that the secret society should continue in existence for the term of the provisional government, that was to say for between eight and ten years, 'so as to create a new attitude in people's minds to fit them for the new order'. Certain members of the Society were alarmed at this proposal, seeing Pestel as a new dictator, for he was thought ambitious and cruel. The northern section transferred Trubetskoy to Kiev to keep an eye on 'this ambitious rogue, who is not another Washington but a Bonaparte.'

Pestel was the most radical and the most far-sighted of all the Decembrists. Herzen, who came under his direct influence, called him 'a socialist before the days of socialism'.

Pestel was, in fact, opposed to parliamentarism. 'The essence of our time', he said, 'lies in the conflict between the masses and aristocrats of all kinds whether they owe their position to birth or to wealth.'

Whilst making provision for the emancipation of the serfs, Pestel wanted the freed land to be owned collectively. He was the first to speak of work as 'the poor people's capital', and he planned that the future government should protect the poor against the rich, pointing out that poor people fall ill too and become unable to work, and at the end of their days have no means of earning a livelihood.

Pestel understood the issues in the people's war against the feudal nobility, but he was even more concerned with the rise of 'the aristocracy of wealth', which was socially more harmful as it could buy public opinion and use it to control the masses.

He was not satisfied with constitutional reforms. His aim was to change man's nature by changing his institutions. It was that which made him not merely a republican but also a democrat and a socialist. Believing in the necessity for a strong, united State, he provided for the Russification of every race living on Russian soil, all of whom—with the exception of the Poles, were to be 'fused into a single nation'.

Pestel looked upon Russian Poland as politically and culturally an independent country, and in planning the unification of religion in

Russia, he excluded the Polish Catholics. The constitutionalist, T. N. Turgenev, on the other hand, as well as Prince Orlov and Dimitriev-Mamonov, demanded the integral union with Russia not only of Russian but also of Austrian and German Poland. On the Polish question, Pestel was in agreement with Alexander I, who had respected the Polish Constitution, and even planned to give Poland back her former eastern provinces.

Pestel recognised the national rights only of the larger nations, and considered that the smaller ones should be sacrificed to assist the State's free development. That is why he defended Poland's independence, on condition that she signed a treaty of alliance with Russia and had the same political and social régime. He wanted the suppression of the feudal and plutocratic aristocracies. He refused to recognise the other Slav races, although the 'United Slavs' was affiliated to the southern section of his secret society. Orlov and Dimitriev-Mamonov, however, devised a plan for a Slav Federation attached to Russia, and comprising 'the Hungarians, the Serbs, and all the Slav peoples'.

Pestel was the first to make a thorough study of the Jewish question. Not only was he a 'socialist before socialism' but also a Zionist before the word was thought of. Looking upon the Jews in Russia and Poland as a 'State within a State', he proposed forming a committee composed of an equal number of Jews and Gentiles to find a means of breaking down Jewish particularism. He foresaw the possibility of creating a Jewish State in the Middle-East. There were two million Jews in Poland and Russia and they needed to be helped in this 'gigantic enterprise'. Pestel remarked that 'such a mass of people looking for a country of their own should not have much difficulty in overcoming any obstacle put in their way'.

One subject on which the members of both sections were in agreement was that an armed rising should take place in the capital, and a manifesto should be published demanding the Czar's abdication and the formation of a provisional government.

The revolt broke out on 14 December 1825. Four crack regiments refused to take the oath of loyalty to the new Czar. But Prince Trubetskoy, who was to have led the revolt, was not to be found. The other Decembrists lost their heads, and the soldiers waited for orders that never came. Nicholas, in rage, sent his cavalry against them, but it was driven back. He then ordered the artillery to open fire. When the first casualties fell, the rest stampeded. Several of the leaders were arrested, including the two Muraviev brothers. Bestujev-Riumin and S. Muraviev rescued them, however, and with the troops under their command attacked and captured the town of Vassilchikov. But they were finally defeated near Belaya Tserkov by troops that had remained loyal to the Czar. The revolt was over. It failed because it came too soon, before the revolutionaries had decided on either a common programme or a practicable plan of action. They were also taken unawares by Alexander's death and the army's disobedience.

When the Czar began reprisals, Benckendorff's police arrested one thousand members of the secret societies. The five leaders, Pestel, Ryléev, Bestujev-Riumin, Serge Muraviev and Kakhovsky were condemned to death: three of them to be beheaded and two, Pestel and Ryléev, to be quartered. The Czar changed the sentence on the first three to one of hanging.

The remainder of the hundred and twenty-one accused were sent to prison. The officers were reduced to the ranks, and the ordinary soldiers flogged and sent to Siberia. Those condemned to death were tortured before their execution. It must be added that the wives of the Decembrists played a gallant rôle in the movement. Some years later, round about 1850, some of them saw Dostoevsky in Siberia, and gave him ten roubles hidden in a Bible, the only book allowed to be read in the prison. This Bible had a decisive effect on Dostoevsky's life, for it led him to utopian socialism and popular Christianity.

The Decembrist revolt had only just been smashed when Nicholas was faced with peasant risings. The *moujiks* had heard rumours of what was going on in St Petersburg, but often their informants were the soldiers, and they received distorted versions which they revised to suit their own hopes and wishes. They were told that the capital was in an uproar, their masters had been arrested, and 'Generals were being slapped'; so they thought that the moment had come to rise against the landowners. Divov, who replaced Nesselrode as Minister for Foreign Affairs, wrote in his private diary:

'There is talk of a few peasant revolts. They are refusing to pay their dues to the landowners, saying that the late Emperor had freed them. Such rumours are certainly the result of the Fourteenth of December.'

Divov was not the only one to believe that the Decembrist rising had thrown the country into turmoil. Nicholas I was obliged to publish a proclamation on 12 May 1826 denying that the late Emperor had abolished feudal dues and freed the serfs. Benckendorff remarked that: 'the serfs, encouraged by criminal promises and false hopes, had refused to obey their masters, and in many places they had revolted.'

The situation in the countryside obliged Nicholas I to study the peasant question, and on 6 December 1826 he created a 'secret committee' for this purpose. He then forbade the landowners to split up peasant families and to sell a serf without leaving him his land. He gave the peasants the impression that though they belonged to the nobles, the land belonged to them. But the groping agrarian policy of Nicholas I did not stop the peasants' revolts. The result was quite the opposite: discontent grew from year to year and reached its height in 1848 and 1849. The Minister for the Interior showed how many peasants' revolts there were between 1825 and 1854 in the following table:

1826–30	41
1831–34	44
1835–39	59
1840–44	101
1845–49	172
1850–55	137
	554

This total, though, is far below the true figure, and according to experts should be multiplied many times. There were 1,622 assassinations and attempted assassinations of landowners in 1841 alone.

Throughout his life, Nicholas I was afraid of a revolution. Between the Decembrists' conspiracy and the 1848 Revolution, he saw the risings in Spain in 1820; the risings in Piedmont in 1831; the French Revolution in July 1830; the Polish insurrection from 1830 to 1831; and various riots in France. So Nicholas, who looked upon man as an automaton or a slave, set himself up as the head of the Counter-Revolution in Europe, thereby earning the support and respect of the Austrian and Prussian reactionaries.

His first act as 'the chief *gendarme* of the forces of European reaction' was to ask the British Government to hand over the Decembrist, N. Turgenev. He made his demand first through his Ambassador to Great Britain and then directly to the Duke of Wellington, who was appointed British Ambassador to Russia on 3 March 1826. Nicholas I made this request verbally, so as to leave the British Government free to choose the pretext for expelling Turgenev. The British opposition, however, which was in touch with Turgenev, got wind of the Czar's plan, and Canning did not comply with the Czar's wishes. Nicholas, however, wished to create a precedent and officially informed Wellington that the Decembrist conspiracy was part of the European revolutionary movement, and that Turgenev was a dangerous character, in touch with secret societies in Paris and London.

In 1836 there appeared in *Telescope*, a bi-monthly review published in Moscow, an article headed *A Philosophical Letter*. It was a stinging attack on Uvarov's official ideology and produced the effect of a bomb. Its author was Count Chaadaev, an aristocrat and one of the dandies of the English Club in Moscow, who encouraged Puskhin and was a great friend of the Decembrists. He had, in fact, been accused of having a hand in the rising on 14 December, but was released for want of proof. Before it was published, *The Philosophical Letter* was read in manuscript by his intimate friends; then copies were made and passed from hand to hand—like Griboedov's *Woe from Wit*—some even being sent abroad. It was originally written in French and then translated into Russian. It is a typical example of clandestine writing, and one can see what a storm it produced from contemporary accounts quoted in Charles Quénet's *Tchaadaiev et les lettres philosophiques.* Alexander Herzen who at this time was in exile at Viatka relates in his *Thoughts and Reminiscences:*

'I was sitting quietly at my desk . . . when the postman arrived with the new number of the *Telescope*. One has to live in exile at the back of beyond to know what it means to have something new to read. Naturally I put everything aside and I started on the *Telescope*. "A Philosophical Letter"— written to some woman—no signature. There was a note to say that it had been written by a Russian, but in French and that this was a translation. That put me off, and I started on something else.

'Eventually I turned to the *Letter*. After one or two pages, I was struck by the writer's gravity and intensity of feeling: every word was redolent of a long period of suffering, to which the author was accustomed, but which still hurt. Only people who have had a long time to think things over, and have learnt much not from books but from life, write like that . . . I went on reading and the theme of the letter began to develop: it was an accusation of Russia, the protest of a man who, in return for everything he has suffered, wants to say at least a part of what he had stored up in his heart.

'I had to stop twice for a breathing-space and a chance to let my emotions and thoughts settle; then I went on and on reading. And this thing was translated into Russian from an unknown writer. . . . I was afraid I was going mad. I read it to Vitberg, then to S., a young teacher at the Viatka College, then I read it again to myself.

'It is extremely likely that the same kind of thing was going on in various country towns and big cities and in the houses of the aristocracy. Some months later, I learnt the author's name.'

Further on Herzen describes the impressions these remarkable pages produced on people in the 'forties.

'Chaadaev's letter was in its own way a "last word", a closing of the door, a parting shot fired into the night: maybe a dying word before the cataclysm? Or perhaps an S.O.S., a cry for help? Maybe it heralded the dawn—or proclaimed no dawn would come. Whatever it meant, one was shaken to one's feet.

What significance could there be, one felt, in two or three pages of a monthly review? Yet its message was so imperative, its appeal in columns unused to frank speech so forcible, that Chaadaev's letter shook every thinking person in Russia.'

According to Chaadaev, the world had learnt nothing from the Russians, for individually and collectively they were poverty-stricken—empty—dead. He asserted that any people's existence was only justified when it lived according to some philosophy, and that Russia had not given the world a single new idea, she had no intellectual mainspring.

'In Russia', he said, 'no one has a definite rôle in life; no one cultivates good habits for their own sake or follows a logical line of conduct; there is nothing to sympathise with or warm to; nothing is lasting, everything disappears leaving no impression on the outside world or on oneself.' He complained that Russia in the 'forties was outside the civilised world, and that she had no traditions like western Europe. 'Everyone born in the West learns in his cradle, in his games, in his mother's caresses notions of duty, justice, law and order.' The Russian, on the other hand, learnt nothing. 'He has no links with the past or the future.' He had no sense of continuity, and was a random wanderer in the world. 'He lacks mental balance and a sense of logic.'

Russia had no history, only a series of events, and yet the Russians belonged 'on a social plane to the West', and their future was dependent on that of European society. They would therefore have to become an integral part of it, otherwise they would be 'swept body and soul into the maelstrom'.

'Let us then do all in our power', Chaadaev concludes by saying, 'to lay the foundations of a new life for those that come after us. We cannot bequeath them what we ourselves have never possessed: beliefs, opinions based on experience, a strongly marked personality, and a philosophy developed in the course of a long, active, rich intellectual life. So let us at least leave them a few ideas, which, although they have not been handed down to us from one generation to another, will have at any rate some element of tradition, and therefore a little more force and value than our own thoughts. We shall have thus done something for posterity and not wasted our lives on this earth.'

Chaadaev regarded the history of mankind as simply that of the Christian Church: the process of establishing the 'Kingdom of God' on earth. In spite of all man's faults of omission and commission, Chaadaev still believed that God's Kingdom had in a way been founded, for its principle was one of limitless progress, and it contained the germ of everything it needed for its eventual fulfilment on earth.

But he argued that Russia, owing to her isolation, had been left without culture or religion, for the Russians were Christians only on the surface. They were merely blind, superficial and often clumsy imitators.

'Cut off by our schism, nothing of what was happening in Europe reached us. We stood apart from the world's great venture. Although we called ourselves Christians, when Christianity advanced in majesty along the path traced by its Divine Founder, we stood still. Whilst the entire world was building anew, we created nothing: we remained squatting in our hovels of logs and thatch. We had no part in mankind's new future, and though we were Christians, the fruits of Christianity were not for us.'

Chaadaev wrote his *Philosophical Letter* as the result of the failure of the Decembrist movement and his discovery of the theories of Joseph de Maistre. He may also, according to Charles Quénet, have been influenced by *Le Génie du Christianisme*.

After it had published the 'Letter', *Telescope* was banned, the censor dismissed, and Chaadaev branded a 'monster' by the Church and a 'madman' by Nicholas. The Czar's comment on the article was: 'In my opinion this hotch-potch of insulting absurdities is the work of a madman.' Chaadaev was therefore declared mentally unbalanced and put under police and medical supervision. He was confined to his room, except for one walk a day, and a drunken doctor appointed by the police came each day to see him. Some months later, he was considered to have been sufficiently punished, and the doctor's visits ceased. In the midst of these vicissitudes, Chaadaev learnt of Pushkin's tragic death.

At the period when the *Philosophical Letter* appeared, there were two trends of thought taking shape in Russia: Occidentalism and Slavophilism. Both had previously been ill-defined tendencies, but the *Telescope's* article precipitated their crystallisation. The Occidentalists were represented by Stankevich's Philosophical Society, frequented by Belinsky, Bakunin, Granovsky and Kireevsky (who later became one of the most prominent Slavophiles), and many other writers and propagandists. The Philosophical Society studied the German philosophers with enthusiasm, and claimed kinship with Hegel, whilst Herzen, the future leading spirit of the Occidentalist movement, formed a club to spread the theories of the French socialists. The Slavophiles, Khomyakov, Kireevsky, Aksakov and others, despite their antipathy for Europe, took Schelling's philosophic system as their starting point. Chaadaev's *Letter* encouraged the Slavophiles to turn to the philosophy of history and the development of a Russian philosophy of history, whilst the Occidentalists were occupied with the problem whether Russia, once she followed Europe's lead, would have to pass through the same stages of social development as the West. It was discovered a century later that this was not so: as Russia had never known feudalism, she passed from autocracy to socialism without going through a period of unrestricted capitalism. Henceforth we can say that Occidentalism was rationalist and scientific and was moving towards materialism, whilst the Slavophiles held a religious and traditionalist viewpoint. They took over the slogan 'Orthodoxy—Autocracy—Popular Nationalism (*Narodnost*)', and extolled the virtues of mystic experience and instinctive action.

At the beginning the two movements were clearly connected. Chaadaev himself, who was so attached to Europe and so fierce an opponent of the 'fanatical Slavs', was a religious man. And Tyutchev, the great Russian poet, who as we shall see further on was hostile to the 1848 Revolution, was a Europe-lover. Before the two movements hardened and the split took place, they were united by their faith in the Russian people and its future, by their love of truth, justice and freedom, and by their determination to emancipate the peasantry. They were opponents, but in no wise enemies, for there was sympathy and respect between them. Bakunin was the first to demand a split, which finally took place in 1845.

Thanks to Herzen, Occidentalism took a clearly revolutionary turn. In 1840 Bakunin went abroad, where he threw himself heart and soul into the revolutionary movement in Europe, playing an important part in the 1848 Revolution. Herzen, when he returned from exile, became the leader of the Occidentalists and an extreme left winger. Henceforth Hegel and the French socialists were happy bedfellows. Fourier, Cabet, Louis Blanc and Proudhon were in everyone's hands. They were studied in detail and produced—as Schelling and Hegel had before them—their propagandists, commentators and interpreters, and later on—unlike Schelling and Hegel—their martyrs. In 1843 Herzen reached the conclusion that the revolution was a necessity. 'France', he noted in his *Journal*, 'gave the impetus.'

Belinsky, who had once preached compromise with the facts, was his disciple in this respect when he exclaimed:

'What does the world's life matter to us, when the individual suffers? Why should I care whether or not the genius tastes the joys of Heaven on earth, while the masses grovel in the mire? . . . My heart bleeds when I look at the masses and their representatives. What right has a man in this century to forget himself in his art?'

Herzen and Belinsky turned to revolution as the only means of saving the common man in Russia from humiliations, beatings, hunger, forced labour, conscription and serfdom. That is why the Occidentalists turned away from religion, 'from the whole squalid business of hereditary rights, from the world of traditions which exist only to perpetuate themselves, and from the eternal acceptance as natural of what is not'. It is not surprising that Herzen ended by attacking the Slavophiles and their doctrines at their very roots.

407

BENJAMIN GORIELY

'. . . These supermen are beginning to make me sick: Khomyakov, hale
and hearty at forty after a life spent guffawing with laughter, who has
created this fantastic vision for himself of the Russo-Byzantine Church
becoming universal, and goes on and on saying the same thing, and has
ruined a tremendous ability; and Aksakov, crazy about Moscow, always
waiting for the resurrection of the old Russia and the transference of her
capital and God knows what besides. . . . Even Kireevsky, with all his
nobility, is a strange character. Belinsky is right: there is no hope of an
understanding with people like that.'

At the beginning of 1847 Herzen went abroad. He felt he could no
longer breathe in Russia. Growing tension with his friends in Moscow,
and his intellectual differences with Granovsky made the voyage all the
more welcome. 'We are in a bad way in our country', he said. 'Our
people live with their eyes on the door, closed by the Czar, and it is rarely
that it opens for a moment. Russians dash abroad in a kind of intoxica-
tion.' Soon, however, Herzen was 'cruelly disappointed'. He saw the
middle class as it really was with all its pettiness, vicious egoism, greed,
family despotism, banal interests and hypocritical moral standards. That
was why he was excited by the enthusiasm of the masses at the time of
the European revolutions in 1848 and 1849. He was an eye-witness of the
Paris Revolution and saw 'the appalling unspeakable Days of June'. He
saw the workers crushed and the 'ignoble triumph' of the victors; and
the revolution's failure shook his faith in any attempt to overthrow the
social order by force.

This journey abroad of Herzen's, in the course of which he founded
the first clandestine Russian press in London, marked, like Bakunin's and
Turgenev's departures, the beginning of the first emigration from Russia
for political reasons. From 1848 onward the Russian revolutionary movement became a concrete reality. It was also in 1848 that Occidentalism
and Slavophilism disappeared to give way to radicalism and reaction.

In an article he wrote in 1912, *To the Memory of Herzen*, Lenin
made some clear and profound observations on Herzen's importance
and significance in the history of revolutionary Russia and the 1848
Revolution.

'Herzen, who was inspired by the Decembrist Conspiracy and founded
the Russian free press, hoisted the standard of revolt against Czarist
autocracy. And his deeds were not wasted. The revolutionary movement
to which Herzen gave the first impetus, was taken over by the revolutionaries from the people, from Chernyshevsky to the heroes of *Narodnaya
Volya*, who gave it body and strength and a razor-edge. Herzen played a
great part in the preparation of the Russian Revolution.

'After assimilating Hegel's dialectic, understanding that it was "the algebra of revolution", and becoming entirely won over to "historical materialism", Herzen—in the 'forties, in the Russia of serfdom—attained the stature of the greatest thinkers of his time.

'But although his stature did not diminish, and he remained a whole-hearted revolutionary, Herzen did not escape the "intellectual fiasco" after the defeat of 1848.

'Herzen's intellectual drama reflects that period of the world's history when the revolutionary spirit of middle-class democracy was already dead and the proletariat's revolutionary strength had not yet fully developed.

'Nevertheless, the ground was crumbling under the feet of this son of landed proprietors, with his aristocratic environment; this revolutionary nobleman who founded Russian socialism—the movement that sprang from "love of the people". The ground was too insecure, and Herzen inevitably became a profound sceptic and pessimist, which resulted in his being drawn towards that liberalism which he yet hated and fought against.'

But in spite of all Herzen's oscillations between democracy and liberalism, democracy time and again prevailed, and a year before his death he was attracted by the International—the International directed by Marx.

The Slavophiles looked upon Russia and the West as two diametrically opposed worlds. Russia, they pointed out, was Orthodox and the recipient of revealed truth, whilst the West was Catholic and Protestant. The fact was that the West had strayed from religion by freeing the individual, for Roman Catholicism and to an even greater extent German Protestantism sought the support of individualist rationalism.

Russia followed the Fathers of the Church, whilst the West followed the Schoolmen, who led them to Protestant philosophy. That was why Russian art too was different from western art. In Russia, beauty was synonymous with truth, whilst Europe believed in abstract beauty which naturally led to 'the false world of imagination'.

Kireevsky considered that the basis of the Russian State was the *Mir*, a form of rural community unknown in the West, in which property was held in common. The European States had grown by conquering weaker nations, and modern parliamentarism was based on the same principle, as the majority asserted its will over the opposition. In Russia, on the other hand, there was unity, and the belief of the individual was that of the whole community.

'We find the same antinomy in Law', Kireevsky said. 'Russian justice is based on the opinions of the people, whereas European justice has been created by the rulers and developed Formalism based on the letter of the law.'

As one can see, the Slavophiles glorified Russia as she was before the days of Peter the Great, with Moscow at the dawn of its history; Russia as an agricultural nation, as opposed (Kireevsky pointed out) to industrial Europe; Russia in which life was peaceful, patriarchal and simple. This old Russia, lying on the edge of the western world, troubled constantly by nomadic tribes, had to develop an ability to visualise the world as a whole. The Muscovite princes considered themselves the heirs of the Byzantine emperors, and called Moscow 'the third Rome'. As for the nobles, they were close to the people and the soil. As Berdiaev said: 'The Russian overlords had no aristocratic and artistic refinement to etherealise them.' Khomyakov, and all the other Slavophiles, said: 'We have our city of which we form an integral part, and nothing can detach us from it. That City is the Old Russia, our land, our country, the City of Christ, Holy Russia.' That is why they damned Peter the Great for having made Russia morally and spiritually dependent on the West. It was again Khomyakov who said: 'the reign of that influence is nearing its end, our moral chains are broken and our intellectual freedom is near at hand, but the battle is not yet won.' To sum up, the Slavophiles wanted to put the clock back, which is why they supported Nicholas I in his reactionary policy. Slavophilism was born of the people's injured feelings. Herzen looked upon it as the result of 'an instinctive resistance to exclusively foreign influence', and he saw that Occidentalism 'would never have the full weight of popular support until it had broken down the Slavophile's arguments'.

Both tendencies are still present in Russian philosophical thought, in matters of feelings, temperament and modes of thought, but as political and social forces they were swept away by the events of 1848. As Occidentalism had been defeated in 1825 after the breaking of the Decembrist movement, so Slavophilism was finished by the awakening of the peoples of western Europe in 1848.

At the moment when Petrashevsky's Circle was banned and the censorship was all-embracing, Khomyakov, although stifling in the atmosphere of persecution, condemned revolutionary France, which 'would reap the reward of her folly'. He expected an early victory for Orthodoxy, and believed that the Czar would free the Slavs of the south, who had not been corrupted by 'political protestantism' (communism and socialism), and turned to religion. Khomyakov, who best expresses the Slavophile's position in 1848, looked upon the revolution as a menace to the political framework and the social order. He called on the people to defend Russia against the revolutionary West, but he did not think that Russia should

interfere in European affairs, as many other equally important Slavophiles did.

Tyntchev, in a letter written in 1843 to Doctor Kolb, and published in
1844 in the *Universal Gazette*, wrote:

'What is Russia? What is her place in history? Where has she come
from? Where is she going? Where does she stand? The world, it is true,
gives her a place in the sun, but the philosophy of history has not yet
deigned to do so.' Nevertheless, for three centuries history had won for
her 'all the cases in which she had become involved through her mysterious
destiny'. At the beginning of the nineteenth century, Russia had intervened in Germany's behalf against France, so as to 'ensure the victory
once and for all of legitimacy over revolutionary action'. Russia defended
Germany's cause because it was her own and in so doing she had raised
the German race, 'a whole world', from degradation. Her next task was
to unite the whole of eastern Europe, a task already three-quarters complete, so as to recreate either by natural processes or by force of arms, a
real eastern Empire, whose prototype, the Byzantine Empire, had been
a rough sketch.

The Occidentalists hailed the 1848 Revolution with delight. Granovsky
believed in its successful outcome. We know the reactions of Herzen and
Bakunin. As for Chaadaev, the events of 1848–9 came as a rude shock to
him, and in a letter to Khomyakov he, who all his life had professed so
great a love of Europe, wrote of the West in disgust. Tyntchev, on the
other hand, was greatly excited, and on winning Nicholas I's approval
for his *Letter to Doctor Kolb*, he sent the Czar in July 1848 a memorandum
on *Russia and the Revolution*.

'Russia and the Revolution', wrote this former diplomat, 'are the only
two forces in Europe. The survival of the one will mean the extinction
of the other. The political and religious future of mankind depends
entirely on the result of the struggle between them—the greatest conflict
that the world has ever seen. Russia is Christian and the Revolution is
anti-Christian to the core. Germany is breaking up, Austria is threatened
by the peoples under her dominion, the Catholic Church which accepts,
adopts and glorifies the Revolution either because she believes in it or to
serve her own ends, cannot overcome it. Russia alone can defeat the
Revolution, and not only will she defeat it, but she will benefit by it, for
she will emancipate and unite under the Czar's sceptre all the Slav peoples
whom the Revolution frees from the Austrian and Hungarian yoke. That
is Russia's undoubted mission, and who are we, her children, to show
ourselves sceptical and pusillanimous?'

The Czar read this memorandum at the moment when he was beginning to take heart again. Delighted at the news of Cavaignac's reprisals

against the Parisian proletariat, he ordered Kiselev, his Ambassador in France, to express his profound gratitude to the French General.

Still, he was sceptical concerning Tyntchev's memorandum. Although it was considered of 'high importance' in St Petersburg, Nicholas I considered it was dangerous, and that Russia would be chasing a phantom if she meddled with the affairs of her friendly neighbours. He also condemned pan-Slavism, which he considered would be the ruin of Russia, so that the memorandum was not allowed to be printed. Tyntchev did not lose heart, however, and sent the Czar a further memorandum, but received no reply.

In the meantime, events were going in the reactionaries' favour. In the autumn of 1848 Nicholas, realising that the danger had passed, began to interfere in the affairs of Germany and Austria. He was well satisfied with Schwarzenberg's compliance, and for a long time looked upon him as one of his governors, put in Vienna to carry out his instructions. In 1849, the Czar decided to help Austria against Hungary, fearing that if Kossuth were finally victorious, there would be a rising in Poland. He gave Paskievich the task of organising an expeditionary force. His intervention in Germany was purely diplomatic, and was directed against the democrats' efforts to unite the German States.

The Czar was able to institute a reign of terror within his Empire, and put himself at the head of the European reactionaries principally because of the treachery of the Russian nobles who—like those of Poland and Hungary—were scared of the peasants. Their liberalism had died with the Decembrist movement. The same period saw the rise of the middle class and the appearance of factory workers in the big towns. Towards 1850, Russia already possessed nine thousand factories employing half a million workmen. The opposition consisted of self-made men, but was too weak to have any influence, whilst the intellectuals of noble birth, the Slavophiles, went over after 1848 to the reactionaries. Petrachevsky's followers had been routed, but there was an increasing number of peasant revolts and mutinies in the army. Secret documents have recently been discovered in Moscow showing that there were many officers and men of the Russian Army who refused to take part in the campaign against Hungary.

Just when Nicholas I was about to deal the final blow to European freedom, there arose in Russia a new group of revolutionaries round Chernyshevsky and the poet Nekrasov, who later edited *The Contemporary*. But there was no organisation and no leader had yet appeared. It is not surprising that the hero of Turgenev's novel, *On the Eve*, should be not a Russian but a Bulgarian. Ten years later Dobraliubov commented: 'There are not, should not and cannot be Russians like that in our time.' In the same article, however (which has since become famous), he added that there soon would be Russians capable of action. 'The day will come at last. There is only one night between the evening and the dawn.'

The dawn of the people in 1848 coincided with the darkest hours of the night in Russia. Yet right underneath the surface of Russian society, we have seen that there were men full of idealism, self-sacrifice and nobility of thought and feeling, who—as they were not strong enough to stand up against the reactionary absolutism of Nicholas I—chose the road to prison with sad serenity.

CONCLUSION

FRANÇOIS FEJTÖ

I think the people are magnificent
Flaubert: 'Education Sentimentale'

Hungary lies humbled at Your Majesty's feet' was the message sent by General Paskievich to Nicholas I after the capitulation at Világos. In the autumn of 1849 the tumult of the revolution had died down everywhere. Young Europe had been defeated. 'Yes, we have been beaten and humiliated', Proudhon wrote some time afterwards in his *Confessions*. 'We have all been scattered, imprisoned, disarmed and gagged. The fate of European democracy has slipped from our hands—from the hands of the people—into those of the Praetorian Guard.' But this incorrigible revolutionary hastened to add: 'But that does not make the war on Rome any more just and constitutional. Because Italy, Hungary and Poland protest in silence, it does not mean to say they have been struck off the list of nations. And we democratic socialists are still the party of the future.'

Contemporary observers looked upon the bloody defeat of the liberal, democratic and nationalist movements of 1848 as an historical enigma. Contrary to all expectations, all hopes raised by the 'people's spring', the Austrian, Russian and Prussian reactionaries had come out victorious. The French Republic, which had been born amidst so much bloodshed, became the springboard for a clever and unscrupulous adventurer. Nearly every state in Europe was under police control, informers flourished, and thousands of people were executed and imprisoned. Let us try to discover the reasons for this surprising setback.

John Stuart Mill seems to have hit the nail on the head in his study of the 1848 Revolution in France, when he points out that the bulk of the people were not prepared to accept the Revolution and take advantage of the rights offered them by the insurgents of Paris. This is even more true of the other peoples, for France had a higher cultural level and greater political experience than the rest of Europe. But even the French were incapable of making full use of universal suffrage. Proudhon's prophecies and warnings were justified. In the first elections organised by the Republic, the republican candidates were in the minority, although

CONCLUSION

contemporary observers unanimously declare that these elections were quite free and there was no interference by the authorities. The people simply would not back up their real friends. The republicans realised too late that it was impossible to improvise democracy, and that two months were not enough to make the whole country understand where they were aiming. 'The people are not ready at all', Denis Poulot, the author of *Sublime*, said of the French. The German, Austrian and Hungarian peoples were even less ready, and throughout Europe middle-class and conservative elements formed the majorities in the new constituent assemblies. One can understand the genuine revolutionaries' despair at this unexpected set-back, and how their dissatisfaction with the elections resulted in the risings first at Rouen, then in Paris, Vienna and Budapest.

The political honesty of the French revolutionary leaders—due partly to their idealism and partly to their inexperience—also largely contributed to their defeat. These leaders were limited in what they could do, as they were members of coalition governments, whose opportunism paralysed their efforts. 'Every collective (i.e. coalition) government is weak, hesitant and vacillating', wrote Lamartine in his *Histoire de la Révolution de 1848*. In addition to representatives of working-class interests, the French provisional Government included intellectuals and lower and upper-middle-class republicans. They neutralised one another and the Government's lack of harmony prevented it at the start from winning the confidence of the country, which the revolution had taken completely by surprise. It could only have gained the people's confidence by energetic measures and an unequivocal propaganda for the cause it stood for. Pillersdorf's Government in Austria and Batthyány's in Hungary were powerless for the same reason. The only difference between the coalition governments formed in France and those of other European countries was that only in France were there representatives of working-class interests in the Government: Louis Blanc and Albert. All the various cabinets had failed, through indecision, to reform the machinery of the State, which went on functioning with its old personnel, in the old way.

We have seen that a large part of the middle class joined the revolutionaries not from their own inclinations but because they were driven to do so by the reactionaries. So it is not surprising that the middle-class element, in 1848 as in 1830, having been unable to prevent the revolution, did all it could to stop it as soon as possible. From the start, the middle and working classes had entirely different attitudes towards the revolution. The middle classes looked upon it as a means to strengthen their own authority and bring about the reforms which they considered to be immediately necessary. The people wanted something quite different and much more important: real equality and fraternity; in other words, a revised edition of the 1793 Revolution. The masses of Berlin, Vienna, Milan and Budapest all wanted social justice. But the idealists like Lamartine and Petöfi ran to help the middle classes in their distress. In France the conception of the Republic, and in Eastern Europe the conception of the Nation, were 'the only means of escaping anarchy', as Lamartine said to the terrified deputies when the Chamber was being besieged by the people of Paris. Lamartine pointed out that anarchy would mean poverty, fanaticism and socialism. So when leaflets bearing the magic words: 'The Republic has been proclaimed', were showered down on the mob demonstrating in the streets of Paris, eye-witnesses tell us that 'a hundred thousand men raised their arms, and a single shout arose from the Place de la Grève . . .' The proclamation of a constitutional régime provoked the same enthusiasm in Turin, Berlin, Vienna, Pressburg and Budapest. But it very soon became clear that the words 'Republic' and 'Nation' had different meanings for the moderate and for the democrat, and, as Daniel Stern remarked, it became clear that 'the middle class from reacting against the social revolution ended by reacting against the political one'.

All the 'united fronts', which had won the first victories of the revolution, broke up. Class interests soon appeared and prevailed over flowery speeches and political convictions. In every country, the revolutionaries were split into two camps: the 'reds' who wanted to carry on the work they had begun to its ideological consequences, and the 'blues' who wanted to prevent a social revolution. The two sides clashed in France on 22 June. Those bloody days, which were really caused by the workers' dissatisfaction with the middle-class republic and with exclusively political reforms, sealed the fate of the French Revolution and at the same time had a fatal influence on all the revolutions in Europe. The Czar Nicholas had every reason to rejoice at the catastrophic defeat of the workers in Paris, and to send Cavaignac his congratulations. The reactionaries alone profited by the conflict between the republican middle class and the workers. John Stuart Mill rightly pointed out that there was no cause for surprise in the middle-class National Guard's behaviour in the 'Days of June'. It had already hastened to help the regular army crush the democratic revolts of 1832 and 1834. It was its conduct in February 1848 which had been exceptional, when—to the amazement of Louis Philippe and his Government—it had caught the revolutionary fever.

Some weeks earlier, the British Government had shown how a revolution could be nipped in the bud. This time it was the republican Cavaignac's turn to prove that his vaunted Jacobinism was merely what Marx described as 'the conservatism of the "juste milieu" disguised by a cloak of violence and an affectation of revolutionary spirit'. His action greatly relieved all the moderates in the Government, who were perpetually terrified of the people. It became plain that all those who had yielded to the pressure of the mob had been deluded: they had over-estimated the importance of the barricades. Engels, who was interested in the 1848–9 revolutions not only from a social but also a military point of view, later came to the conclusion that the barricades of 1848 had been primarily of a moral value.

After the June risings had been put down, the Governments of Central Europe set about dealing with their own popular movements with the serenity of men who have shaken off a nightmare. In his chapter on Austria, Doctor Endres mentions a fact which is far from being an isolated phenomenon: Schwarzer, the Minister for Public Works in the Vienna Government, actually provoked a revolt of the masses by lowering wages and making provocative declarations, so as to smash it with the support of public opinion. The reactionaries' reprisals were, in every country, all the more cruel, as they had been so terrified of what they called 'terrorists'—a term under which they included not only Blanqui but men as mild as Cabet. The very existence of the National Workshops in France, and the public works undertaken in Austria to reduce unemployment, appeared to the middle class as violations of the sacred right of property. The French bill to nationalise the railways produced, despite its cautious phrasing, a storm of protest. The following lines, printed by Alexandre Dumas in his newspaper, sum up the middle class's attitude on the eve of the events in June: 'The terrorists are out to destroy the country, the socialists are out to destroy the family, and the communists are out to destroy property.' On 27 May the *Tribune Nationale* gave this picture of the state of the country: 'The nation's finances are in chaos, law and order have been destroyed, everyone is in a state of ferment . . . justice is a matter of politics, ordinary civil rights have gone by the board . . . and all this is the doing of the Provisional Government.' It is thought possible that these words may have been written by Baudelaire, who had been seen at the barricades in February. In June he looked upon the revolution as sheer folly. 'The people are mad and the middle class is mad', he wrote in his diary.

Whilst the middle class was blinded by fear, the people were exasperated by the betrayal of their hopes. In the months following the revolution, class antagonism proved stronger than the ties of republicanism. The republican's lack of discipline (of which Proudhon, too, complained, looking upon it as one of the causes of defeat) assisted their opponents. Men like Louis Blanc and Ledru-Rollin considered that their most dangerous enemy was not the right wing, but Blanqui. Another reason for the left wing's weakness, was that instead of drawing up a definite programme, which would strengthen the Republic, they produced utopian proposals which they hoped would restore life to normal and calm the nation. Whilst the middle-class theorists wanted to bring in free trade at once, others (like Proudhon, whose proposals were accepted by Emile de Girardin) proclaimed the advantages of creating a 'trade bank'; then there was Lamennais wanting the State to help the export trade. . . . This wave of theorising even engulfed the doctrinaires of the Republic, the staff of the *National,* who taking over the left wing's programme also recommended the formation of co-operative societies for production and distribution.

The romantic and unrealistic character of the February Revolution is of course explained by the fact that the working class had asserted itself for the first time, and that its hopes could not be fulfilled even if all the middle-class demands, however radical, were satisfied. The middle class merely wanted political democracy, but the workers also wanted work and food. Marx was the first to point out that revolutionary excesses of highly developed peoples have a disturbing influence on the reformist movements of backward ones. Events in Germany might very well have taken an entirely different turn if the German middle classes had not caught the fear of the workers, of revolution—and above all—of communism. According to Marx, 'their own revolutionary ardour was considerably cooled'. Influenced by the working-class movements in France and, to some extent, in England, the middle classes of more backward countries, although in actual fact they had less reason than their opposite numbers in the west to fear their own proletariat or communism, became political reactionaries before they had completed their historical mission as progressives. Consequently, whilst on the one hand the very fact of the February Revolution breaking out had a stimulating effect on revolutionary movements in either action or preparation, on the other, the social conflicts which were wrecking the French revolutionary movement had the opposite effect of breaking up the united fronts of the various classes and parties representing the forces of progress.

The *volte-face* of an important section of the middle class was probably made easier by the fact that towards the middle of 1848 it was plain that the economic crisis had reached its climax—at any rate in Britain, where it started. The middle class regained confidence in its own economic system and it patiently waited for the end of the revolution and the restoration of law and order. The middle-class citizens of Paris, looking out of their windows on the streets seething with people as though there were a perpetual holiday, thought that the country had gone mad. George Sand, whose extremist articles had done a good deal to scare the middle class, writes in her memoirs: 'There is the sound of a drum and the cries of the newsvendors . . . the *garde mobile* goes by . . . a tree of liberty is planted . . . then there are the delegations, the ceremonies, the bands of priests and soldiers and Poles and Italians.' Such a spectacle daily strengthened the middle-class Parisians' desire to see the return of law and order. 'We must put a stop to it', they were all saying. This desire for social discipline caused a *rapprochement* between the middle-class moderates, both in Paris and other European capitals, with the conservatives and reactionaries; and finally—in Prussia, Austria, Poland and Hungary—with the very government circles they had all been fighting on the eve of the Revolution.

But the revolutions of 1848 did not fail solely because the economic crisis which had helped precipitate them was neither deep-rooted nor lasting, or because the middle class, which appeared to be destined to control these revolutions and consolidate the ground won, deserted them out of fear of the working class. International politics also contributed to the disaster of 1848. Despite the apparent unanimity of these revolutions, which broke out almost simultaneously, they were not co-ordinated. The revolutionaries' solidarity—with rare exceptions like the October Revolution in Vienna—was shown only in proclamations made by the various revolutionary governments and parliaments, which sent each other messages of sympathy. And from the spring of 1848 onward, it came out that the newly awakened national feelings were much harder to conciliate than some of the fanatical exponents of the new doctrines had imagined. Marx and Engels, the editors of the *Neue Rheinische Zeitung*, later on severely criticised Michael Bakunin for saying in his *Appeal to the Slavs*, on the occasion of the pan-Slav Congress of Prague, that he hoped that democratic nationalism would bring peace and freedom to all the people, without exception.

The attitude of the founders of socialism towards racial problems, and especially pan-Slavism, is worth consideration.

The contributors to this book almost unanimously agree that the decline of nationalism into chauvinism was mainly due to the middle-class attempt to solve internal problems by creating antagonism between the different nations. Mazzini gives an excellent analysis of Charles Albert's dilemma over the revolution, in his *Republic and Monarchy in Italy*. The King of Piedmont, he pointed out, was frightened of losing his throne if he were defeated, but he was also afraid of the liberties which the people would demand after fighting for him. Carlo Cattaneo's comment on Charles Albert (in his Memoirs published in 1849) was: 'He is at war to prevent the proclamation of a Republic in Milan.' The unsolved social problems were a major reason why the Hungarian Revolution, one of the most important liberal movements of 1848, degenerated into a racial conflict. Proudhon criticised the liberals among the minor nobility in Hungary for refusing to grant the Slavs and Rumanians within their borders the same national rights that they were so bravely defending against the centralising policy of Vienna. This petty aristocracy claimed that these races were as backward compared with the Hungarian ruling class as the Bretons, Normans and Catalans were by comparison with the French. Marx and Engels, on the other hand, supported the Hungarians' point of view. This was not, however, because they felt any particular sympathy for the Hungarians, or even—as some of their enemies said— out of an unconscious spirit of German imperialism. Marx and Engels clearly showed by their attitude towards the Polish problem that they were capable of subordinating German interests to the wider ones of Europe. But they were convinced that Europe's progress was best served by the great civilised nations such as the Italians, the Germans, the Poles and the Hungarians. As for the small Slav nations—such as the Czechs and the Serbs—Marx and Engels considered that they could not help but be counter-revolutionaries. They believed that the Serbs, the Croats, the Czechs and the Slovaks were historically bound to disappear, becoming part of their more civilised neighbours. Their geographical and economic conditions were such that they could not remain independent nations, and that even their sincerest democrats, once they wished their people to form a nation, were forced to become counter-revolutionaries and the tools of reaction. The real Slav Congress, wrote Marx and Engels, was not the one Windischgrätz's artillery blew to pieces in Prague, but the Austrian Army itself, mainly composed of Slavs, which easily liquidated the democrats of Bohemia and—with rather more difficulty—the patriots of Hungary.

Marx and Engels had no use for the sentimentalists who bewailed the fate of small nations, which, they said, had to give way to the superior needs of the big nations. If the Slavs were to realise their dream of a great Southern Slav State, Hungary, Austria and Germany would lose the outlet they needed on the Adriatic. The founders of scientific socialism quoted the example of the war between the United States and Mexico. The American middle class had annexed Texas, yet who would dream, they asked, of weeping for that country's lost independence? Marx and Engels were so certain that the interests of the small Slav nations clashed with those of the proletariat, that they were not prepared to take the Czechs' and Croats' desire for independence seriously. And they considered that Bakunin's pan-Slavism was directed, whether or not he intended it, against the revolutionary elements in the Austrian Empire, and was therefore 'reactionary from the start and by its very nature'.

Marx and Engels were to maintain this attitude for several decades, and it was only round about the 'eighties that their followers corrected it. In the light of recent events, it would seem that Bakunin was right. He had defended not only the idea of a federation of all the republics in Europe, but he had also predicted that the small Slav nations would play an important part in this vast federation. Like most of their democratic contemporaries, Marx and Engels were dazzled by the heroism of the Hungarian people, by the manufacture of arms in the national workshops, by the introduction of paper money, by the judgments of the revolutionary tribunals, and by that 'permanent revolution' which recalled the triumphs of the Great Revolution in France. But the Hungarian nobles' strict liberalism came too late in 1848, particularly as—even when Hungary's very existence as a nation·was in danger—they refused to grant the lower classes (whether or not they spoke Hungarian) truly equal rights and the complete abolition of serfdom.

So 1848 was not only the spring of living peoples, but also—in the words of the great Rumanian patriot Barnutiu—the time of 'the resurrection of dead races'. But these races—the Rumanians, the Southern Slavs and the Slovaks—were dead only politically speaking: they had retained their own languages and culture throughout centuries of oppression. The truth of George Sand's axiom—'nations can do nothing if they are isolated'—is clearly shown by the manner in which Austria made use of the tragic antagonisms between the different races comprising the Empire. After 1848, all the forces which were to lead to the disintegration of the Austro-Hungarian Empire and the creation of Yugoslavia, Czechoslovakia and Rumania, were very much in evidence. The proposals to create these States were first put forward by Slav theorists at the time of the Revolution. Kossuth, during his exile in Turin in 1862, when he was meditating on his own revolutionary experience, conceived the idea of a free confederation of all the Danubian peoples: Hungary, Transylvania, Rumania, Croatia and Serbia. He envisaged this free confederation as he realised that it would be impossible to create a centralised State in the area between the Carpathians, the Adriatic and the Black Sea. He wrote in a Turin paper:

'It would be no use for a Danubian nation to annex its neighbours' territory; so long as it remained isolated, it would be in danger, and it would fall in the end to a foreign Power. The Magyars, the Yugoslavs and Rumanians must unite and form a Danubian Confederation. Then they will form a first-class power: a rich and powerful State of thirty million inhabitants, with weight in Europe. I honestly and wholeheartedly recommend union, peace and friendship between the Magyars, the Rumanians and the Slavs, as their one means of assuring a successful future.'

The 'united front' of the nations in revolt against European absolutism in 1848 was just as weak as the internal conditions of the progressives within each nation. The revolutionary parliaments and Governments all failed in their duty towards the liberal and democratic sections of the people. Only the extreme left wings·which formed a tiny but powerful minority, fought to the end for brotherhood between the nations. The history of French politics at the time shows the great gulf between the revolutionary Government's theory and its practice. Lamartine's foreign policy differed from Guizot's only in the tone of its announcements, for he was primarily concerned with avoiding a war.[1] It is certain that if France had given her full support to the revolutionary movements in Europe—from Italy to Belgium and from Belgium to Ireland—she would have been involved in a war with Britain. The majority of members of the Provisional Government dared not take the responsibility. And yet the left wing middle-class leaders also wanted to relax the tension within France by undertaking a foreign war.[2]

Henri Martin, in his book on Manin, the leader of the Venetian revolt, strongly criticises the revolutionary Government's non-interventionist policy, which left the Venetians isolated, in impotent rage. Martin was convinced that if the great demonstration in May had taken place on the banks of the Adige instead of the Seine, there would have been no working-class revolts in June. The British Ambassador, Lord Normanby, also thought that the French Republic would be forced to declare war to solve her own problems. The Second Republic's domestic difficulties resulted—even without a war—in Bonapartism. But the real reason for its collapse was neither its failure to declare war nor its inability to resolve social conflicts by a *coup d'état:* it was its middle-class leaders' lack of experience, initiative and cool-headedness. They had not sufficient confidence in themselves to break down all opposition, and smash all the conspiracies, for they had not yet accepted their own creation, the Republic, as the best form of government.

So France left the other revolutionary movements in Europe—particularly those of Venice and Hungary—to their fate, and they accused her of denying her ideals. One wonders, nevertheless, if anyone would have believed in the honesty of France's intentions if she had given military aid to Italy. Palmerston would not have been alone in his suspicions: the Italians themselves were almost as frightened of French intervention as the Austrians. And what about the Germans? Had the Frankfort Assembly really proved its solidarity and political sense by applauding Welcker's plea for 'our brothers in captivity in Alsace'? The few extreme left-wing pronouncements in favour of the Poles or the Italians were received in

---

[1] 'We love Poland, Italy and all oppressed peoples—but first and foremost we love France, and her fate lies in our hands . . .' (Lamartine: *To the Poles,* 19 March 1848)

[2] 'On 15 May, the progressives of the Republican party looked upon a war as a means of distracting attention for the time being from the problem of unemployment'. (Proudhon)

stony silence. Under the majority of the German deputies' liberal phraseology it was not hard to discover their conviction that, as Bismarck put it in 1850, 'the basic principle of a great State is not a romantic attitude but political enigma'. The Pressburg Diet had not shown any higher political morality, when it lacked the courage openly to refuse the Viennese Court's demand for reinforcements for the Austro-Hungarian army fighting in Italy. The majority of revolutionary leaders pursued a traditional foreign policy, which helped to undermine the success of their domestic policy. The middle class succeeded in making the foreign policy of the old order that had been destroyed acceptable to the masses: dynastic egoism became national egoism. Thus were the seeds sown of what was to become, if not a determining factor of the 1871 war and the great wars of the twentieth century, at any rate the pretext for them.

The mistakes made by the masses and immature classes of society greatly facilitated the work of the British and Russian statesmen, who had tried from the start of the revolution to localise the movement and maintain the balance of power in Europe.

I have already said of Great Britain that her very existence, her highly developed social structure and her interior conflicts stimulated the reformists. From that point of view Britain may be said to have been one of the chief agents of the revolution. But one might also fairly say that her very existence as so powerful a country that France dared not oppose her, prevented the revolution from spreading. Britain, under Palmerston, cannot strictly be called reactionary, as her foreign policy was based on the defence of moderate reformist tendencies, but when the choice lay between the revolution and the restoration of the reactionary *status quo*, Britain chose (though admittedly not without some hesitation) the second alternative. Although the reconstitution of a reactionary Europe was not in Britain's commercial interests, it would not, like the revolution, threaten the very existence of the British Empire. Hawkins, the British Consul in Venice, was himself a Tory, but he was undoubtedly expressing the view of the whole of the British ruling class when he said to Manin that if Britain were to admit the justice of the Lombards' claims, she would be in no position to deny the demands for independence of her subjects in India, Ireland, the Ionian Islands and, generally speaking, in all her colonies. So Britain's paradoxical position was that on the one hand she had contributed to the outbreak of the revolutions, and on the other she did all she could to halt their progress and ensure the victory of the reactionaries.

As for the second Great Power, Russia, her attitude towards the democratic movements was clear from the start. Nicholas I had advised the Courts of both Prussia and Austria to crush the revolutionaries, encouraging them in their belief that—as Frederick William IV wrote to Bunsen—'the only way to deal with democrats is by force of arms'. It was on the Czar's advice that Robert Blum, the Viennese representative in the Frankfort Parliament (who, after being involved in the October Revolution, fell into Windischgrätz's hands) was condemned to death and executed. By occupying the Danubian provinces and Transylvania, and later by attacking Hungary in 1849, Czarist Russia had followed the traditions of the Holy Alliance, but she had also—according to Palmerston—acted against her own imperial interests, as she had helped to save her rival, Austria.

The experiences of 1848 thus showed once again that political and social reform in modern Europe was not each nation's private affair, but had international repercussions, especially amongst the Great Powers. Henceforth, Austria and Turkey remained in existence not by virtue of their own Governments' strength, but because the Great Powers considered that their continuation was 'in the public interest'. It was symbolical that the great Austrian Empire had to be assisted by another vast Empire before she could quell the revolution in the little State of Hungary. The close connection between domestic and foreign policy was evident in the widespread opinion that the ideas of freedom and democracy were simply accessories of French propaganda. Britain might have fought with less spirit against the democrats of Europe had she not looked upon them as virtual allies of France. There can be no doubt that the main reason why the 1848 revolutions failed was because of the hostility of the two great European powers which intervened to smash them: Britain by financial and diplomatic means, and Russia by force of arms.

In the autumn of 1849 Europe was much less free than she had been in the spring of 1848. People at the time wondered in their disillusionment what had been the use of the popular risings which had taken place practically everywhere in Europe. Might it not have been better if social and political advances had come gradually, without violent upheavals, simply as the result of the technical, economic and intellectual forces that were so busily at work?

Put like that, the question seems absurd. It presupposes that the leaders and the masses had a far more direct effect on events than they had: as Ledru-Rollin pointed out, they followed rather than led the way. Instead of querying the value of revolutions, it is more sensible to try and discover why they should be necessary. They are cataclysms whose value and significance lies not in their accelerating evolution, but in the fact that they result from the clash between the dynamic force of progress and the static strength of conservatism. Revolutions, like the great tragedies, lift for a moment the veil hiding 'humanity's secret'. This secret is the passionate spirit of the people who appear on the stage of history only when the world is experiencing the birth-pangs of a new phase in its development. Machiavelli, in his *Meditations on Livy*, heavily underlines the need for nations, if they are not to degenerate, to return from time to time to their basic moral principles. Revolutions are justified by the fact that they do return to them.

Eighteen forty-eight in the history of Europe and the world, marks the spread of new ideas and new aims, which thenceforth became common property. If we look at the revolution from the point of view of its ideas and aims, we can say that the reactionaries only appeared to be the victors in 1848 and 1849. Engels and Proudhon almost simultaneously realised that 'the gravediggers of the 1848 revolutions became their executors'. The Chartists were laughed at and the German and French socialists and communists persecuted, but the British House of Commons voted laws to protect the workers which Marx hailed as the first legislation enshrining socialist principles. And under the Second Empire, in spite of the despotic behaviour of the authorities, the working-class movement continued to grow, remaining faithful to the principles of its heroes, now in their graves, in exile or in prison. The movements in Vienna and Hungary were also crushed, but their chief accomplishment, the abolition of serf-dom, remained. And an extraordinary thing was that the reactionary Austrian Governments that came to power after the revolution completed the modernisation (in the middle-class sense of the word) of the executive, thereby fulfilling one of the main tasks that the revolutionaries had set themselves.

The French elections in April and December 1848, and later the result of the plebiscite, did not finally shake the democrats' faith in the people and the universal suffrage they had wanted it to possess. On the contrary, during the next hundred years, the peoples' battle for the extension of the franchise was to take a major place in the history of European politics. The February Revolution, as John Stuart Mill noted, opened new vistas for the people, on the day on which universal suffrage was proclaimed law. The 1848 Revolution clearly showed that the extension of the right to vote and the democrats' efforts to bring about the political emancipa-tion of the ever-growing masses, was no 'middle-class affair', but a fore-taste of the political institutions of the future. The capitalist middle class was not democratic—it was at the most liberal—at the beginning of its struggle for power. Whenever possible, it did its utmost to prevent the introduction of universal suffrage and all the economic, political and educational reforms demanded by the equalitarians. This should not surprise us, for it is in the middle class's vital interest to preserve its

FRANÇOIS FEJTÖ

economic privileges and the political and legal advantages which guarantee
them.

Democracy was connected with the capitalist upper-middle class only
in so far as it drove the masses toward an ideology which served the
interests of the lower-middle class, the peasants, the intellectuals and the
factory workers, none of whom had the advantages of possessing capital.
Although the middle class succeeded, in the countries in which it had
gained social, economic and political control, in making a caricature of
democratic aims, by preventing the social consequences of political
equality, that does not mean to say that democracy was closely linked to
the future of capitalism and the middle class. The upper-middle class of
every country in 1848 showed that it had more important prizes to win
than democracy. But the Revolution did bring about an alliance between
the social reformers and the democrats, between 'the thinkers and the
oppressed'; and that alliance was to become in the course of the next
century, a major historical factor.

But the 'gravediggers' of the revolution who became its 'executors'
were principally concerned with carrying out the national clauses in its
will. Neither Radetzky nor Schwarzenberg nor Nicholas I could stand
in the way of German and Italian unity. Engels, looking back on the
events of 1848 a quarter of a century afterwards, remarked that 'with the
exception of Poland, the great European nations had won independence
and unity'. There remained the small nations in Europe and elsewhere.
For the past hundred years, the ideas of independence abroad in 1848 have
never ceased revolutionising the world; they have affected every race,
starting with the white and going on to the coloured peoples, and they
have threatened all the old empires and prevented any attempt to
create new ones.

Socialism, democracy, nationalism in its best sense, and internationalism
in the sense of a recognition of the nations' interdependence: those were
the predominant themes of the revolutions of 1848. Like all revolutions,
they marked both a beginning and an end. Daniel Stern, one of its most
interesting historians, defined the revolution as 'the final collapse of the
old alliance between the Catholic Church and the monarchies, and the
disappearance of the last trace of the "Divine Right of Kings"' . . . . that
was the political victory of the 1848 Revolution, which the educated
classes won in the name of Liberty. The first attempt to set up modern
government, the foundation of rational, republican unity won by the
working classes in the name of Equality and Fraternity—that was its social
victory. This double character of the 1848 Revolution, political and social,
due to the fact that the interests of the middle class both combined and
clashed with those of the working class, caused its essential contradiction.

426

CONCLUSION

Sometimes it seemed that it had taken place too late and sometimes—as in the case of the proletarian risings and the revolts of the small nations in central Europe—that it had broken out too soon.

The 1848 Revolution was the work of Young Europe: young races, young social classes and young men. The students played a valiant part, and they formed the vanguard of the movement in Paris, Dresden, Vienna, Budapest, Transylvania and the Serbian provinces. That is why there were so many utopian dreams and so much lyrical enthusiasm. The poets, from Lamartine to Petöfi, were in the heart of the battle. Flaubert makes Frédéric Moreau, the hero of *Education Sentimentale*, reel through the streets of Paris in a state of exaltation, 'as though the heart of all mankind beat in his breast'. There were Frédérics in every city in Europe: they were the real heroes of 1848, fighting at the barricades, heedless of their personal safety, applauding the abolition of the death penalty—and demanding the guillotine for the enemies of the Republic.

The most dangerous delusion of the 1848 Revolution was what Proudhon called 'republican mysticism': the belief that by the very fact of its existence, the Republic would produce social harmony and peaceful progress. The 'Days of June' betrayed the illusion of social harmony. The bitterness of the conflict between the workers and the middle class was a shock from which the 'Frédérics' never recovered, for their sacrifices had been made purely so as to effect a reconciliation between the two classes.

The discovery of their irreconcilable antagonism made 1848 a turning-point in modern history. Some never got over their disillusionment, and they were the ones whose bitterness created the 'realist' school of literature and said with Flaubert's young hero that the time had come to be positive. Others, such as the exponents of historical materialism, noted with satisfaction that the events of June justified their theories and taught the professional revolutionaries the necessity of dispensing with illusion, facing facts and continuing to work for social freedom in full knowledge of the long distance they had to travel, and the number of obstacles in their path.

After 1848 the revolutionaries grew tougher, and their naïve optimism gave place to a better understanding of the psychology of the masses.

The failure of the revolutions had a profound influence on European thought, and gave a fresh impulse to the study of historical philosophy and economics. This renascence alone made the 1848 Revolution a period of fertile experience. It seems as though history decided that the tragic themes of the dramas to be enacted in the centuries to come should be summed up in one great prologue. The hero of these dramas was to be, in the words of Baudelaire, 'Mankind in search of happiness'.

GENERAL INDEX

429

INDEX OF PROPER NAMES

INDEX OF PROPER NAMES

GENDER, EQUITY, AND SCHOOLING
POLICY AND PRACTICE

EDITED BY
BARBARA J. BANK
PETER M. HALL

GARLAND PUBLISHING, INC.
NEW YORK AND LONDON
1997